ELITE STUDENT EDITION

5 STEPS TO A ⟩5™

AP Statistics

2024

Jared Derksen
DeAnna Krause McDonald

McGraw Hill

New York   Chicago   San Francisco   Athens   London   Madrid
Mexico City   Milan   New Delhi   Singapore   Sydney   Toronto

1 2 3 4 5 6 7 8 9 LHS 28 27 26 25 24 23
1 2 3 4 5 6 7 8 9 LHS 28 27 26 25 24 23 (Elite Student Edition)

ISBN   978-1-265-26310-2
MHID   1-265-26310-8

e-ISBN   978-1-265-26341-6
e-MHID   1-265-26341-8

ISBN   978-1-265-26353-9 (Elite Student Edition)
MHID   1-265-26353-1

e-ISBN   978-1-265-26389-8 (Elite Student Edition)
e-MHID   1-265-26389-2

McGraw Hill, the McGraw Hill logo, *5 Steps to a 5*, and related trade dress are trademarks or registered trademarks of McGraw Hill and/or its affiliates in the United States and other countries and may not be used without written permission. All other trademarks are the property of their respective owners. McGraw Hill is not associated with any product or vendor mentioned in this book.

AP, Advanced Placement Program, and *College Board* are registered trademarks of the College Board, which was not involved in the production of, and does not endorse, this product.

The series editor was Grace Freedson, and the project editor was Del Franz. Series design by Jane Tenenbaum.

McGraw Hill products are available at special quantity discounts to use as premiums and sales or for use in corporate training programs. To contact a representative, please visit the Contact Us pages at www.mhprofessional.com.

McGraw Hill is committed to making our products accessible to all learners. To learn more about the available support and accommodations we offer, please contact us at accessibility@mheducation.com. We also participate in the Access Text Network (www.accesstext.org), and ATN members may submit requests through ATN.

CONTENTS

Congratulations, you are now an AP Statistics student. AP Statistics is one of the most interesting and useful subjects you will study in school. Sometimes it has the reputation of being easy compared to calculus. However, it can be deceptively difficult, especially in the second half. It is different and challenging in its own way. Unlike calculus, where you are expected to get precise answers, in statistics you are expected to learn to become comfortable with uncertainty. Instead of saying things like "The answer is ..." you will more often find yourself saying things like "We are confident that ..." or "We have evidence that ..." It's a new and exciting way of thinking.

How do you do well on the AP exam? By understanding statistical principles. Keep up on the material during your AP Statistics class and read this book to review and prepare for the exam. Note that the questions on the AP exam are generally quite conceptual. In addition to doing computations, you will need to explain why you did them and what they mean. This also means you must communicate your thoughts clearly. You can always use a calculator, so learn to use it well. But success on the AP Statistics exam will require more than pushing buttons.

This book is self-contained in that it covers all of the material required by the course content description published by the College Board. However, it is not designed to substitute for an in-class experience or for your textbook. Use this book as a supplement to your in-class studies, as a reference for a quick refresher on a topic, and as one of your major resources as you prepare for the AP exam.

This edition extends and updates previous editions. It takes into account changes in thinking about AP Statistics since the publication of the first edition in 2004 and includes some topics that should help you understand what is important when answering questions on the exam.

You should begin your preparations by reading through the Introduction and Step 1. However, you shouldn't attempt the Diagnostic Exam in Chapter 3 until you have been through all the material in the course. Then you can take the exam to help you determine which topics need more of your attention during the course of your review. Note that the Diagnostic Exam simulates the AP exam to a reasonable extent (although the questions are more basic) and the Practice Exams are similar in style and length to the AP exam.

So, how do you get the best possible score on the AP Statistics exam?

- Pick one of the study plans from this book.
- Study the chapters and do the practice problems.
- Take the Diagnostic Exam and the Practice Exams.
- Review as necessary based on your performance on the Diagnostic Exam and the Practice Exams.
- Get a good night's sleep before the exam.

Selected Epigrams About Statistics

All models are wrong, but some of them are useful.
—George Box

Very few people actually use calculus in a conscious, meaningful way in their day-to-day lives. On the other hand, statistics–that's a subject that you could, and should, use on a daily basis.
—Arthur Benjamin

If the statistics are boring, you've got the wrong numbers.
—Edward Tufte

I keep saying the sexy job in the next ten years will be statisticians.
—Hal Varian

The best thing about being a statistician is that you get to play in everyone's backyard.
—John Tukey

The lottery is a tax on people who flunked math.
—Monique Lloyd

So much of the physical world has been explored. But the deluge of data I get to investigate really lets me chart new territory. Genetic data from people living today forms an archaeological record of what happened to their ancestors living 10,000 years ago.
–Pardis Sabeti

As statisticians, we all have important stories to tell. No matter where you work or what you do, I encourage you to TELL OUR STORIES to your employers, to your students, to a high school class, to the media, and to the public. Let's help everyone appreciate statistics!
–Jessica Utts

ACKNOWLEDGMENTS

With gratitude, we acknowledge the following for their assistance and support:

The participants who attended the College Board workshops—I learned as much from them as they did from me (J.D.).

Grace Feedson, for giving us the opportunity to write this book.

My wife and family, who support me without fail. And the RCHS faculty and my AP Stats colleagues, who have inspired me to strive for more than I ever thought I was capable of (J.D.).

The thousands of my former students, especially Katherine, Thomas, and Elizabeth, and to my husband, Michael (D.K.M.).

JARED DERKSEN has been teaching mathematics for more than 30 years. For most of that time he has taught Advanced Placement Statistics, a program he started and grew to include more than 180 students annually. He has contributed to many different resources, including writing exercises for the Bock/Velleman/DeVeaux series of textbooks. As an AP Consultant, he has trained hundreds of teachers from California to Chengdu, China. He likes math so much, he majored in it twice; once for a BS and again for an MA. In sunny Southern California, he enjoys good food, great books, and Dodger victories.

DeAnna Krause McDonald has been teaching for 35 years and taught Advanced Placement Statistics for 20 years at Palo Verde and University high schools in Tucson, Arizona. She currently teaches statistics courses for the University of Arizona Department of Mathematics from which she has a BS and MA in Mathematics and Teacher Education. Her youngest daughter is now a math teacher as well and is also teaching AP Statistics.

INTRODUCTION: THE FIVE-STEP PROGRAM

The Basics

Sometime, probably last spring, you signed up for AP Statistics. Now you are looking through a book that promises to help you achieve the highest grade in AP Statistics: a 5. Your in-class experiences are all-important in helping you toward this goal but are often not sufficient by themselves. In statistical terms, we would say that there is strong evidence that specific preparation for the AP exam beyond the classroom results in significantly improved performance on the exam. If that last sentence makes sense to you, you should probably buy this book. If it didn't make sense, you should definitely buy this book.

Introducing the Five-Step Preparation Program

This book is organized as a five-step program to prepare you for success on the exam. These steps are designed to provide you with the skills and strategies vital to the exam and the practice that can lead you to that perfect 5. Each of the five steps will provide you with the opportunity to get closer and closer to that level of success. Here are the five steps.

Step 1: Set Up Your Study Program

In this step you will read an overview of the AP Statistics exam (Chapter 1). Included in this overview are: an outline of the topics included in the course; the percentage of the exam that you can expect to cover each topic; the format of the exam; how grades on the exam are determined; the calculator policy for Statistics; and what you need to bring to the exam. You will also learn about a process to help determine which type of exam preparation you want to commit yourself to (Chapter 2):

1. Full School Year: September through mid-May
2. One Semester: January through mid-May
3. Basic Training: Six weeks prior to the exam

Step 2: Determine Your Test Readiness

In this step you will take a diagnostic exam in statistics (Chapter 3). This pretest should give you an idea of how prepared you are to take both of the Practice Tests in Step 5 as you prepare for the real exam. The Diagnostic Exam covers the material on the AP exam, but the questions are more basic. Solutions to the exam are given, as well as suggestions for how to use your results to determine your level of readiness. You should go through the Diagnostic Exam and the given solutions step by step and question by question to build your confidence level.

Step 3: Develop Strategies for Success

In this step, you'll learn strategies that will help you do your best on the exam (Chapter 4). These cover general strategies for success as well as more specific tips and strategies for both the multiple-choice and free-response sections of the exam. Many of these are drawn from our many years of experience as graders for the AP exam; others are the collected wisdom of people involved in the development and grading of the exam.

Step 4: Review the Knowledge You Need to Score High

This step represents the major part, at least in length, of this book. You will review the statistical content you need to know for the exam. Step 4 includes Chapters 5–13 and provides a comprehensive review of statistics as well as sample questions relative to the topics covered in each chapter. If you thoroughly review this material, you will have studied all that is tested on the exam and hence have increased your chances of earning a 5. A combination of good effort all year long in your class and the review provided in these chapters should prepare you to do well.

Step 5: Build Your Test-Taking Confidence

In this step you'll complete your preparation by testing yourself on practice exams. There are two complete sample exams in Step 5 as well as complete solutions to each exam. These exams mirror the AP exam (although they are not reproduced questions from the actual exam) in content and difficulty.

Finally, at the back of this book you'll find additional resources to aid your preparation:

- A summary of formulas related to the AP Statistics exam
- A set of tables needed on the exam
- A brief bibliography
- A short list of websites that might be helpful
- A glossary of terms related to the AP Statistics exam

The Graphics Used in This Book

To emphasize particular skills and strategies, we use several icons throughout this book. An icon in the margin will alert you to pay particular attention to the accompanying text. We use four icons:

 This icon indicates a very important concept that you should not pass over.

 This icon highlights a strategy that you might want to try.

 This icon alerts you to a tip that you might find useful.

 This icon indicates a tip that will help you with your calculator.

Boldfaced words indicate terms included in the glossary at the end of this book.

STEP 1

Set Up Your Study Program

What You Need to Know About the AP Statistics Exam

IN THIS CHAPTER

Summary: Learn what topics are tested, how the test is scored, and basic test-taking information.

Key Ideas

✪ Most colleges will award credit for a score of 4 or 5. Some will award credit for a 3.
✪ Multiple-choice questions account for one-half of your final score.
✪ One point is earned for each correct answer on the multiple-choice section.
✪ Free-response questions account for one-half of your final score.
✪ Your composite score out of a possible 100 on the two test sections is converted to a score on the 1-to-5 scale.

Background Information

The AP Statistics exam that you are taking was first offered by the College Board in 1997. In that year, 7,667 students took the Stats exam (the largest first-year exam ever). Since then, the number of students taking the test has grown rapidly. In 2019, about 225,000 students (of whom 14.5% earned a top grade of a 5) took the AP Statistics exam. Statistics is now one of the 10 largest AP exams.

Some Frequently Asked Questions About the AP Statistics Exam

Why Take the AP Statistics Exam?

Most of you take the AP Statistics exam because you are seeking college credit. Each university makes its own decision about whether and how it recognizes AP credit, but the majority of colleges and universities will accept a 4 or 5 as acceptable credit for their non-calculus-based statistics courses. A small number of schools accept a 3 on the exam. This means you are one course closer to graduation before you even begin. Even if you do not score high enough to earn college credit, the fact that you elected to enroll in AP courses tells admission committees that you are a high achiever and serious about your education. You should contact the admissions office of the university or college you plan to attend and ask them their policy for AP Statistics. In recent years, close to 60% of students have scored 3 or higher on the AP Statistics exam.

What Is the Format of the Exam?

AP Statistics

SECTION	NUMBER OF QUESTIONS	TIME LIMIT
I. Multiple-Choice (50% of exam score)	40	90 minutes
II. Free-Response (50% of exam score)	6 (total)	90 minutes
A. Short Answer (75% of free-response score)	5	60 minutes recommended
B. Investigative Task (25% of free-response score)	1	25 minutes recommended

Approved graphing calculators are allowed during all parts of the test. The two sections of the test are completely separate and are administered in separate 90-minute blocks. Please note that you are not expected to be able to answer all the questions in order to receive a grade of 5. Specific instructions for each part of the test are given in the Diagnostic Exam and the Practice Exams at the end of this book.

You will be provided with a set of common statistical formulas and necessary tables. Copies of these materials are in the Appendices to this book.

Who Writes the AP Statistics Exam?

Development of each AP exam is a multiyear effort that involves many education and testing professionals and students. At the heart of the effort is the AP Statistics Test Development Committee, a group of college and high school statistics teachers who are typically asked to serve for three years. The committee and other college professors create a large pool of multiple-choice questions. With the help of the testing experts at Educational Testing Service (ETS), these questions are then pretested with college students enrolled in Statistics courses for accuracy, appropriateness, clarity, and assurance that there is only one possible answer. The results of this pretesting allow each question to be categorized by degree of difficulty.

The free-response essay questions that make up Section II go through a similar process of creation, modification, pretesting, and final refinement so that the questions cover the necessary areas of material and are at an appropriate level of difficulty and clarity. The committee also makes a great deal of effort to construct a free-response exam that will allow for clear and equitable grading by the AP readers.

At the conclusion of each AP reading and scoring of exams, the exam itself and the results are thoroughly evaluated by the committee and by ETS. In this way, the College Board can use the results to make suggestions for course development in high schools and to plan future exams.

What Topics Appear on the Exam?

The College Board, after consulting with teachers of statistics, develops a curriculum that covers material that college professors expect to cover in their first-year classes. Based on this outline of topics, the exams are written such that those topics are covered in proportion to their importance to the expected statistics understanding of the student. There are four major content themes in AP Statistics: exploratory data analysis, planning and conducting a study, probability and random variables, and statistical inference. The following table is an outline of the curriculum topic areas:

SECTION	TOPIC AREA/ PERCENT OF EXAM	TOPICS
I	Exploring Data • One-Variable: 15–23% • Two-Variable: 5–7%	A. Graphical displays of distributions of one-variable data (dotplot, stemplot, histogram, ogive). B. Summarizing distributions of one-variable data (center, spread, position, boxplots, changing units). C. Comparing distributions of one-variable data. D. Exploring two-variable data (scatterplots, linearity, regression, residuals, transformations). E. Exploring categorical data (tables, mosaic plots, bar charts, marginal and joint frequencies, conditional relative frequencies, comparing distributions from categorical displays).
II	Sampling and Experimentation (12%–15%)	A. Methods of data collection (census, survey, experiment, observational study). B. Planning and conducting surveys (populations and samples, randomness, sources of bias, sampling methods—SRS, stratified, and cluster sampling). C. Experiments (treatments and control groups, random assignment, replication, sources of bias, confounding, placebo effect, blinding, completely randomized design, randomized block design). D. Generalizability of results and types of conclusions.
III	Anticipating Patterns (Probability and Random Variables and Sampling Distributions) • Probability, Random Variables, and Probability	A. Probability (long-run relative frequency, law of large numbers, addition and multiplication rules, conditional probability, independence, random variables, simulation, mean and standard deviation of a random variable). B. Combining independent random variables (means and standard deviations).

Continued

SECTION	TOPIC AREA/ PERCENT OF EXAM	TOPICS
	Distributions: 10–20% • Sampling Distributions: 7–12%	C. The normal distribution. D. Sampling distributions (mean, proportion, differences between two means, difference between two proportions, central limit theorem, simulation, t-distribution, chi-square distribution).
IV	Statistical Inference • Proportions: 12–15% • Means: 10–18% • Chi-Square: 2–5% • Slopes: 2–5%	A. Estimation (population parameters, margin of error, point estimators, confidence interval for a proportion, confidence interval for the difference between two proportions, confidence interval for a mean, confidence interval for the difference between two means, confidence interval for the slope of a least-squares regression line). B. Tests of significance (logic of hypothesis testing, Type I and Type II errors, the concept of the power of a test, tests for means and proportions, chi-square test, test for the slope of a least-squares line).

Who Grades My AP Statistics Exam?

Every June a group of statistics teachers (roughly half college professors and half high school teachers of statistics) gather for a week to assign grades to your hard work. Each of these Faculty Consultants spends several hours getting trained on the scoring rubric for each question they grade (an individual reader may read two to three questions during the week). Because each reader becomes an expert on that question, and because each exam book is anonymous, this process provides a very consistent and unbiased scoring of that question. During a typical day of grading, a random sample of each reader's scores is selected and cross-checked by other experienced Table Leaders to ensure that consistency is maintained throughout the day and the week. Each reader's scores on a given question are also statistically analyzed to make sure they are not giving scores that are significantly higher or lower than the mean scores given by other readers of that question. All measures are taken to maintain consistency and fairness for your benefit.

Will My Exam Remain Anonymous?

Absolutely. Even if your high school teacher happens to randomly read your booklet, there is virtually no way they will know it is you. To the reader, each student is a number, and to the computer, each student is a bar code.

What About That Permission Box on the Back?

The College Board uses some responses to help train high school teachers so that they can help the next generation of statistics students avoid common mistakes. If you check this box, you deny permission to use your exam in this way. All responses are used anonymously. There is no way for anyone to find out whose response it is.

How Is My Multiple-Choice Exam Scored?

The multiple-choice section contains 40 questions and is worth one-half of your final score. Your answer sheet is run through the computer, which adds up your correct responses. Then this score is multiplied by 1.25 to scale it to a maximum of 50 points.

How Is My Free-Response Exam Scored?

Your performance on the free-response section is worth one-half of your final score. There are six questions, and each question is given a score from 0 to 4 (4 = complete response, 3 = substantial response, 2 = developing response, 1 = minimal response, and 0 = insufficient response). Unlike, say, calculus, your response does not have to be perfect to earn the top score. These questions are scored using a carefully prepared rubric to ensure better responses get better scores and that different readers will score the same response the same way.

The raw score on each of questions 1–5 is then multiplied by 1.875 (this forces questions 1–5 to be worth 75% of your free-response score, based on a total of 50) and the raw score on question 6 is multiplied by 3.125 (making question 6 worth 25% of your free-response score). The result is a score based on 50 points for the free-response part of the exam.

How Is My Final Grade Determined, and What Does It Mean?

The scores on the multiple-choice and free-response sections of the test are then combined to give a single composite score based on a 100-point scale. As can be seen from the descriptions earlier, this is not really a percentage score, and it's best not to think of it as one.

In the end, when all of the numbers have been crunched, the Chief Faculty Consultant converts the range of composite scores to the 5-point scale of the AP grades.

The following table gives a typical conversion and, as you complete the practice exams, you may use this to give yourself a hypothetical grade. Keep in mind that the conversion changes every year to adjust for the difficulty of the questions. You should receive your grade in early July.

COMPOSITE SCORING RANGE (OUT OF 100)	AP GRADE	INTERPRETATION OF GRADE
68–100	5	Extremely well qualified
54–67	4	Well qualified
41–53	3	Qualified
32–40	2	Possibly qualified
0–31	1	No recommendation

There is no official passing grade on the AP Exam. However, most people think in terms of 3 or better as passing.

How Do I Register, and How Much Does It Cost?

If you are enrolled in AP Statistics in your high school, your teacher is going to provide all of these details, but a quick summary wouldn't hurt. After all, you do not have to enroll in the AP course to register for and complete the AP exam. When in doubt, the best source of information is the College Board's website: www.collegeboard.org.

The fee for taking the exam is currently $96 but tends to go up a little each year. A $34 fee reduction may be available for eligible students with financial need, depending on the student's state. Finally, most states offer exam subsidies to cover all or part of the cost. You can learn more about fee reductions and subsidies from the coordinator of your AP program or by checking specific information on the official website: https://apstudent.collegeboard .org/takingtheexam/exam-fees.

There are also several optional fees that must be paid if you want your scores rushed to you or if you wish to receive multiple grade reports.

The coordinator of the AP program at your school will inform you where and when you will take the exam. If you live in a small community, your exam may not be administered at your school, so be sure to get this information.

What Is the Graphing Calculator Policy?

The following is the policy on graphing calculators as stated on the College Board's AP Central website:

Each student is expected to bring to the exam a graphing calculator with statistical capabilities. The computational capabilities should include standard statistical univariate and bivariate summaries, through linear regression. The graphical capabilities should include common univariate and bivariate displays such as histograms, boxplots, and scatterplots.

- You can bring two calculators to the exam.
- The calculator memory will not be cleared but you may only use the memory to store programs, not notes.
- For the exam, you're not allowed to access any information in your graphing calculators or elsewhere if it's not directly related to upgrading the statistical functionality of older graphing calculators to make them comparable to statistical features found on newer models. The only acceptable upgrades are those that improve the computational functionalities and/or graphical functionalities for data you key into the calculator while taking the examination. Unacceptable enhancements include, but aren't limited to, keying or scanning text or response templates into the calculator.

During the exam, you can't use minicomputers, pocket organizers, electronic writing pads, or calculators with QWERTY (i.e., typewriter) keyboards.

You may use a calculator to do needed computations. However, remember that the person reading your exam needs to see your reasoning in order to score your exam. Your teacher can check for a list of acceptable calculators on AP Central.

What Should I Bring to the Exam?

- Several #2 pencils (and a pencil sharpener) and a good eraser that doesn't leave smudges
- Black or blue colored pens for the free-response section; some students like to use two colors to make their graphs stand out for the reader
- One or two graphing calculators with fresh batteries
- A watch so that you can monitor your time
- Your school code
- A simple snack if the test site permits it

- Your photo identification and Social Security number
- A light jacket if you know that the test site has strong air conditioning
- Tissues
- Your quiet confidence that you are prepared

What Should I NOT Bring to the Exam?

- A calculator that is not approved for the AP Statistics Exam (for example, anything with a QWERTY keyboard)
- A phone, smartwatch, tablet, or anything else that communicates with the outside world
- Books, a dictionary, study notes, flash cards, highlighting pens, correction fluid, any other office supplies
- Scrap paper
- Portable music of any kind: no iPods, MP3 players, or CD players

Handwriting on the Free-Response Portion of Your Exam

Prior to 2020, Faculty Consultants had access to the physical booklets in which students wrote their free-response answers. If a student's handwriting style was very unusual, we would find a colleague who could decipher the response. This could consist of looking at impressions in the paper, tipping the booklet a bit so that the light caught the penmanship in a different way, or paging through the booklet looking for similar, yet legible, words and or letters.

Going forward, your free-response booklets will be scanned, and Faculty Consultants will grade the scans on a laptop, not the physical copies of your responses. We cannot look at paper impressions, nor tip our computer screens to catch light in a different way. In fact, when some students erase part of a response and rewrite over that erased portion, the scanner might pick up shadows that make it difficult to decide what is the actual response and what was the erased response. The scans of responses from students using #2.5 pencils (0.5 lead) or those who use light pressure when they write can also be a challenge to read on the scanned copies of your exam.

Thus, for the very first time, it is possible that handwriting may create a situation where your response may be misinterpreted to such an extent that your score is lower than deserved. Please consider the following advice:

- If you write with a heavy hand, consider crossing out instead of erasing.
- If you write with a light hand, consider using a #2 pencil (or one with 0.7 lead).
- Take seven (7!!) sharpened pencils with you, one for each of the free-response questions and one for all the multiple choice.
- Finally, mind your penmanship. Your classroom teacher can probably give you advice on whether yours is challenging to read.

CHAPTER 2

How to Plan Your Time

IN THIS CHAPTER

Summary: The right preparation plan for you depends on your study habits and the amount of time you have before the test.

Key Idea

✪ Choose the study plan that's right for you.

Three Approaches to Preparing for the AP Statistics Exam

No one knows your study habits, likes, and dislikes better than you. So, you are the only one who can decide which approach you want and/or need to adopt to prepare for the AP Statistics exam. This may help you place yourself in a particular prep mode. This chapter presents three possible study plans, labeled A, B, and C. Look at the brief profiles below and try to determine which of these three plans is right for you.

You're a full-school-year prep student if:

1. You are the kind of person who likes to plan for everything far in advance.
2. You arrive at the airport two hours before your flight.
3. You like detailed planning and everything in its place.
4. You feel that you must be thoroughly prepared.
5. You hate surprises.

If you fit this profile, consider **Plan A**.

You're a one-semester prep student if:

1. You get to the airport one hour before your flight is scheduled to leave.
2. You are willing to plan ahead to feel comfortable in stressful situations, but you are okay with skipping some details.
3. You feel more comfortable when you know what to expect, but a surprise or two is okay.
4. You are always on time for appointments.

If you fit this profile, consider **Plan B**.

You're a six-week prep student if:

1. You get to the airport at the last possible moment.
2. You work best under pressure and tight deadlines.
3. You feel very confident with the skills and background you've learned in your AP Statistics class.
4. You decided late in the year to take the exam.
5. You like surprises.
6. You feel okay if you arrive 10–15 minutes late for an appointment.

If you fit this profile, consider **Plan C**.

Summary of the Three Study Plans

MONTH	PLAN A (FULL SCHOOL YEAR)	PLAN B (1 SEMESTER)	PLAN C (6 WEEKS)
September–October	Chapters 5 and 6		
November	Chapter 7 Review Ch. 5		
December	Chapter 8 Review Chs. 5 and 6		
January	Chapter 9 Review Chs. 6–8	Chapters 5–7	
February	Chapter 10 Review Chs. 7–9	Chapters 8 and 9 Review Chs. 5–7	
March	Chapters 11 and 12 Review Chs. 8–10	Chapters 10 and 11 Review Chs. 6–9	
April	Chapter 13 Review Chs. 10–12 Diagnostic Exam	Chapters 12 and 13 Review Chs. 8–11 Diagnostic Exam	Review Chs. 5–13 Rapid Reviews 5–13 Diagnostic Exam
May	Practice Exam 1 Practice Exam 2	Practice Exam 1 Practice Exam 2	Practice Exam 1 Practice Exam 2

Calendar for Each Plan

Plan A: You Have a Full School Year to Prepare

SEPTEMBER–OCTOBER (check off the activities as you complete them)

—— Determine into which student mode you would place yourself.

—— Carefully read Chapters 1–4 of this book.

—— Get on the web and take a look at the AP Central website(s).

—— Skim the Comprehensive Review section (these areas will be part of your yearlong preparation).

—— Buy a few highlighters.

—— Flip through the entire book. Break the book in. Write in it. Toss it around a little bit . . . highlight it.

—— Get a clear picture of your school's AP Statistics curriculum.

—— Begin to use the book as a resource to supplement the classroom learning.

—— Read and study Chapter 5–One-Variable Data Analysis.

—— Read and study Chapter 6–Two-Variable Data Analysis.

NOVEMBER

—— Read and study Chapter 7–Design of a Study: Sampling, Surveys, and Experiments.

—— Review Chapter 5.

DECEMBER

—— Read and study Chapter 8–Probability and Random Variables.

—— Review Chapters 6 and 7.

JANUARY (20 weeks have elapsed)

—— Read and study Chapter 9–Binomial Distributions, Geometric Distributions, and Sampling Distributions.

—— Review Chapters 6–8.

FEBRUARY

—— Read and study Chapter 10–Inference: Estimating with Confidence Intervals.

—— Review Chapters 7–9.

—— Look over the Diagnostic Exam.

MARCH (30 weeks have elapsed)

—— Read and study Chapter 11–Inference: Testing Hypotheses.

—— Read and study Chapter 12–Inference for Regression.

—— Review Chapters 8–10.

APRIL

—— Read and study Chapter 13–Inference for Categorical Data: Chi-Square Tests.

—— Read and study Chapter 14–Free Response Question 6: The Investigative Task.

—— Review Chapters 10–12.

—— Take the Diagnostic Exam.

—— Evaluate your strengths and weaknesses.

—— Study appropriate chapters to correct weaknesses.

MAY (first two weeks)

—— Review Chapters 5–14 (that's everything!).

—— Take and score Practice Exam 1.

—— Study appropriate chapters to correct weaknesses.

—— Take and score Practice Exam 2.

—— Study appropriate chapters to correct weaknesses.

—— Get a good night's sleep the night before the exam.

GOOD LUCK ON THE TEST!

Plan B: You Have One Semester to Prepare

Working under the assumption that you've completed one semester of statistics in the classroom, the following calendar will use those skills you've been practicing to prepare you for the May exam.

JANUARY
—— Carefully read Chapters 1–4 of this book.
—— Read and study Chapter 5–One-Variable Data Analysis.
—— Read and Study Chapter 6–Two-Variable Data Analysis.
—— Read and Study Chapter 7–Design of a Study: Sampling, Surveys, and Experiments.

FEBRUARY
—— Read and study Chapter 8–Probability and Random Variables.
—— Read and study Chapter 9–Binomial Distributions, Geometric Distributions, and Sampling Distributions.
—— Review Chapters 5–7.

MARCH
—— Read and study Chapter 10–Inference: Estimating with Confidence Intervals.
—— Read and study Chapter 11–Inference: Testing Hypotheses.
—— Review Chapters 6–9.

APRIL
—— Read and study Chapter 12–Inference for Regression.
—— Read and study Chapter 13–Inference for Categorical Data: Chi-Square Tests.
—— Read and study Chapter 14–Free Response Question 6: The Investigative Task.
—— Review Chapters 8–11.
—— Take Diagnostic Exam.
—— Evaluate your strengths and weaknesses.
—— Study appropriate chapters to correct weaknesses.

MAY (first two weeks)
—— Take and score Practice Exam 1.
—— Study appropriate chapters to correct weaknesses.
—— Take and score Practice Exam 2.
—— Study appropriate chapters to correct weaknesses.
—— Get a good night's sleep the night before the exam.

GOOD LUCK ON THE TEST!

Plan C: You Have Six Weeks to Prepare

At this point, we are going to assume that you have been building your statistics knowledge base for more than six months. You will, therefore, use this book primarily as a specific guide to the AP Statistics Exam.

Given the time constraints, now is not the time to expand your AP Statistics curriculum. Rather, it is the time to limit and refine what you already do know.

APRIL 1–15

—— Skim Chapters 1–4 of this book.
—— Skim Chapters 5–9.
—— Carefully go over the "Rapid Review" sections of Chapters 5–9.

APRIL 16–30

—— Skim Chapters 10–14.
—— Carefully go over the "Rapid Review" sections of Chapters 10–14.
—— Take the Diagnostic Exam.
—— Evaluate your strengths and weaknesses.
—— Study appropriate chapters to correct weaknesses.

MAY (first two weeks)

—— Take and score Practice Exam 1.
—— Study appropriate chapters to correct weaknesses.
—— Take and score Practice Exam 2.
—— Study appropriate chapters to correct weaknesses.
—— Get a good night's sleep the night before the exam.

GOOD LUCK ON THE TEST!

STEP 2

Determine Your Test Readiness

CHAPTER 3   Take a Diagnostic Exam

CHAPTER 3

Take a Diagnostic Exam

IN THIS CHAPTER

Summary: The following diagnostic exam begins with 40 multiple-choice questions. The diagnostic exam also includes five free-response questions and one investigative task much like those on the actual exam. All of these test questions have been written to approximate the coverage of material that you will see on the AP exam but are intentionally somewhat more basic than actual exam questions (which are more closely approximated by the Practice Exams at the end of the book). Once you are done with the exam, check your work against the given answers, which also indicate where you can find the corresponding material in the book. You will also be given a way to convert your score to a rough AP score.

Key Ideas

✪ Practice the kind of questions you will be asked on the real AP Statistics exam.
✪ Answer questions that approximate the coverage of topics on the real exam.
✪ Check your work against the given answers.
✪ Determine your areas of strength and weakness.

AP Statistics Diagnostic Test

ANSWER SHEET FOR SECTION I

1 Ⓐ Ⓑ Ⓒ Ⓓ Ⓔ
2 Ⓐ Ⓑ Ⓒ Ⓓ Ⓔ
3 Ⓐ Ⓑ Ⓒ Ⓓ Ⓔ
4 Ⓐ Ⓑ Ⓒ Ⓓ Ⓔ
5 Ⓐ Ⓑ Ⓒ Ⓓ Ⓔ
6 Ⓐ Ⓑ Ⓒ Ⓓ Ⓔ
7 Ⓐ Ⓑ Ⓒ Ⓓ Ⓔ
8 Ⓐ Ⓑ Ⓒ Ⓓ Ⓔ
9 Ⓐ Ⓑ Ⓒ Ⓓ Ⓔ
10 Ⓐ Ⓑ Ⓒ Ⓓ Ⓔ
11 Ⓐ Ⓑ Ⓒ Ⓓ Ⓔ
12 Ⓐ Ⓑ Ⓒ Ⓓ Ⓔ
13 Ⓐ Ⓑ Ⓒ Ⓓ Ⓔ
14 Ⓐ Ⓑ Ⓒ Ⓓ Ⓔ
15 Ⓐ Ⓑ Ⓒ Ⓓ Ⓔ

16 Ⓐ Ⓑ Ⓒ Ⓓ Ⓔ
17 Ⓐ Ⓑ Ⓒ Ⓓ Ⓔ
18 Ⓐ Ⓑ Ⓒ Ⓓ Ⓔ
19 Ⓐ Ⓑ Ⓒ Ⓓ Ⓔ
20 Ⓐ Ⓑ Ⓒ Ⓓ Ⓔ
21 Ⓐ Ⓑ Ⓒ Ⓓ Ⓔ
22 Ⓐ Ⓑ Ⓒ Ⓓ Ⓔ
23 Ⓐ Ⓑ Ⓒ Ⓓ Ⓔ
24 Ⓐ Ⓑ Ⓒ Ⓓ Ⓔ
25 Ⓐ Ⓑ Ⓒ Ⓓ Ⓔ
26 Ⓐ Ⓑ Ⓒ Ⓓ Ⓔ
27 Ⓐ Ⓑ Ⓒ Ⓓ Ⓔ
28 Ⓐ Ⓑ Ⓒ Ⓓ Ⓔ
29 Ⓐ Ⓑ Ⓒ Ⓓ Ⓔ
30 Ⓐ Ⓑ Ⓒ Ⓓ Ⓔ

31 Ⓐ Ⓑ Ⓒ Ⓓ Ⓔ
32 Ⓐ Ⓑ Ⓒ Ⓓ Ⓔ
33 Ⓐ Ⓑ Ⓒ Ⓓ Ⓔ
34 Ⓐ Ⓑ Ⓒ Ⓓ Ⓔ
35 Ⓐ Ⓑ Ⓒ Ⓓ Ⓔ
36 Ⓐ Ⓑ Ⓒ Ⓓ Ⓔ
37 Ⓐ Ⓑ Ⓒ Ⓓ Ⓔ
38 Ⓐ Ⓑ Ⓒ Ⓓ Ⓔ
39 Ⓐ Ⓑ Ⓒ Ⓓ Ⓔ
40 Ⓐ Ⓑ Ⓒ Ⓓ Ⓔ

AP Statistics Diagnostic Test

SECTION I

Time: 1 hour and 30 minutes

Number of questions: 40

Percent of total grade: 50

Directions: Use the answer sheet provided on the previous page. All questions are given equal weight. There is no penalty for unanswered questions. One point is earned for every correct answer. The use of a calculator is permitted in all parts of this test. You have 90 minutes for this part of the test.

1. Jennifer orders 18 items from an online retailer in the month of March. She lives in a small town that has terrible problems with on-time delivery. In her experience, only 40% of the orders arrive on time. What is the probability that exactly seven of the orders are on time in the month of March?

    a. $\binom{18}{7}(0.4)^{11}(0.6)^{7}$

    b. $\binom{18}{11}(0.4)^{7}(0.6)^{11}$

    c. $\binom{18}{7}(0.4)^{7}(0.6)^{11}$

    d. $(0.4)^{7}(0.6)^{11}$

    e. $(0.6)^{17}(0.4)$

2. A survey using a random sample of 1500 households reports that 51% of U.S. households have only mobile phones and no landlines. The survey results have a margin of error of 2.0 percentage points. Which of the following can be said about C, the confidence level?

    a. $C < 90\%$

    b. $90\% < C < 95\%$

    c. $C = 95\%$

    d. $95\% < C < 99\%$

    e. $C = 99\%$

3. You need to construct a 94% confidence interval for a population proportion. What is the upper critical value of z to be used in constructing this interval?

    a. 0.9699

    b. 1.96

    c. 1.555

    d. −1.88

    e. 1.88

GO ON TO THE NEXT PAGE

4. For each patient visiting a doctor's office, the nurse records the patient's body temperature. The plot above shows the temperatures of 28 patients for one particular day. Which of the following statements is true about the distribution of body temperatures?

   a. The distribution is skewed to the left.
   b. The median temperature could be 98.2°F.
   c. The median temperature could be 98.4°F.
   d. The minimum temperature is exactly 97.0°F.
   e. The distribution is normal.

5. The student council at a high school surveyed students about a variety of questions. Which of the following displays would be appropriate to display the number of males and females in each grade who plan to attend prom?

   a. Side-by-side bar chart
   b. Scatterplot
   c. Histogram
   d. Dotplot
   e. Boxplot

6. Victoria is working for an advertising company that is analyzing the amount of engagement on social media influencers. She randomly selects 80 posts that the target audience might view. For each post she finds the number of people who actively engaged with the post and then computes the average. The sampling distribution of this average will be...

   a. approximately normal, because averages are always normal.
   b. approximately normal, because the sample size is large.
   c. approximately normal, because the standard deviation of the sampling distribution has a small value.
   d. skewed right, because the population is certainly skewed right.
   e. skewed left, because social media influencers can't have low numbers of engagements.

Use the following computer output for a least-squares regression for Questions 7 and 8.

The regression equation is dependent variable: Minutes				
Predictor	Coef	St Dev	t ratio	P
Constant	22.94	11.79	1.95	0.088
x Number of Practice Rounds	−0.6442	0.5466	−1.18	—
s = 2.866	R-sq = 14.8%		R-sq(adj) = 4.1%	

7. This regression uses the number of times a new worker has spent practicing a task (measured in Number of Practice Rounds) to predict how much time is needed to complete one round of the task (measured in Minutes). What is the equation of the least-squares regression line?

   a. $\widehat{Rounds} = -0.6442 + 22.94\ Minutes$

   b. $\widehat{Rounds} = 22.94 + 0.5466\ Minutes$

   c. $\widehat{Minutes} = 22.94 + 2.866\ Rounds$

   d. $\widehat{Minutes} = 22.94 - 0.6442\ Rounds$

   e. $\widehat{Minutes} = -0.6442 + 0.5466\ Rounds$

8. Assuming that the conditions have been met, which of the following would give you a 95% confidence interval for the true slope of the regression line, given that the sample size is 10?

   a. $-0.6442 \pm 2.228(0.5466)$

   b. $-0.6442 \pm 2.262(0.5466)$

   c. $-0.6442 \pm 2.262(0.5466/\sqrt{10})$

   d. $-0.6442 \pm 2.306(0.5466)$

   e. $-0.6442 \pm 2.306(0.5466)$

9. "A hypothesis test yields a *P*-value of 0.20." Which of the following best describes what is meant by this statement?

   a. The probability of getting a statistic at least as extreme as that observed by chance alone if the null hypothesis is true is 0.20.

   b. The probability of getting a statistic as extreme as that observed by chance alone from repeated random sampling is 0.20.

   c. The probability is 0.20 that our statistic is significant.

   d. The probability of getting this statistic is 0.20.

   e. The statistic we observed will occur in fewer than 20% of repeated trials of this study.

10. A random sample of 25 adults over 50 years old and a separate random sample of 25 adults under 30 years old are selected to answer questions about attitudes toward abortion. The answers were categorized as "pro-life" or "pro-choice." Which of the following is the proper null hypothesis for this situation?

    a. The variables "age group" and "attitude toward abortion" are related.

    b. The proportion of "pro-life" older adults is the same as the proportion of "pro-life" younger adults.

    c. The proportion of "pro-life" older adults is related to the proportion of "pro-life" younger adults.

    d. The proportion of "pro-choice" older adults is the same as the proportion of "pro-life" younger adults.

    e. The variables "age group" and "attitude toward abortion" are independent.

11. A sports talk show asks people to call in and give their opinion of the officiating in the local basketball team's most recent loss. Overwhelmingly, the callers complain that the officials were unfair and that the local team deserved to win. Based on the callers, the announcer declares that everyone agrees that the officials were unfair. The announcer's conclusion is unwarranted because...

    a. the announcer needed to use blocking to select his callers.

    b. the announcer failed to use blinding when collecting his sample.

    c. the callers are more likely to be upset and favor the local team, creating voluntary response bias.

    d. the callers are all respondents and some people won't be chosen to answer, causing nonresponse bias.

    e. the callers will be biased and will lie because they aren't with the surveyor, causing response bias.

12. Last year, the level of support for a yearly community event was estimated to be 83%. Officials would like to estimate the level of support this year with 95% confidence and a margin of error no larger than 4%. Which of the following is the smallest sample size that would do so?

    a. 30

    b. 300

    c. 350

    d. 610

    e. 1000

GO ON TO THE NEXT PAGE

13. A sample of size 35 is to be drawn from a large public high school. Each student's ID number is placed into a computer. ID numbers are selected, without replacement, until 35 students have been chosen. What name is given to this type of sample?

    a. Systematic sample
    b. Cluster sample
    c. Simple random sample
    d. Random sample
    e. Because sampling is done without replacement, this method is biased.

14. A teachers' union and a school district are negotiating salaries for the coming year. The teachers want more money, and the district, claiming, as always, budget constraints, wants to pay as little as possible. The district, like most, has a large number of moderately paid teachers and a few highly paid administrators. The salaries of all teachers and administrators are included in trying to figure out, on average, how much the professional staff currently earn. Which of the following would the teachers' union be most likely to quote during negotiations?

    a. The mean of all the salaries
    b. The variance of all the salaries
    c. The standard deviation of all the salaries
    d. The interquartile range of all the salaries
    e. The median of all the salaries

15. A computerized sewing machine has four independent parts: mechanical, circuit board, touch screen, and power control. The probability that each will fail within the first year is 0.01, 0.02, 0.001, and 0.03, respectively. If one of them fails, then the machine does not work. What is the approximate probability that the machine is still working at the end of the first year?

    a. 0.930
    b. 0.939
    c. 0.940
    d. 0.960
    e. greater than 99%

16. David is a huge fan of fishing. On a 10-day fishing trip, he decides to carefully compare his homemade fishing lures to his store-bought lures. Each day he flips a coin. If he flips heads, he uses the homemade lure in the morning and the store-bought in the evening. If he flips tails, the order is reversed. Each day he compares the number of fish caught with each type of lure. The homemade lures were slightly better on average, which was his initial impression.

    What pair of hypotheses should David use to test if his results are statistically significant?

    a. $H_0 : \mu_d = 0$; $H_A : \mu_d \neq 0$; where μ_d is the mean difference in growth (homemade lure minus store-bought lure).
    b. $H_0 : \mu_d = 0$; $H_A : \mu_d > 0$; where μ_d is the mean difference in growth (homemade lure minus store-bought lure).
    c. $H_0 : \mu_1 = \mu_2$; $H_A : \mu_1 \neq \mu_2$; where μ_1 is the mean number caught with the homemade lure and μ_2 is the mean number caught with the store-bought lure.
    d. $H_0 : \mu_1 = \mu_2$; $H_A : \mu_1 > \mu_2$; where μ_1 is the mean number caught with the homemade lure and μ_2 is the mean number caught with the store-bought lure.
    e. Because his randomization might result in the treatments being assigned unequally, he should not run a test.

GO ON TO THE NEXT PAGE

17. A child psychologist gets permission to visit the bedrooms of 25 randomly selected children. Among other variables, she counts the number of LEGO pieces she finds on the floor. She finds a mean of 25.5 pieces with a standard deviation of 7.5 pieces. She is going to assume that these values are true about her entire population of interest.

Which of these correctly describes the sampling distribution of this sample mean?

a. $\mu = 25.5$ pieces; $\sigma = 1.3$ pieces
b. $\mu = 25.5$ pieces; $\sigma = 7.5$ pieces
c. $\mu = 5.1$ pieces; $\sigma = 1.3$ pieces
d. $\mu = 5.1$ pieces; $\sigma = 7.5$ pieces
e. The answer is unknown because $25 < 30$.

18. If three fair coins are flipped, P (0 heads) $= 0.125$, P (exactly 1 head) $= 0.375$, P (exactly 2 heads) $= 0.375$, and P (exactly 3 heads) $= 0.125$. The following results were obtained when three coins were flipped 64 times:

# Heads	Observed
0	10
1	28
2	22
3	4

A chi-square goodness-of-fit test is used to test if the coins are behaving as expected. What is the P-value and conclusion for this test?

a. P-value $= 0.343$; there is not sufficient evidence that the coins are not behaving as expected.
b. P-value $= 0.343$; there is evidence that the coins are behaving as expected.
c. P-value $= 0.00005$; there is strong evidence the coins are not behaving as expected.
d. P-value $= 0.00005$; there is no evidence that the coins are behaving differently than expected.
e. Coins are fair, by definition. This test is not appropriate.

19.

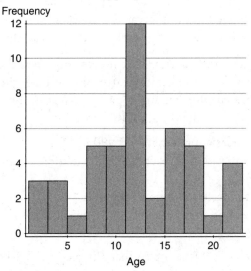

At a party with 47 people, a curious student collects the ages of everyone in attendance. For the histogram pictured above, what is the class interval (boundaries) for the class that contains the median age?

a. $(5, 7)$
b. $(9, 11)$
c. $(11, 13)$
d. $(15, 17)$
e. $(7, 9)$

20. Stefani is ordering fertilizer for her garden. A local garden supply store sells fertilizer by the yard (that really means cubic yard, but that's what they call it). For every yard she orders there is a $15 charge and, in addition, there is a $40 delivery charge. (Total Cost $= \$15(\text{yard}) + \$40$.)

GO ON TO THE NEXT PAGE

If the average order is 4.3 yards with a standard deviation of 2.9 yards, what is the mean and standard deviation of the Total Cost of a typical order?

a. mean = \$4.30; standard deviation = \$2.90
b. mean = \$64.50; standard deviation = \$43.50
c. mean = \$105.50; standard deviation = \$43.50
d. mean = \$105.50; standard deviation = \$83.50
e. Cannot be determined because each order may not be independent

21. A store manager has been tracking the relative frequency of customers who spend more than \$200. These customers he calls Super Customers. In the past, he has observed that 15% of customers meet that requirement. One morning he wants to briefly interview a few of his Super Customers. We will define W to be the number of customers that he will need to observe until he finds his first Super Customer. Which of the following is a false statement?

a. This is a geometric setting.
b. The probability of obtaining his first success on the 5th customer is about 7.8%.
c. The mean of $W = 30$.
d. The mean of $W = 6.67$.
e. The standard deviation of $W = 6.15$.

22. Which of the following is the primary difference between an experiment and an observational study?

a. Experiments are only conducted on human subjects; observational studies can be conducted on nonhuman subjects.
b. In an experiment, the researcher manipulates some variable to observe its effect on a response variable; in an observational study, they simply observe and record the observations.
c. Experiments must use randomized treatment and control groups; observational studies also use treatment and control groups, but they do not need to be randomized.
d. Experiments must be double-blind; observational studies do not need to be.
e. There is no substantive difference—they can both accomplish the same research goals.

23. A scientist calculates a regression equation that successfully uses the amount of alcohol to predict the amount of bacteria that are eliminated. Her scatterplot of bacteria eliminated vs. amount of alcohol appears linear and the residual plot has no apparent pattern. The regression analysis indicates that "R-sq = 98.1%." Which of the following is NOT true?

a. The correlation coefficient is approximately 0.9905.
b. A total of 98.1% of the variation in bacteria eliminated has been successfully described by regression on the amount of alcohol.
c. The alcohol is causing the bacteria to be eliminated.
d. There is a positive correlation that describes this relationship.
e. All of these are correct.

24. A hypothesis test in which $n = 250$ is set up so that P(rejecting H_0 when H_0 is true) = 0.05. Which of the following is true?

a. We can increase the power if we let alpha = 0.05.
b. We can increase the power if we let alpha = 0.01.
c. We can increase the power if we let $n = 200$.
d. We can decrease the power if we let $n = 200$.
e. We can decrease the power if we let $n = 300$.

GO ON TO THE NEXT PAGE

25. For the following observations collected while doing a chi-square test for independence between the two variables Employment Status (Management, Salaried, Hourly) and Workplace Satisfaction (Very Satisfied, Satisfied, Dissatisfied), find the expected value of the cell marked with "**X**."

	Management	Salaried	Hourly
Very Satisfied	5	10(**X**)	11
Satisfied	6	9	12
Dissatisfied	7	8	13

   a. (18*27*36)/100
   b. (8*11)/100
   c. (27*26)/100
   d. (27*26)/81
   e. (8*11)/81

26. A bird-watcher loves it when an American Robin visits his bird feeder. Over the course of the spring, he has tracked the number of American Robins that visit and has developed the probability distribution graphed below. This graph shows the number of American Robins observed each day along with the probability of observing that quantity. What is the mean number of American Robins he observes on a typical day?

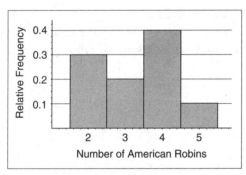

   a. 3.5 American Robins
   b. 4.0 American Robins
   c. 3.7 American Robins
   d. 3.3 American Robins
   e. 3.0 American Robins

27. A psychologist believes that positive rewards for proper behavior are more effective than punishment for bad behavior in promoting good behavior in children. A scale of "proper behavior" is developed. μ_1 = the "proper behavior" rating for children receiving positive rewards, and μ_2 = the "proper behavior" rating for children receiving punishment. If H_0: $\mu_1 - \mu_2 = 0$, which of the following is the proper statement of H_A?

   a. H_A: $\mu_1 - \mu_2 > 0$
   b. H_A: $\mu_1 - \mu_2 < 0$
   c. H_A: $\mu_1 - \mu_2 \neq 0$
   d. Any of the above is an acceptable alternative to the given null.
   e. There isn't enough information given in the problem for us to make a decision.

28. Estrella wants to become a paramedic and takes a screening exam. Scores on the exam have been approximately normally distributed over the years it has been given. The exam is normed with a mean of 80 and a standard

GO ON TO THE NEXT PAGE

deviation of 9. Only those who score in the top 15% on the test are invited back for further evaluation. Estrella received a 90 on the test. What was her percentile rank on the test, and did she qualify for further evaluation?

   a. 13.35; she didn't qualify.
   b. 54.38; she didn't qualify.
   c. 86.65; she qualified.
   d. 84.38; she didn't qualify.
   e. 88.69; she qualified.

29. The table below is a calculation of the grade breakdown of 500 students who are taking introductory psychology at a university. The grades are on a 100-point scale, and the table divides the students into percentiles. Which of these statements is NOT correct?

Percentile	10	20	30	40	50	60	70	80	90	99
Grade	43	55	68	72	75	81	90	92	95	100

   a. This distribution is skewed left.
   b. The mean grade for the 500 students is greater than the median grade.
   c. There are no high outliers among these students.
   d. More students are doing well in the class than are doing poorly in the class.
   e. All of these statements are correct.

30. In a scatterplot, when the point (15,2) is included, the slope of regression line ($y = a + bx$) is $b = -0.54$. The correlation is $r = -0.82$. When the point is removed, the new slope is -1.04 and the new correlation coefficient is -0.95. What name is given to a point whose removal has this kind of effect on statistical calculations?

   a. Outlier
   b. Statistically significant point
   c. Lurking variable
   d. Unusual point
   e. Influential point

31. A one-sided test of a hypothesis about a population mean, based on a sample of size 14, yields a P-value of 0.075. Which of the following best describes the range of t values that would have given this P-value?

   a. $1.345 < t < 1.761$
   b. $1.356 < t < 1.782$
   c. $1.771 < t < 2.160$
   d. $1.350 < t < 1.771$
   e. $1.761 < t < 2.145$

32. A group of students start playing an old-school game called Yahtzee. In this game, five dice are rolled. Each of the five dice has six numbers. If all five dice have the same numbers, the player who rolled yells, "Yahtzee!" and is much closer to winning the game. One of these students has a random digit table and decides to run a simulation to measure the likelihood of rolling a Yahtzee! Which of these methods is appropriate?

   a. Pick five numbers from the table and see if they are the same. If they are, count this as a success. Repeat many times and then calculate the percentage of successes.
   b. Pick the first five numbers from the table. If they are all even or all odd, count this as a success. Repeat many times and then calculate the percentage of successes.
   c. Pick numbers from the table, ignoring 7–0, counting only 1–6. Continue this process until you observe five of the same number. Count this as a success. Repeat many times and then calculate the percentage of successes.

GO ON TO THE NEXT PAGE

    d. Pick numbers from the table, but ignore the odd numbers. If you get five even numbers in a row, count this as a success. Repeat many times and then calculate the percentage of successes.

    e. Pick numbers from the table, ignoring 7–0, counting only 1–6. Once five numbers from 1–6 have been picked, count a success if all five numbers are the same. Repeat many times and then calculate the percentage of successes.

33. A null hypothesis, H_0: $\mu = \mu_0$, is to be tested against a two-sided hypothesis. A sample is taken; $\bar{x}$ is determined and used as the basis for a C-level confidence interval (e.g., $C = 0.95$) for μ. The researcher notes that μ_0 is not in the interval. Another researcher chooses to do a significance test for μ using the same data. What significance level must the second researcher choose in order to guarantee getting the same conclusion about H_0: $\mu = \mu_0$ (that is, reject or not reject) as the first researcher?

    a. $1 - C$

    b. C

    c. α

    d. $1 - \alpha$

    e. $\alpha = 0.05$

34. In an recent election in a small town, polls showed that a local ballot initiative was likely to win. The poll that was taken right before election day predicted that 78% of voters would vote Yes to approve the initiative. On election day, the initiative did pass. In fact, it received 81% Yes votes.

If the preelection polls were based on samples of size 250, which of these describes the sampling distribution of the sample proportion?

    a. $\mu_{\hat{p}} = 0.78$; $\sigma_{\hat{p}} = \sqrt{0.78 * 0.22 * 250}$

    b. $\mu_{\hat{p}} = 0.78$; $\sigma_{\hat{p}} = \sqrt{0.78 * 0.22 / 250}$

    c. $\mu_{\hat{p}} = 0.81$; $\sigma_{\hat{p}} = \sqrt{0.81 * 0.19 / 250}$

    d. $\mu_{\hat{p}} = 0.81$; $\sigma_{\hat{p}} = \sqrt{0.81 * 0.19 * 250}$

    e. None of these

35. X and Y are independent random variables with mean of $X = 3.5$, variance of $X = 7.29$ and mean of $Y = 1.8$, variance of $Y = 0.4225$. What are μ_{X-Y} and σ_{X-Y}?

    a. $\mu_{X-Y} = 1.7$, $\sigma_{X-Y} = 2.6206$

    b. $\mu_{X-Y} = 1.7$, $\sigma_{X-Y} = 2.7770$

    c. $\mu_{X-Y} = 1.7$, $\sigma_{X-Y} = 7.2777$

    d. $\mu_{X-Y} = 1.7$, $\sigma_{X-Y} = 7.3022$

    e. $\mu_{X-Y} = 1.7$, σ_{X-Y} cannot be determined from the information given.

36. A researcher measures the average size of a small insect. Accordingly, as part of her analysis she plans to generate a 95% confidence interval for the mean difference in the male species (which is slightly longer) than the female species, in cm. The interval is determined to be (0.45, 0.80). Which of the following is NOT true? (Assume conditions for inference are met.)

    a. She failed to find evidence of a statistically significant difference.

    b. Her confidence interval contains the difference of the two statistics.

    c. The margin of error is 0.175 cm.

    d. If the researcher subtracted (female – male), both values of the interval would be negative.

    e. All of these are correct.

GO ON TO THE NEXT PAGE

37. A store offers shoppers who make a purchase a scratch card. Each card reveals one number and the probability of each number is listed in the table:

Card	100	50	10	1	0
P(Card)	0.01	0.02	0.03	0.30	0.64

The mean of the distribution of card #s is 2.6 and the standard deviation is 12.1. Once the number has been revealed, the shopper wins a gift card whose value is given by the formula: Value = 10(Card#) + 5. Which of the following is the mean and the standard deviation of Value?

a. mean = 26, standard deviation = 126
b. mean = 26, standard deviation = 121
c. mean = 31, standard deviation = 133
d. mean = 31, standard deviation = 126
e. mean = 31, standard deviation = 121

38. You are developing a new strain of strawberries (say, Type X) and are interested in its sweetness as compared to another strain (say, Type Y). You have four plots of land, call them A, B, C, and D, which are roughly four squares in one large plot for your study (see the figure below). A river runs alongside of plots C and D. Because you are worried that the river might influence the sweetness of the berries, you randomly plant type X in either A or B (and Y in the other) and randomly plant type X in either C or D (and Y in the other). Which of the following terms best describes this design?

a. A completely randomized design
b. A randomized study
c. A randomized observational study
d. A block design, controlling for the strain of strawberry
e. A block design, controlling for the effects of the river

39. The scores on two tests in a statistics class were approximately normally distributed. The first test had a mean of 42 and a standard deviation of 5. For the second test, the mean was 45 with a standard deviation of 6. Jemma earned a 38 on the first test. What score on the second test would be at the same percentile as her score on the first?

a. 38
b. 39
c. 40
d. 41
e. 42

40. A researcher runs an experiment on a water purifier. He has three different chemicals that he can add to make natural water sources safely drinkable for hikers. He is also testing to see if the temperature of the water affects the purity of the water and is running his experiment on both cold and warm water. Which of these is the correct description of this experiment?

a. Three factors (chemical, temperature, and purity) and 12 treatments
b. Two factors (chemical and temperature) and six treatments
c. Two factors (temperature and purity) and four treatments
d. One factor (chemical) and three levels
e. None of these are correct.

GO ON TO THE NEXT PAGE

SECTION II—PART A, QUESTIONS 1–5

Spend about 65 minutes on this part of the exam. Percentage of Section II grade—75.

Directions: Show all your work. Indicate clearly the methods you use because you will be graded on the correctness of your methods as well as on the accuracy of your results and explanation.

1. The ages (in years) and heights (in cm) of 10 girls, ages 2 through 11, were recorded. Part of the regression output and the residual plot for the data are given below.

The regression equation is				
Predictor	Coef	St Dev	*t* ratio	*P*
Constant	76.641	1.188	64.52	0.000
Age	6.3661	0.1672	38.08	0.000
s = 1.518	R-sq = 99.5%		R-sq(adj) = 99.4%	

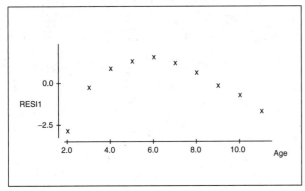

   a. What is the equation of the least-squares regression line for predicting height from age? Please define the variables in your equation.
   b. Interpret the slope of the regression line in the context of the problem.
   c. Suppose you wanted to predict the height of a girl 5.5 years of age. Would the prediction made by the regression equation you gave in (a) be too small, too large, or is there not enough information to tell?

2. You want to determine whether a greater proportion of men or women purchase vanilla lattes (regular or decaf). To collect data, you hire a person to stand inside the local Scorebucks for 2 hours one morning and tally the number of men and women who purchase the vanilla latte, as well as the total number of men and women customers: 63% of the women and 59% of the men purchase a vanilla latte.

   a. Is this an experiment or an observational study? Explain.
   b. Based on the data collected, you write a short article for the local newspaper claiming that a greater proportion of women than men prefer vanilla latte as their designer coffee of choice. A student in the local high school AP Statistics class writes a letter to the editor criticizing your study. What might the student have pointed out?
   c. Suppose you wanted to conduct a study less open to criticism. How might you redo the study?

3. Melanie battles nervousness when she plays basketball. Over the years she has had a 40% chance of making the first shot she takes in a game.

   a. Melanie is curious to know what will probably happen for the first 10 games of the year, with respect to her making her first shot of the game (or not).
   (i) Define the random variable of interest and state how the random variable is distributed.
   (ii) What is the probability that in the these first 10 games Melanie's first shot is made exactly five times?

GO ON TO THE NEXT PAGE

b. If she makes her first shot, her confidence goes way up, and the probability of her making the second shot she takes rises to 70%. But if she misses her first shot, the probability of her making the second shot she takes doesn't change—it's still 40%.

    (i) What is the probability that Melanie makes her second shot?

    (ii) If Melanie does make her second shot, what is the probability that she missed her first shot?

4. A random sample of 72 likely voters taken 3 weeks before the election for school board identified 60 people who planned to vote for Mr. Little. Then a video circulated of Mr. Little screaming at a server at a restaurant. A second random sample of 80 likely voters taken shortly after the video circulated showed that 56 planned to vote for Mr. Little. (a) Does this provide convincing evidence of a drop in support for Mr. Little? Use appropriate statistical reasoning to support your answer. (b) Based on your conclusion from part (a), which of the two errors, Type I or Type II, could have been made? Interpret the consequence of that error in context.

5. A local farmers' market sells grapefruit and claims that the mass of these citrus fruits is approximately normally distributed with a mean of 428.0 grams and a standard deviation of 21.1 grams. You purchase 10 grapefruit, and the average mass of these 10 fruits is 446.2 grams.

a. Describe the sampling distribution of the sample mean, for samples of size 10.

b. You wish to test the claim of the farmers' market, so you begin by using a computer model to simulate drawing 300 samples of size 10 from a population approximately $N(428.0, 21.2)$ grams. Below is the dotplot of the means from these 300 samples.

Mean Mass
(grams)

Explain in simple language how the dotplot shows that the sample mean you are using is an unbiased estimator of the population mean.

c. Given your bag, with its average mass per grapefruit of 446.2 grams, do you think that the farmers' market is correct in its claim? Justify your answer using the dotplot above.

SECTION II—PART B, QUESTION 6

Spend about 25 minutes on this part of the exam. Percentage of Section II grade—25.

Directions: Show all your work. Indicate clearly the methods you use because you will be graded on the correctness of your methods as well as on the accuracy of your results and explanation.

6. A paint manufacturer claims that the average drying time for its best-selling paint is 2 hours. A random sample of drying times for 20 randomly selected cans of paint is obtained to test the manufacturer's claim. The drying times observed, in minutes, were: 123, 118, 115, 121, 130, 127, 112, 120, 116, 136, 131, 128, 139, 110, 133, 122, 133, 119, 135, 109.

a. Obtain a 95% confidence interval for the true mean drying time of the paint.

b. Interpret the confidence interval obtained in part (a) in the context of the problem.

c. Suppose, instead, that a significance test at the 0.05 level of the hypothesis $H_0: \mu = 120$ was conducted against the alternative $H_A: \mu \neq 120$. What is the P-value of the test?

d. Are the answers you got in part (a) and part (c) consistent? Explain.

e. At the 0.05 level, would your conclusion about the mean drying time have been different if the alternative hypothesis had been $H_A: \mu > 120$? Explain.

END OF THE DIAGNOSTIC EXAM

❯ Answers and Explanations

Answers to Diagnostic Test—Section I

1. c	21. c
2. a	22. b
3. a	23. c
4. b	24. d
5. a	25. d
6. b	26. d
7. d	27. a
8. d	28. c
9. a	29. b
10. b	30. e
11. c	31. d
12. c	32. e
13. c	33. a
14. e	34. c
15. c	35. b
16. b	36. a
17. a	37. e
18. a	38. e
19. c	39. c
20. c	40. b

SOLUTIONS TO DIAGNOSTIC TEST—SECTION I

1. From Chapter 9

   The correct answer is (c). If X a **binomial** distribution with parameters n and p, then

   $$P(X = x) = \binom{n}{k} (p)^x (1-p)^{n-x}.$$

   In this problem, $n = 18$, $p = 0.4$, $x = 7$ so that

   $$P(X = 7) = \binom{18}{7}(0.4)^7 (0.6)^{11}.$$

2. From Chapter 10

   The correct answer is (a). You need to solve the equation $0.0175 = z^*\text{sqrt}((0.28)(0.72)/1500)$ for z^*. When you do, you get $z^* = 1.5095$. When you look at table B, you find that 1.5095 is less than 1.645, so z^* is less than 90%.

3. From Chapter 10

   The correct answer is (e). For a 94% z-interval, there will be 6% of the area outside of the interval. That is, there will be 97% of the area less than the upper critical value of z. The nearest entry to 0.97 in the table of standard normal probabilities is 0.9699, which corresponds to a z-score of 1.88. (Using the TI-83/84, we have invNorm(0.97) = 1.8808.)

4. From Chapter 5

   The correct answer is (b). Since there are 28 patients, the median will be between the 14th and 15th data points, which puts it in the bar centered at 98.25°F.

5. From Chapter 8

   The correct answer is (a). These are categorical data. A bar chart is the only one among the choices that is appropriate for categorical data.

6. From Chapter 9

   The correct answer is (b). By the CLT, we know that a sample mean is approximately normally distributed when the sample size is large. In this case, the sample size is 80 (>30), which is more than sufficient.

7. From Chapter 6

   The correct answer is (d). The slope of the regression line, -0.6442, can be found under "Coef" to the right of "Number of Rounds." The intercept of the regression line, 22.94, can be found under "Coef" to the right of "Constant." Rounds is the explanatory variable (x) and Time is the response variable (y).

8. From Chapter 12

   The correct answer is (d). With a sample size of 10, the degrees of freedom for a t-interval are 8. Therefore the t^* value is 2.306. The St Dev in the table has already been divided by the square root of 10. So the margin of error is 2.306 times 11.79.

9. From Chapter 11

   The correct answer is (a). The statement is basically a definition of P-value. It is the likelihood of obtaining, *by chance* alone, a value as extreme or more extreme as that obtained *if* the null hypothesis is true. A very small P-value sheds doubt on the truth of the null hypothesis.

10. From Chapter 13

    The correct answer is (b). Because the samples of men and women represent different populations, this is a chi-square test of homogeneity of proportions: the proportions of each value of the categorical variable (in this case, "pro-choice" or "pro-life") will be the same across the different populations. Had there been only one sample of 50 people drawn, 25 of whom happened to be men and 25 of whom happened to be women, this would have been a test of independence.

11. From Chapter 7

   The correct answer is (c). This is a voluntary response survey and is subject to voluntary response bias. That is, people who feel the most strongly about an issue are those most likely to respond. Because most callers would be fans, they would most likely blame someone besides the team.

12. From Chapter 10

   The correct answer is (c). The formula we use for this is $M > z^*$ times square root $((p)(1 - p)/n)$. z^* for 95% is 1.96 and since we have last year's results we will use $p = 0.83$. Solving for n gives us $n > 338.7811$. The smallest list value greater than this is 350.

13. From Chapter 7

   The correct answer is (c). A random sample from a population is one in which every *member* of the population is equally likely to be selected. A simple random sample is one in which every *sample* of a given size is equally likely to be selected. A sample can be a random sample without being a simple random sample.

14. From Chapter 5

   The correct answer is (e). The teachers are interested in showing that the average teacher salary is low. Because the mean is not resistant, it is pulled in the direction of the few higher salaries and, hence, would be higher than the median, which is not affected by a few extreme values. The teachers would choose the median. The mode, standard deviation, and IQR tell you nothing about the *average* salary.

15. From Chapter 8

   The correct answer is (c). P(still working within one year) means that all four components are still working. You must find the complement for each part of the machine and then, because these components are independent, multiply each. So, P(still working) = $(0.99)(0.98)(0.999)(0.97) = 0.940$.

16. From Chapter 12

   The correct answer is (b). Because David is using each treatment, his experiment is matched pairs. Thus, we need to use hypotheses for the mean difference. Because he thought the homemade lure is better, the alternative is one-sided.

17. From Chapter 9

   The correct answer is (a). The mean of the sampling distribution is the same as the mean of the population. The standard deviation is divided by the square root of the sample size. (Note: assuming you know the parameters is a dubious and risky assumption!)

18. From Chapter 13
    The correct answer is (a).

# Heads	Observed	Expected
0	10	(0.125)(64) = 8
1	28	(0.375)(64) = 24
2	22	(0.375)(64) = 24
3	4	(0.125)(64) = 8

$$\chi^2 = \frac{(10-8)^2}{8} + \frac{(28-24)^2}{24} + \frac{(22-24)^2}{24} + \frac{(4-8)^2}{8} = 3.33.$$

(This calculation can be done on the TI-83/84 as follows: let L1 = observed values; let L2 = expected values; let L3 = (L2-L1)²/L2; then χ² = LIST MATH sum(L3) = 3.33.) In a chi-square goodness-of-fit test, the number of degrees of freedom equals one less than the number of possible outcomes. In this case, df = $n - 1 = 4 - 1 = 3$. The resulting P-value is 34.3%. We fail to reject the null hypothesis (which is that the coin follows the expected distribution), and we conclude that we have failed to find evidence that the coin did not behave as expected.

19. From Chapter 5
    The correct answer is (c). There are 47 terms, so the median is located at the 24th position in an ordered list of terms. From the counts given, the median must be in the interval whose midpoint is 12. Because the intervals are each of width 2, the class interval for the interval whose midpoint is 8 must be (11, 13).

20. From Chapter 5
    The correct answer is (c). When using a linear transformation (Total cost = 15(yard) + 40), the mean is changed by both the multiplication and addition. But the standard deviation is only changed by the multiplication. Mean = 15(4.3) + 40 = $104.50; sd = 15(2.9) = $43.50.

21. From Chapter 9
    The correct answer is (c). The mean of a binomial setting for 200 customers and a 15% chance of success is 30. However, this is a geometric setting, where we are counting how long it takes until we have our first success. The mean and the standard deviation formulas for a geometric random variable are on the formula sheet.

22. From Chapter 7
    The correct answer is (b). In an experiment, the researcher imposes some sort of treatment on the subjects of the study. Both experiments and observational studies can be conducted on human and nonhuman units; there should be randomization to groups in both to the extent possible; they can both be double blind.

23. From Chapter 6
    The correct answer is (c). We cannot make a casual statement like this, even when R sq is very high.

24. From Chapter 10
    The correct answer is (d). You can increase power by increasing the sample size. Conversely, decreasing the sample size to 200 would decrease power.

25. From Chapter 13

The correct answer is (d). There are 81 observations total, 27 observations in the second column and 26 observations in the first row. The expected number in the first row and second column equals

$$\left(\frac{27}{81}\right)(26) = 8.667.$$

26. From Chapter 8

The correct answer is (d).

$$\mu_X = 2(0.3) + 3(0.2) + 4(0.4) + 5(0.1) = 3.3.$$

27. From Chapter 11

The correct answer is (a). The psychologist's belief implies that, if she's correct, $\mu_1 > \mu_2$. Hence, the proper alternative is H_A: $\mu_1 - \mu_2 > 0$.

28. From Chapter 5

The correct answer is (c).

$$z = \frac{90 - 80}{9} = 1.11 \Rightarrow \text{Percentile rank} = \texttt{normalcdf(-100,1.11)} = 0.8665.$$

Because she had to be in the top 15%, she had to be higher than the 85th percentile, so she was invited back.

29. From Chapter 5

The correct answer is (b). This distribution is skewed left. Notice that the spread between the top three percentiles is much smaller than the spread between the bottom three percentiles. In a skewed-right distribution, the mean is much smaller than the median, making (b) the correct answer. In a skewed-left distribution, there the top half of the data is very close together, which means that even a student with a perfect grade of 100 will not be an outlier. And this skewness tells us that more students are doing well and a smaller percentage are doing poorly. Over 60% have scores over 72 while only 30% have low scores.

30. From Chapter 6

The correct answer is (e). An *influential point* is a point whose removal will have a marked effect on a statistical calculation. Because the slope changes from -0.54 to -1.04, it is an influential point.

31. From Chapter 11

The correct answer is (d). df $= 14 - 1 = 13$. For a one-sided test and 13 degrees of freedom, 0.075 lies between tail probability values of 0.05 and 0.10. These correspond, for a one-sided test, to t^* values of 1.771 and 1.350. (If you have a TI-84 with the $\texttt{invT}$ function, $t^* = \texttt{invT(1-0.075,13)} = 1.5299$.)

32. From Chapter 7

The correct answer is (e). Numbers of concern are 1, 2, 3, 4, 5, 6. We ignore the rest. We are interested in when any one of these numbers occurs five times in a row. Only option (e) describes this.

33. From Chapter 10

The correct answer is (a). If a significance test at level α rejects a null hypothesis (H_0: $\mu = \mu_0$) against a two-sided alternative, then μ_0 will not be contained in a $C = 1 - \alpha$ level confidence interval constructed using the same value of $\bar{x}$. Thus, $\alpha = 1 - C$.

34. From Chapter 9

The correct answer is (c). Because 81% was the result in the election, it is the parameter for this scenario. Thus it is the mean and it should be used in the formula for the standard deviation of a sample proportion. That formula is on your formula sheet and is:

$$\sigma\hat{p} = \sqrt{\frac{p(1-p)}{n}}$$

35. From Chapter 8

The correct answer is (b).

μ_{X-Y} is correct for any random variables X and Y. Since the variables X and Y are independent, we add the variances even when we are subtracting! So, σ_{X-Y} = sqrt of (7.29 + 0.4225).

36. From Chapter 10

The correct answer is (a). Because 0 is not in the interval (0.45, 0.80), there is statistically significant evidence of a difference in the averages. A statistic is always in the interval, it is the very middle value. The margin of error is the half the length of the interval. When the order of subtraction is changed, the interval is reversed, and in this case both values will be negative.

37. From Chapter 8

The correct answer is (e). Here we are transforming a random variable. Since Value = 10(Card#) +5, the mean of Value = 10(2.6) + 5 = 31. But the standard deviation is not affected by addition, so stdev of Value = 10(12.1) = 121.

38. From Chapter 7

The correct answer is (e). The choice is made here to treat plots A and B as a block and plots C and D as a block. That way, we are controlling for the possible confounding effects of the river. Hence, the answer is (e). If you answered (d), be careful of confusing the treatment variable with the blocking variable.

39. From Chapter 5

The correct answer is (c).

Since both distributions are approximately normally distributed, equal percentiles will have the same $z =$ scores, so:

$$z_{\text{first test}} = \frac{38-42}{5} = -0.8, \quad z_{\text{2nd test}} = \frac{X-45}{6} = -0.8.$$

Solving the second z-score equation for X gives us 40.

40. From Chapter 7

The correct answer is (b). There are two variables being manipulated: chemical and temperature. Chemical has three levels and temperature has two levels, which creates six different treatments.

SOLUTIONS TO DIAGNOSTIC TEST—SECTION II, PART A

1. a. $\widehat{Height} = 76.641 + 6.3661\,(Age)$
    b. For each additional year of age, the height (in cm) is predicted to increase by 6.36 cm.
    c.

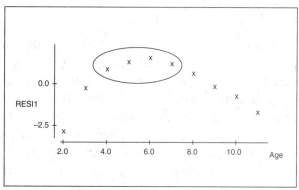

We would expect the residual for 5.5 to be in the same general area as the residuals for 4, 5, 6, and 7 (circled on the graph). The residuals in this area are all positive ⇒ actual − predicted > 0 ⇒ actual > predicted. The prediction would probably be too small.

Scoring Guidelines Free-Response Question 1

Scoring Part (a)

Component 1: Your response correctly has the appropriate values for the slope and the intercept.

Component 2: Your response correctly has the appropriate variables in context including the hat on the response variable.

> If you have both components, score your response as an E for this part.
> If you have one component, score your response as a P.
> Otherwise, score your response as an I.

Scoring Part (b)

Component 1: Your response links an increase of one additional year of age to and increase in height of 6.36 cm.

Component 2: Your response includes the concept of prediction.

Component 3: Your response includes context—year of age and height.

> If you have all three components, score your response as an E for this part.
> If you have component 1 and one of the other two components, score your response as a P.
> Otherwise, score your response as an I.

Scoring Part (c)

Component 1: Your response indicates that the prediction would be too small.

Component 2: Your response justifies this by the location of a prediction in the same area as that of 4, 5, 6, and or 7.

> If you have both components, score your response as an E for this part.
> If you ONLY have component 1 score your response as a P.
> Otherwise, score your response as an I.

Give your response to question 1 an overall score of:

4: EEE (all three parts are essentially correct)
3: EEP in any order
2: EEI, PPP, or EPI in any order
1: EEI or PPI in any order
0: all other combinations

2. a. It is an observational study. The researcher made no attempt to impose a treatment on the subjects in the study. The hired person simply observed and recorded behavior.

   b. • The article made no mention of the sample size. Without that you are unable to judge how much sampling variability there might have been. It's possible that the 63–59 split was attributable to sampling variability.

   • The study was done at *one* Scorebucks, on *one* morning, for a *single* 2-hour period. The population at *that* Scorebucks might differ in some significant way from the patrons at other Scorebucks around the city (and there are many, many of them). It might have been different on a different day or during a different time of the day. A single 2-hour period may not have been enough time to collect sufficient data (we don't know because the sample size wasn't given) and, again, a 2-hour period in the afternoon might have yielded different results.

   c. You would conduct the study at multiple Scorebucks, possibly blocking by location if you believe that might make a difference (i.e., would a working-class neighborhood have different preferences than the ritziest neighborhood?). You would observe at different times of the day and on different days. You would make sure that the total sample size was large enough to control for sampling variability (replication).

Scoring Guidelines Free-Response Question 2

Scoring Part (a)

Component 1: Your response correctly identifies this as an observation.

Component 2: Your response justifies component 1 by noting that no treatments were applied.

   If you have both components, score your response as an E for this part.
   If you ONLY have component 1 score your response as a P.
   Otherwise, score you're your response as an I.

Scoring Part (b)

Component 1: Your response identifies the lack of sample size as an issue of concern.

Component 2: Your response identifies that the study was done at this single Scorebucks, or during this single 2-hour period.

Component 3: Your response either notes that the lack of sample size information leads to lack of information about sampling variability OR your response gives at least one reason that having the study done at this single location/day/time leads to lack of generability to all patrons.

   If you have all three components, score your response as an E for this part.
   If you have two components, score your response as a P.
   Otherwise, score your response as an I.

Scoring Part (c)

Component 1: Your response indicates that the sample size would need to be large enough.

Component 2: Your response indicates that observations would need to be at many different Scorebucks on many different days and at many different times.

> If you have both components, score your response as an E for this part.
> If you have one component, score your response as a P.
> Otherwise, score your response as an I.

Give your response to question 2 an overall score of:

4: EEE (all three parts are essentially correct)
3: EEP in any order
2: EEI, PPP, or EPI in any order
1: EEI or PPI in any order
0: all other combinations

3. a.   (i) Let X = # of games in which Melanie makes her first shot. X is then a binomial random variable with probability of success = 0.4 and the number of trials 10.
        (ii) P(X=5) = 0.2007. (See #1 of the multiple choice section for the formula.)
    b.   From the information given, we have
    - P(hit the first **and** hit the second) = (0.4) (0.7) = 0.28
    - P(hit the first **and** miss the second) = (0.4) (0.3) = 0.12
    - P(miss the first **and** hit the second) = (0.6) (0.4) = 0.24
    - P(miss the first **and** miss the second) = (0.6) (0.6) = 0.36

This information can be summarized in the following table:

		Second Shot	
		Hit	**Miss**
First Shot	**Hit**	0.28	0.12
	Miss	0.24	0.36

(i) P(hit on second shot) = 0.28 + 0.24 = 0.52
(ii) P(miss on first | hit on second) = (0.24)/(0.52) = 6/13 = 0.46.

Scoring Guidelines Free-Response Question 2

Scoring Part (a) (i)

Component 1: Your response correctly identifies the random variable as binomial.
Component 2: Your response correctly identifies the probability of success as 0.04.
Component 3: Your response correctly identifies the number of trials as 10.

> If you have all three components, score your response as an E for this part.
> If you have component 1 and ONLY one of the other components, score your response as a P.
> Otherwise, score your response as an I.

Scoring Part (a) (ii)

Component 1: Your response shows work.
Component 2: Your response has the correct numeric answer.

> If you have both components, score your response as an E for this part.
> If you ONLY have component 1 score your response as a P.
> Otherwise, score you're your response as an I.

Scoring Part (b) (i)

Component 1: Your response shows work.

Component 2: Your response has the correct numeric answer.

If you have both components, score your response as an E for this part.
If you ONLY have component 1 score your response as a P.
Otherwise, score you're your response as an I.

Scoring Part (b) (ii)

Component 1: Your response shows work.

Component 2: Your response has the correct numeric answer.

If you have both components, score your response as an E for this part.
If you ONLY have component 1 score your response as a P.
Otherwise, score you're your response as an I.

Each essentially correct (E) counts as 1 point. Each partially correct (P) counts as ½ point. If your response is between two scores (for example, 2½ points), use a holistic approach to score your response up or down based on the overall strength of the response and communication.

4. a.   Let p_1 be the true proportion who planned to vote for Mr. Little before the video. Let p_2 be the true proportion who plan to vote for him after the video.

$$H_0: p_1 = p_2$$

$$H_A: p_1 > p_2$$

We want to use a 2-proportion z test for this situation. The problem tells us that the samples are random samples.

$$\check{p}_1 = \frac{60}{72} = 0.83, \quad \check{p}_2 = \frac{56}{80} = 0.70.$$

Now, $72(0.83), 72(1 - 0.83), 80(0.70),$ and $80(1 - 0.70)$ are all greater than 5, so the conditions for the test are present.

$$\check{p} = \frac{60+56}{72+80} = 0.76, \quad z = \frac{0.83-0.70}{\sqrt{(0.76)(0.24)\left(\frac{1}{72}+\frac{1}{80}\right)}} = \frac{0.13}{0.069} = 1.88 \Rightarrow P\text{-value} = 0.03.$$

Because P is very low, we reject the null hypothesis. We have reason to believe that the level of support for Mr. Little has declined since his "unfortunate" video.

b.   Because we rejected the null, we could have made a Type I error. That is, support for Mr. Little has not actually declined, but we believe otherwise. As a consequence (for example) people may choose not to volunteer for his campaign.

Scoring Guidelines Free-Response Question 4

Part (a) composes parts I, II, and III of the scoring guidelines for this question.

Scoring Part (I)—Hypotheses and Name of the Test

Component 1: Your response correctly identifies the parameter in context.

Component 2: Your response includes identification of subscripts.

Component 3: Your response correctly lists the null.

Component 4: Your response correctly lists the alternate hypothesis, including direction.

Component 5: Your response identifies the test either by formula or by name.

> If you have four out of the five components, score your response as an E for this part.
> If you have three out of the five components, score your response as a P.
> Otherwise, score your response as an I.

Scoring Part (II)—Validity Conditions and Mechanics

Component 1: Your response states the samples were randomly selected.

Component 2: Your response checks that the sample sizes are large enough as listed in the model solution.

Component 3: Your response checks that for both samples, multiplying by 10 are less than their respective populations as listed in the model solution.

Component 4: Your response lists the correct value of the z-statistic.

Component 5: Your response lists the correct value of the P-value.

> If you have four out of the five components, score your response as an E for this part.
> If you have three out of the five components, score your response as a P.
> Otherwise, score your response as an I.

Scoring Part (III)—Decision

Component 1: Your response links the P-value as being "low" or compares it to a significance level.

Component 2: Your response explicitly or implicitly rejects the null as a consequence of this comparison to the P-value.

Component 2: Your conclusion is in the context of the alternate.

> If you have all three components, score your response as an E for this part.
> If you have two components, score your response as a P.
> Otherwise, score your response as an I.

Part (b) composes part IV of the scoring guidelines for this question.

Scoring Part (IV)—

Component 1: Your response indicates that a Type I error could have been made. (Note, if your response in Part III was to fail to reject the null, then this part should have been that a Type II error have been made.)

Component 2: Your response includes a consequence of Type I error as described in the model solution. (Note, if your response in Part III was to fail to reject the null, then your description must be of a consequence of a Type II error.)

> If you have all three components, score your response as an E for this part.
> If you have two components, score your response as a P.
> Otherwise, score your response as an I.

Each essentially correct (E) counts as 1 point. Each partially correct (P) counts as ½ point. If your response is between two scores (for example, 2½ points), use a holistic approach to score your response up or down based on the overall strength of the response and communication.

5. Grapefruit at the farmers' market:

   a. Because the population is approximately normal, the sampling distribution of the sample mean is also approximately normal with a mean of 428.0 grams and a standard deviation of 6.6724 grams.

   b. Because the center (or mean) of this distribution is approximately equal to the population mean of 428 grams, we have evidence that we are using an unbiased estimator.

   c. There are only two simulated bags out of the 300 simulated samples that have a mean weight of more than 446.2 grams. This is a simulated probability of only 0.0067. Given how small a probability, it seems unlikely that the farmers' market is correct in its claim about the population of bags of grapefruit.

Scoring Guidelines Free-Response Question 5

Scoring Part (a)

Component 1: Your response correctly identifies the mean at 428.0 grams.

Component 2: Your response correctly calculates the standard deviation as $< 21.2/\sqrt{10} >$ or 6.67.

Component 3: Your response correctly identifies the shape of the sampling distribution as approximately normal.

   If you have both components, score your response as an E for this part.
   If you ONLY have component 1 score your response as a P.
   Otherwise, score you're your response as an I.

Scoring Part (b)

Component 1: Your response identifies that the center of the dotplot appears to be about 428.

Component 2: You cite that since the center of this distribution is equal to the population parameter, this is evidence of an unbiased estimator.

   If you have both components, score your response as an E for this part.
   If you have only one component, score your response as a P.
   Otherwise, score your response as an I.

Scoring Part (c)

Component 1: Your response correctly counts the two simulated responses (dots) that are greater than 446.2 grams and calculates a probability of 0.0067 (or 2 out of 300).

Component 2: You said that because this value was small (or less than 5%), it is unlikely that the claim made by the farmer's market about grapefruit is true.

   If you have both components, score your response as an E for this part.
   If you have one component, score your response as a P.
   Otherwise, score your response as an I.

Give your response to question 5 an overall score of:

4: EEE (all three parts are essentially correct)
3: EEP in any order
2: EEI, PPP, or EPI in any order
1: EEI or PPI in any order
0: all other combinations

6. a. $\bar{x} = 123.85$, $s = 9.07$. We are told that the 20 cans of paint have been randomly selected. It is reasonable to assume that a sample of this size is small relative to the total population of such cans. A boxplot of the data shows no significant departures from normality. The conditions necessary to construct a 95% t confidence interval are present.

$$n = 20 \Rightarrow \mathrm{df} = 19 \Rightarrow t^* = 2.093$$

$$123.85 \pm 2.093 \left(\frac{9.07}{\sqrt{20}} \right)$$
$$= 123.85 \pm 2.093(2.03) = (119.60, 128.10).$$

b.   We are 95% confident that the true mean drying time for the paint is between 119.6 minutes and 128.1 minutes. Because 120 minutes is in this interval, we would not consider an average drying time of 120 minutes for the population from which this sample was drawn to be unusual.

c. $t = \dfrac{123.85 - 120}{9.07 \big/ \sqrt{20}} = 1.90 \quad \mathrm{df} = 20 - 1 = 19 \Rightarrow 0.05 < P\text{-value} < 0.10.$

   (On the TI-83/84, we find P-value $= 2 \times$ `tcdf(1.90,100,19) = 0.073`.)

d.   We know that if a two-sided α-level significance test rejects (fails to reject) a null hypothesis, then the hypothesized value of μ will not be (will be) in a $C = 1 - \alpha$ confidence interval. In this problem, 120 was in the $C = 0.95$ confidence interval and a significance test at $\alpha = 0.05$ failed to reject the null as expected.

e.   For the one-sided test, $t = 1.90$, $\mathrm{df} = 19 \Rightarrow 0.025 < P\text{-value} < 0.05$.
   (On the TI-83/84, we find P-value $=$ `tcdf(1.90,100,19) = 0.036`.)

For the two-sided test, we concluded that we did not have evidence to reject the claim of the manufacturer. However, for the one-sided test, we have stronger evidence ($P < 0.05$) and would conclude that the average drying time is most likely greater than 120 minutes.

Scoring Guidelines Free-Response Question 6

Scoring Part (I)—Part (a)

Component 1: Your response states the sample were randomly selected.
Component 2: Your response checks that the sample size is less than 10% of the population.
Component 3: You plot the data and note that it is reasonable to believe that the data comes from a normally distributed population.
Component 4: You either name the interval or list the formula.

Component 5: You include correct confidence interval.

If you have four out of the five components, score your response as an E for this part.
If you have three out of the five components, score your response as a P.
Otherwise, score your response as an I.

Scoring Part (II)—Parts (b) & (c)

Component 1: Your response includes a correct interpretation of the confidence interval as listed in the model solution.

Component 2: Your response includes the interpretation in context.

Component 3: Your response correctly calculates the P-value of 0.073.

If you have all three components, score your response as an E for this part.
If you have two components, score your response as a P.
Otherwise, score your response as an I.

Scoring Part (III)—Parts (d) & (e)

Component 1: Your response notes that since when a two-sided test fails to reject a null, the value hypothesized in the null will be included in the confidence interval. (In the case of the model solution a 95% confidence interval pairs with a significance level of 5%.)

Component 2: Your response continues and notes that since 120 is included in the 95% confidence interval, the interval supports the decision to fail to reject the null.

Component 3: Your response correctly calculates the one-sided P-value of 0.036, which is now less than the significance level of 5%

Component 4: Your response notes that this would give us evidence that the mean drying time is likely greater than 120 minutes.

If you have all four components, score your response as an E for this part.
If you have two or three components, score your response as a P.
Otherwise, score your response as an I.

Give your response to question 6 an overall score of:

4: EEE (all three parts are essentially correct)
3: EEP in any order
2: EEI, PPP, or EPI in any order
1: EEI or PPI in any order
0: all other combinations

Interpretation: How Ready Are You?

Scoring Sheet for Diagnostic Test

Section I: Multiple-Choice Questions

$$\underline{} \times 1.25 = \underline{} = \underline{}$$

number correct   multiple-choice   weighted section I

(out of 40)   score   score (do not round)

Section II: Free-Response Questions

$$\text{Question 1} \frac{}{(\text{out of 4})} \times 1.875 = \frac{}{(\text{do not round})}$$

$$\text{Question 2} \frac{}{(\text{out of 4})} \times 1.875 = \frac{}{(\text{do not round})}$$

$$\text{Question 3} \frac{}{(\text{out of 4})} \times 1.875 = \frac{}{(\text{do not round})}$$

$$\text{Question 4} \frac{}{(\text{out of 4})} \times 1.875 = \frac{}{(\text{do not round})}$$

$$\text{Question 5} \frac{}{(\text{out of 4})} \times 1.875 = \frac{}{(\text{do not round})}$$

$$\text{Question 6} \frac{}{(\text{out of 4})} \times 3.125 = \frac{}{(\text{do not round})}$$

$$\text{Sum} = \underline{}$$

weighted section II score

(do not round)

Composite Score

$$\underline{} + \underline{} = \underline{}$$

weighted section I   weighted section II   composite score

score   score   (round to nearest whole number)

STEP **3**

Develop Strategies
for Success

CHAPTER **4**   Tips for Taking the Exam

Tips for Taking the Exam

IN THIS CHAPTER

Summary: Use these question-answering strategies to raise your AP score.

Key Ideas

Before the Test

✪ Do as many problems as you can on every topic in preparation for the exam.

✪ Know the format of the test in advance.

General Test-Taking Tips

✪ Be aware of time.

✪ If you get stuck on a question, move on. Mark it and come back to it later.

✪ Be neat.

Tips for Multiple-Choice Questions

✪ Read each question carefully.

✪ Try to answer the question yourself before you look at the choices.

✪ If you are unsure of the answer, eliminate as many choices as possible and then guess.

✪ Answer every question.

✪ Drawing a picture can sometimes help.

✪ Go back and read the stem of the question again. Make sure the answer you selected matches the question.

Tips for Free-Response Questions

✪ Read all the questions before you begin writing.

✪ Do not work the problems in order. Answer the easy questions first. Come back to more difficult questions, or parts of questions, later.

✪ Question 1 is often, but not always, the easiest. But be thorough and complete when you answer it!

✪ Don't wait until the end to start Question 6. Start it early. When you get stuck, go back and work on other questions, then come back to this one.

✪ Communicate: make your reasoning clear and in context. Don't ramble.

✪ Calculator syntax is not sufficient for communication. Be sure to clearly identify procedures, distributions, and parameters.

✪ Be consistent from one part of your answer to another.
✪ Draw a graph if one is required. If you refer to a graph you made on your calculator, you must sketch it in your response, and it must be labeled clearly and completely.
✪ Always justify your answers. "Bald answers," that is, numbers without calculations, don't receive full credit.

General Test-Taking Tips

Much of being good at test-taking is experience. Your personal test-taking history and these tips should help you demonstrate what you know (and you know a lot) on the exam. The tips in this section are of a general nature—they apply to taking tests in general as well as to both multiple-choice and free-response questions.

1. *Become familiar with the instructions for the different parts of the exam before the day of the exam.* You don't want to have to waste time figuring out *how* to process the exam. You'll have your hands full using the available time figuring out how to do the questions. Look at the Practice Exams at the end of this book so you understand the nature of the test.

2. *Practice working as many exam-like problems as you can in the weeks before the exam.* This will help you know which statistical technique to choose on each question. It's a great feeling to see a problem on the exam and know that you can do it quickly and easily because it's just like a problem you've practiced on.

3. *Make sure your calculator has new batteries or has been fully charged.* There's nothing worse than a "Replace batteries now" warning at the start of the exam. Bring a spare calculator if you have or can borrow one (you are allowed to have two calculators).

4. *Bring a supply of sharpened pencils to the exam.* You don't want to have to waste time walking to the pencil sharpener during the exam. (The other students will be grateful for the quiet, as well.) Also, bring a good-quality eraser to the exam so that any erasures are neat and complete.

5. *Get a good night's sleep before the exam.* You'll do your best if you are relaxed and confident in your knowledge. If you don't know the material by the night before the exam, you aren't going to learn it in one evening. Relax. Maybe watch an early movie. If you know your stuff and aren't overly tired, you should do fine.

6. *Look over the entire exam first*, whichever part you are working on. Find and do the easy questions first.

7. *Don't spend too much time on any one question.* Remember that you have an average of slightly more than 2 minutes for each multiple-choice question, 12–13 minutes for Questions 1–5 of the free-response section, and 25–30 minutes for the investigative task. Some questions are very short, which will give you extra time to spend on the more challenging questions. At the other time extreme, spending 10 minutes on one multiple-choice question (or 30 minutes on one free-response question) is not a good use of time—you won't have time to finish. *Answer the question and move on.*

8. *Be neat!* On the Statistics exam, communication is very important. This means no smudges on the multiple-choice part of the exam and legible responses on the free-response. A machine may score a smudge as incorrect. Readers work hard to figure out what a response says, but you want to make it easy to see that you know what you're doing.

Tips for Multiple-Choice Questions

There are whole industries dedicated to teaching you how to take a test. In reality, no amount of test-taking strategy will replace knowledge of the subject. If you are on top of the subject, you'll most likely do well even if you haven't paid $500 for a test-prep course. The following tips, when combined with your statistics knowledge, should help you do well.

1. *Read the question carefully before beginning.* A lot of mistakes get made because students don't completely understand the question before trying to answer it. The result is that they will often answer a different question than they were asked.

2. *Try to answer multiple-choice questions before you look at the answers.* Looking at the choices and trying to figure out which one works best is not a good strategy. You run the risk of being led astray by an incorrect answer. Instead, try to answer the question first, as if there was just a blank for the answer and no choices.

3. *Understand that the incorrect answers* (which are called distractors) *are designed to appear reasonable.* Don't get suckered into choosing an answer just because it sounds good! The question designers try to base the distractors on the most common mistakes and misconceptions. For example, suppose you are asked for the median of the five numbers 3, 4, 6, 7, and 15. The correct answer is 6 (the middle score in the ordered list). But suppose you misread the question and calculated the mean instead. You'd get 7 and, be assured, 7 will appear as one of the distractors.

4. *Drawing a picture can often help* visualize the situation described in the problem. Sometimes, relationships become clearer when a picture is used to display them. For example, using Venn diagrams or two-way tables can often help you "see" the nature of a probability problem. Another example would be using a graph or a scatterplot of some given data as part of doing a regression analysis.

5. *Answer every question.* You will earn one point for each correct answer. Incorrect answers are worth zero points, and no points are earned for blank responses. If you aren't sure of an answer, eliminate as many choices as you can, then guess.

6. *Double-check that you have (a) answered the question you are working on*, especially if you've left some questions blank (it's horrible to realize at some point that all your responses are one question off!) *and (b) that you have filled in the correct bubble* for your answer. If you need to make changes, make sure you erase completely and neatly.

Tips for Free-Response Questions

There are many helpful strategies for maximizing your performance on free-response questions, but actually doing so is a learned skill. Students are often too brief or give incomplete responses. Don't assume the reader will fill in the blanks for you. You have to know the material to do well on the free-response, but knowing the material alone is not sufficient—you must also demonstrate *to the reader* that you understand the statistics in the context of the question. Many of the following tips will help you do just that.

1. *Read all parts of a question first before beginning.* There's been a trend in recent years to have more and more subparts to each question (a, b, c, …). The subparts are usually related, and later parts may rely on earlier parts. Students often make the mistake of

answering, say, part (c) as part of their answer to part (a). Understanding the whole question first can help you answer each part correctly.

2. *Communicate clearly, write complete sentences, and organize your solutions.* Make it easy for the reader to follow your line of reasoning. Remember it is your job to demonstrate that you understand the statistics. The reader will not assume you know something unless you say it. Also, answer questions completely but don't ramble. While some irrelevant ramblings may not hurt you as long as the correct answer is there, you *will* be docked if you say something statistically inaccurate or something that contradicts an otherwise correct answer. Answers should be complete but concise. Don't fill space just because it's there. When you've completely answered a question, move on.

3. *Answers alone* (sometimes called "bald" answers) *may receive some credit but usually not much.* If the correct answer is "I'm 95% confident that the true proportion of voters who favor legalizing statistics is between 75% and 95%" and your answer is "(0.75, 0.95)," you simply won't get full credit. Probability questions generally require that you show some calculation, even if it is a simple one. And be sure to include units when appropriate.

4. *Answers must be in context and justified.* A conclusion to an inference problem that says, "Reject the null hypothesis" is simply not enough. A conclusion in context would be something like "Because the P-value of 0.012 is less than $\alpha = 0.05$, we reject the null hypothesis and conclude that there is convincing evidence that a majority of people favor legalizing statistics."

5. *Make sure to answer the question you are being asked.* Brilliant answers to questions no one asked will receive no credit. (Seriously, this is very common—some students think they will get credit if they show that they know something, even if it's not what the question asked.) Another too-common mistake is doing all the calculations needed to support an answer, but never giving the answer! Be sure to look back at the question, then at your response, to be sure you answered the question.

6. *Procedures are to be identified by name or by formula.* Copying the appropriate formula (correctly) will count as identifying your procedure. Correctly substituting the appropriate values into the formula can also save you if you make a calculation error. On the other hand, using an incorrect formula or incorrectly substituting numbers can cost you. Writing the name of the procedure and giving the answer is sufficient but cannot help you if you make a calculation error.

7. If you are using your calculator to do a problem, don't round numbers until you have the final answer. Don't round off at each step of the problem as that creates a cumulative rounding error and can affect the accuracy of your final answer. There is no hard rounding rule, but be reasonable. Don't round means or expected values to whole numbers, but don't keep 8 decimal places, either. A good guideline is to round means to two decimal places beyond the precision of the data and standard deviations one place beyond that. Make sure that any reference to calculator commands has been accompanied by an appropriate explanation of their usage and that all parameters are defined.

8. *Try to answer all parts of every question*—you can't get any credit for a blank answer. On the other hand, you can't fool the readers—your response must be reasonable and responsive to the question. Never provide two solutions to a question and expect the reader to pick the better one. In fact, readers have been instructed to pick the *worse* one. Cross out clearly anything you've written that you don't want the reader to look at.

9. *You don't necessarily need to answer a question in paragraph form.* A bulleted list or algebraic demonstration may work well if you are comfortable doing it that way.

10. *Understand that Question #6, the investigative task, will probably contain questions about material you've never studied.* The goal of such a question is to see how well you think statistically in an unfamiliar situation. The best way to prepare for this question is to practice investigative tasks. Work on applying what you know in a variety of new situations.

Specific Statistics Content Tips

The following set of tips are things that are most worth remembering about specific content issues in statistics. These are things that have been consistent over the years of the reading. This list is *not* exhaustive! The examples, exercises, and solutions that appear in this book are illustrative of the manner in which you are expected to answer free-response problems, but this list is just a sampling of some of the most important things you need to remember.

1. When asked to describe a one-variable data set, always discuss shape, center, and spread in context. That means your answer should mention the variable and include units.
2. If you are asked to compare distributions, use phrases such as *greater than, less than*, and *the same as*. And, again, always answer in context.
3. Understand how skewness can be used to differentiate between the mean and the median.
4. Know how transformations of a data set affect summary statistics.
5. Be careful when using "normal" as an adjective. Normal refers to a specific model, not the general shape of a graph of a data set. It's better to use "mound-shaped and symmetric," etc., instead. You will be docked for saying something like, "The shape of the data set is normal." *No data set is exactly normal.* Save the phrase "approximately normal" for sampling distributions (CLT, remember?).
6. Remember that a correlation does not necessarily imply a causal relationship between two variables. Conversely, the absence of a strong correlation does not mean there is no relationship (it might not be linear).
7. Be able to use a residual plot to help determine if a linear model for a data set is appropriate. Be able to explain your reasoning.
8. Recognize that the correlation coefficient (r) measures the strength and direction of a relation we have reason to believe is linear. The correlation coefficient does NOT tell us that the linear model is an appropriate model.
9. Be able to interpret, in context, the slope and y-intercept of a least-squares regression line. Be sure to include "predicted" or "tends to" in your descriptions of slope and y-intercept.
10. Be able to read computer regression output.
11. Know the definition of a simple random sample (SRS).
12. Know the definition of, and reasons for, choosing to do a stratified random sample instead of a simple random sample.
13. Be able to design an experiment using a completely randomized design. Understand that an experiment that utilizes blocking cannot, by definition, be a *completely* randomized design.
14. Explain the difference between the purposes of randomization and blocking.
15. Be able to describe what blinding and confounding variables are.
16. Clearly describe how to create a simulation for a probability problem.
17. Be clear on the distinction between independent events and mutually exclusive events (and why mutually exclusive events can't be independent).
18. Be able to find the mean and standard deviation of a discrete random variable, especially for binomial and geometric situations (the formulas on the formula sheet).
19. Recognize binomial and geometric situations.
20. Never forget that hypotheses are *always* about parameters, *never* about statistics.

21. Any hypothesis testing procedure involves four steps. Know what they are and that they must always be there. And never forget that your conclusion in context (Step 4) must be linked to your calculations (Step 3) in some way.

22. When doing inference problems, remember that you must *show* that the conditions for the inference procedure are present. It is not sufficient to simply *declare* them present. Realize that you are often not instructed to check the conditions in the question but you must do so anyway.

23. Be clear on the concepts of Type I and Type II errors and the power of a test.

24. If you are required to construct a confidence interval, remember that there are three things you must do to receive full credit: justify that the conditions necessary to construct the interval are present, construct the interval, and interpret the interval in context. You'll need to remember this, because often the only instruction you will see is to construct the interval.

25. If you include graphs as part of your solution, *be sure that axes are labeled and that scales are clearly indicated*. This is part of communication.

STEP 4

Review the Knowledge You Need to Score High

One-Variable Data Analysis

IN THIS CHAPTER

Summary: We begin our study of statistics by considering distributions of data collected on a single variable. This descriptive aspect of statistics is often referred to as *exploratory data analysis* (EDA). "Seeing" the data can often help us understand it, and to that end, we will look at a variety of plots that display or summarize the data and allow us to describe the first important characteristic of a distribution, its **shape**. Following that, we will consider a range of numerical measures for **center** and **spread** (variability) that help complete our description of the distribution. We will learn to describe distributions in terms of these three characteristics: **shape**, **center**, and **spread**, and always **in context**. We will consider ways to describe the dataset itself as an object, as well as ways to describe individual cases within the dataset. A very important model for many distributions, the normal distribution, is considered in some detail.

Key Ideas

✪ Shape of a Distribution
✪ Types of Plots
✪ Measures of Center
✪ Measures of Spread
✪ Five-Number Summary
✪ *z*-Score
✪ Density Curves
✪ Normal Distribution
✪ The 68-95-99.7 Rule

Descriptive Versus Inferential Statistics

Descriptive statistics, often referred to as **exploratory data analysis** (EDA), is concerned with only the data at hand and the story being told by them. **Inferential statistics** involves using our data to make a stronger statement. We want to say something about the population the data come from or that a treatment causes a certain effect. We will begin with descriptive statistics, and we will discuss inferential statistics in later chapters.

Parameters Versus Statistics

Values that describe a sample are called **statistics**, and values that describe a population or population model are called **parameters**. In inferential statistics, we use statistics to estimate parameters. For example, if we draw a sample of 35 students from a large university and compute their mean GPA (that is, the grade point average, usually on a 4-point scale, for each student), we have a statistic. We might want to estimate the mean GPA for *all* students in the university, which is the *parameter*.

Quantitative Versus Categorical (Qualitative) Data

Quantitative data or **numerical data** are measures or counts. They tell us "how much" or "how many."

Categorical data or **qualitative data** are data that can be classified into a group based on a non-quantitative characteristic.

Examples of Quantitative (Numerical) Data: the heights of students in an AP Statistics class; the speeds of cars on a busy expressway; the scores on a final exam; the concentration of lead in the water in each house in a city; the daily temperatures in Death Valley; the number of people jailed for marijuana possession in each jurisdiction.

Examples of Categorical (Qualitative) Data: gender; political party preference; eye color; ethnicity; level of education; socioeconomic level; zip codes. (Even though they are numbers, these just indicate a location.)

There are times that the distinction between quantitative and categorical data is somewhat less clear than in the previous examples. For example, we could view the variable "grade in school" as a categorical variable because it groups people into categories. "Students in grade nine are meeting with guidance counselors today to discuss college options." On the other hand, "grade in school" could be seen as a measure of how many years of education a student has had. In such cases we need to consider how the variable is being used to determine whether we consider it quantitative or categorical.

Discrete and Continuous Variables

Quantitative variables can be either **discrete** or **continuous**. **Discrete variables** take on values with gaps between. Counts, for example, are discrete variables. **Continuous variables** take on any value in an interval. The number of heads we can get on 20 flips of a coin is discrete; the time of day is continuous. The distinction becomes important when we consider the difference between our *data*, which are always discrete (even heights are measured to the nearest inch or centimeter), and *models*, which may be continuous.

If you are given an instruction to "describe" a set of quantitative data, be sure you discuss the *shape* of the data (including gaps and clusters in the data), the *center* of the data (mean, median, mode), and the *spread* of the data (range, interquartile range, standard deviation). And be sure to do all of this *in context*. That means mentioning the cases and variable and units, if there are any.

Graphical Analysis

Our purpose in drawing a graph of data is to get a visual sense of it. We are interested in the **shape** of the data as well as **gaps** in the data, **clusters** of datapoints, and **outliers** (datapoints that lie well outside of the general pattern of the data).

Shape

When we describe **shape**, what we are primarily interested in is the extent to which the graph appears to be **symmetric** (has symmetry around some axis), **mound-shaped** (**bell-shaped**), **skewed** (data are skewed to the left if the tail is to the left; to the right if the tail is to the right), **bimodal** (has more than one location with many scores), or **uniform** (frequencies of the various values are more or less constant).

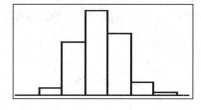

This graph could be described as roughly *symmetric* and *mound-shaped*. Note that it doesn't have to be *perfectly* symmetrical to be classified as symmetric.

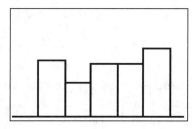

This graph is of a *uniform* distribution. Again, it does not have to be perfectly uniform to be described as *uniform*.

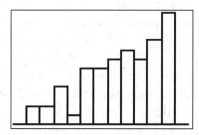

This distribution is **skewed left** because the tail is to the left. If the tail were to the right, the graph would be described at **skewed right**. Note—you might also describe a distribution as **positively skewed** when it is skewed right and **negatively skewed** when the distribution is skewed left.

There are three types of graphs that may help us understand the shape of a distribution: dotplot, stemplot, and histogram. The following 31 scores from a 50-point quiz given to a community college statistics class illustrate these three plots:

28	38	42	33	29	28	41	40	15	36	27	34	22
23	28	50	42	46	28	27	43	29	50	29	32	34
27	26	27	41	18								

Dotplot

A **dotplot** is a very simple type of graph that involves plotting the data values, with dots, above the corresponding values on a number line. A dotplot of the scores on the statistics quiz, drawn by a statistics computer package, looks like this:

[Calculator note: Most calculators do *not* have a built-in function for drawing dotplots. There are online apps that will do so, but you should just get used to drawing one by hand.]

Stemplot (Stem-and-Leaf Plot)

A stemplot is a bit more complicated than a dotplot. Each data value has a *stem* and a *leaf*. There are no mathematical rules for what constitutes the *stem* and what constitutes the *leaf*. Rather, the nature of the data will suggest reasonable choices for the stem and leaves. With the given score data, we might choose the first digit to be the *stem* and the second digit to be the *leaf*. So, the number 42 in a stem and leaf plot would show up as 4 | 2. All the leaves for a common stem are often on the same line. Software typically lists the values ... in increasing order, so the line with stem 4 could be written as 4 | 0112236, although when we make these graphs by hand, we usually don't worry about this. The complete stemplot of the quiz data looks like this:

Score

1	58
2	23677778888999
3	234468
4	0112236
5	00

3 | 5 means 35

Using the 10s digit for the stem and the units digit for the leaf made good sense with this dataset; other choices make sense depending on the type of data. For example, suppose we had a set of gas mileage tests on a particular car (e.g., 28.3, 27.5, 28.1, . . .). In this case, it might make sense to make the stems the integer part of the number and the leaf the decimal part. As another example, consider measurements on a microscopic computer part (0.0018, 0.0023, 0.0021, . . .). Here you'd probably want to ignore the 0.00 (since that doesn't help distinguish between the values) and use the first nonzero digit as the stem and the second nonzero digit as the leaf.

Some data lend themselves to breaking the stem into two or more parts. (Some authors refer to this as *splitting the stems*.) For the statistics quiz data, the stem "4" could be shown with leaves broken up 0–4 and 5–9. Done this way, the stemplot for the scores data would look like this (there is a single "1" because there are no leaves with the values 0–4 for a stem of 1; similarly, there is only one "5" since there are no values in the 55–59 range):

Score

1	58
2	23
2	677778888999
3	2344
3	68
4	011223
4	6
5	00

3 | 5 means 35

The visual image is of data that are slightly skewed to the right (that is, toward the higher scores). We do notice a *cluster* of scores in the high 20s that was not obvious when we used an increment of 10 rather than 5. There is no hard-and-fast rule about how to break up the stems—it's easy to try different arrangements on most computer packages.

Sometimes plotting more than one stemplot, side by side or back to back, can provide us with comparative information. The following stemplot shows the results of two quizzes given for the community college statistics class (one of the quizzes is described on the previous page):

Stem-and-Leaf of Scores 1   **Stem-and-Leaf of Scores 2**

       1 | 33   1 | 58
       2 | 0567799   2 | 23677778888999
       3 | 1125   3 | 234468
       4 | 0235778889999   4 | 0112236
       5 | 00000   5 | 00   KEY: 5 | 0 = score of 50

Or, as a back-to-back stemplot:

            Quiz 1   Quiz 2

               33 | 1 | 58
          9977650 | 2 | 23677778888999
             5211 | 3 | 234468
    999888775320 | 4 | 0112236
            00000 | 5 | 00

It can be seen from this comparison that the scores on Quiz 1 (on the left) were generally higher than for those on Quiz 2—the center of Quiz 1 scores is higher than the center of Quiz 2 scores. Both distributions are reasonably symmetric. The spreads of the two distributions appear to be similar.

[Note: Most calculators do not have a built-in function for drawing stemplots. However, some computer programs do have this ability, and it's quite easy to experiment with various stem increments.]

Histograms and Bar Charts

A **bar chart** is used to illustrate *categorical data*, and a **histogram** is used to illustrate *quantitative data*. The horizontal axis in a *bar chart* contains the categories, and the vertical axis contains the frequencies, or relative frequencies, of each category. The horizontal axis in a *histogram* contains numerical values, and the vertical axis contains the frequencies, or relative frequencies, of the values (often intervals of values). In a bar chart, there is a space between the bars. (It bears repeating that we address the center, shape, and spread for quantitative data only.)

example: A teacher asked his 25 students which social media platform they use the most. Their choices are displayed in the bar chart below:

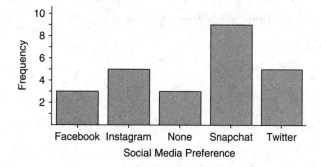

A *histogram* divides the number line into intervals (bins) of equal width. A bar is constructed on each interval, and the height of the bar is the number of cases in that interval. By convention, a value that lies on the boundary between two intervals is included in the interval to the right. So the interval from 25 to 35 contains 25 but not 35.

Consider again the quiz scores we looked at when we discussed dotplots:

28	38	42	33	29	28	41	40	15	36	27	34	22
23	28	50	42	46	28	27	43	29	50	29	32	34
27	26	27	41	18

Because the data are integral and range from 15 to 50, reasonable intervals might be of size 10 or of size 5. The graphs below show what happens with the two choices:

Typically, the interval from 15 to 20 would have class boundaries $15 \leq x < 20$; the interval from 20 to 25 would have class boundaries $20 \leq x < 25$, etc. Notice that a score of 20 would be in the second of those two intervals.

There are no hard-and-fast rules for how wide to make the bars (called "class intervals" or "bins"). You should use computer or calculator software to help you find a picture to which your eye reacts. In this case, intervals of size 5 give us a better sense of the data.

Calculator Tip: When you are specifically asked to draw a graph for a set of data, you should do so without the aid of a calculator. Typing in the raw data is time-consuming and has the potential for entry error. So don't risk it—just neatly draw, label, and scale an appropriate graph.

example: For the histogram below, identify the boundaries for the class intervals.

solution: The midpoints of the intervals begin at 15 and go by increments of 5. So the boundaries of each interval are 2.5 above and below the midpoints. Hence, the boundaries for the class intervals are 12.5, 17.5, 22.5, 27.5, 32.5, 37.5, 42.5, 47.5, and 52.5.

example: For the histogram given in the previous example, what proportion of the scores are less than 27.5?

solution: From the graph we see that there is 1 observation in the first bar, 2 in the second, 6 in the third, etc., for a total of 31 all together. Of these, $1 + 2 + 6 = 9$ are less than 27.5. $9/31 = 0.29$.

example: The heights of 100 college age women are displayed in a stem-and-leaf plot and a histogram. Describe the distribution.

Height

This stem-and-leaf plot breaks the heights into increments of 2 inches:

```
5 | 9
6 | 00001111
6 | 22222333333333333333
6 | 444444444555555555555555555
6 | 6666666666666666666677777777777777
6 | 8888888999
7 | 00                    KEY: 6|2 = 62 inches
7 | 2
```

solution: Both the stem-and-leaf plot and the histogram show symmetric, bell-shaped distributions. The graph is symmetric and centered about 66 inches. In the histogram, the boundaries of the bars are $59 \le x < 61$, $61 \le x < 63$, $63 \le x < 65, \ldots, 71 \le x < 73$. Note that for each interval, the lower bound is contained in the interval, while the upper bound is part of the next larger interval. Also note that the stem-and-leaf plot and the histogram convey the same visual image for the *shape* of the data.

Measures of Center

In the last example of the previous section, we said that the graph appeared to be *centered* at about a height of 66″. In this section, we talk about ways to describe the *center* of a distribution. There are two primary measures of center: the **mean** and the **median**. There is a third measure, the **mode**, but it tells where the most frequent values occur, which may or may not represent the center. In some distributions, the mean, median, and mode will be close in value, but the mode can appear at any point in the distribution, and sometimes there is more than one mode.

Mean

Let x_i represent any value in a set of n values ($i = 1, 2, \ldots, n$). The **mean** of the set is defined as the sum of the x's divided by n. Symbolically, $\bar{x} = \dfrac{\sum x}{n}$. Because the indices on the summation are almost always 1 to n, they are usually omitted. $\sum x$ means "the sum of x" and is defined as follows: $\sum x = x_1 + x_2 + \ldots + x_n$. Think of it as the "add-'em-up" symbol to help remember its definition. $\bar{x}$ is used for the mean of a sample ($\bar{x}$ is a *statistic*). For a population or a theoretical model (such as in Chapters 8 and 9), the mean is a *parameter* symbolized by the Greek letter μ.

(*Note:* In the previous chapter, we made a distinction between *statistics*, which are values that describe sample data, and *parameters*, which are values that describe populations. Unless we are clear that we have access to an entire population or that we are discussing a theoretical model, we use the statistics rather than parameters.)

example: During his major league career, Babe Ruth hit the following number of home runs (1914–1935): 0, 4, 3, 2, 11, 29, 54, 59, 35, 41, 46, 25, 47, 60, 54, 46, 49, 46, 41, 34, 22, 6. What was the *mean* number of home runs per year for his major league career?

$$\text{Solution: } \bar{x} = \frac{\Sigma x}{n} = \frac{0+4+3+2+\cdots+22+6}{22}$$
$$= \frac{714}{22} = 32.45$$

Calculator Tip: While each brand of graphing calculator allows you to type raw data into a list and activate a function that will return statistics such as the mean, it is unlikely that an AP test question would require you to use such a function. Very often, those summary statistics are provided for you.

Median

The **median** of a distribution is the value that cuts the dataset in half. At least 50% of the dataset values are greater than or equal to the median and at least 50% are less than or equal to the median. If the dataset has an odd number of values, the *median* is a member of the set and is the middle value. If there are 3 values, the median is the second value. If there are 5, it is the third, and so on. If the dataset has an even number of values, the median is the mean of the two middle numbers. If there are 4 values, the median is the mean of the second and third values. In general, if there are n values in the ordered dataset, the median is at the $\frac{n+1}{2}$ position. If you have 28 terms in order, you will find the median at position $\frac{28+1}{2} = 14.5$ (that is, between the 14th and 15th terms). Be careful not to interpret $\frac{n+1}{2}$ as the value of the median rather than as the location of the median.

example: Consider once again the data in the previous example from Babe Ruth's career. What was the median number of home runs per year he hit during his major league career?

solution: First, put the numbers in order from smallest to largest: 0, 2, 3, 4, 6, 11, 22, 25, 29, 34, 35, 41, 41, 46, 46, 46, 47, 49, 54, 54, 59, 60. There are 22 scores, so the *median* is found at the 11.5th position, between the 11th and 12th scores (35 and 41). So the *median* is

$$\frac{35+41}{2} = 38.$$

Resistant

Although the mean and the median are both measures of center, the choice of which to use depends on the shape of the distribution. If the distribution is symmetric and mound-shaped, the mean and the median will be close. However, if the distribution has outliers or is strongly skewed, the median is probably the better choice to describe the center. This is because the median is a **resistant statistic,** one whose numerical value is not dramatically influenced by extreme values. By comparison, the mean is not resistant.

> **example:** A group of five teachers in a small school have salaries of $32,700, $32,700, $38,500, $41,600, and $44,500. The mean and the median salaries for these teachers are $38,160 and $38,500, respectively. Suppose the highest paid teacher gets sick, and the school superintendent volunteers to substitute for her. The superintendent's salary is $174,300. If you replace the $44,500 salary with the $174,300 one, the median doesn't change at all (it's still $38,500), but the new mean is $64,120—almost everybody is below average if, by "average," you mean *mean*.

> **example:** For the graph given below, would you expect the mean or the median to be larger? Why?

> **solution:** You would expect the median to be larger than the mean. Because the graph is skewed to the left, and the mean is not resistant, you would expect the mean to be pulled to the left (in fact, the dataset from which this graph was drawn from has a mean of 5.4 and a median of 6, as expected, given the skewness).

Estimating Medians from Grouped Data

If you are given data in the form of a histogram or frequency table in which intervals contain more than one value, you cannot calculate the median, mean, or quartiles precisely. But you can estimate them using reasonable techniques.

example: Noor and Jacob were collecting data for a statistics class. They used a precise scale borrowed from the science department and weighed 100 U.S. pennies. They did not provide the raw data, but these are summarized in a frequency table and a histogram. Estimate the median weight of their sample of pennies.

WEIGHT INTERVAL	FREQUENCY
$2.98 \le x < 3.02$	1
$3.02 \le x < 3.06$	14
$3.06 \le x < 3.10$	29
$3.10 \le x < 3.14$	26
$3.14 \le x < 3.18$	21
$3.18 \le x < 3.22$	7
$3.22 \le x < 2.26$	2

solution: To estimate the median, we recognize that we are looking for the penny in position $\frac{(100+1)}{2}$ = 50.5, or between the 50th and 51st pennies. We need to keep track of the cumulative frequency, the number of pennies that weigh a certain amount or less. You can add a column to the frequency table.

WEIGHT INTERVAL	FREQUENCY	CUMULATIVE FREQUENCY
$2.98 \leq x < 3.02$	1	1
$3.02 \leq x < 3.06$	14	15
$3.06 \leq x < 3.10$	29	44
$3.10 \leq x < 3.14$	26	70
$3.14 \leq x < 3.18$	21	91
$3.18 \leq x < 3.22$	7	98
$3.22 \leq x < 2.26$	2	100

The cumulative frequency of 44 in the third row means that 44 pennies weigh less than 3.10 grams. 29 + 14 + 1 = 44. We know the median is between the 50th and 51st pennies, so that is in the interval $3.10 \leq x < 3.14$. The median is between 3.10 and 3.14 grams. Our estimate could be anywhere in this interval.

You would use a similar technique to estimate the median of the lower half of the data, also known as the first quartile. Since there are 100 pennies, the first quartile is between the 25th and 26th penny in an ordered list. This penny lives somewhere in the interval $3.06 \leq x < 3.10$.

Measures of Spread (Variability)

Simply knowing the center of a distribution doesn't tell you all you might want to know about the distribution. One group of 20 people earning $20,000 each will have the same mean and median as a group of 20 in which 10 people earn $10,000 and 10 people earn $30,000. These two sets of 20 values differ not in terms of center but in terms of spread, or variability. Just as there are measures of center based on the mean and the median, we also have measures of spread based on the mean and the median.

Variance and Standard Deviation

One measure of spread based on the mean is the **variance**. By definition, the variance is the average squared deviation from the mean. That is, it is a measure of spread because the more distant a value is from the mean, the larger will be the square of the difference between it and the mean.

Symbolically, the variance is defined by

$$s^2 = \frac{1}{n-1}\sum(x_i - \bar{x})^2.$$

Note that we average by dividing by $n - 1$ rather than n as you might expect. This is because there are only $n - 1$ independent datapoints, not n, if you know $\bar{x}$. That is, if you know $n - 1$ of the values and you also know $\bar{x}$, then the nth datapoint is determined.

One problem using the variance as a measure of spread is that the units for the variance won't match the units of the original data because each difference is squared. For example, if you find the variance of a set of measurements made in inches, the variance will be in square inches. To correct this, we often take the square root of the variance as our measure of spread.

The square root of the variance is known as the **standard deviation**. Symbolically,

$$s = \sqrt{\frac{1}{n-1}\Sigma(x-\overline{x})^2}.$$

It is more important to understand the formula and what standard deviation measures than to be able to calculate a standard deviation by hand.

Calculator Tip: If you do use the shortcut for summary statistics on the calculator (such as `1-Var Stats` on a TI-83/84), the calculator will, in addition to Sx, return σ_x, which is the standard deviation of a distribution. Its formal definition is $\sigma = \sqrt{\frac{1}{n}\sum(x-\mu)^2}$. Note that this assumes you know μ, the population mean, which you rarely do in practice unless you are dealing with a probability distribution (see Chapter 8). Most of the time in statistics, you are dealing with sample data and not a distribution. Thus, with the exception of the type of probability material found in Chapters 8 and 9, you should use *only s* and not σ.

The definition of *standard deviation* has three useful qualities when it comes to describing the spread (variablity) of a distribution:

- *It is independent of the mean.* Because the standard deviation depends on how far datapoints are from the mean, the actual location of the mean itself is irrelevant.
- *It measures the spread.* The greater the spread, the larger will be the standard deviation. For two datasets with the same mean, the one with the larger standard deviation has more variability.
- *It is independent of n.* Because we are *averaging* squared distances from the mean, the standard deviation will not get larger simply because we add more terms. (The standard deviation *will* get larger if the terms we add are farther from the mean than the current typical distance.)

example: Find the standard deviation of the following 6 numbers: 3, 4, 6, 6, 7, 10.

solution: $\overline{x} = 6 \Rightarrow s = \sqrt{\dfrac{(3-6)^2 + (4-6)^2 + (6-6)^2 + (6-6)^2 + (7-6)^2 + (10-6)^2}{6-1}}$
$= 2.449$

Note that the standard deviation, like the mean, is not *resistant* to extreme values. Because it depends on distances from the mean, it should be clear that extreme values will have a major impact on the numerical value of the standard deviation. Note also that, in practice, you will never have to do the calculation above by hand—you will rely on your calculator or computer software.

Interquartile Range

Although the standard deviation works well in situations where the mean works well (reasonably symmetric distributions), we need a measure of spread that works well when a mean-based measure is not appropriate. That measure is called the **interquartile range**.

Remember that the median of a distribution divides the distribution in two—it is the middle of the distribution. The medians of the upper and lower halves of the distribution, not including the median itself in either half, are called **quartiles**. The median of the lower half is called the **lower quartile**, or the **first quartile** (which is the 25th percentile—**Q1** on the calculator). The median of the upper half is called the **upper quartile**, or the **third quartile** (which is in the 75th percentile—**Q3** on the calculator). The median itself can be thought of as the second quartile or Q2 (although we usually don't).

The **interquartile range (IQR)** is the difference between Q3 and Q1. That is, IQR = Q3 – Q1. When you do `1-Var Stats`, the calculator will return Q1 and Q3 along with a lot of other information. You have to compute the IQR from Q1 and Q3. Note that the IQR comprises the middle 50% of the data.

> **example:** Find Q1, Q3, and the IQR for the following dataset: 5, 5, 6, 7, 8, 9, 11, 13, 17.

> **solution:** Because the data are in order and there is an odd number of values (9), the median is 8. The bottom half of the data comprises 5, 5, 6, 7. The median of the bottom half is the average of 5 and 6, or 5.5, which is Q1. Similarly, Q3 is the median of the top half, which is the mean of 11 and 13, or 12. The IQR = 12 − 5.5 = 6.5.

> **example:** Find the standard deviation and IQR for the number of home runs hit by Babe Ruth in his major league career. The number of home runs was: 0, 4, 3, 2, 11, 29, 54, 59, 35, 41, 46, 25, 47, 60, 54, 46, 49, 46, 41, 34, 22, 6.

> **solution:** Put these numbers into your calculator's list and do `1-Var Stats` on that list. The calculator returns `Sx = 20.21`, `Q1 = 11`, and `Q3 = 47`. Hence, the IQR = Q3 – Q1 = 47 – 11 = 36.

The **range** of the distribution is the difference between the maximum and minimum scores in the distribution. For the home run data, the range equals 60 − 0 = 60. Although this is sometimes used as a measure of spread, it is not very useful because we are usually interested in how the data spread out from the center of the distribution, not in just how far it is from the minimum to the maximum values.

Outliers

We have a pretty good intuitive sense of what an *outlier* is: it's a value far removed from the others. There is no rigorous mathematical formula for determining whether or not something is an outlier, but there are a few conventions that people seem to agree on. Not surprisingly, some of them are based on the mean and some are based on the median!

A commonly agreed-on way to think of outliers based on the mean is to consider how many standard deviations away from the mean a term is. Some texts identify a potential **outlier** as a datapoint that is more than two or three standard deviations from the mean.

In a mound-shaped, symmetric distribution, this is a value that has only about a 5% chance (for two standard deviations) or a 0.3% chance (for three standard deviations) of being as far removed from the center of the distribution as it is. Think of it as a value that is way out in one of the tails of the distribution.

However, most texts now use a median-based measure and identify potential outliers in terms of how far a datapoint is above or below the quartiles in a distribution. To find if a distribution has any outliers, do the following (this is known as the "1.5(IQR) rule"):

- Find the IQR.
- Multiply the IQR by 1.5.
- Find Q1 − 1.5(IQR) and Q3 + 1.5(IQR).
- Any value below Q1 − 1.5(IQR) or above Q3 + 1.5(IQR) is a potential **outlier**.

Some texts call an outlier defined as above a *mild* outlier. An *extreme* outlier would then be one that lies more than 3 IQRs beyond Q1 or Q3.

> **example:** The following data represent the amount of money, in British pounds, spent weekly on tobacco for 11 regions in Britain: 4.03, 3.76, 3.77, 3.34, 3.47, 2.92, 3.20, 2.71, 3.53, 4.51, 4.56. Do any of the regions seem to be spending a lot more or less than the other regions? That is, are there any outliers in the data?

> **solution:** Using a calculator, we find $\bar{x} = 3.62$, $Sx = s = .59$, Q1 = 3.2, Q3 = 4.03.

- Using means: $3.62 \pm 2(0.59) = (2.44, 4.8)$. There are no values in the dataset less than 2.44 or greater than 4.8, so there are no outliers by this method. We don't need to check $\pm 3s$ since there were no outliers using $\pm 2s$.
- Using the 1.5(IQR) rule: Q1 − 1.5(IQR) = 3.2 − 1.5(4.03 − 3.2) = 1.96, Q3 + 1.5(IQR) = 4.03 + 1.5(4.03 − 3.2) = 5.28. Because there are no values in the data less than 1.96 or greater than 5.28, there are no outliers by this method either.

It is important in your work life or research life to investigate outliers. Are they present because your data just happened to contain an unusual value? Did a typographical error occur during data entry? Or is your measuring tool miscalibrated?

Position of a Term in a Distribution

Up until now, we have concentrated on the nature of a distribution as a whole. We have been concerned with the shape, center, and spread of the entire distribution. Now we look briefly at individual cases in the distribution.

Five-Number Summary

There are positions in a dataset that give us valuable information about the dataset. The **five-number summary** of a dataset is composed of the minimum value, the lower quartile, the median, the upper quartile, and the maximum value.

On the TI-83/84, these are reported on the second screen of data when you do `1-Var Stats` as: `minX`, `Q1`, `Med`, `Q3`, and `maxX`.

> **example:** The following data are standard-of-living indices for 20 cities: 2.8, 3.9, 4.6, 5.3, 10.2, 9.8, 7.7, 13, 2.1, 0.3, 9.8, 5.3, 9.8, 2.7, 3.9, 7.7, 7.6, 10.1, 8.4, 8.3. Find the five-number summary for the data.

> **solution:** Put the 20 values into a list on your calculator and do `1-Var Stats`. We find `minX=0.3`, `Q1=3.9`, `Med=7.65`, `Q3=9.8`, and `maxX=13`.

Box-and-Whiskers Plots (Outliers Revisited)

In the first part of this chapter, we discussed three types of graphs: dotplot, stem-and-leaf plot, and histogram. Using the five-number summary, we can add a fourth type of one-variable graph to this group: the **box-and-whiskers plot** (sometimes called a **box-plot**). A box-and-whiskers plot is simply a graphical version of the five-number summary. A box is drawn that contains the middle 50% of the data (from Q1 to Q3) and "whiskers" extend from the lines at the ends of the box (the lower and upper quartiles) to the minimum and maximum values of the data if there are no outliers. If there are outliers, the "whiskers" extend to the last value before the outlier that is *not* an outlier. The outliers themselves are marked with a special symbol, such as a point, a box, or a plus sign.

> **example:** Consider again the standard-of-living indices from the previous example: 2.8, 3.9, 4.6, 5.3, 10.2, 9.8, 7.7, 13, 2.1, 0.3, 9.8, 5.3, 9.8, 2.7, 3.9, 7.7, 7.6, 10.1, 8.4, 8.3. A box-and-whiskers plot of these data look like this (the five-number summary was [0.3, 3.9, 7.65, 9.8, 13]; you would need to add your own horizontal axis and values):

Standard of Living Index

 Calculator Tip: Graphing calculators will display a box-and-whiskers plot. Some allow two types: one that displays outliers based on the $1.5 \times$ IQR rule and one that does not. For AP Statistics, always use the one that displays the outliers.

> **example:** Using the same dataset as the previous example but replacing the 10.2 with 20, which would be an outlier in this dataset (the largest possible non-outlier for these data would be $9.8 + 1.5(9.8 - 3.9) = 18.65$), we get the following graph on the calculator (you would need to add your own horizontal axis and values):

Standard of Living Index

Note that the "whisker" ends at the largest value in the dataset that is **not** an outlier, 13.

Percentile Rank of a Term

The **percentile rank** of a term in a distribution equals the proportion of terms in the distribution less than the term. A term that is *at* the 75th percentile is larger than 75% of the terms in a distribution. If we know the five-number summary for a set of data, then Q1 is at the 25th percentile, the median is at the 50th percentile, and Q3 is at the 75th percentile. Some texts define the percentile rank of a term to be the proportion of terms less than *or equal to* the term. So by this definition, being at the 100th percentile is possible.

z-Scores

One way to identify the position of a term in a distribution is to note how many standard deviations the term is above or below the mean. The statistic that does this is the **z-score:**

$$z_{xi} = \frac{x_i - \overline{x}}{s}.$$

The z-score is positive when x is above the mean and negative when it is below the mean.

example: $z_3 = 1.5$ tells us that the value 3 is 1.5 standard deviations above the mean. $z_3 = -2$ tells us that the value 3 is two standard deviations below the mean.

example: For the first test of the year, Harvey got a 68. The class average (mean) was 73, and the standard deviation was 3. What was Harvey's z-score on this test?

solution: $z_{68} = \dfrac{68 - 73}{3} = -1.67.$

Thus, Harvey was 1.67 standard deviations *below* the mean.

Suppose we have a set of data with mean $\overline{x}$ and standard deviation s. If we subtract $\overline{x}$ from every term in the distribution, it can be shown that the new distribution will have a mean of $\overline{x} - \overline{x} = 0$. If we divide every term by s, then the new distribution will have a standard deviation of $s/s = 1$. Conclusion: If you compute the z-score for every term in a distribution, the distribution of z scores will have a mean of 0 and a standard deviation of 1.

Normal Distribution

We have been discussing characteristics of distributions (shape, center, and spread). Many distributions that have particular interest for us in statistics are roughly symmetric and mound-shaped. The following histogram represents the heights of 100 males whose average height is 70″ and whose standard deviation is 3″.

This is clearly approximately symmetric and mound-shaped. We are going to model these data with a curve that idealizes what we see in this sample of 100. That is, we will model this with a continuous curve that "describes" the shape of the distribution for very large samples. That curve is the graph of the **normal distribution**. A *normal curve*, when superimposed on the earlier histogram, looks like this:

68-95-99.7 Rule

The **68-95-99.7 rule,** or the **empirical rule,** states that *approximately* 68% of the data values in a normal distribution are within one standard deviation of the mean, 95% are within two standard deviations of the mean, and 99.7% are within three standard deviations of the mean. The following three graphs illustrate the 68-95-99.7 rule.

  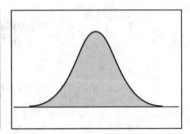

68% within one standard deviation of the mean

95% within two standard deviations of the mean

99.7% within three standard deviations of the mean

Standard Normal Distribution

Because we are dealing with a theoretical distribution, we will use μ and σ, rather than $\bar{x}$ and s, when referring to the normal curve. If X is a variable that has a normal distribution with mean μ and standard deviation σ (we say "X has $N(\mu,\sigma)$"), there is a related distribution we obtain by **standardizing** the data in the distribution to produce the **standard normal distribution**. To do this, we convert the data to a set of z-scores, using the formula

$$z = \frac{x - \mu}{\sigma}.$$

The algebraic effect of this is to produce a distribution of z-scores with mean 0 and standard deviation 1. Computing z-scores is just a linear transformation of the original data, which means that the transformed data will have the same shape as the original distribution. In *this case then*, the distribution of z-scores is normal. We say z has $N(0,1)$.

For the standardized normal curve, the **68-95-99.7 rule** says that approximately 68% of the data points lie between $z = 1$ and $z = -1$, 95% between $z = -2$ and $z = 2$, and 99.7% between $z = -3$ and $z = 3$.

Because many naturally occurring distributions are approximately normal (heights, SAT scores, for example), we are often interested in knowing what proportion of terms lie in a given interval under the normal curve. Problems of this sort can be solved either by use of a calculator or a table of Standard Normal Probabilities (Table A in the appendix to this book). In a typical table, the marginal entries are z-scores, and the table entries are the areas under the curve to the left of a given z-score. All statistics texts have such tables.

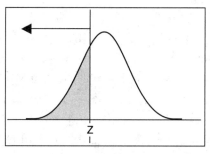

The table entry for z is the area to the left of z and under the curve.

example: What proportion of the area under a normal curve lies to the left of $z = -1.37$?

solution: There are two ways to do this problem, and you should be able to do it either way.

(i) The first way is to use the table of Standard Normal Probabilities. To read the table, move down the left column (titled "z") until you come to the row whose entry is −1.3. The third digit, the 0.07 part, is found by reading across the top row until you come to the column whose entry is 0.07. The entry at the intersection of the row containing −1.3 and the column containing 0.07 is the area under the curve to the left of $z = -1.37$. That value is 0.0853.

(ii) The second way is to use your calculator. It is the more accurate and more efficient way. In the DISTR menu, the second entry is normalcdf (see the next Calculator Tip for a full explanation of the normalpdf and normalcdf functions). The calculator syntax for a standard normal distribution is normalcdf (lower bound, upper bound). In this example, the lower bound can be any large negative number, say, −100. normalcdf(-100,-1.37)=0.0853435081.

Calculator Tip: Part (ii) of the previous example explained how to use normalcdf for standard normal probabilities. The full syntax is normalcdf(lower bound, upper bound, mean, standard deviation). If only the first two parameters are given, the calculator assumes a standard normal distribution (that is, $\mu = 0$ and $\sigma = 1$). The command normalpdf is used to graph a normal curve, but you won't need to worry about using it in this course.

You are almost always interested in the area under the curve and between two points on the number line, so normalcdf is what you will use a lot in this course.

example: What proportion of the area under a normal curve lies between $z = -1.2$ and $z = 0.58$?

solution: (i) Reading from Table A, the area to the left of $z = -1.2$ is 0.1151, and the area to the left of $z = 0.58$ is 0.7190. The geometry of the situation (see below) tells us that the area between the two values is $0.7190 - 0.1151 = 0.6039$.

(ii) Using the calculator, we have `normalcdf(-1.2, 0.58) = 0.603973005`. Round to `0.6040` (difference from the answer in part (i) caused by rounding).

example: In an earlier example, we saw that heights of men are approximately normally distributed with a mean of 70 and a standard deviation of 3. What proportion of men are more than 6′ (72″) tall? Be sure to include a sketch of the situation.

solution: (i) Another way to state this is to ask what proportion of terms in a normal distribution with mean 70 and standard deviation 3 are greater than 72. In order to use the table of Standard Normal Probabilities, we must first convert to z-scores. The z-score corresponding to a height of 72″ is

$$z = \frac{72 - 70}{3} = 0.67.$$

The area to the left of $z = 0.67$ is 0.7486. However, we want the area to the *right* of 0.67, and that is $1 - 0.7486 = 0.2514$.

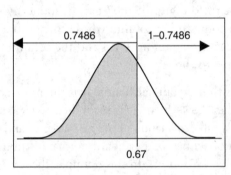

(ii) Using the calculator, we have `normalcdf(0.67,100) = 0.2514`. We could get the answer from the raw data as follows: `normalcdf(72,1000,70,3) = 0.2525`, with the difference being due to rounding. (As explained in the last Calculator Tip, simply add the mean and standard deviation of a nonstandard normal curve to the list of parameters for `normalcdf`.)

example: For the population of men in the previous example, how tall must a man be to be in the top 10% of all men in terms of height?

solution: This type of problem has a standard approach. The idea is to express z_x in two different ways (which are, of course, equal since they are different ways of writing the z-score for the same point): (i) as a numerical value obtained from Table A or from your calculator and (ii) in terms of the definition of a z-score.

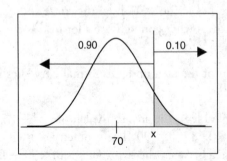

(i) We are looking for the value of x in the drawing. Look at Table A to find the nearest table entry equal to 0.90 (because we know an area, we need to read the table from the inside out to the margins). It is 0.8997 and corresponds to a z-score of 1.28.

So $z_x = 1.28$. But also,

$$z_x = \frac{x-70}{3}.$$

So,

$$z_x = \frac{x-70}{3} = 1.28 \Rightarrow x = 73.84.$$

A man would have to be at least 73.84″ tall to be in the top 10% of all men.

(ii) Using the calculator, the z-score corresponding to an area of 90% to the left of x is given by `invNorm(0.90)` = 1.28. Otherwise, the solution is the same as is given in part (i). See the following Calculator Tip for a full explanation of the `invNorm` function.

Calculator Tip: `invNorm` essentially reverses `normalcdf`. That is, rather than reading from the margins in, it reads from the table out (as in the previous example). `invNorm(A)` returns the z-score that corresponds to an area equal to A lying to the left of z. `invNorm(A, μ, σ)` returns the value of x that has area A to the left of x if x has $N(μ, σ)$.

Math Background

The function that yields the *normal curve* is defined *completely* in terms of its mean and standard deviation. Although you are not required to know it, you might be interested to see that the function that defines the normal curve is

$$f(x) = \frac{1}{\sigma\sqrt{2\pi}} e^{-\frac{1}{2}\left(\frac{x-\mu}{\sigma}\right)^2}.$$

One consequence of this definition is that the total area under the curve, and above the

x-axis, is 1 (for you calculus students, this is because $\int_{-\infty}^{\infty} \frac{1}{\sigma\sqrt{2\pi}} e^{-\frac{1}{2}\left(\frac{x-\mu}{\sigma}\right)^2} dx = 1$).

This fact will be of great use to us later when we consider areas under the normal curve as probabilities.

(**Trivia for calculus students:** one standard deviation from the mean is a *point of inflection*.)

› Rapid Review

1. Describe the *shape* of the histogram below:

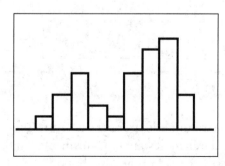

Answer: Bimodal, somewhat skewed to the left.

2. For the graph of problem 1, would you expect the mean to be larger than the median or the median to be larger than the mean? Why?

   Answer: It is difficult to predict. The general guideline that the mean is lower than the median for distributions that are skewed left applies to smooth unimodal distributions. Bimodal distributions don't necessarily follow that pattern.

3. The first quartile (Q1) of a dataset is 12, and the third quartile (Q3) is 18. What is the largest value above Q3 in the dataset that would not be a potential outlier?

   Answer: Outliers lie more than 1.5 IQRs below Q1 or above Q3. Q3 + 1.5(IQR) = 18 + 1.5(18 − 12) = 27. Any value greater than 27 would be an outlier; 27 is the largest value that would not be a potential outlier.

4. A distribution of quiz scores has $\bar{x} = 35$ and $s = 4$. Sara got 40 points on the quiz. What was the associated z-score? What information does that give you if the distribution is approximately normal?

   Answer:

   $$z = \frac{40 - 35}{4} = 1.25.$$

   This means that Sara's score was 1.25 standard deviations above the mean, which puts it at the 89.4th percentile (`normalcdf(-100,1.25)`).

5. In a normal distribution with mean 25 and standard deviation 7, what proportion of terms are less than 20?

   Answer: $z_{20} = \dfrac{20 - 25}{7} = -0.71 \Rightarrow$ Area = 0.2389.

   (By calculator: `normalcdf(-100,20,25,7)=0.2375`.)

6. What are the mean, median, mode, and standard deviation of a *standard normal curve*?

   Answer: Mean = median = mode = 0. Standard deviation = 1.

7. Find the five-number summary and draw the box-and-whiskers plot for the following set of data: 12, 13, 13, 14, 16, 17, 20, 28.

   Answer: The five-number summary is [12, 13, 15, 18.5, 28], and 28 is an outlier (anything larger than 18.5 + 1.5(18.5 − 13) = 26.75 is an outlier by the 1.5(IQR) rule). Since 20 is the largest nonoutlier in the dataset, it is the end of the upper whisker, as shown in the following diagram:

8. A distribution is strongly skewed to the right. Would you prefer to use the mean and the standard deviation or the median and the interquartile range to describe the center and the spread of the distribution?

   Answer: Because the mean is not resistant and is pulled toward the tail of the skewed distribution, you would prefer to use the median and the IQR.

Practice Problems

Multiple-Choice

1. The following list is ordered from smallest to largest: 25, 26, 26, 30, y, y, y, 33, 150. Which of the following statements is (are) true?

    I. The mean is greater than the median.
    II. The mode is 26.
    III. There are no outliers in the data.
        a. I only
        b. I and II only
        c. III only
        d. I and III only
        e. II and III only

2. Megan wonders how the size of her beagle Herbie compares with other beagles. Herbie is 40.6 cm tall. Megan learned on the internet that beagle heights are approximately normally distributed with a mean of 38.5 cm and a standard deviation of 1.25 cm. What is the percentile rank of Herbie's height?

    a. 59
    b. 65
    c. 74
    d. 92
    e. 95

3. The mean and the standard deviation of a normally distributed dataset are 19 and 4, respectively. The value 19 is subtracted from every term in the dataset, and then the result is divided by 4. Which of the following *best* describes the resulting distribution?

    a. It has a mean of 0 and a standard deviation of 1.
    b. It has a mean of 0, a standard deviation of 4, and its shape is normal.
    c. It has a mean of 1 and a standard deviation of 0.
    d. It has a mean of 0, a standard deviation of 1, and its shape is normal.
    e. It has a mean of 0, a standard deviation of 4, and its shape is unknown.

4. The five-number summary for a one-variable dataset is {5, 18, 20, 40, 75}. If you wanted to construct a box-and-whiskers plot for the dataset, what would be the maximum possible length of the right-side "whisker"?

    a. 35
    b. 33
    c. 5
    d. 55
    e. 53

5. A set of 5,000 scores on a college readiness exam are known to be approximately normally distributed with a mean of 72 and a standard deviation of 6. To the nearest integer value, approximately how many scores are between 63 and 75?

    a. 0.6247
    b. 4,115
    c. 3,650
    d. 3,123
    e. 3,227

6. For the data described in problem 5, which score is closest to the 63rd percentile?

   a. 45
   b. 63
   c. 72
   d. 74
   e. 81

7. The following histogram shows the number of students who visited the Career Center each week during the school year.

   The shape of this graph could best be described as

   a. mound-shaped and symmetric.
   b. bimodal.
   c. skewed to the left.
   d. uniform.
   e. skewed to the right.

8. Which of the following statements is (are) true?
   I. The median is resistant to extreme values.
   II. The mean is resistant to extreme values.
   III. The standard deviation is resistant to extreme values.
      a. I only
      b. II only
      c. III only
      d. II and III only
      e. I and III only

9. One of the values in a normal distribution is 43, and its z-score is 1.65. If the mean of the distribution is 40, what is the standard deviation of the distribution?
   a. 3
   b. −1.82
   c. 0.55
   d. 1.82
   e. −0.55

10. Free-response questions on the AP Statistics Exam are graded 4, 3, 2, 1, or 0. Question 2 on the exam was of moderate difficulty. The average score on question 2 was 2.05 with a standard deviation of 1. To the nearest tenth, what score was achieved by a student who was at the 90th percentile of all students on the test? You may assume that the scores on the question were approximately normally distributed.

a. 3.5
b. 3.3
c. 2.9
d. 3.7
e. 3.1

Free-Response

1. Mickey Mantle played with the New York Yankees from 1951 through 1968. He had the following number of home runs for those years: 13, 23, 21, 27, 37, 52, 34, 42, 31, 40, 54, 30, 15, 35, 19, 23, 22, 18. Were any of these years outliers? Explain.

2. Which of the following are properties of the normal distribution? Explain your answers.

   a. It has a mean of 0 and a standard deviation of 1.
   b. Its mean = median = mode.
   c. All terms in the distribution lie within four standard deviations of the mean.
   d. It is bell-shaped.
   e. The total area under the curve and above the horizontal axis is 1.

3. Make a stem-and-leaf plot for the number of home runs hit by Mickey Mantle during his career (from question 1, the numbers are 13, 23, 21, 27, 37, 52, 34, 42, 31, 40, 54, 30, 15, 35, 19, 23, 22, 18). Do it first using an increment of 10, then do it again using an increment of 5. What can you see in the second graph that was not obvious in the first?

4. A group of 15 students were identified as needing supplemental help in basic arithmetic skills. Two of the students were put through a pilot program and achieved scores of 84 and 89 on a test of basic skills after the program was finished. The other 13 students received scores of 66, 82, 76, 79, 72, 98, 75, 80, 76, 55, 77, 68, and 69. Find the z-scores for the students in the pilot program and comment on the success of the program.

5. For the 15 students whose scores were given in question 4, find the five-number summary and construct a boxplot of the data. What are the distinguishing features of the graph?

6. Assuming that the batting averages in Major League Baseball over the years have been approximately normally distributed with a mean of 0.265 and a standard deviation of 0.032, what would be the percentile rank of a player who bats 0.346 (as Mookie Betts did in the 2018 season)?

7. In problem 1, we considered the home runs hit by Mickey Mantle during his career. The following is a stem-and-leaf plot of the number of doubles hit by Mantle during his career. What is the interquartile range (IQR) of this data? (Hint: $n = 18$.)

1	0	8
5	1	1224
(5)	1	56777
8	2	1234
4	2	558
1	3	
1	3	7

Note: The column of numbers to the left of the stemplot gives the cumulative frequencies from each end of the stemplot (e.g., there are 5 values, reading from the top, when you finish the second row). The (5) identifies the location of the row that contains the median of the distribution. It is standard for computer packages to draw stemplots in this manner.

8. For the histogram pictured below, what proportion of the terms are less than 3.5?

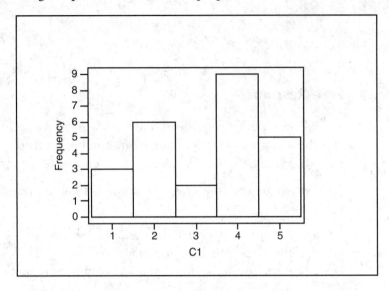

9. The following graph shows boxplots for the number of career home runs for Hank Aaron and Barry Bonds. Comment on the graphs. Which player would you rather have on your team *most* seasons? A season in which you needed a *lot* of home runs?

10. Suppose that being in the top 20% of people with high blood cholesterol level is considered dangerous. Assume that cholesterol levels are approximately normally distributed with mean 185 and standard deviation 25. What is the maximum cholesterol level you can have and not be in the top 20%?

11. The following are the salaries, in millions of dollars, for members of the 2001–2002 Golden State Warriors: 6.2, 5.4, 5.4, 4.9, 4.4, 4.4, 3.4, 3.3, 3.0, 2.4, 2.3, 1.3, 0.3, 0.3. Which gives a better "picture" of these salaries, mean-based or median-based statistics? Explain.

12. The following table gives the results of an experiment in which the ages of 525 pennies from current change were recorded. "0" represents the current year, "1" represents pennies one year old, etc.

Age	0	1	2	3	4	5	6	7	8	9	10	11
Count	163	87	52	75	44	24	36	14	11	5	12	2

Describe the distribution of ages of pennies (remember that the instruction "describe" means to discuss center, spread, and shape). Justify your answer.

13. The mean of a set of 150 values is 35, its median is 33, its standard deviation is 6, and its IQR is 12. A new set is created by first subtracting 10 from every term and then multiplying by 5. What are the mean, median, variance, standard deviation, and IQR of the new set?

14. The following graph shows the distribution of the heights of 300 women whose average height is 65″ and whose standard deviation is 2.5″. Assume that the heights of women are approximately normally distributed. How many of the women would you expect to be less than 5′2″ tall?

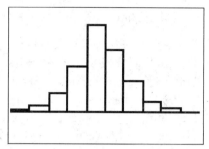

15. Which of the following are properties of the *standard deviation*? Explain your answer.

   a. It's the square root of the average squared deviation from the mean.
   b. It's resistant to extreme values.
   c. It's independent of the number of terms in the distribution.
   d. If you added 25 to every value in the dataset, the standard deviation wouldn't change.
   e. The interval $\bar{x} \pm 2s$ contains 50% of the data in the distribution.

16. Look again at the salaries of the Golden State Warriors in problem 11 (in millions, 6.2, 5.4, 5.4, 4.9, 4.4, 4.4, 3.4, 3.3, 3.0, 2.4, 2.3, 1.3, 0.3, 0.3). Erick Dampier was the highest-paid player at $6.2 million. What sort of raise would he need so that his salary would be an *outlier* among these salaries?

17. Given the histogram below, draw, as best you can, the box-and-whiskers plot for the same data.

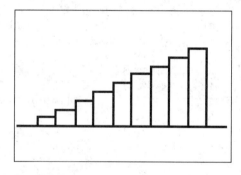

18. On the first test of the semester, the class average was 72 with a standard deviation of 6. On the second test, the class average was 65 with a standard deviation of 8. Nathan scored 80 on the first test and 76 on the second. Compared to the rest of the class, on which test did Nathan do better?

19. What is the mean of a set of data where $s = 20$, $\Sigma x = 245$, and $\Sigma(x - \bar{x})^2 = 13,600$?

Cumulative Review Problems

1. Which of the following are examples of quantitative data?

   a. The number of years each of your teachers has taught
   b. Classifying a statistic as quantitative or categorical

c. The length of time spent by the typical teenager watching television in a month
d. The daily amount of money lost by the airlines in the 15 months after the 9/11 attacks
e. The colors of the rainbow

2. Which of the following are *discrete* and which are *continuous*?

a. The weights of a sample of dieters from a weight-loss program
b. The SAT scores for students who have taken the test over the past 10 years
c. The AP Statistics exam scores for the almost 50,000 students who took the exam in 2009
d. The number of square miles in each of the 20 largest states
e. The distance between any two points on the number line

3. Just exactly what is *statistics*, and what are its two main divisions?

4. What are the main differences between the goals of a *survey* and an *experiment*?

5. Why do we need to understand the concept of a *random variable* in order to do inferential statistics?

Solutions to Practice Problems

Multiple-Choice

1. The correct answer is (a). I is correct since the mean is pulled in the direction of the large maximum value, 150 (well, large compared to the rest of the numbers in the set). II is not correct because the mode is *y*—there are three *y*s and only two 26s. III is not correct because 150 is an outlier (you can't actually compute the upper boundary for an outlier since the third quartile is *y*, but even if you use a larger value, 33, in place of *y*, 150 is still an outlier).

2. The correct answer is (e).

$$z = \frac{40.6 - 38.5}{1.25} = 1.68 \ \rightarrow \text{percentile} = 0.9535 \ (\text{see drawing below}):$$

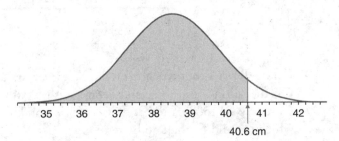

3. The correct answer is (d). The effect on the mean of a dataset of subtracting the same value is to reduce the old mean by that amount (that is, $\mu_{x-k} = \mu_x - k$). Because the original mean was 19, and 19 has been subtracted from every term, the new mean is 0. The effect on the standard deviation of a dataset of dividing each term by the same value is to divide the standard deviation by that value, that is,

$$\sigma_{x/k} = \frac{\sigma_x}{k}.$$

Because the old standard deviation was 4, dividing every term by 4 yields a new standard deviation of 1. Note that the process of subtracting the mean from each term and dividing by the standard deviation creates a set of z-scores

$$z_x = \frac{x - \bar{x}}{s}$$

so that any complete set of z-scores has a mean of 0 and a standard deviation of 1. The shape is normal since any linear transformation of a normal distribution will still be normal.

4. The correct answer is (b). The maximum length of a "whisker" in a box-and-whiskers plot is $1.5(IQR) = 1.5(40 - 18) = 33$.

5. The correct (best) answer is (d). Using Table A, the area under a normal curve between 63 and 75 is 0.6247 ($z_{63} = -1.5 \Rightarrow A_1 = 0.0668$, $z_{75} = 0.5 \Rightarrow A_2 = 0.6915 \Rightarrow A_2 - A_1 = 0.6247$). Then $(0.6247)(5,000) = 3123.5$. Using the TI-83/84, `normal-cdf(63,75,72,6) × 5000 = 3123.3`.

6. The correct answer is (b). Using Table A, a percentile of 63 corresponds to an area 0.63. This gives $z = 0.34$. Solving $0.34 = (x - 72)/6$ yields 74.04. Using the TI-83/84, `invNorm(.63,72,6) = 73.99`.

7. The correct answer is (e). The graph is clearly not symmetric, bimodal, or uniform. It is skewed to the right since that's the direction of the "tail" of the graph.

8. The correct answer is (a). The median is resistant to extreme values, and the mean is not (that is, extreme values will exert a strong influence on the numerical value of the mean but not on the median). II and III involve statistics equal to or dependent upon the mean, so neither of them is resistant.

9. The correct answer is (d). $z = 1.65 = \dfrac{43 - 40}{\sigma} \Rightarrow \sigma = \dfrac{3}{1.65} = 1.82$.

10. The correct answer is (b). A score at the 90th percentile has a z-score of 1.28. Thus, $z_x = \dfrac{x - 2.05}{1} = 1.28 \Rightarrow x = 3.33$.

Free-Response

1. Using the calculator, we find that $\bar{x} = 29.78$, $s = 11.94$, Q1 = 21, Q3 = 37. Using the 1.5(IQR) rule, outliers are values that are less than $21 - 1.5(37 - 21) = -3$ or greater than $37 + 1.5(37 - 21) = 61$. Because no values lie outside of those boundaries, there are no outliers by this rule.

   Using the $\bar{x} \pm 2s$ rule, we have $\bar{x} \pm 2s = 29.78 \pm 2(11.94) = (5.9, 53.66)$. By this standard, the year he hit 54 home runs would be considered an outlier.

2. (a) is a property of the *standard normal distribution*, not a property of normal distributions in general. (b) is a property of the normal distribution. (c) is not a property of the normal distribution—*almost* all the terms are within four standard deviations of the mean but, at least in theory, there are terms at any given distance from the mean. (d) is a property of the normal distribution—the normal curve is the perfect bell-shaped curve. (e) is a property of the normal distribution and is the property that makes this curve useful as a probability density curve.

	Home Runs	**Home Runs**
3.	1	3589	1	3

3.

Home Runs	**Home Runs**
1 | 3589	1 | 3
2 | 12337	1 | 589
3 | 01457	2 | 1233
4 | 02	2 | 7
5 | 24	3 | 014
	3 | 57
	4 | 02
	4 |
	5 | 24

What shows up when done by 5 rather than 10 is the gap between 42 and 52. In 16 out of 18 years, Mantle hit 42 or fewer home runs. He hit more than 50 only twice.

4. $\bar{x} = 76.4$ and $s = 10.17$.

$$z_{84} = \frac{84 - 76.4}{10.17} = 0.75. \quad z_{89} = \frac{89 - 76.4}{10.17} = 1.24.$$

Using the Standard Normal Probability table, a score of 84 corresponds to the 77.34th percentile, and a score of 89 corresponds to the 89.25th percentile. Both students were in the top quartile of scores after the program and performed better than all but one of the other students. We don't know that there is a cause-and-effect relationship between the pilot program and the high scores (that would require comparisons with a pretest), but it's reasonable to assume that the program had a positive impact. You might wonder how the student who got the 98 did so well!

5.

The most distinguishing thing about the graph is that it is quite symmetric. There are no outliers.

6. $z_{0.346} = \dfrac{0.346 - 0.265}{0.032} = 2.53. \Rightarrow$ Area to the left of 2.53 is 0.9943.

That is, Betts's average in 2018 would have placed him in the 99.43th percentile of batters.

7. There are 18 values in the stemplot. The median is 17 (actually between the last two 7s in the row marked by the (5) in the count column of the plot —it's still 17). Because there are 9 values in each half of the stemplot, the median of the lower half of the data, Q1, is the 5th score from the top. So, Q1 = 14. Q3 = the 5th score counting from the bottom = 24. Thus, IQR = 24 − 14 = 10.

8. There are 3 values in the first bar, 6 in the second, 2 in the third, 9 in the fourth, and 5 in the fifth for a total of 25 values in the dataset. Of these, 3 + 6 + 2 = 11 are less than 3.5. There are 25 terms all together, so the proportion of terms less than 3.5 is 11/25 = 0.44.

9. With the exception of the one outlier for Bonds, the most obvious thing about these two is just how similar they are. The medians of the two are almost identical and the IQRs are very similar. The data do not show it, but with the exception of 2001, the year Bonds hit 73 home runs, neither batter ever hit 50 or more home runs in a season. So, for any given season, you should be overjoyed to have either on your team, but there is no good reason to choose one over the other. However, if you based your decision on who had the most home runs in a single season, you would certainly choose Bonds.

10. Let x be the value in question. Because we do not want to be in the top 20%, the area to the left of x is 0.8. Hence $z_x = 0.84$ (found by locating the nearest table entry to 0.8, which is 0.7995 and reading the corresponding z-score as 0.84). Then

$$z_x = 0.84 = \frac{x-185}{25} \Rightarrow x = 206.$$

[Using the calculator, the solution to this problem is given by `invNorm (0.8,185,25)`.]

11. $\bar{x} = \$3.36$ million, $s = \$1.88$ million, *Med* = \$3.35 million, IQR = \$2.6 million. A box-and-whiskers plot of the data looks like this:

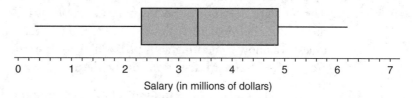

Salary (in millions of dollars)

The fact that the mean and the median are virtually the same, and that the box-and-whiskers plot is more or less symmetric, indicates that either set of measures would be appropriate.

12. The easiest way to do this is to use the calculator. Put the age data in `L1` and the frequencies in `L2`. Then do `1-Var Stats L1,L2` (the calculator will read the second list as frequencies for the first list).

    • The mean is 2.48 years, and the median is 2 years. This indicates that the mean is being pulled to the right—and that the distribution is skewed to the right or has outliers in the direction of the larger values.
    • The standard deviation is 2.61 years. Because one standard deviation to the left would yield a negative value, this also indicates that the distribution extends farther to the right than the left.
    • A histogram of the data, drawn on the TI-83/84, is shown below. This definitely indicates that the ages of these pennies is skewed to the right.

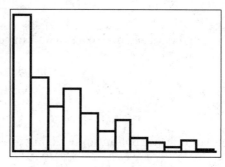

13. The new mean is $5(35 - 10) = 125$.
    The new median is $5(33 - 10) = 115$.
    The new variance is $5^2(6^2) = 900$.
    The new standard deviation is $5(6) = 30$.
    The new IQR is $5(12) = 60$.

14. First we need to find the *proportion* of women who would be less than 62″ tall:

$$z_{55} = \frac{62 - 65}{2.5} = -1.2 \Rightarrow \text{Area} = 0.1151.$$

So 0.1151 of the terms in the distribution would be less than 62″. This means that $0.1151(300) = 34.53$, so you would expect that 34 or 35 of the women would be less than 62″ tall.

15. (a), (c), and (d) are properties of the standard deviation. (a) serves as a definition of the standard deviation. It is independent of the number of terms in the distribution in the sense that simply adding more terms will not necessarily increase or decrease s. (d) is another way of saying that the standard deviation is independent of the mean—it's a measure of spread, not a measure of center.

    The standard deviation is *not* resistant to extreme values (b) because it is based on the mean, not the median. (e) is a statement about the interquartile range. In general, unless we know something about the curve, we don't know what proportion of terms are within 2 standard deviations of the mean.

16. For these data, Q1 = $2.3 million, Q3 = $4.9 million. To be an outlier, Erick would need to make at least $4.9 + 1.5(4.9 - 2.3) = 8.8$ million. In other words, he would need a $2.6 million raise in order to have his salary be an outlier.

17. You need to estimate the median and the quartiles. Note that the histogram is skewed to the left so that the scores tend to pack to the right. This means that the median is to the right of center and that the box-and-whiskers plot would have a long whisker to the left. The box-and-whiskers plot looks like this:

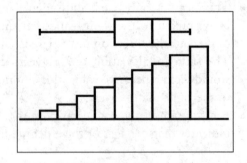

18. If you standardize both scores, you can compare them on the same scale. Accordingly,

$$z_{80} = \frac{80 - 72}{6} = 1.333, z_{76} = \frac{76 - 65}{8} = 1.375.$$

Nathan did slightly, but only slightly, better on the second test.

19.

$$s = 20 = \sqrt{\frac{\sum(x - \overline{x})^2}{n-1}} = \sqrt{\frac{13{,}600}{n-1}}$$

$$20^2 = \frac{13{,}600}{n-1} \Rightarrow n = 35$$

$$\overline{x} = \frac{\sum x}{n} = \frac{245}{35} = 7$$

Solutions to Cumulative Review Problems

1. (a), (c), and (d) are quantitative.

2. (a), (d), and (e) are continuous; (b) and (c) are discrete. Note that (d) could be considered discrete if what we meant by "number of square miles" was the integer number of square miles.

3. Statistics is the science of data. Its two main divisions are *data analysis* and *inference.* Exploratory data analysis (EDA) utilizes graphical and analytical methods to try to see what the data "say." That is, EDA looks at data in a variety of ways in order to understand them. Inference involves using information from samples to make statements or predictions about the population from which the sample was drawn.

4. A survey, based on a sample from some population, is usually given in order to be able to make statements or predictions about the population. An experiment, on the other hand, usually has as its goal studying the differential effects of some treatment on two or more samples, which are often composed of volunteers.

5. Statistical inference is based on being able to determine the probability of getting a particular sample statistic from a population with a hypothesized parameter. For example, we might ask how likely it is to get 55 heads on 100 flips of a fair coin. If it seems unlikely, we might reject the notion that the coin we actually flipped is fair. The probabilistic underpinnings of inference can be understood through the language of random variables. In other words, we need random variables to bridge the gap between simple data analysis and inference.

CHAPTER 6

Two-Variable Data Analysis

IN THIS CHAPTER

Summary: In the previous chapter, we used *exploratory data analysis* to help us understand what a one-variable dataset was saying to us. In this chapter, we extend those ideas to consider the relationships between two variables that might, or might not, be related. In this chapter, and in this course, we are primarily concerned with variables that have a *linear* relationship and, for the most part, leave other types of relationships to more advanced courses. We will spend some time considering nonlinear relationships that, through some sort of transformation, can be analyzed as though the relationship was linear. Finally, we'll consider a statistic that tells the proportion of variability in one variable that can be attributed to the linear relationship with another variable.

Key Ideas

✪ Scatterplots
✪ Linear Models
✪ The Correlation Coefficient
✪ Least Squares Regression Line
✪ Coefficient of Determination
✪ Residuals
✪ Outliers and Influential Points
✪ Transformations to Achieve Linearity

Scatterplots

In the previous chapter, we looked at several different ways to graph one-variable data. By choosing from dotplots, stemplots, histograms, or boxplots, we were able to examine visually patterns in the data. In this chapter, we consider techniques of data analysis for two-variable (**bivariate**) quantitative data. Specifically, our interest is whether or not two variables have a linear relationship and how changes in one variable can allow us to predict changes in the other variable.

> **example:** For an AP Statistics class project, a statistics teacher had her students keep diaries of how many hours they studied before their midterm exam. The following are the data for 15 of the students.
>
> The teacher wanted to know if additional studying is associated with higher grades and drew the following graph, called a **scatterplot**. It seemed pretty obvious to the teacher that students who studied more tended to have higher grades on the exam.

STUDENT	HOURS STUDIED	SCORE ON EXAM
A	0.5	65
B	2.5	80
C	3.0	77
D	1.5	60
E	1.25	68
F	0.75	70
G	4.0	83
H	2.25	85
I	1.5	70
J	6.0	96
K	3.25	84
L	2.5	84
M	0.0	51
N	1.75	63
O	2.0	71

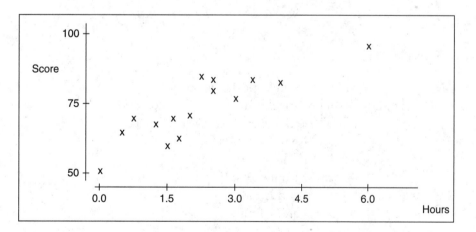

In the previous example, we were interested in seeing whether studying is associated with test performance. To do this we drew a **scatterplot**, which is just a two-dimensional graph of ordered pairs. We put one variable on the horizontal axis and the other on the vertical axis. In the example, the horizontal axis is for "hours studied," and the vertical axis is for "score on test." Each point on the graph represents the ordered pair for one student. If we have an **explanatory variable**, it should be on the horizontal axis, and the **response variable** should be on the vertical axis. It is also common for the horizontal axis to be considered independent, while the other variable is dependent.

We observed that students who study more tend to have higher scores. We say that two variables are **positively associated** if higher-than-average values for one variable are generally paired with higher-than-average values of the other variable. We say they are negatively associated if higher-than-average values for one variable tend to be paired with lower-than-average values of the other variable.

Calculator Tip: In order to draw a scatterplot on your calculator, first enter the data in two lists, say the horizontal-axis variable in L1 and the vertical-axis variable in L2. Then go to STAT PLOT and choose the scatterplot icon from Type. Enter L1 for Xlist and L2 for Ylist. Choose whichever Mark pleases you. Be sure there are no equations active in the Y = list. Then do ZOOM ZoomStat (Zoom-9) and the calculator will draw the scatterplot for you. The calculator seems to do a much better job with scatterplots than it does with histograms, but if you wish, you can still go back and adjust the WINDOW in any way you want.

The scatterplot of the data in the example, drawn on the calculator, looks like this (the window used was [0, 6.5, 1, 40, 105, 5, 1]):

On the AP exam, it is much more efficient to quickly make a sketch of a scatterplot yourself, rather than typing in your data and trying to copy what you see on your calculator screen. Regardless, for any graph you draw, axes must be labeled and must include a scale.

example: Which of the following statements best describes the scatterplot pictured?

  I. A line might fit the data well.
 II. The variables are positively associated.
III. The variables are negatively associated.
    a. I only
    b. II only
    c. III only
    d. I and II only
    e. I and III only

solution: e is correct. The data look as though a line might be a good model, and the y-variable decreases as the x-variable increases so that they are negatively associated.

Correlation

We have seen how to graph two-variable data in a scatterplot. Following the pattern we set in the previous chapter, we now want to do some numerical analysis of the data in an attempt to understand the relationship between the variables better.

In AP Statistics, we are primarily interested in determining the extent to which two variables are *linearly* associated. Two variables are *linearly related* to the extent that their relationship can be modeled by a line. Sometimes, and we will look at this more closely later in this chapter, variables may not be linearly related but can be transformed in such a way that the transformed data are linear. Sometimes the data are related but not linearly (e.g., the height of a thrown ball, t seconds after it is thrown, is a quadratic function of the number of seconds elapsed since it was released).

The first statistic we have to quantify a linear relationship is the Pearson product moment correlation, or, more simply, the **correlation coefficient**, denoted by the letter r. The correlation coefficient is a measure of the *strength* of the linear relationship between two variables as well as an indicator of the *direction* of the linear relationship (whether the variables are positively or negatively associated).

If we have a sample of size n of paired data, say (x,y), and assuming that we have computed summary statistics for x and y (means and standard deviations), the **correlation coefficient r** is defined as follows:

$$r = \frac{1}{n-1}\sum\left(\frac{x_i - \bar{x}}{s_x}\right)\left(\frac{y_i - \bar{y}}{s_y}\right).$$

Because the terms after the summation symbol are nothing more than the z-scores of the individual x and y values, a different way to look at this definition is

$$r = \frac{1}{n-1}\sum z_x z_y.$$

Fortunately, the original formula for the correlation coefficient is found on the formula sheet provided on both the multiple-choice and free-response portions of the statistics exam. And even better, there is almost no chance that you would actually have to use this formula as the results will almost certainly be provided for you.

example: Earlier in the section, we saw some data for hours studied and the corresponding scores on an exam. It can be shown that, for these data, $r = 0.864$ and the scatterplot appears roughly linear. Together, this indicates a strong positive linear relationship between hours studied and exam score. That is, the more hours studied, the higher the exam score. (We will need to confirm that a linear model is appropriate by using a residual plot. More to come on that note.)

The correlation coefficient r has a number of properties you should be familiar with:

- $-1 \le r \le 1$. If $r = -1$ or $r = 1$, the points all lie on a line.
- Although there are no hard-and-fast rules about how strong a correlation is based on its numerical value, the following guidelines might help you categorize r:

VALUE OF r	STRENGTH OF LINEAR RELATIONSHIP
$-1 \le r \le -0.8$	strong
$0.8 \le r \le 1$	
$-0.8 \le r \le -0.5$	moderate
$0.5 \le r \le 0.8$	
$-0.5 \le r \le 0.5$	weak

- If $r > 0$, it indicates that the variables are positively associated. If $r < 0$, it indicates that the variables are negatively associated.
- If $r = 0$, it indicates that there is no linear association that would allow us to predict y from x. It *does not* mean that there is no relationship—just not a linear one.
- It does not matter which variable you call x and which variable you call y. r will be the same. In other words, r depends only on the paired points, not the *ordered* pairs.
- r does not depend on the units of measurement. In the previous example, convert "hours studied" to "minutes studied" and r would still equal 0.864.
- r is not resistant to extreme values because it is based on the mean. A single extreme value can have a powerful impact on r and may cause us to overinterpret the relationship. You must look at the scatterplot of the data as well as r.

example: To illustrate that r is not resistant, consider the following two graphs. The graph on the left, with 12 points, has a marked negative linear association between x and y. The graph on the right has the same basic visual pattern, but as you can see, the addition of the new point has a dramatic effect on r—making what is generally a negative association between two variables appear to have a moderate, positive association.

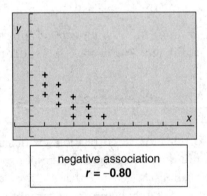

negative association
$r = -0.80$

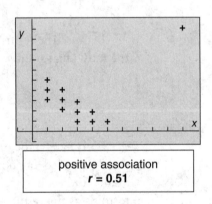

positive association
$r = 0.51$

example: The following computer output, again for the hours studied versus exam score data, indicates R-sq, which is the square of r. Accordingly, $r = \pm\sqrt{0.747} = \pm 0.864$. We will learn how to tell if r is positive or negative using other information. There is a lot of other stuff in the box that doesn't concern us just yet. We will learn about other important parts of the output as we proceed through the rest of this book. Note that we cannot determine the sign of r from R-sq. We need additional information.

The regression equation is
Score = 59.0 + 6.77 hours

Predictor	Coef	St Dev	t ratio	P
Constant	59.026	2.863	20.62	.000
Hours	6.767	1.092	6.20	.000

s = 6.135	R-sq = 74.7%	R-sq(adj) = 72.8%

("R-sq" is called the "coefficient of determination" and has a lot of meaning in its own right in regression. We will consider the coefficient of determination later in this chapter.)

Calculator Tip: In order to find r on your TI calculator, you will first need to change a setting from the factory. Enter CATALOG and scroll down to "Diagnostic On." Press ENTER twice. Now you are ready to find r.

Assuming you have entered the x- and y-values in L1 and L2, enter STAT CALC LinReg(a+bx) [that's STAT CALC 8 on the TI-83/84] and press ENTER. Then enter L1, L2 and press ENTER. You should get a screen that looks like this (using the data from the Study Time vs. Score on Test study):

(Note that reversing L1 and L2 in this operation—entering STAT CALC LinReg(a+bx) L2, L1—will change a and b but will not change r since order doesn't matter in correlation.) If you compare this with the computer output above, you will see that it contains some of the same data, including both r and r^2. At the moment, all you care about in this printout is the value of r.

Correlation and Causation

Two variables, x and y, may have a strong correlation, but you need to take care *not* to interpret that as causation. That is, just because two things seem to go together does not mean that one caused the other—some third variable may be influencing them both. Seeing a fire truck at almost every fire doesn't mean that fire trucks cause fires!

example: The table below shows, for the given years, the per capita consumption of cheese in the United States and the number of doctorates in civil engineering awarded in the United States.

YEAR	U.S. PER CAPITA CHEESE CONSUMPTION (LBS)	NUMBER OF CIVIL ENGINEERING PhDs AWARDED
2000	9.3	480
2001	9.7	501
2002	9.7	540
2003	9.7	552
2004	9.9	547
2005	10.2	622
2006	10.5	655
2007	11	701
2008	10.6	712
2009	10.6	708

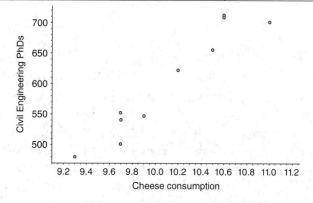

For these data, it turns out that $r = 0.959$.

Is the increase in the amount of cheese consumed in the United States responsible for the increase in civil engineering PhDs? Of course not! Nor the reverse. But you must be careful in situations where a causal relationship might sound more plausible. We still cannot conclude that one causes the other just because we see a correlation between the variables. Even a very strong correlation.

In some cases, there may be a third variable that causes both the variables to change in the same direction. This is discussed more in the next chapter, but in the meantime remember, always remember, that *correlation does not imply causation*.

Linear Models

When we discussed correlation, we learned that it didn't matter which variable we called x and which variable we called y—the correlation r is the same. That is, there is no explanatory and response variable, just two variables that may or may not vary linearly. In this section, we are more interested in predicting, once we've determined the strength of the linear relationship between the two variables, the value of one variable (the response) based on the value of the other variable (the explanatory). In this situation, called linear regression, it matters greatly which variable we call x and which one we call y.

Least-Squares Regression Line

Recall again the data from the study that looked at hours studied versus score on exam:

HOURS STUDIED	SCORE ON EXAM
0.5	65
2.5	80
3.0	77
1.5	60
1.25	68
0.75	70
4.0	83
2.25	85
1.5	70
6.0	96
3.25	84
2.5	84
0.0	51
1.75	63
2.0	71

The scatterplot (see page 97) leads us to believe that the form of this relationship is linear. This, and given $r = 0.864$ for these data, leads us to say that we have a strong, positive, linear association between the variables. Suppose we wanted to predict the score of a person who studied for 2.75 hours. If we knew we were working with a linear model—a line that seemed to fit the data well—we would feel confident about using the equation of the line to make such a prediction. We are looking for a **line of best fit**. We want to find a **regression line**—a line that can be used for predicting response values from explanatory values.

In this situation, we would use the regression line to predict the exam score for a person who studied 2.75 hours.

The line we are looking for is called the **least-squares regression line**. We could draw a variety of lines on our scatterplot trying to determine which has the best fit. Let $\hat{y}$ be the predicted value of y for a given value of x. Then $y - \hat{y}$ represents the error in prediction. We want our line to minimize errors in prediction, so we might first think that $\sum(y - \hat{y})$ would be a good measure ($y - \hat{y}$ is the *actual value* minus the *predicted value*). However, because our line is going to average out the errors in some fashion, we find that $\sum(y - \hat{y}) = 0$. To get around this problem, we use $\sum(y - \hat{y})^2$. This expression will vary with different lines and is sensitive to the fit of the line. That is, $\sum(y - \hat{y})^2$ is small when the linear fit is good and large when it is not.

The **least-squares regression line** (LSRL) is the line that minimizes the sum of squared errors. If $\hat{y} = a + bx$ is the LSRL, then $\hat{y}$ minimizes $\sum(y - \hat{y})^2$.

Digression for Calculus Students Only: It should be clear that trying to find a and b for the line $\hat{y} = a + bx$ that minimizes $\sum(y - \hat{y})^2$ is a typical calculus problem. The difference is that, since $\hat{y}$ is a function of two variables, it requires multivariable calculus to derive it. That is, you need to be beyond first-year calculus to derive the results that follow.

For n ordered pairs (x, y), we calculate: $\bar{x}$, $\bar{y}$, s_x, s_y, and r. Then we have:

If $\hat{y} = a + bx$ is the LSRL, $b = r\dfrac{s_y}{s_x}$, and $a = \bar{y} - b\bar{x}$.

---

example: For the hours studied (x) versus score (y) study, the LSRL is $\hat{y} = 59.03 + 6.77x$. We asked earlier what score would we predict for someone who studied 2.75 hours. Plugging this value into the LSRL, we have $\hat{y} = 59.03 + 6.77(2.75) = 77.63$. It's important to understand that this is the *predicted* value, not the exact value such a person will necessarily get.

example: Consider once again the computer printout for the data of the preceding example:

The regression equation is
Score = 59.0 + 6.77 Hours

Predictor	Coef	St Dev	t ratio	P
Constant	59.026	2.863	20.62	.000
Hours	6.767	1.092	6.20	.000

s = 6.135   R-sq = 74.7%   R-sq(adj) = 72.8%

Exam Tip: An AP Exam question in which you are asked to determine the regression equation from the printout has been common. Be sure you know where the intercept and the slope of the regression line are located in the printout (they are under "Coef").

The regression equation is given as "$\widehat{\text{Score}} = 59 + 6.77$ Hours." The y-intercept, which is the predicted score when the number of hours studied is zero, and the slope of the regression line are listed in the table under the column "Coef."

example: We saw earlier that the calculator output for these data was

The values of a and b are given as part of the output. Remember that these values were obtained by putting the "Hours Studied" data in L1, the "Test Score" data in L2, and doing `LinReg(a+bx)L1,L2`. When using `LinReg(a+bx)`, the explanatory variable *must* come first and the response variable second.

example: An experiment is conducted on the effects of having convicted criminals provide restitution to their victims rather than serving time. The following table gives the data for 10 criminals. The monthly salaries (X) and monthly restitution payments (Y) were as follows:

X	300	880	1000	1540	1560	1600	1600	2200	3200	6000
Y	200	380	400	200	800	600	800	1000	1600	2700

(a) Find the correlation between X and Y and the regression equation that can be used to predict monthly restitution payments from monthly salaries.
(b) Draw a scatterplot of the data and put the LSRL on the graph.
(c) Interpret the slope of the regression line in the context of the problem.
(d) How much would a criminal earning \$1400 per month be expected to pay in restitution?

solution: Put the monthly salaries (x) in L1 and the monthly restitution payments (y) in L2. Then enter `STAT CALC LinReg(a+bx)L1,L2,Y1`.

(a) $r = 0.97$, $\widehat{\text{Payments}} = -56.22 + 0.46$ (Salary). (If you answered $\hat{y} = 56.22 + 0.46x$, you must define x and y so that the regression equation can be understood in the context of the problem. An algebra equation, without a contextual definition of the variables, will not receive full credit.)

(b)

(c) The slope of the regression line is 0.46. This tells us that, for each $1 increase in the criminal's salary, the amount of restitution is predicted to increase by $0.46.

(d) *Payment* = −56.22 + 0.46 (1400) = $587.78.

Residuals

When we developed the LSRL, we referred to $y - \hat{y}$ (the *actual value* − the *predicted value*) as an error in prediction. The formal name for $y - \hat{y}$ is the **residual**. Note that the order is always "actual" − "predicted" so that a positive residual means that the prediction was too small and a negative residual means that the prediction was too large.

> **example:** In the previous example, a criminal earning $1560/month paid restitution of $800/month. The predicted restitution for this amount would be $\hat{y} = −56.22 + 0.46(1560) = \$661.38$. Thus, the residual for this case is $800 − $661.38 = $138.62.

Calculator Tip: The TI-83/84 will generate a complete set of residuals when you perform a LinReg. They are stored in a list called RESID, which can be found in the LIST menu. RESID stores only the current set of residuals. That is, a new set of residuals is stored in RESID each time you perform a new regression.

Residuals can be useful to us in determining the extent to which a linear model is appropriate for a dataset. If a line is an appropriate model, we would expect to find the residuals more or less randomly scattered about the average residual (which is, of course, 0). In fact, we expect to find them approximately normally distributed about 0. A pattern of residuals that does not appear to be more or less randomly distributed about 0 (that is, there is a systematic nature to the graph of the residuals) is evidence that a line is not a good model for the data. If the residuals are small, the line may predict well even though it isn't a good theoretical model for the data. The usual method of determining if a line is a good model is to examine visually a plot of the residuals plotted against the explanatory variable.

Calculator Tip: In order to draw a residual plot on the TI-83/84, and assuming that your x-data are in L1 and your y-data are in L2, first do LinReg(a+bx)L1,L2. Next, you create a STAT PLOT scatterplot, where Xlist is set to L1 and Ylist is set to RESID. RESID can be retrieved from the LIST menu (remember that only the residuals for the most recent regression are stored in RESID). ZOOM ZoomStat will then draw the residual plot for the current list of residuals. It's a good idea to turn off any equations you may have in the Y= list before doing a residual plot or you may get an unwanted line on your plot.

> **example:** The data given below show the height (in cm) at various ages (in months) for a group of children.
> (a) Does a line seem to be a good model for the data? Explain.
> (b) What is the value of the residual for a child of 19 months?

Age	18	19	20	21	22	23	24	25	26	27	28	29
Height	76	77.1	78.1	78.3	78.8	79.4	79.9	81.3	81.1	82.0	82.6	83.5

solution:

(a) Using the calculator (LinReg(a+bx) L1, L2, Y1), we find $\widehat{height} = 64.94 + 0.634(age)$, $r = 0.993$. The large value of r tells us that the points are close to a line. The scatterplot and LSLR are shown below on the graph at the left.

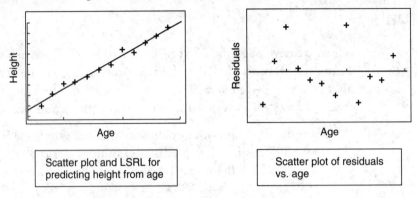

| Scatter plot and LSRL for predicting height from age | Scatter plot of residuals vs. age |

From the graph on the left, a line appears to be a good fit for the data (the points lie close to the line). The residual plot on the right shows no readily obvious pattern, so we have good evidence that a line is a good model for the data and we can feel good about using the LSRL to predict height from age.

(b) The residual (actual minus predicted) for *age* = 19 months is $77.1 - (64.94 + 0.634 \cdot 19) = 0.114$. Note that 77.1 − Y1(19) = 0.112.

Whenever we have graphed a residual plot in this section, the vertical axis has been the residuals and the horizontal axis has been the *x*-variable. On some computer printouts, you may see the horizontal axis labeled "Fits" (as in the graph below) or "Predicted Value."

What you are interested in is the visual image given by the residual plot, and it doesn't matter if the residuals are plotted against the *x*-variable or something else, like "FITS"— the scatter of the points above and below 0 stays the same. All that changes are the horizontal distances between points. This is the way it must be done in multiple regression, since there is more than one independent variable and, as you can see, it can be done in simple linear regression.

On the AP exam, if you need to discuss a residual plot, one will almost certainly be created and provided for you.

If we are trying to predict a value of *y* from a value of *x*, it is called **interpolation** if we are predicting from an *x*-value within the range of *x*-values. It is called **extrapolation** if we are predicting from a value of *x* outside of the *x*-values.

Age	18	19	20	21	22	23	24	25	26	27	28	29
Height	76	77.1	78.1	78.3	78.8	79.4	79.9	81.3	81.1	82.0	82.6	83.5

> **example:** Using the age/height data from the previous example, we are *interpolating* if we attempt to predict height from an age between 18 and 29 months. It is interpolation if we try to predict the height of a 20.5-month-old baby. We are *extrapolating* if we try to predict the height of a child less than 18 months old or more than 29 months old.

If a line has been shown to be a good model for the data and if it fits the line well (i.e., we have a strong *r* and a more or less random distribution of residuals), we can have confidence in interpolated predictions. We can rarely have confidence in extrapolated values. In the previous example, we might be willing to go slightly beyond the ages given because of the high correlation and the good linear model, but it's good practice *not* to extrapolate beyond the data given. If we were to extrapolate the data in the example to a child of 12 years of age (144 months), we would predict the child to be 156.2 inches, or more than 13 feet tall!

Coefficient of Determination

In the absence of a better way to predict *y*-values from *x*-values, our best guess for any given *x* might well be $\bar{y}$, the mean value of *y*.

> **example:** Suppose you had access to the heights and weights of each of the students in your statistics class. You compute the average weight of all the students. You write the heights of each student on a slip of paper, put the slips in a hat, and then draw out one slip. You are asked to predict the weight of the student whose height is on the slip of paper you have drawn. What is your best guess as to the weight of the student?

> **solution:** In the absence of any known relationship between height and weight, your best guess would have to be the average weight of all the students. You know the weights vary about the average and that is about the best you could do.

If we guessed at the weight of each student using the average, we would be wrong most of the time. If we took each of those errors and squared them, we would have what is called the *sum of squares total* (SST). It's the total squared error of our guesses when our best guess is simply the mean of the weights of all students and represents the total variability of *y*.

Now suppose we have a least-squares regression line that we want to use as a model for predicting weight from height. It is, of course, the LSRL we discussed in detail earlier in this chapter, and our hope is that there will be less error in prediction than by using $\bar{y}$. Now, we still have errors from the regression line (called *residuals*, remember?). We call the sum of *those* errors the **sum of squared errors** (SSE). So, SST represents the total error from using $\bar{y}$ as the basis for predicting weight from height, and SSE represents the total error from using the LSRL. SST − SSE represents the benefit of using the regression line rather than $\bar{y}$ for prediction. That is, by using the LSRL rather than $\bar{y}$, we have *explained* a certain proportion of the total variability by regression.

The proportion of the total variability in y that is explained by the regression of y on x is called the **coefficient of determination**. The *coefficient of determination* is symbolized by r^2. Based on the preceding discussion, we note that

$$r^2 = \frac{SST - SSE}{SST}.$$

It can be shown algebraically that this r^2 is actually the square of the familiar r, the correlation coefficient. Many computer programs will report the value of r^2 only (usually as "R-sq"), which means that we must take the square root of r^2 if we only want to know r (remember that r and b, the slope of the regression line, are either both positive or negative so that you can check the sign of b to determine the sign of r if all you are given is r^2). The TI-83/84 calculator will report both r and r^2, as well as the regression coefficient, when you do `LinReg(a+bx)`.

example: Consider the following output for a linear regression:

Predictor	Coef	St Dev	*t* ratio	*P*
Constant	−1.95	21.97	−0.09	.931
x	0.8863	0.2772	3.20	.011
s = 16.57		R-sq = 53.2%		R-sq(adj) = 48.0%

We can see that the LSRL for these data is $\hat{y} = -1.95 + 0.8863x$. $r^2 = 53.2\% = 0.532$. This means that 53.2% of the total variability in y can be explained by the regression of y on x. Furthermore, $r = \sqrt{0.532} = 0.729$ (r is positive since $b = 0.8863$ is positive). We learn more about the other items in the printout later.

You might note that there are two standard errors (estimates of population standard deviations) in the computer printout above. The first is the "St Dev of x" (0.2772 in this example). This is the standard error of the slope of the regression line, s_b, the estimate of the standard deviation of the slope (for information, although you don't need to know this, $s_b = \dfrac{s}{\sqrt{\sum(x-\bar{x})^2}}$). The second standard error given is the standard error of the residuals, the "s" ($s = 16.57$) at the lower-left corner of the table. This is the estimate of the standard deviation of the residuals (again, although you don't need to know this, $s = \sqrt{\dfrac{\sum(y-\breve{y})^2}{n-2}}$).

Outliers and Influential Observations

Some observations have an impact on correlation and regression. We defined an outlier when we were dealing with one-variable data (remember the 1.5 [IQR] rule?). There is no analogous numerical guideline when dealing with two-variable data, but it is the same basic idea: an **outlier** lies outside of the general pattern of the data. Specifically, for regression, an outlier has a large residual. An outlier can certainly influence the correlation and, depending on where it is located, may also exert an influence on the slope of the regression line.

An **influential observation** is one that has a strong influence on the regression model. It may influence the slope, the correlation, the y-intercept, or more than one of these. Its influence, if it doesn't line up with the rest of the data, is on the slope of the regression line. More generally, an influential observation is a datapoint that exerts a strong influence on a measure. Often, the most influential points are extreme in the x-direction. We call these points **high-leverage points**.

example: Graphs I, II, and III are the same except for the point symbolized by the box in Graphs II and III. Graph I below has no outliers or influential points. In Graph II, the point represented by the box would have a large residual and a large influence on the correlation. In Graph III, the point represented by the box would have a small residual but a large influence on the slope. Compare the correlation coefficients and regression lines for each graph. Note that the outlier in Graph II has some effect on the slope and a significant effect on the correlation coefficient. The influential point in Graph III has about the same effect on the correlation coefficient as the outlier in Graph II but is a major influence on the slope of the regression line.

Transformations to Achieve Linearity

Until now, we have been concerned with data that can be modeled with a line. Of course, there are many two-variable relationships that are nonlinear. The path of an object thrown in the air is parabolic (quadratic). Population tends to grow exponentially, at least for a while. Even though you could find an LSRL for nonlinear data, it makes no sense to do so. The AP Statistics course deals only with two-variable data that can be modeled by a line *OR* nonlinear two-variable data that can be *transformed* in such a way that the transformed data can be modeled by a line.

example: The number of a certain type of bacteria present (in thousands) after a certain number of hours is given in the following chart:

HOURS	NUMBER
1.0	1.8
1.5	2.4
2.0	3.1
2.5	4.3
3.0	5.8
3.5	8.0
4.0	10.6
4.5	14.0
5.0	18.0

What would be the predicted quantity of bacteria after 3.75 hours?

solution: A scatterplot of the data and a residual plot [for $\widehat{Number} = a + b(Hour)$] shows that a line is not a good model for these data:

Now, take $ln(Number)$ to produce the following data:

HOURS (L1)	NUMBER (L2)	LN(NUMBER) (L3 = LN (L2))
1.0	1.8	0.59
1.5	2.4	0.88
2.0	3.1	1.13
2.5	4.3	1.46
3.0	5.8	1.76
3.5	8.0	2.08
4.0	10.6	2.36
4.5	14.0	2.64
5.0	18.0	2.89

The scatterplot of *Hours* versus $ln(Number)$ and the residual plot for $ln(\widehat{Number}) = -0.0047 + 0.586(Hours)$ are as follows:

The scatterplot looks much more linear, and the residual plot no longer has the distinctive pattern of the raw data. We have transformed the original data in such a way that the transformed data are well modeled by a line. The regression equation for the transformed data is $ln(\widehat{Number}) = -0.047 + 0.586(Hours)$.

The question asked for how many bacteria are predicted to be present after 3.75 hours. Plugging 3.75 into the regression equation, we have $ln(\widehat{Number}) = -0.0048 + 0.586(3.75) = 2.19$. But that is $ln(\widehat{Number})$, not $\widehat{Number}$. We must back-transform this answer to the original units. Doing so, we have $\widehat{Number} = e^{2.19} = 8.94$ thousand bacteria.

Calculator Tip: You do not need to take logarithms by hand in the preceding example—your calculator is happy to do it for you. Simply put the Hours data in L1 and the Number data in L2. Then let L3 = LN(L2). The LSRL for the transformed data is then found by LinReg(a+bx) L1,L3,Y1.

Remember that the easiest way to find the value of a number substituted into the regression equation is to simply find Y1(#). Y1 is found by entering VARS Y-VARS Function Y1.

Exam Tip: It is *highly unlikely* that you would be asked to try transformations on raw data. Most likely, you will be given a scatterplot, residual plot, and/or a regression output for transformed data, and you will be asked to comment. You may be asked to evaluate the effectiveness of the transformation, or to compare the effectiveness of a couple models.

› Rapid Review

1. The correlation between two variables x and y is 0.85. Interpret this statement.

   Answer: There is a strong, positive, linear association between x and y. That is, as one of the variables increases, the other variable increases as well.

2. The following is a residual plot of a least-squares regression. Does it appear that a line is a good model for the data? Explain.

   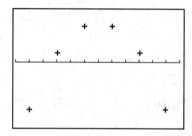

   Answer: The residual plot shows a definite pattern. If a line was a good model, we would expect to see a more or less random pattern of points about 0. A line is unlikely to be a good model for this data.

3. Consider the following scatterplot. Is the point A an outlier, an influential observation, or both? What effect would its removal have on the slope of the regression line?

   Answer: A is not an *outlier* because it would not have a large residual. It is an *influential observation* since its removal would have an effect on a calculation, specifically the slope of the regression line. Removing A would increase the slope of the LSRL.

4. A researcher finds that the LSRL for predicting GPA based on average hours studied per week is $\widehat{GPA} = 1.75 + 0.11$ (*hours studied*). Interpret the slope of the regression line in the context of the problem.

   Answer: A student who studies an hour more than another is predicted to have a GPA 0.11 points higher than the other student.

5. One of the variables that is related to college success (as measured by GPA) is socio-economic status. In one study of the relationship, $r^2 = 0.45$. Explain what this means in the context of the problem.

   Answer: $r^2 = 0.45$ means that 45% of the variability in a college GPA is explained by the regression of GPA on socioeconomic status.

6. Each year of Governor Jones's tenure, the crime rate has decreased in a linear fashion. In fact, $r = -0.8$. It appears that the governor has been effective in reducing the crime rate.

   Answer: Correlation does not necessarily imply causation. The crime rate could have gone down for a number of reasons besides Governor Jones's efforts.

7. What is the regression equation for predicting weight from height in the following computer printout, and what is the correlation between height and weight?

   The regression equation is
   $\widehat{weight} = $ _____ + _____ height

Predictor	Coef	St Dev	*t*-ratio	*P*
Constant	−104.64	39.19	−2.67	.037
Height	3.4715	0.5990	5.80	.001

   s = 7.936   R-sq = 84.8%   R-sq(adj) = 82.3%

   Answer: $\widehat{Weight} = -104.64 + 3.4715(Height)$; $r = \sqrt{0.848} = 0.921$. r is positive since the slope of the regression line is positive and both must have the same sign.

8. In the computer output for Exercise #7 above, identify the standard error of the slope of the regression line and the standard error of the residuals. Briefly explain the meaning of each.

   Answer: The standard error of the slope of the regression line is 0.5990. It is an estimate of the change in the mean response y as the independent variable x changes. The standard error of the residuals is $s = 7.936$ and is an estimate of the variability of the response variable about the LSRL.

Practice Problems

Multiple-Choice

1. Given a set of ordered pairs (x, y) so that $s_x = 1.6$, $s_y = 0.75$, $r = 0.55$. What is the slope of the least-square regression line for these data?

   a. 1.82
   b. 1.17
   c. 2.18
   d. 0.26
   e. 0.78

2.

x	23	15	26	24	22	29	32	40	41	46
y	19	18	22	20	27	25	32	38	35	45

The regression line for the two-variable dataset given above is $\hat{y} = 2.35 + 0.86x$. What is the value of the residual for the point whose x-value is 29?

a. 1.71
b. −1.71
c. 2.29
d. 5.15
e. −2.29

3. A study found a correlation of $r = -0.58$ between hours per week spent watching television and hours per week spent exercising. That is, the more hours spent watching television, the less hours spent exercising per week. Which of the following statements is most accurate?

a. About one-third of the variation in hours spent exercising can be explained by hours spent watching television.
b. A person who watches less television will exercise more.
c. For each hour spent watching television, the predicted decrease in hours spent exercising is 0.58 hrs.
d. There is a cause-and-effect relationship between hours spent watching television and a decline in hours spent exercising.
e. Fifty-eight percent of the hours spent exercising can be explained by the number of hours watching television.

4. A response variable appears to be exponentially related to the explanatory variable. The natural logarithm of each y-value is taken, and the least-squares regression line is found to be $ln(\hat{y}) = 1.64 - 0.88x$. Rounded to two decimal places, what is the predicted value of y when x = 3.1?

a. −1.09
b. −0.34
c. 0.34
d. 0.082
e. 1.09

5. Consider the following residual plot:

Which of the following statements is (are) true?
I. The residual plot indicates that a line is a reasonable model for the data.
II. The residual plot indicates that there is no relationship between the data.
III. The correlation between the variables is probably nonzero.

a. I only
b. II only

    c. I and III only
    d. II and III only
    e. I and II only

6. Suppose the LSRL for predicting weight (in pounds) from height (in inches) is given by $\widehat{Weight} = -115 + 3.6\ (Height)$. Which of the following statements is correct?

  I. A person who is 61 inches tall will weigh 104.6 pounds.
  II. For each additional inch of height, weight will increase on average by 3.6 pounds.
  III. There is a strong positive linear relationship between height and weight.

    a. I only
    b. II only
    c. III only
    d. II and III only
    e. I and II only

7. A least-squares regression line for predicting performance on a college entrance exam based on high school grade point average (GPA) is determined to be $\widehat{Score} = 273.5 + 91.2\ (GPA)$. One student in the study had a high school GPA of 3.0 and an exam score of 510. What is the residual for this student?

    a. 26.2
    b. 43.9
    c. −37.1
    d. −26.2
    e. 37.1

8. The correlation between two variables x and y is −0.26. A new set of scores, x^* and y^*, is constructed by letting $x^* = -x$ and $y^* = y + 12$. The correlation between x^* and y^* is

    a. −0.26
    b. 0.26
    c. 0
    d. 0.52
    e. −0.52

9. A study was done on the relationship between high school grade point average (GPA) and scores on the SAT. The following 8 scores were from a random sample of students taking the exam:

GPA	3.2	3.8	3.9	3.3	3.6	2.8	2.9	3.5
SAT	725	752	745	680	700	562	595	730

What percent of the variation in SAT scores is explained by the regression of SAT score on GPA?

    a. 62.1%
    b. 72.3%
    c. 88.8%
    d. 94.2%
    e. 78.8%

10. A study of mileage found that the least squares regression line for predicting mileage (in miles per gallon) from the weight of the vehicle (in hundreds of pounds) was $\widehat{mpg} = 32.50 - 0.45(weight)$. The mean weight for the vehicles in the study was 2980 pounds. What was the mean miles per gallon in the study?

   a. 19.09
   b. 15.27
   c. −1308.5
   d. 18.65
   e. 20.33

Free-Response

1. Given a two-variable dataset such that $\bar{x} = 14.5$, $\bar{y} = 20$, $s_x = 4$, $s_y = 11$, $r = .80$, find the least-squares regression line of y on x.

2. The data below give the first and second exam scores of 10 students in a calculus class.

Test 1	63	32	87	73	60	63	83	80	98	85
Test 2	51	21	52	90	83	54	73	85	83	46

   (a) Draw a scatterplot of these data.
   (b) To what extent do the scores on the two tests seem related?

3. The following is a residual plot of a linear regression. A line would not be a good fit for these data. Why not? Is the regression equation likely to underestimate or overestimate the y-value of the point in the graph marked with the square?

4. The regional champion in 10 and under 100 m backstroke has had the following winning times (in seconds) over the past 8 years:

Year	1	2	3	4	5	6	7	8
Time	77.3	80.2	77.1	76.4	75.5	75.9	75.1	74.3

   How many years until you expect the winning time to be one minute or less? What's wrong with this estimate?

5. Measurements are made of the number of cockroaches present, on average, every 3 days, beginning on the second day, after apartments in one part of town are vacated. The data are as follows:

Days	2	5	8	11	14
# Roaches	3	4.5	6	7.9	11.5

   How many cockroaches would you expect to be present after 9 days?

6. A study found a strongly positive relationship between number of miles walked per week and overall health. A local news commentator, after reporting on the results of the study, advised everyone to walk more during the coming year because walking more results in better health. Comment on the reporter's advice.

7. Carla, a young sociologist, is excitedly reporting on the results of her first professional study. The finding she is reporting is that 72% of the variation in math grades for girls can be explained by the girls' socioeconomic status. What does this mean, and is it indicative of a strong linear relationship between math grades and socioeconomic status for girls?

8. Which of the following statements are true of a least-squares regression equation?

   (a) It is the unique line that minimizes the sum of the residuals.
   (b) The average residual is 0.
   (c) It minimizes the sum of the squared residuals.
   (d) The slope of the regression line is a constant multiple of the correlation coefficient.
   (e) The slope of the regression line tells you how much the response variable will change for each unit change in the explanatory variable.

9. Consider the following dataset:

x	45	73	82	91
y	15	7.9	5.8	3.5

   Given that the LSRL for these data is $\hat{y} = 26.211 - 0.25x$, what is the value of the residual for $x = 73$? Is the point $(73, 7.9)$ above or below the regression line?

10. Suppose the correlation between two variables is $r = -0.75$. What is true of the correlation coefficient and the slope of the regression line if

    (a) each of the y values is multiplied by -1?
    (b) the x and y variables are reversed?
    (c) the x and y variables are each multiplied by -1?

11. Suppose the regression equation for predicting success on a dexterity task (y) from the number of training sessions (x) is $\hat{y} = 45 + 2.7x$ and that $\frac{s_y}{s_x} = 3.33$.

    What percentage of the variation in y is not explained by the regression on x?

12. Consider the following scatterplot. The highlighted point is both an outlier and an influential point. Describe what will happen to the correlation and the slope of the regression line if that point is removed.

13. The computer printout below gives the regression output for predicting *crime rate* (in crimes per 1000 population) from the *number of casino employees* (in 1000s).

The regression equation is
Rate = _____ + _____ Number

Predictor	Coef	St Dev	t ratio	P
Constant	−0.3980	0.1884	−2.11	.068
Number	0.118320	0.006804	17.39	.000

s = 0.1499   R-sq = 97.4%   R-sq(adj) = 97.1%

Based on the output,

(a) give the equation of the LSRL for predicting *crime rate* from *number*.
(b) give the value of r, the correlation coefficient.
(c) give the predicted *crime rate* for 20,000 casino employees.

14. A study was conducted in a midsize U.S. city to investigate the relationship between the number of homes built in a year and the mean percentage appreciation for that year. The data for a 5-year period are as follows:

Number	110	80	95	70	55
Percent appreciation	15.7	10	12.7	7.8	10.4

(a) Obtain the LSRL for predicting appreciation from number of new homes built in a year.
(b) The following year, 85 new homes are built. What is the predicted appreciation?
(c) How strong is the linear relationship between number of new homes built and percentage appreciation? Explain.
(d) Suppose you didn't know the number of new homes built in a given year. How would you predict appreciation?

15. A set of bivariate data has $r^2 = 0.81$.

(a) x and y are both standardized, and a regression line is fitted to the standardized data. What is the slope of the regression line for the standardized data?
(b) Describe the scatterplot of the original data.

16. Estimate r, the correlation coefficient, for each of the following graphs:

17. The least-squares regression equation for the given data is $\hat{y} = 3 + x$. Calculate the sum of the squared residuals for the LSRL.

x	7	8	11	12	15
y	10	11	14	15	18

18. Many schools require teachers to have evaluations done by students. A study investigated the extent to which student evaluations are related to grades. Teacher evaluations and grades are both given on a scale of 100. The results for Prof. Socrates (y) for 10 of his students are given below together with the average for each student (x).

x	40	60	70	73	75	68	65	85	98	90
y	10	50	60	65	75	73	78	80	90	95

(a) Do you think student grades and the evaluations students give their teachers are related? Explain.

(b) What evaluation score do you think a student who averaged 80 would give Prof. Socrates?

19. Which of the following statements are true?

(a) The correlation coefficient, r, and the slope of the regression line, b, always have the same sign.

(b) The correlation coefficient is the same no matter which variable is considered to be the explanatory variable and which is considered to be the response variable.

(c) The correlation coefficient is resistant to outliers.

(d) x and y are measured in inches, and r is computed. Now, x and y are converted to feet, and a new r is computed. The two computed values of r depend on the units of measurement and will be different.

(e) The idea of a correlation between height and gender is not meaningful because gender is not numerical.

20. A study of right-handed people found that the regression equation for predicting left-hand strength (measured in kg) from right-hand strength is *left-hand strength* = 7.1 + 0.35 (*right-hand strength*).

(a) What is the predicted left-hand strength for a right-handed person whose right-hand strength is 12 kg?

(b) Interpret the intercept and the slope of the regression line in the context of the problem.

Cumulative Review Problems

1. Explain the difference between a statistic and a parameter.

2. True–False. The area under a normal curve between $z = 0.1$ and $z = 0.5$ is the same as the area between $z = 0.3$ and $z = 0.7$.

3. The following scores were achieved by students on a statistics test: 82, 93, 26, 56, 75, 73, 80, 61, 79, 90, 94, 93, 100, 71, 100, 60. Compute the mean and the median for these data and explain why they are different.

4. Is it possible for the standard deviation of a set of data to be negative? Zero? Explain.

5. For the test scores of problem #3, compute the five-number summary and draw a box-plot of the data.

Solutions to Practice Problems

Multiple-Choice

1. The correct answer is (d).

$$b = r \cdot \frac{s_y}{s_x} = (0.55)\left(\frac{0.75}{1.6}\right) = 0.26$$

2. The correct answer is (e). The value of a residual = actual value − predicted value = $25 - [2.35 + 0.86(29)] = -2.29$.

3. The correct answer is (a). $r^2 = (-0.58)^2 = 0.3364$. This is the *coefficient of determination*, which is the proportion of the variation in the response variable that is explained by the regression on the independent variable. Thus, about one-third (33.3%) of the variation in hours spent exercising can be explained by hours spent watching television. (b) is incorrect since correlation does not imply causation. (c) would be correct if $b = -0.58$, but there is no obvious way to predict the response value from the explanatory value just by knowing r. (d) is incorrect for the same reason (b) is incorrect. (e) is incorrect since r, not r^2, is given. In this case $r^2 = 0.3364$, which makes (a) correct.

4. The correct answer is (c). $ln(y) = 1.64 - 0.88(3.1) = -1.088 \Rightarrow y = e^{-1.088} = 0.337$.

5. The correct answer is (c). The pattern is more or less random about 0, which indicates that a line would be a good model for the data. If the data are linearly related, we would expect them to have a non-zero correlation.

6. The correct answer is (b). I is incorrect—the *predicted* weight of a person 61 inches tall is 104.6 pounds. II is a correct interpretation of the slope of the regression line. You could also say that "For each additional inch of height, weight *is predicted to* increase by 3.6 pounds." III is incorrect. It may well be true, but we have no way of knowing that from the information given.

7. The correct answer is (c). The predicted score for the student is $273.5 + (91.2)(3) = 547.1$. The residual is the actual score minus the predicted score, which equals $510 - 547.1 = -37.1$.

8. The correct answer is (b). Consider the expression for r. $r = \frac{1}{n-1}\sum\left(\frac{x - \bar{x}}{s_x}\right)\left(\frac{y - \bar{y}}{s_y}\right)$.

   Adding 12 to each Y-value would not change s_y. Although the average would be 12 larger, the differences $y - \bar{y}$ would stay the same since each y-value is also 12 larger. By taking the negative of each x-value, each term $\frac{x - \bar{x}}{s_x}$ would reverse sign (the mean also reverses sign), but the absolute value of each term would be the same. The net effect is to leave unchanged the absolute value of r but to reverse the sign.

9. The correct answer is (e). The question is asking for the coefficient of determination, r^2 (R-sq on many computer printouts). In this case, $r = 0.8877$ and $r^2 = 0.7881$, or 78.8%. This can be found on your calculator by entering the GPA scores in L1, the SAT scores in L2, and doing STAT CALC 1-Var Stats L1,L2.

10. The correct answer is (a). The point $(\bar{x}, \bar{y})$ always lies on the LSRL. Hence, $\bar{y}$ can be found by simply substituting $\bar{x}$ into the LSRL and solving for $\bar{y}$. Thus, $\bar{y} = 32.5 - 0.45(29.8) = 19.09$ miles per gallon. Be careful: you are told that the equation uses the weights in hundreds of pounds. You must then substitute 29.8 into the regression equation, not 2980, which would get you answer (c).

Free-Response

1. $b = r\dfrac{s_y}{s_x} = (0.80)\left(\dfrac{11}{4}\right) = 2.2$, $a = \bar{y} - b\bar{x} = 20 - (2.2)(14.5) = -11.9$.

   Thus, $\hat{y} = -11.9 + 2.2x$.

2. (a)

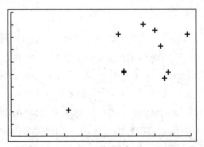

   (b) There seems to be a moderate positive relationship between the scores: students who did better on the first test tend to do better on the second, but the relationship isn't very strong; $r = 0.55$.

3. A line is not a good model for the data because the residual plot shows a definite pattern: the first 8 points have negative residuals, and the last 8 points have positive residuals. The box is in a cluster of points with positive residuals. We know that, for any given point, the residual equals actual value minus predicted value. Because actual − predicted > 0, we have actual > predicted, so the regression equation is likely to underestimate the actual value.

4. The regression equation for predicting time from year is $\widehat{time} = 79.21 - 0.61(year)$. We need $time = 60$. Solving $60 = 79.1 - 0.61(year)$, we get $year = 31.3$. So, we would predict that times will drop under one minute in about 31 or 32 years. The problem with this is that we are extrapolating far beyond the data. Extrapolation is dangerous in any circumstance, and especially so 24 years beyond the last known time. It's likely that the rate of improvement will decrease over time.

5. A scatterplot of the data (graph on the left) appears to be exponential. Taking the natural logarithm of each y-value, the scatterplot (graph on the right) appears to be more linear.

Taking the natural logarithm of each y-value and finding the LSRL, we have $ln(\widehat{\#roaches}) = 0.914 + 0.108\,(days) = 0.914 + 0.108(9) = 1.89$. Then $\widehat{\#roaches} = e^{1.89} = 6.62$.

6. The correlation between walking more and better health may or may not be causal. It may be that people who are healthier walk more. It may be that some other variable, such as general health consciousness, results in walking more and in better health. There may be a causal association, but in general, correlation does not imply causation.

7. Carla has reported the value of r^2, the coefficient of determination. If she had predicted each girl's grade based on the average grade only, there would have been a large amount of variability. But, by considering the regression of grades on socioeconomic status, she has reduced the total amount of variability by 72%. Because $r^2 = 0.72$, $r = 0.85$, which is indicative of a strong positive linear relationship between grades and socioeconomic status. Carla has reason to be happy.

8. (a) is false. $\Sigma(y - \hat{y}) = 0$ for the LSRL, but there is no unique line for which this is true.
   (b) is true.
   (c) is true. In fact, this is the definition of the LSRL—it is the line that minimizes the sum of the squared residuals.
   (d) is true since $b = r\dfrac{s_y}{s_x}$ and $\dfrac{s_y}{s_x}$ is constant.
   (e) is false. The slope of the regression lines tell you by how much the response variable changes *on average* for each unit change in the explanatory variable.

9. $\hat{y} = 26.211 - 0.25x = 26.211 - 0.25(73) = 7.961$. The residual for $x = 73$ is the actual value at 73 minus the predicted value at 73, or $y - \hat{y} = 7.9 - 7.961 = -0.061$. (73, 7.9) is below the LSRL since $y - \hat{y} < 0 \Rightarrow y < \hat{y}$.

10. (a) $r = +0.75$; the slope is positive and is the opposite of the original slope.
    (b) $r = -0.75$. It doesn't matter which variable is called x and which is called y.
    (c) $r = -0.75$; the slope is the same as the original slope.

11. We know that $b = r\dfrac{s_y}{s_x}$, so that $2.7 = r(3.33) \rightarrow r = \dfrac{2.7}{3.33} = 0.81 \rightarrow r^2 = 0.66$. The proportion of the variability that is *not* explained by the regression of y on x is $1 - r^2 = 1 - 0.66 = 0.34$.

12. Because the linear pattern will be stronger, the correlation coefficient will increase. The influential point pulls up on the regression line so that its removal would cause the slope of the regression line to decrease.

13. (a) $\widehat{rate} = -0.3980 + 0.1183\,(number)$.
    (b) $r = \sqrt{0.974} = 0.987$ (r is positive since the slope is positive).
    (c) $\widehat{rate} = -0.3980 + 0.1183(20) = 1.97$ crimes per thousand employees. Be sure to use 20, not 200.

14. (a) $\overline{Percentage\ appreciation} = 1.897 + 0.115\,(number)$.
    (b) $\overline{Percentage\ appreciation} = 1.897 + 0.115(85) = 11.67\%$.
    (c) $r = 0.82$, which indicates a strong linear relationship between the number of new homes built and percent appreciation.
    (d) If the number of new homes built was unknown, your best estimate would be the average percentage appreciation for the 5 years. In this case, the average percentage appreciation is 11.3%. (For what it's worth, the average error [absolute value] using the mean to estimate appreciation is 2.3; for the regression line, it's 1.3.)

15. (a) If $r^2 = 0.81$, then $r = \pm 0.9$. The slope of the regression line for the standardized data is either 0.9 or −0.9.

    (b) If $r = +0.9$, the scatterplot shows a strong positive linear pattern between the variables. Values above the mean on one variable tend to be above the mean on the other, and values below the mean on one variable tend to be below the mean on the other. If $r = -0.9$, there is a strong negative linear pattern to the data. Values above the mean on one variable are associated with values below the mean on the other.

16. (a) $r = 0.8$
    (b) $r = 0.0$
    (c) $r = -1.0$
    (d) $r = -0.5$

17. Each of the points lies on the regression line → every residual is 0 → the sum of the squared residuals is 0.

18. (a) $r = 0.90$ for these data, indicating that there is a strong positive linear relationship between student averages and evaluations of Prof. Socrates. Furthermore, $r^2 = 0.82$, which means that most of the variability in student evaluations can be explained by the regression of student evaluations on student average.

    (b) If y is the evaluation score of Prof. Socrates and x is the corresponding average for the student who gave the evaluation, then $\hat{y} = -29.3 + 1.34x$. If $x = 80$, then $\hat{y} = -29.3 + 1.34(80) = 77.9$, or 78.

19. (a) True, because
    $b = r \dfrac{s_y}{s_x}$ and $\dfrac{s_y}{s_x}$ is positive.

    (b) True. r is the same if explanatory and response variables are reversed. This is not true, however, for the slope of the regression line.

    (c) False. Because r is defined in terms of the means of the x and y variables, it is not resistant.

    (d) False. r does not depend on the units of measurement.

    (e) True. The definition of r, $r = \dfrac{1}{n-1} \sum_{i=1}^{n} \left(\dfrac{x_i - \bar{x}}{s_x} \right) \left(\dfrac{y_i - \bar{y}}{s_y} \right)$,

    necessitates that the variables be numerical, not categorical.

20. (a) $\overline{Left\text{-}hand\ strength} = 7.1 + 0.35(12) = 11.3$ kg.

    (b) **Intercept:** The predicted left-hand strength of a person who has zero right-hand strength is 7.1 kg.
    Slope: On average, left-hand strength increases by 0.35 kg for each 1-kg increase in right-hand strength. Or left-hand strength is predicted to increase by 0.35 kg for each 1-kg increase in right-hand strength.

Solutions to Cumulative Review Problems

1. A *statistic* is a measurement that describes a sample. A *parameter* is a value that describes a population.

2. False. For an interval of fixed length, there will be a greater proportion of the area under the normal curve if the interval is closer to the center than if it is removed from the center. This is because the normal distribution is mound shaped, which implies that the terms tend to group more in the center of the distribution than away from the center.

3. The mean is 77.1, and the median is 79.5. The mean is lower than the median because the mean is not resistant to extreme values, while the median is resistant.

4. By definition, $s = \sqrt{\dfrac{\sum(x-\bar{x})^2}{n-1}}$, which is a positive square root. Since $n > 1$ and $\sum(x-\bar{x})^2 \geq 0$, s cannot be negative. It *can* be zero, but only if $x = \bar{x}$ for all values of x.

5. The 5-number summary is [26, 66, 79.5, 93, 100].

CHAPTER 7

Design of a Study: Sampling, Surveys, and Experiments

IN THIS CHAPTER

Summary: Most chapters in this course are concerned with how to analyze and make inferences from data that have been collected. In this chapter, we discuss how to collect the data in a way that allows us to draw meaningful conclusions. We will discuss surveys and sampling, observational studies, experiments, and the types of problems that can creep into each of them, as well as how to avoid these problems. Once you understand all of this, you will also have the background to understand when and why our inference procedures apply.

Key Ideas
- ✪ Samples and Sampling
- ✪ Surveys
- ✪ Sampling Bias
- ✪ Experiments and Observational Studies
- ✪ Statistical Significance
- ✪ Completely Randomized Design
- ✪ Matched-Pairs Design
- ✪ Blocking

Samples

In the previous two chapters we concentrated on the analysis of data at hand—we didn't worry much about how the data came into our possession. The last part of this book deals with statistical inference—making statements about a population based on samples drawn from the population. In both data analysis and inference, we would like to believe that our analyses, or inferences, are meaningful. If we make a claim about a population based on a sample, we want that claim to be true. Our ability to do meaningful analyses and make reliable inferences is a function of the data we collect. To the extent that the sample data we deal with are representative of the population of interest, we are on solid ground. No interpretation of data that are poorly collected or systematically biased will be meaningful. We need to understand how to gather quality data before proceeding on to inference. In this chapter, we study techniques for gathering data so that we have reasonable confidence that they are representative of our population of interest.

Census

We usually want to know something about the entire population of interest. The way to find this with certainty is to conduct a **census**, a procedure by which every member of a population is selected for study. Doing a census, especially when the population of interest is quite large, is often impractical, too time-consuming, or too expensive. Interestingly enough, relatively small samples can give quite good estimates of population values if the samples are selected properly. For example, it can be shown that approximately 1500 randomly selected voters can give reliable information about the entire voting population of the United States.

The goal of sampling is to produce a **representative sample**, one that has the essential characteristics of the population being studied and is free of any type of bias. We can never be certain that our sample has the characteristics of the population from which it was drawn. Our best chance of making a sample representative is to use some sort of random process in its selection. It is important to note that "bias" does not mean the same thing as "nonrepresentative." Bias refers to a *method* that produces estimates either too high on average or too low on average. Nonrepresentative refers to a particular sample that differs from the population.

Probability Sample

A list of all members of the population from which we can draw a sample is called a **sampling frame**. We would like the sampling frame to be the same set of individuals we are studying. Unfortunately, this is often not the case. (Think, for example, about how selecting individuals from a voter registration list is not the same as all adult residents of a city!) A **probability sample** is one in which each member of the population has a known probability of being in the sample. Each member of the population may or may not have an equal chance of being selected. Probability samples are used to avoid the bias that can arise in a nonprobability sample (such as when a researcher selects the subjects she will use). Probability samples use some sort of random mechanism to choose the members of the sample. The following list includes some types of probability samples:

- **random sample:** Each member of the population is equally likely to be included.
- **simple random sample (SRS):** A sample of a given size is chosen in such a way that every possible sample of that size is equally likely to be chosen. Note that a sample can be a *random sample* but not be a *simple random sample* (SRS). For example, suppose you want a sample of 64 NFL football players. One way to produce a random sample would

be to randomly select two players from each of the 32 teams. This is a random sample but not a simple random sample because not all possible samples of size 64 are possible.

- **systematic sample:** The first member of the sample is chosen according to some random procedure, and then the rest are chosen according to some well-defined pattern. For example, if you wanted 100 people in your sample to be chosen from a list of 10,000 people, you could randomly select, say, the 61st person, and then select every 100th name on the list after that. A systematic sample is random because of the random start, but not a *simple* random sample because not every sample of size n is equally likely. For example, two people right next to each other in the list would never be chosen for the sample.

- **stratified random sample:** This is a sample in which the population is first divided into distinct homogeneous subgroups called *strata* and then a random sample is chosen from each subgroup. For example, you might divide the population of voters into groups by political party and then select an SRS of 250 from each group.

- **cluster sample:** The population is first divided into sections or "clusters." Then we randomly select one or more clusters and include *all* the members of the selected cluster(s) in the sample.

    example: You are going to conduct a survey of your senior class concerning plans for graduation. You want to sample 10% of the class. Describe a procedure by which you could use a systematic sample to obtain your sample and explain why this sample isn't a simple random sample. Is this a random sample?

    solution: One way would be to obtain an alphabetical list of all the seniors. Use a random number generator (such as a table of random digits or a scientific calculator with a random digits function) to select one of the first 10 names on the list. Then proceed to select every 10th name on the list after the first.

    Note that this is not an SRS because not every possible sample of 10% of the senior class is equally likely. For example, people next to each other in the list can't both be in the sample. Theoretically, the first 10% of the list could be the sample if it were an SRS. This clearly isn't possible with this technique.
    Before the first name has been randomly selected, every member of the population has an equal chance to be selected for the sample. Hence, this is a random sample, although it is not a simple random sample.

    example: A large urban school district wants to determine the opinions of its elementary school teachers concerning a proposed curriculum change. The district administration randomly selects three schools from all the elementary schools in the district and surveys each teacher in that school. What kind of sample is this?

    solution: This is a cluster sample. The individual schools represent previously defined groups (clusters) from which we have randomly selected one (it could have been more) for inclusion in our sample.

    example: You are sampling from a population that consists of 45% Engineers, 25% Technicians, 15% Staff, and 15% Administration. How would a *stratified random sample* of 200 people be constructed?

    solution: You want your sample to mirror the population in terms of its distribution. Accordingly, from the Engineers, you would draw an SRS of 90 (that's 45%), an SRS of 50 (25%) from the Technicians, an SRS of 30(15%) from the Staff, and an SRS of 30 (15%) from the Administration.

Of course, not all samples are probability samples. At times, people try to obtain samples by processes that are nonrandom but still hope, through design or faith, that the resulting sample is representative. The danger in all nonprobability samples is that some (unknown) bias may affect the degree to which the sample is representative. That isn't to say that random samples can't be nonrepresentative, just that we have a better chance of avoiding bias. (Remember the difference!) Some types of nonrandom sampling techniques that tend to be biased are

- **self-selected sample** or **voluntary response sample:** People choose whether or not to participate in the survey. A radio call-in show is a typical voluntary response sample.
- **convenience sampling:** The pollster obtains the sample any way he can, usually with the ease of obtaining the sample in mind. For example, handing out questionnaires to every member of a given class at school would be a convenience sample. The key issue here is that the surveyor makes the decision of whom to include in the sample.
- **quota sampling:** The pollster attempts to generate a representative sample by choosing sample members based on matching individual characteristics to known characteristics of the population. This is similar to a stratified random sample, only the process for selecting the sample is nonrandom.

Sampling Bias

We are trying to avoid **bias** in our sampling techniques, which would mean our method chooses samples that produce estimates that are, on average, either too high or too low.

Undercoverage

One type of sampling bias results from **undercoverage**. This happens when some part of the population being sampled is somehow excluded. This can happen when the sampling frame (the list from which the sample will be drawn) isn't the same as the target population.

> **example:** A pollster conducts a telephone survey to gather opinions of the general population about welfare. Persons too poor to be able to afford a telephone are certainly interested in this issue but will be systematically excluded from the sample. The resulting sample will be biased because of the exclusion of this group.

Voluntary Response Bias

Voluntary response bias occurs with self-selected samples. Persons who feel most strongly about an issue are most likely to respond. **Nonresponse bias**, the possible biases of those who choose not to respond, is a related issue.

> **example:** You decide to find out how your neighbors feel about the neighbor who seems to be running a car repair shop on his front lawn. You place a questionnaire in every mailbox within sight of the offending home and ask the people to fill it out and return it to you. About 1/2 of the neighbors return the survey, and 95% of those who do say that they find the situation intolerable. We have no way of knowing the feelings of the 50% of those who didn't return the survey—they may be perfectly happy with the "bad" neighbor. Those who have the strongest opinions are those most likely to return your survey—and they may not represent the opinions of all. Most likely they do not.

> **example:** In response to a question once posed in Ann Landers's advice column, some 70% of respondents (almost 10,000 readers) wrote that they would choose not to have children if they had the choice to do it over again. This is most likely representative only of those parents who were

having a *really* bad day with their children when they decided to respond to the question. In fact, a properly designed opinion poll a few months later found that more than 90% of parents said they *would* have children if they had the chance to do it all over again.

Wording Bias

Wording bias occurs when the wording of the question itself influences the response in a systematic way. A number of studies have demonstrated that welfare gathers more support from a random sample of the public when it is described as "helping people until they can better help themselves" than when it is described as "allowing people to stay on public assistance."

> **example:** Compare the probable responses to the following ways of phrasing a question.
>
> (i) "Do you support using taxpayers' money for sculpture in public spaces?"
>
> (ii) "Do you support beautification of public spaces with sculpture from local artists?"

It's likely that (i) is designed to show that people are against public art and that (ii) is designed to show that people are in favor of public art. The authors of both questions would probably argue that both responses reflect society's attitudes toward public art.

> **example:** Two different Gallup Polls were conducted in Dec. 2003. Both involved people's opinion about the U.S. space program. Here is one part of each poll.
>
> **Poll A:** Would you favor or oppose a new U.S. space program that would send astronauts to the moon? Favor—53%; oppose—45%.
>
> **Poll B:** Would you favor or oppose U.S. government spending billions of dollars to send astronauts to the moon? Favor—31%; oppose—67%.

Response Bias

Response bias arises in a variety of ways. The respondent may not give truthful responses to a question (perhaps they are ashamed of the truth); the respondent may fail to understand the question (you ask if a person is educated but fail to distinguish between levels of education); the respondent desires to please the interviewer (questions concerning race relations may well solicit different answers depending on the race of the interviewer); the ordering of the question may influence the response ("Do you prefer A to B?" may get different responses than "Do you prefer B to A?").

> **example:** What form of bias do you suspect in the following situation? You are a school principal and want to know students' level of satisfaction with the counseling services at your school. You direct one of the school counselors to ask her next 25 counselees how favorably they view the counseling services at the school.
>
> **solution:** A number of things would be wrong with the data you get from such a survey. First, the sample is nonrandom—it is a sample of convenience obtained by selecting 25 consecutive counselees. They may or may not be representative of students who use the counseling service. You don't know.
>
> Second, you are asking people who are seeing their counselor about their opinion of counseling. You will probably get a more favorable view of the

counseling services than you would if you surveyed the general population of the school (would students really unhappy with the counseling services voluntarily be seeing their counselor?). Also, because the counselor is administering the questionnaire, the respondents would have a tendency to want to please the interviewer. The sample certainly suffers from undercoverage—only a small subset of the general population is actually being interviewed. What do those *not* being interviewed think of the counseling?

Experiments and Observational Studies

Statistical Significance

One of the desirable outcomes of a study is to help us determine cause and effect. We do this by looking for differences between groups in an experiment that are so large that we cannot reasonably attribute the difference to chance. We say that a difference between what we would expect to find if there were no treatment and what we actually found is **statistically significant** if the difference is too large to attribute to chance. We discuss numerical methods of determining *significance* in Chapters 10–13.

An **experiment** is a study in which the researcher imposes some sort of treatment on the **experimental units** (which can be human—usually called **subjects** in that case). In an experiment, the idea is to determine the extent to which treatments, the explanatory variable(s), affect outcomes, the response variable(s). For example, a researcher might vary the rewards to different work-group members to see how that affects the group's ability to perform a particular task.

An **observational study**, on the other hand, simply observes and records behavior but does not attempt to impose a treatment in order to manipulate the response. Therefore, in an observational study, we cannot address cause and effect because we have not imposed a treatment. Sample surveys are actually one type of observational study because no treatment is imposed on the subjects of the study.

There are two classes of observational studies: *retrospective* and *prospective*. Retrospective studies examine data for a sample of individuals. Sample surveys are retrospective studies. Prospective studies select a sample of individuals and follow their behavior as time goes on. Sometimes over many years.

> **Exam Tip:** The distinction between an experiment and an observational study is an important one. There is a reasonable chance that you will be asked to show you understand this distinction on the exam. Be sure this section makes sense to you.

example: In order to develop models for predicting risk for cardiovascular disease (CVD) more than 423,000 participants without CVD will be followed over many years to monitor their cardiovascular health. A machine learning algorithm based on 473 variables will be used to identify risk factors for CVD. This is a prospective observational study because participants were selected and will be followed into the future.

example: A group of 60 volunteers who do not exercise are randomly assigned to one of the two fitness programs. One group of 30 is enrolled in a daily walking program, and the other group is put into a running program. After a period of time, the two groups are compared based on their scores on a wellness index. This is an *experiment* because the researcher has imposed the treatment (walking or running) and then measured the effects of the treatment on a defined response.

It may be, even in a controlled experiment, that the measured response is a function of variables present in addition to the treatment variable. A **confounding variable** is one that has an effect on the outcomes of the study but whose effects cannot be separated from those of the treatment variable.

> **example:** A study is conducted to see if Yummy Kibble dog food results in shinier coats on golden retrievers. It's possible that the dogs with shinier coats have them because they have owners who are more conscientious in terms of grooming their pets. Both the dog food and the conscientious owners could contribute to the shinier coats. The variables are **confounded** because their effects cannot be separated.

A well-designed study attempts to anticipate confounding variables in advance and **control** for them. **Statistical control** refers to a researcher holding constant variables not under study that might have an influence on the outcomes.

> **example:** You are going to study the effectiveness of SAT preparation courses on SAT score. You know that better students tend to do well on SAT tests. You could control for the possible confounding effect of academic quality by running your study with groups of "A" students, "B" students, etc.

Control is often considered to be one of the three basic principles of experimental design. The other two basic principles are **randomization** and **replication**.

One purpose of *randomization* is to equalize groups so that the effects of extraneous variables are equalized among groups. *Randomization* involves the use of chance (like putting names in a bin, mixing them, and drawing them) to assign subjects to treatment and control groups. The hope is that the groups being studied will differ systematically *only* in the effects of the treatment variable. Although individuals within the groups may vary, the idea is to make the groups as alike as possible except for the treatment variable. Note that it isn't possible to produce, with certainty, groups free of any confounding variables. It is possible, through the use of randomization, to increase the probability of producing groups that are alike. The idea is to control for the effects of variables you aren't aware of but that might affect the response.

Replication involves applying the treatment to enough subjects (or units) to reduce the effects of chance variation on the outcomes. If each treatment is applied to only one subject, there is no indication of how much the response varies for the treatment (within-treatment variation). To see if there is a difference between treatments, we must be able to compare that to the difference within each treatment.

Completely Randomized Design

A **completely randomized design** for a study involves three essential elements: random allocation of subjects to treatment groups; administration of different treatments to each randomized group (if there is a control group, that is one of the treatment groups); and some sort of comparison of the outcomes from the various groups. A standard diagram of this situation is the following:

There may be several different treatment groups (different levels of a new drug, for example), in which case the diagram could be modified. The control group can either be an older treatment (like a medication currently on the market) or a **placebo**, an inactive treatment. (Note: as a control, placebos are used with human subjects.) A diagram for an experiment with more than two treatment groups might look something like this:

Remember that each group must have enough subjects so that the replication condition is met. The purpose of the *placebo* is to separate genuine treatment effects from possible subject responses due to simply being part of an experiment. Placebos are *not* necessary if a new treatment is being compared to a treatment whose effects have been previously experimentally established. In that case, the new treatment can be compared to the old treatment. A new cream to reduce acne (the treatment), for example, might be compared to an already-on-the-market cream whose effectiveness has long been established.

> **example:** Three hundred graduate students in psychology volunteer to be subjects in an experiment whose purpose is to determine what dosage level of a new drug has the most positive effect on a performance test. There are three levels of the drug to be tested: 200 mg, 500 mg, and 750 mg. Include an additional treatment group to see whether the drug has any effect at all. Design a completely randomized study to test the effectiveness of the various drug levels.

> **solution:** There are three levels of the drug to be tested: 200 mg, 500 mg, and 750 mg. A placebo control can be included, although strictly speaking, it isn't necessary as our purpose is to compare the three dosage levels. We need to randomly allocate the 300 students to each of four groups of 75 each: one group will receive the 200-mg dosage, one will receive the 500-mg dosage, one will receive the 750-mg dosage, and one will receive a placebo (if included). No group will know which treatment its members are receiving (all the pills look the same), nor will the test personnel who come in contact with them know which subjects received which pill (see the definition of "double-blind" given below). Each group will complete the performance test and the results of the various groups will be compared. This design can be diagrammed as follows:

Double-Blind Experiments

In the previous example, it was explained that neither the subjects nor the researchers knew who was receiving which dosage or the placebo. A study is said to be **double-blind** when neither the subjects (or experimental units) nor the evaluators know which group(s) is/are receiving each treatment or control. The reason for this is that, on the part of subjects, simply knowing that they are part of a study may affect the way they respond, and on the part of the evaluators, knowing which group is receiving which treatment can influence the way in which they evaluate the outcomes. Our worry is that the individual treatment and control groups will differ by something other than the treatment unless the study is double-blind. A double-blind study further controls for the placebo effect. Note, however, that somebody has to know which treatment is which. Sometimes students make the mistake of saying things like "Nobody knows which treatment is which."

Randomization

There are several procedures for performing a randomization. They are as follows:

- Tables of random digits. Most textbooks contain tables of random digits. These are usually tables where the digits 0, 1, 2, 3, 4, 5, 6, 7, 8, and 9 appear in random order. That means that, as you move through the table, each digit should appear with probability 1/10, and each entry is independent of the others (knowing what came before doesn't help you make predictions about what comes next).
- Electronic random number generators. Graphing calculators have several random functions: a basic random function (which generates a random real number between 0 and 1), a random integer function (which will generate a list of random integers in a specified range), a random normal function (which will generate random values from a normal distribution with a specified mean and standard deviation), and a random binomial function (which will generate random values from a binomial distribution with a specified number of trials and probability—see Chapter 9). Statistics software and some calculators also have the ability to generate random samples, both with and without replacement, from a fixed population.
- Physical probability generators. Dice, spinners, drawing slips of paper from a bag, and so on are also ways of representing random processes.

Exam questions could ask for descriptions of any of these approaches, and often the approach is left open, so familiarize yourself with these different methods. In general, if you are asked to describe a procedure for selecting a sample or assigning treatments to subjects, be sure to specify the method of randomization, and address whether you are sampling with replacement or without (equivalently, are repeated digits allowed or ignored). And if you are using a random digit table and are using, say, pairs of digits, be clear that 01 is how you represent the number 1, for example.

We will use tables of random digits and/or the calculator in Chapter 8 when we discuss simulation.

Randomized Block Design

Earlier we discussed the need for **control** in a study and identified **randomization** as the main method to control for confounding variables—variables that might influence the outcomes in some way but are not considered in the design of the study (usually because we aren't aware of them). Another type of control involves variables we think might influence the outcome of a study. Suppose we suspect, as in our previous example, that the performance test varies by gender as well as by dosage level of the test drug. That is, we suspect that gender is a *confounding variable* (its effects cannot be separated from the effects of the drug). To control for the effects of gender on the performance test, we utilize what is known as a **block design**. A block design involves doing a completely randomized experiment *within* each block. In this case, that means that each level of the drug would be tested within the group of females and within the group of males. To simplify the example, suppose that we were only testing one level (say, 500 mg) of the drug versus a placebo. The experimental design, blocked by gender, could then be diagrammed as follows:

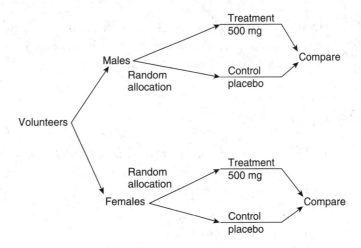

Randomization and block designs each serve a purpose. It's been said that you *block* to control for the variables you know about and *randomize* to control for the ones you don't. Note that your interest here is in studying the effect of the treatment within the population of males and within the population of females, *not* to compare the effects on men and women.

Matched-Pairs Design

A particular block design of interest is the **matched-pairs** design. One possible matched-pairs design involves before and after measurements on the same subjects. In this case, each subject becomes a block on which the experiment is conducted. Another type of matched pairs involves pairing the subjects in some way (matching on, say, height, race, age, etc.).

> **example:** A study is instituted to determine the effectiveness of training teachers to teach AP Statistics. A pretest is administered to each of 23 prospective teachers who subsequently undergo a training program. When the program is finished, the teachers are given a posttest. A score for each teacher is arrived at by subtracting their pretest score from their posttest score. This is a matched-pairs design because two scores are paired for each teacher.

> **example:** One of the questions on the 1997 AP Exam in Statistics asked students to design a study to compare the effects of differing formulations of fish food on fish growth. Students were given a room with eight fish tanks. The room had a heater at the back of the room, a door at the front center of the room, and windows at the front sides of the room. The most correct design involved blocking so that the two tanks nearest the heater in the back of the room were in a single block, the two away from the heater in a second block, the two in the front near the door in a third, and the two in the front near the windows in a fourth. This matching had the effect of controlling for known environmental variations in the room caused by the heater, the door, and the windows. Within each block, one tank was randomly assigned to receive one type of fish food and the remaining tank received the other. The blocking controlled for the known effects of the environment in which the experiment was conducted. The randomization controlled for unknown influences that might be present in the various tank locations.

You will need to recognize paired data, as distinct from two independent sets of data, later on when we study inference. Even though two sets of data are generated in a matched-pairs study, it is the *differences* between the matched values that form the one-sample data used for statistical analysis.

Exam Tip: You need to be clear on the distinction between the purposes of blocking and randomizing. If you are asked to describe an experiment involving blocking, be sure to remember to randomize treatments within blocks.

❯ Rapid Review

1. You are doing a research project on attitudes toward fast food and decide to use as your sample the first 25 people to enter the door at a local hamburger restaurant. Which of the following is (are) true of this sample?

   a. It is a systematic sample.
   b. It is a convenience sample.
   c. It is a random sample.
   d. It is a simple random sample.
   e. It is a self-selected sample.

   Answer: Only (b) is correct. (a), (c), and (d) are all probability samples, which rely on some random process to select the sample, and there is nothing random about the selection process in this situation. (e) is incorrect because, although the sample members voluntarily entered the restaurant, they haven't volunteered to respond to a survey.

2. How does an *experiment* differ from an *observational study*?

   Answer: In an experiment, the researcher imposes some treatment on the subjects (or experimental units) in order to observe a response. In an observational study, the researcher simply observes, compares, and measures, but does not impose a treatment.

3. What are the three key components of an experiment? Explain each.

   Answer: The three components are randomization, control, and replication. You randomize to be sure that the response does not systematically favor one outcome over another. The idea is to equalize groups as much as possible so that differences in response are attributable to the treatment variable alone. Control is designed to hold confounding variables constant (such as the placebo effect). Replication ensures that the experiment is conducted on sufficient numbers of subjects to minimize the effects of chance variation.

4. Your local pro football team has just suffered a humiliating defeat at the hands of its archrival. A local radio sports talk show conducts a call-in poll on whether or not the coach should be fired. What is the poll likely to find?

   Answer: The poll is likely to find that, overwhelmingly, respondents think the coach should be fired. This is a *voluntary* response poll, and we know that such a poll is most likely to draw a response from those who feel most strongly about the issue being polled. Fans who bother to vote in a call-in poll such as this are most likely upset at their team's loss and are looking for someone to blame—this gives them the opportunity. There is, of course, a chance that the coach may be very popular and draw support, but the point to remember is that this is a self-selecting nonrandom sample, and will probably exhibit response bias.

5. It is known that exercise and diet both influence weight loss. Your task is to conduct a study of the effects of diet on weight loss. Explain the concept of *blocking* as it relates to this study.

   Answer: If you did a completely randomized design for this study using diet as the treatment variable, it's very possible that your results would be confounded by the effects of exercise. Because you are aware of this, you would like to control for the effects of exercise. Hence, you *block* by exercise level. You might define, say, three blocks by level of exercise (very active, active, not very active) and do a completely randomized study within each of the blocks. Because exercise level is held constant, you can be confident that differences between treatment and control groups within each block are attributable to diet, not exercise.

6. Explain the concept of a *double-blind* study and why it is important.

   Answer: A study is *double-blind* if neither the subject of the study nor the researchers are aware of who is in the treatment group and who is in the control group. This is to control for the well-known effect of people to (subconsciously) attempt to respond in the way they think they should.

7. You are interested in studying the effects of preparation programs on SAT performance. Briefly describe a matched-pairs design and a completely randomized design for this study.

   Answer: <u>matched pairs</u>: Choose, say, 100 students who have not participated in an SAT prep course. Have them take the SAT. Then have these students take a preparation course and retake the SAT. Do a statistical analysis of the difference between the pre- and postpreparation scores for each student. (*Note* that this design doesn't deal with the influence of retaking the SAT independent of any preparation course, which could be a confounding variable.)

   <u>completely randomized design</u>: Select 100 students and randomly assign them to two groups, one of which takes the SAT with no preparation course and one of which has a preparation course before taking the SAT. Statistically, compare the average performance of each group.

Practice Problems

Multiple-Choice

1. Data were collected in 20 cities on the percentage of women in the workforce. Data were collected in 1990 and again in 1994. Gains, or losses, in this percentage were the measurement upon which the study's conclusions were to be based. What kind of design was this?
   I. A matched-pairs design
   II. An observational study
   III. An experiment using a block design

   (a) I only
   (b) II only
   (c) III only
   (d) I and III only
   (e) I and II only

2. You want to do a survey of members of the senior class at your school and want to select a *simple random sample*. You intend to include 40 students in your sample. Which of the following approaches will generate a simple random sample?

   (a) Write the name of each student in the senior class on a slip of paper and put the papers in a container. Then randomly select 40 slips of paper from the container.
   (b) Assuming that students are randomly assigned to classes, select two classes at random and include those students in your sample.

(c) From a list of all seniors, select one of the first 10 names at random. Then select every *n*th name on the list until you have 40 people selected.

(d) Select the first 40 seniors to pass through the cafeteria door at lunch.

(e) Randomly select 10 students from each of the four senior calculus classes.

3. Which of the following is (are) important in designing an experiment?
   I. Control of all variables that might have an influence on the response variable
   II. Randomization of subjects to treatment groups
   III. Use of a large number of subjects to control for small-sample variability

   (a) I only
   (b) I and II only
   (c) II and III only
   (d) I, II, and III
   (e) II only

4. Your company has developed a new treatment for acne. You think men and women might react differently to the medication, so you separate them into two groups. Then the men are randomly assigned to two groups and the women are randomly assigned to two groups. One of the two groups is given the medication and the other is given a placebo. The basic design of this study is

   (a) completely randomized.
   (b) blocked by gender.
   (c) completely randomized, blocked by gender.
   (d) randomized, blocked by gender and type of medication.
   (e) a matched-pairs design.

5. A *double-blind* design is important in an experiment because

   (a) there is a natural tendency for subjects in an experiment to want to please the researcher.
   (b) it helps control for the placebo effect.
   (c) evaluators of the responses in a study can influence the outcomes if they know which subjects are in the treatment group and which are in the control group.
   (d) subjects in a study might react differently if they knew they were receiving an active treatment or a placebo.
   (e) All of the above are reasons why an experiment should be *double-blind*.

6. Which of the following is not an example of a *probability sample*?

   (a) You are going to sample 10% of a group of students. You randomly select one of the first 10 students on an alphabetical list and then select every 10th student after than on the list.
   (b) You are a sports-talk radio host interested in opinions about whether or not Pete Rose should be elected to the Baseball Hall of Fame, even though he has admitted to betting on his own teams. You ask listeners to call in and vote.
   (c) A random sample of drivers is selected to receive a questionnaire about the manners of Department of Motor Vehicle employees.
   (d) In order to determine attitudes about the Medicare Drug Plan, a random sample is drawn so that each age group (65–70, 70–75, 75–80, 80–85) is represented in proportion to its percentage in the population.
   (e) In choosing respondents for a survey about a proposed recycling program in a large city, interviewers choose homes to survey based on rolling a die. If the die shows a 1, the house is selected. If the dies shows a 2–6, the interviewer moves to the next house.

7. Which of the following is true of an experiment but not of an observational study?

    (a)   A cause-and-effect relationship can be more easily inferred.
    (b)   The cost of conducting it is excessive.
    (c)   More advanced statistics are needed for analysis after the data are gathered.
    (d)   By law, the subjects need to be informed that they are part of a study.
    (e)   Possible confounding variables are more difficult to control.

8. A study showed that persons who ate two carrots a day had significantly better eyesight than those who ate less than one carrot a week. Which of the following statements is (are) correct?
    I.   This study provides evidence that eating carrots contributes to better eyesight.
    II. The general health consciousness of people who eat carrots could be a confounding variable.
    III. This is an observational study and not an experiment.

    (a)   I only
    (b)   III only
    (c)   I and II only
    (d)   II and III only
    (e)   I, II, and III

9. Which of the following situations is a cluster sample?

    (a)   Survey five friends concerning their opinions of the local hockey team.
    (b)   Take a random sample of five voting precincts in a large metropolitan area and do an exit poll at each voting site.
    (c)   Measure the length of time each fifth person entering a restaurant has to wait to be seated.
    (d)   From a list of all students in your school, randomly select 20 to answer a survey about Internet use.
    (e)   Identify four different ethnic groups at your school. From each group, choose enough respondents so that the final sample contains roughly the same proportion of each group as the school population.

Free-Response

1. You are interested in the extent to which ingesting vitamin C inhibits getting a cold. You identify 300 volunteers, 150 of whom have been taking more than 1000 mg of vitamin C a day for the past month and 150 of whom have not taken vitamin C at all during the past month. You record the number of colds during the following month for each group and find that the vitamin C group had significantly fewer colds. Is this an experiment or an observational study? Explain. What do we mean in this case when we say that the finding was *significant*?

2. Design an experiment that employs a *completely randomized design* to study the question of whether of not taking large doses of vitamin C is effective in reducing the number of colds.

3. A survey of physicians found that some doctors gave a placebo rather than an actual medication to patients who experienced pain symptoms for which no physical reason could be found. If the pain symptoms were reduced, the doctors concluded that there was no real physical basis for the complaints. Do the doctors understand *the placebo effect*? Explain.

4. Explain how you would use a table of random digits to help obtain a systematic sample of 10% of the names on an alphabetical list of voters in a community. Is this a random sample? Is it a simple random sample?

5. The *Literary Digest Magazine*, in 1936, predicted that Alf Landon would defeat Franklin Roosevelt in the presidential election that year. The prediction was based on questionnaires mailed to 10 million of its subscribers and to names drawn from other public lists. Those receiving the questionnaires were encouraged to mail back their ballot preference. The prediction was off by 19 percentage points. The magazine received back some 2.3 million ballots from the 10 million sent out. What are some of the things that might have caused the magazine to be so wrong (the same techniques had produced accurate predictions for several previous elections)? (Hint: Think about what was going on in the world in 1936.)

6. Interviewers, after the 9/11 attacks, asked a group of Arab Americans if they trust the administration to make efforts to counter anti-Arab activities. If the interviewer was of Arab descent, 42% responded "yes," and if the interviewer was of non-Arab descent, 55% responded "yes." What seems to be going on here?

7. There are three classes of statistics at your school, each with 30 students. You want to select a simple random sample of 15 students from the 90 students as part of an opinion-gathering project for your social studies class. Describe a procedure for doing this.

8. Question 1 stated, in part, "You are interested in the extent to which ingesting vitamin C inhibits getting a cold. You identify 300 volunteers, 150 of whom have been taking more than 1000 mg of vitamin C a day for the past month and 150 of whom have not taken vitamin C at all during the past month. You record the number of colds during the following month for each group and find that the vitamin C group had significantly fewer colds." Explain the concept of *confounding* in the context of this problem and give an example of how it might have affected the finding that the vitamin C group had fewer colds.

9. A shopping mall wants to know about the attitudes of all shoppers who visit the mall. On a Wednesday morning, the mall places 10 interviewers at a variety of places in the mall and asks questions of shoppers as they pass by. Comment on any bias that might be inherent in this approach.

10. Question 2 asked you to design a *completely randomized experiment* for the situation presented in question 1, that is, to design an experiment that uses treatment and control groups to see if the groups differed in terms of the number of colds suffered by users of 1000 mg a day of vitamin C and those that didn't use vitamin C. Question 8 asked you about possible *confounding variables* in this study. Given that you believe that both general health habits and use of vitamin C might explain a reduced number of colds, design an experiment to determine the effectiveness of vitamin C, taking into account general health habits. You may assume your volunteers vary in their history of vitamin C use.

11. You have developed a weight-loss treatment that involves a combination of exercise and diet pills. The treatment has been effective with subjects who have used a regular dose of the pill of 200 mg, when exercise level is held constant. There is some indication that higher doses of the pill will promote even better results, but you are worried about side effects if the dosage becomes too great. Assume you have 400 overweight volunteers for your study, who have all been on the same exercise program, but who have not been taking any kind of diet pill. Design a study to evaluate the relative effects of a 200-mg, 400-mg, 600-mg, and 800-mg daily dosage of the pill.

12. You are going to study the effectiveness of three different SAT preparation courses. You obtain 60 high school juniors as volunteers to participate in your study. You want to assign each of the 60 students, at random, to one of the three programs. Describe a procedure for assigning students to the programs if

    (a)   you want there to be an equal number of students taking each course.
    (b)   you want each student to be assigned independently to a group. That is, each student should have the same probability of being in any of the three groups.

13. A researcher wants to obtain a sample of 100 teachers who teach in high schools at various economic levels. The researcher has access to a list of teachers in several schools for each of the levels. She has identified four such economic levels (A, B, C, and D) that comprise 10%, 15%, 45%, and 30% of the schools in which the teachers work. Describe what is meant by a *stratified random sample* in this situation, and discuss how she might obtain it.

14. You are testing for sweetness in five varieties of strawberry. You have 10 plots available for testing. The 10 plots are arranged in two side-by-side groups of five. A river runs along the edge of one of the groups of five plots something like the diagram shown below (the available plots are numbered 1–10).

     You decide to control for the possible confounding effect of the river by planting one of each type of strawberry in plots 1–5 and one of each type in plots 6–10 (that is, you block to control for the river). Then, within each block, you randomly assign one type of strawberry to each of the five plots within the block. What is the purpose of randomization in this situation?

15. Look at problem 14 again. It is the following year, and you now have only two types of strawberries to test. Faced with the same physical conditions you had in problem 14, and given that you are concerned that differing soil conditions (as well as proximity to the river) might affect sweetness, how might you block the experiment to produce the most reliable results?

16. A group of volunteers, who had never been in any kind of therapy, were randomly separated into two groups, one of which received an experimental therapy to improve self-concept. The other group, the control group, received traditional therapy. The subjects were not informed of which therapy they were receiving. Psychologists who specialize in self-concept issues evaluated both groups after training for self-concept, and the self-concept scores for the two groups were compared. Could this experiment have been *double-blind*? Explain. If it wasn't *double-blind*, what might have been the impact on the results?

17. You want to determine how students in your school feel about a new dress code for school dances. One group in the student council, call them group A, wants to word the question as follows: "As one way to help improve student behavior at school sponsored events, do you feel that there should be a dress code for school dances?" Another group, group B, prefers, "Should the school administration be allowed to restrict student rights by imposing a dress code for school dances?" Which group do you think favors a dress code, and which opposes it? Explain.

18. A study of reactions to different types of billboard advertising is to be carried out. Two different types of ads (call them Type I and Type II) for each product will be featured on numerous billboards. The organizer of the campaign is concerned that communities

representing different economic strata will react differently to the ads. The three communities where billboards will be placed have been identified as Upper Middle, Middle, and Lower Middle. Four billboards are available in each of the three communities. Design a study to compare the effectiveness of the two types of advertising taking into account the communities involved.

19. In 1976, Shere Hite published a book titled *The Hite Report on Female Sexuality*. The conclusions reported in the book were based on 3000 returned surveys from some 100,000 sent out to, and distributed by, various women's groups. The results were that women were highly critical of men. In what way might the author's findings have been biased?

20. You have 26 women available for a study: Annie, Betty, Clara, Darlene, Edie, Fay, Grace, Helen, Ina, Jane, Koko, Laura, Mary, Nancy, Ophelia, Patty, Quincy, Robin, Suzy, Tina, Ulla, Vivien, Wanda, Xena, Yolanda, and Zoe. The women need to be divided into four groups for the purpose of the study. Explain how you could use a table of random digits to make the needed assignments.

Cumulative Review Problems

1. The five-number summary for a set of data is [52, 55, 60, 63, 85]. Is the mean most likely to be *less than* or *greater than* the median?

2. Pamela selects a random sample of 15 of her classmates and computes the mean and the standard deviation of their pulse rates. She then uses these values to predict the mean and the standard deviation of the pulse rates for the entire school. Which of these measures are *parameters* and which are *statistics*?

3. Consider the following set of values for a dataset: 15, 18, 23, 25, 25, 27, 28, 29, 35, 46, 55. Does this dataset have any *outliers* if we use an outlier rule that

   (a) is based on the median?
   (b) is based on the mean?

4. For the dataset of problem 3, what is z_{55}?

5. A study examining factors that contribute to a strong college GPA finds that 62% of the variation in college GPA can be explained by SAT score. What name is given to this statistic, and what is the correlation (r) between SAT score and college GPA?

Solutions to Practice Problems

Multiple-Choice

1. The correct answer is (e). The data are paired because there are two measurements for each city, so the data are not independent. There is no treatment being applied, so this is an observational study. Matched pairs is one type of block design, but this is NOT an experiment, so III is false.

2. The answer is (a). In order for this to be an SRS, all samples of size 40 must be equally likely. None of the other choices does this [and choice (d) isn't even random]. Note that (a), (b), and (c) are probability samples.

3. The correct answer is (d). These three items represent the three essential parts of an experiment: control, randomization, and replication.

4.   The correct answer is (b). You block men and women into different groups because you are concerned that differential reactions to the medication may confound the results. It is not completely randomized because it is blocked.

5.   The correct answer is (e).

6.   The correct answer is (b). This is an example of a voluntary response and is likely to be biased. Those who feel strongly about the issue are most likely to respond. The other choices all rely on some probability technique to draw a sample. In addition, responses (c) and (e) meet the criteria for a simple random sample (SRS).

7.   The correct answer is (a). If done properly, an experiment permits you to control the variable that might influence the results. Accordingly, you can argue that the only variable that influences the results is the treatment variable.

8.   The correct answer is (d). I isn't true because this is an observational study and, thus, shows a relationship but not necessarily a cause-and-effect one.

9.   The correct answer is (b). (a) is a convenience sample. (c) is a systematic sample. (d) is a simple random sample. (e) is a stratified random sample.

Free-Response

1.   It's an **observational study** because the researcher didn't provide a treatment but simply observed different outcomes from two groups with at least one different characteristic. Participants self-selected themselves into either the vitamin C group or the nonvitamin C group. To say that the finding was significant in this case means that the difference between the number of colds in the vitamin C group and in the nonvitamin C group was too great to attribute to chance—it appears that something besides random variation may have accounted for the difference.

2.   Identify 300 volunteers for the study, preferably none of whom have been taking vitamin C. Randomly split the group into two groups of 150 participants each. One group can be randomly selected to receive a set dosage of vitamin C each day for a month and the other group to receive a placebo. Neither the subjects nor those who administer the medication will know which subjects received the vitamin C and which received the placebo (that is, the study should be *double-blind*). During the month following the giving of pills, you can count the number of colds within each group. Your measurement of interest is the difference in the number of colds between the two groups. Also, placebo effects often diminish over time.

3.   The doctors probably did not understand the placebo effect. We know that, sometimes, a real effect can occur even from a placebo. If people believe they are receiving a real treatment, they will often show a change. But without a control group, we have no way of knowing if the improvement would not have been even more significant with a real treatment. The *difference* between the placebo score and the treatment score is what is important, not one or the other.

4.   If you want 10% of the names on the list, you need every 10th name for your sample. Number the first 10 names on the list 0, 1, 2, . . . , 9. Pick a random place to enter the table of random digits and note the first number. The first person in your sample is the person among the first 10 on the list that corresponds to the number chosen. Then pick every 10th name on the list after that name. This is a random sample to the extent that, before the first name was selected, every member of the population had an equal

chance to be chosen. It is not a simple random sample because not all possible samples of 10% of the population are equally likely. Adjacent names on the list, for example, could not both be part of the sample.

5. This is an instance of *voluntary response bias*. This poll was taken during the depths of the Depression, and people felt strongly about national leadership. Those who wanted a change were more likely to respond than those who were more or less satisfied with the current administration. Also, at the height of the Depression, people who subscribed to magazines and were on public lists were more likely to be wealthy and, hence, Republican (Landon was a Republican and Roosevelt was a Democrat).

6. Almost certainly, respondents are responding in a way they feel will please the interviewer. This is a form of response bias—in this circumstance, people may not give a truthful answer.

7. Many different solutions are possible. One way would be to put the names of all 90 students on slips of paper and put the slips of paper into a box. Then draw out 15 slips of paper at random. The names on the paper are your sample. Another way would be to identify each student by a two-digit number 01, 02, . . . , 90 and use a table of random digits to select 15 numbers. Or you could use the randInt function on your calculator to select 15 numbers between 1 and 90 inclusive. What you *cannot* do, if you want it to be an SRS, is to employ a procedure that selects five students randomly from each of the three classes.

8. Because the two groups were not selected randomly, it is possible that the fewer number of colds in the vitamin C group could be the result of some variable whose effects cannot be separated from the effects of the vitamin C. That would make this other variable a *confounding variable*. A possible confounding variable in this case might be that the group members who take vitamin C might be, as a group, more health conscious than those who do not take vitamin C. This could account for the difference in the number of colds but could not be separated from the effects of taking vitamin C.

9. The study suffers from *undercoverage* of the population of interest, which was declared to be all shoppers at the mall. By restricting their interview time to a Wednesday morning, they effectively exclude most people who work on Wednesday. They essentially have a sample of the opinions of nonworking shoppers. There may be other problems with randomness, but without more specific information about how they gathered their sample, talking about it would only be speculation.

10. We could first administer a questionnaire to all 300 volunteers to determine differing levels of health consciousness. For simplicity, let's just say that the two groups identified are "health conscious" and "not health conscious." Then you would block by "health conscious" and "not health conscious" and run the experiment within each block. A diagram of this experiment might look like this:

11. Because exercise level seems to be more or less constant among the volunteers, there is no need to block for its effect. Furthermore, because the effects of a 200-mg dosage are known, there is no need to have a placebo (although you could)—the 200-mg dosage will serve as the control. Randomly divide your 400 volunteers into four groups of 100 each. Randomly assign each group to one of the four treatment levels: 200 mg, 400 mg, 600 mg, or 800 mg. The study can be and should be double-blind. After a period of time, compare the weight loss results for the four groups.

12. (a) Many answers are possible. One solution involves putting the names of all 60 students on slips of paper, then randomly selecting the papers. The first student goes into program 1, the next into program 2, etc. until all 60 students have been assigned.

    (b) Use a random number generator to select integers from 1 to 3 (like `randInt(1,3)`) on the TI-83/84 or use a table of random numbers assigning each of the programs a range of values (such as 1–3, 4–6, 7–9, and ignore 0). Pick any student and generate a random number from 1 to 3. The student enters the program that corresponds to the number. In this way, the probability of a student ending up in any one group is 1/3, and the selections are independent. It would be unlikely to have the three groups come out completely even in terms of the numbers in each, but we would expect it to be close.

13. In this situation, a *stratified random sample* would be a sample in which the proportion of teachers from each of the four levels is the same as that of the population from which the sample was drawn. That is, in the sample of 100 teachers, 10 should be from level A, 15 from level B, 45 from level C, and 30 from level D. For level A, she could accomplish this by taking an SRS of 10 teachers from a list of all teachers who teach at that level. SRSs of 15, 45, and 30 would then be obtained from each of the other lists.

14. Remember that you block to control for the variables that might affect the outcome that you know about, and you randomize to control for the effect of those you don't know about. In this case, then, you randomize to control for any unknown systematic differences between the plots that might influence sweetness. An example might be that the plots on the northern end of the rows (plots 1 and 6) have naturally richer soil than those plots on the south side.

15. The idea is to get plots that are most similar in order to run the experiment. One possibility would be to match the plots the following way: close to the river north (6 and 7); close to the river south (9 and 10); away from the river north (1 and 2); and away from the river south (4 and 5). This pairing controls for both the effects of the river and possible north–south differences that might affect sweetness. Within each pair, you would randomly select one plot to plant one variety of strawberry, planting the other variety in the other plot.

    This arrangement leaves plots 3 and 8 unassigned. One possibility is simply to leave them empty. Another possibility is to randomly assign each of them to one of the pairs they adjoin. That is, plot 3 could be randomly assigned to join either plot 2 or plot 4. Similarly, plot 8 would join either plot 7 or plot 9.

16. The study could have been double-blind. The question indicates that the subjects did not know which treatment they were receiving. If the psychologists did not know which therapy the subjects had received before being evaluated, then the basic requirement of a double-blind study was met: neither the subjects nor the evaluators who come in contact with them are aware of who is in the treatment and who is in the control group.

If the study wasn't double-blind, it would be because the psychologists were aware of which subjects had which therapy. In this case, the attitudes of the psychologists toward the different therapies might influence their evaluations—probably because they might read more improvement into a therapy of which they approve.

17. Group A favors a dress code; group B does not. Both groups are hoping to bias the response in favor of their position by the way they have worded the question.

18. You probably want to block by community since it is felt that economic status influences attitudes toward advertising. That is, you will have three blocks: Upper Middle, Middle, and Lower Middle. Within each, you have four billboards. Randomly select two of the billboards within each block to receive the Type I ads, and put the Type II ads on the other two. After a few weeks, compare the differences in reaction to each type of advertising within each block.

19. With only 3000 of 100,000 surveys returned, *voluntary response bias* is most likely operating. That is, the 3000 women represented those who felt strongly enough (negatively) about men and were the most likely to respond. We have no way of knowing if the 3% who returned the survey were representative of the 100,000 who received it, but they most likely were not.

20. Assign each of the 26 women a two-digit number, say 01, 02,..., 26. Then enter the table at a random location and note two-digit numbers. Ignore numbers outside of the 01–26 range. The first number chosen assigns the corresponding woman to the first group, the second to the second group, and so on until all 26 have been assigned. This method roughly equalizes the numbers in the group (not quite because 4 doesn't go evenly into 26).

Solutions to Cumulative Review Problems

1. The dataset has an outlier at 85. Because the mean is not resistant to extreme values, it tends to be pulled in the direction of an outlier. Hence, we would expect the mean to be larger than the median.

2. *Parameters* are values that describe populations, and *statistics* are values that describe samples. Hence, the mean and the standard deviation of the pulse rates of Pamela's sample are *statistics*, and the predicted mean and the standard deviation for the entire school are *parameters*.

3. Putting the numbers in the calculator and doing `1-Var Stats`, we find that $\bar{x} = 29.64$, $s = 11.78$, Q1 $= 23$, *Med* $= 27$, and Q3 $= 35$.

   (a) The interquartile range (IQR) $= 35 - 23 = 12$, 1.5(IQR) $= 1.5(12) = 18$. So the boundaries beyond which we find outliers are Q1 $- 1.5$(IQR) $= 23 - 18 = 5$ and Q3 $+ 1.5$(IQR) $= 35 + 18 = 53$. Because 55 is beyond the boundary value of 53, it is an outlier, and it is the only outlier.

   (b) The usual rule for outliers based on the mean is $\bar{x} \pm 3s$. $\bar{x} \pm 3s = 29.64 \pm 3(11.78) = (-5.7, 64.98)$. Using this rule there are no outliers since there are no values less than -5.7 or greater than 64.98. Sometimes $\bar{x} \pm 2s$ is used to determine outliers. In this case, $\bar{x} \pm 2s = 29.64 \pm 2(11.78) = (6.08, 53.2)$. Using this rule, 55 would be an outlier.

4. For the given data, $\bar{x} = 29.64$ and $s = 11.78$. Hence,

$$z_{55} = \frac{55 - 29.64}{11.78} = 2.15.$$

Note that in doing problem 3, we could have computed this z-score and observed that because it is larger than 2, it represents an outlier by the $\bar{x} \pm 2s$ rule that is sometimes used.

5. The problem is referring to the *coefficient of determination*—the proportion of variation in one variable that can be explained by the regression of that variable on another. $r = \sqrt{\text{coefficient of determination}} = \sqrt{0.62} = 0.79$. It should be noted that we have assumed that larger values of SAT scores are associated with larger values of GPA. Therefore, we take the positive square root.

CHAPTER 8

Probability and Random Variables

IN THIS CHAPTER

Summary: We've completed the basics of data analysis, and we now begin the transition to inference. In order to do inference, we need to use the language of probability. In order to use the language of probability, we need an understanding of random variables and probabilities. The next two chapters lay the probability foundation for inference. In this chapter, we'll learn about the basic rules of probability, what it means for events to be independent, and about discrete and continuous random variables, simulation, and rules for combining random variables.

Key Ideas
✪ Probability
✪ Random Variables
✪ Discrete Random Variables
✪ Continuous Random Variables
✪ Probability Distributions
✪ Normal Probability
✪ Simulation
✪ Transforming and Combining Random Variables

Probability

The second major part of a course in statistics involves making *inferences* about populations based on sample data (the first was *exploratory data analysis*). The ability to do this is based on being able to make statements such as "If we assume the null hypothesis to be true, then the probability of getting results such as ours (or more extreme) by chance alone is 0.06." To make sense of this statement, you need to have an understanding of what is meant by the term *probability*, as well as an understanding of some of the basics of probability theory.

A **chance event (random phenomenon)** is an activity whose outcome we can observe or measure but for which we cannot predict the outcome for any single trial. When examining the probability of a particular event, we refer to each occurrence of that event as a "success."

The **probability of an event** is the predicted long-run relative frequency of occurrences of that event. In other words, if we repeat a random process many times, the predicted proportion of outcomes that are "successes" is the probability of success. We can estimate probabilities in a couple of ways: experimentally and theoretically. Because it is a relative frequency, the probability of an event must be between 0 and 1. A probability of 0 means the event is impossible. A probability of 1 means the event is certain.

> **example:** If we roll a six-sided die, we know that we will get a 1, 2, 3, 4, 5, or 6, but we don't know *which* one of these we will get on the next trial. What are two ways we could estimate the probability of rolling a 6?

> **solution:** We could estimate the probability experimentally by rolling a die 300 times. The results of one such set of rolls are shown below.

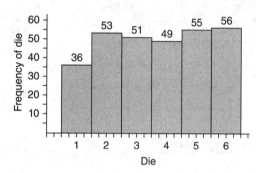

Of the 300 trials, 56 were "successes," so our estimate of the probability based on our experiment is $\frac{56}{300} = 0.187$. We could also estimate the probability theoretically by assuming each possible result is equally likely. If that is the case, then the probability of each number appearing is $\frac{1}{6} = 0.167$. Notice the estimates from the two approaches agree fairly well.

Outcome: One of the possible results of a chance process. Generally we refer to the most basic kind of *occurrences* as outcomes.

Event: A collection of outcomes or simple events.

> **example:** The possible outcomes for the roll of a single die are 1, 2, 3, 4, 5, and 6. Rolling an even number would be an *event* that consists of the *outcomes* 2, 4, and 6.

Sample Spaces and Events

A **sample space** is a **complete** list of **disjoint** outcomes or events. "Complete" means that you have all the possibilities listed. "Disjoint" (also called **mutually exclusive**) means that the events have no outcomes in common. Only one event can happen in a particular trial.

> **example:** Consider the experiment of flipping two coins and noting whether each coin lands heads or tails. A sample space is HH, HT, TH, TT. The list is complete because there is no other possibility for tossing two coins. The list is disjoint because a pair of coin tosses can result in only one of those outcomes.
> If Event B = "at least one coin shows a head," then B is composed of events HH, HT, and TH. Event B is a subset of the sample space S.

example: We could also define a sample space for flipping two coins based on the number of heads. In that case, the sample space is 0, 1, and 2. In this case, however, the outcomes are not equally likely. As the previous example shows, the equally likely outcomes HT and TH both result in one head.

If we let E = the event of interest, and we have defined the sample space with equally likely outcomes, then the probability of E, written $P(E)$, is given by

$$P(E) = \frac{\text{Number of outcomes in E}}{\text{Number of outcomes in the sample space}}$$

The sum of the probabilities of all possible outcomes in a sample space is 1.

The table below represents country of origin and blood type for 500 people attending a large conference. This table of data will be referred to several times over the next couple pages.

COUNTRY	BLOOD TYPE				TOTALS
	O	**A**	**B**	**AB**	
1	150	73	22	5	250
2	46	75	19	10	150
3	29	22	39	10	100
Totals	225	170	80	25	500

example: If we were to randomly select one person from this population of people attending the conference (our repeatable random process), how would you verify that the outcomes in the table define a sample space?

solution: You could check that each person falls into exactly one category in the table. One check for this is to see that the row and column totals are actually the sum of the numbers in the cells. (They are.) If they were not, it would mean that either some people fall into more than one category (the list would not be disjoint) or there would be people not included in the table (the list would not be complete).

example: Using the data above, if you randomly select a person from the population of people attending the conference, what is the probability the person has blood type A?

solution: $P(\text{Type A}) \frac{\textit{Number of type A}}{\textit{Number of people}} = \frac{170}{500} = 0.34$. There is a 34% probability that a randomly selected person attending this conference has blood type A.

The numbers in the total row and the total column are called **marginal frequencies**. The cells in the middle of the table give the **joint frequencies**. Dividing a frequency in a cell by the total gives the proportion of cases in that cell. This is also called the **relative frequency**. If you do this to the marginal frequencies and joint frequencies, you get the **marginal relative frequencies** and the **joint relative frequencies**. If you look at randomly selecting an individual from the population, those relative frequencies give the probability of selecting a person from that cell.

Probabilities of Combined Events

P(A or B): The probability that **either** event A **or** event B occurs (or both). Using set notation, $P(A \text{ or } B)$ can be written $P(A \cup B)$. $A \cup B$ is spoken as "A union B." You won't see set notation much, but it is the way the formula appears on your formula sheet, so it's worth mentioning.

P(A and B): The probability that **both** event A **and** event B occur. Using set notation, $P(A \text{ and } B)$ can be written $P(A \cap B)$. $A \cap B$ is spoken as "A intersect B."

> **example:** Using the same data in that table, if you randomly select a person from the population of people attending the conference, what is the probability the person is from Country 2 **or** has blood type A?

> **solution:** $P(\text{Country 2 or Type A})$ is the sum of all joint frequencies that are either in the column for Type A or in the row for Country 2. The cell that is in both must be counted only once.

COUNTRY	BLOOD TYPE				TOTALS
	O	**A**	**B**	**AB**	
1	150	73	22	5	250
2	46	75	19	10	150
3	29	22	39	10	100
Totals	225	170	80	25	500

The sum of those joint frequencies would be $(46 + 75 + 19 + 10) + (73 + 22)$ or 245. So, $P(\text{Type A or Country \#2}) = \frac{245}{500} = 0.49$.

A shortcut for the previous example is to recognize that you could add the total for Type A and the total for Country 2. But this would count the cell with 75 people twice, so you must subtract that amount from the sum. This is called the **addition rule**.

Addition rule: $P(A \text{ or } B) = P(A) + P(B) - P(A \text{ and } B)$

> **example:** If you randomly select one person from the population above, use the addition rule to find $P(\text{Type A or Country \#2})$.

> **solution:** $P(\text{Type A or Country \#2}) = P(\text{Type A}) + P(\text{Country \#2}) - P(\text{Type A and Country \#2}) = \frac{170}{500} + \frac{150}{500} - \frac{75}{500} = \frac{245}{500} = 0.49$.

> **example:** In the data example above, if you are to randomly select one person, what is $P(\text{Type A or Type O})$?

> **solution:** Because these are disjoint events, $P(\text{Type A and Type O}) = 0$. So the addition rule simplifies to the **addition rule for disjoint events:** $P(A \text{ or } B) = P(A) + P(B)$. In this case, $P(\text{Type A or Type O}) = P(\text{Type A}) + P(\text{Type O}) = \frac{170}{500} + \frac{225}{500} = \frac{395}{500} = 0.79$.

Complement of an event A: Events in the sample space that are not in event A. The complement of an event A is symbolized by $\overline{A}$, or A^c. Furthermore, $P(\overline{A}) = 1 - P(A)$. This can be a useful way to calculate certain probabilities.

> **example:** If you randomly select a person attending this conference, what is the probability that the person has blood type A, O, or AB?

solution: You could add the marginal probabilities for all blood types or you could simply subtract the marginal probability for the one remaining category, Type B, and subtract that from 1. $P(\text{A, O, or AB}) = 1 - P(\text{Type B}) = 1 - \frac{420}{500} = 0.84$.

Conditional Probability

Conditional probability: "The probability of A given B" assumes we have knowledge of an event B having occurred before we compute the probability of event A. This is symbolized by $P(\text{A} \mid \text{B})$.

Conditional probability from a table

example: If you randomly select a person with blood type A, what is the probability that this person is from Country 3?

solution: You know the person has blood type A. That means we do not need to consider the entire population of people attending the conference. We need look only at the relevant column.

	Type A
Country 1	73
Country 2	75
Country 3	22
Total	170

Within the Type A column, 22 of 170 people are from Country 3. So $P(\text{Country 3} \mid \text{Type A}) = \frac{22}{170} = 0.129$.

Conditional probability from a tree diagram

Some conditional probability problems can be solved by using a **tree diagram**. A tree diagram is a schematic way of looking at all possible outcomes.

example: Suppose a computer company has manufacturing plants in three states. Fifty percent of its computers are manufactured in California, and 85% of these are desktops; 30% of computers are manufactured in Washington, and 40% of these are laptops; and 20% of computers are manufactured in Oregon, and 40% of these are desktops. All computers are first shipped to a distribution site before being sent to stores.

a) If you picked a computer at random from the distribution center, what is the probability that it is a laptop?

b) What are the chances that if you randomly selected a laptop from the distribution center, it is a laptop that was manufactured in California?

solution:

a) Note that the final probabilities add to 1 so we know we have considered all possible outcomes. Now, $P(\text{laptop}) = 0.075 + 0.12 + 0.12 = 0.315$.

b) This is a conditional probability question. We have the condition that we selected a laptop. We calculated in part (a) that this will happen 0.315 of the time. The question we are trying to answer is how likely it is that this laptop is from California. Thus, $P(\text{California} \mid \text{laptop}) = (0.075/0.315) = 0.238$.

Independent Events

Independent events: Events A and B are said to be *independent* if and only if the knowledge of one event having occurred does not change the probability that the other event occurs. That is, A and B are independent if the probability of A, given that B occurred, is the same as the probability that A occurred and vice versa. In symbols, A and B are independent if and only if $P(A|B) = P(A)$ or $P(B|A) = P(B)$.

example: Consider drawing one card from a standard deck of 52 playing cards.

Let A = "the card drawn is an ace." $\qquad P(A) = 4/52 = 1/13$.

Let B = "the card drawn is a 10, J, Q, K, or A." $\quad P(B) = 20/52 = 5/13$.

Let C = "the card drawn is a diamond." $\qquad P(C) = 13/52 = 1/4$.

(i) Are A and B independent?

solution: $P(A|B) = P(\text{the card drawn is an ace} \mid \text{the card is a 10, J, Q, K, or A}) = 4/20 = 1/5$ (there are 20 cards to consider, 4 of which are aces). Since $P(A) = 1/13$, knowledge of B has changed what we know about A. That is, in this case, $P(A) \neq P(A|B)$, so events A and B are *not* independent.

(ii) Are A and C independent?

solution: $P(A|C) = P(\text{the card drawn is an ace} \mid \text{the card drawn is a diamond}) = 1/13$ (there are 13 diamonds, one of which is an ace). So, in this case, $P(A) = P(A|C)$ so that the events "the card drawn is an ace" and "the card drawn is a diamond" are independent.

example: If we randomly select a person who attended the conference in the earlier example, are the events from Country 3 and Type A independent?

solution: $P(\text{Country 3}) = \frac{100}{500} = 0.20$. $P(\text{Country 3} \mid \text{Type A}) = \frac{22}{170} = 0.129$. Because these probabilities are not the same, the events *from Country 3* and *Type A* are not independent.

example: If we randomly select a computer from the distribution center (see tree diagram above), are the computer being a laptop and the computer being manufactured in California independent events?

solution: $P(\text{California}) = 0.50$. $P(\text{California} \mid \text{laptop}) = 0.238$. Because these probabilities are not the same, the events California and laptop are not independent.

Probability of A and B or A or B

The Multiplication Rule: $P(A \text{ and } B) = P(A) \cdot P(B|A)$.

Special case of **the multiplication rule:** If A and B are *independent*,

$P(B|A) = P(B)$, so $P(A \text{ and } B) = P(A) \cdot P(B)$.

example: A and B are two mutually exclusive events for which $P(A) = 0.3$ and $P(B) = 0.25$. Find $P(A \text{ or } B)$.

solution: $P(A \text{ or } B) = 0.3 + 0.25 = 0.55$.

example: A basketball player has a 0.6 probability of making a free throw. What is his probability of making two consecutive free throws if

(a) he gets very nervous after making the first shot and his probability of making the second shot drops to 0.4?

solution: P(making the first shot) = 0.6, P(making the second shot | he made the first) = 0.4. So, P(making both shots) = (0.6)(0.4) = 0.24.

(b) the events "he makes his first shot" and "he makes the succeeding shot" are independent?

solution: Since the events are independent, his probability of making each shot is the same. Thus, P(he makes both shots) = (0.6)(0.6) = 0.36.

Segmented Bar Graphs and Mosaic Plots

Often, we want to display categorical data such as that in this example in a graphical format. There are different ways to do so, but two different choices are a segmented bar chart and a mosaic plot. A **segmented bar graph** takes bars of equal length and equal width for each of the groups and divides them up into segments that represent the percentage for each of the categories. To do that, we need to take the frequencies from the data and produce *conditional relative frequencies*.

COUNTRY	BLOOD TYPE				TOTALS
	O	A	B	AB	
1	150	73	22	5	250
2	46	75	19	10	150
3	29	22	39	10	100
Totals	225	170	80	25	500

To produce those relative frequencies, we will take each country as its own group and calculate based on that condition. For example, there are 150 people out of 250 in Country 1 with blood type O, and this would be a conditional relative frequency of 0.60 or 60%.

Once completed, the conditional distribution of blood types by country would produce a table like this. Those conditional frequencies allow us to produce a segmented bar graph.

CONDITIONAL DISTRIBUTION: BLOOD TYPES BY COUNTRY

COUNTRY	BLOOD TYPE			
	O	A	B	AB
1	60%	29.2%	8.8%	2%
2	30.7%	50%	12.7%	6.6%
3	29%	22%	10%	10%

Question: Based on this segmented bar graph, do you believe that blood type and country are independent?

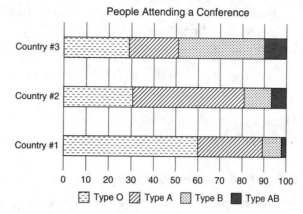

answer: Since the segments are so differently sized in each bar, it does not appear that blood type and country are independent. In fact, if you told me that the person attending the conference was from Country #1, it would be more likely that they were of blood type O.

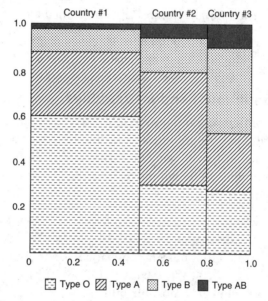

But the conditional frequencies disguise the fact that the sizes of the individual groups are so different. Another type of plot that can be used with these data is a mosaic plot. A **mosaic plot** helps preserve the relative sizes of the groups by keeping the heights the same but making the widths of the bars proportional to the group size. We can still see that a person is more likely to be of blood type O if we find out that they are from Country 1, but with a mosaic plot we can also see that the frequency (that is, the number of people) of people with blood type A is about the same for Countries 1 and 2 because the areas of those rectangles are the same.

Random Variables

Recall our earlier definition of a **probability experiment (random phenomenon)**: An activity whose outcome we can observe and measure but for which we can't predict the result of any single trial. A **random variable**, X, is a numerical value assigned to an outcome of a random phenomenon. Particular values of the random variable X are often given lowercase names, such as x to represent a general value or k to represent a specific value. It is common to see expressions of the form $P(X = x)$ or $P(X = k)$, which refer to the probability that the random variable X takes on the particular value x.

example: If we roll a fair die, the random variable X could be the face-up value of the die. The possible values of X are {1, 2, 3, 4, 5, 6}. $P(X = 2) = 1/6$.

example: The score a college-hopeful student gets on her SAT test can take on values from 200 to 800. These are the possible values of the random variable X, the score a randomly selected student gets on the test.

There are two types of random variables: **discrete random variables** and **continuous random variables**.

Discrete Random Variables

A **discrete random variable (DRV)** is a random variable with a countable number of outcomes. You can think of a discrete random variable as one whose values are separated by gaps. The number of left-handed people in a sample of 100 people, for example, can only take on whole number values from 0 to 100. This is an example of a discrete random variable.

example: the number of votes earned by different candidates in an election.

example: the number of successes in 25 trials of an event whose probability of success on any one trial is known to be 0.3.

Continuous Random Variables

A **continuous random variable (CRV)** is a random variable that takes on values associated with one or more intervals on the number line. The continuous random variable X can assume infinitely many outcomes within an interval. Heights of people, for example, are continuous, although the reported heights may be discrete if they are reported to the nearest inch.

example: Consider the *uniform* distribution $y = 3$ defined on the interval $1 \le x \le 5$. The area under $y = 3$ and above the x axis for any interval corresponds to a continuous random variable. For example, if $2 \le x \le 3$, then $X = 3$. If $2 \le x \le 4.5$, then $X = (4.5 - 2)(3) = 7.5$. Note that there are an infinite number of possible outcomes for X.

Probability Distribution of a Random Variable

A **probability distribution for a random variable** is the possible values of the random variable X together with the probabilities corresponding to those values.

A **probability distribution for a discrete random variable** (DRV) is a list of the possible values of the DRV together with their respective probabilities.

example: Let X be the number of boys in a three-child family. Assuming that the probability of a boy on any one birth is 0.5, the probability distribution for X is

X	0	1	2	3
$P(X)$	1/8	3/8	3/8	1/8

The probabilities P_i of a DRV satisfy two conditions:

(1) $0 \le P_i \le 1$ (that is, every probability is between 0 and 1).

(2) $\Sigma P_i = 1$ (that is, the sum of all probabilities is 1).

(Are these conditions satisfied in the above example?)

The **mean** of a discrete random variable, also called the **expected value**, is given by

$$\mu_X = \sum x \cdot P(x).$$

The **variance of a discrete random variable** is given by

$$\sigma_X^2 = \sum (x - \mu_X)^2 \cdot P(x).$$

The **standard deviation of a discrete random variable** is given by

$$\sigma_X = \sqrt{\sum (x - \mu_X)^2 \cdot P(x)}.$$

example: Given that the following is the probability distribution for a DRV, find $P(X = 3)$.

X	2	3	4	5	6
P(X)	0.15		0.2	0.2	0.35

solution: Since $\sum P_i = 1$, $P(3) = 1 - (0.15 + 0.2 + 0.2 + 0.35) = 0.1$.

example: For the probability distribution given above, find μ_x and σ_x.

solution:

$$\mu_X = 2(0.15) + 3(0.1) + 4(0.2) + 5(0.2) + 6(0.35) = 4.5.$$
$$\sigma_X = \sqrt{(2 - 4.5)^2(0.15) + (3 - 4.5)^2(0.1) + \cdots + (6 - 4.5)^2(0.35)} = 1.432.$$

Calculator Tip: While it's helpful to know the formulas given above, they are given on your formula sheet. In practice it's easier to use your calculator to do the computations. Most calculators have a shortcut for calculation summary statistics of values in a list. For probability distributions you can usually enter the values in one list and the probabilities in the other and set the probability list as your frequency. This feature may make it easier to do homework problems, but on the AP exam you are expected to show your work, as above.

example: Redo the previous example using the TI-83/84, or equivalent, calculator.

solution: Enter the x values in a list (say, L1) and the probabilities in another list (say, L2). Then enter "1-Var Stats L1,L2" and press ENTER. The calculator will read the probabilities in L2 as relative frequencies and return 4.5 for the mean and 1.432 for the standard deviation.

Probability Histogram

A **probability histogram** of a discrete random variable is a way to picture the probability distribution. The following is a TI-83/84 histogram of the probability distribution we used in a couple of the earlier examples.

x	2	3	4	5	6
$p(x)$	0.15	0.1	0.2	0.2	0.35

Probability Distribution for a Continuous Random Variable. When we randomly select a value from a population modeled with a normal distribution, we are using a continuous random variable. Here are a few things to note:

- The probability of any individual value is 0. That is, if a is a point on the horizontal axis, $P(X = a) = 0$.
- To find the probability of an event, you must find the probability that x falls in some given interval. To do this, use the `normalcdf` function on your calculator.
- We will learn about a couple more continuous distributions during the course. The normal distribution is not the only one!

In a normal distribution, the tails of the curve extend to infinity, although there is very little area under the curve when we get more than, say, three standard deviations away from the mean. (The 68-95-99.7 rule stated that about 99.7% of the terms in a normal distribution are within three standard deviations of the mean. Thus, only about 0.3% lie beyond three standard deviations of the mean.)

Areas between two values on the number line and under the normal probability distribution correspond to probabilities. In Chapter 4, we found the proportion of terms falling within certain intervals. Because the total area under the curve is 1, in this chapter we will consider those proportions to be probabilities.

Remember that we *standardized* the normal distribution by converting the data to z-scores

$$\left(z = \frac{x - \bar{x}}{s_x} \right).$$

We learned in Chapter 4 that a standardized normal distribution has a mean of 0 and a standard deviation of 1.

It is generally easiest to use your calculator for calculating normal probabilities, but you can also use the table of Standard Normal Probabilities. It would be best to memorize the values corresponding to the 68-95-99.7 rule.

Normal Probabilities

When we know a distribution is approximately normal, we can solve many types of problems.

> **example:** In a standard normal distribution, what is the probability that $z < 1.5$? (Note that because z is a CRV, $P(X = a) = 0$, so this problem could have been equivalently stated, "What is the probability that $z \leq 1.5$?")

> **solution:** The standard normal table gives areas to the left of a specified z-score. From the table, we determine that the area to the left of $z = 1.5$ is 0.9332. That is, $P(z < 1.5) = 0.9332$. This can be visualized as follows:

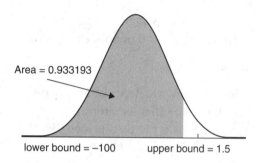

Area = 0.933193

lower bound = –100   upper bound = 1.5

> **example:** It is known that the heights (X) of students at Downtown College are approximately normally distributed with a mean of 68 inches and a standard deviation of 3 inches. That is, X has $N(68, 3)$. Determine

(a) $P(X < 65)$.

> **solution:** $P(X < 65) = P\left(z < \frac{65-68}{3} = -1\right) = 0.1587$ (the area to the left of $z = -1$ from Table A). On the TI-83/84, the corresponding calculation is `normalcdf (-100,-1) = normalcdf (-1000,65,68,30) = 0.1586552596`.

(b) $P(X > 65)$.

> **solution:** From part (a) of the example, we have $P(X < 65) = 0.1587$. Hence, $P(X > 65) = 1 - P(X < 65) = 1 - 0.1587 = 0.8413$. On the TI-83/84, the corresponding calculation is `normalcdf (-1,100) = normalcdf (65,1000,68,3) = 0.8413447404`.

(c) $P(65 < X < 70)$.

> **solution:** $P(65 < X < 70) = P\left(\frac{65-68}{3} < z < \frac{70-68}{3}\right) = P(-1 < z < 0.667) =$
>
> $0.7486 - 0.1587 = 0.5899$ (from Table A, the geometry of the situation dictates that the area to the left of $z = -1$ must be subtracted from the area

to the left of $z = 0.667$). Using the TI-83/84, the calculation is `normal-cdf(-1,0.67) = normalcdf(65,70,68,3) = 0.5889`. This situation is pictured below.

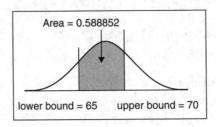

Note that there is some rounding error when using Table A (see the Appendix). In part (c), $z = 0.66667$, but we must use 0.67 to use the table.

(d) $P(70 < X < 75)$.

solution: Now we need the area between 70 and 75. The geometry of the situation dictates that we subtract the area to the left of 70 from the area to the left of 75. This is pictured below.

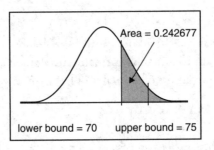

We saw from part (c) that the area to the left of 70 is 0.7486. In a similar fashion, we find that the area to the left of 75 is 0.9901 (based on $z = 2.33$). Thus $P(70 < X < 75)$ = 0.9901 − 0.7486 = 0.2415. The calculation on the TI-83/84 is `normalcdf (70,75,68,3) = 0.2427`. The difference in the answers is due to rounding.

example: SAT scores are approximately normally distributed with a mean of about 500 and a standard deviation of 100. Laurie needs to be in the top 15% on the SAT in order to ensure her acceptance by Giant U. What is the minimum score she must earn to be able to start packing her bags for college?

solution: This is somewhat different from the previous examples. Up until now, we have been given, or have figured out, a z-score, and have needed to determine an area. Now, we are given an area and are asked to determine a particular score. If we are using the table of normal probabilities, it is a situation in which we must read from inside the table out to the z-scores rather than from the outside in. If the particular value of X we are looking for is the lower bound for the top 15% of scores, then there are 85% of the scores to the left of x. We look through the table and find the closest entry to 0.8500 and determine it to be 0.8508. This corresponds to a z-score of 1.04. Another way to write the z-score of the desired value of X is

$$z = \frac{x - 500}{100}.$$

Thus, $z = \dfrac{x - 500}{100} = 1.04$.

Solving for x, we get $x = 500 + 1.04(100) = 604$. So, Laurie must achieve an SAT score of at least 604. While this problem can be done on the calculator as follows: `invNorm(0.85,500,100)`, recent rubrics have required that you list the z-score even if you use this command on your calculator.

Most problems of this type can be solved in the same way: express the z-score of the desired value in two different ways (from the definition, finding the actual value from Table A or by using the `invNorm` function on the calculator), then equate the expressions and solve for x.

Simulation and Random Number Generation

Sometimes probability situations do not lend themselves easily to analytical solutions. In some situations, an acceptable approach might be to run a **simulation**. A simulation utilizes some random process to conduct numerous trials of the situation and then counts the number of successful outcomes to arrive at an estimated probability. In general, the more trials, the more confidence we can have that the relative frequency of successes accurately approximates the desired probability. The **law of large numbers** states that the proportion of successes in the simulation should become, over time, close to the true proportion in the population.

One interesting example of the use of simulation has been in the development of certain "systems" for playing Blackjack. The number of possible situations in Blackjack is large but finite. A computer was used to conduct thousands of simulations of each possible playing decision for each of the possible hands. In this way, certain situations favorable to the player were identified and formed the basis for the published systems.

> **example:** Suppose there is a small island society that places a high value on families having a baby girl. Suppose further that *every* family in the society decides to keep having children until they have a girl and then they stop. If the first child is a girl, they are a one-child family, but it may take several tries before they succeed. Assume that when this policy was decided on that the proportion of girls in the population was 0.5 and the probability of having a girl is 0.5 for each birth. Would this behavior change the proportion of girls in the population? Design a simulation to answer this question.

> **solution:** Use a random number generator, say a fair coin, to simulate a birth. Let heads = "have a girl" and tails = "have a boy." Flip the coin and note whether it falls heads or tails. If it falls heads, the trial ends. If it falls tails, flip again because this represents having a boy. The outcome of interest is the number of trials (births) necessary until a girl is born (if the third flip gives the first head, then $x = 3$). Repeat this many times and determine how many girls and how many boys have been born.

If flipping a coin many times seems a bit tedious, you can also use your calculator to simulate flipping a coin. Let 1 be a head and let 2 be a tail. Then enter MATH PRB rand-Int(1,2) and press ENTER to generate a random 1 or 2. Continue to press ENTER to generate additional random integers 1 or 2. Enter randInt(1,2,n) to generate n random integers, each of which is a 1 or a 2. Enter randInt(a,b,n) to generate n random integers X such that $a \leq X \leq b$.

The following represents a few trials of this simulation (actually done using the random number generator on the TI-83/84 calculator):

TRIAL #	TRIAL RESULTS (H = "GIRL")	# FLIPS UNTIL FIRST GIRL	TOTAL # OF GIRLS AFTER TRIAL IS FINISHED	TOTAL # OF BOYS AFTER TRIAL IS FINISHED
1	TH	2	1	1
2	H	1	2	1
3	TTTH	4	3	4
4	H	1	4	4
5	TH	2	5	5
6	H	1	6	5
7	H	1	7	5
8	H	1	8	5
9	TH	2	9	6
10	H	1	10	6
11	TTTH	4	11	9
12	H	1	12	9
13	H	1	13	9
14	TTTTH	5	14	13
15	TTH	3	15	15

In this limited simulation, the number of boys and girls in the population of 15 families are equal. Based on our simulation, if every familiy kept having children until they have a girl, it would not change the proportion of girls in the population. If the simulation were to be run again, it is unlikely that it would turn out exactly the same. For more reliable estimates, do more trials.

Exam Tip: If you are asked to do a simulation on the AP Statistics exam (and there have been such questions), you may be asked to use a table of random numbers rather than the random number generator on your calculator. This allows the grader to know exactly which numbers you used in your simulation and, therefore, whether you are using them correctly. It is also possible that the question will describe a simulation and you will be asked to interpret the results of the simulation based on a plot of the simulated results.

The following gives 200 outcomes of a typical random number generator separated into groups of 5 digits:

79692	51707	73274	12548	91497	11135	81218	79572	06484	87440
41957	21607	51248	54772	19481	90392	35268	36234	90244	02146
07094	31750	69426	62510	90127	43365	61167	53938	03694	76923
59365	43671	12704	87941	51620	45102	22785	07729	40985	92589

> **example:** A coin is known to be biased in such a way that the probability of getting a head is 0.4. If the coin is flipped 50 times, how many heads would you expect to get?
>
> **solution:** Let 0, 1, 2, 3 be a head and 4, 5, 6, 7, 8, 9 be a tail. If we look at 50 digits beginning with the first row, we see that there are 18 heads (bold-faced below), so the proportion of heads is 18/50 = 0.36. This is close to the expected value of 0.4.
>
> 7969**2** 5**17**07 73274 **123**48 91497 **111**35 81218 79572 **06**484 8744**0**

Sometimes the simulation will be a **wait-time simulation**. In the example above, we could have asked how long it would take, on average, until we get five heads. In this case, using the same definitions for the various digits, we would proceed through the table until we noted five numbers with digits 0–3. We would then write down how many digits we had to look at. Three trials of that simulation might look like this (individual trials are separated by \\):

7969**2** 5**17**07 **732**\\74 **123**48 91497 **11****135** 8**121**\\.

So, it took 13, 14, and 7 trials to get our five heads, or an average of 11.3 trials (the theoretical expected number of trials is 12.5).

Transforming and Combining Random Variables

If X is a random variable, we can transform the data by adding a constant to each value of X, multiplying each value by a constant, or some linear combination of the two. We may do this to make numbers more manageable. For example, if values in our dataset ranged from 8500 to 9000, we could subtract, say, 8500 from each value to get a dataset that ranged from 0 to 500. We would then be interested in the mean and the standard deviation of the new dataset as compared to the old dataset.

Some facts from algebra can help us out here. Let μ_x and σ_x be the mean and the standard deviation, respectively, of the random variable X. Each of the following statements can be algebraically verified if we add or subtract the same constant, a, to or from each term in a dataset ($X \pm a$) or multiply each term by the same constant b (bX) or some combination of these ($a \pm bX$):

- $\mu_{a \pm bX} = a \pm b\mu_x$.
- $\sigma_{a \pm bX} = b\sigma_X$ ($\sigma^2_{a \pm bx} = b^2\sigma^2_X$).

> **example:** Consider a distribution with $\mu_X = 14$, $\sigma_X = 2$. Multiply each value of X by 4 and then add 3 to each. Then $\mu_{3+4X} = 3 + 4(14) = 59$, $\sigma_{3+4X} = 4(2) = 8$.

Rules for the Mean and Standard Deviation of Combined Random Variables

Sometimes we need to combine two random variables. For example, suppose one contractor can finish a particular job, on average, in 40 hours ($\mu_x = 40$). Another contractor can finish a similar job in 35 hours ($\mu_y = 35$). If they work on two separate jobs, how many hours, on average, will they bill for completing both jobs? It should be clear that the average of $X + Y$ is just the average for X plus the average for Y. That is,

$$\mu_{X \pm Y} = \mu_X \pm \mu_Y.$$

The situation is somewhat less clear when we combine variances. In the contractor example above, suppose that

$$\sigma^2_X = 5 \text{ and } \sigma^2_Y = 4.$$

Does the variance of the sum equal the sum of the variances? Well, yes and no. Yes, if the random variables X and Y are independent. No, if the random variables are not independent but are dependent in some way. Furthermore, it doesn't matter if the random variables are added or subtracted, we are still combining the variances. That is,

- $\sigma^2_{X \pm Y} = \sigma^2_X + \sigma^2_Y$, if and only if X and Y are independent.

- $\sigma_{X \pm Y} = \sqrt{\sigma^2_X + \sigma^2_Y}$, if and only if X and Y are independent.

Exam Tip: The rules for means and variances when you combine random variables may seem a bit obscure, but there have been questions on more than one occasion that depend on your knowledge of how this is done.

The rules for means and variances generalize. That is, no matter how many random variables you have: $\mu_{X1 \pm X2 \pm \ldots \pm Xn} = \mu_{X1} \pm \mu_{X2 \pm \ldots} + \mu_{Xn}$ and, if X_1, X_2, ..., X_n are all independent, $\sigma^2_{X_1 \pm X_2 \pm \ldots \pm X_n} = \sigma^2_{X_1} + \sigma^2_{X_2 + \ldots} + \sigma^2_{X_n}$.

example: A private school offers an admission test on the first Saturday of November and the first Saturday of December each year. In 2008, the mean score for hopeful students taking the test in November (X) was 156 with a standard deviation of 12. For those taking the test in December (Y), the mean score was 165 with a standard deviation of 11. What are the mean and the standard deviation of the total score $X + Y$ of all students who took the test in 2008?

solution: We have no reason to think that scores of students who take the test in December are influenced by the scores of those students who took the test in November. Hence, it is reasonable to assume that X and Y are independent. Accordingly,

$$\mu_{X+Y} = \mu_X + \mu_Y = 156 + 165 = 321,$$

$$\sigma_{X+Y} = \sqrt{\sigma^2_X + \sigma^2_Y} = \sqrt{12^2 + 11^2} = \sqrt{265} = 16.28.$$

› Rapid Review

1. A bag has 8 green marbles and 12 red marbles. If you draw one marble from the bag, what is P(draw a green marble)?

   Answer: Let s = number of ways to draw a green marble.

   Let f = number of ways to draw a red marble.

   $$P(E) = \frac{s}{s+f} = \frac{8}{8+12} = \frac{8}{20} = \frac{2}{5}.$$

2. A married couple has three children. At least one of their children is a boy. What is the probability that the couple has exactly two boys?

   Answer: The sample space for having three children is {BBB, BBG, BGB, GBB, BGG, GBG, GGB, GGG}. Of these, there are seven outcomes that have at least one boy. Of these, three have two boys and one girl. Thus, P(the couple has exactly two boys | they have at least one boy) = 3/7.

3. Does the following table represent the probability distribution for a discrete random variable?

X	1	2	3	4
$P(X)$	0.2	0.3	0.3	0.4

Answer: No, because

$$\sum P_i = 1.2.$$

4. In a standard normal distribution, what is $P(z > 0.5)$?

   Answer: From the table, we see that $P(z < 0.5) = 0.6915$. Hence, $P(z > 0.5) = 1 - 0.6915 = 0.3085$. By calculator, `normalcdf (0.5,100) = 0.3085375322`.

5. A random variable X has $N(13, 0.45)$. Describe the distribution of $2 - 4X$ (that is, each datapoint in the distribution is multiplied by 4, and that value is subtracted from 2).

   Answer: We are given that the distribution of X is normal with $\mu_X = 13$ and $\sigma_X = 0.45$. Because $\mu_{a \pm bX} = a \pm b\mu_X$, $\mu_{2-4X} = 2 - 4\mu_X = 2 - 4(13) = -50$. Also, because $\sigma_{a \pm bX} = b\sigma_X$, $\sigma_{2-4X} = 4\sigma_X = 4(0.45) = 1.8$.

Practice Problems

Multiple-Choice

1.

	D	**E**	**Total**
A	15	12	27
B	15	23	38
C	32	28	60
Total	62	63	125

In the table above, what are $P(A \text{ and } E)$ and $P(C|E)$?

(a) 12/125, 28/125
(b) 12/63, 28/60
(c) 12/125, 28/63
(d) 12/125, 28/60
(e) 12/63, 28/63

2.

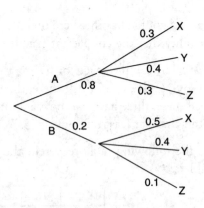

For the tree diagram pictured above, what is $P(B|X)$?

(a) 1/4
(b) 5/17
(c) 2/5
(d) 1/3
(e) 4/5

3. It turns out that 25 seniors at Random High School took both the AP Statistics exam and the AP Spanish Language exam. The mean score on the Statistics exam for the 25 seniors was 2.4 with a standard deviation of 0.6, and the mean score on the Spanish Language exam was 2.65 with a standard deviation of 0.55. We want to combine the scores into a single score. What are the correct mean and standard deviation of the combined scores?

(a) 5.05; 1.15
(b) 5.05; 1.07
(c) 5.05; 0.66
(d) 5.05; 0.81
(e) 5.05; you cannot determine the standard deviation from this information.

4. The GPAs (grade point averages) of students who take the AP Statistics exam are approximately normally distributed with a mean of 3.4 and a standard deviation of 0.3. Using Table A, what is the probability that a student selected at random from this group has a GPA lower than 3.0?

(a) 0.0918
(b) 0.4082
(c) 0.9082
(d) −0.0918
(e) 0

5. The 2000 Census identified the ethnic breakdown of the state of California to be approximately as follows: White: 46%, Latino: 32%, Asian: 11%, Black: 7%, and Other: 4%. Assuming that these are mutually exclusive categories (this is not a realistic assumption), what is the probability that a randomly selected person from the state of California is of Asian or Latino descent?

(a) 46%
(b) 32%
(c) 11%
(d) 43%
(e) 3.5%

6. The students in problem #4 above were normally distributed with a mean GPA of 3.4 and a standard deviation of 0.3. In order to qualify for the school honor society, a student must have a GPA in the top 5% of all GPAs. Accurate to two decimal places, what is the minimum GPA Norma must have in order to qualify for the honor society?

(a) 3.95
(b) 3.92
(c) 3.75
(d) 3.85
(e) 3.89

7. The following are the probability distributions for two random variables, X and Y:

X	$P(X=x)$
3	$\frac{1}{3}$
5	$\frac{1}{2}$
7	$\frac{1}{6}$

Y	$P(Y=y)$
1	$\frac{1}{8}$
3	$\frac{3}{8}$
4	?
5	$\frac{3}{16}$

If X and Y are independent, what is $P(X = 5 \text{ and } Y = 4)$?

(a) $\frac{5}{16}$

(b) $\frac{13}{16}$

(c) $\frac{5}{32}$

(d) $\frac{3}{32}$

(e) $\frac{3}{16}$

8. The following table gives the probabilities of various outcomes for a gambling game.

Outcome	Lose $1	Win $1	Win $2
Probability	0.6	0.25	0.15

What is the player's expected return on a bet of $1?
(a) $0.05
(b) −$0.60
(c) −$0.05
(d) −$0.10
(e) You can't answer this question since this is not a complete probability distribution.

9. You own an unusual die. Three faces are marked with the letter "X," two faces with the letter "Y," and one face with the letter "Z." What is the probability that at least one of the first two rolls is a "Y"?

(a) $\dfrac{1}{6}$

(b) $\dfrac{2}{3}$

(c) $\dfrac{1}{3}$

(d) $\dfrac{5}{9}$

(e) $\dfrac{2}{9}$

10. You roll two regular six-sided dice. What is the probability that the sum is 6 given that one die shows a 4?

(a) $\dfrac{2}{12}$

(b) $\dfrac{2}{11}$

(c) $\dfrac{11}{36}$

(d) $\dfrac{2}{36}$

(e) $\dfrac{12}{36}$

Free-Response

1. Find μ_X and σ_X for the following discrete probability distribution:

X	2	3	4
$P(X)$	1/3	5/12	1/4

2. Given that $P(A) = 0.6$, $P(B) = 0.3$, and $P(B|A) = 0.5$.
   (a) $P(A \text{ and } B) = ?$
   (b) $P(A \text{ or } B) = ?$
   (c) Are events A and B independent?

3. Consider a set of 9000 scores on a national test that is known to be approximately normally distributed with a mean of 500 and a standard deviation of 90.

   (a) What is the probability that a randomly selected student has a score greater than 600?
   (b) How many scores are there between 450 and 600?
   (c) Rachel needs to be in the top 1% of the scores on this test to qualify for a scholarship. What is the minimum score Rachel needs?

4. Consider a random variable X with $\mu_X = 3$, $\sigma_X^2 = 0.25$. Find

   (a) μ_{3+6X}
   (b) σ_{3+6X}

5. Harvey, Laura, and Gina take turns throwing darts at a target. Harvey hits the target 1/2 the time, Laura hits it 1/3 of the time, and Gina hits the target 1/4 of the time. Given that somebody hit the target, what is the probability that it was Laura?

6. Consider two discrete, independent, random variables X and Y with $\mu_X = 3$, $\sigma_X^2 = 1$, $\mu_Y = 5$, and $\sigma_Y^2 = 1.3$. Find μ_{X-Y} and σ_{X-Y}.

7. Which of the following statements is (are) true of a normal distribution?

   I. Exactly 95% of the data are within two standard deviations of the mean.
   II. The mean = the median = the mode.
   III. The area under the normal curve between $z = 1$ and $z = 2$ is greater than the area between $z = 2$ and $z = 3$.

8. Consider the experiment of drawing two cards from a standard deck of 52 cards. Let event A = "draw a face card on the first draw," B = "draw a face card on the second draw," and C = "the first card drawn is a diamond."

   (a) Are events A and B *independent*?
   (b) Are events A and C *independent*?

9. A normal distribution has mean 700 and standard deviation 50. The probability is 0.6 that a randomly selected term from this distribution is above x. What is x?

10. Suppose 80% of the homes in Lakeville have a desktop computer and 30% have both a desktop computer and a laptop computer. What is the probability that a randomly selected home will have a laptop computer given that it has a desktop computer?

11. Consider a probability density curve defined by the line $y = 2x$ on the interval [0,1] (the area under $y = 2x$ on [0,1] is 1). Find $P(0.2 \leq X \leq 0.7)$.

12. Half Moon Bay, California, has an annual pumpkin festival at Halloween. A prime attraction to this festival is a "largest pumpkin" contest. Suppose that the weights of these giant pumpkins are approximately normally distributed with a mean of 125 pounds and a standard deviation of 18 pounds. Farmer Harv brings a pumpkin that is at the 90th percentile of all the pumpkins in the contest. What is the approximate weight of Harv's pumpkin?

13. Consider the following two probability distributions for independent discrete random variable X and Y:

X	2	3	4
$P(X)$	0.3	0.5	?

Y	3	4	5	6
$P(Y)$	?	0.1	?	0.4

If $P(X = 4$ and $Y = 3) = 0.03$, what is $P(Y = 5)$?

14. A contest is held to give away a free pizza. Contestants pick an integer at random from the integers 1 through 100. If the number chosen is divisible by 24 or by 36, the contestant wins the pizza. What is the probability that a contestant wins a pizza?

Use the following excerpt from a random number table for questions 15 and 16:

79692 51707 73274 12548 91497 11135 81218 79572 06484 87440

41957 21607 51248 54772 19481 90392 35268 36234 90244 02146

07094 31750 69426 62510 90127 43365 61167 53938 03694 76923

59365 43671 12704 87941 51620 45102 22785 07729 40985 92589

91547 03927 92309 10589 22107 04390 86297 32990 16963 09131

15. Men and women are about equally likely to earn degrees at City U. However, there is some question whether or not women have equal access to the prestigious School of Law. This year, only 4 of the 12 new students are female. Describe and conduct five trials of a simulation to help determine if this is evidence that women are underrepresented in the School of Law.

16. Suppose that, on a planet far away, the probability of a girl being born is 0.6, and it is socially advantageous to have three girls. How many children would a couple have to have, on average, until they had three girls? Describe and conduct five trials of a simulation to help answer this question.

17. Consider a random variable X with the following probability distribution:

X	20	21	22	23	24
$P(X)$	0.2	0.3	0.2	0.1	0.2

   (a) Find $P(X \leq 22)$.
   (b) Find $P(X > 21)$.
   (c) Find $P(21 \leq X < 24)$.
   (d) Find $P(X \leq 21 \text{ or } X > 23)$.

18. In the casino game of roulette, a ball is rolled around the rim of a circular bowl while a wheel containing 38 slots into which the ball can drop is spun in the opposite direction from the rolling ball; 18 of the slots are red, 18 are black, and 2 are green. A player bets a set amount, say $1, and wins $1 (and keeps her $1 bet) if the ball falls into the color slot the player has wagered on. Assume a player decides to bet that the ball will fall into one of the red slots.

   (a) What is the probability that the player will win?
   (b) What is the expected return on a single bet of $1 on red?

19. A random variable X is normally distributed with mean μ, and standard deviation σ (that is, X has $N(\mu,\sigma)$). What is the probability that a term selected at random from this population will be more than 2.5 standard deviations from the mean?

20. The normal random variable X has a standard deviation of 12. We also know that $P(x > 50) = 0.90$. Find the mean μ of the distribution.

Cumulative Review Problems

1. Consider the following histogram:

   Which of the following statements is true and why?
   I. The mean and median are approximately the same value.
   II. The mean is probably greater than the median.
   III. The median is probably greater than the mean.

2. You are going to do an opinion survey in your school. You can sample 100 students and desire that the sample accurately reflects the ethnic composition of your school. The school data clerk tells you that the student body is 25% Asian, 8% African American, 12% Latino, and 55% Caucasian. How could you sample the student body so that your sample of 100 would reflect this composition, and what is such a sample called?

3. The following data represent the scores on a 50-point AP Statistics quiz:
   46, 36, 50, 42, 46, 30, 46, 32, 50, 32, 40, 42, 20, 47, 39, 32, 22, 43, 42, 46, 48, 34, 47, 46, 27, 50, 46, 42, 20, 23, 42

   Determine the five-number summary for the quiz and draw a boxplot of the data.

4. The following represents some computer output that can be used to predict the number of manatee deaths from the number of powerboats registered in Florida.

Predictor	Coef	St Dev	t ratio	P
Constant	−41.430	7.412	−5.59	.000
Boats	0.12486	0.01290	9.68	.000

   (a) Write the least-square regression line for predicting the number of manatee deaths from the number of powerboat registrations.
   (b) Interpret the slope of the line in the context of the problem.

5. Use the *68-95-99.7 rule* to state whether it seems reasonable that the following sample data could have been drawn from a normal distribution: 12.3, 6.6, 10.6, 9.4, 9.1, 13.7, 12.2, 9, 9.4, 9.2, 8.8, 10.1, 7.0, 10.9, 7.8, 6.5, 10.3, 8.6, 10.6, 13, 11.5, 8.1, 13.0, 10.7, 8.8.

Solutions to Practice Problems

Multiple-Choice

1. The correct answer is (c). There are 12 values in the A *and* E cell out of the total of 125. When we are given column E, the total is 63. Of those, 28 are C.

2. The correct answer is (b).

$$P(X) = (0.8)(0.3) + (0.2)(0.5) = 0.34.$$

$$P(B|X) = \frac{(0.2)(0.5)}{(0.8)(0.3)+(0.2)(0.5)} = \frac{0.10}{0.34} = \frac{5}{17}.$$

(This problem is an example of what is known as Bayes's rule. It's still conditional probability but sort of backward. That is, rather than being given a path and finding the probability of going along that path—$P(X|B)$ refers to the probability of first traveling along B and then along X—we are given the outcome and asked for the probability of having gone along a certain path to get there—$P(B|X)$ refers to the probability of having gotten to X by first having traveled along B. You don't need to know Bayes's rule by name for the AP exam, but you may have to solve a problem like this one.)

3. The correct answer is (e). If you knew that the variables "Score on Statistics Exam" and "Score on Spanish Language Exam" were independent, then the standard deviation would be given by

$$\sqrt{\sigma_1^2 + \sigma_2^2} = \sqrt{(0.6)^2 + (0.55)^2} \approx 0.82.$$

However, you cannot assume that they are independent in this situation. In fact, they aren't because we have two scores on the same people. Hence, there is not enough information.

4. The correct answer is (a).

$$P(X < 3.0) = P\left(z < \frac{3-3.4}{0.3} = -1.33\right) = 0.0918.$$

The calculator answer is `normalcdf(-100,3,3.4,0.3) = 0.0912`. Note that answer (d) makes no sense since probability values must be nonnegative (and, of course, less than or equal to 1).

5. The correct answer is (d). Because ethnic group categories are assumed to be mutually exclusive, $P(\text{Asian or Latino}) = P(\text{Asian}) + P(\text{Latino}) = 32\% + 11\% = 43\%$.

6. The correct answer is (e). The situation is as pictured below:

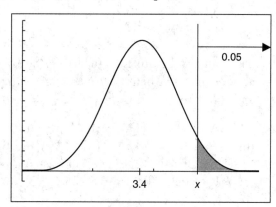

From Table A, $z_x = 1.645$ (also, `invNorm(0.95) = 1.645`).

Hence, $z_x = 1.645 = \dfrac{x - 3.4}{0.3} \Rightarrow x = 3.4 + (0.3)(1.645) = 3.89$. Norma would need a minimum GPA of 3.89 in order to qualify for the honor society.

7. The correct answer is (c). $P(Y = 4) = 1 - \left(\dfrac{1}{8} + \dfrac{3}{8} + \dfrac{3}{16} \right) = \dfrac{5}{16}$. Since they are independent, $P(X = 5 \text{ and } Y = 4) = P(X = 5) \cdot P(Y = 4) = \dfrac{1}{2} \cdot \dfrac{5}{16} = \dfrac{5}{32}$.

8. The correct answer is (c). The expected value is $(-1)(0.6) + (1)(0.25) + (2)(0.15) = -0.05$.

9. The correct answer is (d). $P(\text{at least one of the first two rolls is "Y"}) = P(\text{the first roll is "Y"}) + P(\text{the second roll is "Y"}) - P(\text{both rolls are "Y"}) = \dfrac{1}{3} + \dfrac{1}{3} - \left(\dfrac{1}{3} \right)\left(\dfrac{1}{3} \right) = \dfrac{5}{9}$.

   Alternatively, $P(\text{at least one of the first two rolls is "Y"}) = 1 - P(\text{neither roll is "Y"}) = 1 - \left(\dfrac{2}{3} \right)^2 = \dfrac{5}{9}$.

10. The correct answer is (b). The possible outcomes where one die shows a 4 are highlighted in the table of all possible sums:

	1	2	3	4	5	6
1	2	3	4	*5*	6	7
2	3	4	5	*6*	7	8
3	4	5	6	*7*	8	9
4	*5*	*6*	*7*	*8*	*9*	*10*
5	6	7	8	*9*	10	11
6	7	8	9	*10*	11	12

   There are 11 cells for which one die is a 4 (be careful not to count the **8** twice), 2 of which are 6s.

Free-Response

1. $\mu_x = 2\left(\dfrac{1}{3} \right) + 3\left(\dfrac{5}{12} \right) + 4\left(\dfrac{1}{4} \right) = \dfrac{35}{12} \approx 2.92$

   $$\sigma_X = \sqrt{\left(2 - \dfrac{35}{12} \right)^2 \left(\dfrac{1}{3} \right) + \left(3 - \dfrac{35}{12} \right)^2 \left(\dfrac{5}{12} \right) + \left(4 - \dfrac{35}{12} \right)^2 \left(\dfrac{1}{4} \right)} = 0.759.$$

   This can also be done on the TI-83/84 by putting the X values in `L1` and the probabilities in `L2`. Then `1-Var Stats L1,L2` will give the above values for the mean and standard deviation.

2. (a) $P(A \text{ and } B) = P(A) \cdot P(B|A) = (0.6)(0.5) = 0.30$.
   (b) $P(A \text{ or } B) = P(A) + P(B) - P(A \text{ and } B) = 0.6 + 0.3 - 0.3 = 0.6$
      (Note that the 0.3 that is subtracted came from part (a).)
   (c) $P(B) = 0.3, P(B|A) = 0.5$. Since $P(B) \neq P(B|A)$, events A and B are not independent.

3. (a) Let X represent the score a student earns. We know that X has approximately $N(500, 90)$. What we are looking for is shown in the following graph.

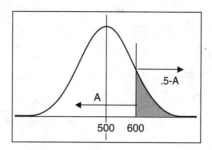

$$P(X > 600) = 1 - 0.8667 = 0.1333.$$

The calculator answer is `normalcdf(600,10,000,500.900)=0.1333` (remember that the upper bound must be "big"—in this exercise, 10,000 was used to get a sufficient number of standard deviations above 600).

(b) We already know, from part (a), that the area to the left of 600 is 0.8667. Similarly we determine the area to the left of 450 as follows:

$$Z_{450} = \frac{450 - 500}{90} = -0.56 \Rightarrow A = 0.2877.$$

Then

$$P(450 < X < 600) = 0.8667 - 0.2877 = 0.5790.$$

There are $0.5790(9000) \approx 5211$ scores.
[This could be done on the calculator as follows: `normalcdf(450,600, 500,90)` `= 0.5775`.]

(c) This situation could be pictured as follows.

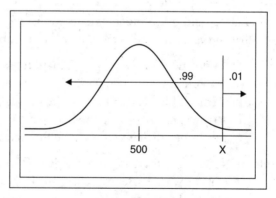

The z-score corresponding to an area of 0.99 is 2.33 (`invNorm(0.99)` on the calculator). So, $z_x = 2.33$. But, also,

$$z_x = \frac{x - 500}{90}.$$

Thus,

$$\frac{x - 500}{90} = 2.33.$$

Solving algebraically for x, we get $x = 709.7$. Rachel needs a score of 710 or higher.

Remember that this type of problem is usually solved by expressing z in two ways (using the definition and finding the area) and solving the equation formed by equating them. On the TI-83/84, the answer could be found as follows: `invNorm(0.99,500, 90)=` `709.37`.

4. (a) $\mu_{3+6X} = 3 + 6\mu_X = 3 + 6(3) = 21$.

(b) Because $\sigma^2_{a+bx} = b^2\sigma^2, \sigma^2_{3+6x} = 6^2\sigma^2_x = 36(0.25) = 9$. Thus,

$$\sigma_{3+6x} = \sqrt{\sigma^2_{3+6X}} = \sqrt{9} = 3.$$

5.

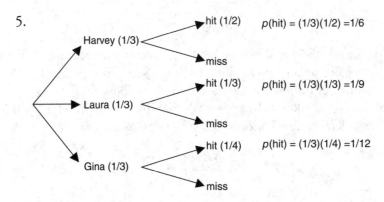

Because we are given that the target was hit, we only need to look at those outcomes. P(the person who hit the target was Laura | the target was hit)

$$= \frac{\frac{1}{9}}{\frac{1}{6} + \frac{1}{9} + \frac{1}{12}} = \frac{4}{13}.$$

6. $\mu_{X-Y} = \mu_X - \mu_Y = 3 - 5 = -2$.

Since X and Y are independent, we have $\sigma_{X-Y} = \sqrt{\sigma^2_X + \sigma^2_Y} = \sqrt{1+1.3} = 1.52$. Note that the variances add even though we are subtracting one random variable from another.

7. I is not true. This is an approximation based on the *68-95-99.7 rule*. The actual value proportion within two standard deviations of the mean, to 4 decimal places, is 0.9545.

II is true. This is a property of the normal curve.

III is true. This is because the bell shape of the normal curve means that there is more area under the curve for a given interval length for intervals closer to the center.

8. (a) No, the events are not independent. The probability of B changes depending on what happens with A. Because there are 12 face cards, if the first card drawn is a face card, then $P(B) = 11/51$. If the first card is not a face card, then $P(B) = 12/51$. Because the probability of B is affected by the outcome of A, A and B are not independent.

(b) $P(A) = 12/52 = 3/13$. $P(A|C) = 3/13$ (3 of the 13 diamonds are face cards). Because these are the same, the events "draw a face card on the first draw" and "the first card drawn is a diamond" are independent.

9. The area to the right of x is 0.6, so the area to the left is 0.4. From the table of Standard Normal Probabilities, $A = 0.4 \Rightarrow z_x = -0.25$. Also

$$z_x = \frac{x - 700}{50}.$$

So,

$$z_x = \frac{x - 700}{50} = -0.25 \Rightarrow x = 687.5.$$

60% of the area is to the right of 687.5. The calculator answer is given by `invNorm(0.4,700,50)=687.33`.

10. Let D = "a home has a desktop computer"; L = "a home has a laptop computer." We are given that $P(D) = 0.8$ and $P(D \text{ and } L) = 0.3$. Thus,

$$P(L \,|\, D) = \frac{P(D \cap L)}{P(D)} = \frac{0.3}{0.8} = \frac{3}{8}.$$

11. The situation can be pictured as shown below. The shaded area is a trapezoid whose area is

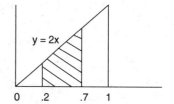

$$\frac{1}{2}(0.7 - 0.2)[2(0.2) + 2(0.7)] = 0.45.$$

12. The fact that Harv's pumpkin is at the 90th percentile means that it is larger than 90% of the pumpkins in the contest. From the table of Standard Normal Probabilities, the area to the left of a term with a z-score of 1.28 is about 0.90. Thus,

$$z_x = 1.28 = \frac{x - 125}{18} \Rightarrow x = 148.04.$$

So, Harv's pumpkin weighed about 148 pounds (for your information, the winning pumpkin at the Half Moon Bay Pumpkin Festival in 2008 weighed over 1528 pounds!). Seven of the 62 pumpkins weighed more than 1000 pounds!

13. Since $\sum P(X) = 1$, we have $P(X = 4) = 1 - P(X = 2) - P(X = 3) = 1 - 0.3 - 0.5 = 0.2$. Thus, filling in the table for X, we have

X	2	3	4
P(X)	0.3	0.5	**0.2**

Since X and Y are independent, $P(X = 4 \text{ and } Y = 3) = P(X = 4) \cdot P(X = 3)$. We are given that $P(X = 4 \text{ and } Y = 3) = 0.03$. Thus, $P(X = 4) \cdot P(Y = 3) = 0.03$. Since we now know that $P(X = 4) = 0.2$, we have $(0.2) \cdot P(Y = 3) = 0.03$, which gives us $P(Y = 3) = \frac{0.03}{0.2} = 0.15$.

Now, since $\sum P(Y) = 1$, we have $P(Y = 5) = 1 - P(Y = 3) - P(Y = 4) - P(Y = 6) = 1 - 0.15 - 0.1 - 0.4 = 0.35$.

14. Let A = "the number is divisible by 24" = {24, 48, 72, 96}. Let B = "the number is divisible by 36" = {36, 72}.

Note that $P(A \text{ and } B) = \dfrac{1}{100}$ (72 is the only number divisible by *both 24 and 36*).

$$P(\text{win a pizza}) = P(A \text{ or } B) = P(A) + P(B) - P(A \text{ and } B) = \frac{4}{100} + \frac{2}{100} - \frac{1}{100} = \frac{5}{100} = 0.05.$$

15. Because the numbers of men and women in the school are about equal (that is, $P(\text{women}) = 0.5$), let an even number represent a female and an odd number represent

a male. Begin on the first line of the table and consider groups of 12 digits. Count the even numbers among the 12. This will be the number of females among the group. Repeat five times. The relevant part of the table is shown below, with even numbers underlined and groups of 12 separated by two slanted bars (\\):

79<u>692</u>   517<u>07</u>   73\\<u>274</u>   12<u>548</u>   91<u>49</u>\\7   11135   8<u>1218</u>

7\\9572   <u>06484</u>   8<u>74</u>\\<u>40</u>   41957   21<u>6</u>07\\

In the five groups of 12 people, there were 3, 6, 3, 8, and 6 women. (*Note:* The result will, of course, vary if a different assignment of digits is made. For example, if you let the digits $0 - 4$ represent a female and $5 - 9$ represent a male, there would be 4, 7, 7, 5, and 7 women in the five groups.) So, in 40% of the trials there were 4 or fewer women in the class even though we would expect the average to be 6 (the average of these 5 trials is 5.2). Hence, it seems that getting only 4 women in a class when we expect 6 really isn't too unusual because it occurs 40% of the time. (It is shown in the next chapter that the theoretical probability of getting 4 or fewer women in a group of 12 people, assuming that men and women are equally likely, is about 0.19.)

16. Because $P(\text{girl}) = 0.6$, let the random digits 1, 2, 3, 4, 5, 6 represent the birth of a girl and 0, 7, 8, 9 represent the birth of a boy. Start on the second row of the random digit table and move across the line until you find the third digit that represents a girl. Note the number of digits needed to get three successes. Repeat 5 times and compute the average. The simulation is shown below (each success, i.e., girl, is underlined and separate trials are delineated by \\).

Start: <u>4195</u>\\7   <u>21607</u>   5\\<u>124</u>\\8   <u>54772</u>   \\<u>19481</u>\\   90392

It took 4, 7, 3, 6, and 5 children before they got their three girls. The average wait was 5. (The theoretical average is exactly 5—we got lucky this time!) As with Exercise 15, the result will vary with different assignment of random digits.

17. (a) $P(x \leq 22) = P(x = 20) + P(x = 21) + P(x = 22) = 0.2 + 0.3 + 0.2 = 0.7$.
    (b) $P(x > 21) = P(x = 22) + P(x = 23) + P(x = 24) = 0.2 + 0.1 + 0.2 = 0.5$.
    (c) $P(21 \leq x < 24) = P(x = 21) + P(x = 22) + P(x = 23) = 0.3 + 0.2 + 0.1 = 0.6$.
    (d) $P(x \leq 21 \text{ or } x > 23) = P(x = 20) + P(x = 21) + P(x = 24) = 0.2 + 0.3 + 0.2 = 0.7$.

18. (a) 18 of the 38 slots are winners, so $P(\text{win if bet on red}) = \dfrac{18}{38} = 0.474$.

    (b) The probability distribution for this game is

Outcome	Win	Lose
X	1	-1
$P(X)$	$18/38$	$20/38$

$$E(X) = \mu_X = \left(\frac{18}{38}\right) + (-1)\left(\frac{20}{38}\right) = -0.052 \text{ or } -5.2\text{¢}.$$

The player will lose 5.2¢, on average, for each dollar bet.

19. From the tables, we see that $P(z < -2.5) = P(z > 2.5) = 0.0062$. So the probability that we are more than 2.5 standard deviations from the mean is $2(0.0062) = 0.0124$. (This can be found on the calculator as follows: 2 normalcdf (2.5,1000).)

20. The situation can be pictured as follows:

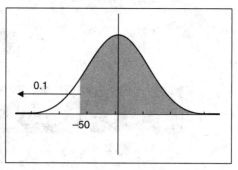

If 90% of the area is to the *right* of 50, then 10% of the area is to the left. So,

$$z_{50} = -1.28 = \frac{50 - \mu}{12} \rightarrow \mu = 65.36.$$

Solutions to Cumulative Review Problems

1. II is true: the mean is most likely greater than the median. This is because the mean, being nonresistant, is pulled in the direction of outliers or skewness. Because the given histogram is clearly skewed to the right, the mean is likely to be to the right of (that is, greater than) the median.

2. The kind of sample you want is a *stratified random sample*. The sample should have 25 Asian students, 8 African American students, 12 Latino students, and 55 Caucasian students. You could get a list of all Asian students from the data clerk and randomly select 25 students from the list. Repeat this process for percentages of African American, Latino, and Caucasian students. Now the proportion of each ethnic group in your sample is the same as its proportion in the population.

3. The five-number summary is [20, 32, 42, 46, 50]. The box plot looks like this:

4. (a) The LSRL line is $\overwidehat{\#\,\text{Manatee deaths}} = -41.430 + 0.12486(\#\text{boats})$.
   (b) For each additional registered powerboat, the number of manatee deaths is predicted to increase by 0.12. You could also say that the number increases, on average, by 0.12.

5. For this set of data, $\bar{x} = 9.9$ and $s = 2.0$. Examination of the 25 points in the dataset yields the following.

	Percentage expected in each interval by the 68-95-99.7 rule	Number of terms from dataset in each interval
$9.9 \pm 1(2) = (7.9, 11.9)$	68% (17/25)	16/25 = 64%
$9.9 \pm 2(2) = (5.9, 13.9)$	95% (23.8/25)	25/25 = 100%
$9.9 \pm 3(2) = (3.9, 15.9)$	99.7% (24.9/25)	25/25 = 100%

The actual values in the dataset (16, 25, 25) are quite close to the expected values (17, 23.8, 24.9) if this truly were data from a normal population. Hence, it seems reasonable that the data could have been a random sample drawn from a population that is approximately normally distributed.

CHAPTER 9

Binomial Distributions, Geometric Distributions, and Sampling Distributions

IN THIS CHAPTER

Summary: In this chapter we finish laying the mathematical (probability) basis for inference by considering the binomial and geometric situations that occur often enough to warrant our study. In the last part of this chapter, we begin our study of inference by introducing the idea of a sampling distribution, one of the most important concepts in statistics. Once we've mastered this material, we will be ready to plunge into a study of formal inference (Chapters 10–13).

Key Ideas

✪ Binomial Distributions
✪ Normal Approximation to the Binomial
✪ Geometric Distributions
✪ Sampling Distributions
✪ Central Limit Theorem

Binomial Distributions

A **binomial experiment** has the following properties:

- The experiment consists of a fixed number, *n*, of identical trials.
- There are only two possible outcomes (that's the "bi" in *binomial*): success (*S*) or failure (*F*).

- The probability of success, p, is the same for each trial.
- The trials are independent (that is, knowledge of the outcomes of earlier trials does not affect the probability of success of the next trial).
- Our interest is in a **binomial random variable** X, which is the count of successes in n trials. The probability distribution of X is the **binomial distribution**.

(Taken together, the second, third, and fourth bullets above are called *Bernoulli trials*. One way to think of a binomial setting is as a fixed number n of Bernoulli trials in which our random variable of interest is the count of successes X in the n trials. You do not need to know the term *Bernoulli trials* for the AP exam.)

The short version of this is to say that a *binomial experiment* consists of n independent trials of an experiment that has two possible outcomes (success or failure), each trial having the same probability of success (p). The *binomial random variable X* is the count of successes.

In practice, we may consider a situation to be binomial when, in fact, the independence condition is not quite satisfied. This occurs when the probability of occurrence of a given trial is affected only slightly by prior trials. For example, suppose that the probability of a defect in a manufacturing process is 0.0005. That is, there is, on average, only 1 defect in 2000 items. Suppose we check a sample of 10,000 items for defects. When we check the first item, the proportion of defects remaining changes slightly for the remaining 9999 items in the sample. We would expect 5 out of 10,000 (0.0005) to be defective. But if the first one we look at is *not* defective, the probability of the next one being defective has changed to 5/9999 or 0.0005005. It's a small change, but it means that the trials are not, strictly speaking, independent. A common rule of thumb is that we will consider a situation to be binomial if the population size is at least 10 times the sample size.

Symbolically, for the *binomial random variable X*, we say X has $B(n, p)$.

> **example:** Suppose Maria is a 65% free-throw shooter. If we assume that repeated shots are independent, we could ask, "What is the probability that Maria makes exactly 7 of her next 10 free throws?" If X is the binomial random variable that gives us the count of successes for this experiment, then we say that X has $B(10, 0.65)$. Our question is then: $P(X = 7) = ?$

> We can think of $B(n, p, x)$ as a particular binomial probability. In this example, then, $B(10, 0.65, 7)$ is the probability that there are exactly 7 successes in 10 repetitions of a binomial experiment where $p = 0.65$. This is handy because it is the same syntax used by the TI-83/84 calculator (`binompdf(n,p,x)`) when doing binomial problems.

If X has $B(n, p)$, then X can take on the values 0, 1, 2, . . . , n. Then,

$$B(n,\ p,\ x) = P(X = x) = \binom{n}{x} p^{x}(1-p)^{n-x}$$

gives the *binomial probability* of exactly x successes for a binomial random variable X that has B(n, p). (Note: This formula is on the formula sheet.)

Now,

$$\binom{n}{x} = \frac{n!}{x!(n-x)!}.$$

Some other notations include

$$\binom{n}{x} = {}_{n}C_{r} = C(n,r).$$

Graphing calculators will have a command for this.

> **example:** Find $B(15, .3, 5)$. That is, find $P(X = 5)$ for 15 trials of a binomial random variable X that succeeds with probability 0.3.

> **solution:**

$$P(X = 5) = \binom{15}{5}(0.3)^5(1 - 0.3)^{15-5}$$

$$= \frac{15!}{5!10!}(0.3)^5(0.7)^{10} = 0.206.$$

Calculator Tip: The solution to the previous example can be found using the *binomial pdf* command on your calculator.

> **example:** Consider once again our free-throw shooter (Maria) from the earlier example. Maria is a 65% free-throw shooter, and each shot is independent. If X is the count of free throws made by Maria, then X has $B(10, 0.65)$ if she shoots 10 free throws. What is the probability she makes exactly seven free throws, that is, $P(X = 7)$?

> **solution:**

$$P(X = 7) = \binom{10}{7}(0.65)^7(0.35)^3 = \frac{10!}{7!3!}(0.65)^7(0.65)^3$$

$$= 0.252.$$

Exam Tip: On binomial probability questions, the expectation is that you identify the distribution (by name or by formula) and parameters. That means, for example, it is enough to write the formula with numbers substituted and the answer. The formula identifies the procedure and parameters. You can also just write "Binomial, $n = 10$, $p = 0.65$. $P(x = 7) = 0.252$."

> **example:** What is the probability that Maria makes *no more than* 5 free throws? That is, what is $P(X \leq 5)$?

> **solution:**

$$P(X \leq 5) = P(X = 0) + P(X = 1) + P(X = 2) + P(X = 3)$$

$$+ P(X = 4) + P(X = 5) = \binom{10}{0}(0.65)^0(0.35)^{10} + \binom{10}{1}(0.65)^1(0.35)^9$$

$$+ \cdots + \binom{10}{5}(0.65)^5(0.35)^5 = 0.249.$$

There is about a 25% chance that she will make 5 or fewer free throws. Graphing calculators have a command to answer such cumulative binomial questions.

> **example:** What is the probability that Maria makes at least 6 free throws?

> **solution:** $P(X \geq 6) = P(X = 6) + P(X = 7) + \cdots + P(X = 10)$
> $= 1 - P(X \leq 5) = 0.751.$

(Note that, in a multipart question on the AP Exam, if you are using the same distribution and parameters as a previous part, you will not need to identify them again. But if the parameters are different, you will need to identify the distribution and parameters again.)

The **mean and standard deviation of a binomial random variable** X are given by $\mu_X = np; \sigma_X = \sqrt{np(1-p)}$. (Note: These formulas are on the formula sheet.) A binomial distribution for a given n and p (meaning you have all possible values of x along with their corresponding probabilities) is an example of a *probability distribution* as defined in Chapter 6. The mean and the standard deviation of a binomial random variable X could be found by using the formulas from Chapter 8:

$$\mu_x = \sum x_i p_i \text{ and } \sigma_x = \sqrt{\sum (x - \mu_x)^2 p_i},$$

but clearly the formulas for the binomial are easier to use. Be careful that you don't try to use the formulas for the mean and standard deviation of a binomial random variable for a discrete random variable that is *not* binomial.

> **example:** Find the mean and the standard deviation of a binomial random variable X that has $B(85, 0.6)$.
>
> **solution:** $\mu_X = (85)(0.6) = 51$; $\sigma_X = \sqrt{85(0.6)(0.4)} = 4.52$.

Geometric Distributions

In the Binomial Distributions section of this chapter, we defined a binomial setting as an experiment in which the following conditions are present:

- The experiment consists of a fixed number, n, of identical trials.
- There are only two possible outcomes: success (S) or failure (F).
- The probability of success, p, is the same for each trial.
- The trials are independent (that is, knowledge of the outcomes of earlier trials does not affect the probability of success of the next trial).
- Our interest is in a **binomial random variable X**, which is the count of successes in n trials. The probability distribution of X is the **binomial distribution**.

There are times we are interested not in the count of successes out of n fixed trials but in the probability that the *first* success occurs on a given trial or in the average number of trials until the first success. A **geometric setting** is defined as follows.

- There are only two possible outcomes: success (S) or failure (F).
- The probability of success, p, is the same for each trial.
- The trials are independent (that is, knowledge of the outcomes of earlier trials does not affect the probability of success of the next trial).
- Our interest is in a **geometric random variable X**, which is the number of trials necessary to obtain the *first* success.

Note that if X is a *binomial*, then X can take on the values 0, 1, 2, . . . , n. If X is *geometric*, then it takes on the values 1, 2, 3, ... There can be zero successes in a binomial, but the earliest a first success can come in a geometric setting is on the first trial.

If X is geometric, the probability that the first success occurs on the *nth trial* is given by $P(X = n) = p(1-p)^{n-1}$. The value of $P(X = n)$ in a geometric setting can be found on the TI-83/84 calculator, in the DISTR menu, as geometpdf(p,n) (note that the order of p and n are, for reasons known only to the good folks at TI, reversed from the binomial). Given the relative simplicity of the formula for $P(X = n)$ for a geometric setting, it's probably just as easy to calculate the expression directly. There is also a geometcdf function that behaves analogously to the binomcdf function, but it is not much needed in this course.

example: Remember Maria, the basketball player whose free-throw shooting percentage was 0.65? What is the probability that the first free throw she manages to hit is on her fourth attempt?

solution: $P(X = 4) = (0.65)(1 - 0.65)^{4-1} = (0.65)(0.35)^3 = 0.028$. This can be done on the TI-83/84 as follows: `geometpdf(p,n)` = `geometpdf(0.65,4)` = 0.028.

example: In a standard deck of 52 cards, there are 12 face cards. So the probability of drawing a face card from a full deck is $12/52 = 0.231$.

(a) If you draw cards with replacement (that is, you replace the card in the deck before drawing the next card), what is the probability that the first face card you draw is the 10th card?

(b) If you draw cards without replacement, what is the probability that the first face card you draw is the 10th card?

solution:

(a) $P(X = 10) = (0.231)(1 - 0.231)^9 = 0.022$. On the TI-83/84: `geometpdf(0.231,10)` = 0.0217.

(b) If you don't replace the card each time, the probability of drawing a face card on each trial is different because the proportion of face cards in the deck changes each time a card is removed. Hence, this is not a geometric setting and cannot be answered by the techniques of this section. It *can* be answered, but not easily, by the techniques of the previous chapter.

Rather than the probability that the first success occurs on a specified trial, we may be interested in the average wait until the first success. The average wait until the first success of a geometric random variable is $1/p$. (This can be derived by summing $(1) \cdot P(X = 1) + (2) \cdot P(X = 2) + (3) \cdot P(X = 3) + \ldots = 1p + 2p(1 - p) + 3p(1 - p)^2 + \ldots$, which can be done using algebraic techniques for summing an infinite series with a common ratio less than 1.)

example: On average, how many free throws will Maria have to take before she makes one (remember, $p = 0.65$)?

solution: Using the formula for the mean found on the formula sheet: $1/p = \dfrac{1}{0.65} = 1.54$.

Since, in a geometric distribution $P(X = n) = p(1 - p)^{n-1}$, the probabilities become less likely as n increases since we are multiplying by $1 - p$, a number less than one. The geometric distribution has a step-ladder graph that looks like this:

Sampling Distributions

Suppose we drew a sample of size 10 from an approximately normal population with unknown mean and standard deviation and got $\bar{x} = 18.87$. Two questions arise: (1) what does this sample tell us about the population from which the sample was drawn, and (2) what would happen if we drew more samples?

Suppose we drew 5 more samples of size 10 from this population and got $\bar{x} = 20.35$, $\bar{x} = 20.04$, $\bar{x} = 19.20$, $\bar{x} = 19.02$, and $\bar{x} = 20.35$. In answer to question (1), we might believe that the population from which these samples was drawn had a mean around 20 because these averages tend to group there (in fact, the six samples were drawn from a normal population whose mean is 20 and whose standard deviation is 4). The mean of the 6 samples is 19.64, which supports our feeling that the mean of the original population might have been 20.

The standard deviation of the 6 samples is 0.68, and you might not have any intuitive sense about how that relates to the population standard deviation, although you might suspect that the standard deviation of the samples should be less than the standard deviation of the population because the chance of an extreme value for an average should be less than that for an individual term (it just doesn't seem very likely that we would draw a *lot* of extreme values in a single sample).

Suppose we continued to draw samples of size 10 from this population until we were exhausted or until we had drawn *all possible samples of size 10*. If we did succeed in drawing all possible samples of size 10 and computed the mean of each sample, the distribution of these sample means would be the **sampling distribution of $\bar{x}$**.

Remembering that a "statistic" is a value that describes a sample, the **sampling distribution of a statistic** is the distribution of that statistic for all possible samples of a given size. It's important to understand that a dotplot of a few samples drawn from a population is not a distribution (it's a *simulation* of a distribution)—it becomes a distribution only when *all* possible samples of a given size are drawn.

Sampling Distribution of a Sample Mean

Suppose we have the sampling distribution of $\bar{x}$. That is, we have formed a distribution of the means of all possible samples of size n from an unknown population (thus, we know little about its shape, center, or spread). Let $\mu_{\bar{x}}$ and $\sigma_{\bar{x}}$ represent the mean and standard deviation of the sampling distribution of $\bar{x}$, respectively.

Then

$$\mu_{\bar{x}} = \mu \text{ and } \sigma_{\bar{x}} = \frac{\sigma}{\sqrt{n}}$$

for any population with mean μ and standard deviation σ.

(*Note:* The formula given for $\sigma_{\bar{x}}$ above is correct only if the sample has true independence between trials, such as when sampling with replacement, or when the population is infinite, such as when tossing a coin. The formula still works well enough if the sample size n is small compared to the population size N. A general rule is that n should be no more than 10% of N to use the formula given for $\sigma_{\bar{x}}$ [that is, $N > 10n$]. This is because, when sampling without replacement, the exact value for the standard deviation of the sampling distribution is actually

$$\sigma_{\bar{x}} = \frac{\sigma}{\sqrt{n}} \sqrt{\frac{N-n}{N-1}}.$$

In practice this usually isn't a major issue because this **Finite Population Correction Factor**

$$\sqrt{\frac{N-n}{N-1}}$$

is close to 1 whenever N is large in comparison to n. (You don't have to know this formula for the AP exam. However, you do need to understand that when our sample size is larger than 10% of the population, an adjustment must be made to the standard deviation formula.)

example: A large population is known to have a mean of 23 and a standard deviation of 2.5. What are the mean and the standard deviation of the sampling distribution of means of samples of size 20 drawn from this population?

solution:

$$\mu_{\bar{x}} = \mu = 23, \ \sigma_{\bar{x}} = \frac{\sigma}{\sqrt{n}} = \frac{2.5}{\sqrt{20}} = 0.559.$$

Central Limit Theorem

The discussion above gives us measures of center and spread for the sampling distribution of $\bar{x}$ but tells us nothing about the *shape* of the sampling distribution. It turns out that the shape of the sampling distribution is determined by (a) the shape of the original population and (b) n, the sample size. If the original population is approximately normal, the shape of the sampling distribution will be approximately normal no matter what the size of the sample.

If the shape of the original population is not normal, or unknown, and the sample size is small, then the shape of the sampling distribution will be similar to that of the original population. For example, if a population is skewed to the right, we would expect the sampling distribution of the mean for small samples also to be somewhat skewed to the right, although not as much as the original population.

When the sample size is large, we have a result known as the **central limit theorem**: When n is sufficiently large, the sampling distribution of $\bar{x}$ will be approximately normal.

A rough rule of thumb for using the central limit theorem is that n should be at least 30. The central limit theorem allows us to use normal calculations to do problems involving sampling distributions without having knowledge of the original population. Note that calculations involving z-procedures require that you know the value of σ, the population standard deviation. Since you will rarely know σ, the large sample size essentially says that the sampling distribution is *approximately*, but not exactly, normal. That is, technically you should not be using z-procedures unless you know σ, but as a practical matter, z-procedures are numerically close to correct for a large n. Given that the population size (N) is large in relation to the sample size (n), the information presented in this section can be summarized in the following table:

example: Describe the sampling distribution of $\bar{x}$ for samples of size 15 drawn from a normal population with mean 65 and standard deviation 9.

	POPULATION	**SAMPLING DISTRIBUTION**
Mean	μ	$\mu_{\bar{x}} = \mu$
Standard Deviation	σ	$\sigma_{\bar{x}} = \dfrac{\sigma}{\sqrt{n}}$
Shape	Normal	Normal
	Undetermined (skewed, etc.)	If n is "small," shape is similar to shape of the population *OR* As n gets "larger," shape becomes more approximately normal (central limit theorem). If $n \geq 30$, the shape of the sampling distribution will generally be approximately normal.

solution: Because the original population is normal, $\bar{x}$ is normal with mean 65 and standard deviation $\dfrac{9}{\sqrt{15}} = 2.32$. That is, $\bar{x}$ has $N\left(65, \dfrac{9}{\sqrt{15}}\right)$.

example: Describe the sampling distribution of $\bar{x}$ for samples of size 15 drawn from a population that is strongly skewed to the left (like the scores on a very easy test) with mean 65 and standard deviation 9.

solution: $\mu_{\bar{x}} = 65$ and $\sigma_{\bar{x}} = 2.32$ as in the above example. However, this time the population is skewed to the left. The sample size is not large enough to argue, based on our rule of thumb ($n \geq 30$), that the sampling distribution is normal. The best we can say is that the sampling distribution is probably more mound-shaped than the original but might still be somewhat skewed to the left.

example: The average adult has completed an average of 11.25 years of education with a standard deviation of 1.75 years. A random sample of 90 adults is obtained. What is the probability that the sample will have a mean

(a) greater than 11.5 years?

(b) between 11 and 11.5 years?

solution: The sampling distribution of $\bar{x}$ has $\mu_{\bar{x}} = 11.25$ and

$$\sigma_{\bar{x}} = \frac{1.75}{\sqrt{90}} = 0.184.$$

Because the sample size is large ($n = 90$), the central limit theorem tells us that large sample techniques are appropriate. Accordingly,

(a) The graph of the sampling distribution is shown below with appropriate values marked:

$$P(\bar{x} > 11.5) = P\left(z > \frac{11.5 - 11.25}{1.75 / \sqrt{90}} = \frac{0.25}{0.184} = 1.36\right) = 0.0869.$$

(b) From part (a), the area to the left of 11.5 is $1 - 0.0869 = 0.9131$. Since the sampling distribution is approximately normal, it is symmetric. Since 11 is the same distance to the left of the mean as 11.5 is to the right, we know that $P(\bar{x} < 11) = P(\bar{x} > 11.5) = 0.0869$. Hence, $P(11 < \bar{x} < 11.5) = 0.9131 - 0.0869 = 0.8262$. The calculator solution is `normalcdf(11,11.5,11,0.184)=0.8258`.

example: Over the years, the scores on the final exam for AP Calculus have been normally distributed with a mean of 82 and a standard deviation of 6. The instructor thought that this year's class was quite dull, and in fact, they only averaged 79 on their final. Assuming that this class is a random sample of 32 students from AP Calculus, what is the probability that the average score on the final for this class is no more than 79? Do you think the instructor was right?

solution:

$$P(\bar{x} \leq 79) = P\left(z \leq \frac{79 - 82}{6/\sqrt{32}} = \frac{-3}{1.06} = -2.83\right) = 0.0023.$$

If this group really were typical, there is less than a 1% probability of getting an average this low by chance alone. That seems unlikely, so we have good evidence that the instructor was correct.

(The calculator solution for this problem is `normalcdf(-1000,79,82,1.06)`.)

Sampling Distributions of a Sample Proportion

If X is the count of successes in a sample of n trials of a binomial random variable, then the **proportion of success** is given by $\hat{p} = X/n$. $\hat{p}$ is what we use for the sample proportion (a statistic). The true population proportion would then be given by p.

> **Digression:** Before introducing $\hat{p}$, we have used $\bar{x}$ and s as statistics, and μ and σ as parameters. Often we represent statistics with English letters and parameters with Greek letters. However, we depart from that convention here by using $\hat{p}$ as a statistic and p as a parameter. There are texts that are true to the English/Greek convention by using p for the sample proportion and π for the population proportion.

We learned in the first section of this chapter that, if X is a binomial random variable, the mean and standard deviation of the sampling distribution of X are given by

$$\mu_X = np, \ \sigma_X = \sqrt{np(1-p)}.$$

We know that if we divide each term in a dataset by the same value n, then the mean and standard deviation of the transformed dataset will be the mean and standard deviation of the original dataset divided by n. Doing the algebra, we find that the mean and standard deviation of the sampling distribution of $\hat{p}$ are given by

$$\mu_{\hat{p}} = p, \ \sigma_{\hat{p}} = \sqrt{\frac{p(1-p)}{n}}.$$

The sampling distribution of $\hat{p}$ will be approximately normally distributed if n and p are large enough. If $\hat{p} = X/n$, then $\hat{p}$ has approximately

$$N\left(p, \sqrt{\frac{p(1-p)}{n}}\right),$$

provided that $np \geq 10$ and $n(1-p) \geq 10$ (or $np \geq 5$ and $n(1-p) \geq 5$).

example: Harold fails to study for his statistics final. The final has 100 multiple-choice questions, each with 5 choices. Harold has no choice but to guess randomly at all 100 questions. What is the probability that Harold will get at least 30% on the test? (*Note:* The probability of successfully guessing for each question is 20%.)

solution: Since 100(0.2) and 100(0.8) are both greater than 10, we can use the normal approximation to the sampling distribution of $\hat{p}$. Since

$$p = 0.2, \ \mu_{\hat{p}} = 0.2 \text{ and } \sigma_{\hat{p}} = \sqrt{\frac{0.2(1-0.2)}{100}} = 0.04.$$

Therefore,

$$P(\hat{p} \geq 0.3) = P\left(z \geq \frac{0.3 - 0.2}{0.04} = 2.5\right) = 0.0062. \text{ The TI-83/84 solution is given by}$$

`normalcdf(0.3,100,0.2,0.040)=0.0062.`

Harold should have studied.

⟩ Rapid Review

1. A coin is known to be unbalanced in such a way that heads only comes up 0.4 of the time.

   (a) What is the probability the first head appears on the 4th toss?
   (b) How many tosses would it take, on average, to flip two heads?

   Answer:

   (a) $P(\text{first head appears on fourth toss}) = 0.4 \ (1 - 0.4)^{4-1} = 0.4(0.6)^3 = 0.0864.$

   (b) Average wait to flip two heads $= 2(\text{average wait to flip one head}) = 2\left(\dfrac{1}{0.4}\right) = 5.$

2. The coin of problem #1 is flipped 50 times. Let X be the number of heads. What is

   (a) the probability of *exactly* 20 heads?
   (b) the probability of *at least* 20 heads?

   Answer:

   (a) $P(X = 20) = \dbinom{50}{20}(0.4)^{20}(0.6)^{30} = 0.115$ [on the TI-83/84: `binompdf(50, 0.4,20)`].

   (b) $P(X \geq 20) = \dbinom{50}{20}(0.4)^{20}(0.6)^{30} + \dbinom{50}{21}(0.4)^{21}(0.6)^{29} + \ldots + \dbinom{50}{50}(0.4)^{50}(0.6)^0$

   $= $ `1-binomcdf(50,0.4,19)=0.554`.

3. A binomial random variable X has $B(300, 0.2)$. Describe the sampling distribution of $\hat{p}$.

   Answer: Since $300(0.2) = 60 \geq 10$ and $300(0.8) = 240 \geq 10$, $\hat{p}$ has approximately a normal distribution with $\mu_{\hat{p}} = 0.2$ and $\sigma_{\hat{p}} = \sqrt{\dfrac{0.2(1-0.2)}{300}} = 0.023.$

4. A distribution is known to be highly skewed to the left with mean 25 and standard deviation 4. Samples of size 10 are drawn from this population, and the mean of each sample is calculated. Describe the sampling distribution of $\bar{x}$.

Answer: $\mu_{\bar{x}} = 25$, $\sigma_{\bar{x}} = \dfrac{4}{\sqrt{10}} = 1.26$.

Since the samples are small, the shape of the sampling distribution would probably show some left-skewness but would be more mound-shaped than the original population.

5. What is the probability that a sample of size 35 drawn from a population with mean 65 and standard deviation 6 will have a mean less than 64?

Answer: The sample size is large enough that we can use large-sample procedures. Hence,

$$P(\bar{x} < 64) = P\left(z < \frac{64 - 65}{\dfrac{6}{\sqrt{35}}} = -0.99\right) = 0.1611.$$

On the TI-83/84, the solution is given by `normalcdf(-100,64, 65, ` $\dfrac{6}{\sqrt{35}}$ `)`.

Practice Problems

Multiple-Choice

1. A binomial event has $n = 60$ trials. The probability of success on each trial is 0.4. Let X be the count of successes of the event during the 60 trials. What are μ_x and σ_x?

   (a) 24, 3.79
   (b) 24, 14.4
   (c) 4.90, 3.79
   (d) 4.90, 14.4
   (e) 2.4, 3.79

2. Consider repeated trials of a binomial random variable. Suppose the probability of the first success occurring on the second trial is 0.25. What is the probability of success on the first trial?

   (a) $1/4$
   (b) 1
   (c) $1/2$
   (d) $1/8$
   (e) $3/16$

3. You form a distribution of the means of all samples of size 9 drawn from an infinite population that is skewed to the left (like the scores on an easy Stats quiz!). The population from which the samples are drawn has a mean of 50 and a standard deviation of 12. Which one of the following statements is true of this distribution?

   (a) $\mu_{\bar{x}} = 50$, $\sigma_{\bar{x}} = 12$, the sampling distribution is skewed somewhat to the left.
   (b) $\mu_{\bar{x}} = 50$, $\sigma_{\bar{x}} = 4$, the sampling distribution is skewed somewhat to the left.
   (c) $\mu_{\bar{x}} = 50$, $\sigma_{\bar{x}} = 12$, the sampling distribution is approximately normal.
   (d) $\mu_{\bar{x}} = 50$, $\sigma_{\bar{x}} = 4$, the sampling distribution is approximately normal.
   (e) $\mu_{\bar{x}} = 50$, $\sigma_{\bar{x}} = 4$, the sample size is too small to make any statements about the shape of the sampling distribution.

4. A 12-sided die has faces numbered from 1–12. Assuming the die is fair (that is, each face is equally likely to appear each time), which of the following would give the exact probability of getting at least 10 threes out of 50 rolls?

(a) $\binom{50}{0}(0.083)^0(0.917)^{50} + \binom{50}{1}(0.083)^1(0.917)^{49} + \ldots + \binom{50}{9}(0.083)^9(0.917)^{41}$.

(b) $\binom{50}{11}(0.083)^{11}(0.917)^{39} + \binom{50}{12}(0.083)^{12}(0.917)^{38} + \ldots + \binom{50}{50}(0.083)^{50}(0.917)^0$.

(c) $1 - \left[\binom{50}{0}(0.083)^0(0.917)^{50} + \binom{50}{1}(0.083)^1(0.917)^{49} + \ldots + \binom{50}{10}(0.083)^{10}(0.917)^{40} \right]$.

(d) $1 - \left[\binom{50}{0}(0.083)^0(0.917)^{50} + \binom{50}{1}(0.083)^1(0.917)^{49} + \ldots + \binom{50}{9}(0.083)^9(0.917)^{41} \right]$.

(e) $\binom{50}{0}(0.083)^0(0.917)^{50} + \binom{50}{1}(0.083)^1(0.917)^{49} + \ldots + \binom{50}{10}(0.083)^{10}(0.917)^{40}$.

5. In a large population, 55% of the people get a physical examination at least once every two years. An SRS of 100 people are interviewed, and the sample proportion is computed. The mean and the standard deviation of the sampling distribution of the sample proportion are

(a) 55, 4.97
(b) 0.55, 0.002
(c) 55, 2
(d) 0.55, 0.0497
(e) The standard deviation cannot be determined from the given information.

6. Which of the following best describes the sampling distribution of a sample mean?

(a) It is the distribution of all possible sample means of a given size.
(b) It is the particular distribution in which $\mu_{\bar{x}} = \mu$ and $\sigma_{\bar{x}} = \sigma$.
(c) It is a graphical representation of the means of all possible samples.
(d) It is the distribution of all possible sample means from a given population.
(e) It is the probability distribution for each possible sample size.

7. Which of the following is not a common characteristic of binomial and geometric experiments?

(a) There are exactly two possible outcomes: success or failure.
(b) There is a random variable X that counts the number of successes.
(c) Each trial is independent (knowledge about what has happened on previous trials gives you no information about the current trial).
(d) The probability of success stays the same from trial to trial.
(e) $P(\text{success}) + P(\text{failure}) = 1$.

8. A school survey of students concerning which band to hire for the next school dance shows 70% of students in favor of hiring The Sand Rubies. What is the approximate

probability that, in a random sample of 200 students, at least 150 will favor hiring The Sand Rubies?

(a) $\binom{200}{150}(0.7)^{150}(0.3)^{50}$.

(b) $\binom{200}{150}(0.3)^{150}(0.7)^{50}$.

(c) $P\left(z > \dfrac{150-140}{\sqrt{200(0.7)(0.3)}}\right)$.

(d) $P\left(z > \dfrac{150-140}{\sqrt{150(0.7)(0.3)}}\right)$.

(e) $P\left(z > \dfrac{140-150}{\sqrt{200(0.7)(0.3)}}\right)$.

Free-Response

1. A factory manufacturing tennis balls determines that the probability that a single can of three balls will contain at least one defective ball is 0.025. What is the probability that a case of 48 cans will contain at least two cans with a defective ball?

2. A population is highly skewed to the left. Describe the shape of the sampling distribution of $\bar{x}$ drawn from this population if the sample size is (a) 3 or (b) 30.

3. In Chapter 8, we had an example in which we asked if it would change the proportion of girls in the population (assumed to be 0.5) if families continued to have children until they had a girl and then they stopped. That problem was to be done by simulation. How could you use what you know about the geometric distribution to answer this same question?

4. At a school better known for football than academics, it is known that only 20% of the scholarship athletes graduate within 5 years. The school is able to give 55 scholarships for football. What are the expected mean and standard deviation of the number of graduates for a group of 55 scholarship athletes?

5. Approximately 10% of the population of the United States is known to have blood type B. What is the probability that between 11% and 15%, inclusive, of a random sample of 500 adults will have type B blood?

6. Which of the following is (are) true of the central limit theorem? (More than one answer might be true.)

   I. $\mu_{\bar{x}} = \mu$.

   II. $\sigma_{\bar{x}} = \dfrac{\sigma}{\sqrt{n}}$ (if $N \geq 10n$).

   III. The sampling distribution of a sample mean will be approximately normally distributed for sufficiently large samples, regardless of the shape of the original population.

   IV. The sampling distribution of a sample mean will be normally distributed if the population from which the samples are drawn is normal.

7. A brake inspection station reports that 15% of all cars tested have brakes in need of replacement pads. For a sample of 20 cars that come to the inspection station,

   (a) what is the probability that exactly 3 have defective brakes?
   (b) what is the mean and standard deviation of the number of cars that need replacement pads?

8. A tire manufacturer claims that his tires will last 40,000 miles with a standard deviation of 5000 miles.

   (a) Assuming that the claim is true, describe the sampling distribution of the mean lifetime of a random sample of 160 tires. Remember that "describe" means discuss center, spread, and shape.
   (b) What is the probability that the mean lifetime of the sample of 160 tires will be less than 39,000 miles? Interpret the probability in terms of the truth of the manufacturer's claim.

9. Crabs off the coast of Northern California have a mean weight of 2 lb with a standard deviation of 5 oz. A large trap captures 35 crabs.

   (a) Describe the sampling distribution for the average weight of a random sample of 35 crabs taken from this population.
   (b) What would the mean weight of a sample of 35 crabs have to be in order to be in the top 10% of all such samples?

10. The probability that a person recovers from a particular type of cancer operation is 0.7. Suppose 8 people have the operation. What is the probability that

    (a) exactly 5 recover?
    (b) they all recover?
    (c) at least one of them recovers?

11. A certain type of lightbulb is advertised to have an average life of 1200 hours. If, in fact, lightbulbs of this type only average 1185 hours with a standard deviation of 80 hours, what is the probability that a sample of 100 bulbs will have an average life of at least 1200 hours?

12. Your task is to explain to your friend Gretchen, who knows virtually nothing (and cares even less) about statistics, just what the sampling distribution of the mean is. Explain the idea of a sampling distribution in such a way that even Gretchen, if she pays attention, will understand.

13. Consider the distribution shown at the right. Describe the shape of the sampling distribution of $\bar{x}$ for samples of size n if

    (a) $n = 3$.
    (b) $n = 40$.

14. After the *Challenger* disaster of 1986, it was discovered that the explosion was caused by defective O-rings. The probability that a single O-ring was defective and would fail (with catastrophic consequences) was 0.003, and there were 12 of them (6 outer and 6 inner). What was the probability that at least one of the O-rings would fail (as it actually did)?

15. Your favorite cereal has a little prize in each box. There are 5 such prizes. Each box is equally likely to contain any one of the prizes. So far, you have been able to collect 2 of the prizes. What is:

    (a) the probability that you will get the third different prize on the next box you buy?
    (b) the probability that it will take three more boxes to get the next prize?
    (c) the average number of boxes you will have to buy before getting the third prize?

16. Opinion polls in 2002 showed that about 70% of the population had a favorable opinion of President Bush. That same year, a simple random sample of 600 adults living in the San Francisco Bay Area showed only 65% had a favorable opinion of President Bush. What is the probability of getting a rating of 65% or less in a random sample of this size if the true proportion in the population was 0.70?

Cumulative Review Problems

1. An unbalanced coin has $p = 0.6$ of turning up heads. Toss the coin three times and let X be the count of heads among the three coins. Construct the probability distribution for this experiment.

2. You are doing a survey for your school newspaper and want to select a sample of 25 seniors. You decide to do this by randomly selecting 5 students from each of the 5 senior-level classes, each of which contains 28 students. The school data clerk assures you that students have been randomly assigned, by computer, to each of the 5 classes. Is this sample

   (a) a random sample?
   (b) a simple random sample?

3. Data are collected in an experiment to measure a person's reaction time (in seconds) as a function of the number of milligrams of a new drug. The least-squares regression line (LSRL) for the data is $\overline{Reaction\ Time} = 0.2 + 0.8(mg)$. Interpret the slope of the regression line in the context of the situation.

4. If $P(A) = 0.5$, $P(B) = 0.3$, and $P(A \text{ or } B) = 0.65$, are events A and B independent?

5. Which of the following is (are) examples of *quantitative data* and which is (are) examples of *categorical data*?

   (a) The height of an individual, measured in inches.
   (b) The color of the shirts in my closet.
   (c) The outcome of a flip of a coin described as "heads" or "tails."
   (d) The value of the change in your pocket.
   (e) Individuals, after they are weighed, are identified as thin, normal, or heavy.
   (f) Your pulse rate.
   (g) Your religion.

Solutions to Practice Problems

Multiple-Choice

1. The correct answer is (a).

$$\mu_X = (60)(0.4) = 24,\ \sigma_X = \sqrt{60(0.4)(0.6)} = \sqrt{14.4} = 3.79$$

2. The correct answer is (c). If it is a binomial random variable, the probability of success, p, is the same on each trial. The probability of not succeeding on the first trial and then succeeding on the second trial is $(1 - p)(p)$. Thus, $(1 - p)p = 0.25$. Solving algebraically, $p = \frac{1}{2}$.

3. The answer is (b).

$$\mu_{\bar{x}} = \mu,\ \sigma_{\bar{x}} = \frac{\sigma}{\sqrt{n}}.$$

For small samples, the shape of the sampling distribution of $\bar{x}$ will resemble the shape of the sampling distribution of the original population. The shape of the sampling distribution of $\bar{x}$ is approximately normal for n sufficiently large.

4. The correct answer is (d). Because the problem stated "at least 10," we must include the term where $x = 10$. If the problem had said "more than 10," the correct answer would have been (b) or (c) (they are equivalent). The answer could also have been given as

$$\binom{50}{10}(0.083)^{10}(0.917)^{40} + \binom{50}{11}(0.083)^{11}(0.917)^{39} + \ldots + \binom{50}{50}(0.083)^{50}(0.917)^{0}.$$

5. The correct answer is (d). $\mu_{\hat{p}} = p = 0.55$, $\sigma_{\hat{p}} = \sqrt{\dfrac{(0.55)(0.45)}{100}} = 0.0497$.

6. The correct answer is (a).

7. The correct answer is (b). This is a characteristic of a binomial experiment. The analogous characteristic for a geometric experiment is that there is a random variable X that is the number of trials needed to achieve the first success.

8. The correct answer is (c). This is actually a binomial situation. If X is the count of students "in favor," then X has $B(200, 0.70)$. Thus, $P(X \geq 150) = P(X = 150) + P(X = 151) + \ldots + P(X = 200)$. Using the TI-83/84, the exact binomial answer equals `1-binomcdf(200,0.7.0,149)=0.0695`. None of the listed choices shows a sum of several binomial expressions, so we assume this is to be done as a normal approximation.

   We note that $B(200, 0.7)$ can be approximated by $N(200(0.7), \sqrt{200(0.7)(0.3)}) = N(140, 6.4807)$. A normal approximation is OK since $200(0.7)$ and $200(0.3)$ are both much greater than 10. Since 75% of 200 is 150, we have $P(X \geq 150) =$
   $$P\left(z \geq \frac{150 - 140}{6.487} = 1.543\right) = 0.614.$$

Free-Response

1. If X is the count of cans with at least one defective ball, then X has $B(48, 0.025)$.
   $$P(X \geq 2) = 1 - P(X = 0) - P(X = 1) =$$
   $$1 - \binom{48}{0}(0.025)^0(0.975)^{48} - \binom{48}{1}(0.025)^1(0.975)^{47} = 0.338.$$

   On the TI-83/84, the solution is given by `1-binomcdf(48,0.025,1)`.

2. We know that the sampling distribution of $\bar{x}$ will be similar to the shape of the original population for a small n and approximately normal for a large n (that's the central limit theorem). Hence,

   (a) if $n = 3$, the sampling distribution would probably be somewhat skewed to the left.
   (b) if $n = 30$, the sampling distribution should be approximately normal.

   Remember that using $n \geq 30$ as a rule of thumb for deciding whether to assume normality is for a sampling distribution just that: a rule of thumb. This is probably a bit conservative. Unless the original population differs markedly from mound-shaped and symmetric, we would expect to see the sampling distribution of $\bar{x}$ be approximately normal for considerably smaller values of n.

3. The average wait for the first success to occur in a geometric setting is $1/p$, where p is the probability of success on any one trial. In this case, the probability of a girl for any one birth is $p = 0.5$. Hence, the average wait for the first girl is $\dfrac{1}{0.5} = 2$. So, we have one boy and one girl, on average, for each two children. The proportion of girls in the population would not change.

4. If X is the count of scholarship athletes that graduate from any sample of 55 players, then X has $B(55, 0.20)$. $\mu_X = 55(0.20) = 11$ and $\sigma_X = \sqrt{55(0.20)(0.80)} = 2.97$.

5. There are two different ways to do this problem: exact binomial or using proportions.

   (i) **Exact binomial.** Let X be the count of persons in the sample that have blood type B. Then X has $B(500, 0.10)$. Also, 11% of 500 is 55 and 15% of 500 is 75. Hence, $P(55 \leq X \leq 75) = P(X \leq 75) - P(X \leq 54) = \texttt{binomcdf(500,0.10,75)} - \texttt{binomcdf(500,0.10,54)} = 0.2475$.

   (ii) **Proportions.** We note that $\mu_X = np = 500(0.1) = 50$ and $n(1-p) = 500(0.9) = 90$, so we are OK to use a normal approximation. Also, $\mu_{\hat{p}} = p = 0.10$ and

   $$\sigma_{\hat{p}} = \sqrt{\frac{(0.1)(0.9)}{500}} = 0.0134. \; P(0.11 \leq \hat{p} \leq 0.15) = P\left(\frac{0.11 - 0.10}{0.0134} \leq z \leq \frac{0.15 - 0.10}{0.0134}\right) =$$

   $P(0.7463 \leq z \leq 3.731) = 0.2276$. On the TI 83/84: $\texttt{normalcdf(0.7463,3.731)}$.

6. All four of these statement are true. However, only III is a statement of the central limit theorem. The others are true of sampling distributions in general.

7. If X is the count of cars with defective pads, then X has $B(20, 0.15)$.

   (a) $P(X = 3)\binom{20}{3}(0.15)^3(0.85)^{17} = 0.243$. On the TI-83/84, the solution is given by $\texttt{binompdf(20,0.15,3)}$.

   (b) $\mu_X = np = 20(0.15) = 3$, $\sigma_X = \sqrt{np(1-p)} = \sqrt{20(0.15)(1-0.15)} = 1.597$.

8. $\mu_{\bar{x}} = 40{,}000$ miles and $\sigma_{\bar{x}} = \dfrac{5000}{\sqrt{160}} = 395.28$ miles.

   (a) With $n = 160$, the sampling distribution of $\bar{x}$ will be approximately normally distributed with mean equal to 40,000 miles and standard deviation 395.28 miles.

   (b) $P(\bar{x} < 39{,}000) = P\left(z < \dfrac{39{,}000 - 40{,}000}{395.28} = -2.53\right) = 0.006$.

   If the manufacturer is correct, there is only about a 0.6% chance of getting an average this low or lower. That makes it unlikely to be just a chance occurrence, and we should have some doubts about the manufacturer's claim.

9. $\mu_x = 2 \text{ lbs} = 32 \text{ oz}$ and $\sigma_x = \dfrac{5}{\sqrt{35}} = 0.845 \text{ oz}$.

   (a) With samples of size 35, the central limit theorem tells us that the sampling distribution of $\bar{x}$ is approximately normal. The mean is 32 oz and standard deviation is 0.845 oz.

   (b) In order for $\bar{x}$ to be in the top 10% of samples, it would have to be at the 90th percentile, which tells us that its z-score is 1.28 [that's $\texttt{InvNorm(0.9)}$ on your calculator]. Hence,

   $$z_{\bar{x}} = 1.28 = \frac{\bar{x} - 32}{0.845}.$$

   Solving, we have $\bar{x} = 33.08$ oz. The mean weight of a sample of 35 crabs has to be at least 33.08 oz, or about 2 lb 1 oz, to be in the top 10% of samples of this size.

10. If X is the number that recover, then X has $B(8, 0.7)$.

    (a) $P(X = 5) = \binom{8}{5}(0.7)^5(0.3)^3 = 0.254$. On the TI-83/84, the solution is given by $\texttt{binompdf(8,0.7,5)}$.

(b) $P(X=8) = \binom{8}{8}(0.7)^8(0.3)^0 = 0.058$. On the TI-83/84, the solution is given by

binompdf(8,0.7,8).

(c) $P(X \geq 1) = 1 - P(X=0) = 1 - \binom{8}{0}(0.7)^0(0.3)^8 = 0.999$. On the TI-83/84, the

solution is given by 1-binompdf(8,0.7,0).

11. $\mu_{\bar{x}} = 1185$ hours, and $\sigma_{\bar{x}} = \dfrac{80}{\sqrt{100}} = 8$ hours.

$$P(\bar{x} \geq 1200) = P\left(z \geq \frac{1200-1185}{8} = 1.875\right) = 0.03.$$

12. The first thing Gretchen needs to understand is that a distribution is just the set of all possible values of some variable. For example, the distribution of SAT scores for the current senior class is just the values of all the SAT scores. We can draw samples from that population if, say, we want to estimate the average SAT score for the senior class but don't have the time or money to get all the data. Suppose we draw samples of size n and compute $\bar{x}$ for each sample. Imagine drawing ALL possible samples of size n from the original distribution (that was the set of SAT scores for everybody in the senior class). Now consider the distribution (all the values) of means for those samples. That is what we call the sampling distribution of $\bar{x}$ (the short version: the sampling distribution of $\bar{x}$ is the set of all possible values of $\bar{x}$ computed from samples of size n).

13. The distribution is skewed to the right.
    (a) If $n = 3$, the sampling distribution of $\bar{x}$ will have some right-skewness but will be more mound-shaped than the parent population.
    (b) If $n = 40$, the central limit theorem tells us that the sampling distribution of $\bar{x}$ will be approximately normal.

14. If X is the count of O-rings that failed, then X has $B(12, 0.003)$.

    P (at least one fails) $= P(X=1) + P(X=2) + \cdots + P(X=12)$

    $$= 1 - P(X=0) = 1 - \binom{12}{0}(0.003)^0(0.997)^{12} = 0.035.$$

    On the TI-83/84, the solution is given by 1-binompdf(12,0.003,0).
    The clear message here is that even though the probability of any one failure seems remote (0.003), the probability of at least one failure (3.5%) is large enough to be worrisome.

15. Because you already have 2 of the 5 prizes, the probability that the next box contains a prize you don't have is $3/5 = 0.6$. If n is the number of trials until the first success, then $P(X=n) = (0.6) \cdot (0.4)^{n-1}$.

    (a) $P(X=1) = (0.6)(0.4)^{1-1} = (0.6)(1) = 0.6$. On the TI-83/84 calculator, the answer can be found by geometpdf(0.6,1).
    (b) $P(X=3) = (0.6)(0.4)^{3-2} = 0.096$. On the calculator: geometpdf(0.6,3).
    (c) The average number of boxes you will have to buy before getting the third prize is $\dfrac{1}{0.6} = 1.67$.

16. If $p = 0.70$, then $\mu_{\hat{p}} = 0.70$ and $\sigma_{\hat{p}} = \sqrt{\dfrac{0.70(1-0.70)}{600}} = 0.019$. Thus, $P(\hat{P} \le 0.65) =$

$P\left(z \le \dfrac{0.65-0.70}{0.019} = -2.63\right) = 0.004$. Since there is a very small probability of getting

a sample proportion as small as 0.65 if the true proportion is really 0.70, it appears that the San Francisco Bay Area may not be representative of the United States as a whole (that is, it is unlikely that we would have obtained a value as small as 0.65 if the true value were 0.70).

Solutions to Cumulative Review Problems

1. The sample space for this event is {HHH, **HHT**, **HTH**, **THH**, HTT, HTH, THH, TTT}. One way to do this problem, using techniques developed in Chapter 8, is to compute the probability of each event. Let $X =$ the count of heads. Then, for example (boldfaced in the list), $P(X = 2) = (0.6)(0.6)(0.4) + (0.6)(0.4)(0.6) + (0.4)(0.6)(0.6) = 3(0.6)^2(0.4) = 0.432$. Another way is to take advantage of the techniques developed in this chapter (noting that the possible values of X are 0, 1, 2, and 3):

$P(X = 0) = (0.4)^3 = 0.064$; $P(X = 1) = \binom{3}{1}(0.6)^1(0.4)^2 = \texttt{binompdf(3,0.6,1)} = 0.288$; $P(X = 2) = \binom{3}{2}(0.6)^2(0.4)^1 = \texttt{binompdf(3,0.6,2)} = 0.432$; and $P(X = 3) = $

$\binom{3}{3}(0.6)^3(0.4)^0 = \texttt{binompdf(3,0.6,3)} = 0.216$. Either way, the probability distribution is then

X	0	1	2	3
P(X)	0.064	0.288	0.432	0.216

Be sure to check that the sum of the probabilities is 1 (it is!).

2. (a) Yes, it is a random sample because each student in any of the 5 classes is equally likely to be included in the sample.
   (b) No, it is not a simple random sample (SRS) because not all samples of size 25 are equally likely. For example, in an SRS, one possible sample is having all 25 come from the same class. Because we only take 5 from each class, this isn't possible.

3. The slope of the regression line is 0.8. For each additional milligram of the drug, reaction time is *predicted* to increase by 0.8 seconds. Or you could say for each additional milligram of the drug, reaction time will increase by 0.8 seconds, *on average*.

4. $P(A \text{ or } B) = P(A \cup B) = P(A) + P(B) - P(A \cap B) = 0.5 + 0.3 - P(A \cap B) = 0.65 \Rightarrow P(A \cap B) = 0.15$. Now, A and B are independent if $P(A \cap B) = P(A) \cdot P(B)$. So, $P(A) \cdot P(B) = (0.3)(0.5) = 0.15 = P(A \cap B)$. Hence, A and B are independent.

5. (a) Quantitative
   (b) Categorical
   (c) Categorical
   (d) Quantitative
   (e) Categorical
   (f) Quantitative
   (g) Categorical

CHAPTER 10

Inference: Estimating with Confidence Intervals

IN THIS CHAPTER

Summary: In this chapter, we begin our formal study of inference by estimating a population parameter. We will learn about confidence intervals, a way of identifying a range of values that we think might contain our parameter of interest. We will develop intervals to estimate a single population proportion and the difference between two population proportions. Then we will introduce the *t* statistic (as an adjustment to *z*) and talk about estimates for means and the difference between two population means.

Key Ideas

✪ Estimation
✪ Confidence Intervals and Margin of Error
✪ Confidence Intervals for a Proportion
✪ Confidence Intervals for a Difference in Proportions
✪ *t* Procedures
✪ Confidence Intervals for a Mean
✪ Confidence Intervals for a Difference in Means
✪ Choosing a Sample Size for a Confidence Interval

Estimation and Confidence Intervals

We have previously described a *statistic* as a value that describes a sample and a *parameter* as a value that describes a population. Now we want use a *statistic* as an **estimate** of a *parameter*. In Chapter 9, we explored sampling distributions to see how a statistic behaves when we repeatedly select random samples from a known population. This helps us understand the tools we use when, in reality, we select *one* sample and we use it to make inferences about the population. What we will do now is develop a process by which we will use our sample to generate a range of plausible population values for the parameter. The statistic itself is called a **point estimate**, and the range of plausible population values from which we might have obtained our estimate is called a **confidence interval**.

> **example:** We survey a random sample of 50 students from a large high school and find that 42% of the students in the sample say they plan to vote for Charlotte for student body treasurer. That is, $\hat{p} = 0.42$ is our *point estimate* for the proportion of *all* students at this school who would say they plan to vote for Charlotte for student body treasurer. But this estimate is almost certainly incorrect. It is extremely unlikely that *exactly* 42% of all students would say this.
>
> So, what is the point of taking a survey if we are almost certain to get an incorrect estimate? To answer that question, we need to go back to what we learned about the sampling distribution of $\hat{p}$. For example, we learned that, with a large enough sample size, about 95% of sample proportions would be within 1.96 standard deviations of the population proportion p. Knowing this allows us to *quantify* our uncertainty in that estimate. In particular, would we be surprised to learn that p is actually, say, 0.39?
>
> If p were 0.39, we would expect about 95% of samples to have a sample proportion $\hat{p}$ within 1.96 standard deviations of 0.39 as represented by the shaded area below. Our sample proportion 0.42 (shown by the vertical line) is clearly in this region, so we would not be surprised to learn that p is 0.39. (Note that here we are defining *surprise* based on whether 0.42 is in the middle 95% of sample proportions.)

> What other values of p would contain $\hat{p} = 0.42$ in the middle 95%? As shown below, if p is anywhere between about 0.30 and about 0.55, then 0.42 is contained in the middle 95% of values.

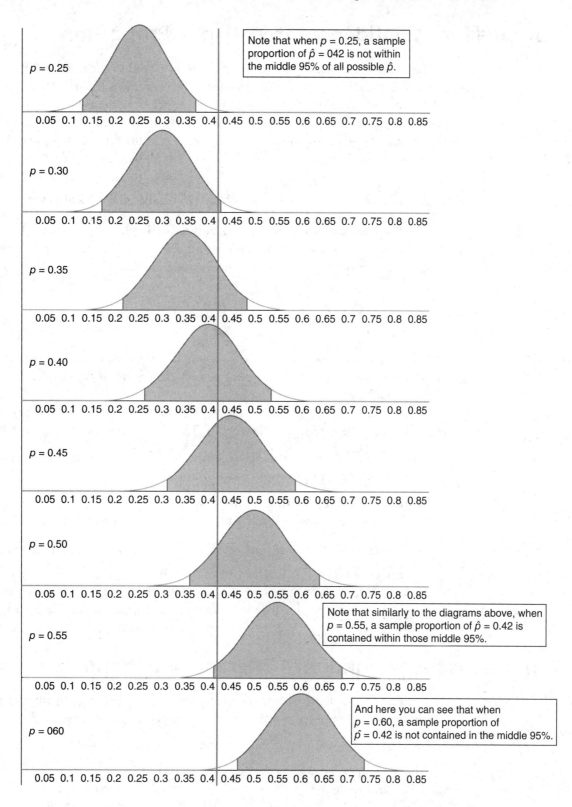

p = 0.25

Note that when p = 0.25, a sample proportion of $\hat{p}$ = 042 is not within the middle 95% of all possible $\hat{p}$.

0.05 0.1 0.15 0.2 0.25 0.3 0.35 0.4 | 0.45 0.5 0.55 0.6 0.65 0.7 0.75 0.8 0.85

p = 0.30

0.05 0.1 0.15 0.2 0.25 0.3 0.35 0.4 | 0.45 0.5 0.55 0.6 0.65 0.7 0.75 0.8 0.85

p = 0.35

0.05 0.1 0.15 0.2 0.25 0.3 0.35 0.4 | 0.45 0.5 0.55 0.6 0.65 0.7 0.75 0.8 0.85

p = 0.40

0.05 0.1 0.15 0.2 0.25 0.3 0.35 0.4 | 0.45 0.5 0.55 0.6 0.65 0.7 0.75 0.8 0.85

p = 0.45

0.05 0.1 0.15 0.2 0.25 0.3 0.35 0.4 | 0.45 0.5 0.55 0.6 0.65 0.7 0.75 0.8 0.85

p = 0.50

0.05 0.1 0.15 0.2 0.25 0.3 0.35 0.4 | 0.45 0.5 0.55 0.6 0.65 0.7 0.75 0.8 0.85

p = 0.55

Note that similarly to the diagrams above, when p = 0.55, a sample proportion of $\hat{p}$ = 0.42 is contained within those middle 95%.

0.05 0.1 0.15 0.2 0.25 0.3 0.35 0.4 | 0.45 0.5 0.55 0.6 0.65 0.7 0.75 0.8 0.85

p = 060

And here you can see that when p = 0.60, a sample proportion of $\hat{p}$ = 0.42 is not contained in the middle 95%.

0.05 0.1 0.15 0.2 0.25 0.3 0.35 0.4 | 0.45 0.5 0.55 0.6 0.65 0.7 0.75 0.8 0.85

That range of *plausible values* of p is called the **95% confidence interval** for p. So we cannot be very certain at all that p is 0.42, but we can be 95% confident that p is between about 0.30 and 0.55. Here, 95% is referred to as the **confidence level**.

Formula for a Confidence Interval for a Proportion

In the earlier diagrams, any value of p that contains 0.42 in the middle 95% of sample proportions is considered a plausible value for p. To be in the middle 95%, $\hat{p} = 0.42$ is within 1.96 standard deviations of that plausible value. That, of course, means that the plausible value is within 1.96 standard deviations of $\hat{p}$. (Those standard deviations are slightly different because they depend on the value we use for p in the formula but not different enough to worry about, so we'll use $\hat{p}$.) We will say that the plausible values of p are in the confidence interval $\hat{p} \pm 1.96\sqrt{\dfrac{\hat{p}(1-\hat{p})}{n}}$. (The 1.96 is called the **critical value**. It is the positive z-score that coincides with the desired confidence level, and is denoted by z^*.)

This allows us to create a more precise interval estimate for p, the proportion of all students at this school who plan to vote for Charlotte for student body treasurer. The interval is

$$\hat{p} \pm z^* \cdot \sqrt{\frac{\hat{p}(1-\hat{p})}{n}} = 0.42 \pm 1.96\sqrt{\frac{0.42(1-0.42)}{50}} = 0.42 \pm 0.137 = (0.28, 0.55).$$

We interpret that interval as follows: *We are 95% confident that the proportion of all students at this school who plan to vote for Charlotte for student body treasurer is between 0.28 and 0.55.*

(*Note:* The part of the formula following the $\pm$ is called the *margin of error*. In this example, we have a margin of error of 0.137, or 13.7 percentage points.)

example: Find the critical value of z required to construct a 98% confidence interval for a population proportion.

solution: We are reading from Table A, the table of Standard Normal Probabilities. Remember that table entries are areas to the left of a given z-score. With $C = 0.98$, we want $\dfrac{1 - 0.98}{2} = 0.01$ in each tail, or 0.99 to the left if z^*. Finding $p = 0.9900$ in the table (the closest we can get is 0.9901), we have $z^* = 2.33$. But note that the bottom two lines of Table B provide the z^* needed for most common confidence levels. With technology, you would use an Inverse Normal function with 0.99 (or 0.01) as the area.

Conditions for a Confidence Interval for a Proportion

Notice that in the figure on the previous page, all the sampling distributions were represented by normal models. Normal models are appropriate here because

$$np = 50 \cdot 0.25 = 12.5 \geq 10 \text{ and } n(1 - p) = 50 \cdot 0.75 = 37.5 \geq 10,$$

and that is the most extreme of the proportions used. It is that normal model that allows us to use 1.96 standard deviations to mark the middle 95% of sample proportions for each possible value of p. Whenever we use a normal model as a basis for our procedure, we have to ensure that it is appropriate to do so. In addition, our model assumes simple random sampling from an infinitely large population (equivalent to sampling with replacement).

We know the sampling distribution is not exactly normal. Ever. We also know that we are not sampling from an infinitely large population and are rarely sampling with replacement. Unfortunately, this means the model we are using is wrong. But, as well-known statistician George Box said, "All models are wrong. But some of them are useful." To see if the model is useful, we check some conditions to see if those assumptions are "close enough" to being met.

ASSUMPTION	CONDITION
We have a simple random sample. This ensures that our model is centered in the correct place, because simple random samples are unbiased.	**Check that we have a simple random sample or its equivalent.** This requires us to look at how the data were collected.
We have a normally distributed sampling distribution. This assures the correct shape of our model.	$n\hat{p}$ **and** $n(1-\hat{p})$ **are both at least 10.** This guideline, along with random sampling, ensures that our sampling distribution is close enough to normal for the normal model to be useful.
We are sampling with replacement or from an infinitely large population. This ensures we have the correct standard deviation of our sampling distribution.	**We are essentially sampling without replacement or our sample size is less than 10% of the population size.** This, in conjunction with random sampling, allows us to use $\sqrt{\dfrac{\hat{P}(1-\hat{P})}{n}}$ as the standard error of the sampling distribution, ignoring the Finite Population Correction Factor described in the previous chapter.

Construct and Interpret a Confidence Interval for a Proportion

Let's revisit the example about Charlotte to see a model response to the following question:

example: We survey a random sample of 50 students from a large high school and find that 42% of the students in the sample say they plan to vote for Charlotte for student body treasurer. Construct and interpret a 95% confidence interval for the proportion of all students at this school who plan to vote for Charlotte for student body treasurer.

solution:

Identify the procedure and check conditions:

We will construct a 1-sample, 95% z confidence interval for a proportion. (*Note:* This identifies the procedure by name.)

- We are told they selected a random sample of 50 students from the school.
- $n\hat{p} = 50 \cdot 0.42 = 21 \geq 10$ and $n(1 - \hat{p}) = 50 \cdot 0.58 = 29 \geq 10$
- We don't know the population of the high school, but we are told it is a large high school. So the population is almost certainly greater than $10n = 10 \cdot 50 = 500$.

Conditions are met for our model to be useful.

Computations:

The 95% confidence interval is

$$\hat{p} \pm z^* \cdot \sqrt{\frac{\hat{p}(1-\hat{p})}{n}} = 0.42 \pm 1.96 \sqrt{\frac{0.42(1-0.42)}{50}} = (0.28, 0.55).$$

(*Note:* The expression above identifies the procedure by formula.)

z^* above is called the **critical value** for z. It is the z-score corresponding to the middle 95% in this case, or whatever confidence level you use.

Interpretation:

We are 95% confident that the proportion of all students at this school who plan to vote for Charlotte for student body treasurer is between 0.28 and 0.55.

Notice that the prompt did not specify to check conditions. But you *must* check conditions as part of the entire process. Learn to do that automatically for every inference procedure.

Confidence Level as a Capture Rate

We saw that we referred to a 95% confidence interval as the set of population proportions that would contain $\hat{p}$ in their middle 95% of sample proportions. There is another important way to think about what that 95% confidence level refers to.

Assume in the situation above that 37% of the student body plans to vote for Charlotte. Notice that the interval earlier, when $\hat{p}$ was 0.42, contains 0.37. We could say that this interval captured the population proportion. But a different sample would result in a different $\hat{p}$ and a different interval. The figure below shows 100 possible samples from this population in which 37% of students plan to vote for Charlotte. The dot in the center shows $\hat{p}$ and the vertical bars show the interval based on that sample proportion. The **dark squares represent** values of $\hat{p}$ whose intervals captured 0.37. The circles represent values whose intervals did not capture 0.37. We can see that six of the intervals did not capture 0.37, so 94 did. In the long run (producing many, many intervals), we expect that 95% of these intervals will capture 0.37.

This gives us a way to interpret a 95% confidence **level**: "If we were to select many samples of 50 students, and construct a confidence interval for each sample, we expect about 95% of the intervals to contain the proportion of all students who plan to vote for Charlotte."

Important: When we say, "We are 95% confident that the true population value lies in an interval," we mean that the *process* used to generate the interval will capture the true population value 95% of the time. We must be careful not to make a probability statement about the interval that has been constructed. Our "confidence" is in the process that generated the interval. When we are discussing the interval itself, there is no longer a repeatable random event. That's why we use the word *confidence* instead of *probability*.

A Confidence Interval for a Mean (*t* Procedures)

General Form of a Confidence Interval

A confidence interval is composed of two parts: a point estimate of a population value and a margin of error. We specify a level of confidence to communicate how certain we are that the interval contains the true population parameter.

A **level** *C* **confidence interval** has the following form: (estimate) ± (margin of error). In turn, the *margin of error* for a confidence interval is composed of two parts: the critical value of z (or t as we shall see) and the standard error. Hence, all confidence intervals take the form

(estimate) ± (margin of error) = (estimate) ± (critical value)(standard error)

This form of the confidence interval is included on the formula sheet.

When we discussed the sampling distribution of $\bar{x}$ in Chapter 9, we knew the population mean and standard deviation. We know the shape of the sampling distribution of $\bar{x}$ is approximately normal if the population is approximately normal, or if n is large enough. The mean of the sampling distribution is μ and the standard error is $\frac{\sigma}{\sqrt{n}}$. In this chapter, we are estimating the population mean from a sample.

For example, pennies (one-cent coins) produced in the United States now have an average mass of 2.5 grams and a standard deviation of 0.05 grams. The masses are approximately normally distributed. Say we randomly select 5 pennies from this population and the masses are 2.47 g, 2.48 g, 2.51 g, 2.59 g, and 2.45 g. We could construct a confidence interval for a mean using a process similar to that for proportions. The mean and standard deviation of this sample are 2.499 g and 0.056 g, respectively. The 90% confidence interval is

$$\bar{x} \pm z^* \frac{\sigma}{\sqrt{n}} = 2.499 \pm 1.645 \frac{0.05}{\sqrt{5}} = (2.462, 2.536).$$

Notice that this interval does indeed capture the population mean of 2.5. In fact, if we select 100 random samples and construct an interval for each, we get this:

Here, 90 of our intervals captured $\mu = 2.5$. In the long run, we'd expect about 90% of our intervals to capture μ.

It is rare to have a situation in which we would know the value of the population standard deviation, σ. If we knew enough about the population to know σ, we'd probably also know μ. In fact, we *need* μ to calculate σ. But, in reality, we generally have to use the sample standard deviation s to estimate σ. That turns our formula for the confidence interval into $\bar{x} \pm z^* \frac{s}{\sqrt{n}}$. But let's see what happens to our capture rate when we do this:

Now only 85 of our intervals captured $\mu = 2.5$. This is because the sample standard deviation s tends to *underestimate* σ, and it means our process doesn't capture the mean as often as we say it will. The way to fix this (as discovered by William Sealy Gosset over 100 years ago!) is to adjust the critical value. The new critical value is called t, and it will always be larger than z. This makes the intervals longer and gets us to the capture rate we specified. In this example, if we wanted a 90% capture rate, we would need a critical value of 2.132.

Using that critical value of 2.132, we have captured the population mean of 2.5 grams for 89 of the intervals. The long-run capture rate is back to the 90% we claimed.

To find the appropriate value of t, we need to know two things: the confidence level and the sample size n, because the larger the sample size, the smaller the adjustment we need to make. (To get that value of t, we need a number called the *degrees of freedom*, which for now is $n - 1$. More on degrees of freedom later!)

A confidence interval for a population mean would take on the form

$$\bar{x} \pm t^* \frac{s}{\sqrt{n}},$$

where t^* depends on the confidence level C and the degrees of freedom, s is the sample standard deviation, and n is the sample size.

Conditions for a Confidence Interval for a Mean

The conditions for a confidence interval for a mean are similar to those for a proportion. The difference is in the condition for normality. The population should be approximately normally distributed or we need a large enough sample size that the Central Limit Theorem can be counted on to give us an approximately normal sampling distribution of the $\bar{x}$. We still need a simple random sample and a sample that is less than 10% of the population size.

The confidence level is often expressed as a percent: a 95% confidence interval means that $C = 0.95$, or a 99% confidence interval means that $C = 0.99$. Although any value of C can be used as a confidence level, typical levels are 0.90, 0.95, and 0.99.

> **example:** Find the critical value of t required to construct a 99% confidence interval for a population mean based on a sample size of 15.

> **solution:** First, we need to know that $df = 15 - 1 = 14$. Using the t distribution table (Table B in the Appendices), we can look at the bottom of the table, locating the column for 99% confidence, and move up the table to the row for 14 df. We find $t^* = 2.977$.

Using technology, you would use an Inverse T command and input the area below the critical value you want. A confidence of 99% refers to the *middle* 99%, which goes from the 0.5 percentile to the 99.5 percentile. So the area would be either 0.005 (for the negative value) or 0.995 (for the positive value). The arguments you would enter would be *area* = 0.005 (or 0.995) and *df* = 14.

example: Why is it incorrect, when interpreting the confidence interval above for the mean weight of a penny, to say the following? "There is a 90% probability that the actual mean weight of a penny is between 2.462 g and 2.536 g."

solution: Because probability is about predicting the long-run relative frequency of a repeatable random event. There is no repeatable random event here. The interval is determined, and the actual mean weight is fixed. This particular interval captures the parameter. (Although we wouldn't know that in reality. If we knew the actual mean, why would we try to estimate it from a sample?) This is why we use the phrase "90% confident." It allows us to talk about our level of certainty without referring to it as a probability.

example: A large airline is interested in determining the average number of unoccupied seats for all of its flights. It selects an SRS of 81 flights and determines that the average number of unoccupied seats for the sample is 12.5 seats with a sample standard deviation of 3.9 seats. Construct and interpret a 95% confidence interval for the true number of unoccupied seats for all flights.

solution:

Conditions:

The problem states that we have a simple random sample of 81 flights. The large sample size (81) justifies the construction of a one-sample confidence interval for the population mean. There are definitely more than $10 \times 81 = 810$ flights for a large airline. Conditions are met for a confidence interval for a mean.

Calculations:

The 95% confidence interval is $\bar{x} \pm t^* \dfrac{s}{\sqrt{n}} = 12.5 \pm 1.99 \dfrac{3.9}{\sqrt{81}} = (11.64, 13.36)$, using t^* for $81 - 1 = 80$ *df.*

Interpretation:

We are 95% confident that the mean number of unoccupied seats for all the airline's flights is between 11.6 and 13.4 seats.

Exam Tip: The rubrics for confidence interval questions generally have three parts. The first is *Check conditions and identify the procedure.* The conditions always include the randomization condition and the normality (large sample size) condition. In addition, since we are sampling without replacement, we must check that the sample size is less than 10% of the population size. Identifying the procedure can be done by name (for example *confidence interval for a mean*) or by formula (for example $\bar{x} \pm t^* \dfrac{s}{\sqrt{n}}$). It is a good idea to get in the habit of doing both so if you forget one, you've still done the other!

Estimating a Difference Between Groups

When we select a random sample and calculate a proportion of successes (or a mean of some measure), $\hat{p}$ (or $\bar{x}$) is a random variable. So if we independently select samples from two populations, the sample statistics are independent random variables and, as we saw in Chapter 8,

- $\mu_{X \pm Y} = \mu_X \pm \mu_Y.$

In other words, the mean of the sum (or difference) of two random variables is the sum (or difference) of the means of the individual variables:

- $\sigma^2_{X \pm Y} = \sigma^2_X + \sigma^2_Y$, if and only if X and Y are independent.
- $\sigma_{X \pm Y} = \sqrt{\sigma^2_X + \sigma^2_Y}$, if and only if X and Y are independent.

In other words, when adding or subtracting independent random variables, variances add.

This tells us what we need to create a confidence interval for the difference of two means or two proportions. The statistic will be the difference in proportions (or means). The standard error for the difference in proportions will be

$$\sqrt{\sigma^2_{\hat{p}_1} + \sigma^2_{\hat{p}_2}} = \sqrt{\frac{\hat{p}_1(1-\hat{p}_1)}{n_1} + \frac{\hat{p}_2(1-\hat{p}_2)}{n_2}},$$

so a confidence interval for a difference in proportions has the form

$$(\hat{p}_1 - \hat{p}_2) \pm z^* = \sqrt{\frac{\hat{p}_1(1-\hat{p}_1)}{n_1} + \frac{\hat{p}_2(1-\hat{p}_2)}{n_2}}.$$

Similarly, the confidence interval for a difference in means is

$$(\bar{x}_1 - \bar{x}_2) \pm t^* = \sqrt{\frac{s_1^2}{n_1} + \frac{s_2^2}{n_2}}.$$

There's an added complication with the difference in means, however. The adjustment needed isn't exactly t, but we can get very close if we use degrees of freedom determined by this really messy formula:

$$df = \frac{\left(\dfrac{s_1^2}{n_1} + \dfrac{s_2^2}{n_2}\right)^2}{\dfrac{1}{n_1 - 1}\left(\dfrac{s_1^2}{n_1}\right)^2 + \dfrac{1}{n_2 - 1}\left(\dfrac{s_2^2}{n_2}\right)^2}.$$

Don't worry! You will NOT need to know or use this formula. But your calculator will use this formula, and it will often result in degrees of freedom that are not a whole number. It will be enough for you to report the *df* that your calculator gives and not be alarmed when you see non-whole-number values.

The conditions for an interval are similar to those before:

- We need *two* simple random samples independently selected from two populations.
- For *proportions*, $n_1 \hat{p}_1, n_1(1-\hat{p}_1), n_2 \hat{p}_2, n_2(1-\hat{p}_2)$ must all be at least 10 (or 5, according to some textbooks).

- For *means*, the populations must be approximately normal or the sample sizes must both be large enough to compensate. (If the sample size is more than 30, most textbooks consider that large enough to proceed.)
- Both samples should be less than 10% of the population size.

example: To see whether a particular candidate's popularity changes as the election approaches, a poll was taken six months before the election in which 850 randomly selected American adults were asked whether they have a positive opinion of the candidate, and another poll was taken two weeks before the election with a random sample of 750 American adults. In the first poll, 503 of those surveyed said they had a positive opinion of the candidate, and in the second poll 416 said so. Construct and interpret a 95% confidence interval for the change in the candidate's popularity over those several months.

solution:

Check conditions:

We have two samples randomly and independently selected from two populations. (The population six months before the election can be considered a different population because the opinion may have changed.)

$n_1 \hat{p}_1 = 503, n_1(1 - \hat{p}_1) = 347, n_2 \hat{p}_2 = 416, n_2(1 - \hat{p}_2) = 334$ are all at least 10.

(Subscript 1 refers to the first poll and 2 refers to the second poll.)

Both samples are less than 10% of the population of American adults. Conditions are met for a confidence interval for a difference in proportions.

Calculations:

The 95% confidence interval is

$$(\hat{p}_2 - \hat{p}_1) \pm z^* \sqrt{\frac{\hat{p}_2(1 - \hat{p}_2)}{n_2} + \frac{\hat{p}_1(1 - \hat{p}_1)}{n_1}} = \left(\frac{416}{750} - \frac{503}{850}\right) \pm 1.96 \sqrt{\frac{\frac{416}{750} \cdot \frac{334}{750}}{750} + \frac{\frac{503}{850} \cdot \frac{347}{850}}{850}} = (-0.086, 0.011)$$

Interpretation:

We are 95% confident that the candidate's popularity in the second poll was between 8.6 percentage points lower and 1.1 percentage points higher than in the first poll. Because 0 is in the confidence interval, it is plausible there was no change in the candidate's popularity.

example: A random sample of 50 male students from a large high school was selected and their temperatures were taken. Another random sample of 50 female students was selected and their temperatures were also taken. The data are summarized in the table below.

GENDER	MEAN TEMPERATURE	STANDARD DEVIATION
Female	98.4	0.75
Male	98.1	0.68

Construct a 90% confidence interval for the difference in mean temperatures for all males and all females at this school.

solution:

Check conditions and identify procedure:

- We have random samples of 50 males and 50 females from their populations at the school.
- Because both sample sizes are $50 \geq 30$, we can assume the sampling distribution of $\overline{x}$ is approximately normal.
- Because this is a large high school, there are probably more than $50 \cdot 10 = 500$ males and 500 females at the school.

Conditions are met for a confidence interval for a difference in means.

Calculations:

$$(\overline{x}_F - \overline{x}_M) \pm t^* \sqrt{\frac{s_F^2}{n_F} + \frac{s_M^2}{n_M}} \quad \text{(This identifies the procedure again, by formula.)}$$

$$= (98.4 - 98.1) \pm t^* \sqrt{\frac{0.75^2}{50} + \frac{0.65^2}{50}} \quad \text{using } t^* \text{ for 97.07 } df \text{ (as reported by my}$$

calculator—you could calculate t^* but you do NOT need to)

$$= (0.062, 0.538)$$

Interpretation:

We are 90% confident that the mean temperature for females at this school is between 0.062°F and 0.538°F more than the mean temperature for males at this school.

> **Exam Tip:** There are three steps to a confidence interval: Check conditions and identify the procedure, compute the interval, and interpret the interval in context. The question may not specifically ask for all three steps, but they are always required unless specifically stated otherwise.

Inference for Experiments

The examples so far have involved confidence intervals for sampling situations. Another situation in which we compare two groups is randomized experiments. If we use a completely randomized design in which each treatment is randomly assigned to half the subjects, the conditions for two-sample procedures are not met. We do not have two samples randomly selected from two populations. We have one population (the subjects in the experiment) and the groups (you could call them samples, but we do not recommend that!) are dependently selected. Once you choose one group to get one treatment, the other group is set. Also, each group is 50% of the "population" so that 10% condition is violated as well.

Both errors affect the standard deviation of the model. The problem of the groups not being independent increases the standard deviation, and the problem of the groups being more than 10% of the total number of subjects decreases the standard deviation (remember that Finite Population Correction Factor?). These two effects almost exactly cancel each other out, and we can (thank goodness!) use the same formulas.

One thing that does change is the conditions. Now there are only these two:

- Treatments must be randomly assigned to subjects.
- The groups must be large enough to meet the normality conditions. So for proportions, $n_1\hat{p}_1, n_1(1 - \hat{p}_1)$, $n_2\hat{p}_2$, and $n_2(1 - \hat{p}_2)$ must all be at least 10 (or 5). For means, the data must be consistent with what we'd expect from an approximately normal population, or we must have large treatment groups.

• PARAMETER • ESTIMATOR	CONDITIONS	FORMULA
• Population mean: μ • Estimator: $\bar{x}$	• SRS • Normal population (or very large sample) • σ known (This is almost never the case. So you can pretty much remember "t for means.") *or* • SRS • σ unknown (This is almost always the case.) • Population approximately normal or large sample size ($n > 30$)	$\bar{x} \pm z^* \dfrac{\sigma}{\sqrt{n}}$ $\bar{x} \pm t^* \dfrac{s}{\sqrt{n}}, df = n - 1$
• Population proportion: p • Estimator: $\hat{p}$	• SRS • Large population size relative to sample size • $n\hat{p} \geq 5, n(1 - \hat{p}) \geq 5$ (or $n\hat{p} \geq 10, n(1 - \hat{p}) \geq 10$)	$\hat{p} \pm z^* \sqrt{\dfrac{\hat{p}(1 - \hat{p})}{n}}$
• Difference of population means: $\mu_1 - \mu_2$ • Estimator: $\bar{x}_1 - \bar{x}_2$	• Independent SRSs • Both populations normal • σ_1, σ_2 known (Again, this is almost never the case.) *or* • Independent SRSs • σ_1, σ_2 unknown. (This is almost always the case.) • Approximately normal populations or n_1 and n_2 both "large"	$(\bar{x}_1 - \bar{x}_2) \pm z^* \sqrt{\dfrac{\sigma_1^2}{n_1} + \dfrac{\sigma_2^2}{n_2}}$ $(\bar{x}_1 - \bar{x}_2) \pm t^* \sqrt{\dfrac{s_1^2}{n_1} + \dfrac{s_2^2}{n_2}}$ $df = $ (computed by software) $df = \min\{n_1 - 1, n_2 - 1\}$ (See explanation below.)
• Difference of population proportions: $p_1 - p_2$ • Estimator: $\hat{p}_1 - \hat{p}_2$	• SRSs from independent populations • Large population sizes relative to sample sizes • $n_1\hat{p}_1 \geq 5, n_1(1 - \hat{p}_1) \geq 5$ $n_2\hat{p}_2 \geq 5, n_2(1 - \hat{p}_2) \geq 5$	$(\hat{p}_1 - \hat{p}_2) \pm z^* \sqrt{\dfrac{\hat{p}_1(1 - \hat{p}_1)}{n_1} + \dfrac{\hat{p}_2(1 - \hat{p}_2)}{n_2}}$

These individual confidence interval formulas are NOT on your formula sheet. However, the individual standard errors and the general form of (estimate) $\pm$ (critical value)(standard error) DO appear on the formula sheet.

Sample Size

It is always desirable to select as large a sample as possible when doing research because sample means of larger samples are less variable than sample means of small samples. However, it is often expensive or difficult to draw larger samples so that we try to find the optimum sample size: large enough to accomplish our goals, small enough that we can afford it or manage it. While the question of optimal sample size comes up in many, many types of situations, the outline of concepts for this course only includes your being able to estimate the sample size necessary for a single population proportion.

Sample Size for Estimating a Population Proportion

The confidence interval for a population proportion is given by

$$\hat{p} \pm z^* \sqrt{\frac{\hat{p}(1-\hat{p})}{n}}.$$

The margin of error is

$$z^* \sqrt{\frac{\hat{p}(1-\hat{p})}{n}}.$$

Let M be the desired maximum margin of error. Then,

$$M \leq z^* \sqrt{\frac{\hat{p}(1-\hat{p})}{n}}.$$

Solving for n,

$$n \geq \left(\frac{z^*}{M}\right)^2 \hat{p}(1-\hat{p}).$$

But we do not have a value of $\hat{p}$ until we collect data, so we need a way to estimate $\hat{p}$. There are two ways to choose a value of p.

1. If we have a $\hat{p}$ from a previous study, we could use that in our estimate. That can be a little risky because if we get a new value of $\hat{p}$ that is closer to 0.5 than the previous one, our standard error will be larger than we planned for, and we may not get the margin of error we want. So a safer approach would be...
2. Use 0.5 in the margin of error calculation. The standard error for a proportion (with all else equal) is largest when $p = 0.5$ so if the margin of error is small enough for $\hat{p} = 0.5$, it will be small enough for any other value of $\hat{p}$. The risk here is that you may end up using a sample size that is larger than you need, which can be more expensive.

> **example:** Historically, about 60% of a company's products are purchased by people who have purchased products from the company previously. The company is preparing to introduce a new product and wants to generate a 95% confidence interval for the proportion of its current customers who will purchase the new product. They want to be accurate within 3%. How many customers do they need to sample?

solution: Based on historical data, choose $\hat{p} = 0.6$. Then

$$n \geq \left(\frac{1.96}{0.03}\right)^2 (0.6)(0.4) = 1024.4.$$

The company needs to sample 1025 customers. (We use 1025 since n must be an integer and greater than 1024.4.) Had it not had the historical data, it would have had to use $\hat{p} = 0.5$.

If $\hat{P} = 0.5$, $n \geq \left(\frac{1.96}{0.03}\right)^2 (0.5)(0.5) = 1067.1$. You need a sample of at least 1068 customers.

By using $\hat{p} = 0.6$, the company was able to sample 43 fewer customers, but they run the risk of too small a sample if $\hat{p}$ turns out to be closer to 0.5.

› Rapid Review

1. True–False. A 95% confidence interval for a population proportion is given as (0.37, 0.52). This means that the probability is 0.95 that this interval contains the true proportion.

   Answer: False. Because this interval has been created, there is no repeatable random event. That's why we say, "We are 95% confident." It avoids improper use of the word *probability*. (The probability is 0.95 that the *process* used to generate this interval *will* capture the true proportion.)

2. You have calculated a 90% confidence interval for the mean number of hours volunteers work each week for a large charity. For each adjustment described below, if all else stayed the same, tell whether the confidence interval would become wider, narrower, or neither one and explain why.

   (a) The sample size is quadrupled.

   (b) The confidence level is changed from 90% to 95%.

   (c) The sample standard deviation was corrected to a smaller value.

   (d) The sample mean was corrected to a larger value.

   Answer:

   (a) Narrower. In the margin of error part of the calculation, you divide s by $\sqrt{n}$. Quadrupling the sample size, you would instead divide by $\sqrt{4n} = 2\sqrt{n}$. And the value of t^* gets slightly smaller, too. So the margin of error, and therefore the interval, will be narrower.

   (b) Wider. The critical value for 95% confidence is wider than for 90%. Or, more intuitively, if you want to be more confident of capturing the parameter, use a bigger net!

   (c) Narrower. The standard deviation is in the numerator of the margin of error calculation. If it gets smaller, the margin of error is smaller. Intuitively, if there is less variability in the sample, you can be more precise in your estimate.

   (d) Neither one. Changing the mean will move the center of the interval, but the margin of error will remain unchanged.

3. What is the critical value of t for a 99% confidence interval based on a sample size of 26?

   Answer: Remember that 99% refers to the *middle* 99%, so 0.5% is below that and 0.05% is above that. So you can use a calculator's inverse t function with an area of 0.005 or 0.995 to get –2.787 or 2.787, respectively. From Table B, t Distribution Critical Values, t^* for 99% confidence and 25 *df* is 2.787.

4. What is the critical value of z for a 98% confidence interval for a proportion?

   Answer: Use the inverse normal command on a calculator with a tail area of 0.01 or 0.99 to get ±2.326. Or use Table A, Standard Normal Probabilities, and look for $p = 0.01$ or 0.99 in the body of the table. The nearest table entry to 0.99 is 0.9901, which corresponds to $z^* = 2.33$.

5. A random sample of American high school students was polled five years ago and asked whether they feel they could go one day without their smartphone. The same question was asked of a random sample of high school students this year. A 95% confidence interval was constructed for the difference in proportions of students who said they could not go a day without their smartphones (*This year – five years ago*) and the interval is (0.024, 0.145). Does this confidence interval provide evidence that, if all American high school students had been asked, the proportion of students this year would say they could not go without their smartphones for a day is different than would have said so five years ago?

   Answer: Yes. Because 0 is not contained in the interval.

6. What is the reason we use t rather than z when creating a confidence interval for a mean?

   Answer: We don't know σ and must estimate with s. The sample standard deviation underestimates σ more often than not, making many of our intervals too narrow if we use z. This reduces the capture rate. We use t as an adjustment to get the correct capture rate.

7. You want to create a 95% confidence interval for a population proportion with a margin of error of no more than 0.05. How large a sample do you need?

   Answer: Because there is no estimate for the population proportion, we will use $p = 0.5$ to ensure that even the largest margin of error is at most 0.05.

   $$0.05 \geq 1.96\sqrt{\frac{0.5\cdot0.5}{n}}$$

   Solve for n to get

   $$n \geq \left(\frac{1.96}{0.05}\right)^2 (0.5)(0.5) = 384.16.$$

   You would need a minimum sample size of 385 subjects. (Always round up to ensure your sample size is large enough.)

8. Why must we check that $n\hat{p}$ and $n(1-\hat{p})$ are at least 10? And why do we care that our sample size is less than 10% of the population size?

   Answer: $n\hat{p}$ and $n(1-\hat{p})$ must be at least 10 to ensure that a normal model will give us reasonable approximation to the sampling distribution of $\hat{p}$. Using z to estimate the middle 95% of a sampling distribution (and, hence, use it in the margin of error calculation for our interval) is based on a normal model being appropriate. The sample being less than 10% of the population allows us to use our standard error formulas for those sampling distributions rather than having to use the Finite Population Correction. The sample being larger than 10% of the population is not a bad thing; it just means the standard error is less than we're saying it is.

Practice Problems

Multiple-Choice

1. You are going to create a 95% confidence interval for a population proportion and want the margin of error to be no more than 0.05. Historical data indicate that the population proportion is about 0.7. What is the minimum size random sample you need to construct this interval?

   a. 385
   b. 322
   c. 274
   d. 275
   e. 323

2. Which of the following would result in a smaller margin of error in a confidence interval for a mean?

   a. Increasing the sample size
   b. Increasing the confidence level
   c. More variability in the sample responses
   d. A smaller sample mean
   e. All of these would result in a smaller margin of error.

3. St. Norbert College in Green Bay conducts an annual survey of Wisconsin residents. In 2011 a random sample of 400 Wisconsin residents was selected and 25% of respondents said the country is headed in the right direction. In a 2016 random sample of 664 residents, 28% said they thought the country was headed in the right direction. Do these samples provide convincing evidence of a change in the proportion of adults who thought the country was headed in the right direction?

   a. No, because the 95% confidence interval for the difference contains 3%.
   b. No, because the 95% confidence interval for the difference contains 0%.
   c. No, because the 95% confidence interval for the difference does not contain 0%.
   d. Yes, because the 95% confidence interval for the difference does not contain 3%.
   e. Yes, because the 95% confidence interval for the difference contains 3%.

4. A 95% confidence interval for the difference between two population proportions is found to be (0.07, 0.19). Which of the following statements is (are) true?
   I. It is unlikely that the two populations have the same proportions.
   II. We are 95% confident that the true difference between the population proportions is between 0.07 and 0.19.
   III. The probability is 0.95 that the true difference between the population proportions is between 0.07 and 0.19.

   a. I only
   b. II only
   c. I and II only
   d. I and III only
   e. II and III only

5. A 99% confidence interval for the true mean weight loss (in pounds) for people on the SkinnyQuick diet plan is found to be (1.3, 5.2). Which of the following is (are) correct?
   I. The probability is 0.99 that the mean weight loss is between 1.3 lb and 5.2 lb.
   II. The probability is 0.99 that intervals constructed by this process will capture the true population mean.
   III. We are 99% confident that the true mean weight loss for this program is between 1.3 lb and 5.2 lb.
   IV. This interval provides evidence that the SkinnyQuick plan is effective in reducing the mean weight of people on the plan.

   a. I and II only
   b. II only
   c. II and III only
   d. II, III, and IV only
   e. All of these statements are correct.

6. A poll was conducted in which Americans were asked whether they approve of the job the president of the United States is doing. The poll reported that 34% approve of the job the president is doing, with a margin of error of 3% and a 95% confidence level. Which of these is the best explanation of what that 3% means?

   a. There is a 3% chance that the 34% estimate is incorrect.
   b. Up to 3% of those sampled may have responded incorrectly.
   c. There is a probability of 3% that the proportion of all Americans who approve of the job the president is doing is not in the confidence interval.
   d. In about 95% of all possible samples of this size, the sample proportion will be within three percentage points of 34%.
   e. In about 95% of all possible samples of this size, the sample proportion will be within three percentage points of the proportion of all Americans who approve of the job the president is doing.

7. A 99% confidence interval for the weights of a random sample of high school wrestlers is reported as (125, 160). Which of the following statements about this interval is true?

   a. At least 99% of the weights of high school wrestlers are in the interval (125, 160).
   b. The probability is 0.99 that the true mean weight of high school wrestlers is in the interval (125, 160).
   c. 99% of all samples of this size will yield a confidence interval of (125, 160).
   d. The procedure used to generate this confidence interval will capture the true mean weight of high school wrestlers 99% of the time.
   e. The probability is 0.99 that a randomly selected wrestler will weigh between 125 and 160 lb.

8. This year's statistics class was small (only 15 students). This group averaged 74.5 on the final exam with a sample standard deviation of 3.2. Assuming that this group is a random sample of all students who have taken statistics and the scores in the final exam for all students are approximately normally distributed, which of the following is an approximate 96% confidence interval for the true population mean of all statistics students?
   a. 74.5 ± 7.245
   b. 74.5 ± 7.197
   c. 74.5 ± 1.871
   d. 74.5 ± 1.858
   e. 74.5 ± 1.772

9. A random sample of 425 residents of a city of 50,000 people was taken, and people were asked whether they consider themselves to be conservative, liberal, or moderate. A 95% confidence interval was constructed for the difference $p_C - p_L$, between the proportion of all city residents who consider themselves to be conservative and those who consider themselves to be liberal. Why is this procedure inappropriate?

   a. The sample size is too small to give a good representation of 50,000 people.
   b. The proportions of liberals and conservatives are not independent.
   c. $n\hat{p}$ or $n(1-\hat{p})$ will almost certainly be less than 10 for one of the groups.
   d. The sample size is less than 10% of the population.
   e. We don't know if the population is approximately normally distributed.

Free-Response

1. You attend a large university with approximately 15,000 students. You want to construct a 90% confidence interval estimate, within 5%, for the proportion of students who favor outlawing country music. How large a sample do you need?

2. The local farmers association in Cass County wants to estimate the mean number of bushels of corn produced per acre in the county. A random sample of 13 one-acre plots produced the following results (in number of bushels per acre): 98, 103, 95, 99, 92, 106, 101, 91, 99, 101, 97, 95, 98. Construct a 95% confidence interval for the mean number of bushels per acre in the entire county. The local association has been advertising that the mean yield per acre is 100 bushels. Do you think it is justified in this claim?

3. Two groups of 40 randomly selected students were selected to be part of a study on dropout rates. Members of one group were enrolled in a counseling program designed to give them skills needed to succeed in school, and the other group received no special counseling. Fifteen of the students who received counseling dropped out of school, and 23 of the students who did not receive counseling dropped out. Construct a 90% confidence interval for the true difference between the dropout rates of the two groups. Interpret your answer in the context of the problem.

4. A hotel chain claims that the average stay for its business clients is 5 days. The manager of one hotel in the chain believes that the true stay at his hotel may actually be different from 5 days. A study conducted by the hotel of 100 randomly selected clients yields a mean of 4.55 days with a standard deviation of 3.1 days.

   (a) Construct and interpret a 95% confidence interval for the mean stay at that hotel.
   (b) Does this interval provide convincing evidence that the mean stay at this hotel is different from 5 days?

5. One researcher wants to construct a 99% confidence interval as part of a study. A colleague says such a high level isn't necessary and that a 95% confidence level will suffice. In what ways will these intervals differ?

6. A 95% confidence interval for the true difference between the mean ages of male and female statistics teachers is constructed based on a sample of 95 males and 62 females. Consider each of the following intervals that might have been constructed:
   I. $(-4.5, 3.2)$
   II. $(2.1, 3.9)$
   III. $(-5.2, -1.7)$

For each of these intervals,

(a) interpret the interval, and

(b) describe the conclusion about the difference between the mean ages that might be drawn from the interval.

7. A 99% confidence interval for a population mean is to be constructed. A sample size of 20 will be used for the study. Assuming that the population from which the sample is drawn is approximately normal, what is the upper critical value needed to construct the interval?

8. Wikipedia has a "random article" link that selects an article at random. For a class project, a group of students wants to estimate the mean length of an article on Wikipedia by randomly selecting 100 articles from the more than 5 million articles currently on Wikipedia. The students will record number of words in each article and construct a confidence interval for the mean number of words. The students got into a discussion about whether this link samples with or without replacement. Explain why, for the purposes of their project, it doesn't make much difference whether it samples with or without replacement.

9. A flu vaccine is being tested for effectiveness. To test this, 350 randomly selected people are given the vaccine and observed to see if they develop the flu during the flu season. At the end of the season, 55 of the 350 did get the flu. Construct and interpret a 95% confidence interval for the true proportion of people who will get the flu despite getting the vaccine.

10. A research study gives a 95% confidence interval for the proportion of subjects helped by a new anti-inflammatory drug as (0.56, 0.65).

(a) Interpret this interval in the context of the problem.

(b) What is the meaning of "95% confidence interval," as stated in the problem?

11. For their statistics class, Bree and Ashling wanted to explore the effect of perceived peer pressure. They designed a paper survey in two versions. Version 1 simply asked, "On a scale of 1 (rarely) to 10 (constantly), how often do you procrastinate?" Version 2 asked the same question, but students could see a list of supposed prior students' responses to the question, and these prior student responses circled numbers at the higher end more often than in the middle or at the lower end. Students were randomly assigned one of the two versions of the question and their results were recorded. Summary statistics for each group are recorded in the table below:

TREATMENT	NUMBER OF SUBJECTS	MEAN	STANDARD DEVIATION
Control—Version 1	36	5.85	2.01
Primed—Version 2	32	7.45	1.76

The confidence interval for the difference in means (Version 2 – Version 1) is (0.687, 2.513). What does this interval tell you about the effect of the "peer pressure" version of the question?

12. A study was conducted to determine if male and female 10th graders differ in performance in mathematics. Twenty-three randomly selected males and 26 randomly selected females were each given a 50-question multiple-choice test as part of the study.

The scores were approximately normally distributed. The results of the study were as follows:

	MALES	FEMALES
Sample size	23	26
Mean	40.3	39.2
Std. deviation	8.3	7.6

Construct a 99% confidence interval for the true difference between the mean score for males and the mean score for females. Does the interval suggest that there is a difference between the true means for males and females?

13. A university wants to conduct a telephone poll of state residents to determine opinions about social trends. They estimate that it will cost $2.50 for each response based on the time it takes student employees to get a response to the survey. Through a private donation for this purpose, they have $1,500 to spend on gathering data for the survey.

    (a) If the donor insists that they estimate all proportions to within a 2% margin of error, will they have the funds to do it?
    (b) What is the *minimum* sample size needed to get the desired precision? What should the university tell the donor?

14. You want to estimate the proportion of Californians who want to outlaw cigarette smoking in all public places. Generally speaking, by how much must you increase the sample size to cut the margin of error in half?

15. The game Rock-Paper-Scissors consists of two people, at the same time, making a symbol with their hands. Each player can form a closed fist (rock), show an open palm (paper), or extend two fingers opened (scissors). The idea is that "paper covers rock, scissors cuts paper, and rock smashes scissors" so that each option has one option that it beats and one option that beats it. It is considered a game of chance, but there are those who insist that there is skill involved. There are actually Rock-Paper-Scissors tournaments. One skeptic wants to see if this is true, and he watches someone who claims to be a champion player and records the proportion of games won out of 100. What value of p, the true probability of this player winning, would the skeptic expect to be in his confidence interval?

16. A preelection poll asked likely voters, "If the election were held today, would you vote for Candidate A or Candidate B?" They randomized the order in which the candidates were listed so there would not be any bias based on the order. They reported that 51% of likely voters said they would vote for Candidate B with a margin of error of three percentage points and referred to it as a statistical tie. What does the term *statistical tie* mean?

17. Based on the 2000 census, the population of the United States was about 281.4 million people, and the population of Nevada was about 2 million. We are interested in generating a 95% confidence interval, with a margin of error of 3%, to estimate the proportion of people who will vote in the next presidential election. How much larger a sample will we need to generate this interval for the United States than for the state of Nevada?

18. Professor Olsen has taught statistics for 41 years and has kept the scores of every test he has ever given. Every test has been worth 100 points. He is interested in the average test score over the years. He doesn't want to put all of the scores (there are thousands of them) into a computer to figure out the exact average, so he asks his daughter, Anna, to randomly select 50 of the tests and use those to come up with an estimate of the population average. Anna has been studying statistics at college and decides to create a 98% confidence interval for the true average test score. The mean test score for the 50 randomly selected tests is 73.5 with a standard deviation of 7.1. What does she tell her father?

19. A certain type of pen is claimed to operate for a mean of 190 hours. A random sample of 49 pens is tested, and the mean operating time is found to be 188 hours with a standard deviation of 6 hours. Construct a 95% confidence interval for the true mean operating time of this type of pen. Does the company's claim seem justified?

20. A young researcher thinks there is a difference between the mean ages at which males and females win Oscars for best actor or actress. The student found the mean age for all best actor winners and all best actress winners and constructed a 95% confidence interval for the mean difference between their ages. Is this an appropriate use of a confidence interval? Why or why not?

Cumulative Review Problems

1. Use a normal approximation to the binomial to determine the probability of getting between 470 and 530 heads in 1,000 flips of a fair coin.

2. A survey of the number of televisions per household found the following probability distribution:

TELEVISIONS	PROBABILITY
0	0.03
1	0.37
2	0.46
3	0.10
4	0.04

What is the mean number of television sets per household?

3. A bag of marbles contains four red marbles and five blue marbles. A marble is drawn, its color is observed, and it is returned to the bag.

   (a) What is the probability that the first red marble is drawn on trial 3?
   (b) What is the average wait until a red marble is drawn?

4. A study is conducted to determine which of two competing weight-loss programs is more effective. Random samples of 50 people from each program are evaluated for losing and maintaining weight loss over a 1-year period. The average number of pounds lost per person over the year is used as a basis for comparison.

   (a) Why is this an observational study and not an experiment?
   (b) Describe an experiment that could be used to compare the two programs. Assume that you have available 100 overweight volunteers who are not presently in any program.

5. The correlation between the first and second statistics tests in a class is 0.78.

    (a) Interpret this value.

    (b) What proportion of the variation in the scores on the second test can be explained by the scores on the first test?

Solutions to Practice Problems

Multiple-Choice

1. The correct answer is (e).

$p = 0.7$, $M = 0.05$, $z^* = 1.96$ (for $C = 0.95$) $\Rightarrow$

$n \geq \left(\dfrac{z^*}{M}\right)^2 (\hat{P})(1 - \hat{P}) = \left(\dfrac{1.96}{0.05}\right)^2 (0.7)(0.3) = 322.7$. You need a sample of at least $n = 323$.

2. The correct answer is (a). Options (b) and (c) would increase the margin of error, and option (d) would not change it.

3. The correct answer is (b). It is not necessary to calculate the interval to answer this question because (b) is the only choice that is logically consistent. The question is whether 0% is in the interval, which leaves only options (b) and (c). And if 0 is in the interval, then there is not convincing evidence of a change. And the interval actually does contain 0.

4. The correct answer is (c). Because 0 is not in the interval (0.07, 0.19), it is unlikely to be the true difference between the proportions. III is just plain wrong! We cannot make a probability statement about an interval we have already constructed. All we can say is that the process used to generate this interval has a 0.95 chance of producing an interval that does contain the true population proportion.

5. The correct answer is (d). I is not correct because you cannot make a probability statement about a found interval—the true mean is either in the interval ($P = 1$) or it isn't ($P = 0$). II is correct and is just a restatement of "Intervals constructed by this procedure will capture the true mean 99% of the time." III is true—it's our standard way of *interpreting* a confidence interval. IV is true. Since the interval constructed does not contain 0, it's unlikely that this interval came from a population whose true mean is 0. Since all the values are positive, the interval does provide statistical evidence (but not proof) that the program is effective at promoting weight loss. It does not give evidence that the amount lost is of practical importance.

6. The correct answer is (e). The margin of error is an estimate of how far off our estimate might be. We expect 95% of sample proportions to lie within three percentage points of the population proportion. So we are pretty sure the correct proportion is between 31% and 37%.

7. The correct answer is (d). A confidence level is a statement about the procedure used to generate the interval, not about any one interval. It's difficult to use the word *probability* when interpreting a confidence interval and impossible when describing an interval that has already been constructed. However, you could say, "The probability is 0.99 that an interval constructed in this manner will contain the true population proportion."

8. The correct answer is (c). For $df = 15 - 1 = 14$, $t^* = 2.264$ for a 96% confidence interval (from Table B; if you have a TI-83/84 with the `invT` function, `invT(0.98,14)=2.264`).

   The interval is $74.5 \pm (2.264)\left(\dfrac{3.2}{\sqrt{15}}\right) = 74.5 \pm 1.871$.

9. The correct answer is (b). We don't have samples independently selected from two populations. We have one sample selected from one population. If the proportion of liberals in our sample is higher than in the population, the proportion of conservatives is likely to be lower. The proportions are not independent.

Free-Response

1. $C = 0.90 \Rightarrow z^* = 1.645$, $M = 0.05$. $n \geq \left(\dfrac{1.645}{0.05}\right)^2 (0.5)(0.5) = 270.6$.

   You would need to survey at least 271 students.

2. The population standard deviation is unknown, and the sample size is small (13), so we need to use a t procedure. The problem tells us that the sample is random. Thirteen is less than 10% of the population. A histogram of the data shows no significant departure from normality:

   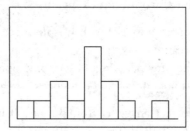

   Now, $\bar{x} = 98.1$, $s = 4.21$, $df = 13 - 1 = 12 \Rightarrow t^* = 2.179$. The 95% confidence interval is

   $$98.1 \pm 2.179\left(\frac{4.21}{\sqrt{13}}\right) = (95.56, 100.64).$$

   Because 100 is contained in this interval, we do not have strong evidence that the mean number of bushels per acre differs from 100, even though the sample mean is only 98.1.

3. This is a two-proportion situation. We are told that the groups were randomly selected and that each sample size is less than 10% of its respective population size, but we need to check that the samples are sufficiently large:

   $$\hat{p}_1 = \frac{15}{40} = 0.375, \quad \hat{p}_2 = \frac{23}{40} = 0.575$$

   $$n_1 \hat{p}_1 = 40(0.375) = 15, \ n_1(1 - \hat{p}_1) = 40(1 - 0.375) = 25.$$

   $$n_2 \hat{p}_2 = 40(0.575) = 23, \ n_2(1 - \hat{p}_2) = 40(1 - 0.575) = 17.$$

   Since all values are greater than or equal to 5, we are justified in constructing a two-proportion z interval. For a 90% z confidence interval, $z^* = 1.645$.

   Thus, $(0.575 - 0.375) \pm 1.645\sqrt{\dfrac{(0.375)(1 - 0.375)}{40} + \dfrac{(0.575)(1 - 0.575)}{40}} = (0.02, 0.38).$

We are 90% confident that the true difference between the dropout rates is between 0.02 and 0.38. Since 0 is not in this interval, we have evidence that the counseling program was effective at reducing the number of dropouts.

4. (a) Check conditions and identify procedure: We have a random sample of clients. Because $n = 100 > 30$, the sample size is large enough to use t procedures. There are probably more than $10 \cdot 100 = 1{,}000$ clients at this hotel. Conditions are met for a confidence interval for a mean.

Compute the interval: The 95% confidence interval is

$$\bar{x} \pm t^* \frac{s}{\sqrt{n}} = 4.55 \pm 1.98 \frac{3.1}{\sqrt{10}} = (3.93, 5.17), \text{ using } t^* \text{ for 99 } df.$$

Interpret the interval: We are 95% confident that the mean stay for clients at this hotel is between 3.93 days and 5.17 days.

(b) Because 5 days is in our interval, we do not have convincing evidence that the mean length of stay is different from 5 days.

5. The 99% confidence interval will be more likely to contain the population value being estimated, but will be wider than a 95% confidence interval.

6. I. (a) We are 95% confident that the true difference between the mean age of male statistics teachers and female statistics teachers is between –4.5 years and 3.2 years.

(b) Since 0 is contained in this interval, we do not have evidence of a statistically significant difference between the mean ages of male and female statistics teachers.

II. (a) We are 95% confident that the true difference between the mean age of male statistics teachers and female statistics teachers is between 2.1 years and 3.9 years.

(b) Since 0 is not in this interval, we do have evidence of a real difference between the mean ages of male and female statistics teachers. In fact, since the interval contains only positive values, we have evidence that the mean age of male statistics teachers is greater than the mean age of female statistics teachers.

III. (a) We are 95% confident that the true difference between the mean age of male statistics teachers and female statistics teachers is between –5.2 years and –1.7 years.

(b) Since 0 is not in this interval, we have evidence of a real difference between the mean ages of male and female statistics teachers. In fact, since the interval contains only negative values, we have evidence that the mean age of male statistics teachers is less than the mean age of female statistics teachers.

7. t procedures are appropriate because the population is approximately normal. $n = 20 \Rightarrow df = 20 - 1 = 19 \Rightarrow t^* = 2.861$ for $C = 0.99$.

8. Because the sample is small compared to the number of articles on Wikipedia (far less than 10% of the population size), sampling without replacement will not change the standard deviation of the sampling distribution of the sample mean enough to notice.

9. $\hat{p} = \frac{55}{350} = 0.157$, $n\hat{p} = 350(0.157) = 54.95 \geq 5$, $n(1-\hat{p})$

$= 350(1 - 0.157) = 295.05 \geq 5.$

The conditions are present to construct a one-proportion z interval.

$$0.157 \pm 1.96 \sqrt{\frac{0.157(1-0.157)}{350}} = (0.119,\ 0.195)$$

We are 95% confident that the true proportion of people who will get the flu despite getting the vaccine is between 11.9% and 19.5%. To say that we are 95% confident means that the process used to construct this interval will, in fact, capture the true population proportion 95% of the time (that is, our "confidence" is in the procedure, not in the interval we found!).

10. (a) We are 95% confident that the true proportion of subjects helped by a new anti-inflammatory drug is (0.56, 0.65).
    (b) The process used to construct this interval will capture the true population proportion, on average, 95 times out of 100.

11. Because 0 is not in the interval and the entire interval of differences is positive, we can conclude that the "peer pressure" version of the question caused people to rate their level of procrastination as 0.687 to 2.513 points higher than the version without the peer pressure.

12. The problem states that the samples were randomly selected and that the scores were approximately normally distributed. Both samples are less than 10% of the populations of males and females in 10th grade, so we can construct a two-sample t interval.

    The interval is $(\bar{x}_M - \bar{x}_F) \pm t^* \sqrt{\dfrac{s_M^2}{n_m} + \dfrac{s_F^2}{n_F}} = (-5.04, 7.24)$, using t^* for 44.9 df. (You do not need to calculate t^* for two-sample procedures on the AP exam. You are sometimes required to report degrees of freedom, which your calculator will give you.) We are 99% confident that male 10th graders score, on average, between 5 points lower and 7 points higher than female 10th graders on this mathematics test. Because 0 is in the interval we cannot conclude that there is a difference in performance between males and females.

13. (a) With a budget of $1,500, they can survey 600 residents. The margin of error if they survey 600 residents is, at most, $1.96\sqrt{\dfrac{0.5 \cdot 0.5}{600}} = 0.04$. They will not have enough funds to meet the donor's goal.
    (b) Solving $1.96\sqrt{\dfrac{0.5 \cdot 0.5}{n}} \leq 0.02, n \geq 2,401$. The donor would need to approximately quadruple the funding for gathering the data to get the desired precision.

14. In the formula for the margin of error, n is in the denominator under the square root. So, for example, doubling the sample size will reduce the margin of error by a factor of $\sqrt{2}$. To cut the margin of error in half, you must multiply n by $2^2 = 4$.

15. The skeptic thinks this player really has a 50% chance of winning any given round, so he would expect 0.5 to be in the interval.

16. A tie would mean that the same proportion of likely voters would say they are voting for Candidate A and Candidate B. Because the two candidates are within three percentage points of each other (the margin of error) it is plausible that the same proportion of people in the population would vote for each candidate. (*Note:* A two-sample procedure here is inappropriate because there are not two independently selected samples from two populations.)

17. Trick question! The population size is not a part of the margin of error formula so you can use the same sample size. (Assuming the sample size is small compared to the population size!)

18. She randomly selected the sample of scores. $n = 50$ so the sample size is large enough to use t procedures. Fifty is less than 10% of the thousands of test scores, so conditions are met for a confidence interval for a mean.

    The interval is $75.5 \pm 2.404 \dfrac{7.1}{\sqrt{50}} = (71.09, 75.91)$.

    She can tell her father that she is 98% confident that the mean score for all his students is between 71.09 and 75.91.

19. The problem states that we have an SRS and $n = 49$. We have a large sample size, but it is less than 10% of the population of all such pens, so we are justified in using t procedures.

    $$188 \pm 2.011 \dfrac{6}{\sqrt{49}} = (186.3, 189.7), \text{ using } t^* \text{ for 95\% confidence and } 48 \, df.$$

    Because 190 is not in this interval, it is not a plausible mean for the population from which we would have gotten this sample. There is some doubt about the company's claim.

20. It is not appropriate because confidence intervals use sample data to make estimates about unknown population values. In this case, the actual difference in the ages of actors and actresses is known, and the true difference can be calculated.

Solutions to Cumulative Review Problems

1. Let $X =$ the number of heads. Then X has $B(1000, 0.5)$ because the coin is fair. This binomial can be approximated by a normal distribution with mean $= 1000(0.5) = 500$ and standard deviation

    $$s = \sqrt{1000(0.5)(0.5)} = 15.81. \; P(470 < X < 530)$$

    $$= P\left(\dfrac{470 - 500}{15.81} < z < \dfrac{530 - 500}{15.81}\right) = P(-1.90 < z < 1.90) = 0.94. \text{ Using the TI-83/84}$$

    calculator, `normalcdf(-1.9,1.9)`.

2. $\mu_x = 0(0.3) + 1(0.37) + 2(0.46) + 3(0.10) + 4(0.04) = 1.75$.

3. (a) $P(\text{draw a red marble}) = 4/9$

    $$G(3) = \dfrac{4}{9}\left(1 - \dfrac{4}{9}\right)^{3-1} = \dfrac{4}{9}\left(\dfrac{5}{9}\right)^2 = 0.137.$$

    (b) Average wait

    $$= \dfrac{1}{p} = \dfrac{1}{\frac{4}{9}} = \dfrac{9}{4} = 2.25.$$

4. (a) It is an observational study because the researchers are simply observing the results between two different groups. To do an experiment, the researcher must manipulate the variable of interest (different weight-loss programs) in order to compare their effects.

   (b) Inform the volunteers that they are going to be enrolled in a weight-loss program and their progress monitored. As they enroll, randomly assign them to one of two groups, say Group A and Group B (without the subjects' knowledge that there are really two different programs). Group A gets one program and Group B the other. After a period of time, compare the average number of pounds lost for the two programs.

5. (a) There is a moderate to strong positive linear relationship between the scores on the first and second tests.

   (b) $0.78^2 = 0.61$. About 61% of the variation in scores on the second test can be explained by the regression on the scores from the first test.

CHAPTER 11

Inference: Testing Hypotheses

IN THIS CHAPTER

Summary: In the last chapter, we concentrated on estimating, using a confidence interval, the value of a population parameter or the difference between two population parameters. In this chapter, we test to see whether some specific hypothesized value of a population parameter, or the difference between two populations' parameters, is plausible or not. We form hypotheses and test to determine the probability of getting a particular result if the null hypothesis is true. We then make decisions about our hypothesis based on that probability.

Key Ideas
✪ Statistical Significance and *P*-Value
✪ The Logic of Hypothesis Testing
✪ Hypothesis-Testing Procedure
✪ A Significance Test for a Population Proportion
✪ Errors in Hypothesis Testing
✪ The Power of a Test
✪ A Significance Test for the Difference between Two Population Proportions
✪ *z*-Procedures versus *t*-Procedures
✪ A Significance Test for a Population Mean
✪ A Significance Test for the Difference between Two Population Means

In the last chapter, we concentrated on estimating the value of a population parameter, using a confidence interval. In this chapter, we form hypotheses and perform a test to determine whether we have convincing evidence that a particular hypothesis is incorrect. To do so, we will be introduced to the logic behind significance testing, the meaning of a *P*-value, the types of errors you have to worry about when testing, and what is meant by the *power* of a test. There's a lot in this chapter, and you will need to work hard to keep it all straight.

Statistical Significance and *P*-Value

Statistical Significance

In the previous chapter, we used confidence intervals to make *estimates* about population values. In one of the examples, we observed that, because 0 was contained in the confidence interval, 0 was a plausible value for the difference in population proportions. In other words, we could NOT conclude that there was a difference in population proportions at all. As we progress through techniques of inference (drawing conclusions about a population from data), we often are interested in whether a sample statistic is likely under a particular assumption.

We begin by making an assumption about the population parameter. This assumption is called the **null hypothesis**. If a sample is not one we would expect based on our null hypothesis, it could be because of sampling variability, or it could be because the sample came from a different population than we thought. If the result is so far from what we expected that we think something other than chance is operating, then the result is said to be **statistically significant**.

> **example:** Todd claims that the average amount of money spent on ride tickets at a county fair is $50. If you have a random group of 50 fairgoers and the average money spent on ride tickets for this group is $49.75, we have little reason to doubt Todd's claim. But if the average for this group is $38, statisticians call this result *statistically significant* meaning that we would be unlikely to have a sample average this low if Todd's claim is true.

In the above example, most people would agree that $49.75 was consistent with Todd's claim (that is, $49.75 was a likely sample mean if the population mean really is $50) and that $38 is inconsistent with the claim (it is *statistically significant*). It is a bit more complicated to decide where between $38 and $49.75 the cutoff is between "reasonably likely" and "unlikely."

There are some general agreements about how unlikely a statistic needs to be, assuming the null hypothesis is true, in order to be statistically significant. Typical significance levels, symbolized by the Greek letter α, are probabilities of 0.1, 0.05, and 0.01. If a result has a lower probability of occurring than the significance level, then the result is statistically significant at that level.

> **example:** A statistics student determined that the probability that a random group of 50 fairgoers would average $38 on county fair ride tickets when Todd's claim of an average of $50 is actually true to be less than 0.00000002. This value is so low that it seems unlikely to have occurred by chance, and so we say that the result is statistically significant. This probability is lower than any of the commonly accepted significance levels.

P-Value

We said that a result is statistically significant if it is unlikely to have occurred by chance given that the null hypothesis is true. The **P-value** is what tells us just *how* unlikely a result actually is under the model based on the null hypothesis. The *P*-value is the probability, based on our model, of getting a sample statistic by chance alone as extreme, or more extreme, as the one we obtained. This requires that we have some expectation about what we ought to get. In other words, the *P*-value is the probability of getting a statistic at least as far removed from expected as we got. A decision about significance can then be made by comparing the obtained *P*-value with a stated value of α.

> **example:** Suppose it turns out that the average amount of money a *random* group of 50 people spend on ride tickets at the county fair is $47.50. What is the probability of getting an observed mean this far below the expected $50 by chance alone (that is, what is the *P*-value) if the true average is $50 (assume the population standard deviation is $8)? Is this finding significant at $\alpha = 0.05$? At $\alpha = 0.01$?

> **solution:** We are assuming the population is normally distributed with mean $50 and standard deviation $8. The sampling distribution for this situation is pictured below:

$$P(\bar{x} < 47.5) = P\left(z < \frac{47.5 - 50}{8/\sqrt{50}} = -2.21\right) = 0.014.$$

This is the *P*-value: it's the probability of getting a sample mean as far below $50 as we did by chance alone, assuming the model based on a mean of $50 is correct. This finding is significant at the 0.05 level but not (quite) at the 0.01 level.

The Hypothesis-Testing Procedure

Now we will want to test whether or not the parameter has a particular value. More accurately, we might ask if we have convincing evidence *against* the hypothesis that $p_1 - p_2 = 0$ or $\mu = 3$, for example. That is, we will test the hypothesis that, say, $p_1 - p_2 = 0$. In the hypothesis-testing procedure, a researcher does NOT look for evidence to support this hypothesis but instead looks for evidence against this hypothesis. The process looks like this:

- *State the null and alternative hypotheses in the context of the problem.* The first hypothesis, the **null hypothesis**, is the hypothesis we are testing. The null hypothesis usually states that there is nothing going on: the claim is correct or that there is no distinction between groups. It is symbolized by H_0. An example of a typical null hypothesis would be $H_0: \mu_1 - \mu_2 = 0$ or $H_0: \mu_1 = \mu_2$. This is the hypothesis that μ_1 and μ_2 are the same, or that populations 1 and 2 have the same mean. Note that μ_1 and μ_2 must be identified in context (for example, $\mu_1 =$ the mean score for all people in the population before training).

  The second hypothesis, the **alternative hypothesis**, is the theory that the researcher wants to confirm by rejecting the null hypothesis. The alternative hypothesis is symbolized by H_A or H_a. There are three possible forms for the alternative hypothesis: $\neq$, $>$, or $<$. If the null is $H_0: \mu_1 - \mu_2 = 0$, then H_A could be

$$H_A: \mu_1 - \mu_2 \neq 0 \text{ (this is called a \textbf{two-sided alternative})}$$

or

$$H_A: \mu_1 - \mu_2 > 0 \text{ (this is a \textbf{one-sided alternative})}$$

or

$$H_A: \mu_1 - \mu_2 < 0 \text{ (also a \textbf{one-sided alternative})}.$$

(In the case of the one-sided alternative, $H_A: \mu_1 - \mu_2 > 0$, the null hypothesis is sometimes written: $H_0: \mu_1 - \mu_2 \leq 0$. This actually makes pretty good sense: if the researcher is wrong in a belief that the difference is greater than 0, then any finding less than or equal to 0 fails to provide evidence in favor of the alternative.)

- *Identify which procedure you intend to use and show that the conditions for its use are present.* We identified the conditions for constructing a confidence interval in the previous chapter. Now, we will want to identify the conditions needed to do hypothesis testing. For the most part, they are similar to those you have already studied. One exception is this: when we are conducting a test for a proportion, we have an assumption about the value of p. This value is referred to as p_0. Because we are creating a model based on p_0, we will use p_0 when checking conditions. Specifically, we check that np_0 and $n(1 - p_0)$ are greater than 10. For a test for a difference in proportions, out null hypothesis is that $p_1 = p_2$. We don't have an estimate for the *value* of p_1 and p_2, so the best we can do is treat the two samples as one big sample to estimate that value. We define $\hat{p}$ as the *pooled proportion*, and we calculate it as the total number of successes over the total sample size. Symbolically,

  $\hat{p} = \dfrac{x_1 + x_2}{n_1 + n_2} = \dfrac{n_1\hat{p}_1 + n_2\hat{p}_2}{n_1 + n_2}$. The condition we must check to ensure that the

  shape of our sampling distribution model for $\hat{p}_1 - \hat{p}_2$ is approximately normal is that $n_1\hat{p}$, $n_1(1 - \hat{p})$, $n_2\hat{p}$, and $n_2(1 - \hat{p})$, are all at least 5 (or 10). If you are going to state a significance level α, it can be done here.

- *Compute the value of the test statistic and the* P*-value.*
- *Give a conclusion, linked to your computations, in the context of the problem.*

Exam Tip: The four steps above have been incorporated into AP exam scoring for any question involving a hypothesis test. Note that for the third item (compute the value of the test statistic and the P-value), the mechanics in the problem are only one part of a complete solution. *All* four steps must be present in order to receive a 4 ("complete response") on the problem.

If you stated a significance level in the second step of the process, the conclusion can be based on a comparison of the P-value with α. If you didn't state a significance level, you can argue your conclusion based on the value of the P-value alone: if it is small, you have evidence against the null; if it is not small, you do not have evidence against the null.

Many statisticians will argue that you are better off to argue directly from the P-value and not use a significance level. One reason for this is the arbitrariness of the P-value. That is, if $\alpha = 0.05$, you would reject the null hypothesis for a P-value of 0.04999 but not for a P-value of 0.05001 when, in reality, there is no practical difference between them.

The conclusion can be (1) that we reject H_0 (because of a sufficiently small P-value) or (2) that we do not reject H_0 (because the P-value is too large). We do **NOT** accept the null: we either reject it or fail to reject it. If we reject H_0, we can say in context that we have convincing evidence in favor of H_A.

> **example:** Consider, one last time, Todd and his claim that the average money spent on fair rides is \$50. A sample was taken and we got \$47.50; we assumed the population standard deviation was \$8. A test of the hypothesis that the average money spent was \$50 on average against the alternative that Todd is incorrect might look something like the following (we will fill in many of the details, especially those in the third part of the process, in the following chapters):

- Let μ be the true average money spent by Todd's fairgoers. H_0: $\mu = \$50$ (or H_0: $\mu \geq \$50$, because the alternative is one sided) and H_A: $\mu < \$50$.
- Because we know the population standard deviation σ, we will use a z-test. We assume the 50 people is an SRS of all the people attending the fair, and the central limit theorem tells us that the sampling distribution of $\overline{x}$ is approximately normal. We will use a significance level of $\alpha = 0.05$.
- In the previous section, we determined that the P-value for this situation (the probability of getting an average as far away from our expected value as we got) is 0.014.
- Because the P-value (0.014) $< \alpha$ (0.05), we can reject H_0. We have good evidence that the true mean amount of money spent on ride tickets is actually less than \$50 (note that we *aren't* claiming anything about exactly how much they do spend on average, just that it's likely to be less than \$50).

Recap of Hypothesis (Significance) Testing

Here's a summary of the logic of hypothesis testing:

I. State hypotheses in the context of the problem. The first hypothesis, the **null hypothesis**, is the hypothesis we are testing. It is symbolized by H_0.

The second hypothesis, the **alternative hypothesis**, is the theory that the researcher hopes to confirm by rejecting the null hypothesis. The alternative hypothesis is symbolized by H_A. There are three forms for the alternative hypothesis: $\neq$, $>$, or $<$. That is, if the null is H_0: $\mu_1 - \mu_2 = 0$, then H_A could be

$$H_A: \mu_1 - \mu_2 \neq 0 \text{ (a \textbf{two-sided alternative})}$$

$$H_A: \mu_1 - \mu_2 > 0 \text{ (a \textbf{one-sided alternative})}$$

$$H_A: \mu_1 - \mu_2 < 0 \text{ (a \textbf{one-sided alternative})}.$$

(In the case of the one-sided alternative H_A: $\mu_1 - \mu_2 > 0$, the null hypothesis is sometimes written H_0: $\mu_1 - \mu_2 \leq 0$.)

II. Identify which procedure you intend to use and show that the conditions for its use are satisfied. If you are going to state a significance level, α, it can be done here.

III. Compute the value of the test statistic and the P-value.

IV. Using the value of the test statistic and/or the P-value, give a conclusion in the context of the problem.

If you stated a significance level, the conclusion can be based on a comparison of the P-value with α. If you didn't state a significance level, you can argue your conclusion based on the relative size of the P-value alone: if it is small, you have evidence against the null hypothesis; if it is not small, you do not have evidence against the null hypothesis.

The conclusion can be (1) that we reject H_0 (because of a sufficiently small P-value) or (2) that we do not reject H_0 (because the P-value is too large). We *never* accept the null hypothesis: we either reject it or fail to reject it. If we reject H_0, we can say that we have convincing evidence in favor of H_A.

Significance testing involves making a decision about whether or not an observed result is statistically significant. That is, is the result sufficiently unlikely, if the null hypothesis were true, so as to provide good evidence for rejecting the null hypothesis in favor of the alternative? The four steps in the hypothesis testing process outlined earlier are the four steps that are required on the AP exam when doing inference problems. In brief, every test of a hypothesis should have the following four steps:

I.   State the null and alternative hypotheses in the context of the problem, defining all symbols. (Make sure that you are using parameters in words and/or symbols!)
II. Identify the appropriate test and check that the conditions for its use are present.
III. Do the correct mechanics, including calculating the value of the test statistic and the P-value.
IV. State a correct conclusion linked to the mechanics in the context of the problem.

> **Exam Tip:** You are not required to *number* the four steps on the exam, but it is a good idea to do so—then you are sure you have done everything required.

Inference for a Single Population Proportion

We are usually more interested in estimating a population proportion with a confidence interval than we are in testing that a population proportion has a particular value. However, significance testing techniques for a particular population proportion exist and follow a pattern similar to those of the previous two sections. The main difference is that the only test statistic is z. The logic is based on using a normal approximation to the binomial, as discussed in Chapter 9.

• **Hypothesis** • **Estimator** • **Standard Error**	**Conditions**	**Test Statistic**
• Null hypothesis: $H_0: p = p_0$ • Estimator: $$\hat{p} = \frac{X}{n},\ \text{where } X \text{ is}$$ the count of successes. • Standard error: $$s_{\hat{p}} = \sqrt{\frac{p_0(1 - p_0)}{n}}$$	• SRS • $np_0 \geq 10$, $n(1 - p_0) \geq 10$ (or $np_0 \geq 5$, $n(1 - p_0) \geq 5$) • $10n <$ Population size	$$z = \frac{\hat{p} - p_0}{\sqrt{\dfrac{p_0(1 - p_0)}{n}}}$$

Notes on the preceding table:

- The standard error for a hypothesis test of a single population proportion is different from that for a confidence interval for a population proportion. The standard error for a confidence interval,

$$s_{\hat{p}} = \sqrt{\frac{\hat{p}(1-\hat{p})}{n}} \ ,$$

is a function of $\hat{p}$, the sample proportion, whereas the standard error for a hypothesis test,

$$s_{\hat{p}} = \sqrt{\frac{p_0(1-p_0)}{n}} \ ,$$

is a function of the hypothesized value of p. This is because a test assumes, for the sake of our model, that $p = p_0$. So we use that hypothesized value in the calculation of the standard error. An interval makes no such assumption.

- Like the conditions for the use of a z-interval, we require that the np_0 and $n(1 - p_0)$ be large enough to justify the normal approximation. As with determining the standard error, we use the hypothesized value of p rather than the sample value. "Large enough" means either $np_0 \geq 5$ and $n(1 - p_0) \geq 5$, or $np_0 \geq 10$ and $n(1 - p_0) \geq 10$ (it varies by textbook, but either 5 or 10 is acceptable).

example: Consider a screening test for prostate cancer that its maker claims will detect the cancer in 85% of the men who actually have the disease. One hundred seventy-five random men who have been previously diagnosed with prostate cancer are given the screening test, and 141 of the men are identified as having the disease. Does this finding provide evidence that the screening test detects the cancer at a rate different from the 85% rate claimed by its manufacturer?

solution:

I. Let $p =$ the true proportion of men with prostate cancer who test positive.

H_0: $p = 0.85$
H_A: $p \neq 0.85$

II. We want to use a one-proportion z-test. We were told that the men were **random**. $175(0.85) = 148.75 > 10$ and $175(1 - 0.85) = 26.25 > 10$ (remember either 5 or 10 can be used to check the sample size condition), and $1750 <$ Population size so the conditions are present to use this test.

III. $\hat{p} = \dfrac{141}{175} = 0.806$.

$$z = \frac{0.806 - 0.85}{\sqrt{\dfrac{0.85(1-0.85)}{175}}} = 1.64 \Rightarrow P\text{-value} = 0.10 \ .$$

Using the TI-83/84, the same answer is obtained by using `1-PropZTest` in the `STAT TESTS` menu. On the AP exam, we recommend that you always make sure to name the test as in Part II, then list the z-value and the P-value reported by your calculator. Add the z-score formula with the correct numbers plugged in (NOT symbolically) if you have time and if you are certain you can write it correctly.

IV. Because the P-value is somewhat large, we do not have sufficient evidence to reject the null hypothesis. There is not convincing evidence to believe that the screening test detects the cancer at a rate different from the 85% rate claimed by its manufacturer.

---

example: Maria has a quarter that she suspects is out of balance. In fact, she thinks it turns up heads more often than it would if it were fair. Maria decides to flip the coin 300 times and count the number of heads. There are 165 heads in the 300 flips. Does this provide evidence at the 0.05 level that the coin is biased in favor of heads? What about at the 0.01 level?

solution:

I. Let p = the true proportion of heads in 300 flips of a fair coin.

H_0: $p = 0.50$ (or H_0: $p \leq 0.50$)
H_A: $p > 0.50$

II. We will use a one-proportion z-test.

We will assume that the 300 flips are a random sample of all flips. $3000 <$ Population and $300(0.50) = 150 > 5$ and $300(1 - 0.50) = 150 > 5$, so the conditions are present for a one-proportion z-test.

III. $\hat{p} = \dfrac{165}{300} = 0.55$, $z = \dfrac{0.55 - 0.50}{\sqrt{\dfrac{0.50(1-0.50)}{300}}} = 1.73 \Rightarrow$ P-value = 0.042.

(This can be done using `1-PropZTest` in the `STAT TESTS` menu of the TI-83/84. We will repeat this many times—on the AP exam, you SHOULD do the mechanics using the test menu from your brand of calculator. Just identify the procedure and list the values reported. Whether you identify the procedure by name or formula, the components of the name of the procedure are all important: one proportion, z, and the word test must be clear.)

IV. The question asked about both $\alpha = 0.05$ and $\alpha = 0.01$. We note that this finding would have been significant at $\alpha = 0.05$ but not at $\alpha = 0.01$. For the two significance levels, the solutions would look something like this:

(1) Because the P-value (0.042) $< \alpha$ (0.05), we reject the null hypothesis. We have evidence that the true proportion of heads is greater than 0.50.

(2) Because the P-value (0.042) $> \alpha$ (0.01), we fail to reject the null hypothesis. We do not have convincing evidence that the true proportion of heads is greater than 0.50.

Type I and Type II Errors and the Power of a Test

When we do a hypothesis test we never really know if we have made the correct decision or not. We can try to minimize our chances of being wrong, but there are trade-offs involved. If we are given a hypothesis, it may be true or it may be false. We can decide to reject the hypothesis or not to reject it. This leads to four possible outcomes:

	Decision	
Hypothesis	*Do not reject*	*Reject*
True		
False		

Two of the cells in the table are errors and two are not. Filling those in, we have

	Decision	
Hypothesis	*Do not reject*	*Reject*
True	OK	Error
False	Error	OK

Note that, in statistics, the term *error* does not mean somebody did something wrong. It refers to variability. An "error" occurs because the sampling variability caused a sample statistic that led us to the wrong decision. The errors have names that are rather unspectacular: If the (null) hypothesis is true, and we mistakenly reject it, it is a **Type I error**. If the hypothesis is false, and we mistakenly fail to reject it, it is a **Type II error**. We note that the probability of a Type I error is equal to α, the significance level. (This is because a *P*-value ***less than*** α causes us to reject H_0. If H_0 is true, and we decide to reject it because we got an unusual sample, we have made a Type I error.) We call the probability of a Type II error β. Filling the table with this information, we have

	Decision	
Hypothesis	*Do not reject*	*Reject*
True	OK	Type I Error $P(Type\ I) = \alpha$
False	Type II Error $P(Type\ II) = \beta$	OK

The cell in the lower right-hand corner is important. The probability of correctly rejecting a false hypothesis (in favor of the alternative) is called the **power of the test**. The power of the test equals $1 - \beta$. Finally, then, our decision table looks like this:

	Decision	
Hypothesis	*Do not reject*	*Reject*
True	OK	Type I Error $P(Type\ I) = \alpha$
False	Type II Error $P(Type\ II) = \beta$	OK [*power* = $1 - \beta$]

Exam Tip: You will not need to know how to actually calculate *P*(*Type II error*) or the power of the rest on the AP exam. You *will* need to understand the concept of each, what affects each, and how they are related.

example: Sticky Fingers is arrested for shoplifting. The judge, in her instructions to the jury, says that Sticky is innocent until proven guilty. That is, the jury's hypothesis is that Sticky is innocent. Identify Type I and Type II errors in this situation and explain the consequence of each.

solution: Our hypothesis is that Sticky is innocent. A Type I error involves mistakenly rejecting a true hypothesis. In this case, Sticky *is* innocent, but because we reject innocence, he is found guilty. The risk in a Type I error is that Sticky goes to jail for a crime he didn't commit.

A Type II error involves failing to reject a false hypothesis. If the hypothesis is false, then Sticky is guilty, but because there was not enough evidence to believe so, we acquit him. The risk in Type II error is that Sticky goes free even though he is guilty.

In life we often have to choose between possible errors. In the earlier example, the choice was between sending an innocent person to jail (a Type I error) or setting a criminal free (a Type II error). Which of these is the more serious error is not a statistical question—it's a social one.

We can decrease the chance of Type I error by adjusting α. By making α very small, we could virtually ensure that we would never mistakenly reject a true hypothesis. However, this would result in a large Type II error because we are making it hard to reject the null under any circumstance, even when it is false.

The probability of making a Type II error is smaller and, hence, the power of the test greater if

- the sample size is increased.
- the standard deviation of our sample data is decreased (this is not always under the control of the researcher but, for example, if more precise measurements are possible the variability in the data could be reduced).
- we choose a larger significance level (α).
- the effect size (the difference between the hypothesized parameter and the true value) is larger. A bigger difference is easier to detect!

example: A pharmaceutical company created a new skin cream to help sunburn heal faster. They are going to conduct a clinical trial (a randomized experiment) to determine if the cream decreases the time for sunburn to heal. Suppose that, in fact, this cream does work. Which of the following is equivalent to the power of the test?

(a) The decrease in the amount of time it takes for the cream to heal the sunburn
(b) The probability that the researchers conclude from the experiment that the cream is ineffective
(c) The probability that the researchers conclude from the experiment that there is no conclusive evidence
(d) The probability that the researchers conclude from the experiment that the cream works
(e) The probability that the null hypothesis is false

solution: The power of the test is the probability of rejecting a false null hypothesis in favor of an alternative—in this case, the hypothesis that the cream doesn't work. If we correctly reject this hypothesis, the researchers will conclude that the cream does, in fact, work. Hence, (d) is the correct answer.

Inference for the Difference Between Two Population Proportions

The logic behind inference for two population proportions is the same as for the others we have studied. As with the one-sample case, there are some differences between z-intervals and z-tests in terms of the computation of the standard error. The following table gives the essential details.

• Hypothesis • Estimator • Standard Error	Conditions	Test Statistic
• Null hypothesis: $H_0: p_1 - p_2 = 0$ (or $H_0: p_1 = p_2$) • Estimator: $\hat{p}_1 - \hat{p}_2$ where $\hat{p}_1 = \dfrac{X_1}{n_1}$ $\hat{p}_2 = \dfrac{X_2}{n_2}$ • Standard error: $s_{\hat{p}_1 - \hat{p}_2} = \sqrt{\hat{p}(1-\hat{p})\left(\dfrac{1}{n_1}+\dfrac{1}{n_2}\right)},$ where $\hat{p} = \dfrac{X_1+X_2}{n_1+n_2}$	• SRSs from independent populations • Each sample size is less than 10% of its population when sampling without replacement $n_1 \cdot \hat{p}, n_1 \cdot (1-\hat{p}),$ $n_2 \cdot \hat{p}, n_2 \cdot (1-\hat{p})$ are all > 5 (or 10)	$z = \dfrac{\hat{p}_1 - \hat{p}_2}{\sqrt{\hat{p}(1-\hat{p})\left(\dfrac{1}{n_1}+\dfrac{1}{n_2}\right)}},$ where $\hat{p} = \dfrac{X_1+X_2}{n_1+n_2}$

example: Two concentrations of a new vaccine designed to prevent infection are developed and a study is conducted to determine if they differ in their effectiveness. Participants were randomly placed into treatment groups, one group receiving Vaccine A and the other Vaccine B. The results from the study are given in the following table.

	Vaccine A	Vaccine B
Infected	102	95
Not infected	123	190
Total	225	285

Does this study provide statistical evidence at the $\alpha = 0.01$ level that the vaccines differ in their effectiveness?

solution:

I. Let p_1 = the population proportion infected after receiving Vaccine A.

Let p_2 = the population proportion infected after receiving Vaccine B.

$H_0: p_1 - p_2 = 0$
$H_A: p_1 - p_2 \neq 0$

II. We will use a two-proportion z-test at $\alpha = 0.01$.

$$\hat{p}_1 = \frac{102}{225} = 0.453, \quad \hat{p}_2 = \frac{95}{285} = 0.333,$$

$$\hat{p} = \frac{102 + 95}{225 + 285} \approx 0.387$$

$$n_1\hat{p} = 225 \cdot 0.387 \approx 87.1, \quad n_1(1 - \hat{p}) = 225 \cdot 0.613 \approx 137.9,$$

$$n_2\hat{p} = 285 \cdot 0.387 \approx 110.3, \quad n_2(1 - \hat{p}) = 285 \cdot 0.613 \approx 174.7$$

Patients were randomly assigned treatments; therefore, we do not check $10n$ < Population.

(All values are larger than 5 and treatments of vaccine have been randomly applied, so the conditions necessary are present for the two-proportion z-test.*)

III. $z = 2.76$ and P-value = 0.0057
On the AP exam, you should simply name the procedure. You can just report the values listed as we did here—especially in the case of a two-sample test such as this.

IV. Because $P = 0.0057 < 0.01$, we reject the null hypothesis. We have convincing evidence that the two vaccines differ in their effectiveness.

---

z-Procedures versus *t*-Procedures

We are going to move from procedures that involve counting and producing proportions to those in which we are measuring and producing means. With proportions, assuming the proper conditions are met, we deal only with large samples—that is, with z-procedures. When doing inference for a population mean, or for the difference between two population means, we typically use t-procedures because we do not know the population standard deviation. We use t-procedures when doing inference for a population mean or for the difference between two populations' means when the following are true about each sample:

(a) The sample is a simple random sample from the population.
    and
(b) The *population* from which the sample is drawn is approximately normally distributed or the sample size is large enough.

When we have not been given information that the population is approximately normally distributed, many textbooks define a large-enough sample size to be greater than or equal to 40.

But what do we do when there is no information given about the distribution of the population and the sample size is not large enough? When using t-procedures we check to see if it is plausible that the data could have come from an approximately normal population!

A stemplot, boxplot, dotplot, or normal probability plot can be used to show that there are no outliers or extreme skewness in the data itself. This gives us reason to believe that the data came from an approximately normal population. (For the exam itself, our preference is a dotplot because they are quick to produce.) t-procedures are **robust** against these assumptions, which means that the procedures still work reasonably well even with some violation of the condition of normality, provided there is not much skewness. Some texts use the following guidelines for sample size when deciding whether or not to use t-procedures:

- $n < 15$. Use t-procedures if a plot of the data shows no outliers and no skewness.
- $15 < n < 40$. Use t-procedures unless there are outliers or marked skewness.
- $n > 40$. Use t-procedures for any distribution.

(For the two-sample case discussed later, these guidelines can still be used if you replace n with n_1 and n_2.)

Inference for a Single Population Mean

In step II of the hypothesis-testing procedure, we need to identify the test to be used and justify the conditions needed. The test can be identified by name or by formula. For example, you could say, "I will do a one-sample t-test for a population mean," to identify the procedure in words. To identify the procedure with a formula, write the formula for the **test statistic,** which will usually have the following form:

$$\text{Test Statistic} = \frac{\text{estimator} - \text{hypothesized value}}{\text{standard error}}.$$

When doing inference for a single mean, the *estimator* is $\bar{x}$, the hypothesized value is μ_0 in the null hypothesis H_0: $\mu = \mu_0$, and the standard error is the estimate of the standard deviation of $\bar{x}$, which is

$$s_{\bar{x}} = \frac{s}{\sqrt{n}} \ (\text{df} = n - 1).$$

• Hypothesis • Estimator • Standard Error	Conditions	Test Statistic
• Null hypothesis: H_0: $\mu = \mu_0$ • Estimator: $\bar{x}$ • Standard error: $s_{\bar{x}} = \dfrac{s}{\sqrt{n}}$	• SRS • σ known • Population normal or large sample size	$z = \dfrac{\bar{x} - \mu_o}{\sigma/\sqrt{n}}$
	• SRS • Large sample *or* population approximately normal	$t = \dfrac{\bar{x} - \mu_o}{s/\sqrt{n}}$, $\text{df} = n - 1$

Note: **Paired samples** (dependent samples) are a special case of one-sample statistics (H_0: $\mu_d = 0$).

example: A study was done to determine if students who want to major in the theater arts differ in self-concept from the average for all high school students. The mean self-concept score for all high school students is known to be 100. A random sample of 49 students who state that they want to major in the theater arts is selected and their self-concept score is measured. The mean score of the students in the sample is 104.5 with a standard deviation of 14.4. Does this finding provide evidence, at the 0.05 level of significance, that the mean self-concept score of students who plan to major in the theater arts differs from the average? Since we were not given the population standard deviation, we will use t-procedures.

solution 1 (test statistic approach): The solution to this problem will be put into a form that emphasizes the format required when writing out solutions on the AP exam.

I. Let $\mu =$ the mean self-concept score of all students who plan to major in theater arts.

H_0: $\mu = 100$
H_A: $\mu \neq 100$
(The alternative is two-sided because the problem wants to know if the mean "differs" from 100. It would have been one-sided if it had asked whether the mean is higher than average.)

II. Since σ is unknown, we will use a one-sample t-test at $\alpha = 0.05$.

Conditions:

- The problem states that we have a random sample.

- Sample size n is large (greater than 40) and $490 <$ Population.

III. $t = \dfrac{104.5 - 100}{14.4 / \sqrt{49}} = 2.19 \Rightarrow P\text{-value} = 0.0336.$

IV. Because P-value $(0.0336) < \alpha$ (0.05), we reject H_0. We have convincing evidence that the mean self-concept score for all students who plan to major in theater arts differs from the mean of all high school students.

Notes on the previous solution:

- Had the alternative hypothesis been one-sided, the P-value would have been 0.0168. We end up with twice as much in step III because we needed to consider the area in *both* tails.
- The problem told us that the significance level was 0.05. Had it not mentioned a significance level, we could have chosen one, or we could have argued a conclusion based only on the derived P-value without a significance level.
- The linkage between the P-value and the significance level must be made explicit in part IV. Some sort of statement, such as "Since P-value $(0.0336) < \alpha$ (0.05) . . ." or, if no significance level is stated, "Since the P-value is small . . .," will indicate that your conclusion is based on the P-value determined in step III.

Using Confidence Intervals for Two-Sided Alternatives

Consider a two-sided significance test at, say, $\alpha = 0.05$ and a confidence interval with $C = 0.95$. A sample statistic that would result in a significant result at the 0.05 level would also generate a 95% confidence interval that does not contain the hypothesized value. Confidence intervals for two-sided hypothesis tests could then be used in place of generating a test statistic and finding a P-value. If the sample value generates a C-level confidence interval that does not contain the hypothesized value of the parameter, then a significance test based on the same sample value would reject the null hypothesis at $\alpha = 1 - C$. Questions sometimes ask for such a decision to be made based on a confidence interval. Beware, however. If a question simply asks if there is statistical evidence to support a hypothesis, the question is asking for a **test**, not an interval. You should *never* use confidence intervals for hypothesis tests involving one-sided alternative hypotheses. (One-sided confidence intervals are not a part of this course.)

solution 2 (confidence interval approach—in this case an appropriate approach but only because H_A is two-sided):

> **I.** Let $\mu =$ the true mean self-concept score of all students who plan to major in theater arts.
>
> H_0: $\mu = 100$
> H_A: $\mu \neq 100$
>
> **II.** We will use a 95% t-confidence interval ($C = 0.95$).
>
> Conditions:
>
> - The sample is random.
> - We have a large sample size ($n = 49$) and $490 <$ Population.
>
> **III.** $\bar{x} = 104.5$, $104.5 \pm t^* \left(\dfrac{14.4}{\sqrt{49}} \right) = (100.36, 108.64)$
>
> We are 95% confident that the mean self-concept score of all students who plan to major in theater arts is in the interval (100.36, 108.64).
>
> **IV.** Because 100 is not in the 95% confidence interval for μ, we reject H_0. We have strong evidence that the true mean self-concept score of all students who plan to major in theater arts differs from the mean of all high school students.

Inference for the Difference Between Two Population Means

The two-sample case for the difference in the means of two independent samples is more complicated than the one-sample case. The hypothesis testing logic is identical, however, so the contrasts are in the mechanics needed to do the problems, not in the process. For hypotheses about the differences between two means, the procedures are summarized in the following table.

• Hypothesis • Estimator • Standard Error	Conditions	Test Statistic
• Null hypothesis: $H_0: \mu_1 - \mu_2 = 0$ *OR* $H_0 : \mu_1 = \mu_2$ • Estimator: $\bar{x}_1 - \bar{x}_2$	• σ_1^2 and σ_2^2 known– Use z-procedures but if unknown use t-procedures • $10n_1 <$ Population 1 • $10n_2 <$ Population 2	$z = \dfrac{\bar{x}_1 - \bar{x}_2}{\sqrt{\dfrac{\sigma_1^2}{n_1} + \dfrac{\sigma_2^2}{n_2}}}$ (rarely used since σ_1^2 and σ_2^2 are rarely known)
• Standard error: $s_{\bar{x}_1 - \bar{x}_2} = \sqrt{\dfrac{s_1^2}{n_1} + \dfrac{s_2^2}{n_2}}$	• Two independent random samples from approximately normal populations *or* large sample sizes ($n_1 \geq 30$ and $n_2 \geq 30$)	$t = \dfrac{\bar{x}_1 - \bar{x}_2}{\sqrt{\dfrac{s_1^2}{n_1} + \dfrac{s_2^2}{n_2}}}$ $df =$ (the often non-integer value given by your calculator) or $df = \min\{ n_1 - 1, n_2 - 1\}$

Note on the above table:

- The "non-integer value" is based on the formula given in Chapter 10.

example: A statistics teacher, Mr. Gosset, gave a quiz to his 8:00 a.m. class and to his 9:00 a.m. class. There were 50 points possible on the quiz. The data for the two classes are in this table:

	n	$\bar{x}$	s
Group 1 (8:00 a.m.)	34	40.2	9.57
Group 2 (9:00 a.m.)	31	44.9	4.86

Before the quiz, some members of the 9:00 a.m. class had been bragging that later classes do better in statistics. Considering these two classes as random samples from the populations of 8:00 a.m. and 9:00 a.m. classes, do these data provide evidence at the 0.01 level of significance that students in 9:00 a.m. classes do better than those in 8:00 a.m. classes?

solution:

> **I.** Let μ_1 = the true mean score for 8:00 a.m. classes.
> Let μ_2 = the true mean score for 9:00 a.m. classes.
> H_0: $\mu_1 - \mu_2 = 0$
> H_A: $\mu_1 - \mu_2 < 0$
>
> **II.** We will use a *two-sample* t-test at $\alpha = 0.01$. We assume these samples are random samples from independent populations. t-procedures are justified because both sample sizes are larger than 30 and 10 times each sample size is less than the population sizes.
>
> (*Note:* If the sample sizes were not large enough, we would need reasonable evidence that the samples were drawn from populations that are approximately normally distributed. To that end, we would examine graphs of the sample data.)
>
> **III.** Using the test menu of our calculator we activate the command for a `2-Sample t Test`: $t = -2.53$, df $= 49.92$, and P-value $= 0.007$.
>
> **IV.** Because P-value $(0.007) < \alpha$ (0.01), we reject the null hypothesis. We have convincing evidence that the true mean for 9:00 a.m. classes is higher than the true mean for 8:00 a.m. classes.

Watch Out for Matched Pairs!

There are problems that appear to need the two-sample procedures as described in the example above. However, the samples are not drawn from independent populations—the data are paired in some way. When you have paired data you should run a one-sample hypothesis test on the *differences*!

> **example:** A company president believes that there are more absences on Monday than on other days of the week. The company has 45 workers. The following table gives the number of worker absences on Mondays and Wednesdays for a random sample of eight weeks from the past two years. Do the data provide evidence that there are more absences on Mondays?

	Week 1	Week 2	Week 3	Week 4	Week 5	Week 6	Week 7	Week 8
Monday	5	9	2	3	2	6	4	1
Wednesday	2	5	4	0	3	1	2	0

> **solution:** Because the data are paired on a weekly basis, the data we use for this problem are the *differences* between the days of the week for each of the eight weeks. Adding a row to the table that gives the differences (absences on Monday minus absences on Wednesday), we have

	Week 1	Week 2	Week 3	Week 4	Week 5	Week 6	Week 7	Week 8
Monday	5	9	2	3	2	6	4	1
Wednesday	2	5	4	0	3	1	2	1
Difference	3	4	−2	3	−1	5	2	0

I. Let μ_d = the true mean difference between number of absences on Monday and absences on Wednesday where d = Mon − Wed:

H_0: $\mu_d = 0$ (or H_0: $\mu_d \le 0$)
H_A: $\mu_d > 0$

II. We will use a one-sample t-test for the difference scores.

Conditions:

A dotplot of the data shows no outliers or severe skewness. Also, we are told that the eight weeks are randomly selected and 80 < Population of all weeks.

III. Using the t Test function on calculator, we find that $t = 1.99$ with $df = 7$ and P-value = 0.044.

IV. The P-value is small. This provides us with convincing evidence that, on average over the past two years, there have been more absences on Mondays than on Wednesdays.

Calculator Tip: The TI-83/84 and other brands can do each of the significance tests described in this chapter, as well as those in Chapters 12 and 13. Graphing calculators will also do all of the confidence intervals we considered in Chapter 10. On the TI-83/84 you get to the tests by entering STAT TESTS. Note that Z-Test and T-Test are what are often referred to as "one-sample tests." The two-sample tests are identified as 2-SampZTest and 2-SampTTest. Most of the tests will give you a choice between Data and Stats. Data means that you have your data in a list, and Stats means that you have the summary statistics of your data. Once you find the test you want, just follow the calculator prompts and enter the values requested.

〉 Rapid Review

1. A researcher reports that a finding of $x = 3.1$ is significant at the 0.05 level of significance. What is the meaning of this statement?

   Answer: Under the assumption that the null hypothesis is true, the probability of getting a value at least as extreme as the one obtained is less than 0.05. It was unlikely to have occurred by chance.

2. Let μ_1 = the mean score on a test of agility using a new training method and let μ_2 = the mean score on the test using the traditional method. Consider a test of H_0: $\mu_1 - \mu_2 = 0$. A large sample significance test finds $P = 0.04$. What conclusion, in the context of the problem, do you report if

   (a) $\alpha = 0.05$?

   (b) $\alpha = 0.01$?

Answer:

(a) Because the *P*-value is less than 0.05, we reject the null hypothesis at the 5% significance level. We have evidence that there is a nonzero difference between the traditional and new training methods.

(b) Because the *P*-value is greater than 0.01, we do not have sufficient evidence to reject the null hypothesis at the 1% significance level. We do not have strong support for the hypothesis that the training methods differ in effectiveness.

3. True–False: In a hypothesis test concerning a single mean, we can use either *z*-procedures or *t*-procedures as long as the sample size is at least 20.

   Answer: False. With a sample size of only 20, we cannot use *z*-procedures unless we know that the population from which the sample was drawn is approximately normal *and* σ is known. We can use *t*-procedures if the data do not have outliers or severe skewness, that is, if it is reasonable to believe based on a graph of the data that the population from which the sample was drawn is approximately normal.

4. We are going to conduct a two-sided significance test for a population proportion. The null hypothesis is H_0: $p = 0.3$. The simple random sample of 225 subjects yields $\hat{p} = 0.35$. What is the standard error, $s_{\hat{p}}$, involved in this procedure if

   (a) you are constructing a confidence interval for the true population proportion?

   (b) you are doing a significance test for the null hypothesis?

   Answer:

   (a) For a confidence interval, you use the value of $\hat{p}$ in the standard error.

   Hence, $s_{\hat{p}} = \sqrt{\dfrac{(0.35)(1-0.35)}{225}} = 0.0318.$

   (b) For a significance test, you use the hypothesized value of *p*. Hence,

   $$s_{\hat{p}} = \sqrt{\dfrac{(0.3)(1-0.3)}{225}} = 0.03055.$$

5. For the following data,

   (a) assuming treatments were randomly assigned, justify the use of a two-proportion *z*-test for H_0: $p_1 - p_2 = 0$.

   (b) what is the value of the test statistic for H_0: $p_1 - p_2 = 0$?

   (c) what is the *P*-value of the test statistic for the two-sided alternative?

	n	*x*	$\hat{p}$
Group 1	40	12	0.3
Group 2	35	14	0.4

   Answer:

   (a) $\hat{p} = \dfrac{12+14}{40+35} = 0.35$

$$n_1 \hat{p} = 40 \cdot 0.35 = 14, \quad n_1(1-\hat{p}) = 40 \cdot 0.65 = 26$$

$$n_2 \hat{p} = 35 \cdot 0.35 = 12.25, \quad n_2(1-\hat{p}) = 35 \cdot 0.65 = 22.75 \text{ are all greater than 5.}$$

Since all values are at least 5, the conditions are present for a two-proportion z-test.

(b) $z = \dfrac{0.3 - 0.4}{\sqrt{0.35(1-0.35)\left(\dfrac{1}{40} + \dfrac{1}{35}\right)}} = -0.91.$

(c) $z = -0.91$, P-value $= 2(0.18) = 0.36$ (from Table A). But of course, you ought to just use your calculator to get these values. On the TI-83/84, you would simply activate the 2-proportion z-test, then list the z- and P-values.

6. You want to conduct a one-sample test (t-test) for a population mean. Your random sample size of 10 yields the following data: 26, 27, 34, 29, 38, 30, 28, 30, 30, 23. Should you proceed with your test? Explain.

Answer: A boxplot of the data shows that the 38 is an outlier. Furthermore, the dotplot of the data casts doubt on the approximate normality of the population from which this sample was drawn. Hence, you should *not* use a t-test on these data.

7. A randomized experiment was conducted to see if adding compost to a potted plant will help the plant to grow taller. Unknown to the researchers, this compost actually does improve the height of plants. But in their experiment, they got a P-value of 0.15 and, thus, failed to reject their null hypothesis. They concluded there was not convincing evidence that the compost helped. What type of error did they make?

Answer: The null hypothesis is false but the researchers failed to reject it. That is a Type II error.

8. Mary comes running into your office and excitedly tells you that she got a statistically significant finding from the data on her most recent research project. What is she talking about?

Answer: Mary means that the finding she got had such a small probability of occurring by chance that she has concluded it probably wasn't just chance variation but a real difference from expected.

9. Which of the following statements is correct?

I. The t distribution has more area in its tails than the z distribution (normal).

II. When constructing a confidence interval for a population mean, you would always use z^* rather than t^* if you have a sample size of at least 30 ($n > 30$).

III. When constructing a two-sample t interval, the "conservative" method of choosing degrees of freedom ($df = $ min $\{n_1 - 1, n_2 - 1\}$) will result in a wider confidence interval than other methods.

Answer:

- I is correct. A t distribution, because it must estimate the population standard deviation, has more variability than the normal distribution.

- II is not correct. It is definitely not correct that you would always use z^* rather than t^* in this situation. A more interesting question is, *Could* you use z^* rather than t^*? The answer to that question is a qualified "yes." The difference between z^* and t^* is small for large sample sizes (e.g., for a 95% confidence interval based on a sample size of 50, $z^* = 1.96$ and $t^* = 2.01$), and while a t interval would have a somewhat larger margin of error, the intervals constructed would capture roughly the same range of values. In fact, many traditional statistics books teach this as the proper method. Now, having said that, the best advice is to *always* use t when dealing with a one-sample situation when s is unknown (confidence interval or hypothesis test), and use z only when you know, or have a very good estimate of, the population standard deviation.

- III is correct. The conservative method ($df = \min\{n_1 - 1, n_2 - 1\}$) will give a larger value of t^*, which, in turn, will create a larger margin of error, which will result in a wider confidence interval than other methods for a given confidence level.

Practice Problems

Multiple-Choice

1. Which of the following will increase the power of a test?
   a. Increase n.
   b. Increase a.
   c. Reduce the amount of variability in the sample.
   d. Consider an alternative hypothesis further from the null.
   e. All of these will increase the power of a test.

2. Under a null hypothesis, a sample value yields a P-value of 0.015. Which of the following statements is (are) true?
   I. This finding is statistically significant at the 0.05 level of significance.
   II. This finding is statistically significant at the 0.01 level of significance.
   III. The probability of getting a sample value as extreme as this one by chance alone if the null hypothesis is true is 0.015.

   a. I and III only
   b. I only
   c. III only
   d. II and III only
   e. I, II, and III

3. In a test of the null hypothesis $H_0: p = 0.35$ with $a = 0.01$, against the alternative hypothesis $H_A: p < 0.35$, a large random sample produced a z-score of -2.05. Based on this, which of the following conclusions can be drawn?
   a. It is likely that $p < 0.35$.
   b. $p < 0.35$ only 2% of the time.
   c. If the z-score were positive instead of negative, we would be able to reject the null hypothesis.
   d. We do not have sufficient evidence to claim that $p < 0.35$.
   e. 1% of the time we will reject the alternative hypothesis in error.

4. A paint manufacturer advertises that one gallon of its paint will cover 400 square feet of interior wall. Some local painters suspect the average coverage is considerably less and decide to conduct an experiment to find out. If μ represents the true average number of square feet covered by the paint, which of the following are the correct null and alternative hypotheses to be tested?

   a. H_0: $\mu = 400$, H_A: $\mu > 400$
   b. H_0: $\mu \geq 400$, H_A: $\mu \neq 400$
   c. H_0: $\mu = 400$, H_A: $\mu \neq 400$
   d. H_0: $\mu \neq 400$, H_A: $\mu < 400$
   e. H_0: $\mu \geq 400$, H_A: $\mu < 400$

5. A school district claims that the average teacher in the district earns $48,000 per year. The teachers' organization argues that the average salary is less. A random sample of 25 teachers yields a mean salary of $47,500 with a sample standard deviation of $2,000. Assuming that the distribution of all teachers' salaries is approximately normally distributed, what is the value of the t-test statistic and the P-value for a test of the hypothesis H_0: $\mu = 48,000$ against H_A: $\mu < 48,000$? (Remember, $df = 25 - 1 = 24$.)

   a. $t = 1.25$, $0.10 < P < 0.15$
   b. $t = -1.25$, $0.20 < P < 0.30$
   c. $t = 1.25$, $0.20 < P < 0.30$
   d. $t = -1.25$, $0.10 < P < 0.15$
   e. $t = -1.25$, $P > 0.25$

6. Which of the following conditions is (are) necessary to justify the use of z-procedures in a significance test about a population proportion?
   I. The samples must be drawn from a normal population.
   II. The population must be much larger (10–20 times) than the sample.
   III. $np_0 \geq 5$ and $n(1 - p_0) \geq 5$.

   a. I only
   b. I and II only
   c. II and III only
   d. III only
   e. I, II, and III

7. A minister claims that more than 70% of the adult population attends a religious service at least once a month. Let $p =$ the proportion of adults who attend church. The null and alternative hypotheses you would use to test this claim would be

   a. H_0: $p \leq 0.7$, H_A: $p > 0.7$
   b. H_0: $m \leq 0.7$, H_A: $m > 0.7$
   c. H_0: $p = 0.7$, H_A: $p \neq 0.7$
   d. H_0: $p \leq 0.7$, H_A: $p < 0.7$
   e. H_0: $p \geq 0.7$, H_A: $p < 0.7$

8. When is it OK to use a confidence interval instead of computing a P-value in a hypothesis test?

   a. In any significance test
   b. In any hypothesis test with a two-sided alternative hypothesis
   c. Only when the hypothesized value of the parameter is *not* in the confidence interval
   d. Only when you are conducting a hypothesis test with a one-sided alternative
   e. Only when doing a test for a single population mean or a single population proportion

9. Which of the following is *not* a required step for a significance test?

   a. State null and alternative hypotheses in the context of the problem.
   b. Identify the test to be used and justify the conditions for using it.
   c. State the significance level for which you will decide to reject the null hypothesis.
   d. Compute the value of the test statistic and the *P*-value.
   e. State a correct conclusion in the context of the problem.

10. Which of the following best describes what we mean when we say that *t*-procedures are *robust*?

    a. The *t*-procedures work well with almost any distribution.
    b. The numerical value of *t* is not affected by outliers.
    c. The *t*-procedures will still work reasonably well even if the assumption of normality is violated.
    d. *t*-procedures can be used as long as the sample size is at least 40.
    e. *t*-procedures are as accurate as *z*-procedures.

11. For a hypothesis test of $H_0: \mu = \mu_0$ against the alternative $H_A: \mu < \mu_0$, the *z*-test statistic is found to be 2.00. This finding is

    a. significant at the 0.05 level but not at the 0.01 level.
    b. significant at the 0.01 level but not at the 0.05 level.
    c. significant at both the 0.01 and the 0.05 levels.
    d. significant at neither the 0.01 nor the 0.05 levels.
    e. not large enough to be considered significant.

12. Two types of tennis balls were tested to determine which one goes faster on a serve. Eight different players served one of each type of ball and the results were recorded:

SERVER	TYPE A	TYPE B
Raphael	120	115
Roger	125	122
Serena	119	114
Venus	110	114
Andy	118	115
Maria	82	91
Lleyton	115	110
Ana	105	106

Assuming that the speeds are approximately normally distributed, how many degrees of freedom will there be in the appropriate *t*-test used to determine which type of tennis ball travels faster?

a. 6
b. 7
c. 16
d. 15
e. 14

13. Two statistics teachers want to compare their teaching methods. They decide to give the same final exam and use the scores on the exam as a basis for comparison. They decide that the value of interest to them will be the proportion of students in each class who score above 80% on the final. One class has 32 students, and one has 27 students. Which of the following would be the most appropriate test for this situation?

   a. Two proportion z-test
   b. Two-sample t-test
   c. Chi-square goodness-of-fit test
   d. One-sample z-test
   e. Chi-square test for independence

Free-Response

1. A university is worried that it might not have sufficient housing for its students for the next academic year. It's very expensive to build additional housing, so it is operating under the assumption (hypothesis) that the housing it has is sufficient, and it will spend the money to build additional housing only if it is convinced it is necessary (that is, it rejects its hypothesis).
   (a) For the university's assumption, what is the risk involved in making a Type I error?
   (b) For the university's assumption, what is the risk involved in making a Type II error?

2. A large high school has been waging a campaign against smoking. Before the campaign began in 2004, a random sample of 100 students from the junior and senior classes found 27 who admitted to smoking (we understand that some students who do so would be reluctant to admit it on a survey). To assess the success of their program, in early 2007 the administration surveyed a random sample of 175 juniors and seniors, and 30 responded that they smoked. Is this good evidence that the use of cigarettes has been reduced at the school?

3. Twenty-six pairs of identical twins are enrolled in a study to determine the impact of training on ability to memorize a string of letters. Two programs (A and B) are being studied. One member of each pair is randomly assigned to one of the two groups and the other twin goes into the other group. Each group undergoes the appropriate training program, and then the scores for pairs of twins are compared. The means and standard deviations for groups A and B are determined as well as the mean and standard deviation for the difference between each twin's score. Is this study a *one-sample* or *two-sample* situation, and how many degrees of freedom are involved in determining the t-value?

4. Which of the following statements is (are) correct? Explain.
   I. A confidence interval can be used instead of a test statistic in any hypothesis test involving means or proportions.
   II. A confidence interval can be used instead of a test statistic in a two-sided hypothesis test involving means or proportions.
   III. The standard error for constructing a confidence interval for a population proportion and the standard error for a significance test for a population proportion are the same.
   IV. The standard error for constructing a confidence interval for a population mean and the standard error for a significance test for a population mean are the same.

5. The average math SAT score at Centennial High School over the years is 520. The mathematics faculty believes that this year's class of seniors is the best the school has ever had in mathematics. One hundred seventy-five seniors take the exam and achieve an average score of 531 with a sample standard deviation of 96. Does this performance provide good statistical evidence that this year's class is, in fact, superior?

6. An avid reader, Booker Worm, claims that he reads books that average more than 375 pages in length. A random sample of 13 books on his shelf had the following number of pages: 595, 353, 434, 382, 420, 225, 408, 422, 315, 502, 503, 384, 420. Do the data support Booker's claim? Test at the 0.05 level of significance.

7. The statistics teacher, Dr. Tukey, gave a 50-point quiz to his class of 10 students, and they didn't do very well, at least by Dr. Tukey's standards (which are quite high). Rather than continuing to the next chapter, he spent some time reviewing the material and then gave another quiz. The quizzes were comparable in length and difficulty. The results of the two quizzes were as follows.

Student	1	2	3	4	5	6	7	8	9	10
Quiz 1	42	38	34	37	36	26	44	32	38	31
Quiz 2	45	40	36	38	34	28	44	35	42	30

Do the data indicate that the review was successful, at the 0.05 level, at improving the performance of the students on this material? Give statistical evidence for your conclusion.

8. The new reality TV show *I Want to Marry a Statistician* has been showing on Monday evenings, and ratings show that it has been watched by 55% of the viewing audience each week. The producers are moving the show to Wednesday night but are concerned that such a move might reduce the percentage of the viewing public watching the show. After the show has been moved, a random sample of 500 people who are watching television on Wednesday night is surveyed and asked what show they are watching. Two hundred fifty-five respond that they are watching *I Want to Marry a Statistician*. Does this finding provide evidence at the 0.01 level of significance that the percentage of the viewing public watching *I Want to Marry a Statistician* has declined?

9. Harvey is running for student body president. A survey is conducted by the AP Statistics class in an attempt to predict the outcome of the election. They randomly sample 30 students, 16 of whom say they plan to vote for Harvey. Harvey figures (correctly) that 53.3% of students in the sample intend to vote for him and is overjoyed at his soon-to-be-celebrated victory. Explain carefully why Harvey should not get too excited until the votes are counted.

10. A company uses two different models, call them model A and model B, of a machine to produce electronic locks for hotels. The company has several hundred of each machine in use in its various factories. The machines are not perfect, and the company would like to phase out of service the one that produces more defects in the locks. A random sample of 13 model A machines and 11 model B machines is tested, and the data for the average number of defects per week are given in the following table.

	n	$\bar{x}$	s
Model A	13	11.5	2.3
Model B	11	13.1	2.9

Dotplots of the data indicate that there are no outliers or strong skewness in the data and that there are no strong departures from normal. Do these data provide statistically convincing evidence that the two machines differ in terms of the number of defects produced?

11. Take another look at the preceding problem. Suppose there were 30 of each model machine that were sampled. Assuming that the sample means and standard deviations are the same as given in problem 9, how might this have affected the hypothesis test you performed in that problem?

12. The directors of a large metropolitan airport claim that security procedures are 98% accurate in detecting banned metal objects that passengers may try to carry onto a plane. The local agency charged with enforcing security thinks the security procedures are not as good as claimed. A study of 250 passengers showed that screeners missed nine banned carry-on items. What is the *P*-value for this test, and what conclusion would you draw based on it?

13. A random sample of 175 married couples is selected to see if women have a stronger reaction than men to videos that contain violent material. At the conclusion of the study, each couple is given a questionnaire designed to measure the intensity of their reaction. Higher values indicate a stronger reaction. The means and standard deviations for all men, all women, and the differences between husbands and wives are as follows:

	$\bar{x}$	s
Men	8.56	1.42
Women	8.97	1.84
Difference (Husband–Wife)	−0.38	1.77

Do the data give strong statistical evidence that wives have a stronger reaction to violence in videos than do their husbands?

14. An election is bitterly contested between two rivals. In a poll of 750 potential voters taken 4 weeks before the election, 420 indicated a preference for candidate Grumpy over candidate Dopey. Two weeks later, a new poll of 900 randomly selected potential voters found 465 who plan to vote for Grumpy. Dopey immediately began advertising that support for Grumpy was slipping dramatically and that he was going to win the election. Statistically speaking (say at the 0.05 level), how happy should Dopey be (i.e., how sure is he that support for Grumpy has dropped)?

15. Consider, once again, the situation of problem 8. In that problem, a one-sided, two-proportion z-test was conducted to determine if there had been a drop in the proportion of people who watch the show *I Want to Marry a Statistician* when it was moved from Monday to Wednesday evenings.

Suppose instead that the producers were interested in whether the popularity ratings for the show had changed in *any* direction since the move. Over the seasons the show had been broadcast on Mondays, the popularity rating for the show (10 high, 1 low) had averaged 7.3. After moving the show to the new time, ratings were taken for 12 consecutive weeks. The average rating was determined to be 6.1 with a sample standard deviation of 2.7. Does this provide evidence, at the 0.05 level of significance, that the ratings for the show have changed? Use a confidence interval, rather than a *t*-test, as part of your argument. A dotplot of the data indicates that the ratings are approximately normally distributed.

Cumulative Review Problems

1. How large a sample is needed to estimate a population proportion within 2.5% at the 99% level of confidence if
   a. you have no reasonable estimate of the population proportion?
   b. you have data that show the population proportion should be about 0.7?

2. Let X be a binomial random variable with $n = 250$ and $p \doteq 0.6$. Use a normal approximation to the binomial to approximate $P(X > 160)$.

3. Write the mathematical expression you would use to evaluate $P(X > 2)$ for a binomial random variable X that has $B(5, 0.3)$ (that is, X is a binomial random variable equal to the number of successes out of 5 trials of an event that occurs with probability of success $p = 0.3$). Do not evaluate.

4. An individual is picked at random from a group of 55 company employees. Thirty of the employees are on-site, and 25 are remote workers. Six of the on-site workers are administrators. Given that the individual picked is on-site, what is the probability the worker is an administrator?

5. A random sample of 25 cigarettes of a certain brand were tested for nicotine content, and the mean was found to be 1.85 mg with a standard deviation of 0.75 mg. Find a 90% confidence interval for the mean number of mg of nicotine in this type of cigarette. Assume that the amount of nicotine in cigarettes is approximately normally distributed. Interpret the interval in the context of the problem.

Solutions to Practice Problems

Multiple-Choice

1. The correct answer is (e).

2. The correct answer is (a). It is not significant at the 0.01 level because 0.015 is greater than 0.01.

3. The correct answer is (d). To reject the null at the 0.01 level of significance, we would need to have $z < -2.33$.

4. The correct answer is (e). Because we are concerned that the actual amount of coverage might be less than 400 square feet, the only options for the alternative hypothesis are (d) and (e) (the alternative hypothesis in (a) is in the wrong direction, and the alternatives in (b) and (c) are two-sided). The null hypothesis given in (d) is not a form we would use for a null (the only choices are $=$, $\leq$, or $\geq$). We might see $H_0 : \mu = 400$ rather than $H_0 : \mu \geq 400$. Both are correct statements of a null hypothesis against the alternative $H_A : \mu < 400$.

5. The correct answer is (d).

$$t = \frac{47500 - 48000}{2000 / \sqrt{25}} = -1.25 \Rightarrow 0.10 < P < 0.15$$

for the one-sided alternative. The calculator answer is $P = 0.112$. Had the alternative been two-sided, the correct answer would have been (b).

6. The correct answer is (c). If the sample size conditions are met, it is not necessary that the samples be drawn from a normal population.

7. The correct answer is (a). Often you will see the null written as $H_0: p = 0.7$ rather than $H_0: p \le 0.7$. Either is correct.

8. The correct answer is (b). In AP Statistics, we consider confidence intervals to be two-sided. A two-sided α-level significance test will reject the null hypothesis whenever the hypothesized value of the parameter is not contained in the $C = 1 - \alpha$ level confidence interval.

9. (c) is not one of the required steps. You can state a significance level that you will later compare to the P-value, but it is not required. You can simply argue the strength of the evidence against the null hypothesis based on the P-value alone—small values of P provide evidence against the null.

10. (c) is the most correct response. (a) is incorrect because t-procedures do not work well with, for example, small samples that come from nonnormal populations. (b) is false because the numerical value of t is, like z, affected by outliers. t-procedures are generally OK to use for samples of size 40 or larger, but this is not what is meant by *robust*, so (d) is incorrect. (e) is not correct since the t-distribution is more variable than the standard normal. It becomes closer to z as sample size increases but is "as accurate" only in the limiting case.

11. The correct answer is (d). The alternative hypothesis, $H_0: \mu = \mu_0$, would require a negative value of z to be evidence against the null. Because the given value is positive, we conclude that the finding is in the wrong direction to support the alternative and, hence, is not going to be significant at *any* level.

12. The correct answer is (b). Because the data are paired, the appropriate t-test is a one-sample test for the mean of the difference in scores. In this case, $df = n - 1 = 8 - 1 = 7$.

13. The correct answer is (a). The problem states that the teachers will record for comparison the number of students in each class who score above 80%. Because the enrollments differ in the two classes, we need to compare the proportion of students who score above 80% in each class. Thus the appropriate test is a two-proportion z-test. Note that, although it is not one of the choices, a chi-square test for homogeneity of proportions could also be used, since we are interested in whether the proportions of those getting above 80% are the same across the two populations.

Free-Response

1. (a) A Type I error is made when we mistakenly reject a true null hypothesis. In this situation, that means that we would mistakenly reject the true hypothesis that the available housing is sufficient. The risk would be that a lot of money would be spent on building additional housing when it wasn't necessary.

(b) A Type II error is made when we mistakenly fail to reject a false hypothesis. In this situation, that means we would fail to reject the false hypothesis that the available housing is sufficient. The risk is that the university would have insufficient housing for its students.

2.

I. Let p_1 = the true proportion of students who admit to smoking in 2004.

Let p_2 = the true proportion of students who admit to smoking in 2007.

H_0: $p_1 = p_2$ (or H_0: $p_1 - p_2 = 0$; or H_0: $p_1 \leq p_2$; or H_0: $p_1 - p_2 > 0$).
H_A: $p_1 > p_2$ (or H_0: $p_1 > p_2$).

II. We will use a two-proportion z-test. The survey involved drawing random samples from independent populations with $1000 < \text{Pop}_1$ and $1750 < \text{Pop}_2$.

$$\hat{p} = \frac{27 + 30}{100 + 175} \approx 0.21$$

$n_1 \hat{p} = 100 \cdot 0.21 = 21$, $n_1(1 - \hat{p}) = 100 \cdot 0.79 = 79$

$n_2 \hat{p} = 175 \cdot 0.21 = 36.75$, $n_2(1 - \hat{p}) = 175 \cdot 0.79 = 138.25$, are all greater than 5 (or 10), so conditions are met for a two-proportion z-test.

III. Using the 2-prop z-test from the test menu on your calculator we find that $z = 1.949$ and the P-value $= 0.026$.

IV. Since the P-value is small (a difference in sample proportions this extreme would occur only about 2.6% of the time if there had been no decrease in usage), we have evidence that the rate of smoking among students (at least among juniors and seniors) has decreased.

---

3. This is a paired study because the scores for each pair of twins are compared. Hence, it is a one-sample situation, and there are 26 pieces of data to be analyzed, which are the 26 difference scores between the twins. Hence, $df = 26 - 1 = 25$.

4. • I is not correct. A confidence interval, at least in AP Statistics, cannot be used in any one-sided hypothesis test—only two-sided tests.

   • II is correct. A confidence interval constructed from a random sample that does not contain the hypothesized value of the parameter can be considered statistically significant evidence against the null hypothesis.

   • III is not correct. The standard error for a confidence interval based on the sample proportions is

$$s_{\hat{p}} = \sqrt{\frac{\hat{p}(1 - \hat{p})}{n}}.$$

   The standard error for a significance test based on the hypothesized population value is

$$s_{\hat{p}} = \sqrt{\frac{p_0(1 - p_0)}{n}}.$$

   • IV is correct.

5.

I. Let μ = the true mean score for all students taking the exam.

H_0: $\mu = 520$ (or, H_0: $\mu \leq 520$)
H_A: $\mu > 520$

II. We will use a one-sample t-test. We consider the 175 students to be a random sample of students taking the exam. The sample size is larger than 40, so the conditions for inference are present. (*Note:* Due to the very large sample size, it is reasonable that the sample standard deviation is a good estimate of the population standard deviation. This means that you would receive credit on the AP exam for doing this problem as a z-test, although a t-test is preferable. But you must explicitly appeal to the very large sample size if you use a z-test.) 1750 < population size.

III. Using the one-sample t-test from the test menu on your calculator, we find that with $\bar{x} = 531$ and $s_x = 96$, $t = 152$, $df = 174$, and P-value = 0.0657.

IV. The P-value, which is greater than 0.05, is not small enough to provide convincing evidence that the current class is superior in math ability as measured by the SAT.

6.

I. Let μ = the true average number of pages in the books Booker reads.

H_0: $\mu \leq 375$
H_A: $\mu > 375$

II. We will use a one-sample t-test test at $\alpha = 0.05$. The problem states that the sample is a random sample. A dotplot of the data shows good symmetry and no outliers. In addition, 130 < population of all books.

The conditions for the t-test are present.

III. Using the one-sample t-test from the test menu on your calculator we find that with $\bar{x} = 412.5$ and $s_x = 91.35$, $t = 1.48$, $df = 12$, and P-value = 0.082.

IV. Because $P > 0.05$, we cannot reject H_0. We do not have convincing evidence to back up Booker's claim that the books he reads actually average more than 375 pages in length.

7. The data are paired by individual students, so we need to test the difference scores for the students rather than the means for each quiz. The differences are given in the following table.

Student	1	2	3	4	5	6	7	8	9	10
Quiz 1	42	38	34	37	36	26	44	32	38	31
Quiz 2	45	40	36	38	34	28	44	35	42	30
Difference (Q2 – Q1)	3	2	2	1	−2	2	0	3	4	−1

> **I.** Let μ_d = the mean of the differences between the scores of students on Quiz 2 and Quiz 1.
>
> H_0: $\mu_d = 0$
> H_A: $\mu_d > 0$
>
> **II.** This is a matched pairs t-test. That is, it is a one-sample t-test for a population mean. We assume that this is a random sample of all students who took both quizzes and that $100 <$ than population size.
>
>
>
> A dotplot of the differences in scores shows outliers or skewness so the conditions to use the one-sample t-test have been met.
>
> **III.** Using the one-sample t-test from the test menu on your calculator we find that with $\bar{x}_d = 1.4$ and $s_d = 1.9$, $t = 2.33$, $df = 9$, and P-value = 0.022.
>
> **IV.** Because $P < 0.05$, we reject the null hypothesis. The data provide convincing evidence at the 0.05 level that the review was successful at improving student performance on the material.

8.

> **I.** Let p = the true proportion of Wednesday night television viewers who are watching *I Want to Marry a Statistician*.
>
> H_0: $p = 0.55$
> H_A: $p < 0.55$
>
> **II.** We want to use a one-proportion z-test at $\alpha = 0.01$. $500(0.55) = 275 > 5$ and $500(1 - 0.55) = 225 > 5$. Also, $5000 <$ population size. Thus, the conditions needed for this test have been met.
>
> **III.** Using the one-sample z-test for proportions from the test menu on your calculator (STAT TESTS 1-PropZTest) with $\hat{p} = 255/500 \Rightarrow x = 255$, $n = 500$ the calculator shows $z = -1.80$ and P-value = 0.036.
>
> **IV.** Because $P > 0.01$, we do not have sufficient evidence to reject the null hypothesis. The evidence is not convincing evidence to conclude at the 0.01 level that the proportion of viewers has dropped since the program was moved to a different night.

9. Let's suppose that the Stats class constructed a 95% confidence interval for the true proportion of students who plan to vote for Harvey (we are assuming that this a random sample from the population of interest, and we note that both $n\hat{p}$ and $n(1 - \hat{p})$ are greater than 10). $\hat{p} = \dfrac{16}{30} = 0.533$ (as Harvey figured). Then a 95% confidence interval for the true proportion of votes Harvey can expect to get is $0.533 \pm 1.96\sqrt{\dfrac{(0.533)(1-0.533)}{30}} = (0.355, 0.712)$. That is, we are 95% confident that between 35.5% and 71.2% of students plan to vote for Harvey. It is certainly possible

for him to have a majority, but there are plausible values for the true proportion that are less than a majority as well. Harvey shouldn't get too complacent! (The argument is similar with a 90% CI: (0.384, 0.683) or with a 99% CI: (0.299, 0.768).)

10.

> **I.** Let μ_1 = the true mean number of defects produced by machine A.
> Let μ_2 = the true mean number of defects produced by machine B.
>
> $H_0: \mu_1 - \mu_2 = 0$
> $H_A: \mu_1 - \mu_2 \neq 0$
>
> **II.** We use a two-sample t-test for the difference between means. These conditions are given in the problem: both samples are simple random samples from independent, approximately normal populations. Additionally, 130 and 110 are both < population sizes.
>
> **III.** Using the two-sample t-test (2SampTTest) from the test menu on your calculator, we find that with $\bar{x}_1 = 11.5$, $s_1 = 2.3$, $n_1 = 13$ $\bar{x}_2 = 13.1$, $s_2 = 2.9$, $n_2 = 11$, $t = -1.478$, $df = 18.99$, and P-value $= 0.1557$.
>
> **IV.** The P-value is too large to reject the null. We do not have convincing evidence that the types of machines actually differ in the number of defects produced.

11. Using a two-sample t-test and increasing the sample sizes to 30 each, steps I and II would not change. Step III would change to

$$t = -2.37, df = 55.14 \Rightarrow P\text{-}value = 0.0214.$$

In step IV, a student could argue that we could reject the null because the P-value is small. This is an example of how larger sample sizes make it easier to detect statistically significant differences.

12. $H_0: p \geq 0.98$, $H_A: p < 0.98$, $\hat{p} = \dfrac{241}{250} = 0.964$.

$$z = \frac{0.964 - 0.98}{\sqrt{\dfrac{(0.98)(0.02)}{250}}} = -1.81, \ P\text{-value} = 0.035.$$

This P-value is lower than an alpha level of 0.05. This provides evidence against the null and in favor of the alternative that security procedures actually detect less than the claimed percentage of banned objects. (However, a different student could argue that this P-value is higher than an alpha level of 0.01 and therefore does NOT provide convincing evidence that the security procedures detect less than 98% of all banned objects.)

13.

> **I.** Let $\mu_d =$ the mean of the differences between the scores of husbands and wives.
>
> H_0: $\mu_d = 0$
> H_A: $\mu_d < 0$
>
> **II.** This is a matched-pairs situation, and we will use a one-sample t-test for a population mean. We are told that this is a random sample of married couples. Because $n = 175 > 30$, t procedures are appropriate.
>
> **III.** Using the one-sample t-test on your calculator, we find that with $\bar{x}_d = -0.38$ and $s_d = 1.77$, $t = -2.84$, $df = 174$, and P-value $= 0.0023$.
>
> **IV.** Because P is very small (smaller than and reasonable value of alpha), we reject H_0. The data provide convincing evidence that women have a stronger reaction to violence in videos than do men.

14.

> **I.** Let $p_1 =$ the true proportion of voters who plan to vote for Grumpy 4 weeks before the election.
>
> Let $p_2 =$ the true proportion of voters who plan to vote for Grumpy 2 weeks before the election.
>
> H_0: $p_1 - p_2 = 0$
> H_A: $p_1 - p_2 > 0$
>
> **II.** We will use a two-proportion z-test for the difference between two population proportions. Both samples are random samples of the voting populations at the time as well as less than 10% of those populations. And
>
> $$\hat{p} = \frac{420 + 425}{750 + 900} \approx 0.536$$
>
> $n_1 \hat{p} = 420 \cdot 0.536 = 225.12$, $n_1(1 - \hat{p}) = 420 \cdot 0.464 = 194.88$
>
> $n_2 \hat{p} = 900 \cdot 0.536 = 482.4$, $n_2(1 - \hat{p}) = 900 \cdot 0.464 = 417.6$
>
> All values are larger than 5, so the conditions needed for the two-proportion z-test are present.
>
> **III.** From the test menu 2-PropZTest yields $z = 1.75$ and a P-value $= 0.039$.
>
> **IV.** Because $P < 0.05$, we can reject the null hypothesis. Candidate Dopey may have cause for celebration—there is convincing evidence that support for candidate Grumpy is dropping.

15.

> **I.** Let μ = the true mean popularity rating for *I Want to Marry a Statistician*.
>
> H_0: $\mu = 7.3$
> H_A: $\mu \neq 7.3$
>
> **II.** We will use a one-sample t confidence interval (at the direction of the problem—otherwise, we would most likely have chosen to do a one-sample t significance test) at $\alpha = 0.05$, which, for the two-sided test, is equivalent to a confidence level of 0.95 ($C = 0.95$). We will assume that the ratings are a random sample of the population of all ratings. The sample size is small, but we are told that the ratings are approximately normally distributed so that the conditions necessary for the inference are present.
>
> **III.** $\bar{x} = 6.1$, $s = 2.7$. For $df = 12 - 1 = 11$ and a 95% confidence interval, $t^* = 2.201$. A 95% t confidence interval from your calculator gives (4.384, 7.816).
>
> **IV.** Since 7.3 is in the interval (4.384, 7.816) and is therefore a plausible value for μ, we cannot reject H_0 at the 0.05 level of significance. We do not have convincing evidence that there has been a significant change in the popularity rating of the show after its move to Wednesday night.
>
> (*Note:* A one-sample t-test for these data yields P-value = 0.15.)

Solutions to Cumulative Review Problems

1. a. $n \geq \left(\dfrac{2.576}{2(0.025)}\right)^2 = 2654.3$; use a sample size ≥ 2655.

    b. $n \geq (0.7)(1-0.7)\left(\dfrac{2.576}{0.025}\right)^2 = 2229.6$; use a sample size ≥ 2230.

2. $\mu_X = (250)(0.6) = 150$, $\sigma_X = \sqrt{(250)(0.6)(0.4)} = 7.75$

    Using the exact binomial given by `1-binomcdf(250,0.6,160)=0.087`, or by using the normal approximation to the binomial,

    $$P(X > 160) = P\left(z > \dfrac{160 - 150}{7.75}\right) = P(z > 1.29) = 0.099.$$

3. You can use the following calculation:

    $$\binom{5}{3}(0.3)^3(0.7)^2 + \binom{5}{4}(0.3)^4(0.7)^1 + \binom{5}{5}(0.3)^5(0.7)^0$$

4. P (the worker is an administrator | the worker is on-site)

$$= \frac{P(\text{A and OS})}{P(\text{OS})} = \frac{6/55}{30/55} = \frac{6}{30} = 0.20.$$

5. A confidence interval is justified because we are dealing with a random sample from an approximately normally distributed population. $df = 25 - 1 = 24$ with $t^* = 1.711$. Using the `Tinterval` from the test menu of our calculator we get (1.5934, 2.1066). Therefore, we are 90% confident that the true mean mg per cigarette for this type of cigarette is between 1.59 mg and 2.11 mg. (Notice the three parts are included: checked conditions, named the procedure with appropriate calculations, and interpreted the results in context.)

Inference for Regression

IN THIS CHAPTER

Summary: In the last two chapters, we've considered inference for population means and proportions and for the difference between two population means or two population proportions. In this chapter, we extend the study of linear regression begun in Chapter 6 to include inference for the slope of a regression line, including both confidence intervals and significance testing. Finally, we will look at the use of technology when doing inference for regression.

Key Ideas
- ✪ Simple Linear Regression (Review)
- ✪ Significance Test for the Slope of a Regression Line
- ✪ Confidence Interval for the Slope of a Regression Line
- ✪ Inference for Regression Using Technology

Simple Linear Regression

When we studied data analysis earlier in this text, we distinguished between *statistics* and *parameters*. Statistics are measurements or values that describe samples, and parameters are measurements that describe populations. We have also seen that statistics can be used to estimate parameters. Thus, we have used $\bar{x}$ to estimate the population mean μ, s to estimate the population standard deviation σ, and so on. In Chapter 6, we introduced the least-squares regression line ($\hat{y} = a + bx$), which was based on a set of ordered pairs. $\hat{y}$ is actually a statistic because it is based on sample data. In this chapter, we study the parameter, μ_y, which is estimated by $\hat{y}$.

Before we look at the model for linear regression, let's consider an example to remind us of what we did in Chapter 6:

example: The following data are pulse rates and heights for a group of 10 statistics students (the scatterplot of the data and a residual plot indicate that a linear model is appropriate):

Height	70	60	70	63	59	55	64	64	72	66
Pulse	78	70	65	62	63	68	76	58	73	53

a. What is the least-squares regression line for predicting pulse rate from height?
b. What is the correlation coefficient between height and pulse rate? Interpret the correlation coefficient in the context of the problem.
c. What is the predicted pulse rate of a 67″ tall student?
d. Interpret the slope of the regression line in the context of the problem.

solution:

a. $\widehat{Pulse\ rate} = 47.17 + 0.302\ (Height)$. (Done on the TI-83/84 with *Height* in L1 and *Pulse* in L2, the LSRL can be found STAT CALC LinReg(a+bx) L1,L2,Y1.)
b. $r = 0.21$. There is a weak, positive, linear relationship between Height and Pulse rate.
c. $\widehat{Pulse\ rate} = 47.17 + 0.302(67) = 67.4$. (On the Ti-83/84: Y1(67) = 67.42. Remember that you can paste Y1 to the home screen by entering VARS Y-VARS Function Y1.)
d. For a statistics student who is one inch taller than another, the pulse rate is predicted to be an additional 0.302 beats per minute.

When doing inference for regression, we use $\hat{y} = a + bx$ to estimate the true population regression line. Similar to what we have done with other statistics used for inference, we use *a* and *b* as estimators of population parameters α and β, the intercept and slope of the population regression, respectively. The conditions necessary for doing inference for regression are:

- For each given value of *x*, the values of the response variable *y*-values are independent and normally distributed.
- For each given value of *x*, the standard deviation, σ, of *y*-values is the same.
- The mean response of the *y*-values for the fixed values of *x* are linearly related by the equation $\mu_y = \alpha + \beta x$.

example: Consider a situation in which we are interested in how well a person scores on an agility test after a fixed number of 3-oz glasses of wine. Let *x* be the number of glasses consumed. Let *x* take on the values 1, 2, 3, 4, 5, and 6. Let *y* be the score on the agility test (scale: 1–100). Then for any given value x_i, there will be a distribution of *y*-values with mean μ_{y_i}. The conditions for inference for regression are that (1) each of these distributions of *y*-values is normally distributed, (2) each of these distributions of *y*-values has the same standard deviation σ, and (3) each of the μ_{y_i} lies on a line.

Remember that a *residual* was the error involved when making a prediction from a regression equation (residual = actual value of y − predicted value of $y = y_i - \hat{y}_i$). Not surprisingly, the standard error of the predictions is a function of the squared residuals:

$$s = \sqrt{\frac{SS_{RES}}{n-2}} = \sqrt{\frac{\sum(y_i - \hat{y}_i)^2}{n-2}}.$$

s is an estimator of σ, the standard deviation of the residuals. Thus, there are actually three parameters to worry about in regression: α, β, and σ, which are estimated by *a*, *b*, and *s*, respectively.

The final statistic we need to do inference for regression is the standard error of the slope of the regression line. Here's the formula for that calculation, but thankfully you will not need to use this formula on the exam:

$$s_b = \frac{s}{\sqrt{\sum (x_i - \bar{x})^2}} = \frac{\sqrt{\dfrac{\sum (y_i - \hat{y}_i)^2}{n-2}}}{\sqrt{\sum (x_i - \bar{x})^2}}$$

In summary, inference for regression depends on estimating $\mu_y = \alpha + \beta x$ with $\hat{y} = a + bx$. For each x, the response values of y are independent and follow a normal distribution with each distribution having the same standard deviation. Inference for regression depends on the following statistics:

- a, the estimate of the y intercept, α, of μ_y
- b, the estimate of the slope, β, of μ_y
- s, the standard error of the residuals
- s_b, the standard error of the slope of the regression line

In the section that follows, we explore inference for the slope of a regression line in terms of a significance test and a confidence interval for the slope.

Inference for the Slope of a Regression Line

Inference for regression consists of either a significance test or a confidence interval for the slope of a regression line. The null hypothesis in a significance test is $H_0: \beta = \beta_0$, but generally you will test $H_0: \beta = 0$. Our interest is the extent to which a least-squares regression line is a good model for the data. That is, the significance test is a test of a linear model for the data.

In theory we could test whether the slope of the regression line is equal to any specific value. However, the usual test is whether the slope of the regression line is zero or not. If the slope of the line is zero, then there is no linear relationship between the x and y variables (remember: $b = r\dfrac{s_y}{s_x}$; if $r = 0$, then $b = 0$).

The alternative hypothesis is often two sided (i.e., $H_A: \beta \neq 0$). However, we could do a one-sided test if we believed that the data were positively or negatively related.

Significance Test for the Slope of a Regression Line

The basic details of a significance test for the slope of a regression line are given in the following table:

• HYPOTHESIS		
• ESTIMATOR		
• STANDARD ERROR	CONDITIONS	TEST STATISTIC
• Null hypothesis: $H_0: \beta = \beta_0$ (most often: $H_0: \beta = 0$) • Estimator: b (from: $\hat{y} = a + bx$) • Standard error of the residuals:	• For each given value of x, the values of the response variable y are independent and normally distributed.	

Continued

$$s = \sqrt{\frac{SS_{RES}}{n-2}} = \sqrt{\frac{\sum(y_i - \hat{y}_i)^2}{n-2}}.$$

(Gives the variability of the vertical distances of the y-values from the regression line)

- Standard error of the slope:

$$s_b = \frac{s}{\sqrt{\sum(x_i - \overline{x})^2}}$$

(Gives the variability of the estimates of the slope of the regression line)

- For each given value of x, the standard deviation of y is the same.

- The mean response of the y-values for the fixed values of x are linearly related by the equation $\mu_y = \alpha + \beta x$.

$$t = \frac{b - \beta_o}{s_b}$$
$$= \frac{b}{s_b} \text{ (if } \beta_o = 0),$$
$$df = n - 2$$

example: The data in the following table give the top 15 states in terms of per-pupil expenditure in 1985 and the average teacher salary in the state for that year.

STATE/SALARY		PER-PUPIL EXPENDITURE
MN	27360	3982
CO	25892	4042
OR	25788	4123
PA	25853	4168
WI	26525	4247
MD	27186	4349
DE	24624	4517
MA	26800	4642
RI	29470	4669
CT	26610	4888
DC	33990	5020
WY	27224	5440
NJ	27170	5536
NY	30678	5710
AK	41480	8349

Test the hypothesis, at the 0.01 level of significance, that there is no straight-line relationship between per-pupil expenditure and teacher salary. Assume that the conditions necessary for inference for linear regression are present.

solution:

> **I.** Let $\beta =$ the true slope of the regression line for predicting salary from per-pupil expenditure.
>
> $$H_0: \beta = 0.$$
>
> $$H_A: \beta \neq 0.$$
>
> **II.** We will use the *t*-test for the slope of the regression line. The problem states that the conditions necessary for linear regression are present.
>
> **III.** The regression equation is
> $$\widehat{Salary} = 12027 + 3.34\, PPE$$
> $$(s = 2281,\ s_b = 0.5536)$$
>
> $$t = \frac{3.34 - 0}{0.5536} = 6.04, \qquad df = 15 - 2$$
> $$= 13 \Rightarrow P - \text{value} = 0.0000.$$
>
> If you need s_b for some reason—such as constructing a confidence interval for the slope of the regression line—and only have access to a calculator, you can find it by noting that, since $t = \dfrac{b}{s_b}$, then $s_b = \dfrac{b}{t}$.
>
> **IV.** Because $P < \alpha$, we reject H_0. We have very strong evidence that the true slope of the regression line is not zero. We have evidence that there is a linear relationship between amount of per-pupil expenditure and teacher salary.

A significance test that the slope of a regression line equals zero is closely related to a test that there is no correlation between the variables. That is, if ρ is the population correlation coefficient, then the test statistic for $H_0: \beta = 0$ is equal to the test statistic for $H_0: \rho = 0$. You aren't required to know it for the AP exam, but the *t*-test statistic for $H_0: \rho = 0$, where r is the sample correlation coefficient, is

$$t = r\sqrt{\frac{n-2}{1-r^2}}, \ \ df = n - 2.$$

Because this and the test for a nonzero slope are equivalent, it should come as no surprise that

$$r\sqrt{\frac{n-2}{1-r^2}} = \frac{b}{s_b}.$$

Confidence Interval for the Slope of a Regression Line

In addition to doing hypothesis tests on H_0: $\beta = \beta_0$, we can construct a confidence interval for the true slope of a regression line. The details follow:

• PARAMETER • ESTIMATOR	CONDITIONS	FORMULA
• Population slope: β • Estimator: b (from: $\hat{y} = a + bx$) • Standard error of the residuals. • Standard error of the slope.	• For each given value of x, the values of the response variable y are independent and normally distributed. • For each given value of x, the standard deviation of y is the same. • The mean response of the y-values for the fixed values of x are linearly related by the equation $\mu_y = \alpha + \beta x$.	$b \pm t^* s_b$, $df = n - 2$ (where t^* is the upper critical value of t for a C-level confidence interval)

example: Consider once again the earlier example on predicting teacher salary from per-pupil expenditure. Construct a 95% confidence interval for the slope of the population regression line.

solution: When we were doing a test of H_0: $\beta = 0$ for that problem, we found that $\widehat{Salary} = 12027 + 3.34\ PPE$. The slope of the regression line for the 15 points, and hence our estimate of β, is $b = 3.34$. We also had $t = 6.04$.

Our confidence interval is of the form $b \pm t^* s_b$. We need to find t^* and s_b. For $C = 0.95$, $df = 15 - 2 = 13$, we have $t^* = 2.160$ (from Table B; if you have a TI-83/84 with the `invT` function, use `invT(0.975,13)`). Now, as mentioned in part III of the previous solution plan, $s_b = \dfrac{b}{t} = \dfrac{3.34}{6.04} = 0.5530$.

Hence, $b \pm t^* s_b = 3.34 \pm 2.160(0.5530) = (2.15, 4.53)$. We are 95% confident that the true slope of the regression line is between 2.15 and 4.53. Note that, since 0 is *not* in this interval, this finding is consistent with our earlier rejection of the hypothesis that the slope equals 0. This is another way of saying that we have statistically significant evidence of a predictive linear relationship between *PPE* and *Salary*.

Inference for Regression Using Technology

If you had to do them from the raw data, the computations involved in doing inference for the slope of a regression line would be daunting.

Would you want to compute $s_b = \dfrac{s}{\sqrt{\sum (x_i - \bar{x})^2}} = \dfrac{\sqrt{\dfrac{\sum (y_i - \hat{y}_i)^2}{n-2}}}{\sqrt{\sum (x_i - \bar{x})^2}}$ by hand?

Fortunately, you may never be required to do this by hand but instead can rely on computer output you are given, or you will be able to use your calculator to do the computations.

Consider the following data that were gathered by counting the number of cricket chirps in 15 seconds and noting the temperature.

Number of Chirps	22	27	35	15	28	30	39	23	25	18	35	29
Temperature (°F)	64	68	78	60	72	76	82	66	70	62	80	74

We want to use technology to test the hypothesis that the slope of the regression line is 0 and to construct a confidence interval for the true slope of the regression line.

First let us look at the computer regression output for these data.

The regression equation is
$\widehat{Temp} = 44.0 + 0.993$ Number

Predictor	Coef	St Dev	t ratio	P
Constant	44.013	1.827	24.09	0.000
Number	0.99340	0.06523	15.23	0.000
$s = 1.538$	R-sq = 95.9%		R-sq(adj) = 95.5%	

You should be able to read most of this table, but you are not responsible for all of it. You see the following table entries:

- The regression equation, $\widehat{Temp} = 44.0 + 0.993$ Number, is the least-squares regression line (LSRL) for predicting temperature from the number of cricket chirps.
- Under "Predictor" are the y-intercept and explanatory variable of the regression equation, called "Constant" and "Number" (for number of chirps) in this example.
- Under "Coef" are the values of the "Constant" (which equals the y-intercept, the a in $\hat{y} = a + bx$; here, $a = 44.013$) and the slope of the regression line (which is the coefficient of "Number" in this example, the b in $\hat{y} = a + bx$; here, $b = 0.99340$).
- For the purposes of this book, we are not concerned with the "Stdev," "t-ratio," or "P" for "Constant"; therefore, only the "44.013" is meaningful for us.
- "Stdev" of "Number" is the standard error of the slope (what we have called s_b, the variability of the estimates of the slope of the regression line, which *equals* here

$\dfrac{s}{\sqrt{\sum (x_i - \bar{x})^2}}$ $s_b = 0.06523$); "t-ratio" is the value of the t-test statistic ($t = \dfrac{b}{s_b}$,

$df = n - 2$; here, $t = \dfrac{0.99340}{0.06523} = 15.23$); and P is the P-value associated with the test statistic assuming a two-sided test (here, $P = 0.000$; if you were doing a *one*-sided test, you would need to divide the given P-value by 2).

- s is the standard error of the residuals, which is the variability of the vertical distances of the y-values from the regression line; $s = \sqrt{\dfrac{\sum(y_i - \hat{y}_i)^2}{n-2}}$ (here, $s = 1.538$).

- "R-sq" is the coefficient of determination (or, r^2; here R-sq $= 95.9\% \Rightarrow 95.9\%$ of the variation in temperature that is explained by the regression on the number of chirps in 15 seconds; note that, here, $r = \sqrt{0.959} = 0.979$ —it's positive since $b = 0.9934$ is positive). You don't need to worry about "R-sq(adj)."

Thankfully, all of the mechanics needed to do a t-test for the slope of a regression line are contained in this printout. You need only to quote the appropriate values in your write-up. Thus, for the problem given earlier, we see that $t = 15.23 \Rightarrow P$-value $= 0.000$.

> **Exam Tip:** You may be given a problem that has both the raw data and the computer printout based on the data. If so, there is *no* advantage to doing the computations all over again because they have already been done for you. The juice just isn't worth the squeeze!

A confidence interval for the slope of a regression line follows the same pattern as all confidence intervals (estimate ± (critical value) × (standard error)): $b \pm t^* s_b$, based on $n - 2$ degrees of freedom. A 99% confidence interval for the slope in this situation ($df = 10 \Rightarrow t^* = 3.169$ from Table B) is $0.9934 \pm 3.169(0.06523) = (0.787, 1.200)$.

If you *have* to do a confidence interval using the calculator and do not have a TI-83/84 with the `LinRegTInt` function, you first need to determine s_b. Because you know that $t = \dfrac{b}{s_b} \Rightarrow s_b = \dfrac{b}{t}$, it follows that $s_b = \dfrac{0.9934}{15.2295} = 0.0652$, which agrees with the standard error of the slope ("St Dev" of "Number") given in the computer printout.

A 95% confidence interval for the slope of the regression line for predicting temperature from the number of chirps per minute is then given by $0.9934 \pm 2.228(0.0652) = (0.848, 1.139)$. $t^* = 2.228$ is based on $C = 0.95$ and $df = 12 - 2 = 10$. (Note that the "s" given in the printout is the standard error of the residuals, not the standard error of the slope.)

> Rapid Review

1. The regression equation for predicting grade point average from number of hours studied is determined to be $\widehat{GPA} = 1.95 + 0.05(Hours)$. Interpret the slope of the regression line.

   Answer: For each additional hour studied, the GPA is predicted to increase by 0.05 points.

2. Which of the following is *not* a necessary condition for doing inference for the slope of a regression line?

   a   For each given value of the independent variable, the response variable is normally distributed.

   b. The values of the predictor and response variables are independent.

   c. For each given value of the independent variable, the distribution of the response variable has the same standard deviation.

   d. The mean response values lie on a line.

Answer: (b) is not a condition for doing inference for the slope of a regression line. In fact, we are trying to find out the degree to which they are not independent.

3. True–False: Significance tests for the slope of a regression line are always based on the hypothesis H_0: $\beta = 0$ versus the alternative H_A: $\beta \neq 0$.

Answer: False. While the stated null and alternative may be the usual hypotheses in a test about the slope of the regression line, it is possible to test that the slope has some particular nonzero value or that the alternative can be one sided (H_A: $B > 0$ or H_A: $\beta < 0$). Note that most computer programs will test only the two-sided alternative by default. The TI-83/84 will test either a one- or two-sided alternative.

4. Consider the following computer printout:

The regression equation is
$\hat{y} = 282 + 0.634\,x$

Predictor	Coef	St Dev	t ratio	P
Constant	282.459	3.928	71.91	0.000
x	0.63383	0.07039	9.00	0.000
s = 9.282	R-sq = 81.0%	R-sq(adj) = 80.0%		

   a. What is the slope of the regression line?

   b. What is the standard error of the residuals?

   c. What is the standard error of the slope?

   d. Do the data indicate a predictive linear relationship between x and y?

Answer:

   a. 0.634

   b. 9.282

   c. 0.07039

   d. Yes, the *t*-test statistic $= 9.00 \Rightarrow$ *P*-value $= .000$. That is, the probability is close to zero of getting a sample slope of 0.634 if, in fact, the true slope was zero.

5. A *t*-test for the slope of a regression line is to be conducted at the 0.02 level of significance based on 18 data values. As usual, the test is two sided. What is the upper critical value for this test (that is, find the minimum positive value of t^* for which a finding would be considered significant)?

Answer: There are $18 - 2 = 16$ degrees of freedom. Since the alternative is two sided, the rejection region has 0.01 in each tail. Using Table B, we find the value at the intersection of the $df = 16$ row and the 0.01 column: $t^* = 2.583$. If you have a TI-83/84 with the `invT` function, `invT(0.99,16)=2.583`. This is, of course, the same value of t^* you would use to construct a 98% confidence interval for the slope of the regression line.

6. In the printout from question #4, we were given the regression equation $\hat{y} = 282 + 0.634x$. The t-test for H_0: $\beta = 0$ yielded a P-value of 0.000. What is the conclusion you would arrive at based on these data?

Answer: Because P is very small, we would reject the null hypothesis that the slope of the regression line is 0. We have strong evidence of a predictive linear relationship between x and y.

7. Suppose the computer output for regression reports $P = 0.036$. What is the P-value for H_A: $\beta > 0$ (assuming the test was in the correct direction for the data)?

Answer: 0.018. Computer output for regression assumes the alternative is two sided (H_A: $\beta \neq 0$). Hence the P-value reported assumes the finding could have been in either tail of the t-distribution. The correct P-value for the one-sided test is one-half of this value.

Practice Problems

Multiple-Choice

1. Which of the following statements is (are) true?

I. In the computer output for regression, s is the estimator of σ, the standard deviation of the residuals.
II. The t-test statistic for the H_0: $\beta = 0$ has the same value as the t-test statistic for H_0: $\rho = 0$.
III. The t-test for the slope of a regression line is always two sided (H_A: $\beta \neq 0$).

   a. I only
   b. II only
   c. III only
   d. I and II only
   e. I and III only

Use the following output in answering questions 2–4:

A study attempted to establish a linear relationship between IQ score and musical aptitude. The following table is a partial printout of the regression analysis and is based on a sample of 20 individuals.

The regression equation is
$\widehat{MusApt} = -22.3 + 0.493 \, IQ$

Predictor	Coef	St Dev	t ratio	P
Constant	−22.26	12.94	−1.72	.102
IQ	0.4925	0.1215		
$s = 6.143$	R-sq = 47.7%	R-sq(adj) = 44.8%		

2. The value of the t-test statistic for H_0: $\beta = 0$ is
   a. 4.05
   b. −1.72
   c. 0.4925
   d. 6.143
   e. 0.0802

3. A 99% confidence interval for the slope of the regression line is
   a. $0.4925 \pm 2.878(6.143)$.
   b. $0.4925 \pm 2.861(0.1215)$.
   c. $0.4925 \pm 2.861(6.143)$.
   d. $0.4925 \pm 2.845(0.1215)$.
   e. $0.4925 \pm 2.878(0.1215)$.

4. Which of the following best interprets the slope of the regression line?
   a. A student with an IQ one point above another student has a Musical Aptitude score 0.4925 points higher.
   b. As IQ score increases, so does the Musical Aptitude score.
   c. A student with an IQ one point above another student is predicted to have a Musical Aptitude score 0.4925 points higher.
   d. For each additional point of Musical Aptitude, IQ is predicted to increase by 0.4925 points.
   e. There is a strong predictive linear relationship between IQ score and Musical Aptitude.

5. A group of 12 students take both the SAT Math and the SAT Verbal. The least-squares regression line for predicting Verbal Score from Math Score is determined to be $\overline{Verbal\ Score} = 106.56 + 0.74(Math\ Score)$. Furthermore, $s_b = 0.11$. Which of the following is a 95% confidence interval for the slope of the regression line?
   a. 0.74 ± 0.245
   b. 0.74 ± 0.242
   c. 0.74 ± 0.240
   d. 0.74 ± 0.071
   e. 0.74 ± 0.199

Free-Response

1–5. The following table gives the ages in months of a sample of children and their mean height (in inches) at that age.

Age	18	19	20	21	22	23	24	25	26	27	28
Height	30.0	30.7	30.7	30.8	31.0	31.4	31.5	31.9	32.0	32.6	32.9

1. Find the correlation coefficient and the least-squares regression line for predicting height (in inches) from age (in months).

2. Draw a scatterplot of the data and the LSRL on the plot. Does the line appear to be a good model for the data?

3. Construct a residual plot for the data. Does the line still appear to be a good model for the data?

4. Use your LSRL to predict the height of a child of 35 months. How confident should you be in this prediction?

5. Interpret the slope of the regression line found in question 1 in the context of the problem.

6. In 2002, there were 23 states in which more than 50% of high school graduates took the SAT test. The following printout gives the regression analysis for predicting SAT Math from SAT Verbal from these 23 states.

The regression equation is

Predictor	Coef	St Dev	t ratio	P
Constant	185.77	71.45	2.60	0.017
Verbal	0.6419	0.1420	4.52	0.000
$s = 7.457$	R-sq = 49.3%		R-sq(adj) = 46.9%	

    a. What is the equation of the least-squares regression line for predicting Math SAT score from Verbal SAT score?

    b. Determine the slope of the regression line and interpret in the context of the problem.

    c. Identify the standard error of the slope of the regression line and interpret it in the context of the problem.

    d. Identify the standard error of the residuals and interpret it in the context of the problem.

    e. Assuming that the conditions needed for doing inference for regression are present, what are the hypotheses being tested in this problem, what test statistic is used in the analysis, what is its value, and what conclusion would you make concerning the hypothesis?

7. For the regression analysis of question 6:

    a. Construct and interpret a 95% confidence interval for the true slope of the regression line.

    b. Explain what is meant by "95% confidence interval" in the context of the problem.

8. It has been argued that the average score on the SAT test drops as more students take the test (nationally, about 46% of graduating students took the SAT). The following data are the computer output for predicting SAT Math score from the percentage taking the test (PCT) for each of the 50 states. Assuming that the conditions for doing inference for regression are met, test the hypothesis that scores decline as the proportion of students taking the test rises. That is, test to determine if the slope of the regression line is negative. Test at the 0.01 level of significance.

The regression equation is $\widehat{SAT\,Math} = 574 - 99.5$ PCT

Predictor	Coef	St Dev	t ratio	P
Constant	574.179	4.123	139.25	0.000
PCT	−99.516	8.832	−11.27	0.000
$s = 17.45$	R-sq = 72.6%	R-sq(adj) = 72.0%		

9. Some bored researchers got the idea that they could predict a person's pulse rate from the person's height (earlier studies had shown a very weak linear relationship between pulse rate and weight). They collected data on 20 college-age women. The following table is part of the computer output of their findings.

The regression equation is

Pulse = [   ] Height

Predictor	Coef	St Dev	t ratio	P
Constant	52. 00	37.24	1.40	0.180
Height	0.2647	0.5687		
$s = 10.25$	R-sq $= 1.2\%$	R-sq(adj) $= 0.0\%$		

a. Determine the t-ratio and the P-value for the test.
b. Construct a 99% confidence interval for the slope of the regression line used to predict pulse rate from height.
c. Do you think there is a predictive linear relationship between height and pulse rate? Explain.
d. Suppose the researchers were hoping to show that there was a positive linear relationship between pulse rate and height. Are the t-ratio and P-value the same as in part (a)? If not, what are they?

Cumulative Review Problems

1. You are testing the hypothesis H_0: $p = 0.6$. You sample 75 people as part of your study and calculate that $\hat{p} = 0.7$.

    a. What is $s_{\hat{p}}$ for a significance test for p?
    b. What is $s_{\hat{p}}$ for a confidence interval for p?

2. A manufacturer of lightbulbs claims a mean life of 1500 hours. A mean of 1450 hours would represent a significant departure from this claim. Suppose, in fact, the mean life of bulbs is only 1450 hours. In this context, what is meant by the power of the test (no calculation is required)?

3. Complete the following table by filling in the shape of the sampling distribution of $\bar{x}$ for each situation.

SITUATION	SHAPE OF SAMPLING DISTRIBUTION
• Shape of parent population: normal • Sample size: $n = 8$	
• Shape of parent population: normal • Sample size: $n = 35$	
• Shape of parent population: strongly skewed to the left • Sample size: $n = 8$	
• Shape of parent population: strongly skewed to the left • Sample size: $n = 35$	
• Shape of parent population: unknown • Sample size: $n = 8$	
• Shape of parent population: unknown • Sample size: $n = 50$	

4. The following is most of a probability distribution for a discrete random variable.

X	2	6	7	9
$p(x)$	0.15	0.25		0.40

Find the mean and the standard deviation of this distribution.

5. Consider the following scatterplot and regression line.

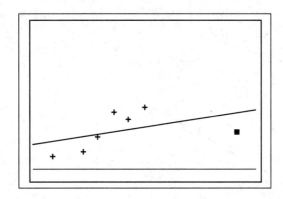

a. Would you describe the point marked with a box as an outlier, influential point, neither, or both?
b. What would be the effect on the correlation coefficient of removing the box-point?
c. What would be the effect on the slope of the regression line of removing the box-point?

Solutions to Practice Problems

Multiple-Choice

1. The correct answer is (d). II is true since it can be shown that $t = \dfrac{b}{s_b} = r\sqrt{\dfrac{n-2}{1-r^2}}$.

    III is not true since, although we often use the alternative $H_A: \beta \neq 0$, we can certainly test a null with an alternative that states that there is a positive or a negative association between the variables.

2. The correct answer is (a). $t = \dfrac{b}{s_b} = \dfrac{0.4925}{0.1215} = 4.05$.

3. The correct answer is (e). For $n = 20$, $df = 20 - 2 = 18 \Rightarrow t^* = 2.878$ for $C = 0.99$.

4. The correct answer is (c). Note that (a) is not correct since it doesn't have "predicted" or "on average" to qualify the increase. (b) is a true statement but is not the best interpretation of the slope. (d) has mixed up the response and explanatory variables. (e) is also true ($t = 4.05 \Rightarrow$ P-value $= 0.0008$) but is not an interpretation of the slope.

5. The correct answer is (a). A 95% confidence interval at $12 - 2 = 10$ degrees of freedom has a critical value of $t^* = 2.228$ (from Table B; if you have a TI-83/84 with the `invT` function, `invT(0.975,10) = 2.228`). The required interval is $0.74 \pm (2.228)(0.11) = 0.74 \pm 0.245$.

Free-Response

1. $r = 0.9817$, height $= 25.41 + 0.261(\text{age})$

   (Assuming that you have put the age data in L1 and the height data in L2, remember that this can be done on the TI-83/84 as follows: STAT CALC LinReg(a+bx) L1,L2,Y1.)

2. The line does appear to be a good model for the data.

   (After the regression equation was calculated on the TI-83/84 and the LSRL stored in Y1, this was constructed in STAT PLOT by drawing a scatterplot with Xlist:L1 and Ylist:L2.)

   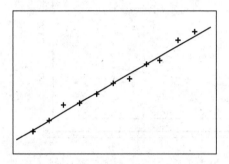

3. The residual pattern seems quite random. A line still appears to be a good model for the data.

   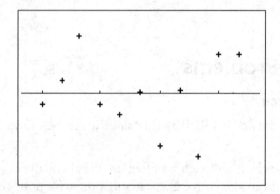

(This scatterplot was constructed on the TI-83/84 using STAT PLOT with Xlist:L1 and Ylist:RESID. Remember that the list of residuals for the most recent regression is saved in a list named RESID.)

4. $\widehat{Height} = 25.41 + 0.261(35) = 34.545$ (Y1(35) = 34.54). You probably shouldn't be too confident in this prediction. Thirty-five is well outside of the data on which the LSRL was constructed and, even though the line appears to be a good fit for the data, there is no reason to believe that a linear pattern is going to continue indefinitely. (If it did, a 25-year-old would have a predicted height of $25.41 + 0.261(12 \times 25) = 103.71''$, or 8.64 feet!)

5. The slope of the regression line is 0.261. This means that, for an increase in age of 1 month, height is predicted to increase by 0.261 inches. You could also say, that, for an increase in age of 1 month, height will increase on average by 0.261 inches.

6. a. $\widehat{Math} = 185.77 + 0.6419(Verbal)$.

    b. $b = 0.6419$. For each additional point scored on the SAT Verbal test, the score on the SAT Math test is predicted to increase by 0.6419 points (or will increase *on average* by 0.6419 points). (Very important on the AP exam: be very sure to say "is predicted" or "on average" if you'd like maximum credit for the problem!)

    c. The standard error of the slope is $s_b = 0.1420$. This is an estimate of the variability of the standard deviation of the estimated slope for predicting SAT Verbal from SAT Math.

    d. The standard error of the residuals is $s = 7.457$. This value is a measure of variation in SAT Verbal for a fixed value of SAT Math.

    e. • The hypotheses being tested are H_0: $\beta = 0$ (which is equivalent to H_0: $\rho = 0$) and H_A $\beta \neq 0$, where β is the slope of the regression line for predicting SAT Verbal from SAT Math.

        • The test statistic used in the analysis is $t = \dfrac{b}{s_b} = \dfrac{0.6419}{0.1420} = 4.52$, $df = 23 - 2 = 21$.

7. a. $df = 23 - 2 = 21 \Rightarrow t^* = 2.080$. The 95% confidence interval is $0.6419 \pm 2.080(0.1420) = (0.35, 0.94)$. We are 95% confident that, for each 1 point increase in SAT Verbal, the true increase in SAT Math is between 0.35 points and 0.94 points.

    b. The procedure used to generate the confidence interval would produce intervals that contain the true slope of the regression line, on average, 0.95 of the time.

8. I. Let β = the true slope of the regression line for predicting SAT Math score from the percentage of graduating seniors taking the test.

$$H_0: \beta = 0$$

$$H_A: \beta < 0$$

    II. We use a linear regression t test with $\alpha = 0.01$. The problem states that the conditions for doing inference for regression are met.

    III. We see from the printout that

$$t = \frac{b}{s_b} = \frac{-99.516}{8.832} = -11.27$$

    based on $50 - 2 = 48$ degrees of freedom. The P-value is 0.000. (*Note:* The P-value in the printout is for a two-sided test. However, since the P-value for a one-sided test would only be half as large, it is still 0.000.)

    IV. Because $P < 0.01$, we reject the null hypothesis. We have very strong evidence that there is a negative linear relationship between the proportion of students taking SAT Math and the average score on the test.

9. a. $t = \dfrac{b}{s_b} = \dfrac{0.2647}{0.5687} = 0.47$, $df = 20 - 2 = 18 \Rightarrow P$-value $= 0.644$.

    b. $df = 18 \Rightarrow t^* = 2.878$; $0.2647 \pm 2.878(0.5687) = (-1.37, 1.90)$.

c. No. The *P*-value is very large, giving no grounds to reject the null hypothesis that the slope of the regression line is 0. Furthermore, the correlation coefficient is only $r = \sqrt{0.012} = 0.11$, which is very close to 0. Finally, the confidence interval constructed in part (b) contains the value 0 as a likely value of the slope of the population regression line.

d. The *t*-ratio would still be 0.47. The *P*-value, however, would be half of the 0.644, or 0.322 because the computer output assumes a two-sided test. This is a lower *P*-value but is still much too large to infer any significant linear relationship between pulse rate and height.

Solutions to Cumulative Review Problems

1. a. $s_{\hat{p}} = \sqrt{\dfrac{(0.6)(0.4)}{75}} = 0.057.$

   b. $s_{\hat{p}} = \sqrt{\dfrac{(0.7)(0.3)}{75}} = 0.053.$

2. The *power of the test* is the probability of correctly rejecting a false hypothesis against a particular alternative. In other words, the *power* of this test is the probability of rejecting the claim that the true mean is 1500 hours against the alternative that the true mean is only 1450 hours.

SITUATION	SHAPE OF SAMPLING DISTRIBUTION
• Shape of parent population: normal • Sample size: $n = 8$	**Normal**
• Shape of parent population: normal • Sample size: $n = 35$	**Normal**
• Shape of parent population: strongly skewed to the left • Sample size: $n = 8$	**Skewed somewhat to the left**
• Shape of parent population: strongly skewed to the left • Sample size: $n = 35$	**Approximately normal (central limit theorem)**
• Shape of parent population: unknown • Sample size: $n = 8$	**Similar to parent population**
• Shape of parent population: unknown • Sample size: $n = 50$	**Approximately normal (central limit theorem)**

4. $P(7) = 1 - (0.15 + 0.25 + 0.40) = 0.20.$

   $\mu_x = 2(0.15) + 6(0.25) + 7(0.20) + 9(0.40) = 6.8.$

$$\sigma_X = \sqrt{(2-6.8)^2(0.15)+(6-6.8)^2(0.25)+(7-6.8)^2(0.20)+(9-6.8)^2(0.40)} = 2.36.$$

(Remember that this can be done by putting the X-values in L1, the $p(x)$-values in L2, and doing STAT CALC 1-Var Stats L1,L2.)

5. a. The point is both an outlier and an influential point. It is an outlier because it is removed from the general pattern of the data. It is an influential observation because it is an outlier in the x direction and its removal would have an impact on the slope of the regression line.

   b. Removing the point would increase the correlation coefficient. That is, the remaining data are better modeled by a line without the box-point than with it.

   c. Removing the point would make the slope of the regression line more positive (and steeper) than it is already.

CHAPTER 13

Inference for Categorical Data: Chi-Squared Tests

IN THIS CHAPTER

Summary: In this final chapter, we will look at inference for categorical variables. Up until now, we have studied data analysis and inference only for one or two numerical variables (those whose outcomes we can measure), and proportions, which are categorical variable with only two possible values (success and failure). The material in this chapter opens up for us a wide range of research topics, allowing us to compare categorical variables across several values. For example, we will ask new questions like "Is there an association between gender and political party preference?"

Key Ideas
- ✪ Chi-Square Goodness-of-Fit Test
- ✪ Chi-Square Test for Independence
- ✪ Chi-Square Test for Homogeneity of Proportions (Populations)
- ✪ χ^2 versus z^2

Chi-Square Goodness-of-Fit Test

Imagine that the following are the approximate percentages for the different blood types among people with blue eyes: A: 40%; B: 11%; AB: 4%; O: 45%. A random sample of 1000 people with brown eyes yielded the following blood type data: A: 270; B: 200; AB: 40; O: 490. Does this sample provide evidence that the distribution of blood types among brown-eyed people differs from that of blue-eyed people, or could the sample values simply be due to sampling variation? This is the kind of question we can answer with the chi-square **goodness-of-fit test**. (*Chi* is the Greek letter χ; chi-square is, logically enough, χ^2.) With the chi-square goodness-of-fit test, we note that there is one categorical variable (blood type) and one population (brown-eyed people). In this chapter we will also encounter a situation in which there is one categorical variable measured across two or more populations (called a chi-square test for homogeneity of proportions) and a situation in which there are two categorical variables measured across a single population (called a chi-square test for independence).

To answer this question, we need to compare the **observed values** in the sample with the **expected values** we would get *if* the sample of people with brown eyes really had the same distribution of blood types as the blue-eyed people. The values we need for this are summarized in the following table:

BLOOD TYPE	PROPORTION OF POPULATION	EXPECTED VALUES	OBSERVED VALUES
A	0.40	$(0.4)(1000) = 400$	270
B	0.11	$(0.11)(1000) = 110$	200
AB	0.04	$(0.04)(1000) = 40$	40
O	0.45	$(0.45)(1000) = 450$	490

It appears that the numbers vary noticeably for types A and B, but not as much for types AB and O. The table can be rewritten as follows:

BLOOD TYPE	OBSERVED VALUES	EXPECTED VALUES
A	270	400
B	200	110
AB	40	40
O	490	450

Before working through this problem, a note on symbols. Often in this book, and in statistics in general, we use English letters for statistics (measurements from data) and Greek letters for parameters (population values). Hence, $\bar{x}$ is a sample mean and μ is a population mean, s is a sample standard deviation, σ is a population standard deviation, and so on. We follow this same convention in this chapter: we will use χ^2 when referring to a population value or to the name of a test and use X^2 when referring to the chi-square statistic.

The chi-square statistic (X^2) calculates the squared difference between the observed and expected values relative to the expected value for each category. The X^2 statistic is computed as follows:

$$X^2 = \sum \frac{(\text{Observed} - \text{Expected})^2}{\text{Expected}} = \sum \frac{(O - E)^2}{E}.$$

The chi-square distribution is based on the number of degrees of freedom, which equals, for the goodness-of-fit test, the number of categories minus 1 ($df = c - 1$). The X^2 statistic follows approximately a unique chi-square distribution, assuming a random sample and a large enough sample, for each different number of degrees of freedom. The probability that a sample has a X^2 value as large as it does can be read from a table of X^2 critical values or determined from a calculator. There is a X^2 table in the back of this book, and you will be supplied a table like this on the AP exam. We will demonstrate both the use of tables and the calculator in the examples and problems that follow.

A hypothesis test for X^2 goodness-of-fit follows the by-now familiar pattern. The essential parts of the test are summarized in the following table.

HYPOTHESES	CONDITIONS	TEST STATISTIC
• Null hypothesis: H_0: p_1 = population proportion for category 1 p_2 = population proportion for category 2 . . . p_n = population proportion for category n This is usually stated in words: "The proportions of the population in each category are the same as those given in the table above" or something like that. • Alternative hypothesis: H_A: at least one of the proportions in H_0 is not equal to the claimed population proportion.	• Observations are based on a random sample. • The number of each expected count is at least 5. (Some texts use the following condition for expected counts: at least 80% of the counts are greater than 5 and none is less than 1. It is acceptable for you to use either of these.)	$X^2 = \sum \dfrac{(O-E)^2}{E}$ $df = c - 1$

Now, let's answer the question posed in the opening paragraph of this chapter. We will use the by now familiar four-step hypothesis-testing procedure introduced in Chapter 11.

example: The following are the approximate percentages for the different blood types among people with blue eyes: A: 40%; B: 11%; AB: 4%; O: 45%. A random sample of 1000 brown-eyed people yielded the following blood type data: A: 270; B: 200; AB: 40; O: 490. Does this sample indicate that the distribution of blood types among people with brown eyes differs from that of the people with blue eyes?

solution:

I. Let p_A = proportion of brown-eyed people with type A blood; p_B = proportion with type B blood; p_{AB} = proportion with type AB blood; p_O = proportion with type O blood. H_0: p_A = 0.40, p_B = 0.11, p_{AB} = 0.04, p_0 = 0.45.

H_A: at least one of these proportions is not as stated.

II. We will use the χ^2 goodness-of-fit test. The problem states that the sample is a random sample. The expected values are type A: 400; type B: 110; type AB: 40; type O: 450. Each of these is greater than 5. The conditions needed for the test are satisfied.

III. The data are summarized in the table:

BLOOD TYPE	OBSERVED VALUES	EXPECTED VALUES
A	270	400
B	200	110
AB	40	40
O	490	450

$$X^2 = \sum \frac{(O-E)^2}{E} = \frac{(270-400)^2}{400} + \frac{(200-110)^2}{110}$$
$$+ \frac{(40-40)^2}{40} + \frac{(490-450)^2}{450} = 119.44,$$
$$df = 4-1 = 3.$$

From the X^2 table (Table C, which is read very much like Table B), we see that 119.44 is much larger than any value for $df = 3$. Hence, the P-value < 0.0005. (A calculator gives a P-value of 1.02×10^{-25}—more about how to do this coming up next.)

IV. Because the P-value is so small, we reject the null hypothesis. We have very strong evidence that the proportions of the various blood types among brown-eyed people differ from the proportions among people with blue eyes.

Calculator Tip: All newer graphing calculators have two χ^2 tests in the test menu. The goodness-of-fit test will require the observed and expected frequencies to be entered into lists. Older calculators that do not have the goodness-of-fit test put you at a slight disadvantage, but the computation is simple enough with list operations. If you put the observed frequencies in the first list, and the expected fewquencies in the second, you can create a third list with the formula $\dfrac{(List1 - List2)^2}{List2}$, then calculate the sum of $List2$ to get the χ^2 statistic. Then use the χ^2 cdf function to calculate the area above the χ^2 statistic.

example: The statistics teacher, Mr. Eicher, used his calculator to simulate rolling a die 96 times and storing the results in a list L1. He did this by entering MATH PRB randInt(1,6,96) → (L1). Next, he sorted the list

(`STAT SortA(L1)`). He then counted the number of each face value. The results were as follows (this is called a one-way table):

FACE VALUE	OBSERVED
1	19
2	15
3	10
4	14
5	17
6	21

Does it appear that the teacher's calculator is simulating a fair die? (That is, are the observations consistent with what you would expect to get *if* the die were fair?)

solution:

I. Let $p_1, p_2, \ldots, p_6$ be the population proportion for each face of the die to appear on repeated trials of a roll of a fair die.

H_0: $p_1 = p_2 = p_3 = p_4 = p_5 = p_6 = \frac{1}{6}$.

H_A: At least one of the proportions is not equal to 1/6.

II. We will use a χ^2 goodness-of-fit test. If the die is fair, we would expect to get

$$\left(\frac{1}{6}\right)(96) = 16$$

of each face. Because all expected values are greater than 5, the conditions are met for this test.

FACE VALUE	OBSERVED	EXPECTED
1	19	16
2	15	16
3	10	16
4	14	16
5	17	16
6	21	16

III. $X^2 = 4.75$ (calculator result), $df = 6 - 1 = 5$ P-value > 0.25 (Table C) or P-value $= 0.45$ (calculator).

(*Remember:* To get X^2 on the calculator, put the Observed values in L1, the Expected values in L2, let L3 = (L1-L2)²/L2, then `LIST MATH SUM (L3)` will be X^2. The corresponding probability is then found by `DISTR` χ^2`cdf(4.75,100,5)`. This can also be done on a TI-83/84 that has the χ^2 `GOF-Test`.)

IV. Because $P > 0.25$, we fail to reject the null hypothesis. We do not have convincing evidence that the calculator is failing to simulate a fair die.

Inference for Two-Way Tables

Two-Way Tables (Contingency Tables) Defined

A **two-way table**, or **contingency table**, for categorical data is simply a rectangular array of cells. Each cell contains the frequencies for the joint values of the row and column variables. If the row variable has r values, then there will be r rows of data in the table. If the column variable has c values, then there will be c columns of data in the table. Thus, there are $r \times c$ cells in the table. (The **dimension** of the table is $r \times c$.) The **marginal totals** are the sums of the observations for each row and each column.

> **example:** A class of 36 students is polled concerning political party preference. The results are presented in the following *two-way* table.

Political Party Preference

		Democrat	Republican	Independent	Total
Gender	**Male**	11	7	2	20
	Female	7	8	1	16
	Total	18	15	3	36

The values of the row variable (Gender) are "Male" and "Female." The values of the column variable (Political Party Preference) are "Democrat," "Republican," and "Independent." There are $r = 2$ rows and $c = 3$ columns. We refer to this as a 2×3 table (the number of rows always comes first). The row marginal totals are 20 and 16; the column marginal totals are 18, 15, and 3. Note that the sum of the row and column marginal totals must both add to the total number in the sample.

In the example earlier, we had one population of 36 students and two categorical variables (gender and party preference). In this type of situation, we are interested in whether or not the variables are independent in the population. That is, does knowledge of one variable provide you with information about the other variable? Another study might have drawn a simple random sample of 20 males from, say, the senior class and another simple random sample of 16 females. Now we have two populations rather than one, but only one categorical variable. Now we might ask if the proportions of Democrats, Republicans, and Independents in each population are the same. Either way we do it, we end up with the same contingency table given in the example. We will look at how these differences in design play out in the next couple of sections.

Chi-Square Test for Independence

A random sample of 400 adult residents of a large western city are polled to determine their attitudes concerning raising taxes to support education. The residents are classified according to age (younger, middle, older) and whether or not they favor such an increase in taxes. The results are presented in the following table.

Attitude Toward Raising Taxes to Support Education

		Favor	Do Not Favor	Total
Age	**Younger**	130	120	250
	Middle	75	35	110
	Older	28	12	40
	Total	233	167	400

We are interested in whether or not, in the adult population of this large city, age and attitude toward education taxes are associated (note that, in this situation, we have one population and two categorical variables). That is, does knowledge of a person's age group give us information about that person's attitude toward education taxes? Another way of asking this is "Are the variables *age group* and *attitude toward education taxes* independent in the population?" As part of a hypothesis test, the null hypothesis is that the two variables are independent, and the alternative is that they are not: H_0: the variables *age group* and *attitude toward education taxes* are independent among all adult residents of this city *vs.* H_A: the variables are not independent among all adult residents of this city. Alternatively, we could say H_0: the variables *age group* and *attitude toward education taxes* are not associated among all adult residents of this city *vs.* H_A: the variables *age group* and *attitude toward education taxes* are associated among all adult residents of this city.

The test statistic for the independence hypothesis is the same chi-square statistic we saw for the goodness-of-fit test:

$$X^2 = \sum \frac{(O-E)^2}{E}.$$

For a two-way table, the number of degrees of freedom is calculated as (*number of rows* − 1)(*number of columns* − 1) = $(r-1)(c-1)$. As with the goodness-of-fit test, we require that we are dealing with a random sample and that the number of expected values in each cell be at least 5 (or some texts say there are no empty cells and at least 80% of the cells have more than 5 expected values).

Calculation of the expected frequencies for chi-square can be labor intensive if there are many cells, but it is *usually* done by technology (see the next Calculator Tip for details). However, you should know how expected frequencies are derived.

example (calculation of expected frequency): Suppose we are testing for independence of the variables (age group and opinion) in the previous example. For the two-way table with the given marginal values, find the expected frequency for the cell marked "Exp."

		Favor	Do Not Favor	Total
	Younger			250
Age	Middle		Exp	110
	Older			40
	Total	233	167	400

solution: There are two ways to approach finding an expected value, but they are numerically equivalent and you can use either. The first way is to find the probability of being in the desired location by chance and then multiplying that value times the total in the table (as we found an expected value with discrete random variables). The probability of being in the "Middle" row is $\frac{110}{400}$, and the probability of being in the "Do Not Favor" column is $\frac{167}{400}$.

Assuming independence, the probability of being in "Exp" by chance is then $\left(\frac{110}{400}\right)\left(\frac{167}{400}\right)$. Thus, Exp $= \left(\frac{110}{400}\right)\left(\frac{167}{400}\right)(400) = 45.925$.

The second way is to argue, under the assumption that there is no relation between age group and opinion, that we'd expect each cell in the "Do Not Favor" column to show the same proportion of outcomes. In this case, each row of the "Do Not Favor" column would contain $\frac{167}{400}$ of the row total. Thus, $\text{Exp} = \left(\frac{167}{400}\right)(110) = 45.925$. Most of you will probably find using the calculator easier. (*Note:* Report your expected counts to at least one decimal place.)

Calculator Tip: The easiest way to obtain the expected values is to use your calculator. To do this, let's use the data from the previous examples:

130	120
75	35
28	12

In mathematics, a rectangular array of numbers such as this is called a matrix. Matrix algebra is a separate field of study, but we are only concerned with using the matrix function on our calculator to find a set of expected values (which we'll need to check the conditions for doing a hypothesis test using the chi-square statistics).

On a TI-84, go to `MATRIX EDIT [A]`. Note that our data matrix has three rows and two columns, so make the dimension of the matrix (the numbers right after `MATRIX [A]`) read 3×2. The calculator expects you enter the data by rows, so just enter 130, 120, 75, 35, 28, 12 in order and the matrix will be correct. Now, `QUIT` the `MATRIX` menu and go to `STAT TESTS` χ^2`-Test` (*Note:* Technically we don't yet know that we have the conditions present to do a χ^2-test, but this is the way we'll find our expected values.) Enter [A] for `Observed` and [B] for `Expected` (you can paste "[A]" by entering `MATRIX NAMES [A]`). Then, choose `Calculate`. The calculator will return some things we don't care about yet ($X^2 = 10.748$, $p = 0.0046$, and $df = 2$). Now return to the `MATRIX` menu and select `NAMES [B]` and press `ENTER`. You should get the following matrix of expected values:

$$\begin{bmatrix} 145.625 & 104.375 \\ 64.075 & 45.925 \\ 23.3 & 16.7 \end{bmatrix}$$

Note that the entry in the second row and second column, 45.925, agrees with our hand calculation for "Exp" in the previous example.

The χ^2-test for independence can be summarized as follows:

HYPOTHESES	CONDITIONS	TEST STATISTIC
• Null hypothesis: H_0: The row and column variables are independent (or they are not associated). • Alternative hypothesis: H_0: The row and column variables are not independent (or they are associated).	• Observations are based on a random sample. • The number of each expected count is at least 5. (Some texts use the following condition: all expected values are greater than 1, and at least 80% of the expected values are greater than 5.)	$X^2 = \sum \frac{(O-E)^2}{E}$ $df = (r-1)(c-1)$

example: A study of 150 randomly selected cities was conducted to determine if crime rate is associated with outdoor temperature. The results of the study are summarized in the following table:

Crime Rate

Temperature		BELOW	NORMAL	ABOVE
	Below	12	8	5
	Normal	35	41	24
	Above	4	7	14

Do these data provide evidence, at the 0.02 level of significance, that the crime rate is associated with the temperature at the time of the crime?

solution:

I.

H_0: The crime rate is independent of temperature (or, H_0: Crime Rate and Temperature are not associated).

H_A: The crime rate is not independent of temperature (or, H_A: Crime Rate and Temperature are associated).

II. We will use a chi-square test for independence.
The cities were randomly selected.
A matrix of expected values (using the TI-83/84 as explained in the previous Calculator Tip) is found to be

$\begin{bmatrix} 8.5 & 9.33 & 7.17 \\ 34 & 37.33 & 28.67 \\ 8.5 & 9.33 & 7.17 \end{bmatrix}$. Since all expected values are greater than 5, the conditions

are present for a chi-square test.

III. $X^2 = \sum \dfrac{(O-E)^2}{E} = \dfrac{(12-8.5)^2}{8.5} + \cdots + \dfrac{(14-7.17)^2}{7.17} = 12.92, df = (3-1)(3-1) = 4$

$\Rightarrow 0.01 < P\text{-value} < 0.02$ (from Table C; or P-value = DISTR X^2cdf (12.92,1000,410) = 0.012).
(Note that the entire problem could be done by entering the observed values in MATRIX [A] and using STAT TESTS X^2-Test.)

IV. Since $P < 0.02$, we reject H_0. We have strong evidence that the number of crimes committed is related to the temperature at the time of the crime.

Chi-Square Test for Homogeneity of Proportions (or Homogeneity of Populations)

In the previous section, we tested for the independence of two categorical variables measured on a single population. In this section we again use the chi-square statistic but will investigate whether or not the values of a single categorical variable are proportional among two or more populations. In the previous section, we considered a situation in which a sample of 36 students was selected and were then categorized according to gender and political party preference. We then asked if gender and party preference are independent in the population. Now suppose instead that we had selected a random sample of 20 males from the population of males in the school and another, independent, random sample of 16 females from the population of females in the school. Within each sample we classify the students as Democrat, Republican, or Independent. The results are presented in the following table, which you should notice is *exactly* the same table we presented earlier when gender was a category.

Political Party Preference

Gender		DEMOCRAT	REPUBLICAN	INDEPENDENT	TOTAL
	Male	11	7	2	20
	Female	7	8	1	16
	Total	18	15	3	36

Because "Male" and "Female" are now considered separate populations, we do not ask if gender and political party preference are independent in the population of students. We ask instead if the proportions of Democrats, Republicans, and Independents are the *same* within the populations of Males and Females. This is the test for homogeneity of proportions (or homogeneity of populations). Let the proportion of Male Democrats be p_1; the proportion of Female Democrats be p_2; the proportion of Male Republicans be p_3; the proportion of Female Republicans be p_4; the proportion of Independent Males be p_5; and the proportion of Independent Females be p_6. Our null and alternative hypotheses are then

H_0: $p_1 = p_2$, $p_3 = p_4$, $p_5 = p_6$.
H_A: At least one of these proportions is not as specified in the null.

It works just as well, and might be a bit easier, to state the hypotheses as follows.

H_0: The proportions of Democrats, Republicans, and Independents are the same among Male and Female students.
H_A: Not all of the proportions stated in the null hypothesis are equal.

For a given two-way table the expected values are the same under a hypothesis of homogeneity or independence.

example: A university dean suspects that there is a difference between how tenured and nontenured professors view a proposed salary increase. She randomly selects 20 nontenured instructors and 25 tenured staff to see if there is a difference. She gets the following results.

	FAVOR PLAN	DO NOT FAVOR PLAN
Tenured	15	10
Nontenured	8	12

Do these data provide good statistical evidence that tenured and nontenured faculty differ in their attitudes toward the proposed salary increase?

solution:

> **I.** Let p_1 = the proportion of tenured faculty who favor the plan and let p_2 = the proportion of nontenured faculty who favor the plan.
> H_0: $p_1 = p_2$
> H_A: $p_1 \neq p_2$
>
> **II.** We will use a chi-square test for homogeneity of proportions. The samples of tenured and nontenured instructors are given as random. We determine that the expected values are given by the matrix $\begin{bmatrix} 12.78 & 12.22 \\ 10.22 & 9.78 \end{bmatrix}$. Because all expected values are greater than 5, the conditions for the test are present.
>
> **III.** $X^2 = 1.78$, $df = (2-1)(2-1) = 1 \Rightarrow 0.15 < P\text{-value} < 0.20$ (from Table C; on the TI-83/84: $P = X^2 \texttt{cdf}(1.78, 1000, 1) = 0.182$).
>
> **IV.** The P-value is not small enough to reject the null hypothesis. These data do not provide strong statistical evidence that tenured and nontenured faculty differ in their attitudes toward the proposed salary plan.

$X^2 = z^2$

The example just completed could have been done as a two-proportion z-test where p_1 and p_2 are defined the same way as in the example (that is, the proportions of tenured and nontenured staff that favor the new plan). Then

$$\hat{p}_1 = \frac{15}{25}$$

and

$$\hat{p}_2 = \frac{8}{20}.$$

MATH FUN FACT! Computation of the z-test statistics for the two-proportion z-test yields $z = 1.333$. Now, $z^2 = 1.78$. Because the chi-square test and the two-proportion z-test are testing the same thing, it should come as little surprise that z^2 equals the obtained value of X^2 in the example. For a 2×2 table, the X^2 test statistic and the value of z^2 obtained for the same data in a two-proportion z-test are the same. Note that the z-test is somewhat more flexible in the case that a one-sided test allows us to consider a particular direction of difference, whereas the chi-square test has only one tail and does not allow us to test for a particular direction of the difference. However, this advantage *only* holds for a 2×2 table since there is no way to use a simple z-test for situations with more than two rows and two columns.

❯ Rapid Review

1. A study yields a chi-square statistic value of 20 ($X^2 = 20$). What is the P-value of the test if

   a. the study was a goodness-of-fit test with $n = 12$?
   b. the study was a test of independence between two categorical variables, the row variable with 3 values and the column variable with 4 values?

   Answer:

   a. $n = 12 \Rightarrow df = 12 - 1 = 11 \Rightarrow 0.025 < P < 0.05$.
      (Using the TI-83/84: X^2cdf $(20,1000,11) = 0.045$.)
   b. $r = 3, c = 4 \Rightarrow df = (3 - 1)(4 - 1) = 6 \Rightarrow 0.0025 < P < 0.005$.
      (Using the TI-83/84: X^2 cdf $(20,1000,6) = 0.0028$.)

2–4. The following data were collected while conducting a chi-square test for independence:

Preference

	BRAND A	BRAND B	BRAND C
Male	16	22	15
Female	18 (X)	30	28

2. What null and alternative hypotheses are being tested?

   Answer:

   H_0: Gender and Preference are independent (or H_0: Gender and Preference are not associated).
   H_A: Gender and Preference are not independent (H_A: Gender and Preference are associated).

3. What is the expected frequency of the cell marked with the X?

   Answer: Identifying the marginals on the table we have the following:

16	22	15	53
18 (X)	30	28	76
34	52	43	129

   Since there are 34 values in the column with the X, we expect to find $\dfrac{34}{129}$ of each row total in the cells of the first column. Hence, the expected value for the cell containing X is $\left(\dfrac{34}{129}\right)(76) = 20.03$.

4. How many degrees of freedom are involved in the test?

   Answer: $df = (2 - 1)(3 - 1) = 2$.

5. The null hypothesis for a chi-square goodness-of-fit test is given as

H_0: $p_1 = 0.2, p_2 = 0.3, p_3 = 0.4, p_4 = 0.1$. Which of the following is an appropriate alternative hypothesis?

a. H_A: $p_1 \neq 0.2, p_2 \neq 0.3, p_3 \neq 0.4, p_4 \neq 0.1$.
b. H_A: $p_1 = p_2 = p_3 = p_4$.
c. H_A: At least one of the proportions is not as stated in the null.
d. H_A: $p_1 \neq p_2 \neq p_3 \neq p_4$.

Answer: c

Practice Problems

Multiple-Choice

1. Find the expected value of the cell marked with the "***" in the following 3×2 table (the boldface values are the marginal totals):

observation	observation	**19**
observation	***	**31**
observation	observation	**27**
45	**32**	**77**

a. 74.60
b. 18.12
c. 12.88
d. 19.65
e. 18.70

2. A χ^2 goodness-of-fit test is performed on a random sample of 360 individuals to see if the number of birthdays each month is proportional to the number of days in the month. X^2 is determined to be 23.5. The P-value for this test is

a. $0.001 < P < 0.005$
b. $0.02 < P < 0.025$
c. $0.025 < P < 0.05$
d. $0.01 < P < 0.02$
e. $0.05 < P < 0.10$

3. Two random samples, one of high school teachers and one of college teachers, are selected and each sample is asked about their job satisfaction. Which of the following are appropriate null and alternative hypotheses for this situation?

a. H_0: The proportion of each level of job satisfaction is the same for high school teachers and college teachers.
   H_A: The proportions of teachers highly satisfied with their jobs is higher for college teachers.
b. H_0: Teaching level and job satisfaction are independent.
   H_A: Teaching level and job satisfaction are not independent.
c. H_0: Teaching level and job satisfaction are associated.
   H_A: Teaching level and job satisfaction are not associated.

d. H_0: The proportion of each level of job satisfaction is the same for high school teachers and college teachers.
H_A: Not all of the proportions of each level of job satisfaction are the same for high school teachers and college teachers.

e. H_0: Teaching level and job satisfaction are independent.
H_A: Teaching level and job satisfaction are not associated.

4. A group separated into men and women are asked their preference toward certain types of television shows. The following table gives the results.

	Program Type A	Program Type B
Men	5	20
Women	3	12

Which of the following statements is (are) true?
   I.   The variables gender and program preference are independent.
   II. For these data, $X^2 = 0$.
   III. The variables gender and program preference are related.

   a. I only
   b. I and II only
   c. II only
   d. III only
   e. II and III only

5. For the following two-way table, compute the value of X^2.

	C	D
A	15	25
B	10	30

   a. 2.63
   b. 1.22
   c. 1.89
   d. 2.04
   e. 1.45

6. The main difference between a X^2 test for independence and a X^2 test for homogeneity of proportions is which of the following?

   a. They are based on a different number of degrees of freedom.
   b. One of the tests is for a two-sided alternative and the other is for a one-sided alternative.
   c. In one case, two variables are compared within a single population. In the other case, two populations are compared in terms of a single variable.
   d. For a given value of X^2, they have different P-values.
   e. There are no differences between the tests. They measure exactly the same thing.

7. A study is to be conducted to help determine if ethnicity is related to blood type. Ethnic groups are identified as White, African American, Asian, Latino, or Other. Blood types are A, B, O, and AB. How many degrees of freedom are there for a chi-square test of independence between Ethnicity and Blood Type?

a. $5 \times 4 = 20$
b. $5 \times 3 = 15$
c. $4 \times 4 = 16$
d. $5 + 4 - 2 = 7$
e. $4 \times 3 = 12$

8. Which of the following statements is (are) correct?

   I. A condition for using a χ^2 test is that most expected frequencies must be at least 5 and that all must be at least 1.

  II. A χ^2 test for goodness of fit tests the degree to which a categorical variable has a specific distribution.

 III. Expected cell values are computed in the same way for goodness of fit tests and tests of independence.

  a.   I only
  b.   II only
  c.   I and II only
  d.   II and III only
  e.   I, II, and III

Free-Response

1. An AP Statistics student noted that the probability distribution for a binomial random variable with $n = 4$ and $p = 0.3$ is approximately given by the following:

n	P
0	0.240
1	0.412
2	0.265
3	0.076
4	0.008

(*Note:* $\Sigma\, p = 1.001$ rather than 1 due to rounding.)

The student decides to test the `randBin` function on her TI-83/84 by putting 500 values into a list using this function (`randBin(4,0.3,500)` → L1) and counting the number of each outcome. (Can you think of an efficient way to count each outcome?) She obtained the following:

n	Observed
0	110
1	190
2	160
3	36
4	4

Do these data provide evidence that the `randBin` function on the calculator is correctly generating values from this distribution?

Calculator Tip: It's a bit of a digression, but if you actually wanted to do the experiment in question 1, you would need to have an efficient way of counting the number of each outcome. You certainly don't want to simply scroll through all 500 entries and tally each one. Even sorting them first and then counting would be tedious (more so if n were bigger than 4). One easy way is to draw a histogram of the data and then TRACE to get the totals. Once you have your 500 values from randBin in L1, go to STAT PLOTS and set up a histogram for L1. Choose a WINDOW something like $[-0.5, 4.5, 1, -1, 300, 1, 1]$. Be sure that Xscl is set to 1. You may need to adjust the Ymax from 300 to get a nice picture on your screen. Then simply TRACE across the bars of the histogram and read the value of n for each outcome off of the screen. The reason for having x go from –0.5 to 4.5 is so that the (integer) outcomes will be in the middle of each bar of the histogram.

2. A chi-square test for the homogeneity of proportions is conducted on three populations and one categorical variable that has four values. Computation of the chi-square statistic yields $\chi^2 = 17.2$. Is this result significant at the 0.01 level of significance?

3. Which of the following best describes the difference between a test for independence and a test for homogeneity of proportions? Discuss the correctness of each answer.

    a. There is no difference because they both produce the same value of the chi-square test statistic.
    b. A test for independence has one population and two categorical variables, whereas a test for homogeneity of proportions has more than one population and only one categorical variable.
    c. A test for homogeneity of proportions has one population and two categorical variables, whereas a test for independence has more than one population and only one categorical variable.
    d. A test for independence uses count data when calculating chi-square and a test for homogeneity uses percentages or proportions when calculating chi-square.

4. Compute the expected value for the cell that contains the frog. You are given the marginal distribution.

	D	E	F	G	Total
A					94
B			🐸		96
C					119
Total	74	69	128	38	309

5. Restaurants in two parts of a major city were compared on customer satisfaction to see if location influences customer satisfaction. A random sample of 38 patrons from

the Big Steak Restaurant in the eastern part of town and another random sample of 36 patrons from the Big Steak Restaurant on the western side of town were interviewed for the study. The restaurants are under the same management, and the researcher established that they are virtually identical in terms of decor, service, menu, and food quality. The results are presented in the following table.

Patrons' Ratings of Restaurants

	Excellent	Good	Fair	Poor
Eastern	10	12	11	5
Western	6	15	7	8

Do these data provide good evidence that location influences customer satisfaction?

6. A chi-square test for goodness of fit is done on a variable with 15 categories. What is the minimum value of χ^2 necessary to reject the null hypothesis at the 0.02 level of significance?

7. The number of defects from a manufacturing process by day of the week are as follows:

	Monday	Tuesday	Wednesday	Thursday	Friday
Number:	36	23	26	25	40

The manufacturer is concerned that the number of defects is greater on Monday and Friday. Test, at the 0.05 level of significance, the claim that the proportion of defects is the same each day of the week.

8. A study was done on opinions concerning the legalization of marijuana at Mountain Vista College. One hundred fifty-seven respondents were randomly selected from a large pool of faculty, students, and parents at the college. Respondents were given a choice of favoring the legalization of marijuana, opposing the legalization of marijuana, or favoring making marijuana a legal but controlled substance. The results of the survey were as follows.

	FAVOR LEGALIZATION	OPPOSE LEGALIZATION	FAVOR LEGALIZATION WITH CONTROL
Students	17	9	6
Faculty	33	40	27
Parents	5	8	12

Do these data support, at the 0.05 level, the contention that the type of respondent (student, faculty, or parent) is related to the opinion toward legalization? Is this a test of independence or a test of homogeneity of proportions?

Cumulative Review Problems

Use the computer output given below to answer Questions 1 and 2.

The regression equation is
$y = -136 + 3.98\,X$

Predictor	Coef	St Dev	t ratio	P
Constant	−136.10	42.47	−3.20	.024
X	3.9795	0.6529	6.09	.002
$s = 8.434$	R-sq = 88.1%		R-sq(adj) = 85.8%	

1. Based on the computer output above, what conclusion would you draw concerning H_0: $\beta = 0$? Justify your answer.

2. Use the computer output above to construct a 99% confidence interval for the slope of the regression line ($n = 8$). Interpret your interval.

3. If you roll two dice, the probability that you roll a sum of 10 is approximately 0.083.

    a. What is the probability that you first roll a 10 on the 10th roll?
    b. What is the average number of rolls until you first roll a 10?

4. An experiment is conducted by taking measurements of a personality trait on identical twins and then comparing the results for each set of twins. Would the analysis of the results assume two independent populations or proceed as though there were a single population? Explain.

5. The lengths and widths of a certain type of fish were measured and the least-squares regression line for predicting width from length was found to be: $\widehat{width} = -0.826 + 0.193\,(length)$. The graph that follows is a residual plot for the data:

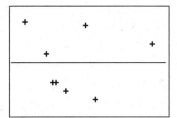

    a. The fish whose width is 3.8 had a length of 25.5. What is the residual for this point?

    b. Based on the residual plot, does a line seem like a good model for the data?

Solutions to Practice Problems

Multiple-Choice

1. The correct answer is (c). The expected value for that cell can be found as follows:

    $$\left(\frac{32}{77}\right)(31) = 12.88\,.$$

2. The correct answer is (d). Since there are 12 months in a year, we have $n = 12$ and $df = 12 - 1 = 11$. Reading from Table C, $0.01 < P\text{-value} < 0.02$. The exact value is given by the TI-83/84 as X^2 cdf$(23.5,1000,11) = 0.015$.

3. The correct answer is (d). Because we have independent random samples of teachers from each of the two levels, this is a test of homogeneity of proportions. It would have been a test of independence if there was only one sample broken into categories (correct answer would be (b) in that case).

4. The correct answer is (b). The expected values for the cells are exactly equal to the observed values; for example, for the 1st row, 1st column, $\text{Exp} = \left(\dfrac{25}{40}\right)(8) = 5$, so X^2 must equal $0 \Rightarrow$ the variables are independent, and are not related.

5. The correct answer is (e). The expected values for this two-way table are given by the matrix: $\begin{bmatrix} 12.5 & 27.5 \\ 12.5 & 27.5 \end{bmatrix}$.

    Then,

    $$X^2 = \frac{(15-12.5)^2}{12.5} + \frac{(25-27.5)^2}{27.5} + \frac{(10-12.5)^2}{12.5}$$
    $$+ \frac{(30-27.5)^2}{27.5} = 1.45.$$

6. The correct answer is (c). In a X^2 test for independence, we are interested in whether or not two categorical variables, measured on a single population, are related. In a X^2 test for homogeneity of proportions, we are interested in whether two or more populations have the same proportions for each of the values of a single categorical variable.

7. The correct answer is (e). Using Ethnicity as the row variable, there are five rows ($r = 5$) and four columns ($c = 4$). The number of degrees of freedom for an $r \times c$ table is $(r - 1)(c - 1)$. In this question, $(5 - 1)(4 - 1) = 4 \times 3 = 12$.

8. The correct answer is (c). In III, the expected value for each category in a goodness-of-fit test is found by multiplying the proportion of the distribution of each category by the sample size. The expected value for a test of independence is found by multiplying the row total by the column total and then dividing by n.

Free-Response

1.
    I. Let $p_1 =$ the proportion of 0s, $p_2 =$ the proportion of 1s, $p_3 =$ the proportion of 2s, $p_4 =$ the proportion of 3s, and $p_5 =$ the proportion of 4s.

    H_0: $p_1 = 0.24$, $p_2 = 0.41$, $p_3 = 0.27$, $p_4 = 0.07$, $p_5 = 0.01$.

    H_A: Not all of the proportions stated in H_0 are correct.

    II. We will use a chi-square goodness-of-fit test. The observed counts and expected values for the 500 trials are shown in the following table:

N	OBSERVED	EXPECTED
0	110	$(0.24)(500) = 120$
1	190	$(0.41)(500) = 205$
2	160	$(0.27)(500) = 135$
3	36	$(0.07)(500) = 35$
4	4	$(0.01)(500) = 5$

Continued

We note that all expected values are at least 5, so the conditions necessary for the chi-square test are present.

III. $X^2 = \sum \frac{(O-E)^2}{E} = \frac{(110-120)^2}{120} + \cdots + \frac{(4-5)^2}{5} = 6.79$, df $= 4 \Rightarrow$

$0.10 < P$-value < 0.15 (from Table C). Using the TI-83/84, X^2 cdf (6.79, 1000,40) = 0.147.

IV. The P-value is greater than any commonly accepted significance level. Hence, we do not reject H_0 and conclude that we do not have good evidence that the calculator is not correctly generating values from $B(4, 0.3)$.

2. For a 3×4 two-way table, $df = (3-1)(4-1) = 6 \Rightarrow 0.005 < P$-value < 0.01 (from Table C). The finding is significant at the 0.01 level of significance. Using the TI-83/84, P-value $= X^2$ cdf (17.2,1000,6) = 0.009.

3. (a) is not correct. For a given set of observations, they both do produce the same value of chi-square. However, they differ in that they are different ways to design a study. (b) is correct. A test of independence hypothesizes that two categorical variables are independent within a given population. A test for homogeneity of proportions hypothesizes that the proportions of the values of a single categorical variable are the same for more than one population. (c) is incorrect. It is a reversal of the actual difference between the two designs. (d) is incorrect. You always use count data when computing chi-square.

4. The expected value of the cell with the frog is $\frac{128}{309}(96) = 39.77$.

5. Based on the design of the study, this is a test of homogeneity of proportions.

I. H_0: The proportions of patrons who rate the restaurant Excellent, Good, Fair, and Poor are the same for the eastern and western sides of town.

H_A: Not all the proportions are the same.

II. We will use the chi-square test for homogeneity of proportions.

Calculation of expected values (using the TI-83/84) yields the following results:

$\begin{bmatrix} 8.22 & 13.86 & 9.24 & 6.68 \\ 7.78 & 13.14 & 8.76 & 6.32 \end{bmatrix}$. Since all expected values are at least 5, the conditions

necessary for this test are present.

III. $X^2 = \sum \frac{(O-E)^2}{E} = \frac{(10-8.22)^2}{8.22} + \cdots + \frac{(8-6.32)^2}{6.32} = 2.86, df = (2-1)(4-1) = 3 \Rightarrow$

P-value > 0.25 (from Table C). X^2 cdf (2.86,1000,3) = 0.414.

IV. The P-value is larger than any commonly accepted significance level. Thus, we cannot reject H_0. We do not have evidence that location influences customer satisfaction.

6. If $n = 15$, then $df = 15 - 1 = 14$. In the table we find the entry in the column for tail probability of 0.02 and the row with 14 degrees of freedom. That value is 26.87. Any value of X^2 larger than 26.87 will yield a P-value less than 0.02.

7.

I. Let p_1 be the true proportion of defects produced on Monday.

Let p_2 be the true proportion of defects produced on Tuesday.

Let p_3 be the true proportion of defects produced on Wednesday.

Let p_4 be the true proportion of defects produced on Thursday.

Let p_5 be the true proportion of defects produced on Friday.

H_0: $p_1 = p_2 = p_3 = p_4 = p_5$ (the proportion of defects is the same each day of the week).

H_A: At least one proportion does not equal the others (the proportion of defects is not the same each day of the week).

II. We will use a chi-square goodness-of-fit test. The number of expected defects is the same for each day of the week. Because there was a total of 150 defects during the week, we would expect, if the null is true, to have 30 defects each day. Because the number of expected defects is greater than 5 for each day, the conditions for the chi-square test are present.

III. $X^2 = \sum \dfrac{(O-E)^2}{E} = \dfrac{(36-30)^2}{30} + \cdots + \dfrac{(40-30)^2}{30} = 7.533$, $df = 4 \Rightarrow 0.10 <$

P-value < 0.15 (from Table C). (X^2 cdf (7.533.1000,4) = 0.11; or, you could use the X^2 GOF-Test in the STAT TESTS menu of a TI-83/84 if you have it.)

IV. The P-value is larger than any commonly accepted significance level. We do not have strong evidence that there are more defects produced on Monday and Friday than on other days of the week.

8. Because we have a single population from which we drew our sample and we are asking if two variables are related *within* that population, this is a chi-square test for independence.

I. H_0: Type of respondent and opinion toward the legalization of marijuana are independent.

H_A: Type of respondent and opinion toward the legalization of marijuana are not independent.

II. We will do a X^2 test of independence. The following table gives the observed and expected values for this situation (expected values are the second row in each cell; the expected values were calculated by using the MATRIX function and the X^2–Test item in the STAT TESTS menu):

17 11.21	9 11.62	6 9.17
33 35.03	40 36.31	27 28.66
5 8.76	8 9.08	12 7.17

Continued

> Since all expected values are at least 5, the conditions necessary for the chi-square test are present.
>
> **III.** $\chi^2 = \sum \dfrac{(O-E)^2}{E} = \dfrac{(17-11.21)^2}{11.21} + \cdots + \dfrac{(12-7.17)^2}{7.17} = 10.27,\ df = (3-1)(3-1) = 4 \Rightarrow 0.025 < P\text{-value} < 0.05$ (from Table C).
>
> (Using the TI-83/84, P-value $= \chi^2\text{cdf}(10.27,1000,4) = 0.036$.)
>
> **IV.** Because $P < 0.05$, reject H_0. We have evidence that the type of respondent is related to opinion concerning the legalization of marijuana.

Solutions to Cumulative Review Problems

1. The t-test statistic for the slope of the regression line (under $H_0: \beta = 0$) is 6.09. This translates into a P-value of 0.002, as shown in the printout. This low P-value allows us to reject the null hypothesis. We conclude that we have strong evidence of a linear relationship between X and Y.

2. For $C = 0.99$ (a 99% confidence interval) at $df = n - 2 = 6$, $t^* = 3.707$. The required interval is $3.9795 \pm 3.707(.6529) = (1.56, 6.40)$. We are 99% confident that the true slope of the population regression line lies between 1.56 and 6.40.

3. a. This is a geometric distribution problem. The probability that the first success occurs on the 10th roll is given by $G(10) = (0.083)(1 - 0.083)^9 = 0.038$. (On the TI-83/84, $G(10) = \text{geometpdf}(0.083,10) = 0.038$.)

   b. $\dfrac{1}{0.083} = 12.05$. On average, it will take about 12 rolls before you get a 10.

   (Actually, it's *exactly* 12 rolls on average since the *exact* probability of rolling a 10 is $\dfrac{1}{12}$, not 0.083, and $\dfrac{1}{1/12} = 12$.)

4. This is an example of a *matched-pairs design*. The identical twins form a block for comparison of the treatment. Statistics are based on the differences between the scores of the pairs of twins. Hence, this is a one-variable situation—one population of values, each constructed as a difference of the matched pairs.

5. a. Residual $=$ actual $-$ predicted $= 3.8 - [-0.826 + 0.193(25.5)] = 3.8 - 4.096 = -0.296$.

   b. There does not seem to be any consistent pattern in the residual plot, indicating that a line is probably a good model for the data.

CHAPTER 14

Free-Response Question 6: The Investigative Task

Question 6 in the Free-Response section is called the **Investigative Task**, and it is different from the other free-response questions in three ways. First, it is expected to take longer. The exam recommends about 25 minutes on that question alone! Second, it is worth more than the other free-response questions. The Investigative Task is worth one-fourth, or 25%, of the free-response grade. Because the free-response part of the exam is half of your overall score, the Investigative Task ends up being one-eighth of the total test score! Third, it will address topics in a way that you may not have seen before.

That is because the Investigative Task is intended to test your ability to apply what you've learned in a new and different situation. It might involve working with or creating a statistic you've never seen, or you may be asked to read a different kind of plot from any you've seen, or use a familiar plot in a different way. No worries! You have been doing and thinking about statistics all year, so trust yourself a bit. Follow where the prompts lead.

Because there is no way to predict what topic will be addressed, you cannot really study for it in the traditional sense. What you can and should do is make sure to have a solid understanding of the topics you've learned and then employ some strategies to help ensure your success.

First, realize that parts of the Investigative Task, usually the first parts, will probably be familiar. They almost always start on familiar ground but then lead you to the investigative portion later in the problem, which is the new stuff. It is this new part where you often have to think critically or apply existing statistical knowledge in a new way.

This is the idea of Question 6—to get you to think for yourself in a new situation. So keep calm and go about doing what the question asks you to do—you have been thinking statistically for almost a year; the concepts in this question are likely to be well within your reach. While only the members of the test development committee can ever predict with any certainty what an Investigative Task will actually look like, here's a stab we took to help you:

Taylor and Harper are twins who want to buy a used car to drive when they go to college. Together, they collect information on the age (in years), miles driven (in thousands of miles), and selling price (in thousands of dollars) of a group of 20 of the same model of a popular car currently offered for sale in their area. This information is provided in the table below:

AGE (YEARS)	MILES (1000s)	$PRICE (1000s)	AGE (YEARS)	MILES (1000s)	$PRICE (1000s)
3	20	16.6	1	11	18.2
3	78	11.0	3	79	13.3
3	47	14.6	3	45	14.3
10	111	8.6	1	5	18.0
8	123	8.0	6	112	10.1
3	59	15.0	5	69	12.1
2	39	17.1	5	40	12.9
2	61	14.2	4	44	14.5
7	91	9.6	9	65	10.6
7	118	9.0	2	19	17.0

Taylor wants to use *Age* to predict the selling price of this car. Here are the summary statistics and appropriate plots for Taylor's linear regression:

$$\widehat{Price}_T = 17.9243 - 1.0780(Age)$$

$$r = -0.8850 \, (r^2 = 0.7832)$$

Harper wants to use *Miles Driven* to predict the selling price of this car. Here are the summary statistics and appropriate plots for Harper's linear regression:

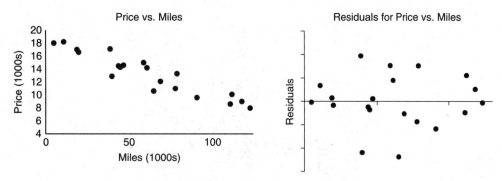

$$\widehat{Price}_H = 18.4598 - 0.0845(Miles)$$

$$r = -0.9370 \,(r^2 = 0.8780)$$

(a) Interpret the value of r^2 for Taylor's regression results in the context of this problem.

(b) Based on the information provided, which linear regression do you think does a better job predicting the price of this car? Explain your answer.

Taylor believes that if they were to include BOTH Age and Miles, they could improve their ability to predict the price of this type of car. To that end, Taylor produces the equation:

$$\widehat{Price} = 18.8674 - 0.4903(Age) - 0.0566(Miles)$$

(c) Use this new regression equation to predict the price of a car that is 4 years old and has 32,000 miles. Show your work.

But Harper points out that to evaluate whether or not this new equation actually is more effective will require some new way to measure how well the model predicts the price of this model of car. So Harper consulted some sources and found a statistic that has the same interpretation as r^2 but can be used with more than one independent variable.

Let r_T = correlation for the linear relationship between Age and Price, r_H = correlation for the linear relationship between Miles and Price, and $r_{A\&M}$ = correlation for the linear relationship between Age and Miles. Harper finds the following formula for the coefficient of determination when you have **two** independent variables:

$$R^2 = \frac{(r_T)^2 + (r_H)^2 - 2(r_T)(r_H)(r_{A\&M})}{1 - (r_{A\&M})^2}$$

Taylor and Harper find that the relationship between Age and Miles appears to be a positive linear relationship with a correlation of 0.7687.

(d) Use this new formula as well as the information provided in the regression output at the beginning of the problem to find the value of R^2 for the twins' sample of cars. Then interpret this value in the context of the problem.

Harper consults a large national database of all cars of this type currently offered for sale with information as to price, age, and miles driven. Harper is able to ask for 200 random samples of 20 cars each and calculate R^2 for predicting Price using both Age and Miles. The dotplot shown below represents the 200 values of R^2 that Harper collected from these samples.

(e) Using Harper's dotplot and the value of $\mathbf{R^2}$ you obtained in part (d), comment on whether you believe the sample of 20 cars the twins used in their analysis is likely a representative sample of all cars of this model currently for sale nationwide.

Solution

First, notice that while the raw data is included in the table, you do not need to type these values into your calculator—all relevant statistical summaries have been provided to help you answer this question.

Part (a): Interpret the value of r^2 for Taylor's regression results in the context of this problem.

First, make sure that you grab the appropriate value. $r^2 = 0.7832$. This should be interpreted in context as follows:

78.32% of the variation in the price of the cars in this sample can be explained by the linear relationship with the miles driven.

Note: This part is not new. You are familiar with interpreting r^2.

Part (b): Based on the information provided above, which linear regression do you think does a better job predicting the price of this car? Explain your answer.

Based on the scatterplots and results, Harper's model seems to do a better job at predicting the price of this car. Harper's model has a stronger correlation ($r = -0.9370$ is closer to negative one than is Taylor's $r = -0.8850$). And it would appear that the residual plot for Harper's model is much more randomly scattered and with less variation in that scatter.

Note: This part should also be familiar.

Part (c): Use this new regression equation to predict the price of a model of this car that is 4 years old and has 32,000 miles. Show your work.

(Hint: Be sure to check back with your graphs and use the appropriate units when you substitute. Note that the mileage is given in 1000s of miles, so you need to use 32 in the appropriate place as well as report the answer in thousands of dollars.)

$$\widehat{PRICE} = 18.8674 - 0.4903(Age) - 0.0566(Miles)$$

$$\widehat{PRICE} = 18.8674 - 0.4903(4) - 0.0566(32)$$

$$\widehat{PRICE} = 15.215$$

We would predict the price for a model of this car that is 4 years old and has 32,000 miles would be about $15,215.

Note: Still nothing new.

Part (d): Use this new formula as well as the information provided in the regression output at the beginning of the problem to find the value of $\mathbf{R^2}$ for the twins' sample of cars. Then interpret this value in the context of the problem.

$$\mathbf{R^2} = \frac{(r_T)^2 + (r_H)^2 - 2(r_T)(r_H)(r_{A\&M})}{1 - (r_{A\&M})^2}$$

$$\mathbf{R^2} = \frac{(-0.8850)^2 + (-0.9370)^2 - 2(-0.8850)(-0.9370)(0.7687)}{1 - (0.7687)^2}$$

$$\mathbf{R^2} = 0.9443$$

In the context of this problem, 94.43% of the variation in the price of the cars in this sample can be explained by the relationship with both age and miles driven.

Note: OK, this looks new. You've probably never seen this statistic before. But relax! You were given a formula, and all you need to do is substitute and evaluate. One wrinkle, the sentence **"Taylor and Harper find that the relationship between Age and Miles appears to be a positive linear relationship with a correlation of 0.7687"** *tells you that the value of* $r_{A\&M}$ *is 0.7687. You need to recognize this based on the phrasing in this sentence. The other leap you need to make is in how this calculation of R^2 is interpreted. You were given a key piece of information at the beginning of part (e):* **"So Harper consulted some sources and found a statistic that has the same interpretation as r², but can be used with more than one independent variable."** *By reading the problem carefully you should be able to nail the interpretation of R^2.*

Part (e): Using Harper's dotplot and the value of R^2 you obtained in part (d), comment on whether you believe the sample of 20 cars the twins used in their analysis is likely a representative sample of all cars of this model.

It would appear that only 2 of the 200 samples produced values of R^2 larger than 0.9443, or only 1% of the samples. This is a very small probability and thus makes it unlikely that the sample the twins used in their analysis is a representative sample of all the cars of this model that are currently for sale nationwide.

Note: This **looks** *new, too. But it's really not. You've dealt with simulated sampling distributions in the past. We are simulating a different statistic, but sampling distributions all work the same way. Just find the location of your value among the simulated values and decide if what you got fits with that distribution or not. In other words, use the simulation to get a simulated P-value.*

General Tips for the Investigative Task

- Relax and remember that the first part of the question is usually familiar.
- As you work through the problem, note that the parts often tie together. You may see a direction that states "based on your answer to part (b)." If you get stuck on part (b), make up a **reasonable** answer (and say that you have done so!). Then when needed, go ahead and use this answer in the parts that follow.

- While each of us is unique in how we approach a test—some of us work the problems in order, others of us skip around until all the problems are completed—many teachers believe that you should not leave the Investigative Task for the very last. Consider doing a couple of the first five free-response questions and then starting the Investigative Task. Get a couple of parts of the Investigative Task completed and then go back and finish the rest of the other free-response questions. Finally, use your remaining time to work on the rest of the parts of the Investigative Task.

STEP 5

Build Your Test-Taking Confidence

AP Statistics Practice Test 1
AP Statistics Practice Test 2

AP Statistics Practice Test 1

ANSWER SHEET FOR SECTION I

1 (A) (B) (C) (D) (E)
2 (A) (B) (C) (D) (E)
3 (A) (B) (C) (D) (E)
4 (A) (B) (C) (D) (E)
5 (A) (B) (C) (D) (E)
6 (A) (B) (C) (D) (E)
7 (A) (B) (C) (D) (E)
8 (A) (B) (C) (D) (E)
9 (A) (B) (C) (D) (E)
10 (A) (B) (C) (D) (E)
11 (A) (B) (C) (D) (E)
12 (A) (B) (C) (D) (E)
13 (A) (B) (C) (D) (E)
14 (A) (B) (C) (D) (E)
15 (A) (B) (C) (D) (E)

16 (A) (B) (C) (D) (E)
17 (A) (B) (C) (D) (E)
18 (A) (B) (C) (D) (E)
19 (A) (B) (C) (D) (E)
20 (A) (B) (C) (D) (E)
21 (A) (B) (C) (D) (E)
22 (A) (B) (C) (D) (E)
23 (A) (B) (C) (D) (E)
24 (A) (B) (C) (D) (E)
25 (A) (B) (C) (D) (E)
26 (A) (B) (C) (D) (E)
27 (A) (B) (C) (D) (E)
28 (A) (B) (C) (D) (E)
29 (A) (B) (C) (D) (E)
30 (A) (B) (C) (D) (E)

31 (A) (B) (C) (D) (E)
32 (A) (B) (C) (D) (E)
33 (A) (B) (C) (D) (E)
34 (A) (B) (C) (D) (E)
35 (A) (B) (C) (D) (E)
36 (A) (B) (C) (D) (E)
37 (A) (B) (C) (D) (E)
38 (A) (B) (C) (D) (E)
39 (A) (B) (C) (D) (E)
40 (A) (B) (C) (D) (E)

AP Statistics Practice Test 1

SECTION I

Time: 1 hour and 30 minutes

Number of questions: 40

Percentage of total grade: 50

Directions: Solve each of the following problems. Decide which is the best of the choices given and answer in the appropriate place on the answer sheet. No credit will be given for anything written on the exam. Do not spend too much time on any one problem.

1. A set of test scores has the following five-number summary:

Minimum	Q1	Median	Q3	Maximum
2	18	22.5	28.5	33

Which statement about outliers must be true?

A. There is exactly one outlier on the lower end.
B. There is at least one outlier on the lower end.
C. There is exactly one outlier on the higher end.
D. There is at least one outlier on the higher end.
E. There are no outliers.

2. The table below shows the regression output for predicting the number of calories from the number of milligrams of sodium for items at a fast-food chain. What percentage of the variation in calories is explained by the regression model, using sodium as a predictor?

Predictor	Coef	SE Coef	t-ratio	p
Constant	147.1427	20.6957	7.110	0.0000
Sodium	0.2457	0.0210	11.673	0.0000

$s = 136.69$ r-sq $= 0.542313$ r-sq (adj) $= 0.538333$

A. 7.36%
B. 54.2%
C. 53.8%
D. 73.4%
E. 73.6%

3. A drug company will conduct a randomized controlled study on the effectiveness of a new heart disease medication called Heartaid. Heartaid is more expensive than the currently used medication. The analysis will include a significance test with H_0: Heartaid and the current medication are equally effective at preventing heart disease and H_a: Heartaid is more effective than the current medication at preventing heart disease. Which of these would be a potential consequence of a Type II error?

A. Patients will spend more money on Heartaid, even though it is actually not any more effective than the current medication.
B. Doctors will begin to prescribe Heartaid to patients, even though it is actually not any more effective than the current medication.
C. Patients will continue to use the current medication, even though Heartaid is actually more effective.
D. Researchers will calculate the wrong P-value, making their advice to doctors invalid.
E. Researchers will calculate the correct P-value, but will misinterpret it in their conclusion.

GO ON TO THE NEXT PAGE

4. Researchers in the Southwest are studying tortoises—a species of animal that is affected by habitat loss due to human development of the desert. A total of 78 tortoises are being studied by researchers at several sites. The data on gender and species of all these tortoises is organized in the table shown below.

Species	Male	Female	Total
Agassiz	18	33	51
Morafka	12	15	27
Total	30	48	78

If a tortoise from this study is to be selected at random, let A = *the tortoise is female* and B = *the tortoise is a Morafka*. Which of the following appropriately interprets the value of $P(B|A)$?

A. 31.3% is the probability that a randomly selected Morafka tortoise is a female tortoise.
B. 31.3% is the probability that a randomly selected female tortoise is a Morafka tortoise.
C. 19.2% is the probability that a randomly selected Morafka tortoise is a female tortoise.
D. 19.2% is the probability that a randomly selected female tortoise is a Morafka tortoise.
E. 31.3% is the probability that a randomly selected tortoise is a Morafka tortoise.

5. The main purpose of blocking in an experiment is to

A. reduce bias.
B. reduce confounding.
C. reduce variation within treatments.
D. reduce variation between treatments.
E. reduce the probability of a Type I error.

6. The midterm scores for a statistics course were approximately normally distributed with a mean of 52 points and a standard deviation of 4 points. The final exam scores were approximately normally distributed with a mean of 112 points and a standard deviation of 10 points. One student had a score of 58 points on the midterm. If she had the same standardized score (z-score) on the final exam, what must her score have been?

A. 15 points
B. 58 points

C. 118 points
D. 122 points
E. 127 points

7. Which of the following is *not* an advantage of stratified random sampling over simple random sampling?

A. When done correctly, a stratified random sample is less biased than a simple random sample.
B. When done correctly, a stratified random sampling process has less variability from sample to sample than a simple random sample.
C. When done correctly, a stratified random sample can provide, with a smaller sample size, an estimate that is just as reliable as that of a simple random sample with a larger sample size.
D. A stratified random sample provides information about each stratum in the population as well as an estimate for the population as a whole, and a simple random sample does not.
E. When done correctly, a stratified random sample can provide a more reliable estimate than a simple random sample using the same sample size.

8. Sean loves music. He uses a social media app and asks 100 people how many playlists they have created in their Spotify account. The distribution is skewed right. Which of the following is a true statement about the sampling distribution of the sample mean?

A. The shape of the sampling distribution is approximately normally distributed.
B. The shape of the sampling distribution is slightly skewed right.
C. The shape of the sampling distribution is unknowable because we don't know the shape of the population.
D. The shape of the sampling distribution is unknowable because we don't know the standard deviation of the population.
E. The shape of the sampling distribution is unknowable because Sean used a biased data collection method.

GO ON TO THE NEXT PAGE

9. Breakfast cereals have a wide range of sugar content. Some cereals contain high fructose corn syrup (HFCS) as a source of sugar and some do not. The boxplots below show the total sugar content of different types of cereal for those containing HFCS and for those that do not. Which statement is true based on the boxplots?

A. The number of cereals with HFCS is about the same as the number of cereals without HFCS.
B. The cereals with HFCS have a greater interquartile range than the cereals without HFCS.
C. The cereals without HFCS have a greater range than the cereals with HFCS.
D About half the cereals without HFCS have less sugar than about three-fourths of the cereals with HFCS.
E. About half the cereals with HFCS have more sugar than about three-fourths of the cereals without HFCS.

10. Semir rolls a six-sided die every morning to determine what he will have for breakfast. If he rolls a 1 or 2, he takes time to cook himself a big breakfast. If he rolls a 3 or larger he grabs a quick lighter breakfast. When he cooks himself a big breakfast, there is a 15% chance he will be late for school. If he has a lighter breakfast, there is a 6% chance he will be late for school. What is the probability Semir will be on time for school any given day?

A. 0.09
B. 0.21
C. 0.80
D. 0.91
E. 0.94

11. A barista at a coffee shop tracks the amount of money spent on each purchase in the week before Christmas. Because of the holiday season, there were more large purchases than normal. The distribution of the purchases had an interesting characteristic. The shape was bimodal. Many customers bought just one or two items, spending \$5 to \$10. Another group of customers bought gifts and/or large orders and spent \$25 to \$40. It was also noted that there was a long tail on the high end of the distribution. Which of the following is **not** true?

A. Using a single mean to describe the distribution is unhelpful.
B. There is probably a gap in the distribution of about \$15 to \$20.
C. The IQR of this distribution will be very large.
D. The overall median amount will be greater than the overall mean.
E. The standard deviation is not a useful measure of spread for this distribution.

12. A polling company has been asked to do a poll to see if the proportion of people that would vote for their candidate has *improved* since the previous poll, as their analyst suspects. Using p_p = the proportion of all voters that would have supported their candidate in the previous poll, and p_c = the proportion of all voters that would support their candidate in the current poll, which is an appropriate pair of hypotheses for a significance test?

A. H_0: $p_c > p_p$
   H_a: $p_c \leq p_p$
B. H_0: $p_c < p_p$
   H_a: $p_c > p_p$
C. H_0: $p_c > p_p$
   H_a: $p_c = p_p$
D. H_0: $p_c = p_p$
   H_a: $p_c > p_p$
E. H_0: $p_c = p_p$
   H_a: $p_c \neq p_p$

13. A public health researcher suspected that there would be a relationship between the proportion of people in a state that engage in binge alcohol use and the proportion of people in the state that smoke cigarettes. A regression analysis was performed and some of the output is shown below.

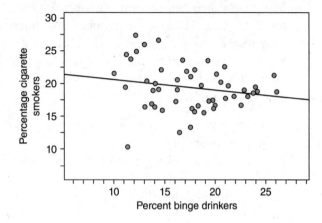

Predictor	Coef	SE Coef	T	P
Constant	22.0758	2.1144	10.441	<0.001
PctBingeDr	−0.1580	0.1174	−1.346	0.1846
S = 3.4605	R-Sq = 0.0356		R-Sq (Adj) = 0.0160	

Which of the following statements is NOT justified by these results?

A. The researcher has proved that an increase in binge drinking results in a decrease in cigarette smoking.
B. The relationship between the variables is weak.
C. The y-intercept is probably an extrapolation.
D. The correlation coefficient is negative.
E. For every 1% increase in binge drinkers the model predicts a 0.16% decrease in cigarette smokers.

14. Marine biologists want to determine whether a small increase in the acidity of seawater would adversely affect marine life. They randomly assigned several *Entacmaea quadricolor*, one species of sea anemone, to one of eight aquariums that had been prepared with environments as similar as possible to the natural habitat. Then they randomly selected four tanks, and gradually increased the acidity of the water. They monitored the health of the anemones for the duration of the study. Which of these statements is NOT true about this study?

A. An advantage of using only one variety of sea anemones is that there should be less variability in the response to each treatment.
B. A disadvantage of using only one variety of sea anemones is that the scope of inference is limited only to that type of anemone.
C. An advantage of using aquariums is that it is easier to maintain control to avoid confounding factors.
D. A disadvantage of using aquariums is that the anemones might respond differently in the ocean than they do in aquariums.
E. If the anemones in the aquariums with increased acidity are less healthy than those without increased acidity, it cannot be determined that the increased acidity *caused* the response.

15. In a large high school, the student council wants to select a sample to survey the student body. They will first select 25 freshmen, then select 25 sophomores, then select 25 juniors, and then finally 25 seniors. This is an example of a

A. cluster sample.
B. stratified sample.
C. simple random sample.
D. convenience sample.
E. systematic sample.

GO ON TO THE NEXT PAGE

16. Listed below are the summary statistics for the daily high temperatures (in degrees F) for the month of September in a midwestern U.S. city. One particular day has a *z*-score of 0.70. What was the likely temperature that day?

Variable	N	Mean	Median	TrMean	StDev	SE Mean
High Temp	30	74.9	75	74.7	7.29	1.33

Variable	Minimum	Maximum	Q1	Q3
High Temp	60	90	69	79

   A. 68
   B. 70
   C. 74
   D. 76
   E. 80

17. In American football, the running back carries the football forward in a quest to score points. Many people create fantasy football teams by selecting players as their "team." These fans analyze data to judge which players are outstanding. The following regression output analyzes the linear relationship between the number of times a running back is given the football (carries) and the total number of yards that player gains in a season for a random sample of 18 running backs.

The regression equation is		
Total yards gained $= 30.947 + 4.3441$(Carries)		
Predictor	Coef	SE Coef
Constant	30.947	7.414
Carries	4.3441	1.811
S $= 56.647$	R-sq $= 45.9\%$	

The appropriate calculation for a 99% confidence interval for the slope of the least squares regression line for the total yards gained versus number of carries in a season for all running backs is

   A. $4.3441 \pm 2.576 \cdot (1.811)/\sqrt{18}$
   B. $4.3441 \pm 2.921 \cdot (1.811)$
   C. $4.3441 \pm 2.921 \cdot (1.811)/\sqrt{18}$
   D. $4.3441 \pm 2.898 \cdot (1.811)$
   E. $4.3441 \pm 2.898 \cdot (1.811)/\sqrt{18}$

18. Above is a cumulative relative frequency plot for the scores of a large university class on a 90-point statistics exam. Which of the following observations is correct?

   A. The median score is at least 60 points.
   B. The distribution of scores is skewed to the right.
   C. The distribution of scores is skewed to the left.
   D. The distribution is roughly symmetric.
   E. If a passing score is 60, most students passed the test.

19. A local politician conducts a simple random of 250 potential voters. The voters are asked if they would support a mayor that is willing to raise taxes. Only 22% of the voters answer Yes to this question. Which of these would be true about the sampling distribution of this sample proportion?

   A. mean = 55; sd = 6.55, shape is skewed right
   B. mean = 55; sd = 6.55, shape is approximately normal
   C. mean = 22%; sd = 1.39%, shape is skewed right
   D. mean = 22%; sd = 2.6%, shape is skewed right
   E. mean = 22%; sd = 2.6%, shape is approximately normal

20. A university sent out a survey to a random sample of 120 recent graduates to see how those graduates feel about the education they received. Thirty-two of the graduates did not respond to the survey. Which of these would be the best way to proceed?

    A. Use the 88 who did respond, using 88 as the sample size in the analysis.
    B. Use the 88 who did respond, using 120 as the sample size in the analysis.
    C. Attempt to contact the 32 who did not respond and get the information from them.
    D. Select 32 more graduates at random and use them to replace the nonresponders.
    E. Start over, sending the survey to more graduates to increase the number of responses.

21. Some health professionals suspect that doctors are more likely to order cardiac tests for men than women, even when women describe exactly the same symptoms. Young doctors, training to work in the emergency room, were randomly assigned to two groups—Group A and Group B—and presented with the exact same description of common symptoms of heart disease. However, those in Group A were told that the patient was a 55-year-old female and those in Group B were told that the patient was a 55-year-old male. All other patient characteristics were exactly the same.

Group	Number of doctors in group	Number of doctors who ordered standard cardiac tests for the patient	Percentage of doctors who ordered standard cardiac tests for the patient
A	60	42	70%
B	40	34	85%

Which of the following is the appropriate statistic to test whether doctors are less likely to order cardiac tests when the patient is female?

A. $z = \dfrac{(0.70) - (0.85)}{\sqrt{(0.70)(0.85)}\sqrt{\dfrac{1}{60} + \dfrac{1}{40}}}$

B. $z = \dfrac{(0.70) - (0.85)}{\sqrt{(0.76)(0.24)}\sqrt{\dfrac{1}{60} + \dfrac{1}{40}}}$

C. $z = \dfrac{(0.70) - (0.85)}{\sqrt{(0.76)(0.24)}\sqrt{\dfrac{1}{42} + \dfrac{1}{34}}}$

D. $z = \dfrac{(0.70) - (0.85)}{\sqrt{\dfrac{(0.70)(0.30)}{60} + \dfrac{(0.85)(0.15)}{40}}}$

E. $z = \dfrac{(0.70) - (0.85)}{\sqrt{\dfrac{(0.70)(0.30)}{42} + \dfrac{(0.85)(0.15)}{34}}}$

22. A study looked at medical records of about 23,000 patients, mostly in Asia. They found that patients who drank at least three cups of green tea per day had a much lower incidence of depression. In an American newspaper article about this study, which of the following statements should **not** be made?

    A. It is possible that people who drink green tea also tend to have healthier lifestyles than those who don't.
    B. It is possible that people who drink green tea also tend to have a more positive outlook on life than those who don't.
    C. Because this is observational data, the association between drinking green tea and a lower incidence of depression is not an indication of a causal relationship.
    D. Because most of these patients lived in Asia, where tea drinking is much more common than in the United States, a similar association may not exist in the United States.
    E. People who want to avoid depression should consider drinking green tea on a daily basis.

23. A polling company wants to estimate, using a 95% confidence interval, the proportion of likely voters that would vote for a particular candidate in the upcoming presidential election. *Of the following choices*, which is the smallest sample size that will ensure a margin of sampling error less than or equal to 2 percentage points?

    A. 250
    B. 950
    C. 1150
    D. 2250
    E. 2450

GO ON TO THE NEXT PAGE

24. The director of a local food bank asks for data on all donations given during the month of November. Of the 100 checks received, the average donation is $155 with a standard deviation of $32. Which of the following is the most appropriate statement?

    A. This November, the average donation is $155.
    B. Fifty percent of all donations this November are more than $155.
    C. We are 95% confident that the average donation in November is between about $91 and $219.
    D. We are 95% confident that the average donation in November is between about $149 and $161.
    E. This November, about 95% of all donations are between $91 and $219.

25. A multiple-choice test has 30 questions, and each question has five options. A student has not studied and will guess on every question. Which calculation shows how to find the probability of getting exactly 15 questions correct?

    A. $\binom{30}{15} 0.2^{15} 0.8^{15}$

    B. $1 - 0.2^{15} 0.8^{15}$
    C. 0.2^{15}
    D. 0.8^{15}
    E. ≈ 0

26. Claire and Max each created a simulated sampling distribution for a test statistic. They each used samples of size 4 from a normal population with the same mean m and standard deviation s. Claire simulated the sampling distribution of $\dfrac{\bar{x} - \mu}{\sigma}$, and Max simulated the sampling distribution of $\dfrac{\bar{x} - \mu}{s}$, where s is the sample standard deviation. Which statement makes a correct comparison of their simulated sampling distributions?

    A. Both simulated sampling distributions are approximately normal.
    B. Both simulated sampling distributions have the same spread.

C. Claire's simulated sampling distribution is skewed to the right, and Max's is roughly symmetric.
D. Claire's simulated sampling distribution is roughly symmetric, and Max's is skewed to the left.
E. Claire's simulated sampling distribution is approximately normal, and Max's is approximately a t-distribution.

27. A dog grooming business has tracked the last 100 transactions and recorded the number of hours that were billed. It is observed that the $IQR^*2 > Range$. The hours that are billed are converted into the cost charged using the following formula: $Cost = \$30(hours) + \$15$. Which of the following statements must be true?

    A. The IQR^*2 is now less than the $Range$.
    B. A mistake has been made. IQR^*2 must be smaller than the $Range$.
    C. The IQR of cost is 30 times bigger than the IQR of hours.
    D. Both the IQR and the $Range$ are increased by 15.
    E. The IQR is increased by a factor of 30, but the $Range$ is not.

28. A test for heartworm in dogs shows a positive result in 96% of dogs that actually have heartworm, and shows a negative result in 98% of dogs with no heartworm. If heartworm actually occurs in 10% of dogs, what is the probability that a randomly selected dog that tested positive for heartworm actually has heartworm?

    A. 11%
    B. 18%
    C. 84%
    D. 88%
    E. 96%

29. A recent poll reported that 43% of Americans approve of the job the president is doing, with a margin of sampling error of ±3.2% at a 95% level of confidence. Which of these correctly interprets that margin of error?

    A. There is a 3.2% chance that the proportion of all Americans who approve of the job the president is doing is not 43%.
    B. There is a 95% chance that the proportion of all Americans who approve of the job the president is doing is 43%.
    C. About 95% of polls conducted in this way will find that between 39.8% and 46.2% of those sampled approve of the job the president is doing.
    D. About 95% of polls conducted in this way will give a sample proportion within 3.2 percentage points of the actual proportion of all Americans who approve of the job the president is doing.
    E. About 3.2% of all Americans approve of 95% of what the president does.

30. Two events A and B each have a nonzero probability. If A and B are independent, which of the following statements is true?

    A. $P(A \text{ and } B) = P(A) \cdot P(B)$
    B. $P(A) = 1 - P(B)$
    C. A and B must be mutually exclusive.
    D. $P(A|B) = P(B|A)$
    E. $P(A \text{ and } B) = 0$

31. Players in the National Football League weigh, on average, about 248 pounds with a standard deviation of about 47 pounds. If four players are to be selected at random, the expected value of the random variable W, the total combined weight of the four players, is 992 pounds. We assume the four players are independent from each other in weight. The standard deviation of W is approximately

    A. 47 pounds
    B. 67 pounds
    C. 94 pounds
    D. 141 pounds
    E. 188 pounds

32. When a patient complains to the doctor about a certain set of symptoms, the doctor diagnoses the patient with Condition A 15% of the time. If a patient with these symptoms is diagnosed with Condition A, the patient is diagnosed with Condition B 70% of the time. A patient with these symptoms that is not diagnosed with Condition A is diagnosed with Condition B 10% of the time. What is the probability that a patient with this set of symptoms will be diagnosed with at least one of these conditions?

    A. 0.235
    B. 0.250
    C. 0.765
    D. 0.850
    E. 0.950

33. A doctor hopes that a new surgery technique will shorten the recovery time compared to the standard technique. To test this, he designed an experiment in which patients who required this type of surgery were randomly assigned to the standard technique or the new technique. Then the mean recovery time for each treatment group was compared. Assuming conditions for inference were met, which analysis should be used?

    A. A t-test for a mean
    B. A t-test for a difference in means
    C. A z-test for a mean
    D. A z-test for a difference in means
    E. A z-test for a difference in proportions

GO ON TO THE NEXT PAGE

34. For a class project, a student wants to see if boys and girls at their large high school differ in the number of contacts they have stored in their phone. The student conducts a survey of 50 randomly sampled boys and 40 randomly selected girls and asks them to report the number of contacts. Which of the following is true about this situation?

    A. Because the population standard deviations are not known and conditions are met, the student *should* use a two-sample *t*-test.
    B. Because the sample sizes are different, the student should *not* use a two-sample *t*-test.
    C. Because the sample sizes are both greater than 30, the student should *not* use a two-sample *t*-test.
    D. Because the shape of the population distribution is not known, the student should *not* use a two-sample *t*-test.
    E. Because np and $n(1 - p)$ are both at least 10, the student *should* use a two-proportion *z*-test.

35. Which of these is the best description of a *P*-value?

    A. The probability of making a Type I error
    B. The probability of making a Type II error
    C. The probability of rejecting the null hypothesis if it is, in fact, false
    D. The probability of getting a test statistic at least as extreme as the observed test statistic, if the null hypothesis is true
    E. The probability of getting a test statistic at least as extreme as the observed test statistic, if the null hypothesis is false

36. A farmer who raises hens for egg production wants his eggs to have a mean mass of 56 grams. He is considering the purchase of a different type of hen, so he took a random sample of 18 eggs laid by this type of hen. The distribution of the masses is symmetric and mound-shaped with a mean of 54.1 grams and no outliers. The farmer conducted a *t*-test to see if there is evidence that the eggs from these hens have a mean mass that is different from 56 grams and got a test statistic of $t = -1.973$. If he uses a 5% significance level, which is the correct conclusion and reason?

    A. Because *t* is more extreme than ± 1.96, he should reject the null hypothesis. He has convincing evidence at the 5% significance level that the mean mass of eggs from these hens is different from 56 grams.
    B. Because *t* is less extreme than the critical value of *t* for 17 degrees of freedom, he should not reject the null hypothesis. He does not have convincing evidence at the 5% significance level that the mean mass of eggs from these hens is different from 56 grams.
    C. Because *t* is less extreme than the critical value of *t* for 18 degrees of freedom, he should not reject the null hypothesis. He does not have convincing evidence at the 5% significance level that the mean mass of eggs from these hens is different from 56 grams.
    D. Because *t* is more extreme than the critical value of *t* for 18 degrees of freedom, he should reject the null hypothesis. He has convincing evidence at the 5% significance level that the mean mass of eggs from these hens is different from 56 grams.
    E. Because the sample mean was less than 56, he should use a one-sided alternative hypothesis. Thus, *t* is more extreme than the critical value of *t* for 17 degrees of freedom, and he should reject the null hypothesis. He has convincing evidence at the 5% significance level that the mean mass of eggs from these hens is different from 56 grams.

GO ON TO THE NEXT PAGE

37. An experiment is conducted in which the response variable is the average gain in participants' performance in the long jump. A two-sample t-test with a 5% level of significance will be used to analyze the results. If all else is kept the same, which of the following descriptions of a possible change in procedure is true?

    A. Change from equal size treatment groups to very different size treatment groups would increase the power of the test.
    B. Change from a 5% significance level to a 1% significance level would increase the power of the test.
    C. Taking more careful measurements to reduce variability in the response would increase the power of the test.
    D. Increasing the sample size would reduce the probability of a Type I error.
    E. Increasing the sample size would increase the probability of a Type I error.

38. Researchers wish to test how rangelands growth is affected by wildfire. A very large open area is divided into 28 equally sized plots and subjected to a controlled burn. One year later, the researchers calculate the percentage of grass returned in each plot after the fire damage. The average percentage return for these 28 plots was 58.5% with a standard deviation of 6.5%. Which of the following represents a 95% confidence interval to estimate the average proportion of grass return one year after a fire?

    A. $0.585 \pm 1.96(0.065/\sqrt{27})$
    B. $0.585 \pm 2.052(0.065/\sqrt{27})$
    C. $0.585 \pm 2.052(0.065/\sqrt{28})$
    D. $0.585 \pm 1.96(0.065/\sqrt{28})$
    E. $0.585 \pm 2.052\sqrt{(0.585)(0.415)/27}$

39. A clothing store stocks a popular sweater in five different colors. They have records for the proportion of each color that was sold over the last several years. The ordering manager is concerned that the sales in first month of sales season reflect a change in preference. Which color makes the greatest contribution to the appropriate test statistic?

Color	Black	Blue	Green	Tan	Gray
Proportion	0.32	0.15	0.12	0.27	0.14

Color	Black	Blue	Green	Tan	Gray
Frequency	113	75	44	120	35

    A. Black
    B. Blue
    C. Green
    D. Tan
    E. Gray

40. Tucson, Arizona, hosts the world's largest gem and mineral show every February. A government official claims that more than 50% of city residents have been to the Gem Show at least once. You decide to test this theory, take a simple random sample of 200 Tucson residents, and discover that 108 have attended. Which of the following is the appropriate calculation of the test statistic for the hypothesis proposed by the government official?

    A. $z = \dfrac{0.54 - 0.50}{\sqrt{(0.54)(0.46)/200}}$

    B. $z = \dfrac{0.54 - 0.50}{\sqrt{(0.50)(0.50)/200}}$

    C. $z = \dfrac{0.54 - 0.50}{\sqrt{(0.54)(0.46)/108}}$

    D. $z = \dfrac{0.54 - 0.50}{\sqrt{(0.50)(0.50)/108}}$

    E. $z = \dfrac{0.54 - 0.50}{\sqrt{(0.54)(0.50)/200}}$

END OF SECTION I

AP Statistics Practice Test 1

SECTION II

Time: 1 hour and 30 minutes

Number of questions: 6

Percentage of total grade: 50

General Instructions

There are two parts to this section of the examination. Part A consists of five equally weighted problems that represent 75% of the total weight of this section. Spend about 65 minutes on this part of the exam. Part B consists of one longer problem that represents 25% of the total weight of this section. Spend about 25 minutes on this part of the exam. You are not necessarily expected to complete all parts of every question. Statistical tables and formulas are provided.

- Be sure to write clearly and legibly. If you make an error, you may save time by crossing it out rather than trying to erase it. Erased or crossed-out work will not be graded.
- Show all your work. Indicate clearly the methods you use because you will be graded on the correctness of your methods as well as the accuracy of your final answers. Correct answers without support work may not receive credit.

Statistics, Section II, Part A, Questions 1–5

Spend about 65 minutes on this part of the exam; percentage of Section II grade: 75.

Directions: Show all your work. Indicate clearly the methods you use because you will be graded on the correctness of your methods as well as on the accuracy of your results and explanation.

1. In response to drought, some plants react with reduced biological nitrogen fixation (BNF), hindering their ability to grow at a typical rate. Scientists are working to develop techniques to supplement crops so that the BNF rate is not as greatly reduced during drought. One promising treatment is to be compared to standard growing conditions on randomly selected acres of soybeans. The following summary data are for the bushels per acre of soybeans for each group:

Variable	N	Mean	StDev	Min	Q1	Med	Q3	Max
Treatment	30	43.555	3.937	36.46	40.52	42.78	46.46	51.50
Control	38	35.813	6.576	27.14	31.99	35.60	42.60	46.27

   a. The maximum yield of the treated acres was 51.50 bushels of soybeans. Is this an unusually high yield compared to the other treated acres? Justify your answer.
   b. How does the variability in bushels per acre compare for the treatment vs. the control? Use at least two different statistical measures of variation to justify your response.
   c. Field workers report to the scientists that the machine to measure the yield in the treatment group was poorly calibrated—each of the bushel values was over-reported by 0.5 bushels. So each of the measures should be reduced (subtracted) by 0.5 bushels. Describe the impact doing so would have on the mean, median, standard deviation, and interquartile range of the treatment group.

GO ON TO THE NEXT PAGE

2. A particular bottle-filling machine is supposed to put 16 ounces of water into a bottle. The amount actually dispensed is approximately normal with mean 16.1 ounces and a standard deviation of 0.12 ounces. A bottle is rejected by quality control if it contains less than 15.7 ounces or more than 16.3 ounces.

   a. What is the probability that a randomly selected bottle gets rejected by quality control?

   b. A quality control engineer is instructed to take a random sample of 20 bottles and find the number that will be rejected.
      (i) Define the random variable of interest and state how the random variable is distributed.
      (ii) What is the probability that, out of 20 randomly selected bottles, at least 2 are rejected by quality control?

   c. What is the probability that a set of 5 randomly selected bottles contains, on average, more than 16.2 ounces of water?

3. A student was curious about a news article that reported the percentage of Americans who believe that a "higher power" affects who wins sporting events. With the assumption that the percentage reported in the article is correct, she simulated selecting samples of 100 Americans and calculating the percentage of those that believe a higher power has a hand in who wins a sporting event. The results of 200 trials are shown below.

Percent Who Believe That a "Higher Power" Influences
the Results of a Sporting Event

   a. The student looked further into how the data was collected. She found this information about the survey, "The random sample was collected via phone calls made on three different Sunday mornings. The randomized phone numbers covered all area codes in the United States."
      (i) Is it appropriate generalize this survey to all Americans?
      (ii) Describe how the day of the week the survey was conducted may have resulted in a bias.

   b. Based on the results of these trials, what appears to be the reported percentage of Americans that believes the results of a sporting event are influenced by a "higher power"? Explain.

   c. Another student believes that the proportion reported in the article is too low. He takes a random sample of 100 Americans and finds that 34% believe in the influence of a "higher power" on the outcome of a sporting event. Based on the dotplot above, does it appear the percentage in the article is correct? Explain why or why not.

GO ON TO THE NEXT PAGE

4. A local hospital is interested in reducing the anxiety that patients experience when they need to provide a blood sample. They plan on recruiting 200 volunteers. The volunteers will be randomly sorted into two groups of 100. The first 100 volunteers will have their blood drawn in the current manner, while the other group will have the nurse engage the volunteer in casual conversation about their plans for the day during the blood draw. After the blood has been drawn, the patients will rate their anxiety on a scale of 1 to 10.
   a. Is this an experiment or an observational study? Why?
   b. An administrator at the hospital comments that double-blinding should be used.
      (i) Explain why it is important that blinding be used on the patient.
      (ii) Explain why would be double-blinding difficult to use.
   c. It is also suggested that a block design would useful. The proposal is that volunteers be sorted into two groups, those that have had a blood draw in the last year and those who have not. Would this modification be an improvement? Explain why or why not.

5. New formulas of gel nail polish have recently been introduced. A local salon wished to test number of days of wear of the new formula against the old formula as a control. Identical bottles of both formulas are prepared, and 14 clients have their nails polished on their first visit with one formula (chosen at random) and then the next visit with the other formula. The number of days of wear is then compared.

Client	A	B	C	D	E	F	G	H	I	J	K	L	M	N
New Gel Polish	18	19	21	19	17	14	16	19	12	15	18	16	14	14
Control—Old Version	15	21	19	16	13	17	12	18	12	13	12	18	15	14

   a. Do these data provide evidence that the mean number of days of wear is greater for the new formula of gel nail polish than for the old? Use $\alpha = 0.05$.
   b. Based on your conclusion from part (a), which of the two errors, Type I or Type II, could have been made? Interpret the consequence of the error in context.

Statistics, Section II, Part B, Question 6

Spend about 25 minutes on this part of the exam; percentage of Section II grade: 25.

   Directions: Show all of your work. Indicate clearly the methods you use because you will be graded on the correctness of your methods as well as on the accuracy of your results and explanation.

6. Overuse of lawn chemicals causes environmental problems when runoff gets into waterways. Researchers tested three types of fertilizer spreaders typically used by homeowners: drop spreaders, handheld broadcast rotary spreaders, and push rotary spreaders. The goal was to determine if the type of spreader influenced the ability of the user to apply the correct amount of fertilizer.

   Fifteen volunteers who were homeowners with no particular training in the use of this equipment operated the spreaders. Each spreader was randomly assigned to a 1,000-square-foot plot of lawn. The researchers prepared the spreaders by correctly setting the dispensation amount and providing the same amount of fertilizer in each spreader. The spreader with fertilizer was weighed before and after the fertilizer was applied to determine the amount dispensed.

   a. What were the experimental units? The treatments? The response variable?
      The plot below shows the amounts dispensed by each type of spreader in kg/100 m².

GO ON TO THE NEXT PAGE

b.   Based on the plot alone, comment on the strength of evidence of a difference in the amount of fertilizer dispensed by the three types of spreaders.

Volunteers with no particular training were used because regular homeowners are the population of interest. However, one researcher points out that there may be very different skill levels among the volunteers. He suggests using a randomized block design, with each volunteer as a block. Each volunteer will use all three spreaders in a randomized order. They ran the experiment with just five volunteers using this design. The results, along with the operator of the spreader, are displayed below.

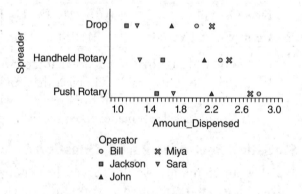

c.   Based on the plot above, comment on the association between the operator of the spreader and the amount of fertilizer dispensed.

To remove the effect of the operators' skill levels on the response variable, the researchers calculated the mean amount dispensed for each operator. Miya's amounts dispensed are given in the table below.

Type of Spreader	Amount Dispensed
Drop	2.2 kg/100 m²
Handheld Rotary	2.4 kg/100 m²
Push Rotary	2.7 kg/100 m²

GO ON TO THE NEXT PAGE

d. To adjust the amount dispensed for Miya, calculate the mean amount of fertilizer she dispensed in her three trials, and subtract that mean from each of her amounts dispensed. Show all computations.

Type of Spreader	Amount Dispensed	Adjusted Amount Dispensed
Drop	2.2 kg/100 m^2	
Handheld Rotary	2.4 kg/100 m^2	
Push Rotary	2.7 kg/100 m^2	

The plot below shows the Adjusted Amount Dispensed for the other four volunteers.

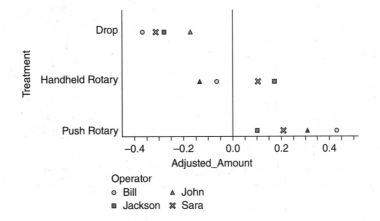

e. Add Miya's Adjusted Amount Dispensed for each type of spreader to the plot above. Then comment on what this new plot reveals about the differences in amounts dispensed between the types of spreaders.

END OF SECTION II

› Answers to Practice Test 1, Section I

1. B
2. B
3. C
4. B
5. C
6. E
7. A
8. A
9. E
10. D
11. D
12. D
13. A
14. E
15. B
16. E
17. B
18. B
19. E
20. C
21. B
22. E
23. E
24. A
25. A
26. E
27. C
28. C
29. D
30. A
31. C
32. A
33. B
34. A
35. D
36. B
37. C
38. C
39. E
40. B

› Solutions to Practice Test 1, Section I

1. (B) Using the outlier guideline, any value above $Q3 + 1.5 \cdot IQR = 28.5 + 1.5 \cdot 10.5 = 44.25$ or below $Q1 - 1.5 \cdot IQR = 18 - 1.5 \cdot 10.5 = 2.25$ is considered an outlier. Because the maximum is 33, there are no values above 44.25. The minimum of 2 is an outlier. There may be more than one value below 2.25, so all we can say is that there is at least one outlier on the lower end.

2. (B) You should recognize that this is the interpretation of r^2. According to the printout, that value is 0.542313, or about 54.2%.

3. (C) A Type II error means that the null hypothesis is false, but we fail to reject it. In this case, a false null hypothesis means that Heartaid actually does work better. Failing to reject that null hypothesis means they don't have convincing evidence that Heartaid is better, so they won't use it.

4. (B) This is asking for a conditional probability. $P(\text{Morafka}|\text{Female})$. Out of the 48 female tortoises, 15 are Morafka. $15/48 = 0.3125$, or about 31.3%.

5. (C) Randomization is what fights against confounding by making the groups as alike as possible. With blocking, similar units are grouped together so the effect of being in that group can be accounted for in the analysis.

6. (E) On the midterm, the z-score is $\dfrac{58 - 52}{4} = 1.5$.

   So she scored 1.5 standard deviations above the mean. To achieve the same standardized score on the final exam, she must score 1.5 standard deviations, or $1.5 \cdot 10 = 15$ points, above the mean on that exam. $112 + 15 = 127$ points.

7. (A) A simple random sample is already unbiased. A stratified random sample cannot improve on that.

8. (A) By the CLT, because the sample is large (100), the sampling distribution is approximately normal.

9. (E) The median of the HFCS group is the same as Q3 of the No HFCS group.

10. (D) $\dfrac{1}{3} \cdot 0.15 + \dfrac{2}{3} \cdot 0.06 = 0.09.\ 1 - 0.09 = 0.91$.

11. (D) Because of the long tail on the high end of the distribution, the median will be less than the mean.

12. (D) The null hypothesis always contains equality. Because they are interested in whether the candidate's support has improved, the alternative hypothesis is one-sided.

13. (A) This is an observational study and cannot make a causal conclusion.

14. (E) Because this is a properly conducted randomized experiment, a causal relationship can be determined. E is the choice that is not true.

15. (B) The population is divided into homogeneous subgroups, and a random sample is selected from each.

16. (E) $z = 0.70 = \dfrac{x - 74.9}{7.29}$, $x \approx 80$.

17. (B) The formula for the confidence interval for the slope is $b_1 \pm t^* \cdot s_{b_1}$. From the printout $b_1 = 4.3441$ and $s_{b_1} = 1.811$. t^* for $18 - 2 = 16$ degrees of freedom and 99% confidence is 2.921.

18. (B) The steeper part of the graph corresponds to the higher bars on a histogram. So the higher bars would be on the left with a tail stretching toward the right.

19. (E) $\text{mean}(\hat{p}) = p = 22\%$; $\text{sd}((\hat{p}) = \sqrt{\dfrac{0.22 * 0.78}{250}}$ $= 0.026$; np & $n(1-p) > 10$, so $\approx$ normal.

20. (C) Nonresponse bias is a problem because the kind of people who don't respond might feel differently from those who do. Getting responses from more of the people who do respond won't fix the problem.

21. (B) Under the null hypothesis, the proportions are the same, so the standard error formula is based on the pooled proportion $\hat{p} = \dfrac{x_1 + x_2}{n_1 + n_2}$.

22. (E) Choice E implies a causal relationship, which is not justified because this is an observational study.

23. (E) The margin of error is largest for $\hat{p} = 0.5$, so if $\hat{p} \neq 0.5$, the margin of error will be even smaller. So use $0.02 = 1.96\sqrt{\dfrac{0.5 \cdot 0.5}{n}}$. Solve for n and round up.

24. (A) They have all the data for November, so there is no inference to do. 50% of the donations are above the median, not the mean. A is the only conclusion we can make.

25. (A) This is a binomial situation, and choice A correctly applies the binomial calculation.

26. (E) Using s in the denominator makes Max's an approximate t-distribution. It has heavier tails and more spread than Claire's approximately normal distribution.

27. (C) Multiplying affects both measures of location and spread. Adding affects only measures of location. It is reasonable that the middle of 50% of the data can have a larger spread than the tails, making $2*IQR > Range$.

28. (C) This is easiest to see in a two-way table.

29. (D) The confidence interval is based on one sample of many possible samples. The process has a 95% chance of capturing the true proportion of all Americans within the interval created. But there is nothing special about that one interval.

30. (A) That is the multiplication rule for independent events.

31. (C) Since these are four independent occurrences of W, the variances add. So the standard deviation is $\sqrt{47^2 + 47^2 + 47^2 + 47^2} = 94$.

32. (A) The bottom path in the tree diagram shows that the probability that a patient has neither condition is $0.85 \cdot 0.90 = 0.765$. $1 - 0.765 = 0.235$.

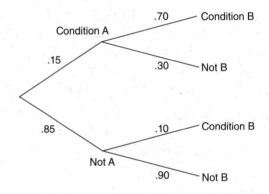

33. (B) They are comparing means without a known population standard deviation.

	Positive Test	Negative Test	Total
Heartworm present	$0.96 \cdot 0.1 = 0.096$	$0.1 - 0.096 = 0.004$	0.1
Heartworm not present	$0.9 - 0.882 = 0.018$	$0.98 \cdot 0.9 = 0.882$	$1 - 0.1 = 0.9$
Total	$0.096 + 0.018 = 0.114$	$0.004 + 0.882 = 0.886$	1

The required probability is $0.096/0.114 = 0.842$.

34. (A) They are comparing means, so a *t*-test would be the appropriate test. The students were randomly selected. With such large sample sizes, population shapes are not a concern. Conditions are met.

35. (D) That is the definition of a *P*-value.

36. (B) The critical value of *t* for $n - 1 = 17$ degrees of freedom is ± 2.11. His test statistic was not outside those values.

37. (C) Reducing measurement variability would give a lower standard error of the mean and, therefore, a greater test statistic (in absolute value). Thus, the probability of rejecting the null hypothesis increases.

38. (C) This is a confidence interval for a mean with unknown σ, so *t* for 27 degrees of freedom is used rather than *z*. The standard error of the mean is $\dfrac{s}{\sqrt{n}} = \dfrac{0.065}{\sqrt{28}}$.

39. (E) The chi-square component for gray is ≈ 6.79, which is the largest of the five components.

40. (B) The official should use the hypothesized value of *p*, which is 0.5, in the calculation. Also, $n = 200$, not 108.

› Solutions to Practice Test 1, Section II, Part A

Free-response questions are scored in parts, with each part designated as either E for essentially correct, P for partially correct, or I for incorrect. A scoring guide for each of these questions is given below the solution.

1. a. The 1.5*IQR* guideline can be used. $IQR = 46.46 - 40.52 = 5.94$. $1.5IQR = 8.91$ bushels. The largest possible nonoutlier would be $46.46 + 8.91 = 55.37$ bushels. The maximum of 51.5 bushels is below this value, so it is not an unusually high soybean yield.
   (It would be acceptable to use the mean + 2 standard deviations, which is $43.555 + 2 \cdot 3.937 = 51.249$. Using this guideline, the maximum is more than 2 standard deviations from the mean, so one might consider it unusual.)
   b. The standard deviation of the control group is larger than that of the treatment group. The IQR of the control group (10.61) is also larger than that of the treatment group (4.94). Finally, the range of the range of the control group (19.13) is greater than that of the treatment group (15.04).
   c. The mean and median would both decrease by 0.5 bushels. The standard deviation and interquartile range would be unchanged.

Scoring Part (a)

Component 1: Your response includes an application of an algorithm for calculating unusual observations. For example, taking 1.5(IQR) and adding it to the third quartile to get 55.37.

Component 2: Your response justifies a conclusion that 51.50 is or is not an unusually high yield based on your application in component #1. For example, saying 51.50 is not an unusually high yield because it is less than 55.37.

> If you have both components, score your response as an E for part (a).
> If you have only one component, score your response as a P.
> Otherwise, score your response as an I.

Scoring Part (b)

Score your response as an E for part (b) if you used two out of the three measures of variability in a correct comparison.
> Otherwise, score your response as an I.

Scoring Part (c)

Component 1: Your response notes that the mean and median BOTH decrease by 0.5 bushels.

Component 2: Your response notes that the standard deviation AND the interquartile range would remain unchanged.

> If you have both components, score your response as an E for part (a).
> If you have only one component, score your response as a P.
> Otherwise, score your response as an I.

Give your response to this question an overall score of:

4: EEE (all three parts essentially correct)
3: EEP in any order
2: EEI or EPI in any order

1: EII or PPI in any order
0: all other combinations

2. a. Using a normal model with $\mu = 16.1$ and $\sigma = 0.12$, the z-score for $15.7 = \dfrac{15.7 - 16.1}{0.12} = -3.33$. The

z-score for $16.3 = \dfrac{16.3 - 16.1}{0.12} = 1.67$. $1 - P(15.7 < x < 16.3) =$ Since we want the area that is

outside of those two values (not between), the probability is $1 - P(-3.33 < z < 1.67) = 0.048$.

b. (i) This is a binomial situation with $n = 20$ and $p = 0.048$ (from part a).

(ii) $P(x \geq 2) = 1 - P(x \leq 1) = 1 - \begin{pmatrix} 20 \\ 0 \end{pmatrix} 0.048^0 \cdot 0.952^{20} - \begin{pmatrix} 20 \\ 1 \end{pmatrix} 0.048^1 \cdot 0.952^{19} \approx 0.25$.

c. This is the sampling distribution of $\bar{x}$, which will be approximately normal with $\mu_{\bar{x}} = \mu = 16.1$, and

$\sigma_{\bar{x}} = \dfrac{\sigma}{\sqrt{n}} = \dfrac{0.12}{\sqrt{5}} = 0.0537$.

$P(\bar{x} > 16.2) = P\left(z > \dfrac{16.2 - 16.1}{0.0537} = 1.86\right) = 0.03$

Scoring Part (a)

Component 1: A normal distribution is shown by name, by sketch, or by using the letter z.
Component 2: The mean and standard deviation are labeled in a formula or on a sketch.
Component 3: The answer region is shaded or described, with boundaries labeled.
Component 4: The correct answer is calculated.

If you have all four components, score your response as an E for part (a).
If you have two or three components, score your response as a P.
Otherwise, score your response as an I.

Scoring Part (b)

Component 1: Your response specifies the fixed number of trials by listing $n = 20$, the probability being $p = 0.048$, and this being a binomial situation either in words (as in the model solution) OR in a statement of a binomial calculation where those numeric values are identified by variables as well. For example: BinomialCDF($n = 20$, $p = 0.049$, $x = 1$).

Component 2: Your response includes a correct value for the probability with work shown.

If you have both components, score your response as an E for part (b).
If you have only one component, score your response as a P.
Otherwise, score your response as an I.

Scoring Part (c)

Component 1: A normal distribution is shown by name, by sketch, or by using the letter z.
Component 2: The mean and standard deviation are labeled in a formula or on a sketch.
Component 3: The answer region is shaded or described, with boundaries labeled.
Component 4: The correct answer is calculated.

If you have all four components, score your response as an E for part (a).
If you have two or three components, score your response as a P.
Otherwise, score your response as an I.

Give your response an overall score of:

4: EEE (all three parts essentially correct)
3: EEP in any order
2: EEI, PPP, or EPI in any order
1: EII or PPI in any order
0: all other combinations

3. a. (i) It would not be appropriate to generalize this to all Americans because not all Americans have telephones.
   (ii) The day of the week may have resulted in bias because many people might be unavailable to answer their phones due to their attendance at religious services.
   b. Based on these trials, it would appear that approximately 25% believe that the results of a sporting event are influenced by a higher power since the center of the dotplot is at roughly 25%.
   c. If we assume that the percent in the article is correct and thus the dotplot is a simulated sampling distribution for that percent, then the P-value would be 19.5% (39 out of 200 dots). This is so large that we cannot reject the claim in the newspaper.

Scoring Part (a)

Component 1: You said that it would not be appropriate and gave an appropriate reason, such as given in the model solution.

Component 2: You gave a reasonable explanation for why Sunday would cause bias.

   If you have both components, score your response as an E for part (a).
   If you have only one component, score your response as a P.
   Otherwise, score your response as an I.

Scoring Part (b)

Component 1: Your response includes a value of either 25%, 26%, or 27%.

Component 2: Your response justifies your value because it is the mean or center of the simulated distribution.

   If you have both components, score your response as an E for part (b).
   If you have only one component, score your response as a P.
   Otherwise, score your response as an I.

Scoring Part (c)

Component 1: Your response includes a reference to the conditional nature of how the dotplot was produced. (If the newspaper article is correct.)

Component 2: Your response found the appropriate P-value.

Component 3: Your response includes an appropriate response based on the P-value.

   If you have all three components, score your response as an E for part (b).
   If you have two out of three components, score your response as a P.
   Otherwise, score your response as an I.

Give your response to this question an overall score of:

4: EE (Both parts essentially correct)
3: EP in any order
2: EI in any order or PP
1: PI in any order
0: any other combination

4. a. This study is an experiment because volunteers were randomly assigned to treatments.
   b. (i) The patients should not know what the treatments actually are because they may expect to be more or less anxious as a result. Then we would not know if the treatment or the expectation was the reason for the results.
      (ii) Since the treatment itself is the nurse, it would be impossible to keep the nurse blind to being the treatment.
   c. A block design as suggested would be an improvement because volunteers who have recently had a blood draw would remember their experience more strongly and their response to the treatment or control may have less variation.

Scoring Part (a)

Component 1: You said that this was an experiment.

Component 2: Your response justifies the choice of an experiment because the volunteers were randomly assigned to treatments.

> If you have both components, score your response as an E for part (a).
> Otherwise, score your response as an I.

Scoring Part (b)

Component 1: Your response explains why volunteers should not know which treatment they are assigned to that is related to the response variable of anxiety.

Component 2: Your response explains that the treatment itself cannot be blind to their participation as the treatment.

> If you have both components, score your response as an E for part (b).
> If you have only one component, score your response as a P.
> Otherwise, score your response as an I.

Scoring Part (c)

Component 1: Your response notes that recent donors have prior experience.

Component 2: Your response notes that volunteers with prior experience may respond with less variation to the treatments.

> If you have both components, score your response as an E for part (b).
> If you have only one component, score your response as a P.
> Otherwise, score your response as an I.

Give your response to this question an overall score of:

4: EEE (All parts essentially correct)
3: EEP in any order
2: EEI, EPP, EPI (in any order), or PPP
1: PPI, EII (in any order)
0: any other combination

5. a. This is a matched pairs design with Difference = New − Old and μ = mean of the differences.

   <u>Hypotheses:</u> $H_0: \mu_{diff} = 0$

   $H_a: \mu_{diff} \neq 0$

   <u>Check conditions:</u>
   Treatments are assigned to subjects in a random order.

The plot of the differences is reasonably symmetric with no outliers.

Conditions are met for a matched pairs *t*-test.

<u>Computations:</u>

$$t = \frac{\mu_{diff} - 0}{s_{diff}} = 1.705$$

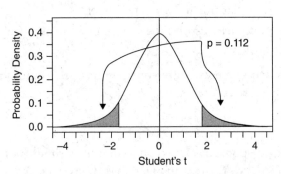

Comparing to a *t* distribution with 13 degrees of freedom, the *P*-value is 0.112.

<u>Conclusion:</u>

Because the *P*-value = 0.112 > α = 0.05, we fail to reject the null hypothesis. We do not have convincing evidence that the mean number of days of wear is greater for the new formula of gel nail polish than for the old.

b. Because we failed to reject the null, we could have made a Type II error—failing to reject the null when the null is actually false. One consequence could be that the new gel polish supported by the industry and consumers miss out on a superior product.

Scoring Part (I)—The hypotheses step is scored as follows:

Component 1: Your response defined the direction of subtraction.

Component 2: Your response includes a definition of the parameter using μ.

Component 3: Your response correctly states both hypotheses using μ.

If you have all three components, score your response as an E for this part.
If you have two components, score your response as a P.
Otherwise, score your response as an I.

Scoring Part (II)—The conditions step is scored as follows:

Component 1: Your response states that the treatments were applied in random order.

Component 2: Your response includes a plot of the differences AND notes that the differences do not give us reason to doubt we have met the normal condition.

Component 3: You have named the test as either a *t*-test OR included the correct equation for a one-sample *t*-test with or without numeric substitutions.

If you have all three components, score your response as an E for this part.
If you have two components, score your response as a P.
Otherwise, score your response as an I.

Scoring Part (III)—The mechanics step is scored as follows:

Essentially correct (E) if you have listed the correct t-value, degrees of freedom, and P-value
Partially correct (P) if you are only missing the degrees of freedom
Incorrect (I) for all other responses

Scoring Part (IV)—The decision step is scored as follows:

Component 1: Your response includes an explicit comparison of the P-value to the significance level.
Component 2: Based on that comparison, you came to a correct decision.
Component 3: Your response is written in the context of the alternate.

> If you have all three components, score your response as an E for this part.
> If you have two components, score your response as a P.
> Otherwise, score your response as an I.

Each essentially correct (E) counts as 1 point. Each partially correct (P) counts as ½ point. If your response is between two scores (for example, 2 ½ points), use a holistic approach to score your response up or down based on the overall strength of the response and communication.

❯ Solutions to Practice Test 1, Section II, Part B

6. a. The experimental units are the plots of land. The treatments are the three types of spreaders. The response variable is the amount of fertilizer dispensed.
   b. There seems to be a slight difference in the amounts dispensed, but with the large amount of overlap between the groups it is not very convincing evidence of a difference.
   c. There seems to be a strong association between the operator and the amount dispensed. Jackson and Sara dispensed smaller amounts with all three spreaders than the other operators. Bill and Miya dispensed larger amounts.
   d. Miya's mean amount dispensed is $\dfrac{2.2 + 2.4 + 2.7}{3} = 2.43$.

Type of Spreader	Amount Dispensed	Adjusted Amount Dispensed
Drop	2.2 kg/100 m^2	2.2 − 2.43 = −0.23
Handheld Rotary	2.4 kg/100 m^2	2.4 − 2.43 = −0.03
Push Rotary	2.7 kg/100 m^2	2.7 − 2.43 = 0.27

e.

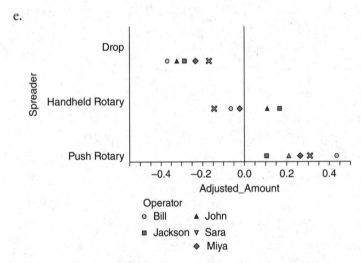

There is now much less overlap between the treatments. With the variability of the operator accounted for, the evidence of a difference is more convincing. With drop spreaders, users tend to dispense the least fertilizer, and with push rotary spreaders, they tend to dispense the most.

Scoring Parts (a) and (b) together

Component 1: The experimental units are the plots of land.

Component 2: The treatments are the three types of spreaders.

Component 3: The response variable is the amount of fertilizer used.

Component 4: Your response cites the overlap in saying that there is not convincing evidence of a difference.

> If you have all four components, score your response as an E for this part.
> If you have two or three components, score your response as a P.
> Otherwise, score your response as an I.

Scoring Part (c)

Component 1: Your response states that there appears to be a strong association.

Component 2: You cite specific evidence from the plot—for example, noting that Sara and Jackson seem to dispense smaller amounts.

If you have both components, score your response as an E for this part.

If you have one component, score your response as a P.

Otherwise, score your response as an I.

Scoring Parts (d) and (e) together

Component 1: Your response correctly calculates the mean amount of 2.43 and then subtracts it from each of the values in the table with work shown.

Component 2: Your response takes the values listed in the adjusted amount dispensed column and plots them on the provided graph. (*Note:* The plot should reflect the values in the table, whatever those values may be.)

Component 3: Your response notes that there is much less overlap (or less variation).

Component 4: Your response cites a specific spreader dispensing more/less fertilizer.

If you have all four components, score your response as an E for this part.

If you have three components, score your response as a P.

Otherwise, score your response as an I.

Give your response to this question an overall score of:

4: EEE (All parts essentially correct)
3: EEP in any order
2: EEI, EPP, EPI (in any order), or PPP
1: PPI, EII (in any order)
0: any other combination

Now that you have scored each of your questions, those scores combine to produce an overall assessment of your performance. Transfer the number of correct multiple-choice questions and the score for each of the free-response questions to the appropriate place in the box below. After you do all your arithmetic, you will have a composite score. Use that composite as a guide to your projected overall exam performance. Keep in mind that this is merely a guide! While we have seen plenty of exam questions, both multiple choice and free response, this practice exam is not an actual AP exam.

Section I: Multiple Choice		
_____ × 1.25 = _____		
# Correct		**Score Section I**
		(Do Not Round)
Section II: Free Response		
	Raw score Multiplier Weighted Score	
Question 1	× 1.875 =	(Do not round)
Question 2	× 1.875 =	(Do not round)
Question 3	× 1.875 =	(Do not round)
Question 4	× 1.875 =	(Do not round)
Question 5	× 1.875 =	(Do not round)
Question 6	× 3.125 =	(Do not round)
	SUM of the weighted scores = _____	
		Score Section II
		(Do Not Round)
Your Composite Score:		
Section I **Score Section II** _____ + _____ = _____		**Score Composite**

Your composite score	Your projected overall score on the exam
100—70	5
69—57	4
56—44	3
43—33	2

AP Statistics Practice Test 2

ANSWER SHEET FOR SECTION I

1 (A) (B) (C) (D) (E)
2 (A) (B) (C) (D) (E)
3 (A) (B) (C) (D) (E)
4 (A) (B) (C) (D) (E)
5 (A) (B) (C) (D) (E)
6 (A) (B) (C) (D) (E)
7 (A) (B) (C) (D) (E)
8 (A) (B) (C) (D) (E)
9 (A) (B) (C) (D) (E)
10 (A) (B) (C) (D) (E)
11 (A) (B) (C) (D) (E)
12 (A) (B) (C) (D) (E)
13 (A) (B) (C) (D) (E)
14 (A) (B) (C) (D) (E)
15 (A) (B) (C) (D) (E)

16 (A) (B) (C) (D) (E)
17 (A) (B) (C) (D) (E)
18 (A) (B) (C) (D) (E)
19 (A) (B) (C) (D) (E)
20 (A) (B) (C) (D) (E)
21 (A) (B) (C) (D) (E)
22 (A) (B) (C) (D) (E)
23 (A) (B) (C) (D) (E)
24 (A) (B) (C) (D) (E)
25 (A) (B) (C) (D) (E)
26 (A) (B) (C) (D) (E)
27 (A) (B) (C) (D) (E)
28 (A) (B) (C) (D) (E)
29 (A) (B) (C) (D) (E)
30 (A) (B) (C) (D) (E)

31 (A) (B) (C) (D) (E)
32 (A) (B) (C) (D) (E)
33 (A) (B) (C) (D) (E)
34 (A) (B) (C) (D) (E)
35 (A) (B) (C) (D) (E)
36 (A) (B) (C) (D) (E)
37 (A) (B) (C) (D) (E)
38 (A) (B) (C) (D) (E)
39 (A) (B) (C) (D) (E)
40 (A) (B) (C) (D) (E)

AP Statistics Practice Test 2

SECTION I

Time: 1 hour and 30 minutes

Number of questions: 40

Percentage of total grade: 50

Directions: Solve each of the following problems. Decide which is the best of the choices given and answer in the appropriate place on the answer sheet. No credit will be given for anything written on the exam. Do not spend too much time on any one problem.

1. Sixty-two students were asked to complete a number puzzle. The number of minutes each student needed to complete the puzzle was recorded and the times are displayed in the histogram below. Which of the following describes the distribution?

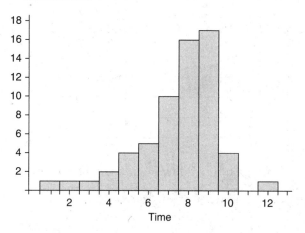

A. The distribution is approximately normal.
B. The distribution is roughly symmetric.
C. The distribution is bimodal.
D. The distribution is skewed left.
E. The distribution is skewed right.

2. The table below shows the regression output for predicting the number of calories from the number of milligrams of sodium for items at a fast-food chain. Which is a correct interpretation of the slope of the regression line?

Predictor	Coef	SE Coef	t-ratio	p
Constant	147.1427	20.6957	7.110	0.0000
Sodium	0.2457	0.0210	11.673	0.0000

s = 136.69   r-sq = 0.542313   r-sq (adj) = 0.538333

A. Every milligram of sodium contains 0.2457 calories.
B. A food item with one more milligram of sodium than another tends to have 0.2457 more calories.
C. A food item with one more milligram of sodium than another tends to have 136.69 more calories.
D. A food item with one more milligram of sodium than another tends to have 147.1427 more calories.
E. A food item with one more calorie than another tends to have 147.1427 more milligrams of sodium.

GO ON TO THE NEXT PAGE

3. A new fertilizer is to be tested on tomato plants to determine if it increases the production of the plants. The available land is divided into eight plots. Four of the plots are on a hill, and four are in a valley, as shown. The plots in the valley are expected to get more water due to the influence of gravity, and those on the hill will get more direct sunlight. A randomized block design will be used, using two blocks of four plots each. Which of the following blocking schemes would be most appropriate?

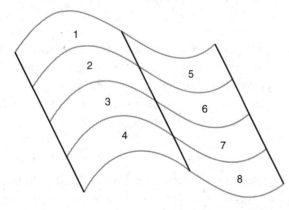

A. Plots 1, 2, 3, and 4 in one block and plots 5, 6, 7, and 8 in the other
B. Plots 1, 2, 5, and 6 in one block and plots 3, 4, 7, and 8 in the other
C. Plots 1, 4, 5, and 8 in one block and plots 2, 3, 6, and 7 in the other
D. Plots 1, 3, 6, and 8 in one block and plots 2, 4, 5, and 7 in the other
E. The plots should be randomly assigned to blocks.

4. At a large hospital, the durations of emergency room visits, from check-in to discharge, are approximately normally distributed with a mean of 167 minutes and a standard deviation of 76 minutes. Which interval, to the nearest minute, contains the middle 80% of durations?

A. 15 minutes to 319 minutes
B. 53 minutes to 281 minutes
C. 70 minutes to 264 minutes
D. 91 minutes to 243 minutes
E. 103 minutes to 231 minutes

5. Aliana works 6-hour weekend shifts at an area chain restaurant as a hostess, and she wants to explore whether customer preferences are influenced by how you ask them about seating. Aliana's questioning strategy is as follows:

Question	Asked of all customers
A. Would you prefer a booth or a table?	. . . in the first two hours of her shift
B. Would you prefer a table or a booth?	. . . in the middle two hours of her shift
C. Where would you like to sit?	. . . in the last two hours of her shift

Aliana collected data over the course of several weekends, and her results are in the table below:

	Question Aliana asked:			
Party requested to sit at	A	B	C	Totals
Table	4	22	18	44
Booth	15	23	21	59
Totals	19	45	39	103

Which of the following is a true statement?

A. The number of degrees of freedom for the χ^2 is 102.
B. The sample size is a large enough size because it is bigger than 30.
C. We do not meet the conditions for a χ^2 test because the Table/Question A cell is less than 5.
D. We do not meet the conditions for a χ^2 because Aliana did not randomly assign treatments to subjects.
E. We do not meet the conditions for a χ^2 test because Aliana did not ask the same number of customers each of the three questions.

6. A small business owner hopes that her clients will pay for their bills within 30 days. At the end of the year, she takes a random sample of her accounts. She calculates a 95% confidence interval to estimate the proportion that paid within 30 days. That interval was calculated to be (78.5%, 84.8%). Which of the following statements is correct?

   A. There is a 95% probability that the population proportion is in the interval.
   B. If she collected a larger sample, the margin of error would be larger.
   C. If she used a 99% confidence level, the margin of error would be smaller.
   D. She is 95% confident that the sample proportion is in the interval.
   E. If she wants to have a more precise estimate, she could increase her sample size.

7. An infrared thermometer measures the surface temperature of an object from a distance. The measurement errors for one particular model are approximately normally distributed with a mean of 0 degrees C and a standard deviation of 1.3 degrees C. If the temperature of an object is 20 degrees C, what is the probability that the thermometer will report the temperature as less than 18 degrees C?

   A. 0.023
   B. 0.062
   C. 0.097
   D. 0.903
   E. 0.938

8. A study was conducted to test a new style of keyboard in preventing repetitive stress disorders. Volunteers who have had problems with such injuries were randomly assigned to use either a traditional keyboard or the new design. A significance test was conducted with the alternative hypothesis that a smaller proportion of those using the new keyboard will suffer injuries than those using the traditional keyboard. The resulting P-value was 0.07. Which is a correct interpretation of this P-value?

   A. The null hypothesis should be rejected.
   B. The null hypothesis should be accepted.
   C. There is a 7% chance that the null hypothesis is correct.
   D. There is a 7% chance of getting a difference between the two groups at least as large as the observed difference if the new keyboard is really no better at preventing injuries.
   E. There is a 7% chance that the observed difference is due to chance.

9. For a class project, Charlotte recorded the heights of all 28 students in her class and calculated several statistics. She then realized she made an error recording the height of the tallest person in the class. She correctly had him listed as the tallest but needed to add two inches to his recorded height to correct it. Which of these measures of spread must remain unchanged?

   A. Mean absolute deviation
   B. Standard deviation
   C. Variance
   D. Interquartile range
   E. Range

10. A large company grants its hourly employees pay raises after their six-month performance review. The amounts of the raises average $0.25 per hour, with a standard deviation of $0.05 per hour. Let $\hat{y}$ represent the average pay raise of 50 randomly selected hourly employees. Which calculation would give the approximate probability that $\hat{y}$ is at least $0.30 per hour?

A. $P(z \geq 0.30)$

B. $P\left(z \geq \dfrac{0.30 - 0.25}{0.05 / \sqrt{50}}\right)$

C. $P\left(z \geq \dfrac{0.30 - 0.25}{0.05 / 50}\right)$

D. $P\left(z \geq \dfrac{0.30 - 0.25}{0.05}\right)$

E. This probability cannot be calculated because no information is given about the shape of the distribution of all pay raises.

11. The table below shows the daily high temperatures for the month of October for two cities in different regions of the country.

Hendersonville		Sheboygan
	4	68
2	5	00234
76	5	55777779
411110	6	011122444
988765	6	699
332211	7	123
8777766	7	9
430	8	

Which of the following statements is true?

A. The range of the October temperatures for Hendersonville is greater than the range of October temperatures for Sheboygan.
B. The median October temperature for Hendersonville is less than the median October temperature for Sheboygan.
C. The median of the October temperatures for Hendersonville is greater than the third quartile of the October temperatures for Sheboygan.

D. The mean of the October temperatures for Hendersonville is less than the mean of the October temperatures for Sheboygan.
E. The interquartile range of the October temperatures for Hendersonville is about the same as the interquartile range of the October temperatures for Sheboygan.

12. Elizabeth operates a sushi store. She sells an all-you-can-eat option. In an effort to control her costs, she tracks the average number of pieces ordered by an all-you-can-eat customer. In the past, she estimated that the typical customer ate an average of 21 pieces. She will track her orders for the next three days to determine if the mean number has changed. Which is the appropriate set of hypotheses for her to use?

A. $H_0: \mu = 21$; $H_A: \mu > 21$
B. $H_0: \mu < 21$; $H_A: \mu = 21$
C. $H_0: \bar{x} = 21$; $H_A: \bar{x} > 21$
D. $H_0: \mu = 21$; $H_A: \mu \neq 21$
E. $H_0: \bar{x} = 21$; $H_A: \bar{x} \neq 21$

13. A woman who works for a department store wants to sue the company for discrimination based on gender. Her reasoning is that women seem less likely to get promoted than men. She presented this table showing the employees eligible for promotion divided by both gender and whether they were promoted or not. Does the table provide some evidence to support her claim?

	Men	Women	Total
Promoted	9	12	21
Not Promoted	15	31	46
Total	24	43	67

A. No, because more women than men were promoted.
B. No, because the proportion of women who were promoted is the same as the proportion of men who were promoted.
C. No, because the proportion of women who were promoted is less than the proportion of men who were promoted.
D. Yes, because the proportion of women who were promoted is less than the proportion of men who were promoted.
E. Yes, because the proportion of women who were promoted is less than the proportion of women who were not promoted.

GO ON TO THE NEXT PAGE

14. Students in a statistics class, as part of an activity, measured the length of their hair in inches. Summary statistics are shown below.

Variable	N	Mean	Median	TrMean	StDev	SE Mean
Hair Length	41	9.18	3.5	8.75	8.91	1.39

Variable	Minimum	Maximum	Q1	Q3
Hair Length	0	29	2	18.5

Which of the following statements is true?

A. Seventy-five percent of the students had hair at least 18.5 inches long.
B. Fifty percent of the students had hair between 9.18 and 29 inches long.
C. Fifty percent of the students had hair between 2 and 18.5 inches long.
D. The distribution of hair lengths can be appropriately modeled by a normal distribution.
E. The distribution of hair lengths has at least one outlier.

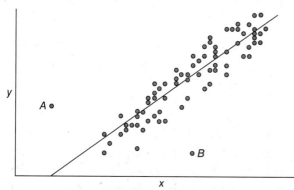

15. The scatterplot above shows data points and the regression line for predicting y from x. Which statement is true about the effect of removing point A or B on the regression model?

A. Removing A would decrease the slope, but removing B would increase the slope.
B. Removing A would increase the slope, but removing B would have little effect on the slope.
C. Removing A would decrease the correlation, but removing B would increase the correlation.
D. Removing point A would increase the correlation, and removing point B would not change the correlation.
E. Removing point A would increase the y-intercept, and removing point B would decrease the y-intercept.

16. A local shopping mall is curious to find out if their potential customers will drive to the mall for holiday shopping or if they will stay home and shop using online options. To conduct a survey, they send several employees to local supermarkets and survey people as they enter the stores. Which of the following is a correct statement?

A. Undercoverage bias is a concern because people who shop online will not be at supermarkets.
B. Response bias is a concern because some people will lie.
C. Nonresponse bias is a concern because some people will decline to participate in the survey.
D. Voluntary response bias is a concern because people will have to volunteer to answer the survey.
E. Convenience bias is a concern because the employees are staying in the area by the mall.

17. After graduation, you have the opportunity to open a local pizza restaurant. But to cover all your expenses as well as pay yourself a salary, you need an average revenue of about $9,000 per month. Anything less and you risk losing your business. You take a random sample of 30 different pizza restaurants similar to the one you hope to open and get data on their monthly sales. For the hypotheses

$$H_0: \mu = \$9,000 \quad H_a: \mu > \$9,000$$

describe a Type I error and its consequence.

A. The consequences of a Type I error cannot be determined without an α-level.
B. You believe the average sales of pizza restaurants like yours is more than $9,000, so you open a pizza restaurant and have a high risk of losing your business.
C. You believe the average sales of pizza restaurants like yours is more than $9,000, so you open a pizza restaurant and have a high probability of a successful business.
D. You believe the average sales of pizza restaurants like yours is $9,000 or less, so you do not open a pizza restaurant yourself and will miss out on an opportunity to own a successful business.
E. You believe the average sales of pizza restaurants like yours is $9,000 or less, so you do not open a pizza restaurant because other pizza places are not successful.

GO ON TO THE NEXT PAGE

18. A particular crop of one variety of onion has weights that are approximately normally distributed with mean 9.8 oz and standard deviation 2.1 oz. How does an onion in the 28th percentile for weight compare to the mean?

A. 1.22 ounces below the mean
B. 0.59 ounces below the mean
C. 0.59 ounces above the mean
D. 1.22 ounces above the mean
E. 2.26 ounces above the mean

19. A pharmaceutical company wants to test a new cholesterol-reducing drug against the previous drug. It does not anticipate much association between cholesterol level and gender, but it does anticipate an association between cholesterol level and the amount of exercise a person gets. For a randomized block design, it should

A. block on gender because it is not associated with cholesterol level.
B. block on gender because males and females are different.
C. block on the type of drug because it may be associated with cholesterol level.
D. block on exercise level because it is associated with cholesterol level.
E. block on both gender and exercise because blocking on more variables gives more reliable estimates.

20. A high school sent a survey to a randomly selected sample of 75 of last year's graduating class. 27 of those selected did not return the survey. The best plan of action would be to

A. use the surveys that were returned and change the sample size to 48 for the analysis.
B. use the surveys that were returned and leave the sample size at 75 for the analysis.
C. randomly select 27 additional class members and send the survey to them.
D. start over with a new sample but use a larger sample size.
E. follow up with those that did not return the survey to encourage them to respond.

21. A baseball fan is hoping to see his favorite player hit a home run. This player has been on a hot streak recently and has hit a home run one out every eight times he has an at-bat. That is, the fan is assuming the chances he hits a home run is $\frac{1}{8}$. What are the chances that the fan will have to watch 10 at-bats until finally seeing a home run on the player's 11th attempt?

A. $\binom{11}{1}\left(\frac{1}{8}\right)^1\left(\frac{7}{8}\right)^{10}$

B. $\binom{11}{1}\left(\frac{7}{8}\right)^1\left(\frac{1}{8}\right)^{10}$

C. $\left(\frac{1}{8}\right)^{10}\left(\frac{7}{8}\right)^1$

D. $\left(\frac{7}{8}\right)^{10}\left(\frac{1}{8}\right)^1$

E. $1-\left(\frac{7}{8}\right)^{11}$

22. The president of an online music streaming service whose customers pay a fee wants to gather additional information about customers who have joined in the past 12 months. The company plans to send out an email survey to a sample of current customers with a link that gives participants a month of streaming service for free once the survey has been completed. They know that musical tastes vary by geographical region. Which of the following sample plans would produce the most representative sample of its customers?

A. Choose all the customers who joined in the last month.
B. Make a list of all the customers who joined in the last 12 months and choose a random sample of customers on this list.
C. From the list of all customers who joined in the last 12 months, classify customers by the state in which they live, then choose 10 customers from each state.
D. From the list of all customers who joined in the last 12 months, classify customers by the state in which they live, then choose 3% of the customers from each state.
E. Make a list of all customers who joined in the last 12 months and choose every 10th customer on this list.

GO ON TO THE NEXT PAGE

23. The reason we check that np and $n(1-p)$ are at least 10 when calculating probabilities in a binomial situation is to

    A. ensure that $\hat{p}$ has a binomial distribution.
    B. be sure the sample is random enough.
    C. make sure the sampling distribution of $\hat{p}$ is symmetric enough to use a normal approximation.
    D. get an unbiased estimate for p.
    E. be able to use $\sqrt{\dfrac{p(1-p)}{n}}$ as the standard deviation of $\hat{p}$.

24. A maker of breakfast cereals plans to run a promotion in which an action figure is included in each box of cereal. The more popular figures will appear in fewer boxes. The probability of getting a box with each kind of toy is shown in the table below.

Toy	Serenity	Blackstar	Spartan	Kropp
Probability	0.12	0.18	0.30	0.40

    What is the probability that the first two randomly selected boxes contain Serenity and Blackstar?

    A. 0.0216
    B. 0.0432
    C. 0.0468
    D. 0.2784
    E. 0.3000

25. A department store has a promotion in which it hands out a "scratchcard" at the checkout register, with a percentage discount concealed by an opaque covering. The customer scratches off the covering and reveals the amount of the discount. The table below shows the probability that a randomly selected card contains each percent discount.

Percentage of discount	5%	10%	15%	25%	50%
Probability	0.45	0.25	0.15	0.10	0.05

    If customers spend an average of $40, how many dollars can the store expect to discount, on average?

    A. $2
    B. $4.80
    C. $6
    D. $8.40
    E. $16

26. In basketball, an offensive rebound occurs when a player shoots and misses, and a player from the same team recovers the ball. For the 176 players on the roster for one season of professional men's basketball, the third quartile for the total number of offensive rebounds for one season was 143. If five players are selected at random (with replacement) from that season, what is the approximate probability that at least three of them had more than 143 rebounds that season?

    A. 0.0127
    B. 0.0879
    C. 0.1035
    D. 0.8965
    E. 0.9121

27. A new smartwatch is manufactured in one part of a factory, then secured for shipping in another, independent part of the factory. The weight of the smartwatch has a mean of 62 grams and a standard deviation of 1.0 grams. The weight of the packaging (box, user's guide, bubble wrap, etc.) has a mean of 456 grams and a standard deviation of 6 grams. Together, the distribution of the weight of the smartwatch and its packaging would have the following mean and standard deviation:

    A. Mean 518 grams; standard deviation 7.0 grams
    B. Mean 518 grams; standard deviation 3.5 grams
    C. Mean 518 grams; standard deviation 6.1 grams
    D. Mean 394 grams; standard deviation 6.1 grams
    E. Mean 394 grams; standard deviation 3.5 grams

28. Students in a small high school were asked to vote for a meal for a school event. The results of the survey and the grades of the students are summarized below.

	Hot dogs	Pizza	Tacos	**Total**
Freshmen	45	54	52	**151**
Sophomores	41	42	45	**138**
Juniors	37	48	59	**144**
Seniors	41	51	60	**152**
Total	**174**	**195**	**216**	**585**

Are the events *Student is a junior* and *Student chose pizza* independent?

A. Yes, because the proportion of juniors who chose pizza is the same as the proportion of all students who chose pizza.

B. Yes, because the proportion of students that preferred pizza who are juniors is different from the proportion of all students who are juniors.

C. No, because the proportion of juniors who chose pizza is the same as the proportion of all students who chose pizza.

D. No, because the proportion of students who are juniors that preferred pizza is different from the proportion of all students who are juniors.

E. No, because the proportion of juniors who chose pizza is different from the proportions of other grades who chose pizza.

29. The total cholesterol level in a large population of people is strongly skewed right with a mean of 210 mg/dL and a standard deviation of 15 mg/dL. If random samples of size 16 are repeatedly drawn from this population, which of the following appropriately describes the sampling distribution of these sample means?

A. The shape is unknown with a mean of 210 and a standard deviation of 15.

B. The shape is somewhat skewed right with a mean of 210 and a standard deviation of 3.75.

C. The shape is approximately normal with a mean of 210 and a standard deviation of 15.

D. The shape is approximately normal with a mean of 210 and a standard deviation of 3.75.

E. The shape is now skewed left with a mean of 210 and a standard deviation of 3.75.

30. In one metropolitan region, technical writers have an annual salary that is approximately normally distributed with a mean of $55,800. The first quartile of salaries is $48,815. What is the standard deviation?

A. $6,984
B. $10,356
C. $10,476
D. $13,968
E. $20,709

31. Which of these explains why t should be used instead of z for inference procedures for means?

A. The Central Limit Theorem applies to proportions but not means.

B. We use z for proportions because proportions are approximately normal. Means are not.

C. We use z for proportions because the sampling distribution of sample proportions is approximately normal, but that is not the case for the sampling distribution of sample means.

D. The sampling distribution of sample means is a t-distribution, not a z-distribution.

E. When using the sample standard deviation to estimate the population standard deviation, more variability is introduced into the sampling distribution of the statistic.

32. Which of the following is *least* likely to reduce bias in a sample survey?

A. Following up with those who did not respond to the survey the first time

B. Asking questions in a neutral manner to avoid influencing the responses

C. Using stratified random sampling rather than simple random sampling

D. Selecting samples randomly

E. Allowing responses to be anonymous

33. A school yearbook is curious to know which color palette students prefer for the cover of the yearbook. They show students three different color choices. They also compare the responses of the lower classmen to those of the upper classmen.

	Lower	Upper
Red	15	22
Blue	28	8
Green	20	14

How many degrees of freedom should be used in a test of independence of class and color preference?

A. 2
B. 3
C. 5
D. 6
E. 106

GO ON TO THE NEXT PAGE

34. A local library has a scanner to detect library materials that have not been checked out. Each item has a chip somewhere inside. Upon checkout, the chip is deactivated so the scanner will not set off the alarm. The scanner has a 98% chance of detecting an active chip (meaning the material has not been checked out) and setting off the alarm. The scanner also has a 3% chance of sounding the alarm when someone passes through without an active chip. It is estimated that 0.5% of library customers actually try to leave the library with an active chip. What is the probability that, if the alarm sounds, the patron leaving the library has an item with an active chip?

    A. 0.0049
    B. 0.0348
    C. 0.1410
    D. 0.9700
    E. 0.9800

35. Which of the following is the best description of the power of a significance test?

    A. The probability that the null hypothesis is true.
    B. The probability of getting a Type I error.
    C. The probability of getting a Type II error.
    D. The probability of getting a test statistic at least as extreme as the actual test statistic, if the null hypothesis is true.
    E. The probability of rejecting the null hypothesis if it is, in fact, false.

36. A school board of a large school district is proposing a new dress code for students. Some students feel that this dress code unfairly targets female students. To see if there is a difference between boys and girls in their opposition to the new dress code, they conduct a poll of 60 randomly selected male and 70 randomly selected female high school students in the district. They find that 66 females oppose the dress code and 50 males oppose the dress code. Which of the following explains why a two-proportion z-test is not appropriate?

    A. The sample sizes are different.
    B. The sample sizes are too large.
    C. The number of successes and the number of failures for the two groups are not all large enough.

    D. The shapes of the population distributions are not known.
    E. The population standard deviations are not known.

37. Researchers are conducting an experiment using a significance level of 0.05. The null hypothesis is, in fact, false. If they modify their experiment to use twice as many experimental units for each treatment, which of the following would be true?

    A. The probability of a Type I error and the probability of a Type II error would both decrease.
    B. The probability of a Type I error and the power would both increase.
    C. The probability of a Type II error and the power would both increase.
    D. The probability of a Type I error would stay the same and the power would increase.
    E. The probability of a Type II error would stay the same and the power would increase.

38. A producer of skin care products has created a new formula for its cream to cure acne. To compare the effectiveness of the new cream to that of the old cream, it conducted a double-blind randomized experiment. Volunteers with acne tried the old formula on one side of their face and the new formula on the other, and which side got which formula was determined randomly. The response variable was the difference in the number of pimples (old formula − new formula). Which is the correct significance test to perform?

    A. A two-proportion z-test
    B. A two-sample t-test
    C. A matched pairs t-test
    D. A chi-square test of independence
    E. A chi-square goodness-of-fit test

GO ON TO THE NEXT PAGE

39. Smartphones with larger screens tend to be more expensive than smartphones with smaller screens. A random sample of currently available smartphones was selected. A 95% confidence interval for the slope of the regression line to predict price from screen size is (61, 542). Which of the following statements concerning this interval is correct?

    A. If many samples of this size were taken, about 95% of confidence intervals for the slope based on those samples would contain the slope of the line for all smartphones that are currently available.
    B. If many samples of this size were taken, about 95% of those samples would have a regression line with a slope between 61 and 542.
    C. There is convincing evidence that the size of the screen is the reason for the difference in price.
    D. Because this interval is so large, there is no convincing evidence of a relationship between screen size and price.
    E. There is not enough information to make a statement about the relationship between screen size and price because memory capacity and other features must also be taken into account.

40. In the 50 states of the United States, the financial climate for people living in retirement varies. Some states are very tax friendly to retirees. Other states are much less tax friendly to retirees. As a member of the Oregon state legislature, you wonder if Oregon's tax policies are driving older, retired people to move to other states. You have a cousin in Florida with the opposite idea—that the tax-friendly nature of Florida attracts more retirees. Each of you takes a random sample of the adults in your respective states and finds the statistics in the table below.

State	Sample Size	Mean Age	Standard Deviation
Oregon	31	40.63	19.78
Florida	41	44.65	20.60

The 99% confidence interval for the difference in the mean age of adults in Oregon and adults in Florida is (−16.73, 8.69). Does this interval provide convincing evidence that the mean ages of adults in the two states differ?

    A. Yes, because 0 is in the interval.
    B. No, because 0 is in the interval.
    C. Yes, because the mean ages are different in the two samples.
    D. No, because the mean ages of the samples are less than one standard deviation apart.
    E. Yes, because this is a t-interval for a difference in means.

END OF SECTION I

AP Statistics Practice Test 2

SECTION II

Time: 1 hour and 30 minutes

Number of questions: 6

Percentage of total grade: 50

General Instructions

There are two parts to this section of the examination. Part A consists of five equally weighted problems that represent 75% of the total weight of this section. Spend about 65 minutes on this part of the exam. Part B consists of one longer problem that represents 25% of the total weight of this section. Spend about 25 minutes on this part of the exam. You are not necessarily expected to complete all parts of every question. Statistical tables and formulas are provided.

- Be sure to write clearly and legibly. If you make an error, you may save time by crossing it out rather than trying to erase it. Erased or crossed-out work will not be graded.
- Show all your work. Indicate clearly the methods you use because you will be graded on the correctness of your methods as well as the accuracy of your final answers. Correct answers without support work may not receive credit.

Statistics, Section II, Part A, Questions 1–5

Spend about 65 minutes on this part of the exam; percentage of Section II grade: 75.

Directions: Show all your work. Indicate clearly the methods you use because you will be graded on the correctness of your methods as well as on the accuracy of your results and explanation.

1. Universities generally post the rosters of all their student athletes, including which sport they play and their heights. The boxplots below show the distributions of the men and women athletes.

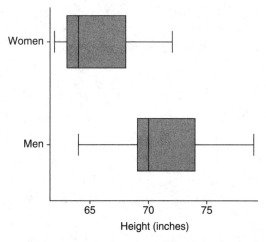

a. Write a few sentences comparing the heights of the men to the heights of the women.
b. The median of the women's heights is much closer to first quartile than it is to the third quartile. What does this tell you is probably true about the shape of the distribution?
c. What can you say is likely to be true about the relationship between the mean and the median of the women's heights?

GO ON TO THE NEXT PAGE

2. In the fictional story *The Legend of Sleepy Hollow*, the Headless Horseman chases Ichabod Crane through the New England countryside. A video game based on this legend has Crane choosing his route randomly, with a probability of 15% that he stays on the road and 85% that he cuts through the forest. If he stays on the road, there is a 90% chance of the Horseman catching Ichabod. If he cuts through the forest, there is only a 64% change of being caught.

   a. What is the probability that Ichabod Crane is caught?
   b. Given that the Horseman will catch him, what are the chances that it was a game where Mr. Crane cut through the forest?
   c. Are the events being caught and choosing a path independent? Explain,

3. A small town is interested to see how frequently the town park is used by the citizens. The mayor of the town collects a random sample of 450 citizens who are asked, "Have you used the town park in the last month?" Out of the 450 polled, 123 stated that they had used the park in the last month.

   a. Construct and interpret a 95% confidence for the percentage of the town's citizens that have been to the park in the last month.
   b. One of the local newspapers claims that improvements to the park should only be paid for if one-third of the town's citizens are using the park. Based on your interval in part (a), what conclusion should the newspaper make about the improvements?

4. Cortisol is a hormone produced by the body to control inflammation. People with chronic inflammation and, hence, chronically elevated cortisol levels can develop problems with their immune system. To explore this, 100 adult volunteers with chronic inflammation will participate in a study to compare the effect of black tea versus coffee on cortisol levels. Each volunteer will be assigned at random to one of the two groups and provided with daily capsules that contain a concentrated form of either black tea or coffee. Each will also have his or her cortisol levels measured at the beginning of the study and then 20 weeks later.

   a. Describe how you would assign the 100 volunteers to the two groups in such a way as to allow a statistically valid comparison of the two treatments.
   b. Explain a *statistical* advantage to using capsules rather than having participants actually drink coffee or tea.
   c. Is it reasonable to generalize the findings of this study to all adults with chronic inflammation? Explain.

GO ON TO THE NEXT PAGE

5. A large school district is planning an enrichment program for next summer. It is planning four course options for students: Music, Sports, Drama, or Academic Enrichment. For planning purposes, the district selected a random sample of 100 freshmen, a random sample of 100 sophomores, and a random sample of 100 juniors. (Since seniors will have graduated, they were not surveyed.) The selected students were asked which program they would choose to attend. The results for each class are shown in the graph below:

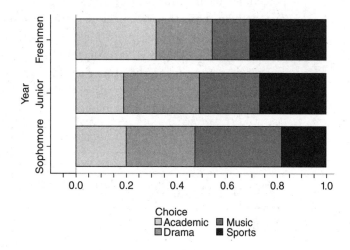

a. Describe any associations you see between year in school and choice of program.
b. District administrators want to determine if there is convincing evidence that students in different years have different preferences for programs throughout the whole district.
    i. Identify the hypothesis test they should use by name.
    ii. Write the null and alternative hypotheses appropriate for this test.
    iii. State the degrees of freedom for this test.
c. The *P*-value from the test is 0.0082. What conclusion should the administrators reach?

Statistics, Section II, Part B, Question 6

Spend about 25 minutes on this part of the exam; percentage of Section II grade: 25.

Directions: Show all your work. Indicate clearly the methods you use because you will be graded on the correctness of your methods as well as on the accuracy of your results and explanation.

6. In 1937, the United States passed the Wagner-Steagall Act, also known as the National Housing Act. This piece of legislation was intended to remedy the unsafe housing conditions in which many low-income families were living. The National Housing Act contributed to today's common wisdom that when a household devotes more than 30% of its income to housing expenses that household is said to be burdened. A household that devotes more than 50% of its income to housing expenses is said to be severely burdened.

A graduate student interning at a nonprofit organization that addresses affordable housing has received a grant to study this issue. However, the grant will only cover in-depth investigation of eight households. The table below represents the percentage

GO ON TO THE NEXT PAGE

of income devoted to housing expenses (rent, utilities, etc.) for each of eight randomly selected low-income households.

Subject	A	B	C	D	E	F	G	H
%	46.3	59.1	70.4	52.2	54.5	47.0	51.9	53.4

a. Local officials say that for low-income households in this community the median percentage of income spent on housing is 48%. The graduate student would like to test the hypothesis that the mean percentage is actually higher than 48. If the graduate student wants to use a t-test for this hypothesis, are the conditions for inference satisfied? Briefly explain your answer.

b. Rather than a test using the numeric values, the graduate student decides to turn the data into categorical data by noting whether each subject's income is above or below the hypothesized median percentage of 48. Fill out the table appropriately to reflect the graduate student's change of the data:

Subject	A	B	C	D	E	F	G	H
%	46.3	59.1	70.4	52.2	54.5	57.0	51.9	53.4
Data Change								

c. Explain how the graduate student's decision to change the nature of the data addresses any issues raised in part (a).

d. If it were true that the median percentage of income devoted to housing expenses was 48%, then we would expect half of the population to spend less than 48% on housing expenses. Using the information in the table above, calculate the approximate probability that one or fewer clients would have a housing expense percentage of less than 48%.

e. Based on your answer to part (d), do you have convincing evidence that the graduate student's hypothesis is correct? Explain your answer.

END OF SECTION II

〉 Answers to Practice Test 2, Section I

1. D	21. D
2. B	22. D
3. A	23. C
4. C	24. B
5. D	25. B
6. E	26. C
7. B	27. C
8. D	28. A
9. D	29. B
10. B	30. B
11. C	31. E
12. D	32. C
13. D	33. A
14. C	34. C
15. B	35. E
16. A	36. C
17. B	37. D
18. A	38. C
19. D	39. A
20. E	40. D

> Solutions to Practice Test 2, Section I

1. (D) The location of the tail indicates skew. The tail is located toward the smaller values of time; therefore, we call this distribution skewed left (since smaller values are to the left of larger values).

2. (B) Slope, traditionally written as $\Delta y / \Delta x$, becomes $\Delta CaloriesPredicted / \Delta Sodium = 0.2457/1$. So, every item with 1 additional mg of sodium tends to have 0.2457 more calories.

3. (A) Since water and sunlight also influence plant growth, we block on those variables. Plots 1, 2, 3, and 4 all get more direct sunlight. Plots 5, 6, 7, and 8 all get increased water.

4. (C) The middle 80% of durations symmetrically straddles the mean of 167 minutes. That leaves 10% of the durations in each tail. Using Standard Normal Probabilities (Table A in the Appendix to this book), we find a z-score that corresponds to a 10% tail area that is ± 1.28. Solving the equations $\pm 1.28 = (x - 167)/76$ gives us approximately 70 minutes and 264 minutes.

5. (D) Aliana's customers were not randomly selected. But neither did she randomly assign customers to her treatments—she spilt her shift into three parts and applied the treatment to all customers during the period.

6. (E) There is no probability once the interval is created. Options B and C are backwards. The sample proportion is in the center of the interval.

7. (B) Measurement errors are values calculated using the expression Thermometer Reading $-20°C$. If the reading is $18°C$, then the error would be $-2°C$. We then need to calculate the probability that the error is less than $-2°C$. Using Table A (see Appendix), we find
$$P\left(z < \frac{-2-0}{1.3}\right) = 0.062.$$

8. (D) The definition of a P-value is the probability, in repeated sampling, of obtaining results at least as large/small as ours when the null hypothesis is actually true. Therefore, a P-value in this case says that there is a 7% chance of a difference at least as large if the new keyboard is no better than the old.

9. (D) Changing the largest value in a data set, in this case increasing it by two inches, would not affect either Q1 or Q3; therefore, the IQR remains unchanged.

10. (B) The sampling distribution of the sample mean is approximately normal because $n = 50 > 30$.
$$\mu_{\bar{x}} = \mu = 0.25, \text{ and } \sigma_{\bar{x}} = \frac{\sigma}{\sqrt{n}} = \frac{0.05}{\sqrt{50}}.$$

11. (C) The median for Hendersonville is 71 degrees. The third quartile for Sheboygan is 64 degrees.

12. (D) The 71% refers to r^2. So $r = \pm\sqrt{0.71} \approx \pm 0.84$. Because the association is positive, $r = +0.84$.

13. (D) In this case $12/43 = 0.28$ women were promoted and $9/24 = 0.38$ men were promoted. The table does provide some evidence since these values are so different. It remains to be seen whether this difference is statistically significant.

14. (C) The values 2 and 18.5 represent Q1 and Q3, respectively. Approximately 50% of the values would be between Q1 and Q3.

15. (B) Point A "pulls up" on the left end of the line. Removing it would drop the left end, increasing the slope. Point B is pulling down near the mean value of x. Removing it would have little impact on the slope.

16. (A) Only option A correctly describes a bias that will systematically leave out a group of people that we strongly suspect will be different in shopping habits than those that are surveyed.

17. (B) A Type I error means the null hypothesis is true, but you reject it. That means pizza places, on average, do not make over $9,000 per month, but you believe they do. You might open a business and do poorly.

18. (A) We need to find the z-score that corresponds to a lower-tail area/probability of 0.2800. Using Table A (see Appendix), that z-score is -0.58. $-0.58 \cdot 2.1$ ounces $= -1.22$ ounces, so this onion is 1.22 ounces below the mean.

19. (D) Because there is an association between exercise and cholesterol, we need to block on level of exercise.

20. (E) If we are to use the data that were returned, then we have to find a way to overcome nonresponse by getting survey results from those who did not return the survey.

21. (D) The setting is a geometric probability. There are 10 "failures" (7/8) and then one "success" (1/8).

22. (D) The key phrase in this question is "most representative sample of its customers." Choice (D) ensures that the sample selects customers from each state and that selection is proportional to the number of customers from each state. For example, if 25% of the customers are from California, then 25% of the sample will be from California.

23. (C) In order to use a normal approximation to a binomial model such as this, we should see if np and $n(1 - p)$ are both at least 10. (Note, some authors will check to see if both are at least 5 and others will check to see if both are at least 15.)

24. (B) We need to calculate P(Serenity in first box, Blackstar in second box) as well as P(Blackstar in first box, Serenity in second box) and then add them. This would be $(0.12)(0.18) + (0.18)(0.12) = 0.0432$.

25. (B) Using the expected value formula for a probability function we get $(0.05)(0.45) + (0.10)(0.25) + (0.15)(0.15) + (0.25)(0.10) + (0.50)(0.05) = 0.12$, or 12%. 12% of $40 is $4.80.

26. (C) The probability of selecting a player above the third quartile is 0.25 because we are sampling with replacement, this situation meets the conditions of a binomial variable with $n = 5$ and probability of success $= 0.25$. Therefore, $P(x \geq 3) = P(3) + P(4) + P(5)$. Using the formula $P(x = k) = \binom{n}{k} p^k (1 - p)^{n-k}$ we get $P(3) + P(4) + P(5) = 0.1035$.

27. (C) The mean of the total weight is the same as the sum of the individual means, or 62 grams + 456 grams = 518 grams. We are told that the shipping is secured in an independent part of the factory, so therefore the variance of the total weight is given by $(1.0 \text{ grams})^2 + (6 \text{ grams})^2$. We find the standard deviation of the total weight by taking the square root of that variance, or $\sqrt{1^2 + 6^2} = 6.1$ grams.

28. (A) Recall that two events A and B are independent if $P(A|B) = P(A)$. The proportion of juniors in the group who vote for pizza is $48/144 = 0.33333$. The proportion of all students who vote for pizza is $195/585 = 0.3333$. Since these are the same value, *Student is a junior* and *Student chooses pizza* are independent.

29. (B) Because $\bar{x}$ is an unbiased estimator of the mean, the sampling distribution of those sample means has the same value as the population. Therefore, mean = 210. The standard deviation of the sampling distribution is given by $\sigma/\sqrt{n} = 15/\sqrt{4} = 3.75$. However, the population is substantially skewed right and the sample size is very small. Therefore, we cannot say that the shape of the sampling distribution is approximately normal.

30. (B) The z-score for the first quartile ($p = 0.25$) is -0.674. $z = \dfrac{48,815 - 55,800}{s} = -0.67449$. So $s = \dfrac{48,815 - 55,800}{-0.67449} = 10,356$.

31. (E) The correct option provides the explanation.

32. (C) The question asks which is least likely to reduce bias in a sample survey. Simple random sampling is unbiased, so using a stratified random sample would not improve on that. You can take a representative sample but still introduce bias unless you address the actions in choices (A), (B), (D), and (E).

33. (B) Degrees of freedom are calculated by (rows − 1)(columns − 1). In this case, $(3 − 1)(2 − 1) = 2$.

34. (C) This can be done using a two-way table.

	Active chip	No active chip	Total
Alarm	$0.98 \cdot 0.005 = 0.0049$	$0.03 \cdot 0.995 = 0.02985$	$0.0049 + 0.02985 = 0.03475$
No alarm	$0.005 - 0.0049 = 0.0001$	$0.995 - 0.02985 = 0.96515$	$0.0001 + 0.96515 = 0.96525$
Total	0.005	0.995	1

The required probability is $0.0049/0.03475 = 0.1410$.

35. (E) That is the definition of power.

36. (C) The number of successes and failures each needs to be greater than 10 for both males and females. Since the success/failure numbers for females are 66/4, we do not meet this condition.

37. (D) We did not change the significance level, which is the probability of making a Type I error. Increasing the sample size is one way to increase the power of the test.

38. (C) Each volunteer behaves as his or her own block. Therefore, a matched pairs test is appropriate.

39. (A) This choice correctly interprets the confidence level of 95%. When you take many, many, many samples of the same size, 95% of the confidence intervals you build around your sample results will contain the parameter you hope to estimate.

40. (B) Since zero is contained in the interval, zero (representing no difference in the means) is a plausible value. So, we do not have convincing evidence that there is a difference.

› Solutions to Practice Test 2, Section II

For these questions on this practice exam we recommend that you read through the model solutions and then try scoring your own responses. You can then check using the scoring guides that follow question 6.

1. Fencing Team

   a. The men's height has a higher center and a larger spread than the women's height. Women's height appears skewed right while the men's height appears more symmetrical (although complete information about shape cannot be determined from a boxplot).

   b. Because the median is closer to the first quartile than the third quartile, this is likely to indicate that the distribution of women's heights is skewed to the right. The lower half of the data is in a smaller range than the top half of the data.

   c. Because the women's heights are skewed right, this will increase the mean of the distribution and it is almost certain that the mean will be larger than the median.

2. Using the tree diagram below:

   a. $P(\text{caught}) = (0.15)(0.90) + (0.85)(0.64) = 0.679$

   b. $P\left(\text{Taking Forest given Caught}\right) = \dfrac{(0.85)(0.64)}{(0.15)(0.90) + (0.85)(0.64)} = 0.8012$

   c. The probability of being caught given that he takes the road is 0.90 but from part (a) the probability of being caught in general is 0.679. (Similarly for taking the forest route.) Since these are different, being caught and the choosing a path are not independent.

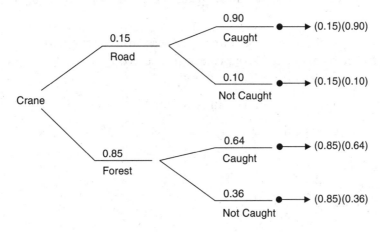

3. A small-town park survey.

   a. The sample was randomly selected and 450 is most likely less than 10% of the town's population. Both 123 and 327 are greater than 10. So, we have met the conditions necessary to calculate a 95% confidence interval of:

   $$0.2733 \pm 1.96\sqrt{(0.2733)(0.7267)/450} = 0.2733 \pm 0.4118 = (0.2321, 0.3145)$$

   Therefore, we are 95% confident that the percentage of all the town's citizens who have been to the park in the past month is between 23.2% and 31.4%.

   b. Since one-third (or 0.333) is not in the interval and therefore not a plausible value for the population proportion, the newspaper would be justified in not supporting improvements to the park.

Scoring Guidelines:

Scoring Part (a)

Component 1: Your response notes that the sample was randomly selected.

Component 2: Your response checks that $10(450) <$ Population of the town.

Component 3: Your response checks that 123 and 327 are both greater than 10.

> If you have all three components, score your response as an E for this part.
> If you have two components, score your response as a P.
> Otherwise, score your response as an I.

Scoring Parts (a) and (b)

Component 1: You have listed the equation or the name of procedure to calculate an interval to estimate a population proportion.

Component 2: Your response includes the correct interval endpoints. (This component may be met in component 3.)

Component 3: Your response correctly interprets the interval as listed in the model solution.

Component 4: Your interpretation of the interval includes context.

> If you have all four components, score your response as an E for this part.
> If you have component two or three components, score your response as a P.
> Otherwise, score your response as an I.

Scoring Part (c)

Component 1: Your response says that the newspaper would be justified in NOT supporting improvements to the park.

Component 2: Your response justifies this conclusion because one-third (or 0.3333) is not included in the interval.

> If you have both components, score your response as an E for this part.
> If you ONLY have component 1 score your response as a P.
> Otherwise, score your response as an I.

Give your response to question 1 an overall score of:

4: EEE (all three parts are essentially correct)
3: EEP in any order
2: EEI, PPP, or EPI in any order
1: EEI or PPI in any order
0: all other combinations

4. Cortisol
   a. Put all 100 volunteers' names on equally sized pieces of paper into a hat and mix thoroughly. Then draw the names one at a time out of the hat. The first 50 names drawn are the volunteers who will receive the black tea capsules. The remaining 50 names are the volunteers who will receive coffee capsules.
   b. Using capsules keeps the volunteers blind to which treatment they are receiving so that any effect can be attributed to the treatment (tea or coffee concentrate) rather than perhaps the placebo effect.
   c. It is not reasonable to generalize the results of this study to all adults. The sample was a voluntary one, not a random one.

5. Summer enrichment program
   a. There appears to be an association between course option choices and age as the distributions are so different. Specifically, the proportion of sophomores who chose music is higher than that of juniors and much higher than that of the freshmen. The proportion of juniors who chose academics is about the same as that of sophomores, but much lower than that of the freshmen.
   b. i. Chi-square test for homogeneity
      ii. H_0: Choice of enrichment program is the same for the populations of freshmen, sophomores, and juniors.

      H_a: Choice of enrichment program is not the same for all three populations.
      iii. $(2-1)(4-1) = 3$ degrees of freedom.

   c. Since the P-value is so low, lower than any reasonable value of alpha, the district administrators should reject the null hypothesis. It appears that the choice of enrichment program is not the same for all three populations of students.

6. Affordable housing
   a. The graduate student should not use a t-test for this hypothesis because the sample is so small and contains one outlier of 70.4%.
   b. The table should be filled in as follows:

Subject	A	B	C	D	E	F	G	H
%	46.3	59.1	70.4	52.2	54.5	57.0	51.9	53.4
Data Change	Below	Above	Above	Above	Above	Above	Above	Above

   c. Once the variable has been changed to a categorical variable (above/below), the outlier ceases to be an issue.
   d. This is now a binomial probability with $n = 8$ and $P(\text{below the median}) = 0.50$. The approximate probability that 1 or fewer clients would have a housing expense percentage of less than 48 is found by $P(0) + P(1)$, calculated using the formula $P(x = k) = \binom{n}{k} p^k (1-p)^{n-k}$ once for each probability.

   This is $0.00391 + 0.03125 = 0.03516$.
   e. Since the probability is greater than an alpha level of 0.01, I do not have convincing evidence that the graduate student's hypothesis is correct. (Alternatively: Since the probability is less than an alpha level of 0.05, I do have convincing evidence that the graduate student's hypothesis is correct.)

Free-Response Question 1

Scoring Part (a)

Component 1: Your response includes a correct comparison of center using comparison words.

Component 2: Your response includes a correct comparison of spread using comparison words. (Examples of comparison words are higher, bigger, smaller, more than, less than. *Note:* "While" is not a comparison word.)

Component 3: Your response includes a correct description of the shape of each distribution without definitive language—for example, saying "the distribution of heights is symmetrical" is definitive. Using the phrase "appears symmetrical" is a correct description of a shape.

If you have all three components, score your response as an E for part (a).
If you have only two components, score your response as a P.
Otherwise, score your response as an I.

Scoring Part (b)

Component 1: Your response notes that the distribution is likely to be skewed right.

Component 2: Your response justifies by either citing the relationship of the median to the quartiles OR cites the range of the lower half in comparison to the range of the upper half.

> If you have both components, score your response as an E for part (a).
> If you have only one component, score your response as a P.
> Otherwise, score your response as an I.

Scoring Part (c)

Component 1: Your response says that the mean is likely larger than the median.

Component 2: Your response justifies by citing that in a skewed right distribution, the mean is generally larger than the median.

> If you have both components, score your response as an E for part (a).
> If you have only one component, score your response as a P.
> Otherwise, score your response as an I.

Give your response to question 1 an overall score of:

4: EEE (all three parts essentially correct)
3: EEP in any order
2: EEI, PPP, or EPI in any order
1: EII or PPI in any order
0: all other combinations

Free-Response Question 2

Scoring Part (a)

Component 1: Your response has the correct probability of 0.679.

Component 2: Your response includes work shown; for example, using a table or tree diagram, etc.

> If you have both components, score your response as an E for part (a).
> If you have only one component, score your response as a P.
> Otherwise, score your response as an I.

Scoring Part (b)

Component 1: Your response has the correct probability of 0.8012.

Component 2: Your response includes work shown; for example, using a table or tree diagram, etc.

> If you have both components, score your response as an E for part (b).
> If you have only one component, score your response as a P.
> Otherwise, score your response as an I.

Scoring Part (c)

Component 1: You say "no," these events are not independent.

Component 2: Your response justifies using an example similar to the model solution.

> If you have both components, score your response as an E for part (a).
> If you have only one component, score your response as a P.
> Otherwise, score your response as an I.

Give your response to question 2 an overall score of:

4: EEE (all three parts essentially correct)
3: EEP in any order
2: EEI, PPP, or EPI in any order
1: EII or PPI in any order
0: all other combinations

Free-Response Question 3

Scoring Part (a)

Component 1: Your response identifies the center of the distribution at about 428 grams.

Component 2: You cite that since the center of the distribution is equal to the population parameter, this is evidence of an unbiased estimator.

> If you have both components, score your response as an E for part (a).
> If you have only one component, score your response as a P.
> Otherwise, score your response as an I.

Scoring Part (b)

Component 1: Your response correctly counts the two simulated responses (dots) that are greater than 446.2 grams and calculates a probability of 0.0067 (or 2 out of 300).

Component 2: You said that because this value was small (or less than 5%), it is unlikely that the claim made by the farmer's market about grapefruit is true.

> If you have both components, score your response as an E for part (b).
> If you have only one component, score your response as a P.
> Otherwise, score your response as an I.

Give your response to question 3 an overall score of:

4: EE (Both parts essentially correct)
3: EP in any order
2: EI in any order or PP
1: PI in any order
0: any other combination

Free-Response Question 4

Scoring Part (a)

Component 1: Your response uses an acceptable method of identifying each of the subjects; for example, names on papers or numbering an ordered list of names from 001 to 100.

Component 2: Your response then uses your method to randomly choose 50 unique subjects (not numbers!) for the first group and therefore assigns the remaining 50 subjects to the second group.

> If you have both components, score your response as an E for part (a).
> If you have only one component, score your response as a P.
> Otherwise, score your response as an I.

Scoring Part (b)

Component 1: Your response recognizes that the capsules keep the subjects from knowing which treatment they have been assigned.

Component 2: Your response cites that the reason for doing so is to control for the placebo effect.

> If you have both components, score your response as an E for part (b).
> If you have only one component, score your response as a P.
> Otherwise, score your response as an I.

Scoring Part (c)

Component 1: Your response says no, it is not reasonable.

Component 2: You justify the answer by citing that this is not a random sample of the population.

> If you have both components, score your response as an E for part (a).
> If you have only the first component, score your response as a P.
> If you said "yes," score your response as an I.

Give your response to question 4 an overall score of:

4: EEE (all three parts essentially correct)
3: EEP in any order
2: EEI, PPP, or EPI in any order
1: EII or PPI in any order
0: all other combinations

Free-Response Question 5

Scoring Part (a)

Component 1: Your response says that there appears to be an association because these distributions are so different.

Component 2: You cite at least one specific difference between the groups.

> If you have both components, score your response as an E for part (a).
> If you have only one component, score your response as a P.
> Otherwise, score your response as an I.

Scoring Part (b)

Component 1: You name the test correctly.

Component 2: Your null hypothesis is correctly worded.

Component 2: Your alternate hypothesis is correctly worded.

Component 2: You have listed the correct degrees of freedom.

> If you have all four components, score your response as an E for part (b).
> If you have only two or three components, score your response as a P.
> Otherwise, score your response as an I.

Scoring Part (c)

Component 1: Your response includes an explicit comparison of the P-value to a significance level of either 0.01 or 0.05 OR to the magnitude of the P-value as being low.

Component 2: Based on that comparison, you came to a correct decision.

Component 3: Your response is written in the context of the alternate.

> If you have all three components, score your response as an E for this part.
> If you have two components, score your response as a P.
> Otherwise, score your response as an I.

Give your response to question 5 an overall score of:

4: EEE (all three parts essentially correct)
3: EEP in any order
2: EEI, PPP, or EPI in any order
1: EII or PPI in any order
0: all other combinations

Free-Response Question 6

Scoring Part (a)

Component 1: You provide a dotplot of the data values.
Component 2: You say "no," the graduate student should not use a t-procedure.
Component 3: You cite as evidence the presence of the outlier as justification.

> If you have all three components, score your response as an E for this part.
> If you have two components, score your response as a P.
> Otherwise, score your response as an I.

Scoring Parts (b) and (c) together

Component 1: Your table is correctly filled in.
Component 2: You cite that the outlier ceases to be an issue once the variable has been changed.

> If you have both components, score your response as an E for this part.
> If you have one component, score your response as a P.
> Otherwise, score your response as an I.

Scoring Part (d)

Component 1: Your response specifies the fixed number of trials by listing $n = 8$, the probability being $p = 0.5$, and this being a binomial situation either in words (as in the model solution) OR in a statement of a binomial calculation where those numeric values are identified by variables as well. For example: BinomialCDF($n = 8$, $p = 0.5$, $x = 1$).
Component 2: Your response includes a correct value for the probability with work shown.

> If you have both components, score your response as an E for this part.
> If you have one component, score your response as a P.
> Otherwise, score your response as an I.

Scoring Part (e)

Component 1: Your response includes an explicit comparison of the P-value calculated in part (d) to a significance level of either 0.01 or 0.05 OR to the magnitude of this P-value as being low or high.
Component 2: Based on that comparison, you came to a correct decision.
Component 3: Your response is written in the context of the alternate.

> If you have all three components, score your response as an E for this part.
> If you have two components, score your response as a P.
> Otherwise, score your response as an I.

Each essentially correct (E) counts as 1 point. Each partially correct (P) counts as ½ point. If your response is between two scores (for example, 2 ½ points), use a holistic approach to score your response up or down based on the overall strength of the response and communication.

5 Minutes to a 5

180 Daily Questions and Activities

5 Minutes a Day

INTRODUCTION

Welcome to *5 Minutes to a 5: 180 Questions and Activities!* This bonus section is another tool for you to use as you work toward your goal of achieving a 5 on the AP exam in May. It includes 180 AP questions and activities that cover the most essential course materials and are meant to be completed in conjunction with the *5 Steps* book.

One of the secrets to excelling in your AP class is spending a bit of time *each day* studying the subject(s). The questions and activities offered here are designed to be done one per day, and each should take 5 minutes or so to complete, although there might be exceptions. (Depending on the exam—some exercises may take a little longer, some a little less.) You will encounter stimulating questions to make you think about a topic in a big way, and some very subject-specific activities, which cover the main book's chapters; some science subjects will offer at-home labs, and some humanities subjects will offer ample chunks of text to be read on one day, with questions and activities for follow-up on the following day(s). There will also be suggestions for relevant videos for you to watch, websites to visit, or both. Most questions and activities are linked to the specific chapters of your book so that you are constantly fortifying your knowledge.

Remember—approaching this section for 5 minutes a day is much more effective than bingeing a week's worth in one sitting! So if you practice all the extra exercises in this section and reinforce the main content of this book, we are certain you will build the skills and confidence needed to succeed on your exam. Good luck!

—Editors of McGraw Hill

Check off each activity as it is completed.

1. ❑	46. ❑	91. ❑	136. ❑
2. ❑	47. ❑	92. ❑	137. ❑
3. ❑	48. ❑	93. ❑	138. ❑
4. ❑	49. ❑	94. ❑	139. ❑
5. ❑	50. ❑	95. ❑	140. ❑
6. ❑	51. ❑	96. ❑	141. ❑
7. ❑	52. ❑	97. ❑	142. ❑
8. ❑	53. ❑	98. ❑	143. ❑
9. ❑	54. ❑	99. ❑	144. ❑
10. ❑	55. ❑	100. ❑	145. ❑
11. ❑	56. ❑	101. ❑	146. ❑
12. ❑	57. ❑	102. ❑	147. ❑
13. ❑	58. ❑	103. ❑	148. ❑
14. ❑	59. ❑	104. ❑	149. ❑
15. ❑	60. ❑	105. ❑	150. ❑
16. ❑	61. ❑	106. ❑	151. ❑
17. ❑	62. ❑	107. ❑	152. ❑
18. ❑	63. ❑	108. ❑	153. ❑
19. ❑	64. ❑	109. ❑	154. ❑
20. ❑	65. ❑	110. ❑	155. ❑
21. ❑	66. ❑	111. ❑	156. ❑
22. ❑	67. ❑	112. ❑	157. ❑
23. ❑	68. ❑	113. ❑	158. ❑
24. ❑	69. ❑	114. ❑	159. ❑
25. ❑	70. ❑	115. ❑	160. ❑
26. ❑	71. ❑	116. ❑	161. ❑
27. ❑	72. ❑	117. ❑	162. ❑
28. ❑	73. ❑	118. ❑	163. ❑
29. ❑	74. ❑	119. ❑	164. ❑
30. ❑	75. ❑	120. ❑	165. ❑
31. ❑	76. ❑	121. ❑	166. ❑
32. ❑	77. ❑	122. ❑	167. ❑
33. ❑	78. ❑	123. ❑	168. ❑
34. ❑	79. ❑	124. ❑	169. ❑
35. ❑	80. ❑	125. ❑	170. ❑
36. ❑	81. ❑	126. ❑	171. ❑
37. ❑	82. ❑	127. ❑	172. ❑
38. ❑	83. ❑	128. ❑	173. ❑
39. ❑	84. ❑	129. ❑	174. ❑
40. ❑	85. ❑	130. ❑	175. ❑
41. ❑	86. ❑	131. ❑	176. ❑
42. ❑	87. ❑	132. ❑	177. ❑
43. ❑	88. ❑	133. ❑	178. ❑
44. ❑	89. ❑	134. ❑	179. ❑
45. ❑	90. ❑	135. ❑	180. ❑

Day 1

CHAPTER 5. ONE-VARIABLE DATA ANALYSIS

Identify each variable as categorical or quantitative.

a. Heights of girls on the school basketball team.

b. The favorite movie genres at your school.

c. The age of the customers at a restaurant.

d. The income level of the citizens in a city, divided into three groups, low, middle, and high income.

The distribution below represents $n = 62$ observations. Describe this distribution.

Day 3

A distribution of observations is roughly symmetrical with no apparent outliers. Which measures of center/spread would be appropriate to describe this distribution?

The boxplot below represents the wait time in minutes of a sample of 27 customers who called for tech support from their Internet provider.

6   10   14   18   22

Which of the following statements is/are true?

A. The range of wait times for this group of customers is 16 minutes.

B. The mean wait time for these customers is 14 minutes.

C. About 50% of the time, these customers waited 14 minutes or more.

D. The distribution of wait times for this group of customers is symmetric.

In a set of 15 observations, the mean is equal to 27. In another set of 20 observations, the mean is equal to 33. What is the mean of all the observations?

Day 6

Decide what shape each of the following distributions would have. Would it be symmetric or skewed? If skewed, which direction? Mound-shaped? Would there be outliers? A wall?

a. The areas of all Minnesota lakes

b. Amounts of retirement savings families have as they approach retirement: http://www.usatoday.com/story/sponsor-story/motley-fool/2016/05/03/average-savings-for-those-nearing-retirement/83833804/

c. Weights of National Football League players

d. Heights of National Football League players

e. Ages of sitting U.S. senators

Day 7

A manufacturer creates a package that has a mean weight of 530 grams and a standard deviation of 4 grams. Interpret the standard deviation in this context.

A dataset of 24 observations produces the following summary data:

N	MIN	Q1	MEDIAN	Q3	MAX
23	29	31	37	45	75

Describe the distribution of data based on the summary data.

Day 9

Which quantitative graph is a poor choice for seeing the shape of a distribution? Which graph(s) are best for preserving the original data? How many graphs can you name for displaying quantitative data?

The distribution of household incomes in a particular state has a mean of $57,200 and a standard deviation of $45,500. Based on this, is it reasonable to think the incomes in this state are approximately normally distributed?

A group of 39 students were asked how many times they posted or replied on a class discussion board. The histogram is shown below with the frequency listed above each bar. Describe the distribution.

Day 12

Define "percentile." What does it mean if your height is at the 80th percentile? What does it mean if your reading score is at the 41st percentile?

The cumulative relative frequency plot below shows household incomes for a random sample of households. Create a boxplot of this distribution.

Day 14

There are two groups of workers at a factory. Data is collected on how many minutes it takes them to complete a certain task. Compare the distributions.

↑ 5 Minutes to a 5

Day 15

Which of the following statements is/are true?

A. The standard deviation is a resistant measure of variability.

B. If all values in a dataset are exactly the same, then the standard deviation will be equal to 1.

C. The standard deviation of every dataset will be positive.

D. To find the variance of a dataset, take the square root of the standard deviation.

E. The standard deviation should always be a positive number.

Day 16

Stephen was disappointed in his grade on a recent statistics test. He calculated his z-score and found that it was −0.45. What percent of students scored below Stephen's score?

Day 17

At a farm where customers come to pick their own vegetables, the distribution of the weight of a box of vegetables has a mean of 220 ounces with a standard deviation of 15 ounces. Interpret the standard deviation in the context of this problem.

Day 18

Shown below are some summary statistics for the scores on a test for a statistics class.

MEAN	MEDIAN	StDEV	MIN	Q1	Q3	MAX	N
22.4	22.5	6.68	2	18	28.5	33	33

Alyssa's score was 24.5 points. Calculate her z-score and interpret the z-score in this context.

Otis is 57 inches tall. His brother Acer is 45 inches tall. For Otis's age group, the mean height is 54.5 inches with a standard deviation of 2.4 inches. For Acer's age group, the mean height is 41.5 inches with a standard deviation of 2.7 inches. Which of the brothers is taller, relatively speaking?

The following data are collected from a group of people: country of origin and blood type. Construct an appropriate graph to compare the distribution of blood types within the peoples of these two countries. Does there appear to be an association between country of origin and blood type? Justify your answer.

| | BLOOD TYPE | | | | |
	O	A	B	AB	TOTAL
Australia	74	57	15	4	150
Finland	56	79	31	14	180
Total	130	136	46	18	330

The graph below is a cumulative relative frequency plot showing the number of days spent on the market before the sale of a used car. Approximate the interquartile range.

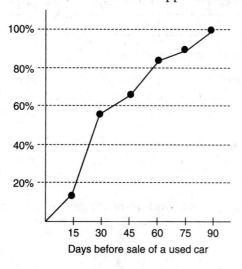

Days before sale of a used car

5 Minutes to a 5

The following are summary statistics for a certain dataset:

N	MEAN	StDEV	MIN	Q1	MEDIAN	Q3	MAX
25	18.4	6.95	8	12	15	20	40

Two students make the following observations:

Meredith: This distribution has a center of 18.4 with a spread of 6.95. Because the mean is so much greater than the median, it is reasonable to say that the distribution is skewed to the left.

Margaret: This distribution has a center of 18.4 with an IQR of 8. There is at least one outlier at the right because 40 is greater than $Q3 + 1.5(IQR)$ but no outliers to the left. Because of this, it is reasonable to say that the distribution is skewed to the right.

Comment on what is correct and/or incorrect about each student's comments.

Day 23

The stemplot below contains the test scores for 30 students. Calculate and interpret the percentile for the student who scored 92.

STEM	LEAF
6	5 8
7	0 1 1
7	5 6 9 9
8	1 2 2 3 4 4
8	5 5 6 6 7 8 8
9	0 1 2 3
9	5 5 8 9

The median of a dataset is 36. One value of the dataset was mistakenly listed at 42 when it should have been 82. Once the correction is made, what is the new median?

Day 25

The website fivethirtyeight.com declared Detroit to be the worst sports city in America. As a part of that calculation, they calculated that the Detroit Redwings, the city's professional hockey team, won fewer games than average. Specifically, the journalist calculated a z-score of -3.29 for the 2020 hockey season. How would you interpret this value?

The summary statistics below are for the length of songs (in minutes) on the first five studio albums of a pop singer. Given the data, is it reasonable to believe that the distribution of the length of songs is approximately normally distributed? Explain your answer.

N	MEAN	StDEV	MIN	Q1	MEDIAN	Q3	MAX
67	4.0996	0.7055	2.92	3.65	3.97	4.35	6.72

An approximately normal distribution has a mean of 48 and a standard deviation of 6. Approximately what percentage of the distribution is between 36 and 60?

The table below lists the summary statistics for the length, in minutes, for a sample of songs played on a popular radio station.

MEAN	StDEV	MIN	Q1	MEDIAN	Q3	MAX
3.90	0.56	2.92	3.56	3.85	4.08	5.48

The sound engineer at a radio station needs information in seconds, not minutes. Describe the effect of transforming from minutes to seconds on the following statistics: mean, variance, IQR, and median.

Day 29

A certain species of adult flamingo has heights that are approximately normally distributed with a mean of 4.8280 feet and a standard deviation of 0.453 feet. One of these flamingos at a local zoo is 5.625 feet tall. What percentile does a flamingo of this height represent?

A certain population has a mean of 200 and a standard deviation of 15. A value of 240 therefore has a z-score of 2.67. Explain why you cannot calculate the percentile for a value of 240.

The life span of a new lithium-ion battery is approximately normally distributed with a mean of 30 months and a standard deviation of 3.5 months. How long do the top 10% of these batteries last?

A national organization to certify if firefighter candidates are physically able has developed a new test of physical abilities. The organization publishes that the new test scores are approximately normally distributed with a mean of 28 and a standard deviation of 12. As a budding statistician, you believe that there is a typo in the press release. What evidence supports your belief?

CHAPTER 6. TWO-VARIABLE DATA ANALYSIS

In a random sample of father–daughter pairs, the slope of the regression line predicting the daughter's height from the father's height is 0.441. For each of the following interpretations of the slope, comment on whether it is appropriate, and if not, how it could be improved.

A. For every inch added to the father's height, the daughter's height is typically predicted to go up by 0.441 inches.

B. A father who is taller than another father is predicted to have a daughter who is taller than the other father's daughter.

C. A father who is 1 inch taller than another father will have a daughter who is 0.441 inches taller than the other father's daughter.

In a random sample of father–daughter pairs, the slope of the regression line predicting the daughter's height from the father's height is 0.441. For each of the following interpretations of the slope, comment on whether it is appropriate, and if not, how it could be improved.

A. A daughter who is 0.441 inches taller than another daughter is predicted to have a father who is 1 inch taller than the other daughter's father.

B. A father who is 1 inch taller than another father tends to have a daughter who is approximately 0.441 inches taller than the other father's daughter on average.

C. A father who is 1 inch taller than another father will have a daughter who is approximately 0.441 inches taller than the other father's daughter.

5 Minutes to a 5

Day 35

In a random sample of father–daughter pairs, the slope of the regression line predicting the daughter's height from the father's height is 0.441. For each of the following interpretations of the slope, comment on whether it is appropriate, and if not, how it could be improved.

A. A father who is 1 inch taller than another father is predicted to have a daughter who is approximately 0.441 inches taller than the other father's daughter.

B. For every inch of the father's height, the daughter's height is predicted to be 0.441 inches.

C. The *y*-value is predicted to go up by 0.441 whenever the *x*-value goes up by 1.

You have data on several brands of breakfast cereal, and you find a strong linear relationship between the number of calories per serving and the amount of carbohydrates per serving. You fit a regression line to the data with carbohydrates per serving as the explanatory variable. The cereals in your sample range from 22 g to 50 g of carbohydrates per serving. The y-intercept of the regression line is 2 calories. For each statement about the y-intercept, decide whether it is correct, and if not, how it could be improved.

A. This means that a cereal with no carbohydrates would have 2 calories per serving.

B. This value is meaningless because a cereal would not have 0 grams of carbohydrates.

C. This value is not reliable because it requires extrapolating outside the range of our data.

Day 37

Is the correlation coefficient r a resistant measure of the strength of a linear association between two variables? If the correlation coefficient is high, are you certain that the data follows a linear model?

What does it mean to say that a residual is large and positive? Small and negative? Draw a sketch and show an example of each.

Day 39

Match the values of the correlation coefficient with the statements that best describe those values.

CORRELATION COEFFICIENT	STATEMENT
A. −0.97	**1.** A perfect positive correlation
B. 0.13	**2.** Somebody made a mistake
C. −0.83	**3.** A very weak correlation
D. −1.08	**4.** A moderately strong negative correlation
E. 1.00	**5.** A very strong correlation

Use the scatterplot shown to describe the relationship between the median income versus the number of times households reported they went to the park over the course of a year.

# of visits to
public parks

Median Income

Based on the residual plot below, comment on the appropriateness of a linear relationship between your two variables.

y = 0

Explain what an ideal residual plot looks like to confirm the linearity of a dataset. What else can be revealed in a residual plot?

Which of the following would represent a relatively strong negative linear relationship?

A. $r = 0.23$, $y = 16.5332 - 0.4451x$

B. $r = -0.93$, $y = 16.5332 + 0.4451x$

C. $r = 0.93$, $y = 16.5332 + 0.4451x$

D. $r = -0.83$, $y = 16.5332 - 0.4451x$

A least-squares regression line has been computed to predict the hand span (cm) of a male student from his height in cm. The equation is $\widehat{handspan} = -11.2570 + 0.1781(height)$. One student is 189 cm tall and has a 22 cm hand span. What is the residual for this student?

Day 45

A least-squares regression line has been computed to predict the hand span (cm) of a male student from his height in cm. The equation is $\widehat{handspan} = -11.2570 + 0.1781(height)$. Jeremy sits behind you in class and remarks that his residual is −0.75 cm. Interpret Jeremy's residual.

The regression printout below shows the relationship between the number of mishandled bags per 1,000 passengers and the percent of on-time arrivals for all U.S. airlines.

Predictor	Coefficient	Std Error	t	P	ΔR^2
Constant	7.0890	3.9305	1.804	0.1015	
PctOnTimeArrivals	−0.0525	0.0505	−1.038	0.3236	0.0973

Source	DF	SS	MS	F	P	ΔR^2
Regression	1	1.6722	1.6722	1.078	0.3236	0.0973
Residual	10	15.5101	1.5510			
Total	11	17.1823				

R^2: **0.0973186**
Adjusted R^2: **0.00705048**
Std dev error: **1.2454**

a. Write the regression equation. Define the variables in context.

b. Interpret the slope and the y-intercept in this context.

The regression printout below shows the relationship between the number of mis-handled bags per 1,000 passengers and the percent of on-time arrivals for all U.S. airlines.

Predictor	Coefficient	Std Error	t	P	ΔR^2
Constant	7.0890	3.9305	1.804	0.1015	
PctOnTimeArrivals	–0.0525	0.0505	–1.038	0.3236	0.0973

Source	DF	SS	MS	F	P	ΔR^2
Regression	1	1.6722	1.6722	1.078	0.3236	0.0973
Residual	10	15.5101	1.5510			
Total	11	17.1823				

R^2: **0.0973186**
Adjusted R^2: **0.00705048**
Std dev error: **1.2454**

a. What is the correlation coefficient?

b. What percentage of the variation in mishandled bags per thousand customers is explained by the regression model with the percentage of on-time arrivals as a predictor?

c. What do these two values tell you about this relationship?

Day 48

The regression printout below shows the relationship between the number of mis-handled bags per 1,000 passengers and the percentage of on-time arrivals for all U.S. airlines. One airline had 80.8% on-time arrivals and 3.92 mishandled bags per 1,000 customers.

Predictor	Coefficient	Std Error	t	P	ΔR^2
Constant	7.0890	3.9305	1.804	0.1015	
PctOnTimeArrivals	−0.0525	0.0505	−1.038	0.3236	0.0973

Source	DF	SS	MS	F	P	ΔR^2
Regression	1	1.6722	1.6722	1.078	0.3236	0.0973
Residual	10	15.5101	1.5510			
Total	11	17.1823				

R^2: **0.0973186**
Adjusted R^2: **0.00705048**
Std dev error: **1.2454**

a. What is the residual for this airline?

b. Interpret that residual in context.

5 Minutes to a 5

Below is part of the regression printout for the relationship between the number of mishandled bags per 1,000 passengers and the percent of on-time arrivals for all U.S. airlines. It shows that the standard deviation of the error (the residuals) is 1.2454. Interpret this number in context.

R^2: **0.0973186**
Adjusted R^2: **0.00705048**
Std dev error: **1.2454**

A professor in a statistics course informs his students that over the course of many years he has developed a regression equation that predicts a student's final exam score using their midterm score.

$$\widehat{final} = 2.53 + 0.85\,(midterm)$$

a. What is the predicted final exam score for a student who scored 88 on the midterm?

b. As a student, would you hope for a positive residual or a negative residual? Explain.

Consider the scatterplot below. Your study partner calls the observation in the box an *outlier*. Explain what your study partner means.

In the scatterplot below, describe the effect of removing the observation in the box on the slope and on the correlation.

5 Minutes to a 5

The relationship between the median income in a zip code (MedIncome) and the percentage of households served (%) by a social service agency is not linear. However, transforming both variables produces a linear relationship that is quite strong and one for which the residual plot has random scatter. The regression for the transformation is $\widehat{\log(\%)} = 9.4294 - 2.2542\log(MedIncome)$. Predict the percentage of residents who would need services in a zip code where the median income is \$20,000.

Day 54

CHAPTER 7. DESIGN OF A STUDY: SAMPLING, SURVEYS, AND EXPERIMENTS

A researcher wants to know about how teens use social media. One question asks whether they have made a new friend through social media. They use a cluster random sample, selecting school districts at random from around the country, and ask all teenagers in those school districts to complete a survey. They find that 59% of teens surveyed say they have made a new friend through social media.

a. What is the population?

b. What is the sample?

c. What is the parameter?

d. What is the statistic?

Day 55

For each statement below, decide whether it is a reason to select a random sample rather than do a census.

A. A sample is cheaper and easier than a census.

B. A sample is more accurate than a census.

C. Sometimes the sample must be destroyed.

D. A census can be biased, and a random sample is not.

E. A sample can allow you to spend more time with each subject and get more accurate information.

What are the three best ways to protect against confounding in an experiment?

Explain the difference between stratified random sampling and cluster random sampling. What is a main benefit of each?

Day 58

Explain the difference between stratification and blocking.

You want to take a random sample of 100 adults from your city to ask whether they feel the library is important. You decide to do a door-to-door survey. You randomly select 10 city blocks and survey all 10 houses on each block. You conduct your survey from 9 a.m. to 1 p.m. on a Wednesday.

a. What kind of survey method is being used?

b. Describe how undercoverage created by time and day will create a biased estimate.

A student said that "bias" and "nonrepresentative" mean the same thing. Explain to the student the difference between them.

Day 61

A group of runners are curious if a new style of shoe will improve comfort and foot pain. The runners flip a coin. If they flip heads, they will try the new shoes for two weeks and then their old shoes for two weeks. Those that flip tails will reverse the order. At the end of each two-week period, the runners will report any injuries and measure their pain on a 10-point scale. What type of experimental design is this?

Day 62

A researcher would like to get a random sample of 1,000 adults living in a particular state. To that end, the researcher takes the list of all people with driving licenses and numbers the list. Using the random number generator, the researcher chooses 1,000 numbers without repeats. The 1,000 adults with those numbers will be in the sample. Will this sampling design accomplish the goal of the researcher?

In a large corporation, 2,000 employees have a bachelor's degree. The other 1,000 employees have a degree beyond a bachelor's. The human resources department takes a random sample of 100 of those with only a bachelor's degree and 50 of those with an advanced degree for a total of 150 employees. The HR department reports that the resulting group is a simple random sample. Is the HR department correct? Why or why not?

5 Minutes to a 5

Researchers interested in improving the turf quality for golf courses did a study to determine whether mowing height and/or herbicides would help control an invasive species of unwanted grass. They tried three different mowing heights: 3 inches, 4 inches, and 5 inches. Three herbicides (A, B, and C) were tested, as well as leaving the plot untreated. Forty-eight plots of land were used for the study, and each combination of mowing height and herbicide was randomly assigned to 4 plots.

a. What are the factors?

b. Describe the levels for each of the factors.

c. What are the treatments?

d. What are the experimental units?

5 Minutes to a 5

Day 65

A survey question reads as follows: "The plastic rings that hold together a six-pack of soda cans are so strong that, once entangled around the neck of any animal, choke the animal to death within three minutes. Would you support regulation to reduce the strength of plastic soda can rings?" Of a simple random sample surveyed, 84% answered "yes."

Describe a concern you have about the accuracy of this statistic.

To compare the effect of a new pesticide to that of the current pesticide, a large food company plants spinach in 8 different garden plots. Four plots are randomly assigned to each type of pesticide. At the end of the growing season, the amount of damage due to insects will be measured on each plant, and the mean amount of damage for the plants using each pesticide will be compared. Your study partner says that this type of design involves blocking. Is your study partner correct?

To measure the average height of a saguaro cactus, a researcher divides a very large plot of desert land into hundreds of 10-meter-by-10-meter plots. She chooses 10 of these plots at random and measures all of the saguaros in those plots. Which of the following represents the sampling plan this researcher used?

A. Simple random sampling

B. Stratified random sampling

C. Systematic sampling

D. Cluster sampling

E. Convenience sampling

Identify the type of sampling in each of the following situations. State whether the method is unbiased or biased.

a. A teacher asks her students how many hours of television they watch per week to estimate the amount of television high school students typically watch.

b. A talk radio host asks a question and directs listeners to text their response.

c. A public interest research group wants to estimate the amount of support in their city for a new proposal. They randomly select 50 city blocks and then visit every household on each of those blocks.

Day 69

Identify the type of sampling in each of the following situations. State whether the method is unbiased or biased.

a. An employer sends out an anonymous survey to its employees to measure job satisfaction. The survey is sent out in an email to all the employees in the company. Employees are politely asked to fill out the survey.

b. A political party has a list of likely voters in their city. They have a computer randomly select 100 people from the list, and they have volunteers call them and ask whom they will vote for.

c. A social worker wants to estimate the change in the percentage of clients in the county who report domestic abuse. To get an estimate from several years ago, before data were stored on computers, she finds the files from that year, randomly selects a number from 1 to 15, and selects that file. Then she selects every 15th file after that.

Explain how to select a simple random sample of 200 students from a large high school.

Explain how to select a stratified random sample of about 200 students from a large high school.

Explain how to select a cluster random sample of about 200 students from a large high school.

A recent study showed a link between higher caffeine intake and reduced odds of developing dementia or cognitive impairment in women over the age of 60 years. Over a 10-year period, researchers had more than 6,000 women keep track of what they drank each day. When the results were released, one Internet health blogger reported that caffeine prevents dementia. Is the blogger statistically correct?

A researcher seeking to improve the health of dogs suffering from arthritis designs a study in the following manner. A random group of dogs is given a new drug, and their owners are to measure the activity level of their dogs. What design flaw would prevent researchers from drawing a conclusion about whether the new drug is effective?

An organization of mathematics teachers is conducting research to compare two teaching methods for a particular topic. They randomly assign the teaching techniques to all the classes of the teachers who have volunteered for the study. They will compare the methods by comparing the mean test scores of the students at the end of the unit. What are the experimental units?

A student describes how to randomly assign 60 subjects for an experiment to compare two drugs, R and X, as follows: Number the list of subjects from 1 to 60. Using a random number generator, ignoring repeats, put the first 30 numbers generated into treatment R. The remaining 30 numbers will be placed in treatment X.

This student's response is not essentially correct. Why not?

In a study to see whether women who stay in the hospital for two days after giving birth recover more quickly than women who stay in the hospital one day after giving birth, two hospitals participated in the study. One hospital was selected at random to be the hospital that sends all its patients home after one day, and the other sent all its patients home after two days (unless complications warranted a longer stay). At the end of the study, it turns out the women who stayed two days did recover more quickly. Explain how which hospital the women stayed at is a confounding variable.

Day 78

A local sportscaster wants to know how the taxpayers of a southwestern city feel about tax breaks proposed to bring a hockey franchise to the area. The sportscaster reports that 67% of those viewers who called in or responded on social media do not support the proposed tax breaks. Would it be appropriate to generalize these results to all taxpayers?

CHAPTER 8. PROBABILITY AND RANDOM VARIABLES

The probability of two independent events, A and B, is given by $P(A) = 0.40$ and $P(B) = 0.32$. Find $P(A \text{ or } B)$.

A random sample of 1,000 adults was classified by pet ownership (pets/no pets) and educational attainment (less than high school, high school only, college). The results are summarized in the table below:

	PETS	NO PETS	TOTAL
Less than high school	362	240	602
High school only	235	40	275
College	63	60	123
Total	660	340	1,000

Suppose that you selected one of these individuals at random. What is the probability that this person is a pet-owning person with only high school educational attainment?

A sample space can be defined as a *complete* list of disjoint events. What is meant by this?

Explain why the sum of probabilities in a sample space must add to 1.

A random sample of 1,000 adults was classified by pet ownership (pets/no pets) and educational attainment (less than high school, high school only, college). The results are summarized in the table below:

	PETS	NO PETS	TOTAL
Less than high school	362	240	602
High school only	235	40	275
College	63	60	123
Total	660	340	1,000

Suppose that you selected one of these individuals at random. Given that this person has a college level of educational attainment, what is the probability that they do *not* have pets?

Day 84

For disjoint events, the addition rule is $P(A \text{ or } B) = P(A) + P(B)$. For other events, the addition rule is $P(A \text{ or } B) = P(A) + P(B) - P(A \text{ and } B)$. Why are there two different rules?

According to a survey, 59% of teens have made a new friend on social media. A different survey finds that 70% of teens own a smartphone. A student uses this information to calculate that the probability that a randomly selected teen has made a new friend on social media *and* owns a smartphone is $0.59 \cdot 0.70 = 0.413$. Is this student correct?

For independent events, the multiplication rule is $P(A \text{ and } B) = P(A) \cdot P(B)$. For dependent events, the addition rule is $P(A \text{ and } B) = P(A) \cdot P(B|A)$. Why are there two different rules?

Day 87

The following chart contains the values of a random variable X and the probabilities associated with those values. Is this a legitimate probability distribution? Explain your answer.

X	14	10	8	6	5	1
P(X)	0.03	0.11	0.18	0.31	0.24	0.16

The table below has marginal probabilities for events *A* and *B*.

	A	Not *A*	Total
B			0.4
Not *B*			0.6
Total	0.3	0.7	1.0

Complete the table if events *A* and *B* are independent.

Day 89

The table below has marginal probabilities for events A and B.

	A	Not A	Total
B			0.4
Not B			0.6
Total	0.3	0.7	1.0

Complete the table if events A and B are disjoint.

The table below has marginal probabilities for events A and B.

	A	Not A	Total
B			0.4
Not B			0.6
Total	0.3	0.7	1.0

Complete the table if events A and B are neither disjoint nor independent.

5 Minutes to a 5

Day 91

The following chart contains the values of a random variable X and the probabilities associated with those values. The mean and the standard deviation of X are 9.88 and 3.314, respectively. Find the missing value.

X	8	15	a	12	10	7
P(X)	0.16	0.20	0.24	0.20	0.12	0.08

A brand of cereal is running a promotion in which they include an autographed collector's card of one of five popular singers, including Katy GooGoo. A man goes to the store and buys five boxes of this cereal, hoping at least two of them contain pictures of Katy GooGoo, the favorite singer of his twin daughters. Design a simulation to estimate the probability that he will be successful.

Day 93

The table below shows ice cream flavor preferences and age groups for youth and counselors at a summer camp.

	CHOCOLATE	VANILLA	BUTTER PECAN	TOTAL
Children 12 or under	48	24	5	77
Teens 13–18	17	14	6	37
Adults	8	13	9	30
Total	73	51	20	144

One person from the camp will have their name drawn at random to win a prize. Explain, in words, the difference between P(*a child 12 or under* and *prefers vanilla*), P(*a child 12 or under* or *prefers vanilla*), P(*a child 12 or under | prefers vanilla*), and P(*prefers vanilla | a child 12 or under*). Then calculate each of those probabilities.

The students at a large high school were classified by sex and by class. Are the events "Is a freshman" and "Is a female" independent? Justify your answer appropriately.

	CLASS				
	FRESHMAN	SOPH	JUNIOR	SENIOR	TOTAL
Female	165	145	120	105	550
Male	135	105	130	95	450
Total	300	250	250	200	1000

Day 95

The students at a large high school were classified by sex and by class. Are the events "Is a male" and "Is a senior" independent? Justify your answer appropriately.

	CLASS				
	FRESHMAN	SOPH	JUNIOR	SENIOR	TOTAL
Female	165	145	120	105	550
Male	135	105	130	95	450
Total	300	250	250	200	1000

A manufacturer of toy hot air balloons packages the balloon in a box that is independently produced in a separate facility. The weight of the balloons is approximately normally distributed with a mean and standard deviation of 42 and 5 ounces, respectively, and the weight of the empty boxes is also approximately normally distributed with mean and standard deviation of 8 and 2 ounces, respectively. How would you describe the shape, center, and spread of the distribution of the boxes containing a toy hot air balloon?

Day 97

CHAPTER 9. BINOMIAL, GEOMETRIC, AND SAMPLING DISTRIBUTIONS

At a certain coffee shop there is a 5% chance that any customer will be randomly awarded with a free drink. What is the probability that in a group of 20 customers, fewer than 3 of them will earn a free drink?

In a recent upswing, 32% of 18- to 24-year-olds in the United States now live with their parents. Say you are to take a random sample of seven 18- to 24-year-olds. Make a probability distribution table for the number of people in your sample who live with their parents.

Your favorite basketball player makes 85% of his free throws. The announcer state that this player usually takes 10 free throws. One might think that you can easily find the probability that he makes exactly 7 out of 10. That is, all you have to do is multiply 0.85 seven times and then 0.15 three times.

What is wrong with that calculation?

Once again, we are thinking about our favorite basketball player that makes 85% of his free throws. But now he is shooting 15 per game. What is the mean and the standard deviation of the number of shots you expect him to make?

Day 101

The weights of sacks of flour are approximately normally distributed with a mean of 200 pounds and a standard deviation of 4 pounds. You select two sacks at random and add their weights. So W = Sack1 + Sack2. Describe the distribution of W.

The weights of sacks of flour are approximately normally distributed with a mean of 200 pounds and a standard deviation of 4 pounds. You select two sacks at random and add their weights. So W = Sack1 + Sack2. What is the probability that the total weight of the two sacks is more than 410 pounds?

The probability that a person in a certain population has type A blood is 10%. In an extremely large, random group from this population, what is the probability that it takes until the fifth person to find a person with type A blood?

$P(A) = 0.64$ and $P(B) = 0.25$, and the events A and B are independent. What is $P(A \text{ or } B)$?

When asked, 10% of people will donate to a particular cause. If people are randomly selected to be called, what is the expected number of calls that need to be made to find someone who will donate? What is the standard deviation of the distribution of how many calls it will take to find a donor?

Members of the school choir are asked to sell an expensive discount book. Based on experience, the vendor gives the choir director the probability distribution for the sales of these books listed below.

Number of discount books sold per student (X)	1	2	3	4
$P(X)$	0.05	0.15	0.36	0.44

There are 86 members of the choir, and each will participate in this fundraiser. What is the total expected number of books that the director will expect the members to sell?

Day 107

Explain what it means when we say that a statistic is an unbiased estimator.

We use the term "unbiased" to describe an estimator and a sampling method. How are the two uses of the word similar?

Day 109

In a geometric distribution, why is 1 the most likely number of trials?

Day 110

A certain very, very large population has a mean of 270 and a standard deviation of 25. Its shape is severely skewed to the left. Random samples of size 16 are repeatedly taken, and the mean of the sample is calculated. Describe the sampling distribution of those sample means.

In a role-playing game, one of the adventurers rolls a 20-sided die to determine how many gold coins he will earn for playing a game of chance. The table below shows the distribution. What is the mean and the standard deviation of this distribution?

Coins	1	2	5	10	15	20	50	100
P(C)	0.10	0.15	0.25	0.20	0.10	0.10	0.05	0.05

Ten percent of people are left-handed. If you are going to randomly select people one at a time until you find your first left-handed person, give two ways to calculate the probability that you will need to select at least five people.

A statistics teacher has a bucket of pennies in his classroom. Students mixed the pennies, selected 4 of them, and created a simulated sampling distribution of the mean ages with 200 samples. A dotplot of the sampling distribution is shown below.

What does each dot represent? And, in particular, what does the second dot from the right show?

In a popular statistics activity based on German tanks in World War II, students selected a sample of seven numbered counters from a bag of sequentially numbered counters and, based on the numbers on the counters they selected, had to estimate how many were in the collection. Students came up with different methods for estimating.

It turns out there were 342 counters in the bag, and students did simulations to compare their methods for estimating. Comment on the quality of each of the estimators based on the simulated sampling distributions below. The vertical line is at 342 tanks, which is their target.

5 Minutes to a 5

A statistics teacher has a bucket of pennies in his classroom. Students mixed the pennies, selected 4 of them, and created a simulated sampling distribution of the mean ages with 200 samples. A dotplot of the sampling distribution is shown below.

Explain the difference between the sample size and the number of samples.

A statistics teacher has a bucket of pennies in his classroom. Students mixed the pennies, selected 4 of them, and created a simulated sampling distribution of the mean ages with 200 samples. A dotplot of the sampling distribution is shown below.

What would happen to this distribution if the sample size was increased? What would happen if the number of samples was increased?

5 Minutes to a 5

In a role-playing game, one of the adventurers rolls a 20-sided die to determine how many gold coins she will earn for playing a game of chance. The table below shows the distribution. The mean and the standard deviation of the number of gold coins is 14.7 coins and 22.4 coins, respectively. What percentage of the coins is within one standard deviation of the mean?

Coins	1	2	5	10	15	20	50	100
P(C)	0.10	0.15	0.25	0.20	0.10	0.10	0.05	0.05

When do we use the *t*-distribution, and why?

The percentage of a certain large population that takes vitamin supplements is 73%. You take repeated samples of size 50 and calculate the sample proportion that take supplements. Describe the sampling distribution of those sample proportions.

CHAPTER 10. INFERENCE: ESTIMATING WITH CONFIDENCE INTERVALS

George Box, the famous statistician, once said, "All models are wrong. But some of them are useful." What did he mean?

One of the conditions for a confidence interval for a proportion is that np and $n(1 - p)$ be greater than 10. What is the reason for that condition?

Day 122

One of the conditions for inference when selecting a random sample from a population is that the sample size be less than 10% of the population size. What is the result of violating this condition?

5 Minutes to a 5

Day 123

Survey results are reported in the following manner: "We are 99% confident that the percentage of the population who favors increasing funding for schools is between 73% and 81%." Explain in simple terms what the "99% confident" phrase means.

A research institute publishes that the estimate for the proportion of the population who have already been infected with a mosquito-borne virus is 35% with a margin of error of 3%. Explain in simple terms what this means.

Day 125

If you have constructed a 95% confidence interval for a population mean, why is it incorrect to say, "There is a 95% chance that the population mean is in this interval"?

If you have constructed a 95% confidence interval for a population mean, why is it incorrect to say, "There is a 95% chance that the sample mean is in this interval"?

Day 127

A non-profit organization wants to estimate the proportion of people who need its services with a margin of error no larger than 2%. How large a sample size would be necessary to do so with 99% confidence?

A national poll was conducted before the U.S. presidential election. A total of 1,136 people were polled, and 46% of those polled said they would be likely to vote for the Democratic candidate, 42% of those polled said they would be likely to vote for the Republican candidate, 8% said they would most likely vote for a third-party candidate, and 4% said they were undecided. A student took these results to calculate a 95% confidence interval for the difference in proportions of all U.S. voters likely to vote for the Democrat and those likely to vote for the Republican using the following formula:

$$CI = 0.04 - 1.96\sqrt{\frac{0.46(1-0.46)}{1136} + \frac{0.42(1-0.42)}{1136}}.$$

Explain why this is inappropriate.

Explain how the confidence level is related to the idea of a "capture rate."

A student does a project to see what sample proportions are likely from a population with 32% successes and conducts a simulation using technology. Using samples of size 500 and a population proportion of 0.32, the student finds that 95% of sample proportions are between 0.28 and 0.36. Explain why the interval (0.28, 0.36) is not a 95% confidence interval in this situation.

Day 131

What is the difference between interpreting a confidence interval and interpreting a confidence level?

A researcher claims that the high histamine levels in certain foods can contribute to health problems such as migraines. A random sample of 24 avocados is available to estimate the average histamine level. If the researcher wants to create a 95% confidence interval, what critical value will be used?

In a random sample of 1,500 bags of coffee beans, 120 showed signs of mold. Which of the following would produce the 95% confidence interval to estimate the proportion of all bags of coffee that are moldy?

A. $0.08 \pm 1.96(0.08)(0.92) / \sqrt{1500}$

B. $0.08 \pm 1.96\sqrt{(0.08)(0.02) / 1500}$

C. $120 \pm 1.96(120)(1380) / \sqrt{1500}$

D. $120 \pm 1.96 \pm \sqrt{(120)(1380) / 1500}$

There are four important symbols when dealing with quantitative samples. They are:
$$\mu, \sigma, \overline{x}, s_x$$
Define each of these symbols.

Which of the following would cut the size of a confidence interval in half while leaving the confidence level the same?

A. Double the size of the sample.

B. Take a sample half the size of before.

C. Quadruple the size of the sample.

D. Take a sample one-fourth the size of before.

A company that makes breakfast cereal has a machine that fills the boxes. One size box is labeled as 21 oz net weight, but the amount actually dispensed has a mean of 21 oz and a standard deviation of 0.4 oz. After adjusting the machine, the quality control manager is looking for convincing evidence that the machine will be more consistent. He plans to select a random sample of these boxes and weigh the contents. What is an appropriate set of hypotheses to use?

Hint: This problem is a bit of a challenge. You are being asked to write a different set of hypotheses than you have learned about, but you should be able to do so.

An organization that investigates the support for political candidates publishes a poll that a particular candidate is favored by 52% of likely voters. The reporter who mentions this poll says there is a margin of error of ±3%. In this case, which of the following statements is true?

A. Three percent of voters could change their minds come election day, and the candidate will only get 49% of the vote.

B. There is a 3% chance that the poll is inaccurate.

C. If this poll were to be conducted again, there is a 3% chance that the results would be different.

D. Because the reasonable estimate for support goes as low as 49%, we cannot say that the candidate is favored by a majority of likely voters.

Do test prep courses help? The owners of an ACT preparation course say that their program helps students perform better on the ACT. They have data that show that students who take their course, on average, outperform the overall population of students, with a *P*-value of 0.00023. Is this evidence that their course improves student performance on the ACT?

Day 139

Match each "everyday language" description with the "statistical language" translation:

Everyday Language

A. The stronger evidence you require, the easier it is to miss the fact that the treatment was effective.

B. The easier you are to convince, the more likely you are to mistakenly think an ineffective treatment is effective.

C. If you are more skeptical, the less likely you are to detect the effectiveness of the treatment.

D. The more effective the treatment is, the easier it is to see its effect.

Statistical Language

1. If alpha is lower, the test has less power.

2. The higher the alpha level, the greater the risk of a Type I error.

3. The larger the effect size, the higher the power.

4. The lower the significance level, the greater the probability of a Type II error.

Day 140

Explain why the power of a test is a concern at the design stage of the study. And, because it is, why wasn't it included in the chapter on designing studies?

CHAPTER 11. INFERENCE: TESTING HYPOTHESES

In a study to investigate whether the claim that in a certain community over 75% get the flu shot, the hypotheses tested were $H_o{:}p = 0.75$ and $H_a{:}p > 0.75$ and resulted in a P-value of 0.08. In the sample taken from the community, 82% of those surveyed had the flu shot. Interpret the P-value.

Day 142

After collecting sample results and verifying conditions, a researcher testing a two-sided hypothesis calculated a z-value of -2.04. What is the P-value associated with this test?

In a study to investigate whether the average time customers spend on hold when they call their Internet service provider is greater than 12 minutes, researchers found a sample average wait time of 14.04 minutes with a *P*-value of 0.0184. Rian and Alex look at the results of the study and make the following comments:

Rian: While the results of this study provide evidence that the average wait time for all customers is more than 12 minutes, the evidence is not convincing enough to say that the average wait time for all customers actually is more than 12 minutes.

Alex: The results of this study provide convincing evidence that the average wait time for all customers is more than 12 minutes.

Alex and Rian were looking at exactly the same results, including the same *P*-value. Which of the following is/are true?

A. Rian must have been using a larger alpha level than Alex.

B. Rian must have been more willing to make a Type 1 error.

C. Alex must have been using a larger alpha level than Rian.

D. Alex must have been more willing to make a Type 2 error.

When conducting a significance test for a population mean, what happens to the test statistic if the sample size increases but everything else remains the same?

When conducting a significance test for a population mean, what happens to the test statistic if the sample standard deviation increases but everything else remains the same?

When conducting a significance test for a population mean, what happens to the test statistic if the sample mean gets closer to the hypothesized mean but everything else remains the same?

Researchers designed an experiment to compare a new method of applying fertilizer to a lawn with a current popular method. Their alternative hypothesis was that the new application method will improve the rate at which grass grows over the current method. After their experiment, they did a significance test for a difference in mean growth rate and found a *P*-value of 0.17. Interpret this *P*-value in the context of this experiment.

Day 148

Under what conditions is a matched-pairs design likely to result in a more powerful test than a test using a difference of independent means?

5 Minutes to a 5

Fifty (50) subjects are available to test at the $\alpha = 0.05$ level that the mean cholesterol level of people who limit their dairy intake is less than 185 mg/dl. Which of the following would result in the increase of the power of the hypothesis test?

A. Reduce the number of subjects to 30.

B. Randomly assign the subjects to treatments.

C. Reduce the alpha level to 0.01.

D. Keep the subjects blind to the purpose of the study.

E. Increase the number of subjects to 60.

By some estimates only 36% of American high school students eat breakfast. A random sample of 200 students is selected from this population. Assuming that 36% is accurate, what is the probability that over 40% of students in the sample will say that they eat breakfast?

In testing whether a new medication improves a condition faster than the old medication, the null hypothesis was "The mean time for the new medication to improve the condition is the same as the mean time for the old medication." With a *P*-value of 0.23, explain why it is incorrect to conclude that the mean times for the two medications are the same.

Researchers are trying to establish whether diets that are low in sodium are healthier for people who do not have problems with high blood pressure. They randomly assign a low-sodium diet or a normal diet to people with low blood pressure who have volunteered to be part of the study. The null hypothesis is that the low-sodium diet has no impact on measures of health, and the alternative hypothesis is that the low-sodium diet improves measures of health. What would constitute a Type I error in this context, and what would be the consequence of making a Type I error?

Researchers are trying to establish whether diets that are low in sodium are healthier for people who do not have problems with high blood pressure. They randomly assign a low-sodium diet or a normal diet to people with low blood pressure who have volunteered to be part of the study. The null hypothesis is that the low-sodium diet has no impact on measures of health, and the alternative hypothesis is that the low-sodium diet improves measures of health. What would constitute a Type II error, and what would be the consequence of making a Type II error?

An appliance manufacturer claims that the average yearly energy cost to operate its refrigerator in your area is \$134. Local energy experts dispute this claim, believing the average yearly cost is actually higher. Which of the following is the appropriate set of hypotheses to test this claim?

A. $H_0 : \mu = \$134$ $H_a : \bar{x} > \$134$

B. $H_0 : \mu \neq \$134$ $H_a : \mu > \$134$

C. $H_0 : \mu = \$134$ $H_a : \mu \neq \$134$

D. $H_0 : \mu = \$134$ $H_a : \mu > \$134$

E. $H_0 : \mu = \$134$ $H_a : \mu < \$134$

One of the conditions required to run a test of significance for a population mean is that of normality. Suppose that you are running a test and your sample size is only 18. A plot of the sample data shows the following:

Has the normal condition been met? Explain your answer.

Describe how the *t*-distribution has the same characteristics as the standard normal distribution. How is it different?

A real estate developer collects a random sample of 250 local home prices. She wants to test if the average home price has declined. Her sample is strongly skewed right. Does this skewness invalidate any attempt at inference? Explain.

In a test of the claim that the average debt carried by a recent college graduate is greater than \$24,000, researchers tested the hypotheses H_o: $\mu = \$24,000$ vs. H_a: $\mu > \$24,000$ at $\alpha = 0.05$ and found a sample mean of \$25,015 with a P-value $= 0.065$. Explain what this P-value means in plain terms.

In a test of the claim that the average debt carried by a recent college graduate is greater than $24,000, researchers tested the hypotheses H_o: $\mu = \$24{,}000$ vs. H_a: $\mu > \$24{,}000$ at $\alpha = 0.05$ and found a sample mean of $25,015 with a P-value $= 0.065$. What decision is appropriate in this instance?

The population of adult American males is approximately normally distributed with a mean weight of 187 pounds and a standard deviation of 29 pounds. A log ride in an amusement park can hold 8 passengers with a maximum weight of 1,600 pounds. Assume that a log is filled with 8 males and you want to know the probability that the log is over its maximum weight. Describe the conditions for testing this question and whether each has been met.

Your best friend wants to test the hypotheses H_o: $\mu = 6$ vs. H_a: $\mu > 6$ by constructing and using a confidence interval. Is your friend correct in wanting to do so?

CHAPTER 12. INTERFERENCE FOR REGRESSION

The plot above shows three rectangles. Imagine taking a random sample of five points within each rectangle and calculating the regression line.

In each plot below, the rectangles we'll "sample" from are different from those above. For each one, state what is different from the original plot, and decide whether the variability in the slope of the regression line increases or decreases.

The following computer output represents the summary statistics for a regression analysis that links the economic welfare of a community (EW) with its literacy rate from a random sample of 35 communities.

The regression equation is

LiteracyRate = 58.624 + 0.0018 EW

Predictor	Coef	SE Coef	T	P
Constant	58.6238	28.1845	2.08	0.0454
EW	0.00181	0.00117	1.55	0.1306

S = 12.17743   R-Sq = 55.7%   R-Sq(adj) = 49.6%

Interpret the value of the slope.

The following computer output represents the summary statistics for a regression analysis that links the economic welfare of a community (EW) with its literacy rate from a random sample of 35 communities.

The regression equation is
LiteracyRate = 58.624 + 0.0018 EW

Predictor	Coef	SE Coef	T	P
Constant	58.6238	28.1845	2.08	0.0454
EW	0.00181	0.00117	1.55	0.1306

S = 12.17743   R-Sq = 55.7%   R-Sq(adj) = 49.6%

Interpret the value of the intercept.

The following computer output represents the summary statistics for a regression analysis that links the economic welfare of a community (EW) with its literacy rate from a random sample of 35 communities.

> The regression equation is
> LiteracyRate = 58.624 + 0.0018 EW
>
> | Predictor | Coef | SE Coef | T | P |
> |-----------|---------|---------|------|--------|
> | Constant | 58.6238 | 28.1845 | 2.08 | 0.0454 |
> | EW | 0.00181 | 0.00117 | 1.55 | 0.1306 |
>
> S = 12.17743   R-Sq = 55.7%   R-Sq(adj) = 49.6%

Interpret the value of S = 12.17743.

The following computer output represents the summary statistics for a regression analysis that links the economic welfare of a community (EW) with its literacy rate from a random sample of 35 communities.

The regression equation is
LiteracyRate = 58.624 + 0.0018 EW

Predictor	Coef	SE Coef	T	P
Constant	58.6238	28.1845	2.08	0.0454
EW	0.00181	0.00117	1.55	0.1306

S = 12.17743   R-Sq = 55.7%   R-Sq(adj) = 49.6%

Find and interpret the residual for a community with an economic welfare of 830 and a literacy rate of 65.

Which of the following plots would be appropriate to check the condition that the residuals are approximately normal? For each, explain their strengths and weaknesses.

A. The scatterplot of the original data

B. A residual plot

C. A dotplot of the residuals

D. A histogram of the residuals

E. A boxplot of the residuals

F. A normal probability plot of the residuals

The following computer output represents the summary statistics for a regression analysis that links the economic welfare of a community (EW) with its literacy rate from a random sample of 35 communities.

The regression equation is

LiteracyRate = 58.624 + 0.0018 EW

Predictor	Coef	SE Coef	T	P
Constant	58.6238	28.1845	2.08	0.0454
EW	0.00181	0.00117	1.55	0.1306

S = 12.17743   R-Sq = 55.7%   R-Sq(adj) = 49.6%

Assume the conditions for inference have been met. What are the correct hypotheses to determine if there is convincing evidence of a linear relationship between literacy rate and EW for the population of communities?

Day 169

The following computer output represents the summary statistics for a regression analysis that links the economic welfare of a community (EW) with its literacy rate from a random sample of 35 communities.

The regression equation is
LiteracyRate = 58.624 + 0.0018 EW

Predictor	Coef	SE Coef	T	P
Constant	58.6238	28.1845	2.08	0.0454
EW	0.00181	0.00117	1.55	0.1306

S = 12.17743   R-Sq = 55.7%   R-Sq(adj) = 49.6%

Assume the conditions for inference have been met. The hypotheses to test whether there is a useful linear relationship between literacy rate and EW are $H_o: \beta = 0$ and $H_a: \beta \neq 0$. Is there convincing evidence at the $\alpha = 0.05$ level that there is a linear relationship between literacy rate and EW for all communities in the population?

The following computer output represents the summary statistics for a regression analysis that links the economic welfare of a community (EW) with its literacy rate from a random sample of 35 communities.

The regression equation is
LiteracyRate = 58.624 + 0.0018 EW

Predictor	Coef	SE Coef	T	P
Constant	58.6238	28.1845	2.08	0.0454
EW	0.00181	0.00117	1.55	0.1306

S = 12.17743   R-Sq = 55.7%   R-Sq(adj) = 49.6%

Find and interpret a 95% confidence interval for the slope of the regression line.

Below is a scatterplot of a variable *y* versus a variable *x* for a random sample from a large population, along with a residual plot and a univariate plot of the residuals.

Based on these plots, are conditions met for inference for the slope of the regression line?

Day 172

CHAPTER 13. INFERENCE FOR CATEGORICAL DATA: CHI-SQUARE

For each statement, determine whether it is a characteristic of the chi-square distribution.

A. The area under the chi-square distribution equals 1.

B. Chi-square is symmetric for all degrees of freedom.

C. The value of the chi-square distribution is always positive.

D. Chi-square is used to compare the means of several populations.

Name the conditions required to run a chi-square test.

A breakfast cereal company puts one of five different prizes in its boxes and claims those prizes are distributed at random in the following fashion:

1	2	3	4	5
Kangaroo	Dolphin	Fox	Penguin	Bunny
25%	20%	10%	20%	25%

You obtain a random sample of 500 boxes of this cereal to test whether or not the company's claim about the prize distribution is accurate. What are the appropriate hypotheses to test this claim?

The following data represent the number of calls to the district tech support line during one random week:

Monday	Tuesday	Wednesday	Thursday	Friday
23	18	19	24	16

The district would like to test the hypothesis that the number of calls is the same for each day of the week. Calculate the value of the chi-square statistic for this test.

A random sample of 400 working adults was taken, and each member of the sample was asked to classify themselves by their education and where they went to high school. Partial results are listed in the table below:

	NO COLLEGE	SOME COLLEGE	4-YEAR DEGREE	ADVANCED DEGREE	TOTAL
Rural					50
Suburban					150
Urban					200
Total	100	60	200	40	400

What is the expected value for the cell that corresponds to Rural/Advanced Degree?

5 Minutes to a 5

The marketing department for a television station is trying to figure out how to target ads for their television shows using social media. They wonder if people of different political beliefs would be interested in different types of crime dramas. They send out surveys to a random sample of television viewers and ask their political affiliation (3 options). It also asks them which of four hypothetical plot lines would be most likely to interest them. The null hypothesis is that there is no association between political affiliation and preferred type of television show. They calculated a chi-square statistic of 15.7. What conclusion should they reach at the 5% significance level?

A random sample of 50 male students and a separate random sample of 50 female students asked the following question: When you take a shower, do you face away from the showerhead or toward it? The results are summarized in the table below.

	MALE	FEMALE	TOTAL
Toward	38	19	57
Away	12	31	43
Total	50	50	100

Calculate the χ^2 statistic and P-value. Then calculate the test statistic for a difference-in-proportions z-test (for either the proportion toward or the proportion away) and the P-value. What do you notice?

Day 179

A random sample of 400 working adults was taken, and each member of the sample was asked to classify themselves by their education and where they went to high school. Partial results are listed in the table below:

	NO COLLEGE	SOME COLLEGE	4-YEAR DEGREE	ADVANCED DEGREE	TOTAL
Rural					50
Suburban					150
Urban					200
Total	100	60	200	40	400

Calculate the number of degrees of freedom for the chi-square test to see if there is an association between education level and where people attended high school.

A random sample of medical records from a local hospital classified people according to the variables shown in the table below.

	UNDER RECOMMENDED WEIGHT RANGE	WITHIN RECOMMENDED WEIGHT RANGE	OVER RECOMMENDED WEIGHT RANGE	TOTAL
Never smoked cigarettes				
Used to smoke cigarettes				
Currently smokes cigarettes				
Total				

a. What would be the appropriate significance test for these data to see if there is an association between smoking and weight?

b. If the *P*-value turns out to be low, can we conclude that cigarette smoking causes differences in weight?

Answers

Day 1

a. Numerical. Heights are measurements.

b. Categorical. Favorite movie is a categorical variable where (relative) frequencies are totaled for each selection.

c. Quantitative. Age is a quantity, usually measured in years.

d. Categorical. While income can be expressed as a quantity, the decision has been made to sort into three categories.

Day 2

There are 62 observations, so the median is halfway between observations 31 and 32. (See the boxes on the dotplot.) Q1 will be observation 16. Q3 will be observation 47. (Each is circled on the dotplot.) This distribution has a center (median) of 20.5 with a spread (IQR) of $23 - 18 = 5$. It appears to be slightly skewed to the right, and there do not appear to be any outliers or gaps.

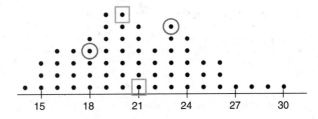

Day 3

Because this distribution is symmetric with no outliers, it would be appropriate to use the mean and the standard deviation to describe the center and spread.

Day 4

A. This is a true statement. Twenty-two minutes (max) minus 6 minutes (min) is 16 minutes.

B. This statement cannot be confirmed true without knowing the actual values.

C. This is a true statement. About 50% of the data will be greater than or equal to the median.

D. This statement is not necessarily true. While the shape of the boxplot itself is symmetric, this is no guarantee that the distribution of the data is also symmetric. For example, below is a dotplot of some possible values of 27 wait times that would produce the boxplot.

Day 5

The sum of the 15 observations is $15 \times 27 = 405$. The other sum is $20 \times 33 = 660$. The overall mean is $(405 + 660)/35 = 30.43$.

Day 6

More important than the right answer is the discussion. But here are the answers.

a. Extremely skewed right. Lake Superior is an extreme outlier.

b. Skewed right with a wall at 0. (A wall is a maximum or minimum value that the data "piles up against.")

c. Bimodal. The upper mode is mostly middle linemen.

d. Mound-shaped and very slightly skewed left.

e. Mound-shaped and symmetric.

Day 7

The typical distance of the packages from the mean of 530 grams is 4 grams. *Note:* You will learn about many more standard deviations. Be ready to use this idea (typical distance from the mean) on more days in the future!

Day 8

The distribution of data has a center (median) of 37 with a spread (IQR) of 14. One and a half times the IQR is 21. Adding 21 to Q3 yields 66. Subtracting 21 from Q1 yields 10. There is at least one outlier because 75 is greater than 66. There are no values less than 10; therefore, there are no outliers on the left. In addition, because there is an outlier only on the right, it is reasonable to also describe the distribution as somewhat skewed to the right.

Day 9

Boxplots are poor graphs for shape as they reduce the entire dataset to only 5 key points. Stem-and-leaf plots will always show the original data. Sometimes a dotplot will, but it depends on the scale, the number of dots, and other factors. The other quantitative graphs are histograms and cumulative frequency plots.

Day 10

No. In an approximately normal distribution, 2.5% of the data would be more than 2 standard deviations below the mean. But that would mean a fair number of households would be below −$33,800. That is not reasonable. A negative income is possible but is quite rare. Zero is only 1.26 standard deviations below the mean. In an approximately normal distribution, 10% of values would lie below that value. But it is unreasonable to think that 10% of households have negative incomes.

Day 11

As annotated on the diagram below, the median (center) is between 12 and 13 discussion posts. The IQR (spread) is between 3 and 5 posts. The shape is somewhat skewed to the right, and there do not appear to be any outliers.

Day 12

A percentile is a measure of the percentage of a distribution that is at or below the given point. If your height is at the 80th percentile, then 80% of the population are at your height or shorter than you. If your reading score is at the 41st percentile, then 41% of the population have reading scores at or below your score.

Day 13

Draw a horizontal line from the 25th, 50th, and 75th percentiles to the graph, then straight down from each of those to find the values for those percentiles. These will define the box. Based on this, Q1 appears to be about 25,000 and Q3 about 80,000, for an IQR of about 55,000. Outliers will be any points below $Q1 - 1.5IQR = 25,000 - 1.5(55,000)$, which is clearly far below zero (no outliers on the low end), or above $Q3 + 1.5IQR = 80,000 + 1.5(55,000) = 162,500$. There are many values above this, which should be marked by individual dots.

The boxplot is as shown:

Day 14

The workers in group B have a faster median time than the workers in group A. The IQR of group B is less than the IQR of group A. Group B has one high outlier (very slow worker!). Group B is probably skewed right. Remember that complete shape information cannot be determined from a boxplot, so sometimes the AP rubrics do not score your shape comments about the shape of a boxplot. However, it is the safest path to include this information.

Day 15

A. False. Because the standard deviation calculation uses the mean, which itself is not resistant to the influence outliers, the standard deviation is not resistant either.

B. False. If all the values were exactly the same there would be no variation, and therefore the standard deviation would be zero, not 1.

C. True. The standard deviation calculation measures typical distance from the mean without regard to direction and is therefore always positive.

D. False. To find the variance we square the standard deviation.

E. True. The standard deviation measures distance, not direction.

Day 16

We have no information about the shape of the distribution of test scores, so it is impossible to know what percent of students scored below Stephen's score.

Day 17

Typically, a box of vegetables will differ from the mean weight by 15 ounces.

Day 18

$z = \dfrac{24.5 - 22.4}{6.68} = 0.314$. Alyssa's score was 0.314 standard deviations above the mean score of 22.38 points.

Day 19

Finding a z-score for each brother would help answer this question.

For Otis: $z(Otis) = \dfrac{57 - 54.5}{2.4} = 1.04$ For Acer: $z(Acer) = \dfrac{45 - 41.5}{2.7} = 1.30$

Acer is 1.30 standard deviations above the mean for his age, while Otis is only 1.04 standard deviations above the mean height for his age. Therefore, one could say that relative to their respective age groups, Acer is taller than Otis.

Day 20

Construct a segmented bar chart. Because the segments are so different, there appears to be an association between country of origin and blood type.

Exam Hint 1: This is categorical data in frequencies by country/blood type. Calculate the relative frequencies (percentages) of the condition **country**, and then construct your segmented bar charts accordingly.

	BLOOD TYPE				
	O	A	B	AB	TOTALS
Australia	74/150 = 49%	57/150 =38%	15/150 =10%	4/150 =3%	150
Finland	56/180 =31%	79/180 =44%	31/180 =17%	14/180 =8%	180

Exam Hint 2: When you are asked to justify an answer, remember to answer the question (there appears to be an association) linked to the work that you produced (because the bar charts are so different) and do so in the context (country of origin and blood type) of the problem.

Day 21

From the graph below, you can see that the estimates for Q3 and Q1 are 17 and 6. Thus, the IQR is about 11 days.

Days before sale of a used car

Day 22

Meredith has used a correct pair of statistics to describe the center and spread of the distribution of these data. However, she incorrectly identified the direction of the skew. Meredith should have said that it is reasonable to say the distribution is skewed to the *right*.

Margaret is correct about 40 being a value that can be called an outlier, as well as saying this distribution is skewed to the right. However, she incorrectly paired the IQR with the mean. Instead, Margaret should have paired the IQR with the *median*.

Day 23

The percentile for the student who scored 92 is $\frac{24}{30} = 0.80$, or the 80th percentile. This means that the student with the 92 scored better than 80% of the class.

Day 24

The median remains 36. Because the old value 42 and its corrected value 82 are both on the same side of the median, the median remains unchanged.

Day 25

The Redwing's winning percentage was 3.29 standard deviations below the mean winning percentage for the 2020 season.

Day 26

The z-score of the minimum value is found by $z = (2.92 - 4.0996)/0.7055$ or $z = -1.67$. If this distribution was approximately normally distributed, there should be roughly 4.75% of the observations below this score. Because there are no values less than 2.92 minutes, it is not reasonable to believe that this distribution is approximately normally distributed.

Day 27

Because 36 and 60 are two standard deviations above and below the mean, respectively, by the empirical rule, approximately 95% of the distribution is between 36 and 60.

Day 28

Each and every value of song length would be multiplied by 60. The statistics would be effected thusly:

STATISTIC	TRANSFORMED VALUE
Mean	(60) • (old mean)
Variance	$(60) \cdot (\text{old StDev})^2$
IQR	$60 \cdot Q3 - 60 \cdot Q1 = 60 \cdot (Q3 - Q1)$
Median	(60) • (old median)

The mean, IQR, and median would be multiplied by 60. The variance would be multiplied by 3,600.

Day 29

Because this distribution is approximately normally distributed with a mean of 4.828 and a standard deviation 0.453 feet, we can use a normal calculation* to find the area under the curve less than 5.625 feet. As you can see in the diagram, this flamingo would represent the 96th percentile.

normalcdf (lower bound, upper bound, mean, stdv)

normalcdf (−100000000, 5.625, 4,828, 0.453) = 0.9607

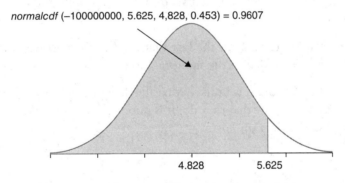

Exam Hint: You should never use the abbreviations from your calculator unless you have explained what the numbers in your "calculator-speak" stand for. In the above question, it would be required that you include the information noted by the asterisk (*) to get full credit for a response.

Day 30

You can calculate a z-score for any value for which the mean and standard deviation of a population are known. But you can only use a normal calculation to find the area/ probability if the population is approximately normally distributed.

Exam Hint: Distributions are described by shape, center, and spread. Unless you can describe the shape as approximately ***normally*** distributed, you cannot use the standard ***normal*** table.

Day 31

We need to find the value marked x on the diagram. Using the standard normal table, the z-score that corresponds most closely to the 10% upper tail area is $z = 1.28$. We solve the equation $z = \dfrac{x - \mu}{\sigma}$ for x. This looks like $1.28 = \dfrac{x - 30}{3.5} \cdot x = (1.28)(3.5) + 30 = 34.48$. So the top 10% of batteries last 34.48 months or longer.

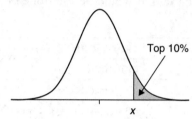

Day 32

According to the 68-95-99.7% rule, for an approximately normal distribution, approximately 68% of the data are within one standard deviation of the mean, 95% are within two, and approximately 99.7% are within three standard deviations. Three standard deviations below the mean of 28 would be a score of –8. It seems unlikely that the test would score negative, so there must be a typo of some sort.

Day 33

A. This might be counted as correct, but we really aren't adding height to the father or the daughter. We are comparing heights of different people, and our interpretation should reflect that.

B. This is a good interpretation of the fact that the slope is positive, but the value of the slope must be included in the interpretation.

C. This is too deterministic. It is unlikely that the data points lie exactly on a line, and this interpretation implies that they do. It is important not to make a statement that is stronger than our data support.

Day 34

A. This makes it sound as though we can use our model to predict the father's height from the daughter's height. But our model works the other way around.

B. This is pretty good. The "tends to" and "on average" show that the model describes the general trend, not the change for every father–daughter pair.

C. This is too deterministic. The word "approximately" does not change the fact that this statement says the daughter's height *will be* greater if the father's height is greater. That will probably not be the case with many father–daughter pairs.

Day 35

A. This is an excellent interpretation. It makes clear that it is the model's prediction that the 0.441 applies to.

B. This makes it sound as though the heights are proportional. In other words, as if the *y*-intercept in our model is 0. But we have no reason to think that is the case. It is important to interpret the slope as the predicted *difference* between two *y*-values for a *difference* of one unit in the *x*-value.

C. There is no context here. This is a good interpretation of what a slope of 0.441 means in general terms, but nothing applies it to heights of daughters and fathers in this sample.

Day 36

A. Too deterministic. A cereal with no carbohydrates is *predicted* to have 2 calories per serving.

B. "Meaningless" might be a bit strong. But since cereals are made with grains as their main ingredient, the essence of this statement is correct.

C. This is true. Extrapolating beyond the range of the data makes predictions very unreliable.

Day 37

The correlation coefficient is not resistant. One outlier can dramatically affect the value of the correlation. Correlation by itself does not confirm that data is linear. Data can follow a curved model, but still have a high correlation. A scattered residual plot is important for verifying a linear model.

Day 38

A large positive residual is far above the regression line, circled in the plot below. A small negative residual is below the regression line and close to the line, shown with a square around it in the plot. ("Large" and "small" are relative terms.)

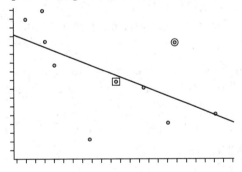

Day 39

ANSWERS
A. −0.97 is (5) A very strong correlation
B. 0.13 is (3) A very weak correlation
C. −0.83 is (4) A moderately strong negative correlation
D. −1.08 is outside the possible interval, so (2) Somebody made a mistake
E. 1.00 is (1) A perfect positive correlation

Day 40

There is a somewhat strong, negative, nonlinear relationship between the median income and the number of visits to a public park in a year.

Exam Hint: You need to address F = form, D = direction, and S = strength whenever you are asked to describe the relationship between the two variables in a bivariate set.

Day 41

The residual plot shows a distinctive pattern; therefore, a linear relationship between the two variables is inappropriate.

Day 42

If there is a linear relationship between two variables, then the residual plot will be randomly scattered above and below the horizontal line at zero. A residual plot can help reveal outliers that are farther away from the regression line than other points. Finally, the residual plot will show if the variation about the line is varying at a constant rate as x increases.

Day 43

D. Although the correlation coefficient in (B) is stronger, the slope in the equation itself must match the direction of the supposed correlation. This makes D the appropriate answer.

Day 44

The residual is calculated as $y - \hat{y}$. In this case the predicted hand-span is $-11.2570 + 0.1781(189) = 22.4039$. So the residual for this student is $22 - 22.4039$ or -0.4039 cm.

Day 45

A residual of -0.75 cm means that Jeremy's hand span is -0.75 cm less than predicted by the linear regression.

Exam Hint: If you remember that a residual is calculated as *Actual – Predicted*, then you'll be better able to interpret what a negative residual means in context.

Day 46

a. $\widehat{Bags} = 7.089 - 0.0525 OnTimeArrivals$

b. The slope means that an airline with an on-time arrival rate that is 1 percentage point higher than another would be predicted to have 0.0525 fewer mishandled bags per 1,000 customers. The y-intercept means that an airline with no on-time arrivals would be predicted to have 7.089 mishandled bags per 1,000 customers. This is not reasonable because no airline with zero on-time arrivals would have customers.

Exam Tip: Don't write regression equations with x and y. Instead use the context words as shown in the answer to part (a). And don't forget a "hat" on the output variable. This indicates that the model is predicting that output variable.

Day 47

a. The correlation coefficient r is the square root of r^2. But the slope is negative, so r must also be negative. $r \approx -0.312$.

b. This sentence describes r^2, so about 9.73% of the variation in mishandled bags per thousand customers is explained by the regression model with the percentage of on-time arrivals as a predictor.

c. They tell you that the linear relationship is quite weak.

Day 48

a. The predicted mishandled baggage rate is $7.089 - 0.0525 \cdot 81.5 = 2.81$. The actual rate is 3.92. The residual is $3.92 - 2.81 = 1.11$ bags.

b. The actual rate of mishandled baggage is 1.11 bags higher than predicted.

Day 49

The regression line predicts the number of mishandled bags per 1,000 passengers, and those predictions are typically off by about 1.2454 bags per 1,000 passengers.

Day 50

a. Plugging 88 into the equation results in a predicted final exam score of about 77.

b. A positive residual is preferred. That would mean you scored higher than predicted by the professor's model.

Day 51

The point in the box is called an outlier because it will have a much larger residual than the rest of the data points.

Day 52

The slope would increase a bit. The point "pulls up" on the left side of the line. Removing it would drop the left end of the line, causing the slope to increase. The correlation would increase as well. The observation in the box has a high residual, which makes the overall relationship weaker. This point has high-leverage because it is extreme in the x-direction.

Day 53

$\widehat{\log(\%)} = 9.4294 - 2.2542 \log(20000) = -0.2660$. But $\widehat{\log(\%)} = -0.2660$ needs to be solved by rewriting the log using its exponential form: $10^{-0.2660} = \widehat{(\%)}$. Thus, $\widehat{(\%)} = 0.5420$. We would predict that in a zip code where the median income was $20,000, roughly 54% of the households would need services.

Exam Hint: We were not given the data that produced this regression so we have no idea if predicting for $20,000 represents an extrapolation.

Day 54

a. The population is all teens in the United States.

b. The sample is teens at the schools selected in the cluster sample.

c. The parameter is the proportion of *all* teens in the United States who have made a new friend through social media. We don't know this proportion exactly.

d. The statistic is the proportion of teens in the sample who have made a new friend through social media. We know this to be 59%.

Day 55

A. Yes.

B. No. A census gives you the population parameter the sample is trying to estimate.

C. Yes. When testing life span of lightbulbs, or taste-testing cookies, the products tested are destroyed.

D. No. A census is not estimating anything so bias does not apply. Also, bias does not apply to a sample, but a sampling method.

E. Yes.

Day 56

1. The best three ways to protect against confounding in an experiment are as follows:
- Randomly assign treatments to subjects. Then the groups should be as alike as possible, and any differences will be due to the random assignment, and we have a model for assessing that.
- Control. Treatment groups should be treated identically except for the treatment.
- Blocking. We mainly use blocking to reduce the effect of the variability within each treatment. But if one subset of subjects will have a different mean response than another, to ensure they are equally split between the treatments we could block on that variable.

Day 57

Stratifying can be thought of as dividing the population into "layers" so each layer is homogenous. These layers are called strata. Then a simple random sample is taken from each layer to ensure that each group is represented in the sample. That is one benefit. Another is that each sample will look more like the population because each group will be proportionally represented. Clusters are naturally existing groups, usually based on location. Several locations are selected randomly, and those locations are easy to visit, and then everyone in each cluster is surveyed. A benefit of cluster sampling is that it is easy (and, therefore, cheap) to survey a lot of people. Both techniques are unbiased methods.

Day 58

One difference is that they are used in different kinds of studies. Stratification is a *sampling* technique, and blocking is a technique for designing *experiments*. Both use the idea of grouping similar subjects together for the purpose of reducing variability, so there is often confusion between the two. But stratifying can be thought of as dividing the population into "layers" so each layer is homogenous. These layers are called strata. Then a simple random sample is taken from each layer. Blocking in an experiment groups similar subjects together, and treatments are randomly assigned to the subjects in each group, or block.

Day 59

a. This is a cluster sample where the city blocks are the clusters.

b. Here is one idea. People who already have graduated from school and have jobs won't be home at this time. Those people won't need the library as much. This will create an underestimate of the parameter.

Exam tip: Answers about bias follow three steps. A description of what the people creating the bias are like. Then connect what they are like to the parameter of interest. And, finally, how this connection creates either an over- or an underestimate of the parameter.

Day 60

A *sample* can be nonrepresentative, meaning it does not represent the population well. "Bias" refers to a *method* of gathering information that results in estimates that are too high on average or too low on average.

Day 61

This is a matched-pairs design. Each runner has tried both treatments. When the data are analyzed, researchers should look at the *difference* in the comfort rating for each type of shoe.

Day 62

No. While this sample design will absolutely produce a random sample of 1,000 people with driving licenses, it will not be a sample of adults living in the state. The plan leaves out those adults without a license and, because people under the age of 18 can have a driving license, it includes people who are not adults.

Day 63

The HR department is not correct. While the sample taken is random, it is not a simple random sample because not every sample of size 150 is equally likely to be chosen. For example, using this method, a sample that consisted of 75 of each group would never be chosen.

Exam Hint: When justifying your answer, use the definition of the term referenced in the stem of the question. In this case, the term is *simple random sample*.

Day 64

a. The factors are *mowing height* and *type of herbicide*.

b. The levels for *mowing height* are 3 inches, 4 inches, and 5 inches. The levels for *type of herbicide* are A, B, C, and untreated.

c. The 12 treatments are the combinations of mowing heights and herbicide:
   - 3 inches with A, 3 inches with B, 3 inches with C, 3 inches with untreated
   - 4 inches with A, 4 inches with B, 4 inches with C, 4 inches with untreated
   - 5 inches with A, 5 inches with B, 5 inches with C, 5 inches with untreated

d. The experimental units are the plots of land.

Day 65

The first part of the question paints a brutal picture and might influence people's responses. The 84% is probably too high an estimate.

Exam Hint: The specific vocabulary term in this question is *response bias*, but you do not have to use the actual term. In fact, describing what might be inappropriate is often easier than accurately recalling the correct vocabulary term. In addition, you should indicate the direction (in this case, *too high* an estimate) to earn a complete response.

Day 66

Your study partner is not correct. This design has assigned the pesticides to the plots randomly. To be a block design, the researcher would have divided up the plots by some similar characteristic (thus creating blocks of plots) that also might influence insect damage and then randomly assigned some of the plots in each block to each type of pesticide.

Day 67

The correct answer is (D) cluster sampling.

Day 68

a. Convenience sample. Biased.

b. Voluntary response sample. Biased.

c. Cluster random sample. Unbiased.

Day 69

a. Voluntary response sample. Biased.

b. Simple random sample. Unbiased.

c. Systematic sample with a random start. Unbiased.

Day 70

Get a list of all students at the school. Number them from 1 to N, the number of students at the school. Use a random number generator to generate 200 distinct integers between 1 and N, inclusive. Select the students corresponding to those numbers.

Day 71

Get a list of all students at the school sorted by, for example, grade. Number them from 1 to N, the number of students in that grade. Use a random number generator to generate 50 distinct integers between 1 and N, inclusive, for each grade. Select the students corresponding to those numbers. This ensures the same number of students in each grade are selected. If the number of students in each grade is quite different, the number of students selected at each grade may be adjusted to reflect the proportion in the population of all students at the school.

Day 72

Get a list of all classrooms at the school. Number them from 1 to N, the number of classrooms at the school. Use a random number generator to generate, say, 8 distinct numbers from 1 to N. (This number may vary if class sizes tend to be different from about 25.) Visit the corresponding classrooms, and survey everyone in those classrooms.

Day 73

Because this is an observational study in which these women were not assigned a treatment but chose to ingest the caffeine themselves, we cannot establish a cause-and-effect relationship between caffeine and the prevention of dementia.

Day 74

An experiment needs to have a comparison group, either one with no treatment or one with a different treatment. This experiment has only one group. Researchers would not be able to say if the new drug is effective without this comparison.

Day 75

Because the treatments are assigned to the classes, the classes are the experimental units.

Day 76

The student has implied that the numbers are being assigned to treatments, not the patients themselves. A complete response would have said, "Put the *subjects* with the first 30 numbers generated into treatment R. The remaining 30 *subjects* will be placed in treatment X."

Day 77

There could be other things about the hospital that sent women home after two days that influenced the recovery time. Maybe the women who went to that hospital received better prenatal care. Or better care during their childbirth. Or maybe they were healthier, on average, to begin with. Because there were only two experimental units (the hospitals), there was no replication, and confounding is present.

Day 78

It would not be appropriate to generalize these results because this is not a random sample of taxpayers. The viewers who called in or responded via social media chose to do so. Volunteers tend to be those with very strong opinions, so 67% may be too high an estimate for those taxpayers who would not support the tax breaks.

Day 79

Using the formula $P(A \text{ or } B) = P(A) + P(B) - P(A \text{ and } B)$, and the fact that because A and B are independent, $P(A \text{ and } B) = P(A) \cdot P(B)$, we get $P(A \text{ or } B) = 0.40 + 0.32 - (0.40)(0.32) = 0.592$.

Exam Hint: You will find probability formulas on the formula sheet in section II. However, these formulas use the mathematical symbols $\cup$ for the word "or" and $\cap$ for the word "and." You should be able to use both the words and the symbols correctly.

Day 80

We need this person to have both characteristics, pet-owning AND high school only. Therefore, the probability of selecting such an individual is 235/1,000 or 23.5%.

Day 81

A complete list means that every possible outcome is included in the list. "Disjoint events" means that no two events listed can happen in the same trial. So each trial will result in exactly one of the events.

Day 82

You can apply the addition rule for disjoint events. The probability that one of the events in the list happens is the sum of the individual probabilities. Because exactly one of the events *must* happen, the probability of one of the events happening is 1.

Day 83

We already know that the person has a college level of educational attainment, so we restrict ourselves to that group only. The probability of selecting a non–pet owner out of the college group is 60/123 or roughly 48.8%.

Day 84

There aren't two different rules. They are the same rule. It's just that if A and B are disjoint, then $P(A \text{ and } B) = 0$. The rule for disjoint events is just a simplified version of the general addition rule.

Day 85

Probably not. If the events *has made a friend on social media* and *owns a smartphone* are independent, this would be correct. But we don't know they are independent, and, if we think about it, they probably aren't. It seems reasonable that teens who own a smartphone are more likely to make a friend on social media than teens who do not own a smartphone.

Day 86

There aren't. They are the same rule. It's just that if A and B are independent, then $P(B|A) = P(B)$. The rule for independent events is just a simplified version of the general multiplication rule.

Day 87

The sum of the probabilities $0.03 + 0.11 + 0.18 + 0.31 + 0.24 + 0.16 = 1.03$ is more than 1.00. Therefore, this is not a legitimate probability distribution.

Day 88

If A and B are independent, then $P(A \text{ and } B) = P(A) \cdot P(B) = 0.12$. Then the rest of the table can be computed by subtracting.

	A	Not A	Total
B	0.12	0.28	0.4
Not B	0.18	0.42	0.6
Total	0.3	0.7	1.0

Day 89

If A and B are disjoint, then $P(A \text{ and } B) = 0$. Then the rest of the table can be computed by subtracting.

	A	Not A	Total
B	0	0.4	0.4
Not B	0.3	0.3	0.6
Total	0.3	0.7	1.0

Day 90

If A and B are independent, then $P(A \text{ and } B) = P(A) \cdot P(B) = 0.12$. If disjoint, $P(A \text{ and } B) = 0$. If they are neither disjoint nor independent, then $P(A \text{ and } B)$ can be any other probability, although it has to be less than or equal to 0.3 for the totals to work out in this example. Then the rest of the table can be computed by subtracting.

	A	Not A	Total
B	0.2	0.2	0.4
Not B	0.1	0.5	0.6
Total	0.3	0.7	1.0

Day 91

The formula to calculate the mean of a probability distribution such as this is given on the formula sheet in section II: $E(X) = \mu_x = \sum x_i p_i$. Solving the equation $8(0.16) + 15(0.20) + a(0.24) + 12(0.20) + 10(0.12) + 7(0.08) + 9.88$ yields $a = 6$.

Exam Hint: Not all information provided in the stem of the problem is necessary. In this instance, the standard deviation of 3.314 is extraneous.

Day 92

Using a random number generator, select 5 random integers from 1 to 5. Let 5 represent Katy GooGoo. Repeated digits are allowed. Record whether the set of five numbers contains at least two 5s. Repeat this 100 times. The proportion of trials that contain at least two 5s is the estimate of the probability that he will be successful.

Day 93

- $P(a\ child\ 12\ or\ under\ and\ prefers\ vanilla)$ is the probability that, out of the 144 people, the one selected is one of the 24 who is 12 or under and prefer vanilla. The probability is $\frac{24}{144}$.
- $P(a\ child\ 12\ or\ under\ or\ prefers\ vanilla)$ is the probability that, out of the 144 people, the one selected is one of the 24 who is 12 or under or prefer vanilla or both. The probability is $\frac{48+24+5+14+13}{144} = \frac{77+51-24}{144} = \frac{104}{144}$.
- $P(a\ child\ 12\ or\ under \mid prefers\ vanilla)$ is the probability that, given the student is one of the 51 people who prefer vanilla, the one selected is one of the 24 who are 12 or under. This probability is $\frac{24}{51}$.
- $P(prefers\ vanilla \mid a\ child\ 12\ or\ under)$ is the probability that, given the student is one of the 77 people who are 12 or under, the one selected is one of the 24 who prefer vanilla. This probability is $\frac{24}{77}$.

Day 94

The probability of a random student chosen being a freshman is 300/1,000 or 30%. If we know that the random student is a female, then the probability that this student is a freshman is 165/550 or 30%. Because these two probabilities are equal, the events "Is a freshman" and "Is a female" are independent. In symbolic terms, it looks like this:

$$P(Freshman) = P(Freshman \setminus Female).$$

Day 95

The probability of a random student chosen being a male is 450/1,000 or 45%. If we know that the random student is a senior, then the probability that this student is a male is 95/200 or 48.5%. Because these two probabilities are not equal, the events "Is a male" and "Is a senior" are not independent. In symbolic terms, it looks like this:

$$P(Male) \neq P(Male \setminus Senior).$$

Day 96

Because both distributions are approximately normally distributed, then the sum of a box and a balloon will also have a distribution that is approximately normal. The mean of this sum will be 42 oz plus 8 oz, or 50 ounces. Because these two variables are independent, the standard deviation can be found by adding the variances and taking the square root, or $\sqrt{5^2 + 2^2} = \sqrt{29} \approx 5.39$ ounces.

Day 97

This is a binomial situation with $n = 20$ and $P(\text{success}) = 0.05$. We want to know the $P(X < 3)$. One straightforward way to find this is to use the formula $P(x = k) = \binom{n}{k} p^k (1-p)^{n-k}$ and calculate $P(x = 0) + P(x = 1) + P(x = 2)$. In doing so, $P(X < 3) = 0.9246$.

Day 98

NO. OF PEOPLE LIVING WITH PARENTS	PROBABILITY
0	$\binom{7}{0} \cdot 0.32^0 \cdot 0.68^7 = 0.06723$
1	$\binom{7}{1} \cdot 0.32^1 \cdot 0.68^6 = 0.06723$
2	$\binom{7}{2} \cdot 0.32^2 \cdot 0.68^5 = 0.06723$
3	$\binom{7}{3} \cdot 0.32^3 \cdot 0.68^4 = 0.06723$
4	$\binom{7}{4} \cdot 0.32^4 \cdot 0.68^3 = 0.06723$
5	$\binom{7}{5} \cdot 0.32^5 \cdot 0.68^2 = 0.06723$
6	$\binom{7}{6} \cdot 0.32^6 \cdot 0.68^1 = 0.06723$
7	$\binom{7}{7} \cdot 0.32^7 \cdot 0.68^0 = 0.06723$

Day 99

This is a binomial calculation. There are many different ways that he can make 7 and miss 3 shots. So that probability must be multiplied by the number of different ways that this can happen. Happily, the binomial probability distribution button on our calculators does this automatically. If you're curious, you can use the combinations button to find out how many different rearrangements there are.

Day 100

This question is asking for the mean and standard deviation of a binomial random variable. Both of these formulas are on the formula sheet.

$\mu = np = (15)(0.85) = 12.75$ made shots and $\sigma = \sqrt{np(1-p)} = \sqrt{15 \times 0.85 \times 0.15} = 1.38$ made shots

Day 101

W = Sack1 + Sack2. The mean of W is equal to Mean(Sack1) + Mean(Sack2), or 400 pounds. Because the sacks were selected randomly, their weights are independent. Therefore, the variance of W is equal to Var(Sack1) + Var(Sack2); in this case 16 + 16, or 32. So, the distribution of the weights of TWO sacks of flour (W) is approximately normally distributed with a mean of 400 pounds and a standard deviation of $\sqrt{32} = 5.66$ pounds.

Day 102

The distribution of the sum is approximately normal with a mean of 400 pounds and a standard deviation of about 5.66 pounds. $P(\text{Sum} > 410) = P\left(z > \dfrac{410 - 400}{5.66} \approx 1.77\right) = 0.038$. There is about a 3.8% chance that the total weight will exceed 410 pounds.

Day 103

This is an example of a geometric probability. Think of it like this: you must first encounter four people in a row who are not of type A and then the fifth person with type A blood.

$$(0.9)(0.9)(0.9)(0.9)(0.1) = 0.06561$$

Day 104

We can use $P(A \text{ or } B) = P(A) + P(B) - P(A \text{ and } B)$. When two events are independent, $P(A \text{ or } B) = P(A)P(B)$. Because our events are independent, $P(A \text{ or } B) = (0.64)(0.25) = 0.16$. And thus $P(A \text{ or } B) = P(A) + P(B) - P(A \text{ or } B) = 0.64 + 0.25 - 0.16 = 0.73$.

Day 105

For a geometric distribution, $E(X) = \dfrac{1}{p} = \dfrac{1}{0.10} = 10$. $\sigma(X) = \dfrac{\sqrt{1-p}}{p} = \dfrac{\sqrt{1-0.10}}{0.10} = 9.49$.

Day 106

The expected number of books per student = $1(0.05) + 2(0.15) + 3(0.36) + 4(0.44) = 3.19$.

The total expected number of books $= (3.19)(86) = 274.34$ books.

Exam Hint: Resist the temptation to round your answer to the nearest whole number.

Day 107

The mean of the sampling distribution of that statistic is the same as the parameter we are using it to estimate.

Day 108

In both cases, the word "unbiased" is talking about being correct *on average*. In sampling, we want a method of selecting the sample that results in correct estimates of the parameter on average. When talking about an estimator, we also want a technique that gives correct predictions on average.

Day 109

The probability of a success on the first trial is p. To find the probability that the first success happens on the second trial, we multiply p by $(1 - p)$, which is less than 1. So the probability that two trials are needed must be less than the probability that one trial is needed. And for each subsequent number of trials, we keep multiplying by $(1 - p)$, so the probabilities keep getting smaller.

Day 110

Because the sample mean $\bar{x}$ is an unbiased estimator of μ, the mean of the sampling distribution is 270. Because the sample size is less than 10% of the very, very large population, the standard deviation of the sampling distribution is $\sigma/\sqrt{n}$ or 6.25. However, 16 is not a large enough sample size to meet the normal condition, so the sampling distribution is likely still somewhat skewed to the left.

Day 111

$$\text{Mean} = \sum x_i \cdot p_i = 1(0.10) + 2(0.15) + 5(0.25) + \ldots = 14.65 \text{ gold coins}$$

$$\text{StDev} = \sqrt{\sum (x_i - \mu_x)^2 \cdot p_i} = 22.36 \text{ gold coins from the following calculation:}$$

$$\sqrt{(1 - 14.65)^2 + (2 - 14.65)^2 + \cdots}$$

Exam Hint: If you just need the mean, it is fastest to just do the multiplying and adding "by hand." But if you also need the standard deviation, the 1-variable statistics command on your calculator will do the heavy lifting for you. You should still show the first few terms of both formulas. Finally, remember that these formulas are on your formula sheet.

Day 112

One possibility would be to calculate the infinite sum $0.9^4 \cdot 0.1 + 0.9^5 \cdot 0.1 + 0.9^6 \cdot 0.1 + \ldots$, but that requires mathematics that isn't a prerequisite for AP Statistics! Another approach would be to calculate the probability of getting the first left-handed person on the first, second, third, or fourth attempt, and subtract from 1. That's $1 - (0.1 + 0.9 \cdot 0.1 + 0.9^2 \cdot 0.1 + 0.9^3 \cdot 0.1) = 0.6561$. A third way would be to recognize that if it requires at least five people, that means the first four are failures. $0.9^4 = 0.6561$.

Day 113

Each dot represents a set of four pennies selected by a student. The second dot from the right shows that that particular set of four pennies had a mean age of just over 38 years. The fact that it is second from the right indicates that this was a particularly high mean age compared to the rest of the samples of pennies.

Day 114

Double mean and double median are unbiased, but double mean has lower spread, so it is the better estimator. Maximum and mean plus 2(SD) are both biased. The maximum, though it does estimate too low almost all the time, does have a low spread compared to all the other estimators so still might not be a terrible estimator. (As it turns out, multiplying the maximum by $\frac{n+1}{n}$ shifts it, so it is unbiased and still has a really low spread!)

Day 115

The sample size is the number of pennies in each sample: $n = 4$. The number of samples is the number of dots. In this simulated sampling distribution, there were 200 samples taken.

Day 116

Increasing the sample size would mean each student would select more pennies each time they took a sample. If they did that, the sampling distribution would become more symmetric and less spread out, with the center remaining the same. Increasing the number of samples would mean there are more than 200 dots, and the plot would fill in more and smooth out, giving a better prediction of what the actual sampling distribution looks like.

Day 117

Using a bit of rounding, 15 ± 22, or -7 to 37, is within one standard deviation of the mean. All of the coins from 1 to 20 are in this interval. Only 50 and 100 coins are not in this range. So, $6/8 = 75\%$ are within one standard deviation of the mean.

Exam Hint: Do NOT use the normal distribution for problems like these! Notice that the answer is NOT 68%.

Day 118

We use the t-distribution when we are estimating or testing a population mean, and we don't know the population standard deviation. When we estimate the population standard deviation with the sample standard deviation, we tend to underestimate. So our confidence intervals capture the population mean less often than advertised, and our significance tests reject the null hypothesis more often than they should. The t-distribution adjusts for this by increasing the capture rate of a confidence interval by making the interval wider and by putting more values of the test statistic in the tails, making it harder to reject the null hypothesis.

Day 119

Because $\hat{p}$ is an unbiased estimator of p, the mean of the sampling distribution will be 0.68. Because the sample size of 50 is less than 10% of the population, the standard deviation of the sampling distribution will be $\sqrt{\frac{p(1-p)}{n}} = \sqrt{\frac{0.73(1-0.73)}{50}} = 0.0638$.

Because both $np > 10$ and $n(1-p) > 10$ [$50(0.73) = 36.5$ and $50(0.27) = 13.5$], the sampling distribution of $\hat{p}$ will be approximately normally distributed.

Day 120

The models we use, such as the normal model, the linear regression model, the *t*-distribution, and so on, are never exactly correct for any set of data. The models are always "wrong." But, as long as our data fit the models reasonably well, the models provide reasonably accurate estimates, which makes them useful.

Day 121

This is to ensure that sample size is large enough for the shape of the sampling distribution of $\hat{p}$ to be approximately normal.

Day 122

The formula for the standard error, $\frac{\sigma}{\sqrt{n}}$ or $\sqrt{\frac{p(1-p)}{n}}$, is only technically correct for sampling without replacement. It is "close enough" to correct as long as the sample size is less than 10% of the population. So if we violate that 10% condition, the formula for the standard error will be incorrect.

Day 123

If many, many surveys were taken in the same way as this one, 99 out of 100 of the confidence intervals we created would capture the actual population percentage of people who favor increasing funding for schools.

Day 124

It is reasonable to believe that the true proportion of the population who have been infected with the mosquito-borne virus is anywhere from 32% to 38%.

Day 125

Because the interval has been created, and the population mean is fixed, there is no repeatable random event. Either the mean is in the interval or it is not. But there is no 95% probability associated with it.

Day 126

Because there is a 100% chance the sample mean is in the interval. The interval was built around the sample mean. The sample mean will be in the exact center of the interval. It is the population mean we are trying to estimate.

Day 127

We need to use the equation $Margin\ of\ Error = z^* \sqrt{\frac{p(1-p)}{n}}$. The z^* value for 99% confidence is 2.576, and we'll use a conservative value of $p = 0.5$. Solving $0.02 = 2.576 \sqrt{\frac{(0.5)(0.5)}{n}}$ results in $n = 4147.36$. So the sample size necessary is 4,148 or more.

Exam Hint: When you are asked for sample size, remember that you must be within the margin of error given. The value 4,147.36 will give you exactly a margin of error of 2%. But you cannot take a sample of partial subjects. Because increasing the sample size decreases the margin of error, you should round your answer up.

Day 128

One of the conditions for the confidence interval for a difference in proportions is that there are two samples randomly and independently selected from two populations. That allows us to add variances to get the formula for the SE of the difference. Here we have one sample selected from one population, so there is not independence. If more people in a sample support one candidate, there are fewer remaining who could support the other candidate.

Day 129

The confidence level states the proportion of random samples that will contain the population parameter within the confidence interval. In other words, it is the proportion of intervals that would "capture" the population parameter.

Day 130

A confidence interval determines which population proportions would contain a particular sample proportion in the middle 95% of their sampling distribution. Here, the 32% is the population proportion, not a sample proportion, and the interval shows the *sample proportions* that would be expected from that one population.

Day 131

Interpreting the confidence interval means stating what the particular calculated interval means. We must state what we think is in that interval (identify the parameter) and how confident we are. Interpreting the confidence level is not about the particular interval but the process.

Day 132

Assuming that all conditions for inference have been met, we must find t^* for $df = 23$ with 95% confidence. Looking in the table yields $t^* = 2.069$.

Day 133

The correct answer is (B). We need to use the formula $\hat{p} \pm z^* \sqrt{\hat{p}(1-\hat{p})/n}$, where $\hat{p} = \dfrac{120}{1500} = 0.08$ and the critical value for a 95% confidence interval $z^* = 1.96$.

Day 134

The first two symbols, μ and σ, are the mean and standard deviation of the population. We sometimes have a theory about what the mean might be (this is our null hypothesis) and we usually do not know what the standard deviation of the population is.

The symbols $\bar{x}$ and s_x are the mean and standard deviation of the data we have. They are the sample statistics that we have calculated from our sample. They are, hopefully, reasonable estimates of μ and σ. However, we know that for small samples, s_x tends to over-estimate σ.

Day 135

The correct answer is (C). In the calculation of any confidence interval you divide by the square root of the sample size. To cut the size of the interval in half, you would need to divide by twice your square root of n. Putting 2 back in the square root results in $\sqrt{4n}$ being in your denominator. Thus, you should quadruple your sample size to cut your confidence interval in half.

Day 136

If the goal is to see whether the machine is more consistent, they want the standard deviation to decrease. An appropriate set of hypotheses would be

$$H_0: \sigma = 0.4$$
$$H_a: \sigma = 0.4$$

Day 137

The correct answer is (D). Any value that is $\pm 3\%$ of 52% is a reasonable estimate of what percentage of likely voters would support the candidate.

Day 138

No. Remember, association does not imply causation! One possible alternative explanation is that students who are more concerned about their test score will take the course. But those students would possibly outperform the general population anyway.

Day 139

A-4, B-2, C-1, D-3. The alpha level relates to the level of evidence we require to reject the null hypothesis. A low alpha (say, 1% rather than 5%) requires a result to be farther out in the tails before we will reject H_0, making it more difficult to reject.

Day 140

Before conducting an experiment, which can be time-consuming and expensive, it is wise to have some idea how likely you are to detect a difference if there is one. Generally, researchers would have some preliminary data or some experience that might give them an estimate of the size of the treatment's effect and (if appropriate) the standard deviation of the responses. Based on these estimates, the researcher can see how many subjects would be needed to detect a difference of that size at a specified significance level. If they can't afford enough subjects, they may be better off abandoning or redesigning their experiment rather than wasting time and money on a study that is unlikely to detect the effect.

We didn't include this in the chapter on designing studies because you had not yet learned what a significance test was. It wouldn't have made any sense. Hopefully it does now!

Day 141

If it were true that 75% of the population get the flu shot, then we would see results like 82% or even more extreme in repeated sampling about 8% of the time.

Day 142

The *P*-value is equal to $2 \cdot P(z < -2.04) = 0.0414$.

Day 143

A. False. 14.04 minutes is greater than 12 minutes, so Rian is correct that there is evidence the average wait time for all customers of this Internet provider is more than 12 minutes. However, Rian must have been using an alpha level less than 0.0184 to state that the evidence was not convincing. (Let's say Rian was using $\alpha = 0.01$. In the same vein, Alex must have been using an alpha level greater than 0.0184 to find the evidence convincing; for example, $\alpha = 0.05$.)

B. False. The alpha level is the probability of making a Type 1 error. Rian's alpha level is smaller than Alex's; therefore, Rian must have been less willing to make a Type 1 error.

C. True by the reasoning above.

D. False. The relationship between alpha level and Type 2 error is such that increasing alpha decreases the probability of a Type 2 error. Alex's larger alpha level would result in a smaller Type 2 probability. Thus, Alex must have been less willing than Rian to make a Type 2 error.

Day 144

Looking at the formula for the test statistic $t = \dfrac{\bar{x} - \mu_0}{s/\sqrt{n}}$, as n increases, $s/\sqrt{n}$ decreases, so the whole test statistic must increase in absolute value.

Day 145

Looking at the formula for the test statistic $t = \dfrac{\bar{x} - \mu_0}{s/\sqrt{n}}$, as s increases, $s/\sqrt{n}$ also increases, so the whole test statistic must decrease in absolute value.

Day 146

Looking at the formula for the test statistic $t = \dfrac{\bar{x} - \mu_0}{s/\sqrt{n}}$, as $\bar{x} - \mu_0$ gets closer to zero, the whole test statistic must decrease in absolute value.

Day 147

If there is really no difference in mean growth rate for the new method and the current method, there is a 17% chance that an experiment would result in a difference as large or larger than the difference that occurred in the actual experiment. (Other statements, such as "They should fail to reject the null hypothesis" or "They do not have convincing evidence that the new method works better," may be true, but they are not interpretations of the *P*-value.)

Day 148

When pairs are created so that the individuals in each pair are similar to each other with respect to the response variable.

Day 149

The answer is (E). When you increase the sample size, you decrease the standard deviation calculation in the test statistic. This creates a distribution of the test statistic that is narrower (has less variation itself) and makes it more likely that your test will correctly reject a false null hypothesis.

Day 150

We meet the conditions that allow us to use a normal approximation in this situation. Randomness is stated in the stem of the problem, independence because 10(200) is less than the population of all American high school students, and normality because 0.36(200) and 0.64(200) are both more than 10. Therefore, we can calculate

$$P\left(z > \frac{0.40 - 0.36}{\sqrt{\frac{(0.36)(0.64)}{200}}}\right) = 0.1193.$$

Day 151

We can conclude that we don't have convincing evidence that the new medication works better. That is not the same as saying we have evidence that the medications are equal. It is very possible that the new medication does work better, but the difference was too small for us to detect it. "No difference" is one of many possible models that might explain the difference we saw, so we don't accept that one particular model. (We never accept the null hypothesis!)

Day 152

A Type I error would be rejecting the null hypothesis when it is true. In this context, that means the researchers would conclude that the low-sodium diet improves health when, in fact, it does not. The consequence of that would be that they would recommend low-sodium diets to people when it would not actually help them.

Day 153

A Type II error would be failing to reject the null hypothesis when it is false. In this context, that means the researchers would conclude that they do not have evidence that the low-sodium diet improves health when, in fact, it does. The consequence of that would be that they would not recommend low-sodium diets to people when it would actually help them.

Day 154

The correct answer is (D).

Day 155

The normal condition is met when the population is approximately normally distributed or the sample size is large enough (generally, greater than 30). Because the sample size is less than 30 and we were not told anything about the shape of the distribution, we MUST use the plot. In this case, because the plot of the sample data is relatively symmetric with no outliers, it is reasonable to believe that these sample data come from an approximately normal population. You might choose to say, "The graph gives no offense to normality."

Exam Hint: It's the population that needs to be approximately normally distributed, not the sample data.

Day 156

Both are bell-shaped. Both are symmetric about the mean. In both, the mean, median, and mode are located at the center of the distribution. Neither curve touches its horizontal axis.

The t-distribution is actually a family of curves, each member of which is identified by degrees of freedom. The t-distribution is more spread out than the standard normal distribution. As the sample size increases, the t-distribution approaches the standard normal distribution.

Day 157

No. The Central Limit Theorem states that for large sample sizes ($n = 250$), the sample mean will be approximately normally distributed. The skewness of the sample is not a problem.

Day 158

If it were true that the average debt carried by a recent college graduate equals $24,000 we would see a sample mean of $25,015 or more in repeated sampling 6.5% of the time.

Day 159

While there is evidence that the average debt carried by a recent college graduate is greater than $24,000, this evidence is not statistically convincing because the P-value (0.065) is greater than alpha (0.05). Therefore, we fail to reject H_o.

Day 160

Randomness—it is highly unlikely that a log will be filled with a random group of 8 adult American males. People wait in line in friend/family groups. This would violate the random condition.

Independence—8 is less than 10% of the population of all males.

Normality—the population is described as being approximately normally distributed, so we have met the normal condition.

Day 161

No, a confidence interval should not be used in a one-sided test. (*Note*: It is possible to create a confidence interval for a one-sided test, but doing so is beyond the scope of AP Statistics.)

Answers

Day 162

Below, the lines with maximum and minimum slopes are shown on the original plot and both modified plots.

In the first modified plot, the variability in y for each value of x decreased. As the lines indicate, there is less variability in the slopes. In the second modified plot, the variability in the x-values decreased. This resulted in *greater* variability in the slope. This helps to explain why the variability in y is in the numerator of the formula for the standard error of the slope, and the variability in x is in the denominator.

Day 163

For a community with one additional unit of EW, it is predicted that the literacy rate would be 0.000117 higher typically.

Day 164

The intercept is 58.6238. In a community with an EW of zero, we would expect a literacy rate of 58.6238. This may not be reasonable; in a community with a zero rating of economic welfare, we would expect a lower literacy rate.

Day 165

S is the standard deviation of the residuals. The typical difference between the actual literacy rate and that predicted by the linear regression with EW is about 12.17743.

Day 166

Plugging 830 into the regression equation gives a predicted literacy rate of 60.118. The residual is $(65 - 60.118) = 4.882$.

This community has a literacy rate 4.882 higher than was predicted, given its EW.

Day 167

A. It is very difficult to see the shape of the distribution of the residuals in the scatterplot, so this would not be the most appropriate. You would have to give a pretty convincing explanation to justify this from a scatterplot.

B. As in the scatterplot, the shape of the distribution is difficult to see.

C. This is ideal. The shape is very apparent from a dotplot.

D. Also ideal. As long as the bin widths are appropriate for seeing the shape.

E. Not ideal. The boxplot is a rough summary, and the shape is impossible to determine from a boxplot. However, since the main concerns with the t-procedures are that the distribution is roughly symmetric and there are no outliers, a boxplot could conceivably give enough information to check this condition.

F. This is ideal. It takes more practice to interpret deviations from normality, but if the plot is pretty linear, you should be good to go!

Day 168

We want to know if we have convincing evidence that the slope of the regression between literacy rate and EW is something other than zero for the population of communities. So the correct hypotheses should be

$$H_o: \beta = 0$$
$$H_a: \beta \neq 0$$

where β = the slope of the regression line relating literacy and EW for the population of communities.

Day 169

The P-value for the slope is read directly from the table as 0.1306. (This P-value represents that of a two-sided test.) Because the P-value (0.1306) is greater than α (0.05), there is not enough evidence to reject the null hypothesis. There is not convincing evidence that there is a linear relationship between literacy rate and EW for all communities in the population.

Day 170

The formula for the confidence interval is $\hat{y} \pm t^* \cdot s_b$ using t^* for $35 - 2 = 33$ df. The interval is $0.00181 \pm 2.035 \cdot 0.00117 = (-0.000571, 0.004191)$. We are 95% confident that the slope of the regression line for the relationship between literacy rate and economic welfare for all communities in the population is between -0.000571 and 0.004191. Because 0 is contained in this interval, we do not have convincing evidence that there is a relationship between these variables in the population of all communities.

Day 171

No. The scatterplot and residual plot both seem to indicate a linear relationship. However, the variability in y-values is not consistent across x-values as indicated by the "fan-shaped" residual plot. Also, the residuals are not close to normally distributed as shown by the univariate plot of residuals.

Day 172

A. Yes. As a population density function, the area underneath the curve of chi-square is 1.

B. No. For all values of degrees of freedom, chi-square is right-skewed, although it gets more symmetric (approaching a normal distribution) as the number of degrees of freedom increases.

C. Yes (mostly). If a distribution of frequencies matches exactly what is hypothesized, the value of chi-square equals 0. Otherwise, it is positive.

D. No. Chi-square is not used to compare means; it is used to compare several proportions.

Day 173

The sample is random, the sample size is less than 10% of the population size, and the expected values are all greater than or equal to 5.

Day 174

$$H_0: p_1 = 0.25, \ p_2 = 0.2, p_3 = 0.1, p_4 = 0.2, p_5 = 0.25$$

$$H_a: \text{At least one of these proportions is different}$$

Day 175

If the number of calls is the same for each day of the week, then we would expect that these 100 calls would be equally distributed. So the expected value for each day would be 20 calls. The calculation for chi-square is as follows:

$$\chi^2 = \frac{(23-20)^2}{20} + \frac{(18-20)^2}{20} + \frac{(19-20)^2}{20} + \frac{(24-20)^2}{20} + \frac{(16-20)^2}{20} = 2.3$$

Day 176

$$\text{Expected cell count} = \frac{(row\ total)(column\ total)}{(grand\ total)} = \frac{(50)(40)}{(400)} = 5$$

Day 177

This requires a χ^2 with $(3{-}1)(4{-}1) = 6$ df. A calculator will show that this gives a P-value of 0.018. Alternatively, the χ^2 table shows that, with 6 df, a 5% significance level corresponds to a χ^2 critical value of 12.59. In fact, 15.3 falls between tail probabilities of 0.02 and 0.01. The conclusion should be *Because the P-value of 0.018 is less than 0.05* (or *Because the P-value is between 0.02 and .01, which is less than 0.05* or *Because the χ^2 statistic of 15.3 is greater than the critical value of 12.59) we reject the null hypothesis. We have convincing evidence that there is an association between political affiliation and preferred type of television show.*

Day 178

$\chi^2 = 14.7287$, P-value $= 0.000124$; $z = 3.8378$, P-value $= 0.000124$. The P-values are equal. Less obvious is that the χ^2 statistic is the square of the test statistic from the z-test!

Day 179

In a two-way table, the number of degrees of freedom is calculated using the formula $df = (columns - 1)(rows - 1)$. In this case, $df = (4 - 1)(3 - 1) = 3 \cdot 2 = 6$.

Day 180

a. A chi-square test for independence.

b. No. There were no randomly assigned treatments, so causation cannot be established.

Appendixes

Formula Sheet
Tables
Bibliography
Websites
Glossary

FORMULA SHEET

I. Descriptive Statistics

$$\bar{x} = \frac{1}{n}\sum x_i = \frac{\sum x_i}{n} \qquad s_x = \sqrt{\frac{1}{n-1}\sum(x_i - \bar{x})^2} = \sqrt{\frac{\sum(x_i - \bar{x})^2}{n-1}}$$

$$\hat{y} = a + bx \qquad \bar{y} = a + b\bar{x}$$

$$r = \frac{1}{n-1}\sum\left(\frac{x_i - \bar{x}}{s_x}\right)\left(\frac{y_i - \bar{y}}{s_y}\right) \qquad b = r\frac{s_y}{s_x}$$

II. Probability and Distributions

$$P(A \cup B) = P(A) + P(B) - P(A \cap B) \qquad P(A|B) = \frac{P(A \cap B)}{P(B)}$$

PROBABILITY DISTRIBUTION	MEAN	STANDARD DEVIATION
Discrete random variable, X	$\mu_x = E(X) = \Sigma x_i P(x_i)$	$\sigma_x = \sqrt{\sum(x_i - \mu_x)^2 P(x_i)}$
If X has a binomial distribution with parameters n and p, then $$P(X = x) = \binom{n}{x}p^x(1-p)^{n-x},$$ where $x = 0, 1, 2, \ldots, n$.	$\mu_x = np$	$\sigma_x = \sqrt{np(1-p)}$
If X has a geometric distribution with parameters p, then $P(X = x) = (1-p)^{x-1}p$, where $x = 1, 2, \ldots,$	$\mu_x = \dfrac{1}{p}$	$\sigma_x = \dfrac{\sqrt{1-p}}{p}$

III. Sampling Distributions and Inferential Statistics

$$\text{Standard Test Statistic: } \frac{\text{statistic} - \text{parameter}}{\text{standard error of the statistic}}$$

$$\text{Confidence interval: statistic} \pm (\text{critical value})(\text{standard error of statistic})$$

$$\text{Chi-square statistic: } \chi^2 = \sum\frac{(\text{observed} - \text{expected})^2}{\text{expected}}$$

Table 1 **Sampling distributions for proportions**

RANDOM VARIABLE	PARAMETERS OF SAMPLING DISTRIBUTION	STANDARD ERROR* OF SAMPLE STATISTIC
For one population: $\hat{p}$	$\mu_{\hat{p}} = p \qquad \sigma_{\hat{p}} = \sqrt{\dfrac{p(1-p)}{n}}$	$s_{\hat{p}} = \sqrt{\dfrac{\hat{p}(1-\hat{p})}{n}}$
For two populations: $\hat{p}_1 - \hat{p}_2$	$\mu_{\hat{p}1-\hat{p}2} = p_1 - p_2$ $\sigma_{\hat{p}1-\hat{p}2} = \sqrt{\dfrac{\hat{p}_1(1-\hat{p}_1)}{n_1} + \dfrac{\hat{p}_2(1-\hat{p}_2)}{n_2}}$	$s_{\hat{p}1-\hat{p}2} = \sqrt{\dfrac{\hat{p}_1(1-\hat{p}_1)}{n_1} + \dfrac{\hat{p}_2(1-\hat{p}_2)}{n_2}}$ When $p_1 = p_2$ is assumed, $s_{\hat{p}1-\hat{p}2} = \sqrt{\hat{p}_c(1-\hat{p}_c)\left(\dfrac{1}{n_1}+\dfrac{1}{n_2}\right)}$, where $\hat{p}_c = \dfrac{X_1+X_2}{n_1+n_2}$.

*Standard deviation is a measurement of variability from the theoretical population. Standard error is the estimate of the standard deviation. If the standard deviation of the statistic is assumed to be known, then the standard deviation should be used instead of the standard error.

Table 2 **Sampling distributions for means**

RANDOM VARIABLE	PARAMETERS OF SAMPLING DISTRIBUTION	STANDARD ERROR* OF SAMPLE STATISTIC
For one population: $\bar{X}$	$\mu_{\bar{X}} = \mu \qquad \sigma_{\bar{X}} = \dfrac{\sigma}{\sqrt{n}}$	$s_{\bar{X}} = \dfrac{s}{\sqrt{n}}$
For two populations: $\bar{X}_1 - \bar{X}_2$	$\mu_{\bar{X}_1-\bar{X}_2} = \mu_1 - \mu_2$ $\sigma_{\bar{X}_1-\bar{X}_2} = \sqrt{\dfrac{\sigma_1^2}{n_1} + \dfrac{\sigma_2^2}{n_2}}$	$s_{\bar{X}_1-\bar{X}_2} = \sqrt{\dfrac{s_1^2}{n_1} + \dfrac{s_2^2}{n_2}}$

Table 3 **Sampling distributions for simple linear regression**

RANDOM VARIABLE	PARAMETERS OF SAMPLING DISTRIBUTION	STANDARD ERROR* OF SAMPLE STATISTIC
For slope b	$\mu_b = \beta \qquad \sigma_b = \dfrac{\sigma}{\sigma_x \sqrt{n}}$, where $\sigma_x = \sqrt{\dfrac{\sum(x_i-\bar{x})^2}{n}}$	$s_b = \dfrac{s}{s_x\sqrt{n-1}}$, where $s = \sqrt{\dfrac{\sum(y_i-\hat{y}_i)^2}{n-2}}$ and $s_x = \sqrt{\dfrac{\sum(x_i-\bar{x})^2}{n-1}}$

TABLES

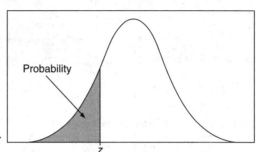

Table entry for z is the probability lying below z.

Probability

z

TABLE A   Standard Normal Probabilities

z	.00	.01	.02	.03	.04	.05	.06	.07	.08	.09
−3.4	.0003	.0003	.0003	.0003	.0003	.0003	.0003	.0003	.0003	.0002
−3.3	.0005	.0005	.0005	.0004	.0004	.0004	.0004	.0004	.0004	.0003
−3.2	.0007	.0007	.0006	.0006	.0006	.0006	.0006	.0005	.0005	.0005
−3.1	.0010	.0009	.0009	.0009	.0008	.0008	.0008	.0008	.0007	.0007
−3.0	.0013	.0013	.0013	.0012	.0012	.0011	.0011	.0011	.0010	.0010
−2.9	.0019	.0018	.0018	.0017	.0016	.0016	.0015	.0015	.0014	.0014
−2.8	.0026	.0025	.0024	.0023	.0023	.0022	.0021	.0021	.0020	.0019
−2.7	.0035	.0034	.0033	.0032	.0031	.0030	.0029	.0028	.0027	.0026
−2.6	.0047	.0045	.0044	.0043	.0041	.0040	.0039	.0038	.0037	.0036
−2.5	.0062	.0060	.0059	.0057	.0055	.0054	.0052	.0051	.0049	.0048
−2.4	.0082	.0080	.0078	.0075	.0073	.0071	.0069	.0068	.0066	.0064
−2.3	.0107	.0104	.0102	.0099	.0096	.0094	.0091	.0089	.0087	.0084
−2.2	.0139	.0136	.0132	.0129	.0125	.0122	.0119	.0116	.0113	.0110
−2.1	.0179	.0174	.0170	.0166	.0162	.0158	.0154	.0150	.0146	.0143
−2.0	.0228	.0222	.0217	.0212	.0207	.0202	.0197	.0192	.0188	.0183
−1.9	.0287	.0281	.0274	.0268	.0262	.0256	.0250	.0244	.0239	.0233
−1.8	.0359	.0351	.0344	.0336	.0329	.0322	.0314	.0307	.0301	.0294
−1.7	.0446	.0436	.0427	.0418	.0409	.0401	.0392	.0384	.0375	.0367
−1.6	.0548	.0537	.0526	.0516	.0505	.0495	.0485	.0475	.0465	.0455
−1.5	.0668	.0655	.0643	.0630	.0618	.0606	.0594	.0582	.0571	.0559
−1.4	.0808	.0793	.0778	.0764	.0749	.0735	.0721	.0708	.0694	.0681
−1.3	.0968	.0951	.0934	.0918	.0901	.0885	.0869	.0853	.0838	.0823
−1.2	.1151	.1131	.1112	.1093	.1075	.1056	.1038	.1020	.1003	.0985
−1.1	.1357	.1335	.1314	.1292	.1271	.1251	.1230	.1210	.1190	.1170
−1.0	.1587	.1562	.1539	.1515	.1492	.1469	.1446	.1423	.1401	.1379
−0.9	.1841	.1814	.1788	.1762	.1736	.1711	.1685	.1660	.1635	.1611
−0.8	.2119	.2090	.2061	.2033	.2005	.1977	.1949	.1922	.1894	.1867
−0.7	.2420	.2389	.2358	.2327	.2296	.2266	.2236	.2206	.2177	.2148
−0.6	.2743	.2709	.2676	.2643	.2611	.2578	.2546	.2514	.2483	.2451
−0.5	.3085	.3050	.3015	.2981	.2946	.2912	.2877	.2843	.2810	.2776
−0.4	.3446	.3409	.3372	.3336	.3300	.3264	.3228	.3192	.3156	.3121
−0.3	.3821	.3783	.3745	.3707	.3669	.3632	.3594	.3557	.3520	.3483
−0.2	.4207	.4168	.4129	.4090	.4052	.4013	.3974	.3936	.3897	.3859
−0.1	.4602	.4562	.4522	.4483	.4443	.4404	.4364	.4325	.4286	.4247
−0.0	.5000	.4960	.4920	.4880	.4840	.4801	.4761	.4721	.4681	.4641

Continued

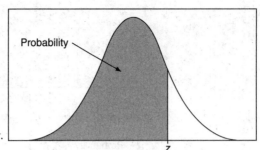

Table entry for z is the
probability lying below z.

Probability

z

TABLE A   Standard Normal Probabilities (*continued*)

z	.00	.01	.02	.03	.04	.05	.06	.07	.08	.09
0.0	.5000	.5040	.5080	.5120	.5160	.5199	.5239	.5279	.5319	.5359
0.1	.5398	.5438	.5478	.5517	.5557	.5596	.5636	.5675	.5714	.5753
0.2	.5793	.5832	.5871	.5910	.5948	.5987	.6026	.6064	.6103	.6141
0.3	.6179	.6217	.6255	.6293	.6331	.6368	.6406	.6443	.6480	.6517
0.4	.6554	.6591	.6628	.6664	.6700	.6736	.6772	.6808	.6844	.6879
0.5	.6915	.6950	.6985	.7019	.7054	.7088	.7123	.7157	.7190	.7224
0.6	.7257	.7291	.7324	.7357	.7389	.7422	.7454	.7486	.7517	.7549
0.7	.7580	.7611	.7642	.7673	.7704	.7734	.7764	.7794	.7823	.7852
0.8	.7881	.7910	.7939	.7967	.7995	.8023	.8051	.8078	.8106	.8133
0.9	.8159	.8186	.8212	.8238	.8264	.8289	.8315	.8340	.8365	.8389
1.0	.8413	.8438	.8461	.8485	.8508	.8531	.8554	.8577	.8599	.8621
1.1	.8643	.8665	.8686	.8708	.8729	.8749	.8770	.8790	.8810	.8830
1.2	.8849	.8869	.8888	.8907	.8925	.8944	.8962	.8980	.8997	.9015
1.3	.9032	.9049	.9066	.9082	.9099	.9115	.9131	.9147	.9162	.9177
1.4	.9192	.9207	.9222	.9236	.9251	.9265	.9279	.9292	.9306	.9319
1.5	.9332	.9345	.9357	.9370	.9382	.9394	.9406	.9418	.9429	.9441
1.6	.9452	.9463	.9474	.9484	.9495	.9505	.9515	.9525	.9535	.9545
1.7	.9554	.9564	.9573	.9582	.9591	.9599	.9608	.9616	.9625	.9633
1.8	.9641	.9649	.9656	.9664	.9671	.9678	.9686	.9693	.9699	.9706
1.9	.9713	.9719	.9726	.9732	.9738	.9744	.9750	.9756	.9761	.9767
2.0	.9772	.9778	.9783	.9788	.9793	.9798	.9803	.9808	.9812	.9817
2.1	.9821	.9826	.9830	.9834	.9838	.9842	.9846	.9850	.9854	.9857
2.2	.9861	.9864	.9868	.9871	.9875	.9878	.9881	.9884	.9887	.9890
2.3	.9893	.9896	.9898	.9901	.9904	.9906	.9909	.9911	.9913	.9916
2.4	.9918	.9920	.9922	.9925	.9927	.9929	.9931	.9932	.9934	.9936
2.5	.9938	.9940	.9941	.9943	.9945	.9946	.9948	.9949	.9951	.9952
2.6	.9953	.9955	.9956	.9957	.9959	.9960	.9961	.9962	.9963	.9964
2.7	.9965	.9966	.9967	.9968	.9969	.9970	.9971	.9972	.9973	.9974
2.8	.9974	.9975	.9976	.9977	.9977	.9978	.9979	.9979	.9980	.9981
2.9	.9981	.9982	.9982	.9983	.9984	.9984	.9985	.9985	.9986	.9986
3.0	.9987	.9987	.9987	.9988	.9988	.9989	.9989	.9989	.9990	.9990
3.1	.9990	.9991	.9991	.9991	.9992	.9992	.9992	.9992	.9993	.9993
3.2	.9993	.9993	.9994	.9994	.9994	.9994	.9994	.9995	.9995	.9995
3.3	.9995	.9995	.9995	.9996	.9996	.9996	.9996	.9996	.9996	.9997
3.4	.9997	.9997	.9997	.9997	.9997	.9997	.9997	.9997	.9997	.9998

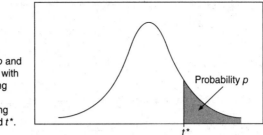

Table entry for p and C is the point t* with probability p lying above it and probability C lying between −t* and t*.

Probability p

t*

TABLE B   t Distribution Critical Values

					TAIL PROBABILITY P							
df	.25	.20	.15	.10	.05	.025	.02	.01	.005	.0025	.001	.0005
1	1.000	1.376	1.963	3.078	6.314	12.71	15.89	31.82	63.66	127.3	318.3	636.6
2	.816	1.061	1.386	1.886	2.920	4.303	4.849	6.965	9.925	14.09	22.33	31.60
3	.765	.978	1.250	1.638	2.353	3.182	3.482	4.541	5.841	7.453	10.21	12.92
4	.741	.941	1.190	1.533	2.132	2.776	2.999	3.747	4.604	5.598	7.173	8.610
5	.727	.920	1.156	1.476	2.015	2.571	2.757	3.365	4.032	4.773	5.893	6.869
6	.718	.906	1.134	1.440	1.943	2.447	2.612	3.143	3.707	4.317	5.208	5.959
7	.711	.896	1.119	1.415	1.895	2.365	2.517	2.998	3.499	4.029	4.785	5.408
8	.706	.889	1.108	1.397	1.860	2.306	2.449	2.896	3.355	3.833	4.501	5.041
9	.703	.883	1.100	1.383	1.833	2.262	2.398	2.821	3.250	3.690	4.297	4.781
10	.700	.879	1.093	1.372	1.812	2.228	2.359	2.764	3.169	3.581	4.144	4.587
11	.697	.876	1.088	1.363	1.796	2.201	2.328	2.718	3.106	3.497	4.025	4.437
12	.695	.873	1.083	1.356	1.782	2.179	2.303	2.681	3.055	3.428	3.930	4.318
13	.694	.870	1.079	1.350	1.771	2.160	2.282	2.650	3.012	3.372	3.852	4.221
14	.692	.868	1.076	1.345	1.761	2.145	2.264	2.624	2.977	3.326	3.787	4.140
15	.691	.866	1.074	1.341	1.753	2.131	2.249	2.602	2.947	3.286	3.733	4.073
16	.690	.865	1.071	1.337	1.746	2.120	2.235	2.583	2.921	3.252	3.686	4.015
17	.689	.863	1.069	1.333	1.740	2.110	2.224	2.567	2.898	3.222	3.646	3.965
18	.688	.862	1.067	1.330	1.734	2.101	2.214	2.552	2.878	3.197	3.611	3.922
19	.688	.861	1.066	1.328	1.729	2.093	2.205	2.539	2.861	3.174	3.579	3.883
20	.687	.860	1.064	1.325	1.725	2.086	2.197	2.528	2.845	3.153	3.552	3.850
21	.686	.859	1.063	1.323	1.721	2.080	2.189	2.518	2.831	3.135	3.527	3.819
22	.686	.858	1.061	1.321	1.717	2.074	2.183	2.508	2.819	3.119	3.505	3.792
23	.685	.858	1.060	1.319	1.714	2.069	2.177	2.500	2.807	3.104	3.485	3.768
24	.685	.857	1.059	1.318	1.711	2.064	2.172	2.492	2.797	3.091	3.467	3.745
25	.684	.856	1.058	1.316	1.708	2.060	2.167	2.485	2.787	3.078	3.450	3.725
26	.684	.856	1.058	1.315	1.706	2.056	2.162	2.479	2.779	3.067	3.435	3.707
27	.684	.855	1.057	1.314	1.703	2.052	2.158	2.473	2.771	3.057	3.421	3.690
28	.683	.855	1.056	1.313	1.701	2.048	2.154	2.467	2.763	3.047	3.408	3.674
29	.683	.854	1.055	1.311	1.699	2.045	2.150	2.462	2.756	3.038	3.396	3.659
30	.683	.854	1.055	1.310	1.697	2.042	2.147	2.457	2.750	3.030	3.385	3.646
40	.681	.851	1.050	1.303	1.684	2.021	2.123	2.423	2.704	2.971	3.307	3.551
50	.679	.849	1.047	1.299	1.676	2.009	2.109	2.403	2.678	2.937	3.261	3.496
60	.679	.848	1.045	1.296	1.671	2.000	2.099	2.390	2.660	2.915	3.232	3.460
80	.678	.846	1.043	1.292	1.664	1.990	2.088	2.374	2.639	2.887	3.195	3.416
100	.677	.845	1.042	1.290	1.660	1.984	2.081	2.364	2.626	2.871	3.174	3.390
1000	.675	.842	1.037	1.282	1.646	1.962	2.056	2.330	2.581	2.813	3.098	3.300
∞	.674	.841	1.036	1.282	1.645	1.960	2.054	2.326	2.576	2.807	3.091	3.291
	50%	60%	70%	80%	90%	95%	96%	98%	99%	99.5%	99.8%	99.9%

Confidence level C

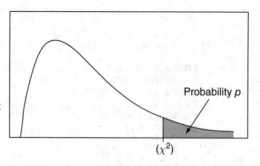

Table entry for p is the point (χ^2) with probability p lying above it.

TABLE C χ^2 **Critical Values**

df	\multicolumn{12}{c}{TAIL PROBABILITY P}
	.25	.20	.15	.10	.05	.025	.02	.01	.005	.0025	.001	.0005
1	1.32	1.64	2.07	2.71	3.84	5.02	5.41	6.63	7.88	9.14	10.83	12.12
2	2.77	3.22	3.79	4.61	5.99	7.38	7.82	9.21	10.60	11.98	13.82	15.20
3	4.11	4.64	5.32	6.25	7.81	9.35	9.84	11.34	12.84	14.32	16.27	17.73
4	5.39	5.99	6.74	7.78	9.49	11.14	11.67	13.28	14.86	16.42	18.47	20.00
5	6.63	7.29	8.12	9.24	11.07	12.83	13.39	15.09	16.75	18.39	20.51	22.11
6	7.84	8.56	9.45	10.64	12.59	14.45	15.03	16.81	18.55	20.25	22.46	24.10
7	9.04	9.80	10.75	12.02	14.07	16.01	16.62	18.48	20.28	22.04	24.32	26.02
8	10.22	11.03	12.03	13.36	15.51	17.53	18.17	20.09	21.95	23.77	26.12	27.87
9	11.39	12.24	13.29	14.68	16.92	19.02	19.68	21.67	23.59	25.46	27.88	29.67
10	12.55	13.44	14.53	15.99	18.31	20.48	21.16	23.21	25.19	27.11	29.59	31.42
11	13.70	14.63	15.77	17.28	19.68	21.92	22.62	24.72	26.76	28.73	31.26	33.14
12	14.85	15.81	16.99	18.55	21.03	23.34	24.05	26.22	28.30	30.32	32.91	34.82
13	15.98	16.98	18.20	19.81	22.36	24.74	25.47	27.69	29.82	31.88	34.53	36.48
14	17.12	18.15	19.41	21.06	23.68	26.12	26.87	29.14	31.32	33.43	36.12	38.11
15	18.25	19.31	20.60	22.31	25.00	27.49	28.26	30.58	32.80	34.95	37.70	39.72
16	19.37	20.47	21.79	23.54	26.30	28.85	29.63	32.00	34.27	36.46	39.25	41.31
17	20.49	21.61	22.98	24.77	27.59	30.19	31.00	33.41	35.72	37.95	40.79	42.88
18	21.60	22.76	24.16	25.99	28.87	31.53	32.35	34.81	37.16	39.42	42.31	44.43
19	22.72	23.90	25.33	27.20	30.14	32.85	33.69	36.19	38.58	40.88	43.82	45.97
20	23.83	25.04	26.50	28.41	31.41	34.17	35.02	37.57	40.00	42.34	45.31	47.50
21	24.93	26.17	27.66	29.62	32.67	35.48	36.34	38.93	41.40	43.78	46.80	49.01
22	26.04	27.30	28.82	30.81	33.92	36.78	37.66	40.29	42.80	45.20	48.27	50.51
23	27.14	28.43	29.98	32.01	35.17	38.08	38.97	41.64	44.18	46.62	49.73	52.00
24	28.24	29.55	31.13	33.20	36.42	39.36	40.27	42.98	45.56	48.03	51.18	53.48
25	29.34	30.68	32.28	34.38	37.65	40.65	41.57	44.31	46.93	49.44	52.62	54.95
26	30.43	31.79	33.43	35.56	38.89	41.92	42.86	45.64	48.29	50.83	54.05	56.41
27	31.53	32.91	34.57	36.74	40.11	43.19	44.14	46.96	49.64	52.22	55.48	57.86
28	32.62	34.03	35.71	37.92	41.34	44.46	45.42	48.28	50.99	53.59	56.89	59.30
29	33.71	35.14	36.85	39.09	42.56	45.72	46.69	49.59	52.34	54.97	58.30	60.73
30	34.80	36.25	37.99	40.26	43.77	46.98	47.96	50.89	53.67	56.33	59.70	62.16
40	45.62	47.27	49.24	51.81	55.76	59.34	60.44	63.69	66.77	69.70	73.40	76.09
50	56.33	58.16	60.35	63.17	67.50	71.42	72.61	76.15	79.49	82.66	86.66	89.56
60	66.98	68.97	71.34	74.40	79.08	83.30	84.58	88.38	91.95	95.34	99.61	102.7
80	88.13	90.41	93.11	96.58	101.9	106.6	108.1	112.3	116.3	120.1	124.8	128.3
100	109.1	111.7	114.7	118.5	124.3	129.6	131.1	135.8	140.2	144.3	149.4	153.2

BIBLIOGRAPHY

Advanced Placement Program Course Description. New York: The College Board, 2010–2016.

Bock, D., Velleman, P., De Veaux, R. 2015. *Stats*: *Modeling the World*, 4th ed. Boston: Pearson.

Moore, David S. 2007. *Introduction to the Practice of Statistics*, 6th ed. New York: W.H. Freeman and Company.

Peck, R., Olsen, C., Devore, J. 2011. *Introduction to Statistics and Data Analysis*, 4th ed. Belmont, CA: Duxbury/Thomson Learning.

Starnes, D., Tabor, J., Yates, D., Moore, D. 2014. *The Practice of Statistics*, 5th ed. New York: W. H. Freeman and Company.

Utts, J., Heckard, R. 2011. *Mind on Statistics,* 4th ed. Belmont, CA: Duxbury/Thomson Learning.

Watkins, A., Scheaffer, R., Cobb, G. 2008. *Statistics in Action*: *Understanding a World of Data*, 2nd ed. Kendall-Hunt Press.

Yates, D., Starnes, D., Moore, D. 2009. *Statistics Through Applications*, 2nd ed. New York: W.H. Freeman and Company.

WEBSITES

Here is a list of websites that contain information and links that you might find useful in your preparation for the AP Statistics exam:

AP Central: http://apcentral.collegeboard.com/home

AP Classroom: http://myap.collegeboard.com

Bureau of the Census: http://www.census.gov/

Data and Story Library (DASL): http://lib.stat.cmu.edu/DASL/

Statkey: http://lock5stat.com/statkey/

Art of Statistics: https://artofstat.com

Rossman/Chance applets: http://www.rossmanchance.com/applets/

GLOSSARY

Alternative hypothesis—the theory that the researcher hopes to confirm by rejecting the null hypothesis

Association—when some of the variability in one variable can be accounted for by the other

Bar chart—graph in which the frequencies or relative frequencies of categories are displayed with bars

Bimodal—distribution with two most common values

Binomial distribution‡—independent observations, each of which succeeds or fails with the same probability, p, over a fixed number of trials, n; the number of successes is the variable of interest

Bivariate data—having to do with two variables

Block—a group of experimental units thought to be homogenous with respect to the response variable

Block design—procedure by which experimental units are put into homogeneous groups in an attempt to reduce variability due to the group on the response variable

Boxplot (box-and-whisker plot)—graphical representation of the five-number summary of a dataset; outliers are also shown

Categorical data—data whose values range over categories

Census—attempt to contact every member of a population

Center—the "middle" of a distribution; either the mean or the median

Central limit theorem—theorem that states that the sampling distribution of a sample mean becomes approximately normal when the sample size is large

Chi-square (χ^2) dsitribution‡—compares a set of observed categorical values to a set of expected values under a set of hypothesized proportions for the categories:

$$\chi^2 = \sum \frac{(O-E)^2}{E}$$

Cluster sample—population is first divided into sections or "clusters"; then we randomly select an entire cluster, or clusters, and include all of the members of the cluster(s) in the sample

‡ The formula sheet has information about this term.

Coefficient of determination (r^2)—measures the proportion of variation in the response variable explained by regression on the explanatory variable

Complement of an event—set of all outcomes in the sample space that are not in the event

Completely randomized design—when all subjects (or experimental units) are randomly assigned to treatments in an experiment

Conditional probability‡—the probability of one event succeeding given that some other event has already occurred

Confidence interval‡—an interval that, with a given level of confidence, is likely to contain a population value; (estimate) ± (margin of error)

Confidence level—the probability that the procedure used to construct an interval will generate an interval that does contain the population value

Confounding variable—has an effect on the outcomes of the study but whose effects cannot be separated from those of the treatment variable

Continuous data—data that can be measured, or take on values in an interval; the set of possible values cannot be counted

Continuous random variable—a random variable whose values are continuous data; takes all values in an interval

Control—holding constant variables in an experiment that might affect the response but are not one of the treatment variables

Convenience sample—sample chosen without any random mechanism; chooses individuals based on ease of selection

Correlation coefficient (r)‡—measures the strength and direction of the linear relationship between two quantitative variables

Correlation is not causation—just because two variables correlate strongly does not mean that one caused the other; only experiments can have causal conclusions

Critical value‡—values in a distribution that identify certain specified areas of the distribution

Discrete data—data that can be counted (possibly infinite) or placed in order

Discrete random variable—random variable whose values are discrete data

Dotplot—graph in which data values are identified as dots placed above their corresponding values on a number line

Double blind—experimental design in which neither the subjects nor the study administrators know what treatment a subject has received

Empirical Rule (68-95-99.7 Rule)—states that, in a normal distribution, about 68% of the terms are within one standard deviation of the mean, about 95% are within two standard deviations, and about 99.7% are within three standard deviations

Expected value‡—mean value of a discrete random variable

Experiment—study in which a researcher measures the responses to a treatment variable, or variables, imposed and controlled by the researcher

Experimental units—individuals on which experiments are conducted

Explanatory variable—explains changes in response variable; treatment variable; independent variable

Extrapolation—predictions about the value of a variable based on the value of another variable outside the range of measured values

Extraneous variable—one that has an effect on the outcomes of the study but whose influence was not part of the investigation

First quartile—the value that identifies the 25th percentile Q1

Five-number summary—for a dataset, [minimum value, Q1, median, Q3, maximum value]

Geometric setting‡—independent observations, each of which succeeds or fails with the same probability p; number of trials needed until first success is variable of interest

High-leverage points—are extreme in the x direction compared to the rest of the points in a scatterplot; usually very influential

Histogram—graph in which numerical data are grouped into intervals and the frequencies or relative frequencies within each interval are displayed with bars

Homogeneity of proportions‡—chi-square hypothesis in which proportions of a categorical variable are tested for homogeneity across two or more populations

Independent events—knowing one event occurs does not change the probability that the other occurs; $P(A) = P(A|B)$

Inferential statistics—use of sample data to make inferences about populations

Influential observation—observation, usually in the x direction, whose removal would have a marked impact on the slope of the regression line

Interquartile range—value of the third quartile minus the value of the first quartile

Least-squares regression line‡—of all possible lines, the line that minimizes the sum of squared errors (residuals) from the line

Margin of error—measure of uncertainty in the estimate of a parameter; (critical value) · (standard error of the statistic)

Marginal totals—row and column totals in a two-way table

Matched pairs—experimental units paired by a researcher based on some common characteristic or characteristic

Matched pairs design—experimental design that utilizes each pair as a block; one unit receives one treatment, and the other unit receives the other treatment

Mean‡—sum of all the values in a dataset divided by the number of values

Median—halfway through an ordered dataset, below and above which lies an equal number of data values; 50th percentile

Mosaic plot—a plot similar to a segmented bar chart but that preserves the size of the individual groups via proportional sizes of the width of the bars themselves

Mound-shaped (bell-shaped)—distribution in which data values tend to cluster about the center of the distribution; characteristic of a normal distribution

Mutually exclusive events—events that cannot occur simultaneously; if one occurs, the other doesn't

Negatively associated—larger values of one variable are associated with smaller values of the other

Nonresponse bias—occurs when subjects selected for a sample do not respond

Normal curve‡—bell-shaped density curve; symmetric about its mean; defined in terms of its mean and standard deviation

Normal distribution—distribution of a random variable X so that $P(a < X < b)$ is the area under the normal curve between a and b

‡The formula sheet has information about this term.

Null hypothesis—hypothesis being tested—usually a statement that there is no effect or difference between treatments; what a researcher wants to disprove to support their alternative

Observational study—when variables of interest are observed and measured but no treatment is imposed in an attempt to influence the response

Observed values—counts of outcomes in an experiment or study; compared with expected values in a chi-square analysis

One-sided alternative—alternative hypothesis that varies from the null in only one direction

One-sided test—used when an alternative hypothesis states that the true value is either less than or greater than the hypothesized value but not both

Outcome—simple events in a probability experiment

Outlier—a data value that is far removed from the general pattern of the data

P(A and B)‡—probability that *both* A and B occur; $P(A \text{ and } B) = P(A) \cdot P(A|B)$

P(A or B)‡—probability that *either* A or B occurs; $P(A \text{ or } B) = P(A) + P(B) - P(A \text{ and } B)$

P-value—probability of getting a sample value at least as extreme as that obtained by chance alone assuming the null hypothesis is true

Parameter—measure that describes a population

Percentile rank—proportion of terms in the distributions less than or equal to the value being considered

Placebo—an inactive procedure or treatment

Placebo effect—effect, often positive, attributable to the patient's expectation that the treatment will have an effect

Point estimate—value based on sample data that represents a likely value for a population parameter

Positively associated—larger values of one variable are associated with larger values of the other

Power of a test—probability of rejecting a null hypothesis against a specific alternative

Probability distribution—identification of the outcomes of a random variable together with the probabilities associated with those outcomes

Probability of an event—relative frequency of the number of ways an event can succeed to the total number of ways it can succeed or fail

Proportion—ratio of the count of a particular outcome to the total number of outcomes

Quantitative data—data whose values are numerical

Quartiles—25th, 50th, and 75th percentiles of a dataset

Random phenomenon—unclear how any one trial will turn out, but there is a regular distribution of outcomes in a large number of trials

Random sample—sample in which each member of the sample is chosen by chance and each member of the population has an equal chance to be in the sample

Random variable—numerical outcome of a random phenomenon

Randomization—random assignment of experimental units to treatments

Range—difference between the maximum and minimum values of a dataset

Replication—repetition of each treatment enough times to help control for chance variation

Representative sample—sample that possesses the essential characteristics of the population from which it was taken

Residual—in a regression, the actual value minus the predicted value

Resistant statistic—one whose numerical value is not influenced by extreme values in the dataset; e.g., median, IQR

Response bias—bias that stems from respondents' inaccurate or untruthful response

Response variable—the y-variable of a regression equation or, in an experiment, the variable that the researcher wants to compare after the treatments are applied

Sample space—set of all possible mutually exclusive outcomes of a probability experiment

Sample survey—using a sample from a population to obtain responses to questions from individuals

Sampling distribution of a statistic—distribution of all possible values of a statistic for samples of a given size

Scatterplot—graphical representation of a set of ordered pairs; horizontal axis is first element in the pair, vertical axis is the second

Shape—geometric description of a dataset: mound-shaped; symmetric, uniform; skewed; etc.

Significance level (α)—probability value that, when compared to the *P*-value, determines whether a finding is statistically significant

Simple random sample (SRS)—sample in which all possible samples of the same size are equally likely to be the sample chosen

Simulation—random imitation of a probabilistic situation

‡The formula sheet has information about this term.

Skewed—distribution that is asymmetrical with data bunched at one end and a tail stretching out in the other

Skewed left (right)—asymmetrical with more of a tail on the left (right) than on the right (left)

Spread—variability of a distribution

Standard deviation‡—the typical distance of the data from the mean

Standard error—estimate for the standard deviation of a statistic

Standard normal distribution‡—normal distribution with a mean of 0 and a standard deviation of 1

Statistic—measure that describes a sample (e.g., sample mean)

Statistically significant—a finding that is unlikely to have occurred by chance

Stemplot (stem-and-leaf plot)—graph in which quantitative data are broken into "stems" and "leaves"; visually similar to a histogram

Stratified random sample—groups of interest (strata) chosen in such a way that they appear in approximately the same proportions in the sample as in the population

Subjects—human experimental units

Survey—obtaining responses to questions from individuals

Symmetric—data values distributed equally above and below the center of the distribution

Systematic random sample—probability sample in which one of the first n subjects is chosen at random for the sample and then each nth person after that is chosen for the sample

Test statistic‡—

$$\frac{\text{statistic - parameter}}{\text{standard error of the statistic}}$$

Third quartile—the value that identifies the 75th percentile; Q3

Tree diagram—graphical technique for showing all possible outcomes in a probability experiment; most useful when given conditional probabilities

Two-sided alternative—alternative hypothesis that can vary from the null in either direction; values much greater than or much less than the null provide evidence against the null

Two-way table—table that lists the outcomes of two categorical variables; the values of one category are given as the row variable, and the values of the other category are given as the column variable; also called a contingency table

Type I error—the error made when a true null hypothesis is rejected

Type II error—the error made when a false null hypothesis is not rejected

Unbiased estimate—mean of the sampling distribution of the estimate equals the parameter being estimated

Undercoverage—some groups in a population are not included in a sample from that population

Uniform—distribution in which all data values have (roughly) the same frequency of occurrence

Univariate data—having to do with a single variable

Variance—standard deviation squared

Voluntary response bias—bias inherent when people choose to respond to a survey or poll; bias is typically toward opinions of those who feel most strongly

Voluntary response sample—sample in which participants are free to respond or not to a survey or a poll

Wording bias—creation of response bias attributable to the phrasing of a question; a form of response bias‡

z-score‡—number of standard deviations a term is above or below the mean:

$$z = \frac{x - \bar{x}}{s}$$

---

‡The formula sheet has information about this term.

5 Steps to Teaching AP Statistics

AP Statistics

TEACHER'S MANUAL

Jared Derksen

AP Statistics Teacher at Rancho Cucamonga High School
Rancho Cucamonga, California

Thanks to Greg Jacobs, an AP physics teacher at Woodberry Forest School in Virginia, for developing the 5-step approach used in this teaching guide.

Introduction to the Teacher's Manual

The AP Statistics community is blessed with a multitude of amazing resources. To begin, the textbooks that our course uses are well written and supply us with very helpful supplements. Also, there has long been a vibrant discussion forum that offers answers to any teacher who asks. But in the last few years, the resources have grown at an astonishing rate. Of course, College Board has created the Course and Exam Description, the AP Classroom, and the AP Daily Videos. And as if this wasn't enough, Khan Academy, Stats Medic, and Skew the Script have sprung up—each replete with a ton of ideas and materials for your AP Statistics classroom.

One of the great resources to help your students succeed in AP Statistics is the book you're holding in your hands right now. This text is filled with learning tips that guide students to maximize their scores. The explanations are clear and helpful. And the practice exams are modeled after the most recent AP exams.

This teacher's manual will take you through the five steps of teaching AP Statistics. These five steps are:

- ▶ **Prepare a strategic plan for the course**
- ▶ **Hold an interesting class every day**
- ▶ **Evaluate your students' progress**
- ▶ **Get students ready to take the AP exam**
- ▶ **Become a better teacher every year**

This guide will not only suggest how to use this *5 Steps* book, but it will also include practical advice from my 24 years of teaching AP Statistics. I am including some of my favorite tips and activities on these pages. I hope that you find in this teacher's manual something that will be useful to you.

STEP 1

Prepare a Strategic Plan for the Course

As mentioned in the preceding section, AP Statistics is blessed with many great resources. As you make your plan for the year, my recommendation is that you follow the sequence of your textbook as your first plan. The Course and Exam Description (CED) has an order of topics that is probably very similar to your textbook and there isn't much gain in trying to match that order exactly. Your textbook has a progression of thinking that is embedded in its exercises. I recommend, especially if you are new to the course, that you follow that sequence—it will make your life so much easier.

That said, many teachers start their school year with Unit 3. It lays a strong foundation for the beginning point of statistics—thinking carefully about how data should be collected. Other teachers have moved regression (Unit 2) to the very end of the course, in part to combine it with Unit 9. What's probably more important than the order of the topics is the backwards planning to ensure you have time to cover the entire course. Carefully examining your school's calendar and mapping out the time each topic will take is a crucial task. And also, plan for the unexpected! Leave in some extra days for that lesson that just didn't go as planned or when something prevented you from holding your scheduled class.

The chart below shows the units (according to the CED) and the time I suggest for each unit. The number of class periods is based on a typical 45-minute class. If your school is on a block schedule or other atypical schedule, you will need to adjust the pacing to fit your class needs.

TOPICS	PACING	5 STEPS TO A 5
Unit 1: Exploring One-Variable Data	14–20 Class Periods	Chapter 5
Unit 2: Exploring Two-Variable Data	10–11 Class Periods	Chapter 6
Unit 3: Collecting Data	11–13 Class Periods	Chapter 7
Unit 4: Probability, Random Variables, and Probability Distributions	18–20 Class Periods	Chapters 8 & 9
Unit 5: Sampling Distributions	6–8 Class Periods	Chapter 9
Unit 6: Inference for Categorical Data: Proportions	16–18 Class Periods	Chapters 10 & 11
Unit 7: Inference for Quantitative Data: Means	14–16 Class Periods	Chapters 10 & 11
Unit 8: Inference for Categorical Data: Chi-Square	5–7 Class Periods	Chapter 13
Unit 9: Inference for Quantitative Data: Slopes	2–4 Class Periods	Chapter 12

You should note that these recommended class periods differ from the recommendations in the CED. In our experience, Unit 1 needs more time than the CED recommends and Units 5, 8, and 9 can be taught in less time. Your mileage may vary! But this is our experience: Unit 5 is best taught with just one-sample sampling distributions. The 2-sample distributions can be briefly mentioned as you begin each of those inference topics. Unit 8, chi-square, is very straightforward for students. Their calculators do most of the heavy lifting and the focus can be placed on the correct wording and interpretations. And finally, inference for slope is a very small percentage of the AP exam and can be taught quickly if one simply focuses on computer output.

You'll want to leave some time for review. Teachers usually plan on taking two to four weeks of cumulative review. And don't forget that once AP testing starts, your students will be busy with other exams. Schedule your review so that your last practice exam is in the last week of April—right before exams commence.

Hold an Interesting Class Every Day

Welcome to the most fun math class there is to teach! This is the class where students will never, ever ask you "When am I going use this?" Statistics is the course where the application of the ideas can't be missed. Well, you might miss it, if you choose poorly. How do you choose wisely?

- **Interesting context is king.** Good statistics problems always (yes, always!) begin with an interesting context. Start every lesson not with the theorem or formula of the chapter, but with a data set (or summary statistics) from an interesting context that has real-world applications and naturally leads to asking and answering the questions that you want to focus on.

- **Student-generated data is fantastic.** Begin class with a quick survey. Use the students' answers to build a 2-way table. Maybe use the classroom next door, too. Run a quick experiment on students to collect a set of numbers.

- **Fun activities can be instructive.** There is a very long list of fun activities and experiments you can perform with your classes. Yes, you need to choose wisely. The best activities don't just entertain, they embed important concepts in the minds of your students. And they don't take all period long; they leave time for summarizing and making conclusions. We'll list some of our favorites below.

In the 1950s, statistics education was dull. Contrived data sets were used in order to simplify calculations. And much time is needed to be spent on how to carry out those calculations. However, our students have a handy calculator on their desk every day. There is little value in even one "by hand" calculation. The AP exam is focused on reading, interpreting, and explaining statistical ideas, and that's what you should focus on during class time. This also results in shorter lectures and more time for students to write, explore, and discuss. Don't hear us wrong—there are statistical ideas that you need to communicate. But if you find that your students are growing bored while you are getting a sore throat, it is probably time to reevaluate if everything you're saying is really necessary.

There are many ways to access ideas for keeping your lessons alive and fresh. Both Twitter and Facebook have user groups that share ideas, as does the official College Board discussion board. And, as mentioned, Stats Medic and Skew the Script are two sites that are full of teaching ideas. That said, here are a few of our favorite activities. Many of these activities can be found with a quick Google search. Also, I keep a cloud drive filled with many resources at **mrmathman.com/ stuff**, sorted by each CED unit.

UNIT	RECOMMENDED ACTIVITIES
Unit 1: Exploring One-Variable Data	▶ Day 1 Activity: Smelling Parkinson's. Student watch a video with the true story of a woman claiming to be able to smell Parkinson's disease. A simple simulation is used to test this claim and students begin the process of learning to think statistically (mrtysonstats.com). ▶ Use Census at Schools from the American Statistical Association (ASA) to complete a survey and/or take a random sample of data. ▶ Student groups graph a quantitative variable (e.g., number of photos on their phone) each using one graph type. Then groups compare the pros and cons of the different graphs.
Unit 2: Exploring Two-Variable Data	▶ Create correlation stations. Students create scatterplots by doing a variety of activities (length versus weight of a vine, measuring hand size and foot size, etc.) (bit.ly/rstations).
Unit 3: Collecting Data	See the Unit 3 folder at mrmathman.com/stuff for these activities: ▶ The Bias Project: Students conduct a survey first in an unbiased manner and then create response bias. This project has been a favorite for years. ▶ Students are given three different kinds of chips (chocolate, butterscotch, white chocolate). They time how long it takes each of them to melt in their mouth. ▶ Take students outside where they complete a Statistics Olympics. For each station, they have to describe all the experimental design vocabulary (factor, levels, response variable, etc.). ▶ For matched pairs, students are given two copies of an emoji (the poop emoji makes them smile!). They time how long it takes to trace the emoji with their dominant versus their non-dominant hand. ▶ The Rolling Down the River activity has been a favorite for years. Students take random samples and stratified samples from a field. The results demonstrate how stratification reduces variability. I created a modern version at bit.ly/riverdocument. ▶ Show Me the Money is an activity that uses box-office earnings of the top 200 movies. Students compare a convenience sample of movies they watched (biased) versus a (unbiased) random sample of movies (mrtysonstats.com). ▶ The Pepsi challenge uses a taste test experiment to see if students can really taste the difference between Coke and Pepsi (mrmathman.com/stuff).
Unit 4: Probability, Random Variables, and Probability Distributions	▶ Students create a game where they calculate the expected value. Students make the rule and pick a mechanism for chance. They have to report the expected values of the game they create (mrmathman.com/stuff). ▶ Casino Lab: Students calculate the probability of various games of chance (mrmathman.com/stuff). ▶ 12 Days of Christmas review worksheet is a probability review using a well-known Christmas carol (mrmathman.com/stuff).
Unit 5: Sampling Distributions	▶ The Penny Lab: Students collect random samples from a bucket of pennies. They compare the distribution of samples of sizes 1, 5, and 25; easy to Google. ▶ Sampling distributions with car prices: Students use a Google spreadsheet that contains data on 1,500 used cars. The random samples that students collect are used to explain sampling distributions (bit.ly/carprices2020).
Unit 6: Inference for Categorical Data: Proportions	▶ Flipping Hershey's Kisses: Students flip Hershey's kisses and record the percentage that land on their base. Then they are guided to construct a confidence interval for this percentage (mrmathman.com/stuff). ▶ Card Trick to introduce hypothesis testing (bit.ly/statscardtrick). ▶ Power Dominos: Challenging puzzle requiring an understanding of errors, power, and significance level (bit.ly/powerdom).

(continued)

UNIT	RECOMMENDED ACTIVITIES
Unit 7: Inference for Quantitative Data: Means	▶ Use a website that tests students' reaction time. Build a confidence interval or compare different groups within your class (bit.ly/statsreact).
Unit 8: Inference for Categorical Data: Chi-Square	▶ Use a box of Froot Loops to test for goodness of fit to see if the color distribution is uniform. ▶ Collect data from your students to construct a 2-way table (you pick the variables).
Unit 9: Inference for Quantitative Data: Slopes	▶ Use this unit to launch a cumulative AP review with Unit 2 review. Start the Super 6 (see Step 4 below) at this time (bit. ly/statsuper6). ▶ Focus on reading computer output! This saves time and helps students practice AP-style questions. Students are not going to need to run these types of problems from data on their calculator.

The *5 Steps* cross-platform site/app can be a helpful tool for student practice. Students can use the Flashcards and the GameCenter to drill themselves or a partner. They can also use the app to study the chapter that corresponds to the unit they are studying in class. They can use practice multiple-choice questions at the end of each chapter to check their understanding of the chapter. For instructions to access the cross-platform site, see the back cover of this book.

The *5 Steps to Teaching AP Statistics: Elite Edition* provides additional questions that can be used in your class. It contains 180 questions that require five minutes a day or less. While they are primarily intended to be used by students studying for the test, you can use these as daily warm-ups in your course or assign them as homework or classwork/group work. To do this, you will need the table below, which organizes these questions and activities by unit.

UNIT	QUESTIONS IN THE ELITE EDITION (Days are listed below)
Unit 1: Exploring One-Variable Data	Days 1–32
Unit 2: Exploring Two-Variable Data	Days 33–53
Unit 3: Collecting Data	Days 54–78
Unit 4: Probability, Random Variables, and Probability Distributions	Days 79–119
Unit 5: Sampling Distributions	Days 107–119
Unit 6: Inference for Categorical Data: Proportions	Days 120–161
Unit 7: Inference for Quantitative Data: Means	Days 120–161
Unit 8: Inference for Categorical Data: Chi-Square	Days 172–180
Unit 9: Inference for Quantitative Data: Slopes	Days 162–171

STEP 3

Evaluate Your Students' Progress

As you make progress through the course, it is critical that you assess your students' understanding. Let's begin this section by noting that the multiple-choice items on the AP Statistics exam are challenging questions. They are not simple recall questions and they contain question stems that require careful reading. Providing students with multiple-choice practice and feedback is thereby essential.

Multiple-Choice Questions

AP classroom quizzes (Topic Questions and Personal Progress Checks) are a useful resource. But don't forget that these questions are meant to be formative in nature and are written on a lower level compared to AP exam questions. Nonetheless, formative assessment is extremely valuable! So, make good use of this resource.

Note that this book is filled with high-quality AP-style multiple-choice items. Before a unit test, part of our review is multiple-choice practice. Students ask for it! They know that each of our unit tests will have some of these challenging questions. Use the chapter-by-chapter multiple-choice items to help students prepare for each unit test.

After a unit test, do not stop evaluating student strengths and weaknesses. I recommend selecting the two or three most missed questions and discussing them thoroughly after each unit test. Then inform students that these same concepts/questions will be seen again on the next test. Sometimes it takes a third time until I am satisfied that enough students have achieved understanding of an important concept.

If your school affords you an item analysis of your multiple-choice tests, make sure to identify which distractor was most successful. I then recommend the following conversation to guide the learning: "Please examine question 3. Most of you thought that D was the right answer. Please figure out with your neighbor why D is, in fact, incorrect."

Finally, at the end of this teacher's manual is a handout for an activity for improving multiple-choice testing skills called "You Finish It!" In these exercises, students are given incomplete multiple-choice items. They are instructed to finish the question. First, make answer option (a) correct. And then answer option (b) is correct. And so on. This forces students to think about the structure in the various answer options. Instead of seeing a jumble of numbers or words, they look for the structures in the numbers and/or think about the definitions of the terms. This is one of our favorite techniques for helping students decipher multiple-choice test items.

Free-Response Questions (FRQ)

When it comes to free-response questions, you have many great resources. While the CED has clarified the AP Statistics curriculum, the changes were rather minor. Thus, the past free-response questions from old exams are a valuable treasure trove of practice problems. Josh Tabor maintains a spreadsheet that sorts the free-response questions by the textbook. Many of us use this spreadsheet to track which questions we have used throughout the course of the school year. See **mrmathman.com/stuff** (folder: Released Exam Resources) for the latest version.

Pick a few free-response questions for the unit you're teaching and use one of them on your unit test. You can use it exactly as is, or you might choose to modify it. Enhancing an AP question with extra parts is a wonderful way to improve your unit test. An AP question typically has no more than four parts, often only three. But your goal on a unit test is to thoroughly measure your students' learning. So, to use regression as an example, an old question might have questions about the slope, the residual plot, and an outlier. You might choose to add a few more questions, for example, asking students about R^2 and asking them to describe the scatterplot. One of the side benefits of these added questions is that any student who is cheating will never find your new, special version of this question!

You also want to use free-response questions in a formative manner. This process has been named the FRAPPY! (Free-Response AP Problem Yay!) process in the AP Statistics community (thanks, Jason!). This process can be varied in many ways. Here's the basic idea:

1. **Students are given an old FRQ**

2. **A 12-minute[1] timer is set**

3. **Students complete the problem**

4. **AP rubric for scoring is explained**

5. **Students grade their own paper**

6. **Students grade each other's papers and/or student samples**

I usually choose to spend about 30 minutes on this activity. Turning the official AP scoring guidelines into a more student-friendly set of slides is recommended. Sometimes it is best if you create your own "student sample" where you write a response that has a common error. Then you can see if students find the error(s). For example, write a student response that is perfect in every way— except leave out all context and just write about "the data." Most students won't see the mistake!

Our friend, Robin Levine-Wissing, recommends that students score their work and student samples *before* they see the rubric. This can be a useful variation after students have done a few FRAPPYs and have some ideas of what AP Statistics requires. Then you can reveal the rubric and students will see if they are correctly anticipating what is expected in their responses.

I cannot overemphasize that the FRAPPY! process is *formative*. Long-time AP Statistics consultant Penny Smeltzer likes to say, "High rigor, low stress!" Students need to feel comfortable making mistakes, admitting that they learned from those mistakes, and sharing that process with their classmates and with you. Students can show you that they have completed the FRAPPY in a variety of ways. They can send you a picture of their work (with corrections in a different color) or they can fill out a short Google form sharing their scoring and what they learned. But, above all, you need to encourage a classroom atmosphere where students try, *even when the work is not worth any points.* If that is not a reality in your classroom, I would encourage you to just try it. And if some students don't work, a frank but positive class discussion about the value of being a learning community together may help set the tone.

See **mrmathman.com/stuff** and look in the FRAPPY folder for a starter set of these resources.

---

[1] Students actually have 13 minutes per FRQ. However, on the actual test there is time wasted with turning pages, etc. And a FRAPPY is usually more straightforward because students know what they are about to write about. Thus, I train my students on 12-minutes per FRQ.

STEP 4

Get Students Ready to Take the AP Exam

As you finish teaching the course, it will be time to transition to preparing your students for the AP exam. I usually plan on using most of April for this task. As a starting point, it is important to realize that you have two important, but somewhat conflicting, goals during this time:

▶ **Reviewing the content of the entire course**

▶ **Scrambled practice where students have to decide which skill they should use**

My favorite method for reviewing the course is a document affectionately titled "The Super 6" (**bit.ly/statsuper6**). I took six free-response questions and made them super long! That is, I kept adding parts until I had covered all (or almost all) of the topics in the CED. I start assigning the Super 6 as the course is winding up. The class completes the regression question as a way to prepare for Unit 9 (inference for slope). There is usually a test in early April on the Super 6 to encourage students to study all six problems. This relatively compact set of questions will help students review almost all of the course (except for inference).

At the same time you are reviewing everything they forgot, you *must* scramble all your practice exercises so that they have to determine what to do. When students are completing the Super 6, they are thinking "Oh, now I'm doing regression. Now I'm doing probability." To give them practice in deciding which operation they should perform, every day in April, grab an old FRQ (or a question from this book), do *not* tell them the topic, set a 12-minute timer, and GO!

Give your students a bar graph. Smile and watch them talk about center, shape, and spread. Give them a sampling distribution probability question and watch them try to use the t-distribution. My good friend Doug Tyson observed, "In calculus it easy to know what you're supposed to do, the hard part is to do it. In statistics, the hard part is to decide what to do. Once you decide, doing it is usually pretty easy." In short, you need to help them remember all the vocabulary and the formulas from the whole book while you scramble and mix up all sorts of practice that forces them to decide when to use the right statistical tool.

Reviewing inference is not a small thing. Students confuse the various formulas and the conditions for each procedure. There are three great websites for practice at choosing the right inference procedure:

▶ Larry Green's website lets students pick which procedure(s) they are ready to recognize. (**bit.ly/namethattest**; this site includes prediction intervals and ANOVA, which are not AP topics. Just have students never select these options.)

▶ Khan Academy has an excellent set of practice problems. (**bit.ly/namethattest2**)

▶ I have also put together a set of documents to help with this skill. They can be found at **bit.ly/namethattest3**. These documents include three sets of old FRQs and a description of how to use them.

When you first start teaching inference, there are only a few formulas and students are focusing on the concepts. However, as the number of formulas grows, student confusion increases. Near the end of this teaching guide, you will find a graphic organizer for all inference procedures. There is both a blank organizer for students and a completed one for your reference. Filling it out is a very valuable activity for students. It is easy to find this information; it is almost certainly in your textbook, and it is certainly in this text. Students should be encouraged to complete this organizer using only the AP formula sheet.

Finally, you need to give students practice exams while you review. I recommend having students complete a full 40-question multiple-choice exam as quickly as possible. There are three exams in this book you can choose from. I tell students that they need to get about 50% right if they're going to pass the AP exam (with a 3) and about 75% correct if they want a 5. This rough rule of thumb lets them know how much work they need to put in to achieve their goal.

As April comes to a close and the time is running out, devote class time to a final mock exam. Depending on your school's schedule, it may need to be only 20 multiple-choice items one day and three FRQs the next. Having students come in after school or on a Saturday to complete a full exam can be valuable, but it is not always imperative, especially if your students already have experience with other AP tests and have developed testing stamina.

Finally, I will observe that test prep can become boring. Varying review activities is imperative. The CED is filled with different instructional practices, as are many of the discussion forums. Strategies like Gallery Walks, Pass the Pen, and rotating through different practice stations are important to ensure student engagement in a month where senioritis and prom are working against you!

STEP 5

Become a Better Teacher Every Year

If you're teaching this course for the first time, congratulations! You are beginning an amazing journey. Every year will get easier. Your explanations will become clearer and you will figure out which activities work with your teaching style. Be patient with yourself! Not every unit will be perfect. You should consider attending an AP summer institute (APSI). Many teachers report that they can better process and absorb the ideas from an APSI when they attend after their first or second year.

AP Statistics is a course that should have a low barrier for entry. That is, there really isn't much in the way of true prerequisites apart from the willingness to work hard combined with critical thinking skills. Because of that, you shouldn't measure your success solely based on your test scores. You should also examine who is taking your course. The kid on the honors math track is going to pass the AP Statistics exam. But what about the student that is not an honor student and only takes one other AP class? Are they finding your course accessible? And maybe you are able to help many of those students earn a passing score! Running a program that is inclusive and includes many different types of students is a goal worth working toward.

As AP teachers, we have one part of our work made easy: the learning targets for our students are clearly set. How do we help more students reach that goal? One thing to consider is rewarding growth over time. Too many of our students develop the bad habit of cramming for a test and then forgetting everything the next day. But our goal as teachers is for students to remember all the statistics they learn by constantly reviewing and retesting in some way.

You might be saying to yourself, "But this is an AP class! They should get it the first time!" Well, if you want a small program filled with only honors students, that will work. But if you want to build a program that includes a wide variety of students from your school, consider giving students multiple opportunities to demonstrate learning.

Additional Resources for Teachers

Here is a list of useful websites for AP Statistics. Please note that the first site on this list will take you to many other useful sites. Included on my page are links to the CED resources that accompany the two most popular textbooks. There are also links to Desmos bookmarks collections, which are useful even if you're not teaching on a distance-learning model.

USEFUL WEBSITES

- ▶ **mrmathman.com/links** contains many of the most popular AP Statistics resources.

- ▶ **mrmathman.com/stuff** is a cloud drive with many useful resources.

- ▶ **bit.ly/statsmyway** contains my lesson plans and ideas.

- ▶ **statsmedic.com** provides lesson plans and a review course for AP Statistics.

- ▶ **skewthescript.org** offers relevant lessons that cover the entire AP Statistics curriculum.

- ▶ Census at School (**https://ww2.amstat.org /censusatschool/index.cfm**) contains activities for the classroom. It is part of the website of the ASA.

- ▶ **fivethirtyeight.com** is a great site for data-based journalism.

- ▶ **pewresearch.org** has surveys of American life and more.

- ▶ **khanacademy.org** is a great source for independent practice.

- ▶ **askgoodquestions.blog** is the blog of former chief reader, Alan Rossman—well worth your time!

- ▶ **bit.ly/Gaisestats** is an excellent document with guidelines for statistics education by the ASA.

Organizer for Inference Procedures

CATEG OR QUANT	# OF SAMPLES	PARAMETER	STATISTIC	SAMPLE SIZE CONDITION	CONFIDENCE INTERVAL	HYPOTHESIS TEST STATISTIC	T/Z/χ^2	DF
Categ	1	p	$\hat{p}$	$n\hat{p}$ & $n(1-\hat{p}) \geq 10$ or np_0 & $n(1-p_0) \geq 10$	$\hat{p} \pm z^* \sqrt{\dfrac{\hat{p}(1-\hat{p})}{n}}$	$z = \dfrac{\hat{p} - p_0}{\sqrt{p_0(1-p_0)\big/n}}$	z	N/A
Categ	2	p_1, p_2	$\hat{p}_1, \hat{p}_2$	$n\hat{p}$ & $n(1-\hat{p}) \geq 10$ -with both samples for interval -with p_c for hyp. test	$(\hat{p}_1 - \hat{p}_2) \pm z^* (SE)$ $SE = \sqrt{\dfrac{\hat{p}_1(1-\hat{p}_1)}{n_1} + \dfrac{\hat{p}_2(1-\hat{p}_2)}{n_2}}$	$z = \dfrac{\hat{p}_1 - \hat{p}_2}{\sqrt{\hat{p}_c(1-\hat{p}_c)\left(\dfrac{1}{n_1} + \dfrac{1}{n_2}\right)}}$	z	N/A
Quant	1	μ	$\bar{x}$	symmetrical graph or $n \geq 30$	$\bar{x} \pm t^* \dfrac{s}{\sqrt{n}}$	$t = \dfrac{\bar{x} - \mu}{\frac{s}{\sqrt{n}}}$	t	$n-1$
Quant	2	μ_1, μ_2	$\bar{x}_1, \bar{x}_2$	symmetrical graphs or $n \geq 30$	$(\bar{x}_1 - \bar{x}_2) \pm t^* SE$ $SE = \sqrt{\dfrac{s_1^2}{n_1} + \dfrac{s_2^2}{n_2}}$	$t = \dfrac{(\bar{x}_1 - \bar{x}_2) - 0}{SE}$	t	from technology
Quant	1-mp	μ_d	$\bar{x}_d$	symmetrical graph or $n \geq 30$	$\bar{x}_d \pm t^* \dfrac{s}{\sqrt{n}}$	$t = \dfrac{\bar{x}_d - \mu_d}{\frac{s}{\sqrt{n}}}$	t	$n-1$
Categ	1	Goodness of Fit	N/A	Expected counts ≥ 5	N/A	$\chi^2 = \sum \dfrac{(Obs - Exp)^2}{Exp}$	χ^2	# categ -1
Categ	1	Independence	N/A	Expected counts ≥ 5	N/A	$\chi^2 = \sum \dfrac{(Obs - Exp)^2}{Exp}$	χ^2	$(r-1)(c-1)$
Categ	2+	Homogeneity	N/A	Expected counts ≥ 5	N/A	$\chi^2 = \sum \dfrac{(Obs - Exp)^2}{Exp}$	χ^2	$(r-1)(c-1)$
Quant	1	β	b	linear data, scattered residual plot, $\approx$ normal residuals	$b \pm t^* SE$ SE on computer output	$t = \dfrac{b - \beta}{SE}$	t	$n-2$

Organizer for Inference Procedures

CATEG OR QUANT	# OF SAMPLES	PARAMETER	STATISTIC	SAMPLE SIZE CONDITION	CONFIDENCE INTERVAL	HYPOTHESIS TEST STATISTIC	T/Z/ χ^2	DF

Finish It!

The following multiple-choice questions are unfinished. Your task is to finish them. Repeatedly! That is, first finish the questions so that answer (a) is correct. Then finish the questions so that (b) is correct. And so on. Good luck!

1. Christmas tree lights can be beautiful. But sometimes they don't work. You are working with a string of 50 lights. Suppose that in a string of lights each bulb has a 3% chance of failure. You can assume that each bulb is independent of the next.

   a. $(0.97)^{50}$

   b. $1-(1-0.03)^{50}$

   c. $(0.97)^{49}(0.03)^{1}$

   d. $\binom{50}{4}(0.03)^{4}(0.97)^{46}$

2. A worker at a local ski resort is often amused by the attempts of skiers to smoothly use the ski lift. He reads that 7% of skiers have a problem using a ski lift. We assume that each skier is independent of the next.

   a. $(0.07)^{13}$

   b. $(0.93)^{13}$

   c. $1-(1-0.07)^{13}$

   d. $(0.93)^{12}(0.07)^{1}$

   e. $\binom{13}{5}(0.07)^{5}(0.93)^{8}$

3. A city planner needs to collect data from a neighborhood of approximately 5,000 homes. He will conduct a survey asking residents various financial questions related to home costs. The homes are roughly in a square grid, divided by streets that intersect in quarter-mile blocks. The planner knows that the homes in the southern section are generally more expensive.

   a. Census

   b. Simple random sample

   c. Stratified random sample

   d. Systematic random sample

   e. Cluster sample

4. The yearbook class on campus asks students a variety of survey questions.

   a. Bar chart

   b. Parallel boxplots

   c. A histogram

   d. Scatterplot

5. In a database of book prices, the List Price of a book is used to compare to the Amazon Price. A linear model is found to be appropriate, with $R^2 = 90.3\%$ and a regression equation: $\widehat{AmazonPrice} = -2.41 + 0.83(ListPrice)$

   a. For every $1 increase in List Price, there is a $0.83 increase in the predicted Amazon Price.

   b. For every $1 increase in Amazon Price, there is a $0.83 increase in the predicted List Price.

   c. For every $1 increase in List Price, there is a $2.41 decrease in the predicted Amazon Price.

   d. 90.3% of the variation in List Price has been successfully explained by Amazon Price.

   e. 90.3% of the variation in Amazon Price has been successfully explained by List Price.

   Note: Eliminate the distractors that are meaningless/incorrect. Finish the question only for the valid options.

6. A financial services company collects data on the earned income of 250 individuals *and* also from the siblings of those 250 individuals.

   a. 1-sample *t*-test

   b. Matched-pairs *t*-test

   c. 2-sample *t*-test

   d. Chi-square test of independence

Finish It! Answer Key

1a. What is the probability that all 50 lights work?

1b. What is the probability that at least 1 of the 50 bulbs fails?

1c. What is the probability that the first failure is the very last bulb checked?

1d. What is the probability that exactly 4 out of 50 bulbs fail?

2a. What is the probability that all 13 have problems?

2b. What is the probability that none of the 13 have problems?

2c. What is the probability that at least 1 of the 13 have problems?

2d. What is the probability that none of the skiers have problems until the 13th?

2e. What is the probability that exactly 5 of the 13 skiers have problems?

3a. The city planner surveys all 5,000 homes.

3b. 100 homes are randomly chosen using a random number generator.

3c. 50 homes are randomly selected from the south and 50 from the north.

3d. Every 50th house is selected from a list of homes in the neighborhood.

3e. 10 quarter-mile blocks are randomly selected. Homes on those blocks are surveyed.

4a. The yearbook asks students to name their favorite subject.

4b. Upper- and lower class students are asked how many minutes they study in a week.

4c. Students are asked how many hours they sleep each night.

4d. Students are asked how much money they earn each week and how much they spend on eating out.

5b, 5c, and **5d** are nonsense.

5a. Interpret the slope in context.

5d. Interpret R^2 in context.

6a and **6c** are not possible because these samples are *not* from independent populations.

6b. Does an older sibling make more money, on average, than their younger sibling?

6d. Divide income into four different income brackets. Compare older to younger siblings to test if income level is independent of birth order.